Herman Melville

—⟨⟩—

A to Z

HERMAN MELVILLE

A TO Z

The Essential Reference to His Life and Work

CARL ROLLYSON and LISA PADDOCK

Facts On File, Inc.

Herman Melville A to Z: The Essential Reference to His Life and Work

Facts On File, Inc.
11 Penn Plaza
New York NY 10001

Library of Congress Cataloging-in-Publication Data

Rollyson, Carl E. (Carl Edmund)
Herman Melville A to Z: the essential reference to his life and work / Carl Rollyson and Lisa Paddock.
p. cm.
Includes bibliographical references (p.) and index.
ISBN 0-8160-3851-1 (hardcover : alk. paper) — ISBN 0-8160-4160-1 (pbk. : alk. paper)
1. Melville, Herman, 1819–1891—Encyclopedias. 2. Authors, American—19th
century—Biography—Encyclopedias. I. Paddock, Lisa Olson. II. Title.

PS2386 .A24 2000
813′.3—dc21

[B]   00-035338

Facts On File books are available at special discounts when purchased in bulk quantities for businesses, associations, institutions or sales promotions. Please call our Special Sales Department in New York at
(212) 967-8800 or (800) 322-8755.

You can find Facts On File on the World Wide Web at http://www.factsonfile.com

Paperback cover design by Nora Wertz
Jacket design by Cathy Rincon
Family tree drawn by Jeremy Eagle

Printed in the United States of America

VB Hermitage 10 9 8 7 6 5 4 3 2 1
(pbk) 10 9 8 7 6 5 4 3 2 1

This book is printed on acid-free paper.

CONTENTS

INTRODUCTION
VII

CHRONOLOGY
IX

A-TO-Z ENTRIES
1

GENEALOGY OF HERMAN MELVILLE
225

CATEGORICAL INDEX
229

BIBLIOGRAPHY
237

INDEX
243

INTRODUCTION

According to the journal *American Literature,* Herman Melville is now the American author studied most frequently. One can think, perhaps, of greater American novelists—William Faulkner, for example—but is there another American author who has distinguished himself in so many different genres and written within those genres such diverse work? Melville wrote few great short stories, yet his greatest, "Bartleby the Scrivener" and "Benito Cereno," rival the short fiction of any major American writer. Henry James may be our finest practitioner of the novella, but he wrote nothing that surpasses the haunting and anguished tale *Billy Budd.* Undoubtedly *Moby-Dick* is a masterpiece of American literature, but few novelists can claim to have produced novels as distinctive as *Typee, Pierre, Israel Potter,* and *The Confidence Man.* The playful style of *Typee* seems a universe away from the wry, acerbic wit of *Israel Potter,* itself a far cry from the parodic romantic prose of *Pierre. The Confidence Man,* with a trickster figure at its center, marks a departure from Melville's earlier work even as it looks forward to the idea of role-playing and of shifting American identities that Ralph Ellison probes so deftly in *Invisible Man.* As poet, Melville distinguished himself in both the short, terse poems of his Civil War series, *Battle Pieces,* and the long narrative epic, *Clarel,* a work as ambitious as Chaucer's *Canterbury Tales* and Milton's *Paradise Lost.* The only genre he did not attempt is the drama, although a good deal of *Moby-Dick* seems written for the Shakespearean stage.

Even in *Moby-Dick,* it has to be acknowledged that Melville is an uneven writer. He often wrote in an excess of exuberance, a mark of the man as well as of the writer. He apparently wanted to bowl over his readers as he sometimes bowled over his friends and family. As a result, he tried too hard. *Pierre* is relentless with "thees" and "thous" and pseudo-poeticisms that alien-

ated and fatigued not only his own generation but subsequent readers as well. Yet on a second reading this novel gains in stature, especially when the reader is willing to explore with Melville the nature of love and of art and (again with Melville) forsake the craving for a realistic style and story.

It is the magnitude of Melville's ambition, the fact that he succeeded so many times in spite of his failures, that makes his work an inexhaustible study. Each of Melville's writings raises questions about style, structure, the meaning of literature, and the meaning of life. No American writer surpasses Melville in portraying the very act of writing itself as an adventure, a quest. And the more that is discovered about his biography, the more remarkable his career—much of it spent in obscurity—seems.

That Melville should have been rediscovered in the 1920s seems, in retrospect, inevitable. After the late 1850s he largely dropped out of sight as far as the literary establishment and the common reader were concerned. His work was too ambiguous, too skeptical, and even too morose for the late 19th century, which was more willing to be entertained by the mordant humor of Mark Twain and the mild realism of William Dean Howells. In the 1920s, such writers as William Faulkner and Ernest Hemingway—not to mention critics such as Raymond Weaver and Lewis Mumford—were searching for an indigenous literary tradition that would support their evolving sense of modernism, which combined a critical look at America with an aspiration to compete on equal terms with innovative European writers such as James Joyce and Marcel Proust. Herman Melville became the inspiration for this new generation of American writers, the touchstone for their own creative and critical quests.

Melville seems no less relevant today. There are plans to make a movie of his troubling novel, *Pierre,* and director John Huston turned *Moby-Dick* into a memorable film in 1956. More recently, Melville's "great whale" of a book has been transformed into a made-for-television movie. *Billy Budd* has been adapted both for film and an opera by Benjamin Britten. Playwright Tony Kushner has said of Melville: "I used him unconsciously and consciously when I was writing the second part of 'Angels in America.' I said to myself, 'Herman would approve of this.'" Kushner suggests the enormousness of Melville's authority in the realm of the American imagination. Writers as diverse as Jack London, William Faulkner, Robert Penn Warren, and Norman Mailer have paid homage to Melville's magnificent poetry and prose.

The recent discovery of more than 500 Melville family letters radically altered Melville scholarship, delaying Hershel Parker's definitive biography by several years, and making possible the first full Melville biography by Laurie Robertson-Lorant in 1996. As Robertson-Lorant observes in her appendix, fundamental issues about Melville's identity as a man and as a writer are just beginning to be discussed. New discoveries do not make the earlier criticism and biography irrelevant, but there is a pressing need for an up-to-date and accessible reference guide free of the jargon of specialized scholarship, a guide that does not presuppose familiarity with Melville's body of work and Melville studies, while at the same time organizing a wealth of information about Melville in a form scholars, too, will find useful to consult.

All entries in *Herman Melville A to Z* are complete in themselves, containing a discussion of how a character, term, place, historical figure, allusion, or reference functions in one or more of Melville's works. There is no need to constantly consult charts or tables while reading an individual entry. We cross-reference entries by using small capital letters. Thus, for example, in a synopsis of *Clarel*, PLATO refers to an entry on Plato that will be found in the P section.

In addition to incorporating information of the kind to be found in earlier Melville reference books, we have made a diligent effort to annotate his work with biographical information. Entries on his friends and family are extensive. As the first fully illustrated reference book on Herman Melville, this volume reproduces drawings and photographs that help to recapture the look and feel of his world.

Herman Melville A to Z draws upon many useful earlier works of reference, literary criticism, and biography. For example, *A Companion to Melville Studies*, edited by John Bryant (1986), contains an introduction describing the Melville renaissance, as well as separate sections on "Melville's World," "Melville's Work," "Melville's Thought," "Melville's Art," and "Melville's Mark." The history of Melville's reception is documented in *Melville: The Critical Heritage*, edited by Watson G. Branch (1974). Generations of Melville students have relied on *Melville: A Collection of Critical Essays*, edited by Richard Chase (1962), which covers the major work, contains some discussion of the life, and includes a chronology of important dates. More recent collections of criticism include *Critical Essays on Herman Melville's Moby-Dick*, edited by Brian Higgins and Hershel Parker (1992), and collections of criticism on all Melville's major works. There are numerous specialized studies and monographs, such as Joyce Sparer Adler's *War in Melville's Imagination* (1981) and Charles R. Anderson's *Melville in the South Seas* (1966). The trend of recent scholarship is evident in James Creech's *Closet Writing/Gay Reading: The Case of Melville's "Pierre"* (1993). The cultural context of Melville's writing is explored in monographs such as Marvin Fisher's *Going Under: Melville's Short Fiction and the American 1850s* (1977). Other reference works include Kathleen K. Kier's *Melville Encyclopedia: The Novels* (1990). All Melville scholars are indebted to Jay Leyda for his day-by-day chronology, *The Melville Log: A Documentary Life of Herman Melville, 1819–1891* (1951, revised 1969), currently being updated and revised by Hershel Parker for CD-ROM.

The chronology and bibliography in *Melville A to Z* provide detailed records of Melville's life and career and of the most important scholarship on a writer who still seems to be evolving, and who wrote with a capacity to reach generations beyond his own—generations who continue to make Melville modern or, rather, to make what seems "modern" a project that involves understanding Herman Melville.

CHRONOLOGY

Melville's Life and Times*

1774

Thomas Melvill (1751–1832), Melville's paternal grandfather, marries Priscella Scollay (1755–1833), Melville's paternal grandmother.

1776

Thomas Melvill becomes an artillery officer in the U.S. Navy and distinguishes himself fighting at Bunker Hill.

1778

Peter Gansevoort (1749–1812), Melville's maternal grandfather, marries Catherine Van Schaick (1751–1830), Melville's maternal grandmother. He descended from Harmen Harmense Van Gansevoort, a master brewer who emigrated from the Netherlands around 1656 and settled in Fort Orange, later named Albany, New York. Peter takes command of Fort Schuyler (later named Fort Stanwix), at a strategic point overlooking the route from the Hudson and Mohawk valleys to the Great Lakes. Gansevoort repels the British and their Indian allies, gaining a formidable reputation as a ruthless Indian fighter who burned Indian villages and starved their inhabitants.

1796

George Washington appoints Thomas Melvill naval officer of the Port of Boston.

1781

Lemuel Shaw, Melville's father-in-law, is born.

1782

Allan Melvill, Melville's father, is born.

1791

Maria Gansevoort, Melville's mother, is born.

1809

Washington Irving, under the pseudonym Diedrich Knickerbocker, publishes *A History of New York*.

1814

October 14: Allan Melvill marries Maria Gansevoort.

1815

December 6: Gansevoort Melville, Melville's brother, is born.

1816

Evert Duyckinck is born.

1817

August: Helen Maria Melville Griggs, Melville's sister, is born.

William Cullen Bryant publishes "Thanatopsis."

1818

New York surpasses Boston and Philadelphia in the volume of trade with Europe and the Far East. First steamboat travels on the Great Lakes.

1819

Melville's father, Allan, borrows $6,500 to start a business selling fancy dry goods.

July: A crowd gathers in the sweltering heat to witness the hanging of Rose Butler, a black woman accused of setting fire to combustibles in a stairwell where she worked.

August 1: **Melville is born in New York City. He is the third child (second son) of Allan Melvill (of Scottish descent) and Maria Gansevoort, daughter of**

---

* Events that concern Melville directly appear in bold; other events in regular type.

General Peter Gansevoort, American Revolutionary War hero, a slave owner, and head of a powerful Albany, New York, family. Melville's mother takes the family to Albany by an upriver steamer, hoping to avoid New York City's yellow fever epidemic.

November: The family returns to New York City. The robust American economy takes a temporary downturn. Walt Whitman is born.

1820

Allan Melvill moves his store to 134 Pearl Street near the family's home in the Battery. But his wife spends more time in Albany, keeping her children away from New York City's unsanitary streets with pigs and rats rooting in the garbage.

September: Allan finds a new house at 55 Cortlandt Street with more spacious accommodations.

Missouri Compromise: Maine enters Union as a free state, and Missouri as a slave state (in 1821). Washington Colonization Society founds Liberia in Africa for repatriation of slaves and free black men.

1821

August 24: Augusta, Melville's sister, is born.
Santa Fe Trail opens.

1822

As soon as the first yellow fever case of the summer is reported in New York City, Allan Melvill takes his family to Boston for a two-month stay.

1823

April 24: Allan, Melville's brother, is born.
October: The whole family falls ill with winter viruses.

December 2: Monroe Doctrine proclaimed opposing any European power colonizing any independent nation in the Western Hemisphere.

1824

March: Still hoping to find a house away from the damp of downtown New York City, Allan Melvill moves his family to 33 Bleecker Street, between Broadway and the Bowery. They spend the summer in their new home, an improvement over clammy Cortlandt Street.

1825

July: The first American ascends in a hot air balloon. Catherine, Melville's sister, is born.

1825

September: Melville begins four years at New York Male High School.

The Erie Canal opens, establishing a connection between New York City and the West.

1826

Melville and two of his sisters contract scarlet fever. The disease will impair his vision for the rest of his life.

Summer: Herman is sent to Albany, where he learns about the patroons of the Hudson Valley.

July 4: Both Thomas Jefferson and John Adams die, marking the end of the American Revolutionary War generation.

1827

August 26: Frances, Melville's sister, is born. Melville visits paternal grandparents in Boston.

1828

Herman Melville is named best speaker in the high school's Introductory department.

April 28: Allan Melvill moves his family into an elegant house at 675 Broadway, close to the Astors and other prominent members of New York society.

Noah Webster publishes the *American Dictionary of the English Language.* The Working Men's Party is founded in New York. The Baltimore and Ohio Railroad becomes the first passenger railroad in the U.S.

1829

July: Melville visits paternal grandparents in Boston.

The new administration of President Andrew Jackson inaugurates the spoils system, handing out jobs to prominent government supporters. Slavery is abolished in Mexico. David Walker's *Appeal,* a widely distributed pamphlet against slavery, appears.

1829–30

Melville attends Columbia Grammar School in New York.

1830

September: Allan Melvill's business fails.

October: Family moves to Albany and settles in a house at 338 North Market Street.

January 24: Thomas, Melville's youngest brother, is born. Herman attends Albany Academy for a year.

Revolution in Paris, Louis Philippe (1773–1850) becomes the French "citizen King." Fur trappers explore the Rocky Mountains. Emily Dickinson is born. Sir Charles Lyell's *Principles of Geology* is published.

1831

Allan Melvill borrows $2,000 from Peter Gansevoort to establish a fur-and-cap store at 364 South Market Street.

December: On a trip to New York City Allan Melvill fails to find customers for his new business. He arrives home exhausted and ill after exposure to subzero temperatures on the deck of a Hudson River steamer.

Charles Darwin (1809–82) sails as a naturalist on a surveying expedition in H.M.S. *Beagle* to South America, New Zealand, and Australia. William Lloyd

Garrison begins publishing the abolitionist periodical the *Liberator* in Boston. The first horse-drawn buses appear in New York City. Cyrus McCormick invents the reaper.

1832

January 28: **Allan Melvill dies in debt.**

Summer: **A cholera epidemic in Albany spurs Maria Melvill to take her family to Pittsfield, Massachusetts.**

New England Anti-Slavery Society founded in Boston. First horse-drawn trolleys appear in New York City.

1832–34

Melville is employed as clerk at the New York State Bank in Albany. Sometime during this period Melville's mother adds the final *e* to the family's name, hoping to separate the family from her husband's failures.

1833

Melville visits Pittsfield briefly.

Shipping magnate Frederic Tudor invents a way to ship ice to the tropical outposts of the British Empire. The *New York Sun,* the first successful penny daily newspaper, is founded. The General Trades Union is founded. Slavery is abolished in the British Empire.

1834–35

Melville works on his uncle Thomas's farm near Pittsfield, Massachusetts.

1835

Melville returns to Albany as bookkeeper and clerk in his brother's fur business. Enrolls in Albany's Classical School. Joins Albany's Young Man's Association.

Anti-abolitionist riots in New York City. Texas declares its right to secede from Mexico. Samuel Colt patents a revolving pistol. Samuel Clemens (Mark Twain) is born.

1836

Davy Crockett is killed at the Alamo. Texas wins independence from Mexico. Ralph Waldo Emerson publishes "Nature."

1836–37

September 1–March 1: **Melville attends Albany Academy again. Joins Ciceronian Debating Society.**

1837

April: **Melville's brother Gansevoort's business fails in the Panic of 1837. Banks tighten credit in a depression that lasts five years. Herman obtains position as teacher in Sikes District School near Pittsfield for the fall term, then returns to Albany.**

June: **Melville's Uncle Thomas moves to Galena, Illinois, hoping to recoup his fortune as a farmer.**

Nathaniel Hawthorne's *Twice-Told Tales* becomes a best-seller.

1838

March 24: **Melville publishes satirical remarks on the area's debating clubs in the *Albany Microscope*.**

May: **Confronted with mounting debts, Maria Melville moves her family to a less expensive two-family house in Lansingburgh, a small but elegant village 10 miles north of Albany. Herman works briefly on his uncle's farm in the summer and fall.**

November: **Herman returns to Lansingburgh and studies at the Lansingburgh Academy, receiving a certificate as a surveyor and engineer. Becomes president of Philo Logos debating society.** Underground Railroad begins transport of slaves to Canada. The Wilkes expedition sets out to circumnavigate the globe, to explore the South Polar region, to take soundings and make scientific observations. It is an age of discovery, with much of the world still to be mapped. England has 90 ships of the line, Russia 50, France 49, America 15.

1839

May: **Melville publishes "Fragments from a Writing Desk," signed L.A.V., in the *Democratic Press and Lansingburgh Advertiser*.**

May 23: **Maria Melville writes to her brother Peter Gansevoort, urging him to help her pay the balance of her rent.**

June 5–October 1: **Melville serves as crew member aboard the trading ship *St Lawrence*, which sails from New York to Liverpool and back. Under the name of "Harry the Reefer," publishes a sketch ("The Death Craft") that prefigures certain aspects of "Benito Cereno."**

American traveler John Lloyd Stephens (1805–52) discovers and explores the antiquities of the ancient Maya culture in Central America. Two British ships, the *Erebus* and the *Terror,* set off on an expedition to the Antarctic. Shipping magnate Samuel Cunard (1787–1865) establishes the British and North-American Royal Mail Steam Packet Company (later called the Cunard Line). Charles Goodyear (1800–60) invents "vulcanization," which makes the commercial production of rubber feasible. George D. Weed publishes influential antislavery pamphlet, "Slavery As It Is."

1839–40

Melville is a schoolteacher in Greenbush, New York, but has to leave when the school's board informs him they cannot pay his salary. Teaches as substitute in Brunswick, New York.

1840

Summer: **Travels to see his uncle Thomas in Galena, Illinois, taking with him a friend, Eli Fly. On their** way east they take a Mississippi River steamer (described in *The Confidence Man*). They visit St. Louis, explore Indian mounds, and then return to New York seeking employment (without success). Herman spends Christmas with his family in Lansingburgh.

Nelson's Column is erected in Trafalgar Square, London, to commemorate his great victory over the French fleet in 1805. The Blue Riband is awarded to the S.S. *Britannia* for the fastest crossing of the Atlantic. The United States has 2,816 miles of railroad in operation. The bicycle is invented.

1841

January 3: **Melville sails from New Bedford, Massachusetts, on the whaling ship *Acushnet*.**

March: **Stops at Rio de Janeiro. Experiences his first whale hunt off the coast of Brazil.**

April: **Rounds Cape Horn.**

May: **Stopping for 10 days at Callao, the *Acushnet* has 200 barrels of oil in its hold.**

June: **Visits Peru.**

August: **The *Acushnet* adds another 350 barrels of oil to its hold. Fall and winter are spent cruising the Galápagos Islands.**

December: **Captain Pease, the *Acushnet*'s captain, falls ill and treats his men badly. Melville meets William Henry Chase, son of Owen Chase, author of *Narrative of the Most Extraordinary and Distressing Shipwreck of the Whale-Ship Essex* (1821), who loans Melville a copy of the book, which Melville has been eager to read for some time.**

U.S.S. *Creole* is taken over by slaves on a trip from Virginia to Louisiana. They sail into Nassau and declare themselves free. Overland migration to California begins. Ralph Waldo Emerson publishes *Essays, First Series*. P. T. Barnum opens the "American Museum" in New York City. The *New York Tribune* begins publishing. The first university degrees are granted to American women.

1842

July 9: **Melville deserts with Richard Tobias Greene at Nuku Hiva in the Marquesas. Lives for a month in the Taipi valley.**

August 9: **Melville departs on the Australian whaler, *Lucy-Ann*. Twelve of the 32–man crew had already deserted on this poorly equipped and badly run ship. Their captain, Ventom, was described as a "petty tyrant" with a "nasty temper." Melville later drew on this appalling episode for *Omoo*. He is shackled and put off the ship in Tahiti as a mutineer. His British jailer allows him freedom during the day if he promises to return at night when authorities come to inspect the jail.**

October: **Escapes by canoe with John B. Troy and explores Tahiti and Eimeo. Works on a potato farm.**

November 7: **Sails on Nantucket whaler *Charles & Henry*. A cousin, Guert Gansevoort, puts down a mutiny aboard the U.S. brig *Somers*.** Charles Dickens publishes *American Notes*. Henry Wadsworth Longfellow publishes *Poems of Slavery*. Washington Irving is appointed ambassador to Spain. Boston and Albany are connected by railroad. Anesthesia is first used in surgery.

1843

May 2: **Melville is discharged in Lahaina, Hawaii.**

July 13: **In Honolulu, begins work as a clerk-book-keeper at an annual salary of $150 to be paid quarterly. He is also provided with board, lodging, and laundry. He sells supplies and takes inventory.**

August 19: **Enlists in the U.S. Navy and sails on the frigate *United States*. Meets and befriends John J. Chase. Visits Marquesas, Tahiti, Valparaiso, Callao.**

October 6: **In Nuku Hiva (the Marquesas) Melville observes the gangs of convicts the French have brought in to construct a fortress and to supply an arsenal. Reads Charles Darwin's *Narrative of the Surveying Voyages of His Majesty's ships Adventure and Beagle*, George's *History of the United States*, and Hough's *Military Law Authorities*. Befriends ship-mate Ephraim Curtiss Hine, author of *The Haunted Barque and Other Poems* (1848). Melville would later draw on Hine for his depiction of "Lemsford the Poet" in *White Jacket*.**

S.S. *Great Britain*, the first propeller-driven ship to cross the Atlantic, is launched at Bristol. Congress grants Samuel Morse $30,000 to build the first telegraph line between Washington and Baltimore.

1844

January: **Melville visits Lima.**

Spring: **Visits Mazatlán.**

Summer: **Visits Rio de Janeiro.**

October 2: **Sails around Race Point into Cape Cod Bay. Melville tastes fresh cod for the first time in four years.**

October 3: **Arrives in Boston. Visits the Bunker Hill Monument, an Egyptian obelisk 221 feet high, situated on a hill overlooking Charlestown. Melville writes a dedication to the monument in *Israel Potter*.**

October 14: **Discharged from the navy. Melville would later write about the navy as the "asylum for the perverse, the home of the unfortunate." Returns to his mother's home in Lansingburgh.**

First message by Morse's telegraph is sent. Emerson's *Essays, Second Series* is published.

1845

Melville begins work on *Typee*. Takes over his mother's big attic as his writing den. Peruses Charles S. Stewart's *A Visit to the South Seas, in the U.S. Ship Vincennes, During the Years 1829 and 1830*, William

Ellis's *Polynesian Researches*, and Captain David Porter's *Journal of a Cruise Made to the Pacific Ocean in the U.S. Frigate Essex.*

July: Gansevoort Melville is appointed secretary to the American legation in London by the new Polk administration. Herman submits manuscript of *Typee* to Harper & Brothers, which rejects it.

November/December: Travels to Boston, either to visit his intended wife's relatives or to look for a job in the Custom House where his grandfather had worked. Gansevoort, advised by a friend at Harper's, shows the manuscript to the British publisher John Murray, who accepts the book on December 13. Murray offers the neophyte author a contract for a two-volume edition of 1,000 copies. Melville is to receive an advance of £100 at half profits.

Edgar Allan Poe publishes *The Raven and Other Poems.* U.S. Naval Academy at Annapolis is opened.

1846–48

Mexican War.

1846

January: Washington Irving, American minister in Madrid, visits London, and Gansevoort tells him about his brother's book. Gansevoort reads excerpts to Irving, who admires the author's "graphic" style and "exquisite" descriptions.

February 27: Murray publishes *Typee* in London.

March 4: Murray confesses to Gansevoort that he suspects *Typee* is more fiction than fact. He proposes tempering the book's more sensational aspects. Gansevoort falls ill with a severe headache, followed by partial blindness. Several of his teeth are also extracted, but his illness worsens.

March 20: Wiley & Putnam publish *Typee* in New York.

April 3: Gansevoort writes Herman that he fears he is "breaking up." His request to relinquish his embassy duties is granted.

May 12: Gansevoort, Melville's brother, dies of tubercular meningitis in London. A memorial service is held in Westminster Abbey. Twelve people, mostly Americans, attend.

May 29: Herman and his family learn of Gansevoort's death. By steamer Herman takes a 20-hour trip to New York to take charge of his brother's body. He apparently reacts to the death with restraint, writing to Peter Gansevoort about removing the "remains" to Albany. In Buffalo, Richard Tobias Greene publicly supports Melville's version of events in *Typee.*

August: A revised edition of the book appears in New York with an addition, "The Story of Toby," Melville's response to his friend's public account and to the charge that the book is really fiction.

November: Travels to New York City and confers with Evert Duyckinck about *Omoo,* asking his advice

as a "friend," not as an editor at Wiley & Putnam. Duyckinck approves of Melville's work and recommends it to his brother George, remarking "his account of the church building there [in Tahiti] is very much in the spirit of Dickens's humorous handling of sacred things in Italy."

December 18: Melville signs a contract with Harper & Brothers to publish *Omoo.*

President Polk declares war on Mexico. Brigham Young leads the Mormons to the Great Salt Lake in Utah. The Smithsonian Institution is founded in Washington, D.C. Famine in Ireland is precipitated by the failure of the potato crop. Elias Howe invents the sewing machine.

1847

January: Evert Duyckinck is named chief editor of a new weekly, the *Literary World.* He asks Melville if he can publish a part of *Omoo,* but Melville prefers to wait for book publication and instead writes a review of J. Ross Browne's *Etchings of a Whaling Cruise* and Captain Ringbolt's *Sailor's Life and Sailor's Yarns.* Neither book quite satisfies Melville: the former presents just facts without a compelling style; the latter is pleasant but lacks profundity.

February 1: Ships proof sheet of *Omoo* to his agent John Brodhead in London; attends Donizetti opera *Lucia di Lammermoor* at Palmo's Opera House. Murray offers £150 in promissory notes provided that sales are good.

February 4: Melville travels to Washington, D.C., to see federal officials whom Gansevoort had supported in the 1844 campaign. He hopes to secure a position in the Treasury Department, but given Melville's lack of political experience and his brother's death, nothing is done to find him employment.

March 9: Travels to Boston, evidently to ask Judge Lemuel Shaw for his daughter Elizabeth's hand in marriage. Shaw, Chief Justice of the Massachusetts Supreme Court and an old friend of the Melvilles, is concerned about Herman's prospects as a writer, but he is also impressed by the young man's openness and drive.

March 27: John Murray publishes 4,000 copies of *Omoo* in London. The first printing sells out in one week.

May 1: Harper publishes *Omoo* in New York.

May 4: Melville visits New York and sees Thomas Cole's epic painting series *The Course of Empire.* Cole's amalgamation of historical and allegorical motifs will figure in Melville's next book, *Mardi and a Voyage Thither.*

July 30: Dines with Evert Duyckinck, who confides to his diary that Melville, a writer in the vein of Washington Irving, is about to be married and is "cheerful company." The next evening Melville's friends treat him to a bachelor party.

August 4: **Marries Elizabeth Shaw in Boston. The couple honeymoon in New Hampshire and Canada, and then move in with Melville's mother in Lansingburgh.**

October: **Finding Lansingburgh too confining and wanting access to New York City's literary life, Melville and his brother Allan purchase a brownstone at 103 Fourth Avenue, between 11th and 12th Streets. Their mothers and sisters also move in. Melville befriends literary figures Evert Duyckinck and Cornelius Matthews and writes for their journals,** *Literary World and Yankee Doodle.* **Evert Duyckinck takes Melville to the opening of the American Art-Union. The novelist sees more of Cole's work as well as that of the painters Edward Hicks and Thomas Sully. At the exhibition Melville meets the poet William Cullen Bryant and the genre painter William Sydney Mount. Duyckinck observes that Melville seems very happy in his new family arrangement. The novelist devotes himself to a life structured around his new work.**

Christmas Eve: **Melville and his wife attend the Astor Place Theater. When her brother arrives, they take him to see the view from Trinity Church and then they go to a performance of Donizetti's** *Lucrezia Borgia* **and to a party of friends afterward.**

1848–49
California gold rush.

1848
February 14: **Herman and Elizabeth Melville attend poet Anna Charlotte Lynch's annual Valentine party. There they meet several literary lights: Fitz-Greene Halleck, Nathaniel Parker Willis, Bayard Taylor, Charles Fenno Hoffman, Parke Godwin, Henry T. Tuckerman, Felix Darley, G. P. A. Healy, Seba Smith, Caroline Kirkland, Grace Greenwood, William Cullen Bryant, Catharine Maria Sedgwick, the renowned preacher Dr. Orville Dewey, and the engraver and painter Asher Durand.**

May 5: **Elizabeth Melville shows the first strains of living with an intense, dedicated author. This usually confident woman seems distracted and less than articulate in her letters. Her proximity to authorship (she has been copying the final pages of her husband's manuscript) takes its toll. Part of the problem is that Melville's new work,** *Mardi,* **is taking a new direction, and his publisher, John Murray, is reluctant to publish what he deems a "romance."**

June: **Melville purchases a translation of Dante's** *Divine Comedy,* **which helps him to extend the allegorical approach of** *Mardi.*

August: **Husband and wife travel to Pittsfield for a vacation. They stay at Melvill House, an inn owned by Melville's aunt Mary, the widowed wife of his uncle Thomas. Melville leaves his pregnant wife at** her parents' home while he returns to New York to finish his book. He reads William Makepeace Thackeray's *Vanity Fair* during breaks from writing.

The New York State legislature passes the Married Woman's Property Act, under which a married woman could retain her personal property if she could prove charges of abuse by her husband. Without a judgment in her favor, however, a woman could lose everything. Lucretia Mott and Elizabeth Cady Stanton organize a convention of women in Seneca Falls, New York, announcing a "Declaration of Sentiments" comparing male domination to British repression and women's rights a principle as important as the liberties fought for in the American Revolution. John Jacob Astor, the wealthiest landlord in New York, dies.

Louis Philippe's reign in France ends and revolutionary fervor sweeps Europe. Austrians demand greater autonomy from their absolutist system of government. The Magyars (Hungarians) agitate for complete independence and the end of the Austro-Hungarian Empire. Editor Horace Greeley dispatches Margaret Fuller to report on the revolution in Rome for the *New York Daily Tribune.* Karl Marx and Friedrich Engels publish *The Communist Manifesto.* Serfdom is abolished in Austria. In England, the Chartists demand democratic changes such as a secret ballot and universal male suffrage, but their program is not adopted by Parliament.

In America, the presidential campaign year is marked by debates over the Wilmot Proviso, which proposes a ban on slavery in the new territories captured from Mexico. In New York, antislavery Democrats hold their own convention opposing the majority position of the party, which tolerates slavery as a means of preserving the Union. The New York News Agency (in 1856 renamed the Associated Press) is established. Lewis Temple, an African-American blacksmith in New Bedford, invents a new harpoon, a vast improvement over the traditional barbed spear. Indians had used stone-headed spears and arrows to hunt whales. Temple perfected the toggle iron, with blades that expanded on impact, ripping and grasping whale flesh.

1849
January: **Melville ships proofs of** *Mardi* **to John Murray. Requests £200. He rejoins his wife in Boston and attends one of Ralph Waldo Emerson's lectures. Expecting to find Emerson "full of transcendentalisms, myths & oracular gibberish," Melville is surprised to find him "quite intelligible." He also attends a reading by the acclaimed British actress Fanny Kemble. Her interpretation of Desdemona is like that of a "boarding school miss," he protests, but she is a "glorious Lady Macbeth."**

He finds her curiously masculine, and wonders what a private examination of her would reveal. His biographer, Laurie Robertson-Lorant, calls this an "uncharacteristically crude remark." The expectant parents spend two months in Boston. Melville reads Emerson's essays, Seneca's moral philosophy, and essays by Eastlake and Hazlitt on the methods of modern painters and principles of aesthetics. Begins work on *Redburn*.

February 16: Malcolm, a son, is born in Boston.

March 16: Richard Bentley publishes *Mardi* in London.

April 14: Harper publishes *Mardi* in New York.

May 7: At the Astor Place Theater, a mob protests the performance of Macbeth by the English actor William Macready. They are incensed that their favorite, the renowned actor Edwin Forrest, also performing Macbeth, should have to contend with this foreign interloper. Melville joins 47 prominent New Yorkers—among them Washington Irving and Evert Duyckinck—defending Macready's right to appear. In spite of their signed petition, a crowd of Forrest supporters storms the theater three days later, attempting to disrupt Macready's performance. The violence begins with the throwing of bottles and stones. As the mob gathers strength, the militia is mustered. Soldiers fire into the crowd estimated at 25,000, and 22 people are killed, with 36 more wounded. Altogether, the riot injures 100 people. Eighty-six men are incarcerated.

Summer: Melville works through a steamy summer in New York, finishing *White-Jacket* near the end of September, undaunted by a cholera epidemic. At a New York bookstall, Melville becomes intrigued with a small book of memoirs, *The Life and Remarkable Adventures of Israel R. Potter (A Native of Cranston, Rhode Island), Who was a Soldier in the American Revolution.*

September 29: Richard Bentley publishes *Redburn*, a popular success, in London.

October 11: Travels to London to see his publishers, asking for $500 for *White-Jacket*. Bentley gives Melville £100 owing him for *Redburn* and £200 for the first one thousand copies of *White-Jacket*. Worried about piracy, Bentley feels he can offer no more and reminds Melville that the firm did not make a profit on *Mardi*.

November 13: Before dawn a crowd gathers to witness the execution of George and Maria Manning, a married couple. They had conspired to murder a friend and then turned against each other when apprehended. Melville commented on the "brutish crowd" and the unusual spectacle of this couple being "hung side by side—still unreconciled to each other." How so much must have changed, he speculated, from the day they had married. Melville does not know that in the crowd another writer, Charles Dickens, also watches the event, finding the crowd nearly as wicked as the condemned couple.

November 14: Harper's publishes *Redburn* in New York.

November 17: Visits a gallery "full of gems," including Guido Reni's *St. John in the Wilderness*, Nicholas Poussin's *Assumption of the Virgin*, Joshua Reynold's portraits as well as work by Titian and the Dutch and Flemish masters. The genre paintings in particular are like strolling through "green meadows & woodlands steeped in haze," comments Melville, who feels a "profound calm."

November 24: Enjoying his success in London, Melville puts down in his journal that he had returned to his rooms at midnight with "an indefinite quantity of Champaigne [sic] Sherry, Old Port, Hock, Madeira, & Claret in me."

November 27: He embarks to tour the Continent, taking a Channel steamer, the *Emerald* for Boulogne. By late afternoon his train has arrived in Paris. He finds the city's sites alternately beautiful and bizarre.

Edgar Allan Poe dies.

1850

January 23: Bentley publishes *White-Jacket* in London.

February: Melville returns to New York.

March: Reviews James Fenimore Cooper's novel *The Red Rover* in *The Literary World*. Like the work Melville is beginning to contemplate, Cooper's novel centers on a character who embodies the ambiguities of identity.

March 21: Harper publishes *White-Jacket* in New York.

April 29: Melville renews his membership in the New York Society Library and begins reviewing work he has read on sea voyages. He is attracted to the story of Mocha Dick, a whale, a story the *Knickerbocker* published in 1839.

July: The Melvilles move to Pittsfield for the summer. At the end of the month Melville returns to New York to escort his mother and sisters to Pittsfield. At the same time, he invites his literary colleagues Evert Duyckinck and Cornelius Matthews to Melvill House for a week.

August 5: Meets and befriends Nathaniel Hawthorne; publishes "Hawthorne and His Mosses" in the *Literary World*.

August 9: Melville begins work on his review of Hawthorne's *Mosses from an Old Manse*.

August 10: Duyckinck takes the review back to New York for publication in the *Literary World*, it appears in two parts on August 17 and 24.

September 14: With help from his father-in-law Melville purchases a 160-acre farm near Pittsfield. By early October his family is in residence at what he calls Arrowhead. The Compromise of 1850 limits the spread of slavery, but Congress also enacts the Fugitive Slave Law, forcing Northerners to return slaves escaping from the South. Judge Shaw, who opposes slavery, and who has judged cases on the state level refusing to return slaves, is put in an uncomfortable position. He decides not to resign his judgeship, disappointing some of his fervent abolitionist friends.

October 4: Ex-slave Frederick Douglass speaks at Faneuil Hall in Boston, stimulating the formation of the Boston Vigilance Committee headed by Richard Dana Jr. Eighty members vow to aid fugitive slaves. The Astor family collects $100,000 a year in rents. **The narrator of "Bartleby, the Scrivener" accords Astor reverential respect.** Nathaniel Hawthorne publishes *The Scarlet Letter.* Emerson publishes "Representative Men." *Harper's Magazine* is founded.

1851

March: **Melville learns that his old friend Eli James Murdock Fly is destitute and invalided. Melville escorts Fly to Springfield, Massachusetts, where he embarks on a train for Brattleboro, Vermont, to try the "water-cure."**

April 11: **Melville helps deliver a clock and bedstead to Nathaniel Hawthorne.**

August 1: **Melville pays a surprise call on the Hawthornes. The two writers "talk about time and eternity, things of this world and of the next, and books, and publishers, and all possible and impossible matters, that lasted pretty deep into the night." (Robertson-Lorant)**

October 18: **Bentley publishes a handsome three-volume edition of *Moby-Dick* in London.**

November 14: **Harper publishes *Moby-Dick* (dedicated to Hawthorne) in New York. The American edition is also sumptuous: 2,915 copies embossed with gilt life preservers. Reviewers complain about the $1.50 price—very high for the period.**

October 22: **Stanwix, a second son, is born.** James Fenimore Cooper dies. Hawthorne publishes *The House of the Seven Gables.* The schooner *America* wins the race around the Isle of Wight and brings the America's Cup to the U.S. The *New York Times* publishes its first issue.

1852

July: **After visiting Melville at Arrowhead, Judge Shaw takes him to New Bedford and Nantucket to meet some of his friends.**

August 6: **Harper publishes *Pierre* in New York.**

November: **Sampson Low publishes *Pierre* in London.**

Winter: **Works on a novella, "The Isle of the Cross." Along with Washington Irving and William Cullen Bryant, as well as other writers, Melville peti-**tions Congress to institute international publishing agreements to protect the copyrights of authors, but Congress takes no action.**

Harriet Beecher Stowe's *Uncle Tom's Cabin* is published and sells a record 300,000 copies in one year. Hiram Powers's sculpture *The Greek Slave* causes a sensation when it is put on display in New York's Crystal Palace.

1853

May 22: **Elizabeth, a daughter, is born. Melville's health suffers. Friends and family try (unsuccessfully) to secure a consulship for him. Financial difficulties, strains in the marriage and family life, and sickness mark the Melville household for the next 25 years. At Harper's, a fire destroys many of Melville's unsold books.**

June: **Melville travels to New York to show his manuscript of "The Isle of the Cross" to Harper's.**

1854

Melville promises Harper's the delivery of several manuscripts based on stories he is writing. Plans for several books, however, including "The Isle of the Cross," never fructify.

March: **During a period of harsh storms Melville works at the sketches that will form part of *The Piazza Tales*.**

May: Thomas Wentworth Higginson and other militant abolitionists storm a Boston jail to free Anthony Burns, a fugitive slave, even as Judge Shaw is hearing arguments in the case. Higginson and his forces fail to obtain Burns's release and a deputy is killed in the melee. Higginson, along with Theodore Parker and Wendell Phillips, are charged with obstruction of justice. Their case is thrown out of court. Judge Shaw rules that Burns be returned to his owner. William Lloyd Garrison burns copies of the United States Constitution, the Fugitive Slave Law, and Shaw's court decision.

September 24: **Melville drives through a snowstorm to visit his cousin Priscilla, a seamstress.**

U.S. Senate ratifies Gadsden Purchase for acquisition of parts of southern New Mexico and Arizona. "War for Bleeding Kansas" between pro- and antislavery forces. The Republican Party is formed. S.S. *Brandon* is launched as the first ship with compound expansion engines. The railroad reaches the Mississippi. Henry David Thoreau publishes *Walden, or Life in the Woods. Putnam's Monthly Magazine* is founded.

1854–55

July–March: Israel Potter **is serialized in *Putnam's Monthly Magazine.***

1855

February: **Melville suffers acutely from sciatica. Nevertheless, he attends a literary party in honor of the visiting William Makepeace Thackeray.**

March: **Putnam publishes *Israel Potter* in New York. Frances, a second daughter, is born (March 2). Melville is afflicted with both rheumatism and sciatica and is treated by Oliver Wendell Holmes.**

April: **The *Albany Evening Journal* and other eastern newspapers are full of accounts of one William Thompson, a man of many aliases and a swindler par excellence. He is referred to as a "confidence-man." He is undoubtedly one of the models for Melville's character by the same name.**

May: **George Routledge publishes *Israel Potter* in London.**

Spring: **Melville nears completion of "Benito Cereno."**

The first iron Cunard steamer crosses the Atlantic in nine and a half days. Walt Whitman publishes *Leaves of Grass;* he also calls New York the most radical city in America. **Evert Duyckinck publishes the *Cyclopaedia of American Literature,* which includes an entry on Melville.**

1856

May: **Dix & Edwards publishes *The Piazza Tales* in New York; Sampson Low distributes this edition in London.**

October 11: **With financial help from his father-in-law, Melville embarks on a journey to the Holy Land, stopping first in Glasgow. He also visits Hawthorne in Liverpool. "Herman Melville came to see me at the Consulate," Hawthorne wrote, "looking much as he used to do (a little paler, and perhaps a little sadder), in a rough outside coat, and with his characteristic gravity and reserve of manner. . . . Melville has not been well, of late; he has been affected with neuralgic complaints in his head and limbs, and no doubt has suffered from too constant literary occupations, pursued without much success, latterly; and his writings, for a long while past, have indicated a morbid state of mind." Melville resumes his trip, departing for the Middle East, Greece and Italy.**

New Year's Eve: **Melville and one of his fellow travelers, Dr. Lockwood, ride donkeys toward the Valley of the Nile.**

New York's *Weekly Times* decries the Fillmore administration's support of William Walker, an American soldier of fortune who invades Nicaragua and declares himself its president. Massacre of Potawatomie Creek, Kansas. Proslavery gang murders antislavery agitators for admission of Kansas as a free state.

1857

New Year's Day: **Melville returns to Alexandria to arrange passage to the Holy Land.**

January 6: **Melville's ship lands at Jaffa and he proceeds immediately to Jerusalem.**

January 18: **Leaves Jerusalem with a question: "Is the desolation of the land the result of the fatal embrace of the Deity?"**

February 5: **Melville journeys through Rhodes "afflicted with the great curse of modern travel— skepticism."**

April 1: **Dix & Edwards publish *The Confidence Man* in New York; Longman, Brown, Green, Longmans & Roberts publish *The Confidence Man* in London. Melville arrives in the city by the end of April. He walks through Hyde Park and Kensington Gardens, visits Madame Tussaud's wax museum and the Crystal Palace (built for the 1851 Great Exhibition and lavishly praised as a noble structure by others). Melville finds it "a vast toy" and "overdone."**

May 4: **Returns to Liverpool for voyage to New York. He declares in a poem of this time: "We sham, we shuffle while faith declines."**

May 20: **Arrives in New York.**

October: **Melville begins a three-year effort to make a living as a lecturer, with meager results.**

Europe and America experience high inflation. The gold rush has set off frantic speculation in land and railroad stocks; the Crimean War has stimulated overproduction of staples such as grain. There is panic on Wall Street. Businesses go bankrupt. Tensions over slavery worsen with the passage of the Kansas-Nebraska Act.

William Walker is hailed as a hero after he returns to the U.S., having been expelled from Nicaragua.

The Dred Scott case is decided by the Supreme Court: The ruling stipulates that slaves cannot bring legal actions. Not only is Scott's case thrown out, but he also is ordered back to his owner in Missouri. (Scott argued that his domicile in a free territory rendered his reenslavement unconstitutional.)

American engineer E. G. Otis installs the first safety elevator in New York. The transatlantic cable between New York and London is laid.

1858

Melville lectures in the South (Tennessee area) and in the Midwest (Ohio area).

Lincoln-Douglas debates take place. New York Symphony Orchestra gives its first concert. S.S. *Great Eastern,* the largest ship of its time (27,000 tons), is launched. First stagecoach line from Missouri to Pacific Coast is established.

1859

Melville lectures in Baltimore, Wisconsin, New York, and Massachusetts.

First oil well in U.S. is drilled in Titusville, Pennsylvania. The steamroller and the first practical storage battery are invented. Gold is discovered in Colorado and Nevada. Charles Darwin's *Origin of Species* is published. Washington Irving dies.

1860

May 28: **Melville travels on the clipper ship** *Meteor* **to San Francisco as a guest of the captain, his brother Thomas.**

November 12: **Returns to New York via Panama. His brother Allan tells him that his book of poems has not found a publisher.**

The New York population numbers 813,699 citizens. Twelve thousand are free blacks, slavery having been outlawed in 1827. The city relies on the cotton trade, which nets $200 million a year. Western wheat is another important staple. Seventy-five percent of the nation's imports are handled by the city's port. New York bankers dread a war if Southern planters, squeezed by Republican antislavery policies, cannot repay bank loans. In the city there is a deep division between abolitionists and a populace now full of immigrants, especially the Irish, who fear the idea of freedom for all blacks, who would then flood the labor market working for cheap wages. Banker Richard Lathers assembles members of the Democratic Vigilant Association to extend an appeal to the South, proposing that slaves gradually be emancipated and returned to Africa. He fears, as do other bankers, that England would enter an American Civil War on the side of the South because of the importance of cotton to the British economy.

On February 15, Abraham Lincoln arrives in New York to give a speech at Cooper Union. Over 1,500 show up in spite of a snowstorm. He argues eloquently for opposing the spread of slavery and for preserving the Union. Gathering support in New York, he begins to make progress toward the Republican nomination. He is elected president in November. South Carolina secedes from the Union in protest.

The Marble Faun, Hawthorne's last novel, is published. American inventor Christopher L. Sholes invents the first typewriter. The Pony Express runs from Missouri to California.

1861

February 18: Jefferson Davis is inaugurated as president of the Confederacy. President-elect Lincoln travels through New York on the way to Washington amidst rumors of a Southern plot to stop him from taking office.

March 12: **Melville travels to Washington, attends one of Lincoln's receptions. He reports to his wife: "Ladies in full dress by the hundred. A steady stream of two-&-twos wound thro' the apartments shaking hands with 'Old Abe' . . . without cessation for an hour & a half. Of course I was one of the shakers. Old Abe is much better looking [than] I expected & younger looking. He shook hands like a good fellow—working hard at it like a man sawing wood at so**

much per cord. Mrs. Lincoln is rather good looking I thought. The scene was very fine altogether. Superb furniture—flood of light—magnificent flowers—full band of music & c." Melville is seeking a consular appointment. Judge Shaw dies and has an Easter funeral.**

Washington Peace Convention tries to preserve the Union, but the Congress of Montgomery forms the Confederate States of America with South Carolina, Georgia, Alabama, Mississippi, Florida, and Louisiana.

April 13: Walt Whitman, walking down Broadway after the opera, hears the news of the Confederate onslaught against Fort Sumter. The next day, Lincoln calls on the state militias, asking for 75,000 men to defend Washington, D.C. West Virginia separates from Virginia and remains loyal to the Union. Telegraph links East and West. **Henry Sanford Gansevoort, Melville's cousin, is in New York's Seventh Regiment.**

June: **Melville and Evert Duyckinck visit Guert Gansevoort, now on shore duty at the Brooklyn Navy Yard.**

July 21: Early Confederate victories like Bull Run convince many New York businessmen that the Union cannot win the war.

August: **Melville travels to Boston, where his wife has been staying, and the family reassembles in Albany. The Melvilles live in New York during the winter but celebrate Christmas and New Year's in Boston. Melville again suffers from rheumatism.**

Elizabeth Cady Stanton lobbies the New York legislature to abolish the "legalized slavery" of women. Specifically, she wants wife-beating made grounds for divorce. The legislature rejects the proposed law, and New York is one of six states that do not allow divorce or separation because of cruelty.

1862

Melville lives briefly in Pittsfield and is badly injured when he is thrown from a wagon.

Union forces capture Fort Henry, Roanoke Island, Fort Donelson, Jacksonville, and New Orleans; they are defeated at second Battle of Bull Run and Fredericksburg. R. J. Gatling (1818–1903) invents the 10-barrel gun, named after him. Henry David Thoreau dies.

1863

January 1: President Lincoln issues the Emancipation Proclamation, freeing slaves in states rebelling against the Union.

February: **Melville is slowly recovering from a bout of rheumatism.**

Summer: **The Melvilles are in the Berkshires and celebrate July 4 with fireworks.**

July 11: The draft lottery is announced.

July 12: New York City protestors take to the streets to oppose the draft and the despotism of the federal government. On Broadway, whites march with a "No Draft" banner. Irish gangs begin a spree of violence, tearing up railroad tracks, smashing windows with paving stones, and ripping down telegraph wires. The rioters loot an arms factory. The damage spreads from lower to upper Manhattan as lower-class whites and immigrants vent their rage against African Americans and wealthier Americans who can buy their way out of the draft. Draft offices are burned. Even the mayor's home is attacked, provoking a call for federal troops.

July 14: Federal troops are brought into New York City from the Brooklyn Navy Yard and West Point. **Melville writes a poem, "The House-top: A Night Place," from the perspective of a man watching the riots: "No sleep. The sultriness pervades the air / And binds the brain—a dense oppression, such / As tawny tigers feel in matted shades, / Vexing their blood and making apt for ravage."**

August: **Husband and wife leave their children for a vacation / second honeymoon, touring Bash-Bish Falls, Mount Everett, Copake, Great Barrington, Monterey, and the hill towns of Becket, Savoy, and Cummington. Elizabeth Melville writes: "We passed through some of the wildest and most enchanting scenery, both mountain and valley and I cannot sufficiently congratulate myself that I have seen it before leaving Berkshire."**

October: **Family leaves Arrowhead in a swap for a New York house (104 East 26th Street) owned by Melville's brother Allan.**

Fifth Avenue becomes the most fashionable street in the city, supplanting Broadway. Confederate victories at Chancellorsville, Virginia; defeats at Gettysburg, Pennsylvania, and Vicksburg, Mississippi; surrender at Fort Hudson; further defeat at Chattanooga, Tennessee; victory at Chickamauga, Georgia. Lincoln delivers the Gettysburg Address at the dedication of a military cemetery.

1864

February: **Melville pays off his Harper's debt. His mother falls ill.**

March: **George Duyckinck dies.**

April: **Visits his cousin, Colonel Henry Gansevoort, in an army camp on the Virginia front.**

May 19: Nathaniel Hawthorne dies. Admiral Farragut sinks the Confederate ironclad *Tennessee.* He is said to exclaim, "Damn the torpedoes! Full speed ahead!" General Philip Sheridan routs Jubal Early's forces at Cedar Creek. General Ulysses S. Grant succeeds General Halleck as commander in chief of the Union armies. General Sherman marches his army from Chattanooga through Georgia; defeats

Confederate army at Atlanta; occupies Savannah. Confederate agents set Barnum Museum and Astor House on fire as part of plot to burn down New York City.

1865

January 21: Congress passes the Thirteenth Amendment, abolishing slavery.

February 2: John Rock, an African-American attorney and physician, is admitted to practice before the Massachusetts Supreme Judicial Court.

February 6: Robert E. Lee is given supreme command over the weakening Confederate armies. Confederate currency has become worthless. Food is scarce in the South's devastated areas. People are eating their pets.

March 3: Abraham Lincoln takes the oath of office for his second term, urging his countrymen to "bind up the nation's wounds; to care for him who shall have borne the battles, and for his widow, and his orphan—to do all which may achieve and cherish a just and lasting peace, among ourselves, and with all nations." Union fleet takes Charleston; Richmond, Virginia, surrenders to Grant; Jefferson Davis appoints Robert E. Lee general in chief of the Confederate army.

April 9: Lee surrenders to Grant at Appomattox.

April 14: Lincoln is assassinated. Jefferson Davis, president of the Confederacy, is captured and imprisoned.

May: *Drum-Taps,* Walt Whitman's sequence of Civil War poems, is published.

May 26: The Civil War ends.

Summer: **Intensely involved with writing his Civil War poems, Melville nevertheless takes frequent breaks for exercise and to help family members. He assists his sister Augusta in distributing cakes and other sweets to the Sabbath (Sunday) schools. His health has improved considerably.**

The Ku Klux Klan is founded. The first train holdup occurs, at North Bend, Ohio. The Atlantic cable is completed. Joseph Lister initiates antiseptic surgery by using carbolic acid on a compound wound. First oil pipeline (six miles) is constructed in Pennsylvania. The first railroad sleeping cars are designed by George Pullman. Matthew Arnold publishes *Essays in Criticism.* The *San Francisco Examiner* and *San Francisco Chronicle* are founded.

Maria Mitchell, possibly the model for Urania in Melville's poem "After the Pleasure Party," is the first woman appointed as professor of astronomy at Vassar College.

1866

August 17: **Harper's publishes Melville's *Battle-Pieces and Aspects of the War* in New York. It is dedicated to "the memory of the three hundred thousand who in**

the war for the maintenance of the Union fell devotedly under the flag of their fathers." An item in the *New York Herald* includes the comment: "For ten years the public has wondered what has become of Melville."

December 5: Melville is appointed deputy inspector of customs at the port of New York. He takes an oath, swearing that he has "never voluntarily borne arms against the United States." He signs an affidavit affirming that he will "support the Constitution of the United States." He is issued a numbered tin badge to be worn on his lapel and "a set of government locks, a record book or two, forms and stationery." The position requires him to work six days a week. His only time off is for national holidays and a two-week vacation. He is paid $4 a day or approximately $1,200 a year, "a pittance," one of his relatives remarked. It was the same salary Hawthorne received during his employment at the Salem Custom-House in 1846. Even on his low salary, Melville was expected to contribute two percent of his salary to the Republican State Committee.

The National Labor Union is established. It advocates "equal pay for equal work" and the inclusion of women and African Americans in the labor movement. The Fourteenth Amendment is passed, prohibiting voting discrimination, denying public office to certain Confederates, and repudiating Confederate war debt.

1867

May: A legal separation is discussed after Melville's wife and minister conclude he is mentally unbalanced. Given the laws of the time, Elizabeth Melville would forfeit everything—children, home, and all property—if she should leave her husband. Rumors circulate that Melville sometimes beats his wife.

September 10: Malcolm, the Melvilles' son, stays out until 3:00 A.M. His anxious mother asks him where he has been. He has been out with a friend to parties and a nightclub, he replies. She chides him for coming home so late but kisses him goodnight, and he goes to bed. He has not been drinking, as far as his mother can tell.

September 11: Malcolm does not appear in the morning. He answers his sister's call, but he does not come out of his room. Melville, apparently in a temper, tells the family to leave Malcolm alone: if he is late for work, he will have to pay the consequences. Malcolm remains in his room all day. Melville returns quite late from work, finds his son's door locked, and breaks into the room. Malcolm is curled up on his bed in his nightclothes with a pistol in his right hand. Melville sees the bullet hole in his son's right temple. Melville summons the coroner, who declares the death a suicide. The Melvilles find their son's death mysterious and cannot accept the verdict

of suicide. Apparently no one heard the shot, or no one was willing to acknowledge it.

September 14: At Malcolm's funeral, the Melvilles, suffering from shock, do not cry. Herman, so often a stoic, looks "quite composed."

November: Melville's brother, Thomas, is appointed governor of the Sailor's Snug Harbor, a Staten Island complex including dormitories, a seaman's chapel, a domed Renaissance memorial church and music hall, and other buildings.

Matthew Arnold publishes *Culture and Anarchy.* Mark Twain visits New York City and is appalled to find that 100,000 people have only cellars for homes and that tenements with a capacity to house eight families are crammed with as many as 300 people. Elizabeth Cady Stanton campaigns for the abolition of "all discrimination on account of sex or race."

1868

July 15: Guert Gansevoort dies. George Adler, Melville's old friend, dies.

Christmas: There is a family reunion at Snug Harbor. Melville's mother enjoys seeing her seven children and six of her seven grandchildren. She calls Snug Harbor "a very social place little family whist parties, private Billiard tables, or I should say perhaps Billiard tables in private houses—are very general." Herman and Elizabeth stay the night and return to the city the next day, where they host a party for Elizabeth's nephew Oakes Shaw, who closely resembles Malcolm.

President Andrew Johnson is impeached. U. S. Grant is elected president. Herbert Spencer coins the phrase "the survival of the fittest." Congress approves eight-hour day for federal employees.

Meat-packing factory of P. D. Armour opens in Chicago. Mark Twain visits New York and calls it a "splendid desert." The pace of life in the city was killing: "There is something in this ceaseless buzz, the hurry, and hustle, that keeps a stranger in a state of unwholesome excitement all the time, and makes him restless and weary."

1869

Melville reads Matthew Arnold's *Essays in Criticism* and is struck by Arnold's observation that the "literary career seems to me unreal, both in its essence and in the rewards which one seeks from it, and there fatally marred by a secret absurdity." Melville comments: "This is the finest verbal statement of a truth which every one who thinks in these days must have felt."

June: The Melvilles celebrate Elizabeth's 47th birthday at Snug Harbor. Melville's family and friends often gather at this comfortable place.

September: Elizabeth suffers from "neuralgia & weakness." (Robertson-Lorant). Stanwix leaves home

and embarks on desultory travels.

The young French statesman Georges Clemenceau visits the United States and calls Reconstruction "Darwinian." The *Atlantic Monthly* states that it is "tired of the Negro question." Jim Fisk and Jay Gould conspire to control the New York gold market, bribing President Grant's brother-in-law to restrict the Treasury's gold bullion, causing the price of gold to rise. While other investors are ruined, Fisk and Gould make huge profits. In New York, corruption is even worse, for the city is ruled by the regime of Boss Tweed and Tammany Hall, which bilks the city coffers of enormous sums—estimated at between $50 million and $200 million. Fisk and Gould escape prosecution, but Tweed is eventually convicted of 204 of the 220 charges against him. The Knights of Labor is established and campaigns for an eight-hour workday. The vacuum cleaner is invented. The transcontinental railroad is completed. Wyoming passes first U.S. woman-suffrage law.

1870

The Supreme Court overturns provisions of a civil rights bill, canceling protections for African American voters. **The Dictionary of American Biography is issued. Melville is not in it.** John D. Rockefeller founds Standard Oil.

1871

The Commune in Paris rules for two months. The Supreme Court overturns another civil rights bill, further destroying the rights of African-American voters. Charles Darwin publishes *The Descent of Man*. Simon Ingersoll invents the pneumatic rock drill. P. T. Barnum opens his circus, "The Greatest Show on Earth," in Brooklyn. Chicago is devastated by the Great Fire. S.S. *Oceanic,* the first of the modern luxury liners, is launched.

Christmas: **Increasingly reclusive, Melville nonetheless celebrates with his family at Snug Harbor. His mother is in fine form; his wife is depressed about the loss of Malcolm.**

1872

So many scandals plague the Grant administration that it is doubted he can be reelected. The economy takes a downturn. **Melville fears losing his job, but the crisis ebbs.**

February: **Allan, Melville's youngest brother, dies of tuberculosis. Allan had often been Herman's companion and adviser. Maria Gansevoort Melville, Melville's mother, dies.**

November: **Fire destroys Elizabeth Melville's Boston property.** The U.S. General Amnesty Act pardons former Confederates. William Thompson, later Lord Kelvin, invents a machine by which ships can take accurate soundings while at sea. American engi-

neer George Westinghouse (1846–1916) perfects automatic railroad air brake.

1873

February: **Stanwix returns from trips through Arkansas and Mississippi to New Orleans and Havana. He had also been in Costa Rica and Nicaragua. Herman comes down with a severe illness that lasts almost two months.**

May: **Melville begins work again as a customs inspector. The home life of the Melvilles seems to have settled down into a comfortable pattern, husband and wife apparently reconciled. Elizabeth writes to a relative: "When Herman is gone all day, or the largest part of it, the house seems utterly desolate—it is quite a new sensation for me to have the days seem so *long*—We are counting the days for going to Pittsfield and think with longings of the refreshing breezes from hill-tops."**

August: **A visit to Arrowhead proves to be a tonic. Elizabeth writes about "walking, or driving, or sitting out doors . . . as if we could not get enough of the reviving air, after being nearly suffocated in the heat and *smell* of New York."** There is a stock market panic and the economy falters. Six thousand small businesses go bankrupt. The streets are full of beggars.

1874

March: **Stanwix finds a job on a sheep ranch in California at a salary of $25 a month.**

Christmas: **Stanwix comes home at his mother's urging. He has little to show for his ranching period and is embarrassed.**

The first American zoo is established in Philadelphia. The Society for the Prevention of Cruelty to Children is founded by E. T. Gerry in New York. A. T. Still (1828–1917) founds osteopathy in Kansas. H. Solomon introduces pressure-cooking methods for canning foods, so that steam under pressure cooks food quickly and preserves it.

1875

Mark Twain publishes *The Adventures of Tom Sawyer.* Helena Blavatsky founds the Theosophical Society in New York.

1875–76

By the end of 1875 Stanwix moves to San Francisco. Melville works intensively on *Clarel*. His wife worries over his health and confides to a relative: "The fact is, that Herman, poor fellow, is in such a frightfully nervous state, & particularly now with such an added strain on his mind, that I am actually *afraid* to have any one here for fear that he will be upset entirely, & not be able to go on with the printing—He was not willing to have his own sisters here, and I had to write Augusta before she left Albany to that effect— that was the reason she changed her plan, and went

to Tom's—If ever this dreadful *incubus* of a *book* (I call it so because it has undermined all our happiness) gets off Herman's shoulders I do hope he may be in better mental health—but at present I have reasons to feel the gravest concern & anxiety about it—to put it in mild phrase—please do not speak of it—you know how such things are exaggerated—& I will tell you more when I see you."

1876

April 4: Augusta, Melville's sister, dies. In late March she had suffered an internal hemorrhage. Herman hurried to Snug Harbor and found her at the point of death. She has been a fount of energy, caring for her family, doing good works in her parish, as well as being an ardent novel reader and amanuensis for her brother.

April 7: Herman takes Augusta's body by boat to Albany to be buried in the family plot. He had done the same for his brother Gansevoort 30 years earlier. By the end of the month *Clarel* has been set in type, and a relieved Elizabeth writes to a friend: "I shall be thankful when it is all finished and off of his mind and cannot help hoping that his health will improve when he is released from this long continual mental strain."

May 10: The Centennial Exhibition opens in Philadelphia.

June 3: Putnam publishes *Clarel* in New York and distributes the edition in England; it is paid for by Melville's uncle, Peter Gansevoort, to whom Melville dedicates the book. It was published in two volumes, described by Laurie Robertson-Lorant as "bound in fine-ribbed cloth embossed with a gilt Jerusalem cross cradled by palm trees and crested with three crowns beneath a star stamped on its cover."

November: The Centennial Exhibition closes, having attracted 10 million visitors, who are able to view George Washington's false teeth and the work of Edmonia Lewis, the first African-American sculptor of note. The Plains Indians re-create their sacred dances, and various artifacts on display show the "primitive stage of civilization." Guards attempt to stop Frederick Douglass from entering the fairgrounds. When they learn of his identity, he is admitted to the exhibition.

The presidential election is undecided. Samuel Tilden (Democrat) has 184 electoral votes while Rutherford B. Hayes (Republican) has 165. Tilden wins the popular vote, but 20 electoral votes are in dispute.

A reformatory is established for juvenile offenders in Elmira, New York. Women now constitute 20 percent of America's workforce. Lieutenant Colonel Custer and 265 men are killed at Little Bighorn, Montana. Alexander Graham Bell patents the telephone.

1877

Melville continues to work at the Custom House surrounded by corruption and incompetence. His salary remains at $1,200 a year, and he will never receive a raise.

Rutherford B. Hayes takes office in a contested election that he wins by one vote in the House of Representatives. The Republicans agree to restrain Reconstruction in exchange for the presidency. Federal troops are withdrawn from the South. "How about President Hayes?" Melville writes to a cousin. "What's the use? life is short, and Hayes' term is four years, each of 365 days." At the end of the year Melville receives a royalty statement from Harper's. *Omoo, Redburn, White-Jacket,* and *Moby-Dick* together account for 192 copies sold, for which the author receives $64.38. He spends most of his royalties on prints and books. By New Year's he is suffering from erysipelas, a painful inflammation sometimes called "Saint Anthony's fire," since the saint suffered from this form of skin irritation. Melville's hands are temporarily paralyzed and his joints ache. It is impossible to write in this condition.

Public phones are introduced in the U.S.

1878

Melville's wife inherits a large amount of money from the estate of her aunt, Martha Marett.

July 4: The Melvilles celebrate at Snug Harbor.

August: Evert Duyckinck dies. Melville is the last one to see him alive. Stanwix writes from Sacramento where he is hospitalized. It is not clear what ails him, but the family is relieved to know where he is, since he has not been in contact with them for a long time.

Edison patents phonograph.

1879

A family friend visits Elizabeth and Herman and finds them feeling rather depleted.

Mary Baker Eddy becomes pastor of the Church of Christ, Scientist, Boston.

1880

Frances Melville marries Henry B. Thomas.

Thomas Edison perfects the electric light bulb. First important gold strike in Alaska.

1881

President Garfield is assassinated. New York's population reaches 1,200,000.

1882

February 24: Eleanor Melville Thomas, Melville's first grandchild, is born.

Summer: Elizabeth spends time with family at Overlook Mountain in Woodstock, New York, where Herman joins her for a week. Stanwix writes his mother often but complains of a chronic cough. In fact, he has contracted tuberculosis.

The U.S. bans Chinese immigration for 10 years. Thomas Edison designs the first hydroelectric plant.

1883

Robert, one of Melville's cousins, dies, and the circle of friends and family around Melville begins to shrink rapidly. Forty-five percent of all industrial workers makes less than $500 a year. Twelve million families make less than Melville's annual $1,200 salary.

Melville becomes a member of All Souls' Church. Although his skepticism seems not to have relaxed, his membership may simply reflect his continual search for religious inspiration and his belief in the "intersympathy of creeds."

The Brooklyn Bridge opens. The U.S. Civil Service is reformed. The first skyscraper is constructed in Chicago. Buffalo Bill (William Cody) organizes his first "Wild West Show."

1884

March: **Thomas Melville, Melville's brother, dies of a heart attack.**

April: **Judge Shaw's son dies, as does Melville's Aunt Mary.**

Hiram Maxim invents machine gun. Steam turbine invented.

1885

May: **Melville publishes a poem, "The Admiral of the White," in the** *New York Daily Tribune* **and the** *Boston Herald.*

August: **Elizabeth presents Herman with a copy of a book on Balzac. Melville underlines a statement of Balzac's that to have a strong life means to "forget life's misfortunes." Melville travels to Pittsfield while Elizabeth goes to New Hampshire for relief from her hay fever. An old friend finds Melville content: "He did not evince the slightest aversion to society but appeared to enjoy the hearty welcome which it gave him."**

December 31: **Resigns position as customs inspector. Frances Priscilla Melville, Melville's sister, dies. Melville receives a royalty check from Harper's for $223.73 covering the sale of all of his books. Stanwix's tubercular condition worsens, and he moves to southern California to take advantage of the drier climate.**

Cornelius Vanderbilt dies with a fortune estimated at $200 million. In Haymarket Square, Chicago police gun down laborers demonstrating for decent wages and working conditions.

1886

A Dutch visitor to the city meets Melville and comments that he is "a delightful talker when in the mood," but that he also is a genius who has to be "handled with care."

February 23: **Stanwix dies in San Francisco. Melville's reaction is not known.**

October: **Melville's brother-in-law John Hoadley dies. He had become a good friend of Herman's and shared a love of literature. A poet, Hoadley was one of Melville's most sympathetic readers.**

New York celebrates completion of the Statue of Liberty. Emily Dickinson dies. Henry James publishes *The Bostonians.* Hydroelectric installations are begun at Niagara Falls. The American Federation of Labor is founded.

1887

March 4: **Melville receives his final royalty statement from Harper's, for $50.02.** *Typee, Mardi, Redburn, Pierre,* **and** *Battle-Pieces* **remain in stock, but sales are minuscule.** *Omoo, White-Jacket,* **and** *Moby-Dick* **are out of print.**

1888

Melville receives a bequest of $3,000 from his sister Frances Priscilla. In March, he uses part of the money to visit Bermuda. The rest will be spent on private printings of his poetry. De Vinne Press produces a private printing of 25 copies of *John Marr and Other Sailors.* **Melville writes "Billy in the Darbies," the genesis of** *Billy Budd.* **Helen Maria Melville Griggs, Melville's sister, dies.**

May: **The** *American Magazine* **publishes an article attempting to exonerate the officers who condemned the mutineers on the Somers. Melville produces a 70-page draft of** *Billy Budd.* **Not feeling well, he writes: "I, Herman Melville, declare this to be my will. Any property, of whatever kind, I may die possessed of, including money in banks, and my share in the as yet undivided real estate at Gansevoort, I bequeathe to my wife. I do this because I have confidence that through her our children and grand-children will get their proportion of any benefit that may accrue. —I appoint my wife executrix of this will. — In witness, whereof I have hereunto set my hand and seal this 11th day of June 1888."**

First electric trolley line opens.

1889

March: **Melville continues working on** *Billy Budd,* **which he has expanded to 350 pages.**

November: **Professor Archibald MacMechan of Dalhousie University in Nova Scotia writes to Melville craving more information than the meager amount that is available in Evert Duyckinck's** *Cyclopaedia,* **which appeared in 1855. Melville replies: "You do not know, perhaps, that I have entered my eighth decade. After twenty years nearly, as an outdoor Custom House officer, I have lately** come into possession of unobstructed leisure, but only just as, in the course of my nature, my vigor sensibly declines. What little of it is left I husband for certain matters as yet incomplete, and which indeed may never be completed."

The new Madison Square Garden, designed by Stanford White, is completed.

1890

December: **Melville is afflicted with a respiratory infection, which turns out to be bronchitis.**

Iron and steel workers strike in the U.S. The first cans of pineapple are produced. The first entirely steel-framed building is erected in Chicago. W. L. Judson invents the clothing zipper. Rubber gloves are used for the first time in surgery at Johns Hopkins Hospital in Baltimore. First automatic telephone switchboard is introduced. Rudolf Diesel patents his first combustion engine.

1891

May: **Caxton Press produces a private printing of 25 copies of *Timoleon*.**

June 13: **Herman presents Elizabeth with a copy of *Timoleon* in which he writes: "To Her—without whose assistance both manual and literary Timoleon**

& c could not have passed through the press—with her name I gratefully and affectionately inscribe this volume."

August: **Elizabeth makes a fair copy of *Weeds and Wildings: With a Rose or Two* for the printer. Melville is failing fast but still plays with his grandchildren.**

September: **Toward the end of the month Melville declines rapidly.**

September 28: **Just after midnight Melville suffers a heart attack and dies, leaving *Billy Budd* and several poems, including *Weeds and Wildings*, in manuscript. Elizabeth keeps the papers in a tin breadbox.** Congress finally passes a law respecting international copyright, nearly 40 years after Melville and other writers agitated for its passage.

1892

Walt Whitman dies.

1906

Catherine Gansevoort Melville Hoadley, Melville's sister, dies. Fanny and Eleanor, Melville's grandchildren, become custodians of his papers.

1924

Billy Budd is published.

HERMAN MELVILLE

A TO Z

A, I, and O ("The Polysyllables," "The Vowels")
Minor characters in *MARDI*. The three daughters of NIMNI and his wife, OHIRO MOLDONA Fivona, aristocrats of the isle of Pimminee, are collectively known as "The Polysyllables" or "The Vowels." The brevity of their names is said to indicate their innate gentility.

abbot, the Character in *CLAREL*. *See* CHRISTODULUS.

Abdon Minor character in *CLAREL*. The host of the inn in JERUSALEM where CLAREL stays, this orthodox Jew represents the persistence of old religious beliefs. Traveling from India to Amsterdam to Jerusalem, Abdon, a trader, has found his resting place, unlike Clarel and his fellow pilgrims.

abolitionists Under the leadership of figures such as William Lloyd Garrison and Wendell Phillips, a vocal minority of Northerners agitated for the abolition of slavery throughout the North American continent. Prominent in the radical faction of the Republican Party, abolitionists were uncompromising and often inflammatory. Garrison, for example, burned the American Constitution in public. Moderate and conservative Americans, regardless of political affiliation, opposed outright abolition and thought of the abolitionists as troublemakers. Abolitionism was particularly strong in New England. Both Ralph Waldo EMERSON and Henry David Thoreau supported abolitionist protests—and even the violence of agitators like John BROWN. Other writers, including Melville and Nathaniel HAWTHORNE, were sympathetic toward the abolitionists, but they were not political activists and were wary of the fanatical devotion to a cause. Melville's position on slavery, judging from his fiction such as "BENITO CERENO," was unequivocal: slavery was an evil that blinded men to justice and freedom. Certainly Melville was in sympathy with his father-in-law, Judge Lemuel Shaw, who at first ruled against returning fugitive slaves—although later he had to bow to the Supreme Court's decision in the Dred Scott case, which endorsed the return of the escaped slaves to their Southern owners.

Abrazza Minor character in *MARDI*. Abrazza is the "carefree bachelor" ruler of the island of Bonovona. Hailing MEDIA as a "fellow demigod and king," Abrazza makes TAJI and his party welcome, debating with the philosopher BABBALANJA over the merits of the poet Lombardo's masterwork, the *Kostanza*. Abrazza's judgment—that the *Kostanza* "lacks cohesion"—is thought to be Melville's own tongue-in-cheek attempt to forestall critical attacks on *Mardi*.

Acushnet Whaling ship of which Herman Melville was a crew member between 1841 and 1843. The *Acushnet* carried Melville to the South Seas and the adventures that would form the basis for his first two novels. When he was 21 years old and at loose ends, Melville signed on as a common sailor with the crew of the *Acushnet*, the newest of America's whaling fleet. The ship set sail from Fairhaven, Massachusetts, on January 3, 1841, commanded by Captain Valentine Pease II, with a crew of 25, only eight of whom completed the grueling four years that made up a whaling voyage. Melville himself lasted for 18 months, deserting the ship when it reached Nuku Hiva in the MARQUESAS. His reasons for doing so included the harsh conditions on board, the captain's dictatorial behavior, the paucity of the catch, and the allure of the Marquesas. In *TYPEE*, the novel that reflected his time among the natives there, the *Acushnet* is renamed the *Dolly*, and Captain Pease is transformed into the tyrannical Captain Vangs.

"Adieu" (1947) Poem. One of the more than 40 poems Melville left uncollected or unpublished when he died, "Adieu" serves as a kind of epitaph for this artist unheralded in his own lifetime:

> Ring down! The curtain falls and ye
> Will go your ways. Yet think of me.
> And genie take what's genie given
> And long be happy under heaven.

Adler, George (1821–1868) A native of Leipzig, he taught German philology at the University of the City of New York (later New York University). Melville met Adler on his way to Europe in 1849, and they spent time at sea discussing "Fixed Fate, Free Will, foreknowledge absolute," Melville reported. They also talked over Immanuel KANT and Emanuel SWEDENBORG. In London, they visited and dined at places Dr. Johnson had made famous. Then Adler proposed visiting art galleries, which Melville delighted in. Adler was eventually hospitalized for a mental disorder and died in 1868 without recovering his mind.

"The Admiral of the White"   *See* "THE HAGLETS."

"The Æolian Harp: *At the Surf Inn*" (1888) Poem in "JOHN MARR." For the Romantic poets, the Æolian harp—a stringed instrument placed near a window, where it could be played by the breezes—was a benevolent emblem of the universal spirit or of poetic inspiration. Melville's harp, on the other hand, shrieks "up in mad crescendo— / Dying down with plaintive key!" reminding the speaker of a ghost ship, dismasted and adrift, that once threatened his ship. Whereas TRAN-SCENDENTALISTS saw the instrument as wholly benevolent, in Melville's poem it summons up images of nature's destructive power.

Afretee Minor character in *OMOO*. Afretee is the wife of Ereemear PO-PO and the mother of LOO. She and her husband play host for several days to the narrator and LONG GHOST in Partoowye.

African Americans Melville's fiction and poetry portray slavery as an evil and attacks whites for their failure to accord slaves the same amount of humanity as they accorded themselves. Melville did not become directly involved in politics, however, even though members of his family and his friends did. Like even the most fervent abolitionists, he rarely saw African Americans as full-fledged human beings. Instead, he thought Northerners should practice "paternal guardianship" of former slaves. Frederick DOUGLASS, an escaped slave and militant abolitionist, chafed under this kind of patronization and advocated immediate and unequivocal freedom and equal rights for African Americans.

"After the Pleasure Party. Lines Traced Under an Image of Amor Threatening" (1891) Poem in *TIMO-LEON.* This extraordinary poem opens with an epigraph that warns virgins not to be overly proud of their purity and to beware of love. In the poem itself, Melville adopts the persona of a woman, an astronomer named Urania (perhaps based on Maria Mitchell, America's first female astronomer, whom Melville met on Nantucket, Massachusetts, in 1852). In a dramatic monologue delivered on the terrace of a Mediterranean villa, Urania describes the turmoil she has undergone in trying to resolve her conflicting desires to pursue her interest in science and to give in to sexual desire—the latter aroused after attending a pleasure party, or rural outing, where she sees a man to whom she is attracted walking with a peasant girl.

Unable to reconcile her desires, she moves to Rome, where she becomes enraptured with classical statuary. Later, a picture of the Virgin Mary inspires her to consider entering a nunnery. Instead of doing so, however, Urania invokes the goddess Athena to arm her against Eros. The poet then interjects the warning that "art" cannot save Urania from desire, which is itself the most profound source of creativity.

Melville's poem shows influences not only of his own appreciative examination of Roman statuary during his trip to Italy in 1857 and his struggles with his own probable BISEXUALITY, but also of his reading about the myth of the adrogyne in PLATO's *Symposium* and Arthur SCHOPENHAUER's "Metaphysics of the Love of the Sexes."

Agar Minor character in *CLAREL*. Agar, Ruth's mother, has come to Jerusalem with her husband Nathan and her two children. She is a passive, traditional woman who does her Zionist husband's bidding. She and Ruth die of grief when Nathan is murdered.

Agath Character in *CLAREL*. The pilgrims meet this Greek timoneer (pilot) at MAR SABA. He accompanies them as far as BETHLEHEM. He is a kind of Job figure, a symbol of human suffering, but he is also a survivor whom the pilgrims respect.

"The Age of Antonines" (1891) Poem in *TIMOLEON*. In 1877, Melville sent an earlier copy of this poem to his brother-in-law, John Chapman Hoadley, the husband of his sister Catherine. With the poem he enclosed a note indicating that the verse had been inspired by Edward Gibbon's *History of the Decline and Fall of the Roman Empire* (1788). Gibbon portrays the age of Antoninus Pius, who ruled the Roman Empire from 138–161 A.D., as a singularly happy period of prosperity, civility, and political stability. In the version of the poem that appears in *Timoleon,* this classical period is pictured as similarly golden and contrasted with the commercial avarice and Christian religiosity that provide poor modern analogues.

Ahab Character in *MOBY-DICK*. Captain of the *PEQUOD*, this strong, broadly formed man has a mythical air about him, as though he were a god bursting out of a violent natural catastrophe. He is a man of overbearing grimness, restless and full of rage because the whale has taken his leg and the universe permits such mutilation. In the Bible (1 Kings 16:33), Ahab is a king of Israel who "did more to provoke the Lord God of Israel to anger than all the kings of Israel that were before him." Melville's Ahab is said to be modeled on Charles WILKES, whose famous sea explorations Melville read about. Ahab's Shakesperean soliloquies set him apart from Melville's other major characters. Like Hamlet, he questions the meaning of life. Like Othello he is extraordinarily proud. His quest for Moby-Dick mesmerizes even as it terrorizes his crew.

Akenside, Mark (1721–1770)   English poet and physician, best known for his *Pleasures of Imagination* (1744), which the CONFIDENCE MAN claims to be reading when he comes upon the COLLEGIAN reading TACITUS. The confidence man favors imagination in Akenside because it is an antidote to cynicism and distrust in Tacitus, for the latter attitudes prevent people from trusting their fellow human beings.

Alanno   *See* ALLEN, WILLIAM.

Albany, New York   State capital of New York and home of Herman Melville's mother, Maria Gansevoort MELVILLE. Located in eastern New York State on the west bank of the Hudson River, Albany was first a Dutch fur-trading post established in 1613, four years after explorer Henry Hudson visited the site. In 1624, several Walloon families settled permanently in the Dutch outpost called Fort Orange, which was renamed Albany 40 years later when the English took control of the area. After the Revolutionary War, the state capital moved to Albany from New York City, and with the opening of the Champlain and Erie canals in the 1820s Albany—which had remained crucial to the fur trade—grew into a center for other types of trade, such as lumber and grain. The Albany that Herman Melville knew as a young boy was dominated by high-minded but comfort-loving Dutch patroons like his uncle Peter GANSEVOORT, whose home Melville visited in 1826, a time when his father described him as an "honest hearted double rooted Knickerbocker of the true Albany stamp."

In 1830, business reversals forced Melville's family to relocate from New York City to Albany in order to take advantage of the aid and comfort afforded by proximity to Maria's family. Eleven-year-old Herman, together with his older brother, Gansevoort, was enrolled at Albany Academy, a college preparatory school, where their studies included English literature and world religions. They did not stay long, however, for Albany in the early 1820s was in the grip of a deep economic recession. Already mired in debt, Allan MELVILL borrowed money from Peter Gansevoort to set up an ill-fated fur-and-cap store. Only a year after he was enrolled at Albany Academy, Herman was withdrawn. After Allan Melvill died the following January, Herman's brother Gansevoort, too, withdrew from school in order to take over his father's business. Melville and his family would remain in Albany until May 1838, when penury exacerbated by an illness that prevented Gansevoort from working forced them to seek less expensive accommodations in LANSINGBURGH, 10 miles up the Hudson River.

Albatross   In chapter 52 of MOBY-DICK, the PEQUOD meets the *Albatross*. This wreck of a ship is a visible reminder of the ship described in RIME OF THE ANCIENT MARINER by Samuel Taylor Coleridge. AHAB and his crew try to communicate with the *Albatross*, but the two ships pass without exchanging an intelligible word about whether the whale Moby-Dick has been sighted. ISHMAEL speculates that Ahab avoids the gam (a social meeting of whale ships) because he does not want to encounter a captain who may lack news about the whale and sympathy for Ahab's quest. The *Pequod*, no less than the ship in Coleridge's poem, is doomed—in part because it violates nature in its pursuit of the whale, enacting Ahab's desire for revenge and destruction.

Aleema   Minor character in MARDI. Aleema is the old priest who imprisoned the maiden YILLAH on the island of Amma. He is killed by TAJI while traveling to the island of Tedaidee when Taji discovers that the priest's cargo includes Yillah, whom the priest plans to sacrifice. Ever afterward, Taji is pursued by three of the priest's warrior sons, who attempt repeatedly to avenge their father's murder.

Allen, Ethan (1738–1789)   Born in Litchfield, Connecticut, on January 10, 1738, Allen moved to Vermont in 1772. During the Revolutionary War he captured Fort Ticonderoga and was then captured by the British in September 1775. In a prisoner exchange, the British released Allen on May 6, 1778, and he returned to Vermont, where he died on February 12, 1789. Allen appears in ISRAEL POTTER as a British captive and a type of American indomitability, a fitting parallel to John Paul JONES, who also appears in the novel.

Allen, William (1803–1879)   Politician who appears as a minor character named Alanno in MARDI. William Allen was a lawyer practicing in Chillicothe, Ohio, when he ran for a seat in the United States House of Representatives in 1832. He served as a Democrat in the House from 1833 to 1835, then in the U.S. Senate from 1843 to 1849. After temporarily retiring from politics to work on his Ohio fruit farm, Allen served as the state's governor from 1874 to 1876. From 1843 to 1849, Allen was chairman of the Senate Committee on Foreign Relations, where he supported the expansionism of President John Tyler, and then that of Tyler's successor, James K. Polk. The major political battlegrounds during this period were the slaveholding territory of Texas—the annexation of which the Senate refused to endorse—and the Oregon Territory. Allen is said to have written the Democratic Party's 1844 election slogan, "Fifty-Four Forty or Fight," which helped elect Polk and gained approval for the annexation of Oregon up to the latitude of fifty-four degrees, forty minutes.

Allen's commitment to what would become the doctrine of "manifest destiny," the belief that America had a natural right to colonize the entire continent—and beyond, is reflected in Melville's caricature of Alanno of Hio-Hio in *Mardi*. Alanno is a tall, gaunt figure who bombastically holds forth against King BELLO of Dominora (the embodiment of England, America's opponent in the struggle over the Oregon Territory) in the Temple of Freedom in Vivenza.

Almanni   Minor character in *MARDI*. A stern-eyed, resolute warrior who is related to King MEDIA of Odo, Almanni is appointed regent during Media's voyage through the Mardian isles with TAJI.

"Always with Us!" (1924)   Poem in *WEEDS AND WILDINGS*. In this five-stanza poem from the "The Year" section of the volume, Melville describes the robin as a "wise guest" who knows that "absence endears." In contrast, the crow, an "Inconsiderate fowl," is ever with us. Regardless of the season, the crow's foreboding call can be heard issuing from the "blasted hemlock"—presumably a memento mori.

"The Ambuscade" (1924)   Poem in *WEEDS AND WILDINGS*. Part of the "As They Fell" sequence in the second half of the volume, "A Rose or Two," "The Ambuscade" presents a "white nun" whose chaste dress disguises a passionate nature:

> Custodian of love's slumbering germ—
> Nay, nurtures it, till time disclose
> How frost fed Amor's burning rose.

Female sexuality, Melville implies, is late-blooming, but all the more passionate for the delay.

"America" (1866)   Poem in *BATTLE-PIECES*. As the last of the "battle-pieces" that form the main part of this volume of CIVIL WAR poetry, "America" stands as a kind of coda for the whole. In this four-part poem, "America" is pictured as a heroic, larger-than-life mother figure, first seen with "the exulting heart / Of young maturity," and finally, after the Civil War, with "Law on her brow and empire in her eyes."

"The American Aloe on Exhibition" (1924)   Poem in *WEEDS AND WILDINGS*. Like other pieces in the "This, That and the Other" section of the volume, this poem opens with a bit of prose, in this case to deny the "floral superstition" that the so-called century plant blooms but once every hundred years. Melville had seen the century plant on display at the Philadelphia Exposition, where in 1876 people had paid "Ten cents admission" to see "bon-bons of the hour." Here the author adopts the persona of the aloe, which decidedly is not one of the "bon-bons," but instead an "aged stem." The aloe has outlived the roses that accounted it little more than a weed. So, Melville implies, will his writings—unpopular in his day—someday be accounted as fine and rare as the delayed blossoming of the century plant.

"Amoroso" (1924)   Poem in *WEEDS AND WILDINGS*. This is the first poem in the second half of the volume "A Rose or Two," which itself is divided into two parts, the first bearing the title "As They Fell." "Amoroso" is a vivid reminder that this collection was dedicated to Elizabeth MELVILLE, who seems to be the Rosamond of this love poem that speaks of "a plighted pair" of spouses "wooing in the snows!"

Ancient Mariner   *See* RIME OF THE ANCIENT MARINER.

Anna   Character in "I AND MY CHIMNEY" and "THE APPLE-TREE TABLE." In both stories she is one of the narrator's two daughters.

Annatoo   Character in *MARDI*. Annatoo is the Polynesian native wife of SAMOA, navigator of the *Parki*. When the narrator and his companion, JARL, come aboard the ravaged brigantine, Samoa and Annatoo are the only survivors of an earlier attack on the ship by pirate Cholos. Annatoo is deeply attached to any item she can pilfer from the ship—and she pilfers many, sometimes to the point of endangering the safety of her fellow passengers. She has a rather Punch-and-Judy relationship with her husband, develops a crush on Jarl that later turns to loathing, and shares a relationship of mutual dislike with the narrator of the novel. During a storm at sea, she is conveniently struck in the head and washed overboard, thus allowing Samoa, Jarl, and the narrator to get on with their adventures free of her interference.

Antone   Minor character in *OMOO*. Antone is a Portuguese sailor from the Cape Verde Islands who is one of the narrator's shipmates aboard the *Julia*. He is one of the signatories to the round-robin list of grievances that lands most of the crew in jail in Papeetee.

"Apathy and Enthusiasm. (1860–1.)" (1866)   Poem in *BATTLE-PIECES*. As grim November passes and "the winter died despairing," apathy about civil war is transformed into enthusiasm. With the arrival of spring, "the young were all elation / Hearing Sumter's cannon roar." In an allusion to Milton's *Paradise Lost*, Melville imbues the young with a sense of being on God's side, identifying with the gigantic archangel Michael and underestimating Satan. The poem ends ominously with a quotation from an Iroquois proverb: *"Grief to every graybeard / When young Indians lead the war."* From the outset, Melville implies, Northern elders knew that the war would not soon be over and were reluctant to take on such a formidable enemy as the Confederacy. This two-part poem juxtaposes the wariness of the old with the reckless enthusiasm of the young men who rushed into battle.

"The Apparition. (A Retrospect.)" (1866) Poem in *BATTLE-PIECES*. On July 30, 1864, the army of Ulysses S. Grant blew up a mine near Petersburg, Virginia, as part of a futile attempt to take the city. Recalling that disaster, Melville warns that something similar can happen again; that is, if the peace that followed Appomattox does not go well, another "convulsion" can convert green fields into a "goblin-mountain."

"The Apparition. (The Parthenon uplifted on its rock first challenging the view on the approach to Athens.)" (1891) Poem in *TIMOLEON*. One of the poems in the section labeled "Fruit of Travel Long Ago," "The Apparition" grew out of Melville's sojourn in Athens in 1857, when he noted in his journal, "Parthenon elevated like cross of Constantine." Later, when he wrote "The Apparition," he remembered both that the Parthenon dominates Athens from atop the citadel of the Acropolis, and that this supreme physical and spiritual achievement had been supplanted by the cross that converted Emperor Constantine I (A.D. 280?–337) of Rome to Christianity. Such is the power of the Parthenon, though, that had the Cynic philosopher Diogenes (412?–323 B.C.) lived to see it, even he "might have swerved / In mood nor barked so much at Man." This is a pun on "cynic," which in Greek means "dog," and was also the name of an ancient Greek school of thought that believed virtue to be the only good and to be only achievable through self-control.

"The Apple-Tree Table; Or, Original Spiritual Manifestations" (1856) Short story. Probably written in the autumn of 1855, "The Apple-Tree Table" bears some resemblance to another story Melville wrote around the same time, "I AND MY CHIMNEY." Both feature male narrators whose households consist of a wife, two daughters named JULIA and ANNA, and a maid named BIDDY. The same configuration also appears in another "domestic" tale, "JIMMY ROSE," written the year before, although in this story the daughters are not named.

All three of these stories—together with "THE PIAZZA," probably written early in 1856—are "domestic" tales set in old houses. Like "Jimmy Rose," "The Apple-Tree Table" takes place in an old urban mansion. One day in his garden, the narrator discovers a rusty old key that happens to open the locked door of an old garret in the house, long rumored to be haunted. In the garret, the narrator finds two items that attract his atten-

tion: a cloven-footed table and a copy of Cotton Mather's *Magnalia Christi Americana* (1702), both of which he brings downstairs. Both of his daughters are distressed by the look of the table, but his wife sets it up to be used at breakfast and teatime. That night, the narrator sits at the table reading Mather when he hears an odd ticking sound, which makes him uncomfortable both with the devilish-looking table and with Mather's tales of witchcraft. The next morning his practical wife sets about looking for the source of the odd noise, which is discovered that night when the narrator, again reading beside the table, notices a gorgeous bug emerging from a crack in the wood. He inverts a tumbler over it, but by the morning the maid has disposed of the creature. That night the narrator, his wife, and their daughters all gather around the table, which has begun ticking again. At 6 A.M., another beautiful bug emerges from a hole in the table, apparently having lain dormant in the wood for some 150 years. Julia, previously convinced that the table was inhabited by spirits, now claims that the glorious creature is an emblem of the resurrection.

Melville had access to several sources for his tale, beginning with Mather's *Magnalia* (a kind of "History of New England Witchcraft," as Washington IRVING called it in "The Legend of Sleepy Hollow") and the vogue for SPIRITUALISM. The story of a beautiful bug emerging from an applewood table is told toward the end of Henry David Thoreau's *Walden* (1854), as well as in at least one other work, Timothy Dwight's *Travels in New-England and New-York* (1821), which Melville made use of in his essay "HAWTHORNE AND HIS MOSSES." Published anonymously in *Putnam's Monthly Magazine* in May 1856, "The Apple-Tree Table" is Melville's penultimate effort at short fiction. Its only known successor is "The Piazza," composed specifically to serve as an introduction to the collection of reprinted stories that bears its name.

Aranda, Alexandro Character in "BENITO CERENO." By the time the action of the story opens, Aranda, the owner of the slave cargo aboard the *San Dominick,* is dead, a victim of a bloody shipboard slave revolt. His skeleton is lashed to the ship's prow as a grisly figurehead above the ironic legend, "Follow your leader," that is crudely painted underneath.

"The Archipelago" (1891) Poem in *TIMOLEON*. Part of the "Fruit of Travel Long Ago" section of the volume, "The Archipelago" reflects some of Melville's observations about Greek islands in the Aegean, which he sailed in 1856. He found them sterile and dry, and in his diary he wrote that the barrenness of the island of Patmos, where Saint John is said to have written the Book of Revelation, made him "afflicted with the great curse of modern travel—skepticism." He found he simply could not believe that John had ever experienced revelations in such a place. The Greek archipelago, he thought, compared unfavorably with the islands of Polynesia, still "fresh as at their first creation." But in the poem, he recalls the Greek islands as still possessing traces of their former glory: "They still retain in outline true / Their grace of form when earth was new / And primal." They are, he says, "Polynesia reft of palms."

Arheetoo   Minor character in OMOO. A clever and intelligent native of Tahiti, Arheetoo argues with Long Ghost about which Sabbath to keep and asks the narrator to draft a set of forged papers attesting to his character. The papers are intended to permit him access to the dirty linens generated by various incoming ships, the laundering of which would afford a good income.

"The Armies of the Wilderness. (1863–4.)" (1866)   Poem in BATTLE-PIECES. The Battle of the Wilderness took place in northern Virginia over two days in May 1864 and cost some 12,000 lives. Melville's poem is set before the fighting begins and focuses on the common humanity of the opposing sides. Through field glasses, Union soldiers watch the enemy playing baseball. As the poet observes, "They could have joined them in their sport / But for the vale's deep rent." Much of the poem dwells on just such diurnal detail: Union soldiers kindle their fires with Confederate books and bonds; they use a headstone as a hearth stone on which to boil water for punch. These passages are, however, interspersed with italicized verses that meditate on the meaning of this war, *this strife of brothers.*"

Arnaut, the   Character in CLAREL. A huge Albanian warrior who works as an escort for pilgrims. A Muslim, descended from ancient nobility, he has fought for the czar and the sultan. His heroic stature attracts the pilgrims, particularly ROLFE. He seems a kind of natural man immune to the corruptions and tormenting doubts of civilization.

Arnold, Matthew (1822–1888)   Born in Laleham, Middlesex, England, this Victorian poet exerted much influence on the intellectual and literary life of England and America. His poetry often addressed the loss of faith in the modern world emerging from scientific study, especially from Darwin's study of evolution. As an essayist he explored wide-ranging social, literary, and cultural issues. Melville read Arnold avidly and was influenced by both his poetry and criticism. Arnold's greatest poem, "DOVER BEACH," is one of the key influences on CLAREL. But no less important is CULTURE AND ANARCHY, Arnold's groundbreaking book on the Greek and Hebrew heritage of Western civilization.

Arrowhead   Herman Melville's home from 1850–63. In mid-September 1850, Melville bought a 160-acre farm near Pittsfield, Massachusetts. He wanted to be near his friend Nathaniel HAWTHORNE—then living in Lenox, Massachusetts—whom Melville considered a great writer and a role model. Melville lived at Arrowhead for 14 years, writing poems about the place, farming, and rearing his children. He gloried in the sunrises and sunsets, the woods, and the change of seasons, recapturing some of the "wild sublimity" he said he had experienced at sea. In 1855, however, Melville found himself unable to keep up with the mortgage payments and the physical labor required on the farm. He put Arrowhead up for sale. There were no takers until April 1863, when his brother Allan offered to pay him three-quarters of the farm's assessed value of $4,000. Herman, in turn, agreed to buy Allan's New York City residence for $7,750.

"Art" (1891)   Poem in TIMOLEON. Melville condensed his theory of art into this brief poem. Art is, he says, the product of opposites in conflict. Like sexual union, these opposites "pulsed life create," but the struggle is like the biblical Jacob's wrestling match with an angel, which left him with a wound in the thigh, symbolically emasculated.

Aster, China   Character in THE CONFIDENCE MAN. Aster is the subject of a long story told by EGBERT, the disciple of Mark WINSOME. Aster, a candle maker, comes to grief when he relies on a loan from a friend. Egbert relates Aster's fate as an object lesson to the cosmopolitan (a.k.a. the CONFIDENCE MAN), who is asking for a loan.

Astor, John Jacob (1763–1848)   Fur trader and financier. Born John Jakub Ashdour in Waldorf, Germany, Astor came to the United States in 1783. Arriving penniless, within a few years he had opened a small store in New York City that sold musical instruments and furs. Astor soon parlayed his knowledge of the fur business into a near monopoly of the fur trade, then of trade with China. He made more money by lending funds to the U.S. government in 1814. Shrewd real estate investments in New York brought him further wealth. At the time of his death he was the richest man in America, with a fortune estimated at $20 million. A bequest of $350,000 was used to establish the Astor Library, which later became the New York Public Library. Astor's will, which was published on April 5, 1848, in the New York *Herald*, was a complex affair that Melville satirized in MARDI. Melville evoked Astor again in "BARTLEBY, THE SCRIVENER" which is narrated by a Wall Street lawyer who is "not unemployed" by "the late John Jacob Astor."

Astor Place riots   On May 7, 1849, a mob of fanatical American nationalists protested the appearance of the

On September 14, 1850, Melville purchased a 160-acre farm near Pittsfield, Massachusetts, and called it Arrowhead. (Herman Melville's Arrowhead)

English actor William Macready at the Astor Place Theater in New York City. Macready was performing the title role in *Macbeth* at the same time as the American actor Edwin Forrest's production was running in the city. Melville was one of several prominent New Yorkers to sign a petition defending Macready's right to appear in New York. Nevertheless, on the evening of May 9, violence broke out as Forrest's backers tried to storm the Astor Place Theater and prevent Macready from performing. Although their assault was unsuccessful, the rioting led to widespread destruction in a melee that involved 25,000 people and led to the deaths of 22, with an additional 36 injured. Eighty-six arrests were made.

"At the Cannon's Mouth. Destruction of the Ram Albemarle by the Torpedo-launch. (October, 1864)." (1866)   Poem in *BATTLE-PIECES*. Inspired by a successful attack on October 27, 1864, at the mouth of the Roanoke River, "At the Cannon's Mouth" praises the daring—like that "which brave poets own"—displayed by Lieutenant William Barker Cushing in the CIVIL WAR. Cushing drove his launch into the Confederate ship *Albemarle,* and although he survived his "mad dash at

death," most of his 15-man crew did not. Melville clearly sees in Cushing a kindred spirit: "That scorn of life which earns life's crown; / Earns, but not always wins."

"At the Hostelry" *See* "THE BURGUNDY CLUB SKETCHES."

"The Attic Landscape" (1891)   Poem in *TIMOLEON*. Part of the "Fruit of Travel Long Ago" section of the volume, "The Attic Landscape" acts as a kind of travelers' advisory: in Greece, where empty hillsides and mountaintop temples face one another, "Art and Nature lodged together" in "sculptural grace." In "THE SAME," a quatrain that continues this poem, Melville writes that the Attic landscape evokes thoughts of Plato and "authenticates" the philosopher's ideas.

Atufal   Character in "BENITO CERENO." Atufal is the majestic former African king enslaved by Alexandro Aranda, the owner of the *San Dominick*'s slave cargo. In the slave revolt that results in Aranda's murder, Atufal is one of the chief henchmen of Babo, the revolutionary leader. When Captain Amasa DELANO visits the ship,

Atufal is hourly brought in chains before Captain Don Benito CERENO, ostensibly to beg his pardon for an offense. Instead, Atufal's silence on these occasions mocks Don Benito's true status as Babo's slave.

Aunt Dorothea In *PIERRE; OR, THE AMBIGUITIES*, Pierre's aunt who tells him the story of how Ralph Winwood, a cousin of Pierre's father, painted a portrait of Pierre's father at a time when his father was said to be in love with a French woman. This story contributes to Pierre's strong feeling that Isabel BANFORD is indeed his sister by the very woman his father ultimately rejected.

Aunt Llanyllyn In *PIERRE*, Lucy TARTAN's aunt, a "pensive, childless, white-turbaned widow."

"Aurora-Borealis. Commemorative of the Dissolution of Armies at the Peace. (May, 1865.)" (1866) Poem in *BATTLE-PIECES*. This piece consists of an extended metaphor that likens the demobilization of troops at the end of the CIVIL WAR to God's "disbanding" the Northern Lights, the "million blades that glowed."

"Authentic Anecdotes of 'Old Zack' [Reported for *Yankee Doodle* by his special correspondent at the seat of War]" (1847) This series of nine satiric sketches of Zachary TAYLOR was Melville's first published correspondence to the humor magazine *YANKEE DOODLE*, whose staff Melville joined in the summer of 1847. An introductory section testifies to the "authenticity" of what follows and concludes with a "certificate" to that effect ostensibly signed by Major General Taylor.

"Anecdote I" concerns Taylor's supposed manual defusing of a Mexican mortar shell. A "P.S." states that P. T. BARNUM, who happened to learn of the incident from the *Yankee Doodle* correspondent, demands that a search party look for the shell, even as he orders a duplicate made to exhibit in his museum. In "Anecdote II," the correspondent reports seeing Taylor washing and mending his own clothes—many of which he needs to let out because of his increasing girth. "Anecdote III" purports to show Taylor's "insensibility

to bodily pain" by relating an incident in which the general rode all day sitting on a tack placed in his saddle on a dare by a drummer boy. When the general dismounts that night, he leaves the seat of his pants attached to the saddle. Once again, Barnum begs for the relic so that he can display it in his museum. A pseudoscientific description of the general's physical appearance is laid out in fulsome detail by "a Surgeon of the Army in Mexico." "Anecdote IV" includes what is billed as a "private letter" "most probably traced with the point of a ram-rod on a drum head" by the general to his Mexican counterpart, Santa Anna, expressing sympathy for the latter's loss at the Battle of Buena Vista. "Anecdote V" describes how an enemy shot causes a freshly baked chicken pie to land on the general's head. "Anecdote VI" consists of a letter from Barnum offering the general a job when his military service ends. "Anecdote VII" contains the "steamboat story," which holds that the general, having given up his berth to a sick soldier, passed a night before and even inside the oven of the boat. "Anecdote VIII" consists of a letter—itself consisting primarily of a graphic representation of the Stars and Stripes, purported typeset by the general himself—responding to *Yankee Doodle*'s inquiry about his political ambitions.

In "Anecdote IX," the correspondent describes Taylor's active eating habits.

Published anonymously in seven weekly installments between July 24 and September 11, 1847, Melville's satires were meant to burlesque the exaggerated accounts of Taylor's war exploits that were being circulated to promote his candidacy in the upcoming presidential election.

"The Avatar" (1924) Poem in *WEEDS AND WILDINGS*. Part of the "This, That and the Other" section of the volume, "The Avatar" has a decidedly religious cast. It declares that when the "rose-god" came to earth he took not the lovely and exalted form of a rose, but instead that of "Sweet-Briar, a wilding or weed."

Azzageddi *See* BABBALANJA.

B

Babbalanja Character in *MARDI*. Babbalanja, a philosopher, is one of four members of King MEDIA's court to accompany the king and TAJI on their quest through the Mardian isles for the elusive YILLAH. Babbalanja, as his name suggests, babbles on at length about life, death, and everything between as the party sails ever onward. His tendency to argue both sides of an issue, he declares, is the product of his inner demon, which he calls *Azzageddi.* At the end of the novel, Babbalanja decides to stay on Serenia to embrace the heavenly peace that is both a religion and a way of life on the island.

Babo Character in "BENITO CERENO." Babo, who acts as Captain CERENO's attentive body servant during Amasa DELANO's time aboard the *San Dominick,* is in truth the leader of the successful slave revolt that has murdered most of the ship's Spanish officers and crew and enslaved Cereno himself. When Cereno attempts a desperate escape, Babo tries equally desperately to kill him. Finally Babo is subdued, tried, and executed for his crimes. His head is then exhibited on a pike in the plaza of Lima, Peru, and seems to meet "unabashed, the gaze of the white," as well as to look toward the final resting places of his dead slave master and Benito Cereno.

Bachelor In chapter 115 of *MOBY-DICK,* the *PEQUOD* meets the *Bachelor.* Returning from a successful whaling trip, the merry crew of the *Bachelor* does not suit the brooding, monomaniac AHAB. It is as if the *Bachelor* inhabits another universe: the ship's captain has neither seen nor bothered himself with the whale Moby-Dick.

Bacon, Francis (1561–1626) English lawyer, politician, and philosopher in the Elizabethan period. A wily intriguer versed in the stratagems of survival at court, Bacon also propounded a philosophy that situated human knowledge as the product of systematic scientific inquiry. Bacon sought, in other words, to describe all phenomena on the basis of precise observation and categorization. His reliance on logic and law irritated Melville, who saw the world in much more ambiguous terms. Bacon is specifically criticized in *PIERRE,* where he appears as an example of the "watchmaker" mind,

aware only of the phenomena under his local control, so to speak. Bacon is also referred to slightingly by the CONFIDENCE MAN, who suspects the MISSOURIAN is reading Bacon and thus is treating the ideas of trust and confidence in human nature with too much skepticism and rationality.

Baldy Minor character in *WHITE-JACKET.* Baldy is one of WHITE-JACKET's messmates, a captain of the mizzentop, who, when ordered to move too quickly in a sail-furling contest with neighbor ships, jumps to obey. His actions result in a precipitous fall to the deck that cripples him for life. This episode mirrors one that happened in October 1843 on board the *United States* during Melville's tenure.

"Ball's Bluff. A Reverie. (October, 1861.)" (1866) Poem in *BATTLE-PIECES.* Written in the form of a dramatic monologue, this poem concerns a Union defeat on October 21, 1861, at Ball's Bluff, Virginia, where four Union regiments were ambushed by Confederates. More than 1,000 Union soldiers ultimately died, and this defeat crushed Union morale, as the poem illustrates. Just weeks earlier, the speaker recalls, he had witnessed young Union troops beneath his window marching lustily off to war. Now those same soldiers have met their fate by the cliffs of the Potomac.

Baltimore Minor character in *OMOO.* Baltimore is an African American ship's cook—and a native of Baltimore, Maryland, from which he has fled as a runaway slave—on board the *Julia.* An old man, Baltimore is flummoxed when his cook shed, set atop the deck of the *Julia,* is lifted from its moorings during a gale. But Baltimore is known for his good nature, and when the crew signs its "round robin" protest over conditions aboard ship, the cook is nominated to take it ashore to the British consul.

Banford, Isabel Pierre's putative sister in *PIERRE.* At first, certain that Isabel is his half-sister, Pierre commits his life to protecting her and to shielding his father's reputation from the scandal that acknowledging her publicly would bring to the Glendinning family. As she becomes more involved in his life, however, Pierre has second thoughts, questioning his own rush to believe in her story. The melancholy, intense, and demanding Isabel requires more and more proof of Pierre's loyalty, hastening his own tragic downfall.

banker, the   Character in *CLAREL*. The banker is one of the pilgrims, on his way to conduct a business deal in Beirut. He leaves the pilgrims when they reach the Wilderness. He has not taken the religious nature of the journey seriously; indeed, he represents the materialist world that is antithetical to religious belief.

Bannadonna   Character in "THE BELL-TOWER." Bannadonna is the "great mechanician" whose great ambition is realized when he builds a clock- and bell tower 300 feet high. Just as the creation is inaugurated, however, its creator is killed by an automaton he has built to ring the hours on a gigantic, but fatally flawed, bell.

barber, the   Character in *THE CONFIDENCE MAN*. The barber's sign, "No trust," provokes the CONFIDENCE MAN into a long discourse about why it is necessary to place trust in humanity. The barber remains skeptical.

Bardianna   Presence in *MARDI*. Although not, strictly speaking, a character in the novel, Bardianna informs so much of the philosopher BABBALANJA's talk that the former seems at times almost to inhabit the latter. Bardianna is an ancient authority of the isles of Mardi, known for his pithy observations. In Bardianna's will—recited in all its weird detail by Babbalanja—Melville sends up the last testament of John Jacob ASTOR.

"Barrington Isle and the Buccaneers"   Sketch Sixth of "THE ENCANTADAS."

Bartleby   Title character of "BARTLEBY, THE SCRIVENER." The neurasthenic but self-possessed young man who repeatedly declares that he would "prefer not" to participate in life's normal activities certainly reflects aspects of Melville's own personality. He also may have been based in part on Melville's boyhood friend, Eli FLY, who worked as a copyist and in later life was an invalid cared for by others.

"Bartleby, the Scrivener: A Story of Wall-Street" (1853)   Short story. An elderly lawyer with a Wall Street practice that specializes in bonds, mortgages, and deeds hires a pallid young man named Bartleby as a copyist, or scrivener. After a time, however, Bartleby informs his employer that he would "prefer not to" copy legal documents any more, instead maintaining a sort of vigil behind a folding screen in the lawyer's office. For all that the lawyer and his three other employees can tell, Bartleby eats almost nothing and seems to spend all of his time staring trancelike out of a window that affords only a view of a blank brick wall. All efforts to rouse him are met with passive resistance. One Sunday when the lawyer happens to stop by his office, he finds his way barred by Bartleby and concludes that the melancholy fellow has been living there. When Bartleby resists his employer's attempts to fire him and force him from the premises, the lawyer packs up his office and moves elsewhere. When the new tenant of the Wall Street office has Bartleby evicted, the former scrivener takes up residence in the building stairwell and sleeps in the office entryway until he is arrested for vagrancy. When the lawyer visits him in the Tombs, the city prison, he finds Bartleby once again staring at a blank wall. Bartleby refuses the special food the lawyer buys for him; when the lawyer returns a few days later, he finds Bartleby slumped at the base of the wall, dead. Unable to shake off Bartleby's strange hold on his conscience, after the scrivener's death the lawyer learns that he had previously worked in the dead letter office in Washington, a revelation that prompts the lawyer to exclaim, "Ah Bartleby! Ah humanity!"

"Bartleby" was first published anonymously in two installments in *PUTNAM'S MONTHLY MAGAZINE* in November and December 1853. It was republished as the second of *THE PIAZZA TALES* in 1855, but its author's identity was known long before that. "Bartleby" bore both the stamp of Melville's manner and traces of his biography—particularly his unwillingness to "copy" then popular literary styles. In recent times, the story has proven to be one of Melville's most frequently studied works, its elusive allegory the source of numerous interpretations. Explicators have declared Bartleby to be, variously, a Christ figure and a schizophrenic, a representation of the TRANSCENDENTALIST Henry David Thoreau and the embodiment of existential philosophy.

Barnum, P[hineas] T[aylor] (1810–1891)   Showman and promoter. Born in Bethel, Connecticut, Barnum worked at a number of professions, including editing an abolitionist newspaper, before discovering his true calling. His career as a promoter began in 1835, when he purchased an octogenarian African American woman named Joice Heth, who purported to be George Washington's 160-year-old former nurse. Barnum exhibited her widely, publishing sensational advertisements as well as anonymous attacks on her veracity by way of promotion. Playing further on the American public's eagerness to be gulled, in 1841 Barnum purchased Scudder's American Museum and Peale's Museum, combining their collections of curiosities to form his own American Museum. It was here that he displayed one of his most successful oddities, the midget he called General Tom Thumb. He also brought the Swedish singing sensation Jenny Lind to the United States in 1850. In 1855, Barnum retired to

Barnum's New Museum in New York's Madison Square caused a sensation in the mid-1800s. References to P. T. Barnum appear in several of Melville's works. (Library of Congress)

his palatial estate, called Iranistan, in Bridgeport, Connecticut, where, after serving as a state legislator from 1867 to 1869, he was elected mayor in 1875. A few years earlier, he had reentered show business, premiering his three-ring circus—"The Greatest Show on Earth"—in 1871. In 1881, he joined forces with his former rival, James A. Bailey, to form the Barnum & Bailey Circus.

P. T. Barnum figures in several works that Melville published in the late 1840s. He is a character in a series of short pieces published in 1847 in the humorous weekly *YANKEE DOODLE*. In *MARDI*, the oddities of Barnum's American Museum are reflected in the relics collected by the eccentric antiquarian, OH OH.

"The Battle for the Bay. (August, 1864.)" (1866)
Poem in *BATTLE-PIECES*. The battle in question is that for Mobile Bay, Alabama, where the Union naval officer David Farragut is said to have declared, "Damn the torpedoes!" Commanding while lashed to a mast, Farragut prevailed over the Confederates in this CIVIL WAR

encounter and earned a promotion to vice admiral. Melville's tribute yet makes clear the costs of this triumph: "But pale on the scarred fleet's decks there lay / A silent man for every silent gun."

"The Battle for the Mississippi. (April, 1862.)" (1866)
Poem in *BATTLE-PIECES*. On April 24–25, 1862, Union admiral David Farragut lashed himself to the rigging of his ship and drove through the floating wrecks guarding the harbor at New Orleans. His assault took the Confederates by surprise, and Farragut managed to take the city without firing a single shot. Melville's poem commemorating the victory is biblical, proclaiming, "The Lord is a man of war!"

"Battle of Stone River, Tennessee. A View from Oxford Cloisters. (January, 1863.)" (1866) Poem in *BATTLE-PIECES*. Melville compares this indecisive battle (also known as the Battle of Murfreesboro, Tennessee) in the CIVIL WAR with two skirmishes in the English Wars of the Roses, another civil war that pitted brother against brother. Taking the long view, he speculates that someday the Battle of Stone River could become legendary, like the English battles at Tewkesbury and Barnet Heath. The poem ends with a hopeful, if not entirely rhetorical question: "Shall North and South their rage deplore, / And reunited thrive amain / Like Yorkist and Lancastrian?"

"A Battle Picture" (1947)   Poem. One of more than 40 poems Melville left uncollected or unpublished when he died, "A Battle Picture" is one of several verses apparently inspired by Melville's observations of particular paintings, many of them viewed during his European tour in 1857.

Battle-Pieces and Aspects of the War (1866)   Collection of poems, with a prose supplement. In 1860, when Melville boarded his brother Tom's sailing ship for what was intended as a year-long voyage, he left behind a volume of poetry, for which his brother Allan was to act as agent. Allan's failure to sell the book to a publisher did not deter Melville from writing more poetry, however. Early in 1866, still searching for a means of making his writing turn a profit, he came to believe that the poems he had been writing about the CIVIL WAR could make a saleable collection. *Battle-Pieces and Aspects of the War,* which ultimately included 72 poems and a prose supplement, marked Melville's introduction to the public as a working poet.

The collection opens with a stand-alone poem, "The Portent (1859)," concerning the martyrdom of the abolitionist John BROWN. This opening piece is followed by 52 "battle-pieces," which Melville dedicates to "the memory of the three hundred thousand who in the war for the maintenance of the Union fell devotedly under the flag of their fathers"—that is, to the Union dead. This section of poems is then followed by another, consisting of 19 "Verses Inscriptive and Memorial." *Battle-Pieces* also includes a section of informational notes about the Civil War and concludes with a prose "Supplement" that is a plea for peace, charity, and common sense during Reconstruction.

Published on August 17, 1866, by HARPER & BROTHERS, *Battle-Pieces* received mixed reviews and sold a mere 486 copies in the two years following its publications. Melville, who had been obliged to subsidize the volume's publication, lost $400 on the venture.

Beauty   *See* CHIPS.

Belex   Minor character in *CLAREL*. The leader of six Arabs from BETHLEHEM, he is a Turk and a tough old warrior. His experience has made him a stoic.

Bell, Mr. and Mrs.   Minor characters in *OMOO*. Mr. Bell, a European whose plantation LONG GHOST and

the narrator visit in Taloo, had a real-life counterpart, also named Bell and also a sugar planter. In the novel, Bell is youthful, handsome, and welcoming, but the narrator expresses his disappointment at not finding Mrs. Bell at home. He has seen this Sydney native earlier in the day and thought her by far the most beautiful white woman he has seen in Polynesia. According to an 1848 journal kept by a naval lieutenant named Henry Augustus Wise, Mrs. Bell had become addicted to drink by the time she met Melville. According to Edward T. Perkins's *Na Motu; or, Reef-Rovings in the South Seas: A Narrative of Adventures at the Hawaiian, Georgian, and Society Islands* (1854), Bell and his wife later moved to the Navigators' Islands (Samoa), where Mrs. Bell drowned.

Bello ("Bello of the Hump")   Minor character in *MARDI*. Bello is the king of Dominora (England). He is bested by Vivenza (America), but manages to put down an internal revolt resembling the Chartists' rebellion of 1848 (see CHARTISM).

Bellows, Henry Whitney   Pastor of the All Souls' Unitarian Church in New York City. Elizabeth MELVILLE rented a pew there and had Bellows baptize her son Malcolm. Later Elizabeth's brother, Sam Shaw, called on Bellows to assist Elizabeth during a difficult period in her marriage. Bellows recommended kidnapping Elizabeth and taking her to Boston. Sam wrote to Bellows, indicating his doubt that his sister would go along with such a plan. Elizabeth nevertheless wrote to Bellows, acknowledging his "active interest," good advice, and "encouraging words."

"The Bell-Tower" (1855)   Short story. Melville's story is, depending on the reader's point of view, either enriched or flawed by his extensive reading. In this allegorical tale he alludes to Greek mythology and the Bible, as well as to works by Benvenuto Cellini, Edmund Spenser, Mary Shelley, and his friend Nathaniel HAWTHORNE, among others. In Renaissance Italy, a "great mechanician" named BANNADONNA builds a massive clock- and bell tower 300 feet high. To crown this monument to his ambition, he has a magnificent bell cast, but in the process he strikes a hesitant worker, killing him and marring the giant bell with some flying human debris generated by the assault. The deed is blamed on "esthetic passion," and Bannadonna's act is excused. The grand clock comprises life-size figures that personify the hours and a cloaked figure that is intended to strike the hours on the enormous bell. When the clock is unveiled to the public at one o'clock in the afternoon, the bell gives off a muffled sound. Rushing to the belfry, the town worthies find Bannadonna bleeding to death under the one-o'clock figure as his bell-ringing automaton stands over him with its clubbed arms uplifted. The great bell, scheduled to be rung at last at Bannadonna's funeral, instead falls to the ground, revealing a fatal flaw. The tower itself falls victim to an earthquake a year later. Melville concludes: "So the creator was killed by the creature. So the bell was too heavy for the tower. So the bell's main weakness was where man's blood had flawed. And so pride went before the fall."

Melville submitted his story to PUTNAM'S MONTHLY MAGAZINE in the late spring or early summer of 1855. The magazine's manuscript adviser at first recommended rejection, then changed his mind. "The Bell-Tower" was published anonymously in *Putnam's* in August 1855. It was later reprinted as the last of THE PIAZZA TALES (1856), and appeared two more times during Melville's lifetime: in Rossiter Johnson's *Little Classics: Third Volume: Tragedy* (1875) and in Edmund C. Stedman and Ellen M. Hutchinson's *A Library of American Literature from the Earliest Settlement to the Present Time,* vol. seven (1889).

Belzoni, Giovanni Battista (1778–1823) Italian archaeologist, adventurer, and showman. From 1803 to 1812 Belzoni lived in England, where he developed a hydraulic device intended to control the annual flooding of the Nile River. In 1815 he introduced the machine to Egypt, where the same year he opened the rock temple of Abu-Simbel and discovered the tomb of Seti I at Thebes. Melville seems to have shared his contemporaries' interest in Belzoni's adventures, referring to the hydraulic device in "THE HAPPY FAILURE" and to his measurements of the pyramids in "I AND MY CHIMNEY."

Bembo ("the Mowree") Character in OMOO. Bembo is the savage Mowree (Maori) New Zealand native who acts as second mate aboard the *Julia.* The narrator tells a tale about Bembo's persistent pursuit of a whale— even to the point of standing on the whale's back in order to plant his harpoon—that prefigures AHAB's pursuit in MOBY-DICK. One night the ship is anchored off Papeete and the crew is restive. Bembo gets into a fight with SYDNEY BEN and bests him, but the Mowree is pulled away before he can damage the other man. In a deep sulk, Bembo then tries to run the ship aground. The *Julia* is saved at the last minute, but Bembo is put in chains and confined below decks, never to be seen by the crew again. He is still in irons when the ship leaves Tahiti. Melville apparently based his character on a sailor named Benbow Byrne, with whom he served on the *LUCY-ANN* in 1842.

Ben *See* SYDNEY BEN.

"The Bench of Boors" (1891) Poem in TIMOLEON. In an 1857 entry in his travel diary, Melville mentions hav-

ing seen in museums in Turin and Amsterdam "tavern scenes" and "Dutch convivial scenes" painted by the Dutch genre painter David Teniers the Younger. Melville seems to have a particular painting in mind in this poem: one of Dutch boors, or peasants, "basking" in the glow of a tavern fire. Their somnolence is contrasted with the poet's own insomnia as he lies in bed, musing on Teniers's painting.

"Benito Cereno" (1855) Short story. Melville's source for this long tale is chapter 18 of Captain Amasa DELANO's autobiographical account of his maritime adventures, *Narrative of Voyages and Travels in the Northern and Southern Hemispheres* (1817), chapter 20 of which also provided Melville with material for another tale, "THE ENCANTADAS." Melville adopted Delano's real encounter in February 1800 aboard the *Perseverance* with a ship named the *Tryal* and captained by a Don Benito CERENO. In doing so, Melville changed not only the names of the ships involved in the incident, but also the characters of the individuals involved, in addition inventing a number of telling details that heighten the ambiguity of the slave rebellion aboard ship. Melville also borrowed outright one of the documents pertinent to the ensuing legal case against the rebels, which

"Benito Cereno," Melville's story of a slave revolt on a ship like this one, is considered one of his finest works. (Library of Congress)

Delano appended to his chapter. With few alterations, Melville likewise appended Don Benito's declaration, letting it speak for itself and serve as a counterbalance to the narrative.

The story opens with Delano, captain of the sealer *Bachelor's Delight,* spotting a ship in trouble in a desolate area off the southern coast of Chile. In an attempt to offer help, he and a small crew of his men row over to the *San Dominick,* a ship with a cargo of Senegalese slaves captained by the Spaniard Don Benito Cereno. Seeing the sad state of affairs aboard the slaver, Delano sends his men back to the *Bachelor's Delight* for additional supplies. Delano himself stays aboard the *San Dominick,* where the dispirited and seemingly disoriented Don Benito, accompanied by his attentive black body servant, BABO, explains that the slaver, buffeted by storms and disease, has lost all of its Spanish officers. As a result, the ship and its human cargo are in a pronounced state of disorder.

Delano, who can see this much for himself, nevertheless cannot make sense of what is happening aboard the *San Dominick.* He finds Don Benito's demeanor especially incomprehensible. When one of the slaves stabs a white sailor, the Spanish captain shrugs off the incident. Don Benito seems similarly indifferent when a magisterial slave, ATUFAL, is brought before him in chains but refuses to beg Benito's pardon for the offense that caused him to be manacled. Other slaves, engaged in polishing hatchets, make threatening gestures that Benito ignores. When Don Benito sullenly refuses Delano's offer of hospitality aboard the *Bachelor's Delight,* the American is almost convinced that the Spaniard is not what he seems. Babo, Delano concludes, is both more polite and more commanding.

It is only at the end of this very long tale that the accuracy of Delano's perceptions becomes the focus of the narrative. As he takes his leave of Don Benito, the Spaniard suddenly leaps into Delano's boat, followed by Babo, who clearly aims to kill his captain. Suddenly Amasa Delano experiences a revelation: as he casts his eyes toward the *San Dominick,* where armed slaves pursue the few remaining Spaniards, he understands that the former have been in control all along. As the appended deposition makes clear, the *San Dominick* had been the scene of a bloody slave revolt led by Babo, who also masterminded the masquerade of subservience played out for Delano's benefit.

A coda to the story, however, gives rise to still more ambiguity. As the two captains sail together toward Lima, Don Benito is unable to shake free from his melancholy. When Amasa Delano inquires, "[W]hat has cast such a shadow upon you?" Benito Cereno replies, "The negro." The master, having been violently forced into the role of a slave, finds himself unable to come to terms with the experience. Published in the bloody, contentious period leading up to the CIVIL WAR, "Benito Cereno" provided commentary on more than what Melville, in "HAWTHORNE AND HIS MOSSES," called "the power of blackness" that derives its force from human depravity and original sin.

Bentham, Jeremy (1748–1832) British philosopher considered to be the founder of UTILITARIANISM. Rather than simply supporting the status quo, laws should be shown to be socially beneficial, Bentham argued. He believed in "the greatest happiness of the greatest number." Benthamites are mentioned in *BILLY BUDD, SAILOR,* where they are regarded as practical minded thinkers who have no room for the kind of glory and idealism epitomized by Admiral Horatio NELSON in his victories over the French during the French revolutionary period.

Bentley, Richard (1794–1871) English publisher. Born in London, Bentley set up his first printing establishment there in 1819 with his brother. In 1829, he joined with Henry Colburn in a publishing firm that specialized in fashionable fiction. The partners split up in 1832, but Bentley continued his success, publishing such American authors as James Fenimore COOPER and Henry Wadsworth Longfellow, and in 1837 starting a magazine he named *Bentley's Miscellany.* When John Murray declined to publish Melville's third novel, *MARDI,* Bentley picked it up, publishing it in 1849 in a lavish edition. *Mardi* sold exceedingly poorly in England, and Bentley never recouped his publication expenses. Still, Bentley agreed to publish Melville's next three novels, *REDBURN, WHITE-JACKET,* and *MOBY-DICK*—albeit on far more modest terms. But Bentley lost money on these ventures as well, and when Melville offered him his next novel, *PIERRE,* in 1852, Bentley demurred, indicating that not only was Melville turning material out too quickly, he also was writing abstrusely. Bentley's suggestion that Melville employ an editor to make judicious cuts prompted the frustrated author to cut off communications for several months. Still, Bentley seems to have held Melville in esteem, for later in 1852 he asked the American writer to contribute to the *Miscellany.* Bentley suffered severe financial reversals in 1859 when the House of Lords nullified his claim to British copyrights of American books. In 1867, after he was injured in a railway accident, he turned his business over to his son, George Bentley.

"The Berg (A Dream.)" (1888) Poem in *JOHN MARR.* In a dream, the speaker sees "a ship of martial build" steer into an iceberg, "Directed by madness." Nothing, perhaps, could so well signify nature's indifference to the fate of man as the "sullen" iceberg, itself "Adrift dissolving, bound for death."

Berkeley, George (1685–1753) Melville refers to this Anglo-Irish philosopher's "airy exaltations" in *PIERRE*. Unlike the philosopher Thomas HOBBES, who sought the origin of human ideas and feelings in the operations of the body, Berkeley stated: *esse est percipi* ("to be is to be perceived"); i.e., there is no external reality independent of humans' perception of that reality. Hobbes's materialism led to determinism and atheism, since, in Berkeley's view, Hobbes advocated a philosophy that imprisoned man in the body. But Melville, a man of the world, found it impossible to accept Berkeley's conclusion, which was to deny the existence of matter and the material world. Pierre is caught in precisely this Berkleyan/Hobbesian dilemma: on one hand, he is insufficiently grounded in the world; on the other, he cannot leave the world to inhabit the higher realm of ideas that Berkeley believed in. In other words, neither idealism nor materialism can serve as Pierre's guide.

Bethlehem South of Jerusalem in what is now the Israel-occupied West Bank of the Jordan, Bethlehem is first mentioned in Egyptian records of the 14th century B.C. It is the native city of King David. It also contains the Church of the Nativity, the reputed site of Christ's birth. The city became a monastic center when St. Jerome came to live there in 384. In *CLAREL,* the pilgrims arrive in Bethlehem after 10 days of traveling. It is the end of their journey. Melville visited the city and the site of Christ's birth. He was shown through the Church of the Nativity by a monk, and he also went out on the roof where his pilgrims view the entire city.

Biddy Minor character in "JIMMY ROSE," "I AND MY CHIMNEY," and "THE APPLE-TREE TABLE." In all three stories, Biddy serves as a maid in the narrator's household. Her largest role comes in the last of these stories, where she displays an active belief in SPIRITUALISM.

Bildad, Captain Minor character in *MOBY-DICK.* Part-owner of the *Pequod,* he interests Ishmael, who wonders how Bildad reconciles his Quaker beliefs in pacifism and nonviolence with his career as a whale hunter.

Billy Budd The handsome sailor in *BILLY BUDD, SAILOR* doomed to be executed precisely because he is so innocent. Beloved of all, including Captain VERE, who feels compelled to execute him, Billy's fate raises questions about predestination and human nature.

Billy Budd, Sailor (1924) Melville's last work of prose fiction. This short novel appears to have grown out of Melville's poem "Billy in the Darbies," which he appended to the ending of *Billy Budd.* He drew on many of facts of the SOMERS MUTINY in creating his narrative. According to Melville biographer Laurie

Robertson-Lorant, Melville had 50 manuscript pages in hand by the spring of 1888. He continued working on the novella through the winter of 1888–89, so that by March he had 350 manuscript pages, having added several scenes and characters.

As in *MOBY-DICK,* the narrative of *Billy Budd* is suffused with conflicting points of view and a highly symbolic handling of events. The history of criticism of the novel suggests Melville meant his work to reflect the profound ambiguity and ambivalence of human motivations. Captain VERE, for example, has been a center of controversy, with critics arguing alternately that Melville intended to support or to condemn the duty-driven officer.

SYNOPSIS

Billy Budd is dedicated to English seaman Jack CHASE, with whom Melville served aboard the U.S. frigate *UNITED STATES* in 1843.

Chapter 1
The story begins with the narrator's description of the phenomenon of the "handsome sailor," a man built so symmetrically that he excites the awe of his fellow seamen. The narrator himself saw such a specimen of perfect humanity in the figure of an African seaman on a dock in Liverpool, a man so beautifully proportioned he would be favored by "Anacharsis Cloots" (see CLOOTZ) as a representative of the human species in the French assembly he proposed after the FRENCH REVOLUTION of 1789. The figure the narrator is recalling has nothing in common with the sailor as dandy; rather, he was a type of the honest, physically powerful man. Such is the Billy or "Baby" Budd of the narrative.

"Toward the close of the 18th century," the 21-year-old English foretopman began his career at sea as an impressed sailor (see IMPRESSMENT), having been taken off a merchant ship, the *RIGHTS OF MAN,* and forced to serve on a British man of war, the *INDOMITABLE.* Billy was the only man selected, and he made no protest, although a protest would not have done him any good anyway. Captain GRAVELING, the shipmaster of the merchantman, tells Lieutenant RATCLIFF of the *Indomitable* that he is taking his best man. Billy had calmed a fractious ship, "sugaring even the sourest man," Graveling points out. Provoked by Billy's sweetness, a sailor called Red Whiskers gave him a hard poke in the ribs, and Billy let fly with his arm, and in less than a minute gave the man a "drubbing." Yet Red Whiskers ever after seemed, as Graveling puts it, in love with Billy.

The lieutenant takes the story as a joke, referring to Billy with his baggage as "Apollo with a portmanteau." So Billy says goodbye to the *Rights of Man,* named after Thomas Paine's famous book—a reply to Edmund BURKE's attack on the French Revolution. The ship's owner, like Stephen GIRARD of Philadelphia, named his ships after philosophers such as VOLTAIRE and DIDEROT, whom he admired. The lieutenant takes Billy's good-natured goodbye to the *Rights of Man* as a sly criticism of his impressment, although the narrator clearly suggests Billy is simply saying goodbye. Billy is no philosopher, though by nature he is something of a fatalist, taking what comes in his stride. The narrator suggests he may even think of the impressment as a welcome adventure.

Chapter 2

On the *Indomitable*, Billy does not enjoy quite the popularity he had on the *Rights of Man*. He seems very young and almost feminine in appearance. But Billy adjusts well, apparently ignoring the ambiguous smiles on some of the seasoned sailor's faces. Because Billy looks like a Greek god, he is questioned about his family. He knows nothing about it, he says simply. A foundling, he is illiterate, but he likes to sing and has a splendid voice. He is, the narrator says, a kind of "upright barbarian," perhaps not much different from Adam before the serpent entered paradise. He is rather like "Caspar Hauser wandering dazed in any Christian capital of our time." (See HAUSER, KASPAR.) Like the beautiful heroine with only one flaw in a minor HAWTHORNE tale, Billy has a defect: he stutters when he is under extreme pressure. Thus Billy is not seen as a "conventional hero" in a story that is "no romance."

Chapters 3–5

The *Indomitable* is on its way to join the Mediterranean fleet. It is the summer of 1797. There have been mutinies at SPITHEAD and NORE, a direct result, the narrator suggests, of the FRENCH DIRECTORY and their proselytizing armies. But England itself is not in danger of revolution, and the mutinies represent a "distempering irruption of fever in a frame constitutionally sound." Indeed, even those among the mutineers would contribute later to Horatio Viscount NELSON's great victories.

The narrator digresses to explain how ships and war have changed since Nelson's day. No longer are ships so picturesque in the age of "ironclads." Nelson himself may seem outmoded to contemporary utilitarians who argue that he unnecessarily exposed his own body to gunfire at the battle that cost him his life. Indeed, had Nelson lived, he might have saved more of his fleet and not just won a naval victory, suggest the Benthamites (see UTILITARIANISM). But *"might-have-been"* is a "boggy ground," the narrator retorts. The narrator notes that the Duke of WELLINGTON, the great British general of the Napoleonic Wars, is not such a "trumpet to the blood" as Nelson, and that may be because Nelson, unlike Wellington, was not so personally prudent. Indeed, in putting on his conspicuous medals in battle, Nelson does nothing more than act out the heroic deeds celebrated in poetry.

Returning to the subject of the mutinies, the narrator emphasizes that they were put down, but that discontent lingered and was likely to break out again. Nelson himself was transferred to a potentially mutinous ship because it was thought that his good patriotic example would inspire the men.

Chapters 6–7

Aboard the *Indomitable* there is no evidence of recent mutinies in the British fleet. The ship's captain, Edward Fairfax Vere, sets the example. He is intrepid and mindful of his men, although he brooks no insubordination. Although he has been favored by the nobility, the narrator suggests he has earned his promotions through intelligent and valiant service. On shore he is unobtrusive—not a physically imposing man and not one to use the language of the sea. He is a sober man, with apparently not much of a sense of humor. Although he has a dreamy side, Vere never allows himself to lose control of his command. He gets his nickname, Starry Vere, from an Andrew MARVELL poem that celebrates the "discipline severe / of Fairfax and the starry Vere."

Something of an intellectual, Vere prefers biography and history to fiction. Unlike a literary man, he is drawn more to the subject than to the style of what he reads. Vere is a conservative, believing that revolution merely upsets the world; it cannot provide a better standard of existence. Although he is liked and respected by his fellow officers, some find him somewhat "pedantic."

Chapter 8

The narrator describes John CLAGGART, the master-at-arms. Originally the title referred to an officer charged with supervising the use of weapons aboard ship. As guns became more sophisticated and hand-to-hand combat became outmoded, however, the master-at-arms became a kind of "chief of police," ensuring discipline. Claggart is about 35, fairly tall, with a good face (well formed), although the narrator mentions a heaviness around the jaw that reminds him of Titus OATES. There is something dark about him that goes well beyond his curly jet-black hair. He also has the air of someone brought up in a higher station of life than a master-at-arms. Nothing is known about his background, and from a slight foreignness in his speech it is surmised that perhaps he was not born English. Indeed, at a time when men were taken out of London jails to serve in the navy, almost anything is possible in Claggart's case. That Claggart might have come from the criminal class is possible, because it is known that in his first tour of duty he had to take the lowest position aboard ship. But his superiority and sobriety, his "austere patriotism," and his "ingratiating deference" to superiors led to his rapid advancement.

Chapters 9–13
Billy's shipmates laugh at his conscientious labor. But he has in mind the experience of watching a man flogged for malingering. Billy vowed never to court such trouble. But aboard the *Indomitable*, he finds himself being chastened for infractions—such as the improper stowing of his bag. Billy goes to a veteran seaman, old DANSKER, for advice. Dansker served with Nelson on the *Agamemnon*. Dansker tells Billy that Claggart is "down on you." Billy is surprised, since he has heard crew members say Claggart refers to him as sweet and charming, and Claggart has always spoken pleasantly to Billy. Dansker insists this is all because he is down on Billy. Billy is dumbfounded as Dansker takes refuge in a "pithy guarded cynicism."

The next day Billy happens to spill a bowl of soup in the path of Claggart, who stifles a hasty comment and smiles ambiguously, saying "Handsome is as handsome did it too." Billy takes the words as another sign that if anything, Claggart favors him. The narrator, however, observes bitterness in Claggart's attitude which he just manages to check in Billy's presence, along with something mysterious and Radcliffian (see RADCLIFFE, MRS. ANN) in Claggart's spontaneous dislike. The narrator suggests there may be no rational explanation for Claggart's behavior; rather, he exhibits the "mania of an evil nature."

The narrator speculates that it is Billy's "significant personal beauty" that agitates Claggart. Billy's innocence also infuriates Claggart, who envies the pure state that Billy exemplifies. Powerless to change his nature, Claggart can only, like the scorpion, follow his predestined form of behavior. Claggart (the narrator supposes) suspects Billy of spilling his soup as a provocation to Claggart. The master-at-arms is encouraged in this line of thinking by SQUEAK, one of his subordinates whom Claggart has encouraged to play tricks on Billy. Squeak adds his own mischief by making up critical things Billy is supposed to have said about Claggart. Thus Squeak and the incident with the soup only spur Claggart on to provoke Billy further.

Chapters 14–16
Billy is startled out of his sleep by a voice that bids him to a meeting, where it is hinted that perhaps Billy could assist in a mutiny if it came to that—although the word *mutiny* is never used. A flustered and then angered Billy warns the man, an afterguardsman, to stop such talk or he will be flung overboard. The man retreats as a forecastleman questions Billy about the ruckus.

Never having been approached before about such an intrigue, Billy is puzzled, especially when the fellow who approached him behaves later as though nothing happened and treats Billy as a genial mate. When Billy tells Dansker about the incident, it only confirms the old man's conviction that Claggart is "down on" Billy.

To an uncomprehending Billy, Dansker only says "cat's paw," implying that the afterguardsman has been in Claggart's employ, for a cat's paw is someone used by another as a dupe or tool.

The narrator suggests that, like many seamen, Billy was not of a mind to be suspicious. It would not occur to Billy that Claggart would have such an animosity toward him or engage in such elaborate efforts to trap him.

Chapters 17–20
Billy now finds he is no longer harassed with mishaps and that Claggart's treatment of him is even better. The narrator, however, describes a Claggart who watches Billy with a yearning, melancholy expression. It is almost as if Claggart is mourning that he cannot be close to Billy, cannot love him. His monomania, however, is disguised by a rational demeanor even as a subterranean disturbance makes it certain that there will be some culmination to Claggart's feelings.

Claggart approaches Captain Vere, feigning reluctance to report that a sailor aboard ship, recently impressed, is a "dangerous character." Claggart implies that the man may be fomenting a mutiny. Vere finds Claggart distasteful, although he is barely conscious of his repugnance. He is surprised to hear the handsome Billy Budd named as the suspicious sailor. Claggart calls Billy a "deep one" who has ingratiated himself with the crew.

Vere, who was expecting to promote Billy, warns Claggart of the penalties of bearing false witness. Trying to keep the matter as quiet as possible until he determines the truth of Claggart's charges, Vere arranges an interview with Billy Budd out of the sight of the crew.

The trusting Billy has no idea of the accusation against him. He comes to the captain's cabin hoping that he will be promoted. Signaled by the captain, Claggart comes close to Billy and repeats his charge. Billy is dumbfounded, and Claggart's expression changes to that of a submarine creature avid for prey. Choked with emotion, Billy finds himself unable to respond to Vere's command that he speak and defend himself. The narrator likens Billy to a "vestal priestess" paralyzed by the sentence of doom. Vere divines that Billy is too upset to talk and tells him to take his time. Unfortunately, his kindly, even fatherly concern only makes Billy feel worse, so that impulsively he lashes out with his fist, striking Claggart, who falls immediately to the floor.

Vere calls Billy a "fated boy," and the two try to pick up Claggart, who feels like a "dead snake." Vere changes from a paternal figure to a "military disciplinarian." Vere calls the SURGEON to verify that Claggart is dead, and when the surgeon confirms the captain's suspicion, Vere blurts out: "Struck dead by an angel of

God! Yet the angel must hang!" Vere tells the surgeon to inform Mr. Mordant, the CAPTAIN OF MARINES, that there is to be a drumhead court and to keep the matter among the officers.

The disconcerted surgeon thinks the idea of a court "impolitic." Why not simply put Billy in confinement and turn him over to the admiral? Has Vere lost his senses? The surgeon briefly considers the possibility but realizes that to oppose Vere at this point is to foment mutiny. When the surgeon informs the other officers they, too, think the matter should be referred to the admiral.

Chapter 21
Whether Captain Vere suffers from a disordered mind has to be deduced, the narrator insists, from the narrative itself. The narrator reveals that subsequently Vere was criticized for acting so quickly and without consulting his superiors. With the Nore mutiny in mind, however, Vere felt it necessary to take action immediately. In calling together the drumhead court of FIRST LIEUTENANT, SAILING MASTER, and Captain of Marines, Vere declares he will be the one to be accountable for their actions, and the narrator makes clear that Vere is not a man to exercise his authority for the mere pleasure of the exercise. Although he sees certain limitations in each officer, the captain retains his faith in them and in the necessity of a swift judgment. When questioned by the first lieutenant, Billy confirms Vere's eyewitness account, stipulating only that he is innocent of the charges Claggart brought against him. The first lieutenant clearly indicates that he believes Billy, and Vere echoes the sentiment. Billy explains that he could not find his tongue and could answer only with a blow, not meaning, however, to kill Claggart. Billy denies knowing anything about a mutiny (suppressing the incident with the man who approached him about a revolt) and says there was no enmity between him and Claggart. As to why Claggart should raise such a foul accusation, Billy replies with bafflement, and Vere interrupts to say that it does not matter. Who can say what Claggart felt? It is the "mystery of iniquity." The point is Billy's blow and its result. The narrator suggests that Vere's words constitute a "prejudgment." Billy has no more to say.

Vere addresses the officers, saying they have a military duty to perform that clashes with their moral scruples and compassion. The natural feeling the men have for Billy has to be counteracted by the fact that they do not serve nature but the king. Even in this exceptional case, they must remember that they "fight at command" and must follow the law. The men become agitated when Vere suggests they must ignore their own consciences in favor of loyalty to the imperial power they serve. The blow is a capital crime—but not an intended one, the captain of marines breaks in. He points out that no mutiny was planned. The

Mutiny Act, Vere replies, does not recognize acts of individual will or conscience. In another kind of court, certainly, the extenuating circumstances of Billy's blow would be considered. Billy's motives, in other words, are irrelevant. The lieutenant suggests that the punishment could be "mitigated," but it is impossible to explain such an action to the ship's crew. Under naval regulations, officers do not explain the reasons for their actions. Even if they did, how would this satisfy sailors who are used to "arbitrary discipline," not finely discriminating judgments? An act of clemency would be interpreted as cowardliness, Vere concludes.

Although the officers have qualms, they also respect Vere's earnestness, no less than the fact that he is their superior. They are keenly aware that clemency may be misinterpreted by mutineers. The narrator, not without some sympathy for Vere's position, cites a much later mutiny that occurred aboard the SOMERS in 1842, which resulted in executions upheld by a naval court of inquiry. It is one thing to have the leisure to judge a situation in retrospect, the narrator emphasizes, and another to feel the urgency of making a decision. In brief, Vere's drumhead court decides that Billy must hang.

Chapter 22
Captain Vere privately communicates the court's judgment to Billy Budd. Although there is no witness to this meeting, the narrator speculates that Vere, old enough to be Billy's father, imparted the verdict and the reasons for Billy's execution with a compassionate, paternal attitude that would have touched Billy, who could see how much the captain liked him. At any rate, the lieutenant observes the captain emerging from Billy's cabin with his face full of anguish.

Chapters 23–24
Although it takes no more than an hour and a half to consider and pronounce judgment, rumors are already rife aboard the *Indomitable*. Vere promptly addresses the men of the ship, briefly relating the circumstances that will lead to Billy's execution the following morning. Vere mentions nothing of mutiny, presuming his actions are more telling than any further words from him. The crew take the captain's speech as if it were a "CALVINISTIC text." The officers keep their misgivings to themselves, even though there is some murmuring among the crew.

Devastated by his encounter with "evil incarnate," Billy is somewhat heartened by Vere's kind treatment of him. The CHAPLAIN tries to instruct and comfort Billy, but there seems little to be done for an innocent young man who resembles one of FRA ANGELICO's seraphs. In his natural state, Billy is like one of those Tahitians of Captain COOK's time. Persuaded of Billy's innocence, the chaplain nevertheless does not try to mitigate the result of martial law. He has put his religion at the service of the state, the narrator suggests.

Chapter 25
Eight bells summon the crew to witness the execution at 4 A.M. Hardly a word is uttered as the men assemble. Billy suddenly cries out "God bless Captain Vere!" Vere is moved, but he stands "erectly rigid." Billy is hanged against the overhanging fleecy white sky, a lamb of God, "ascended" and "took the full rose of the dawn."

Chapter 26 A Digression
The PURSER and the surgeon argue over why Billy's body did not exhibit the usual muscular spasm after he was hanged. It cannot be a question of will power (the purser's theory) because (the surgeon explains) the action of the body is involuntary. The surgeon cannot explain the phenomenon scientifically and soon withdraws from the argument, saying he is needed elsewhere.

Chapter 27
Complete silence greets Billy's execution. The men are ordered to disperse. Vere has followed all the forms of the military code.

Chapters 28–30
Shortly after Billy's execution, Vere is mortally wounded in a battle with a French ship. Thus he is cut off too early to experience the glory of the British naval victories at the Battle of the NILE and at the Battle of TRAFALGAR. He dies murmuring Billy Budd's name.

A naval chronicle reports the execution of "William Budd," misstating the facts by reporting that Billy stabbed Claggart. The chronicle speculates that Budd was no Englishman but an alien opposed to the English. It extolls Claggart's faithful service and concludes that the swift sentence has restored order.

The spar from which Billy is hanged is like a piece of the true cross to the men who saw him executed, the narrator reports. The myth of Billy's innocence is perpetuated in a poem, "Billy in the Darbies." This poem ends the book. It describes the chaplain entering the "Lone Bay" where Billy is kept. Billy thinks of his hanging and the end of his life. Billy imagines his shipmates there to comfort him and the watery grave that awaits him. He thinks he hears a sentry approaching and says "Just ease these darbies at the wrist, / And roll me over fair! / I am sleepy, and the oozy weeds about me twist."

PUBLICATION HISTORY

Melville was still at work on *Billy Budd* when he died. Although the work was substantially finished, he continued to polish it as if he regarded this last work of fiction as his final testament. His wife stored the drafts of his novella in a tin bread box, where they remained until her death in 1906. The manuscripts then were

integrated into Melville's papers, but the work was not published until 1924, just as interest in Melville was renewed. The first edition of *Billy Budd* contained several errors and inconsistencies, some of which may have been intentional if Melville aimed to write a narrative questioning the reliability of his narrator or of history itself. As one of Melville's most suggestive texts, *Billy Budd* continues to provoke widely differing interpretations. See, for example, the edition published by Harrison Hayford and Merton M. Sealts Jr., prepared in 1962. These scholars attempt to date and to annotate all of Melville's drafts as a means of exploring the kind of story he intended to write.

bisexuality A sexual orientation that is characterized by attraction to both males and females. Speculation about Melville's sexual orientation has continued, despite his marriage and four children. Biographers take note of his experiences on sailing ships, traditional havens for the expression of homoerotic feelings. There are also striking descriptions of the beautiful men in TYPEE, and scenes in MOBY-DICK of ISHMAEL and QUEEQUEG sharing a bed and embraces. Certainly Melville had a more relaxed view of sexuality than many of his Victorian contemporaries, but hard evidence of his bisexuality has not been found. Yet biographers such as Laurie Robertson-Lorant assume some sort of homoerotic experience in Melville's early years because of its prevalence in his work and because of his strong attraction to kindred spirits such as Nathaniel HAWTHORNE, who also dealt with homoerotic feelings in *The Blithedale Romance* (1852). The issue of Melville's sexual orientation is complicated because 19th-century men and women often used passionate language to describe intimate relationships that were not necessarily sexual.

Black Dan Minor character in OMOO. A short-tempered sailor on board the *Julia,* he adds his name to the round robin, the petition written in the round, listing the crew's complaints.

Bland Character in WHITE-JACKET. Bland is a marine and the sergeant-at-arms aboard the NEVERSINK. He is responsible for carrying out the odious floggings that are liberally dispensed to the men for every breach of discipline, real or imagined. The common sailors naturally feel antipathy toward Bland, which is compounded by his hypocrisy. Although liquor is prohibited, Bland smuggles it aboard while the ship is harbored in Rio de Janeiro; when he is caught, he is only temporarily relieved of his position. The men are surprised to discover that while he is without rank, Bland is quite a sociable fellow. Melville may have based this character on William McNally, a former master-at-arms and also the author of *Evils and Abuses in the Naval* *and Merchant Service Exposed* (1839), one of the books from which Melville borrowed heavily in writing *White-Jacket.*

Blandmour Character in "POOR MAN'S PUDDING AND RICH MAN'S CRUMBS." In "Picture First: Poor Man's Pudding," the narrator is a guest at the poet Blandmour's country house, where the literary man expatiates about the gifts that nature showers on rich and poor alike, making even the poor man's life a good one and his lack of wealth immaterial.

"The Blue-Bird" (1924) Poem in *WEEDS AND WILDINGS.* This poem, which is part of the section titled "The Year," first mourns the death of the bluebird, who arrived too soon in a garden still beset by shrill March winds. The mildness of June, however, transforms the seemingly lost welkin blue of the bird into the azure of larkspur bells, as "[t]he Bird's transfigured in the flower." Resurrection—Christian or not—was much on Melville's mind in his last years, as *Billy Budd* also evinces.

Blunt, Bill ("Liverpool," "William"?) Minor character in *OMOO.* A sailor aboard the *Julia,* Bill Blunt signs his name to the round robin complaint, adding—after the fashion of seamen who are often known by their place of origin—"alias Liverpool." Bill Blunt is probably also the "William" who is imprisoned with the narrator and other "mutineers" in the CALABOOZA BERETANEE, where he slugs down the liniment sent by Doctor Johnson with instructions to "rub well in."

Blunt, Jack Minor character in *REDBURN.* A 25-year-old member of the crew aboard the *Highlander,* Blunt is known aboard ship as an "Irish Cockney." He takes a romantic view of life at sea—and indeed, of life in general. A believer in witchcraft and magic, potions and pills, he is also the possessor of a "Dream Book" purporting to be a treatise on divination. Melville may have based Blunt on James Johnson, a 20-year-old Irishman who served with him on the *St. Lawrence* in 1839.

Bob, Captain Minor character in *OMOO.* Captain Bob is the rotund, generous, and easygoing Tahitian jailor at the CALABOOZA BERETANEE. Bob is an old man, but not so old as to have known Captain COOK, as he casually proclaims. A journal kept by a naval lieutenant named Henry Augustus Wise indicates that Bob was in fact a real person, but that he was dead by 1848.

Bolton, Harry Character in *REDBURN.* Redburn encounters the beautiful youth Harry Bolton near the Liverpool docks. To the credulous Wellingborough REDBURN, Harry gives every appearance of being what he says he is: the scion of an aristocratic family, able to

converse about "the curricle he used to drive in Hyde Park . . . the measurement of Madame Vestris' ankle." Redburn, however, soon begins to suspect that Harry is other than he seems. After spiriting Redburn away to London for a mysterious night at a luxurious gambling hall where he loses what remains of his money, Harry joins the crew of the *Highlander.* Having been hired largely on the basis of his claimed experience as a midshipman aboard an East India trader, Harry proves incapable even of climbing the rigging. Despite Harry's obvious prevarications, Redburn maintains the friendship, and when the *Highlander* reaches New York, the two celebrate together the end of their voyage. Redburn puts the penniless, friendless Harry in touch with an acquaintance who may help him find a job. When these efforts fail, Redburn loses touch with his friend. Only years later does Redburn learn that Harry died while on a whaling cruise, crushed between the ship and the whale itself.

book publishing In the 19th century, book publishing in the United States began to nurture an indigenous literature. Beginning with such authors as Washington IRVING and James Fenimore COOPER, American publishers were able to sell books based on American settings by American authors. Until the 1830s, most literature was imported or pirated from England; that is, American publishers and printers merely took (without permission from authors or publishers) whatever had been published in England and republished it in America. Authors such as Charles Dickens protested this practice of piracy and agitated for the passage of copyright laws to protect the author's property. Well into the 1840s and 1850s, however, when Melville was most active as a published author, English literature continued to usurp a large share of the American market—as Edgar Allan Poe and Ralph Waldo EMERSON complained. Melville traveled to England in part because he was better able to find publishers, such as John MURRAY and Richard BENTLEY, who were willing to take a chance on a new author in the well-developed British market. English editions of Melville's work were often timed to be nearly simultaneous with American editions so that American pirates could not scoop up works published in England for resale in America.

After his initial successes, Melville found it increasingly hard to write for the market. As his readership fell off, so did the amounts that publishers were willing to advance him. Melville wanted a popular audience, yet at the same time he wanted to write enduring literature. When he found he could not satisfy the critics or the public, he withdrew from novel writing. He continued to receive small royalty checks until his death, but his view of a literary career became increasingly cynical. His disgust over the literary world is clearly evident in *PIERRE,* where the budding author is first lionized and then finds himself increasingly isolated when he is not able to produce work that satisfies himself or the public.

Boomer, Captain Minor character in *MOBY-DICK*. His ship, the *Samuel Enderby* of London, has an encounter with the whale. When AHAB questions Boomer about it, Ahab learns that although Boomer has lost an arm to Moby-Dick, he has no intention of pursuing the whale and is not driven by Ahab's mania for revenge.

Borabolla Minor character in *MARDI*. King of the island of Mondoldo, Borabolla welcomes TAJI and MEDIA, whom he calls his cousin, and their party to a feast. He later sends word that JARL, who stayed behind, has died on Mondoldo.

Boston Until almost the middle of the 19th century, Boston was America's intellectual and literary capital. As a seat of learning, with Harvard University and the New England transcendentalists nearby, the city's only true rival was Philadelphia. But beginning in the 1820s, particularly with the sensational success of Washington IRVING and his Knickerbocker stories, New York grew in importance as a literary capital. By the 1840s, when Melville began publishing, New York was definitely the place to be for a promising author. The large amounts of money flowing into busy New York, the start-up of many new literary magazines, attracted men and women with literary aspirations.

For Melville, the heady atmosphere of New York became too much, and Boston often served as a refuge. Not only could he meet writers there who were steeped in a literary tradition that New Yorkers scorned or were ignorant of, but he also could find peace and encouragement from his wife Elizabeth's family, who welcomed him for many Thanksgiving holidays.

Bradford, Alexander Warfield (1815–1867) Lawyer and Melville family friend. Bradford's family and Melville's had a long association; Bradford's father had served as the Melville family minister in ALBANY, NEW YORK. Bradford himself attended Albany Academy with Melville's older brother, Gansevoort, and subsequently was a successful lawyer and politician, scholar of Native American history, and coeditor of the *American Review*. He was able to help both Gansevoort and Allan Melville professionally and tried to do the same for Herman, possibly offering to publish an article about *TYPEE* in 1846 and recommending Herman Melville to Abraham Lincoln in 1861 as a candidate for a consular appointment. By all accounts, Bradford was both well connected and generous. In *REDBURN*, Melville transforms him into Mr. Jones, the family friend who acts as the protagonist's host in NEW YORK CITY and helps him find a position aboard the *Highlander*.

Braid Beard *See* MOHI.

breadfruit A tree and its edible fruit. A staple of Polynesian life, the breadfruit—a species of mulberry—is cultivated for its fruit, its wood, its milky sap (which can be made into a waterproofing compound), and its bark (which can be made into TAPA cloth). The tree grows to a height of approximately 40 feet and bears fruit the size of small melon, with a rough exterior and white, mealy interior. The pulp is often baked, resulting in a soft, sweet mass. It can also be dried and ground into flour for making biscuits, breads, and puddings. Melville mentions breadfruit in all his books set in the South Seas, but in *TYPEE*, he devotes almost an entire chapter to descriptions of the breadfruit and methods of preparing it.

"Bridegroom-Dick" (1888) Poem in *JOHN MARR*. The titular character, an old salt, relates his past seafaring adventures to his "old woman," Bonny Blue. He tells of sailing aboard a wooden ship off Vera Cruz, scene of the victory of "Guert Gan" (doubtless a reference to Melville's cousin Guert GANSEVOORT, who distinguished himself during the MEXICAN WAR before his naval career was sullied by drink and involvement in the *SOMERS* MUTINY. Dick speaks, too, of the stoicism of a Finnish sailor whose admirable self-control motivates his captain to spare him from a FLOGGING. (Melville was working on the narrative that eventually became *BILLY BUDD* at the same time he was composing the poems in *John Marr*.) Dick recalls the CIVIL WAR and its ironclads, and his participation with Admiral Farragut at the Battle for the Bay, waged at Mobile, Alabama, in August 1864. In the end he begs a kiss from his wife, calling himself a "died-down candle."

Bridewell, Lieutenant Minor character in *WHITE-JACKET*. Bridewell is the first lieutenant aboard the narrator's man-of-war, the *NEVERSINK*.

Bridges, James Minor character in *ISRAEL POTTER*. Along with Horn TOOK and John WOODCOCK, Bridges forms a conspiracy of agents in England who aim to aid the American Revolution. Israel agrees to take to Paris the papers that Bridges and the other agents have to get to Benjamin FRANKLIN.

Brodhead, John Romeyn (1814–1873) American diplomat and historian. The son of a Dutch Reformed Church minister, Brodhead was born in Philadelphia but moved with his family to New York in 1826. He attended the Albany Academy, where he was a schoolmate of Herman Melville's older brother, Gansevoort. After graduating from Rutgers College, Brodhead studied law, which he practiced only briefly in NEW YORK CITY before moving to Saugerties, New York, to care for his ailing father. In 1839 he began a diplomatic career in which he first acted as an archivist for New York State, then succeeded Gansevoort Melville as secretary to the American legation in London. Brodhead also took Gansevoort's place as Herman Melville's British literary agent, helping to secure the publication in England of OMOO after Gansevoort's death. He also steered Melville to the publisher Richard BENTLEY when John MURRAY declined to publish MARDI. Brodhead went on to become an eminent historian, publishing several volumes on the history of New York.

Brown, John (1800–1859) American abolitionist, born in Torrington, Connecticut. His family had a history of mental disease, and Brown was never able to make a success at any form of employment he attempted. He began his militant abolitionism in 1855, when he left Ohio, where he had lived since 1805, to join the free-soil agitators bent on stopping slavery's expansion to Kansas. Brown and his sons were involved in violent confrontations with antislavery forces there. He is most famous for his raid (October 16, 1859) on the federal arsenal at Harper's Ferry. Aided by 16 white and five black men, Brown thought his attack would spur a general uprising of the slaves in Virginia and then in the rest of the South. Brown and his men were apprehended by Colonel Robert E. Lee. Brown's men killed three militia and one marine but lost 10 killed and seven captured, including Brown. He became a cause célèbre for abolitionists and an antislavery martyr after he was hanged. He was lauded by writers such as Ralph Waldo EMERSON and Henry David Thoreau. Melville made no public statement about John Brown, but his respect for Brown's fierce determination to free the slaves is reflected in one of his finest poems, "THE PORTENT."

Browne, J. Ross (1821–1875) This author's *Etchings of a Whaling Cruise* (1846) provided Melville with excellent background material for *MOBY-DICK*. Melville reviewed Browne's book, finding its presentation of "unvarnished facts" without charm or romance. Browne's book is probably one factor that led Melville to believe the subject of whaling was ripe for his imagination.

Browne, Sir Thomas (1605–1682) English physician, philosopher, and essayist. Born in London and educated at Oxford University, Browne traveled widely in Europe before studying medicine at Padua and Montpelier, eventually receiving a doctorate from Leiden. He settled in Norwich, where he practiced medicine and pursued scholarship. His first important work, *Religio Medici* (Religion of a Doctor), a justification of his profession, was probably written in 1635 and was initially published—without his permission—in

1642. His most ambitious work, *Pseudodoxia Epidemica* (commonly known as *Vulgar Errors*), is an unscientific, encyclopedic analysis of human folly that was published in 1646. *Hydriotaphia, or Urn Burial*, a treatise on death and burial, appeared together with *The Garden of Cyrus,* an examination of the mystical significance of the number *5,* in 1658. He was knighted by Charles II in 1671 for his antiquarian scholarship, but it is Browne's richly allusive style that left an impact on future generations. Melville was an avid reader of Browne and called him a "crack'd archangel." Browne's influence can be seen throughout the Melville canon. It is particularly apparent, however, in MARDI, where many of the speeches given the philosopher BABBALANJA echo Browne, and the poet Vavona—whom Babbalanja frequently quotes and whom he refers to as both an "archangel" and a "crack-pated god"—is thought to represent Browne.

Bruat, Armand-Joseph (1796–1855) French naval officer. In 1843, Bruat was appointed governor of the recently annexed islands of the MARQUESAS and Tahiti (see SOCIETY ISLANDS). Headquartered in Papeetee, he had virtually unlimited powers. In OMOO, Melville describes him as Admiral DUPETIT-THOUARS's hated henchman. Bruat encountered numerous difficulties during his sojourn in Tahiti, feuding with British authorities and putting down a native uprising. In 1847 he left Tahiti to take up a post as governor of the Antilles.

Bryant, William Cullen (1794–1878) American poet and editor, born in Cummington, Massachusetts. His first book, *Poems* (1821), established his reputation. He became a leading progressive journalist during his editorship of the New York *Evening Post* from 1829 to 1878. He is best known for his anthologized poems "To A Waterfowl" and "Thanatopsis." A contemporary of Walt Whitman's, he was far better known and more popular. To meet William Cullen Bryant at literary events—as Melville did—was to ratify the sense that a writer had arrived in New York and had achieved some reputation. But Bryant and Melville met rarely, and they have left no record of what they thought of each other.

"Buddha" (1891) Poem in TIMOLEON. This six-line poem opens with an epigraph taken from James 4:14: *"For what is your life? It is even a vapor that appeareth for a little time and then vanisheth away."* The sentiments in the poem are much the same as the biblical ones, with the poet envisioning Nirvana as an annihilation of self achieved by those who aspire to "nothingness." Melville had a lively interest in Buddhism, which he came to via his reading of the philosopher Arthur SCHOPENHAUER.

Bulkington Minor character in *MOBY-DICK*. A mate on board the *PEQUOD,* a figure who represents the "intrepid effort of the soul to keep the open independence of her sea," Bulkington reminds ISHMAEL of why he left the "slavish shore."

Bunger, Dr. Jack Minor character in *MOBY-DICK*. A surgeon on the *Samuel Enderby* of London, Bunger treats Captain BOOMER after an encounter with Moby Dick results in the severing of Boomer's arm.

Bungs Minor character in *OMOO*. Bungs is the cooper aboard the *Julia*. Bungs and CHIPS, the ship's carpenter, are devoted to the bottle, and together they devise a scheme to literally tap into the whaler's stores of spirits. Bungs signs the circular round robin petition, but he is the only one of the signatories who agrees to resume his duties on the ship and therefore does not form part of the pack of "mutineers" hauled off to prison.

Bungs is also a minor character in *WHITE-JACKET*, where he is again cast as a cooper, or barrel maker (the name almost dictates that this be his role). After an argument with Scrimmage, a sheet-anchor man, about the proper making of buoys, Bungs has the bad luck to fall overboard. His poorly made buoys do not save him. While Melville was serving aboard the *UNITED STATES*, a cooper named David Black was similarly lost when he fell overboard, thus providing one basis for the story of Bungs.

Bunker Hill, Battle of Melville dedicates *ISRAEL POTTER* to the monument commemorating the Revolutionary War battle of Bunker Hill, at which Colonel William Prescott's 1,200-strong Massachusetts militia fought 2,500 British troops commanded by Thomas Gage. Although the American side lost 140 men, with 271 wounded and 30 captured, British losses were heavier: 226 killed and 828 wounded. The battle confirmed the American resolve to fight on and foreclosed the possibility of a truce or a British compromise with the rebels.

"The Burgundy Club Sketches" Unfinished collection of poetry and prose sketches. At the time of his death, Melville left unfinished an extensive project that was to focus on European art and history. Much of the work that he had slated for this project was probably begun in 1876–77, during and after his extended trip to Europe and the Levant, but then set aside until many years later. The first of the long works that were to form the core of this collection, "At the Hostelry" (first published in 1924), takes the form of a verse symposium among 30 great European painters presided

over by the genial Marquis de Grandvin, who in a sequel discusses Italian history and politics. The second long work that was to have been part of the project is "Naples in the Time of Bomba" (first published in 1924), a poem related to "PAUSILIPPO (IN THE TIME OF BOMBA)," a shorter work that was published in *TIMOLEON* in 1891. In both works, Melville condemns the repressive reign of the Bourbon King Ferdinand II of the Two Sicilies ("Bomba"); but in the projected "Burgundy Club" poem, Melville adopts the persona of Major Jack Gentian, a patrician American who upholds democratic principles and condemns the tyranny of the monarchy. Gentian is both a disciple of the Marquis and Dean of the Burgundy Club, and his lengthy disquisition on Italian history in "Naples in the Time of Bomba" perhaps indicates that Melville intended to develop portraits of other Burgundians who would act as narrators of other components of the "The Burgundy Club Sketches."

Burke, Edmund (1729–1797) British orator, statesman, and political philosopher, born in Dublin. His most famous work is *Reflections on the Revolution in France* (1790). Although he supported the American Revolution, he was a staunch opponent of the FRENCH REVOLUTION and defended the French royal family. In a pamphlet, *The Rights of Man,* Thomas Paine answered Burke and defended the Revolution. Both Burke and Paine are alluded to in *BILLY BUDD.*

Burton, Robert (1577–1640) English clergyman and author. Born in Leicestershire and educated at Oxford, Burton became vicar of Saint Thomas Church in Oxford in 1616 and a rector in Seagrave, Leicestershire, in 1630. He held both positions for the remainder of his life. His most important work, *The Anatomy of Melancholy* (1621), is a wide-ranging exploration of the phenomenon of melancholy that borrows from fields as diverse as classical studies and politics. The book's complex nature influenced Melville greatly, contributing perhaps most conspicuously to *MARDI* and *MOBY-DICK.*

"Butterfly Ditty" (1924) Poem in *WEEDS AND WILDINGS.* Apparently part of the section titled "The Year," "Butterfly Ditty" marks the juncture when spring gives way to summer, which "comes in like a sea." Prelapsarian creatures like butterflies are granted a bliss and an idleness denied "Man, Eden's bad boy" who "Partakes not the bliss."

"C——'s Lament" (1891) Poem in TIMOLEON. The "C" of the poem is Samuel Taylor COLERIDGE, whose work Melville began reading in the 1840s. Like Coleridge's "Dejection: An Ode" (1802), the sentiments in Melville's poem concern the loss of youth and innocence, when "man and nature seemed divine."

Calabooza Beretanee Location in OMOO. When most of the crew of the *Julia* sign a round robin of complaints and refuse to resume their duties, they are first taken aboard a French man-of-war, then detained in the jail, the Calabooza (from a slang word, "calaboose," meaning dungeon) Beretanee ("British") in Papeetee. The sailors' incarceration is something of a lark, as the sailors are only "locked up" at night with their feet placed between two logs; during the day they are allowed to roam freely about the town.

Calhoun, John C[aldwell] (1782–1850) American statesman. Born in South Carolina and educated at Yale University, Calhoun was admitted to the South Carolina bar in 1807 and immediately thereafter went into politics. After serving in the state legislature from 1808 to 1809, in 1811 he was elected to the United States House of Representatives, where he served three terms. In Congress, Calhoun was one of the "war hawks" who persuaded the House to declare war on Britain in 1812. He served as secretary of war (1817–1825) under President James Monroe and as vice president, first under John Quincy Adams, 1825–29, then under Andrew Jackson, 1829–32. In opposing the Tariff of 1828—which benefited the North but penalized Southern states—Calhoun wrote an essay known as the "South Carolina Exposition," in which he advocated state nullification of federal laws. In part because of the nullification controversy, Calhoun resigned in 1832, becoming the first vice president ever to do so. Serving as a U.S. senator from 1832 to 1843, Calhoun became the leading proponent of states' rights. While serving as secretary of state (1844–45) under President John Tyler, Calhoun helped secure the annexation of Texas, opposed the admission of California as a free state, and took an active role in defeating the Wilmot Proviso. He died in Washington, D.C., on March 31, 1850.

Calhoun makes an appearance in MARDI as NULLI, a gaunt zealot of Southern Vivenza who claims that slaves have no souls.

Calvinistic Adjective applied to adherents of John Calvin (1509–64), French theologian and church reformer. Like other Protestant thinkers, Calvin rooted his ideas in the Bible. Only the word of God could be used to reinforce faith. Man alone could never justify his life or understand God, but he could put his confidence in divine providence and grace. The key term in Calvinism is PREDESTINATION, and it is what Melville has in mind when he invokes Calvin's name in CLAREL. Predestination would seem to take away the agency of free will; that is, if the fate of a human being is determined from the outset, then he is powerless to save himself. But as in the Fall of Adam and Eve, mankind does have the opportunity to redeem himself through his actions and his faith. In other works such as MOBY-DICK, Melville probes the possibility that man is predestined even as he asserts his will to overcome his fate. Similarly, in BILLY BUDD, Captain VERE sees Billy as doomed from the start and explains Billy's fate to the crew of the INDOMITABLE as though he were preaching from a "Calvinist text."

"Camoens 1 (Before)" and "Camoens in the Hospital 2 (After)" (1924) Poem. This two-part poem is among the more than 40 that Melville left uncollected or unpublished when he died. They concern the Portuguese poet Luis Vaz de Camões, or Camoens (1524?–1580), who wrote the bulk of *The Lusiads* (1572), the most celebrated work in Portuguese literature, while serving with the Portuguese army in India and Macao and while imprisoned later in Goa. An epic that focuses on the voyages of explorer Vasco de Gama, *The Lusiads* brought Camoens a measure of fame before he died in poverty of plague in a Lisbon hospital in 1580. Melville read and greatly admired the work of Camoens, as did his hero John J. Chase, who, in the person of Jack CHASE, quotes from *The Lusiads* in Portuguese in WHITE-JACKET. A reference to Camoens also appears in BILLY BUDD, which is dedicated to Jack Chase.

Melville's two verses about the great Portuguese poet picture him first at the height of his powers, driven to capture in words the "world [which] with endless beauty teems," then dying, bitterly asking, "What now avails the pageant verse" in a "base" world dedicated to "useful good."

canallers   Mentioned in *MOBY-DICK*, men who worked on Erie Canal boats.

Canterbury Tales, The   Written between approximately 1387 and 1400 by Geoffrey CHAUCER (c. 1343–1400), this unfinished but great poem of world literature inspired Melville to create both *The CONFIDENCE MAN* and *CLAREL*. Chaucer presents a comic and complex portrait of pilgrims on the way to the cathedral town of Canterbury, the site of the death of the Christian martyr Thomas à Becket. The pilgrims, representatives of medieval society, include a knight, prioress, miller, clerk, cook, merchant, monk, pardoner, physician, nun, squire, and so on. These characters are revealed to be both devout and corrupt, to varying degrees, and Chaucer delights in dramatizing their virtues and vices. They debate religion, the nature of women, the institution of marriage, and many other subjects as they travel toward Canterbury. Similarly, Melville dramatizes a range of characters in *The Confidence Man* and *Clarel* who are at once sincere and fraudulent. In the latter, the characters are pilgrims traveling in the Holy Land, and like Chaucer's characters, they have mixed motives. Some are genuinely motivated by faith, others by the search for faith, and still others by a thirst for adventure or business opportunities. Melville explicitly refers to Chaucer in both *The Confidence Man* and *Clarel*. In the latter he notes that his modern pilgrims do not share the sheer joy and energy of the pilgrimage that Chaucer's so abundantly demonstrate.

"A Canticle: Significant of the national exaltation of enthusiasm at the close of the War." (1866)   Poem in *BATTLE-PIECES*. Throughout the CIVIL WAR, Melville was concerned about jingoists who would have the South utterly decimated for the sin of secession. Now, after General Robert E. Lee's surrender at Appomattox, he wanted his book of poems about the conflict to serve as a reminder that the peace could be as destructive as the war. In this poem Melville demonstrates how, by plunging like a cataract into the pool of war, the nation gave rise to a rainbow of peace. The pool, however, remains occupied by a "Giant . . . his forehead white as wool" that threatens future generations if political stability is not achieved.

Cape Horn   The southernmost point of South America. The tip of the archipelago of Tierra del Fuego and now a part of Chile, it was first discovered in 1616 by the Dutch navigator Willem Schouten, who named his discovery for the city of Hoorn in the Netherlands. Prior to the construction of the Panama Canal at the beginning of the 20th century, Cape Horn provided the only way for sailing ships to travel between the Atlantic and Pacific Oceans. Melville made the voyage in 1844 aboard the U.S.S. *UNITED STATES*, and his recollections of the trip, as revisited in *WHITE-JACKET*, indicate just how difficult a passage it can be. "Rounding the Horn" was always one of the worst trials endured by sailing ships, many of which were lost in the cold and stormy waters off Tierra del Fuego.

captain of marines   Minor character in *BILLY BUDD*. He is one of the officers who try Billy for the crime of killing John CLAGGART. He tries to argue that Billy's punishment should be mitigated because he did not intend to kill Claggart. Captain VERE rejoins that the issue is not intention, but rather the consequences of Billy's blow. The ship's crew will understand only how Billy's act was treated; to try to explain why extenuating circumstances lessen the punishment is futile. The failure to punish quickly will incite others to mutiny, Vere suggests. Like the other officers, the captain of marines defers to Vere's judgment.

Carlo   Minor character in *REDBURN*. Melville devotes an entire chapter to this "rich-cheeked, chestnut-haired Italian boy," one of the immigrant passengers aboard the *Highlander* during her homeward voyage to New York. Carlo is no more than 15 years old, poor and friendless, and yet he manages to pay for his trip—as well as make many friends aboard ship—by playing his hand-organ. In his broken English, he lets Redburn know that he also intends to make his way in the New World by similar means. Indeed, when the ship docks, Carlo is one of the first to make his way to shore, paying the watermen with his music.

Carpegna, Edouard Jules Gabrielle de (1816–1883)   French naval officer. By 1841, when he was assigned to the *Reine Blanche,* then under the command of Admiral Abel Aubert DUPETIT-THOUARS, Carpegna was already a seasoned officer, having circumnavigated the globe. In 1843, he arrived on the *Reine Blanche* in Papeetee, Tahiti, where he fought the natives during an uprising and was eventually named captain of the port. After serving in that role from 1844 to 1845, he returned to France, but not before marrying a Tahitian woman, by whom he had a son in 1844.

In *OMOO*, Carpegna is named as one of the assistants to the new French governor of Tahiti, Armand-Joseph BRUAT.

celibate, the   Minor character in *CLAREL*. A Greek monk living in MAR SABA, he is a type of the ascetic, living primarily by force of will.

Celio   Character in CLAREL. This Italian young man is bitter about his humped back. He has rejected Roman Catholicism, and has come to the Holy Land to find new spiritual inspiration. Clarel encounters Celio twice, but they do not speak to each other. Nevertheless, they share a bond as questers for religious insight. Clarel reads Celio's journal and recognizes his "second self." The self-destructive Celio is one example of the disaster potentially awaiting the seeker of a new spiritual truth, yet he is treated in the poem with great respect.

Cenci, Beatrice (1577–99)   Subject of a famous portrait by Guido Reni which is mentioned near the end of PIERRE. She was the daughter of Francesco Cenci (1549–98), a vicious Roman nobleman. With her mother and two brothers, Beatrice successfully plotted her father's assassination. Because of her beauty and her father's cruelty, Beatrice became a figure of great sympathy. Her plight was dramatized in Percy Bysshe Shelley's tragedy *The Cenci* (1819). In *Pierre,* Isabel BANFORD resembles Beatrice in both looks and temperament.

Cereno, Don Benito   Spanish ship captain and title character of "BENITO CERENO." Cereno was in life the captain of the ill-fated *Tryal,* the scene of a successful slave revolt that ended only with the intervention in 1801 of Captain Amasa DELANO and the crew of the *Perseverance.* Melville borrowed the outlines of his story from Delano's account of these events in chapter 18 of his autobiographical *Narrative of Voyages and Travels* (1817). "Benito Cereno" alters a number of facts taken from Delano, but toward the end of the tale he allows Don Benito to speak for himself by appending, almost verbatim, the captain's declaration in the criminal case against the leaders of the revolt—a document reproduced in Delano's book.

chance stranger   A disguise of the title character in *The* CONFIDENCE MAN. He speaks to the MISSOURIAN about the Philosophical Intelligence Office, an organization that hires out boys to help with various farms and business concerns. Identifying himself as "PITCH," the stranger eventually wears down the Missourian's objections and gets him to employ one of the boys.

chaplain, the   Minor character in BILLY BUDD. He tries to provide Billy with religious solace, but Billy seems immune to the teaching of religion and prepared to accept his death as inevitable.

Charlemont   A St. Louis merchant of French descent, the subject of a story told by the cosmopolitan in *The CONFIDENCE MAN.*

Charles & Henry   Whaling ship that Herman Melville signed on with in November 1842. When Melville and his fellow "mutineer" and companion John B. Troy decided to leave Tahiti (see SOCIETY ISLANDS) after several weeks of working and touring, they joined the crew of the Yankee whaler owned by the Coffin brothers of Nantucket, Massachusetts. But when Melville and Troy reported for duty on board the *Charles & Henry,* Captain Coleman recognized Troy as an ex-convict from Sydney, Australia, and refused to let him on board. Melville served rather happily on the *Charles & Henry* for five months. Although the ship was small, conditions were not bad, because the captain treated his men well. When after three months the ship had failed to capture any whales, Captain Coleman changed course. Instead of turning back toward the Galapagos Islands, he headed toward the Sandwich Islands (see HAWAII) to restock before departing to cruise the whaling grounds off the coast of Japan. Melville left the ship on May 2, 1843, when the *Charles & Henry* reached Lahaina on the island of Maui. In OMOO, in which Melville recounts his Tahitian adventures, the *Charles & Henry* is called the *Leviathan.*

"Charles' Isle and the Dog-King."   Sketch Seventh of "THE ENCANTADAS."

Charlton, Captain Richard   British diplomat. After a career as a sea captain and trader, in 1825 Charlton was named as the first British consul to the Pacific. Given oversight of HAWAII and Tahiti (see SOCIETY ISLANDS), his mission was to increase British influence, particularly with regard to trade, in these areas. His opposition to Protestant missionaries brought him into conflict with G. P. Judd in Hawaii, and his importation of liquor to Tahiti caused him problems there. Eventually, the British government relieved him of his post. In 1843, in transit in Mexico, he complained to Rear Admiral Richard Thomas, commander of the British Pacific Squadron, about Hawaiian discrimination against Britain. Thomas responded by sending Lord George PAULET to Hawaii, where Paulet in turn caused further problems because of his extreme demands.

   In an appendix to the main narrative of TYPEE, Melville mentions Charlton and portrays him as having been unfairly treated by Judd and other Hawaiian authorities.

Chartism   Movement for political reform in Great Britain, lasting from 1838 to 1848. In 1837, a labor organization calling itself the London Working Men's Association submitted a legislative program known as the People's Charter to Parliament. Drafted in reaction to the Reform Bill of 1832 (extending the vote to virtually all members of the middle class) and the Poor Law of 1834 (putting treatment of the poor under national supervision), the People's Charter called for voting by secret ballot, universal male suffrage, and annual parliamentary elections. After Parliament rejected the charter, a petition drive gathered 1,250,000 signatures in support of the Chartists' demands. A second rejection by Parliament resulted in a general strike that degenerated into riots. Bickering among Chartist leaders and the revival of trade unionism caused the Chartist movement to subside until 1848, when plans were made for a mass demonstration leading to the presentation of yet another petition to Parliament. Rain dispersed the demonstrators, Parliament rejected their petition on grounds of fraudulent signatures, and the Chartist movement died a quiet death.

In MARDI, Melville devotes some attention to King BELLO's success in putting down an internal rebellion in Dominora that greatly resembles the last gasp of Chartism. In fact, a considerable amount of evidence suggests that Melville added material concerning political events that took place as he was finishing his third novel in 1848. Included are references to Chartism in Britain, the 1848 French Revolution that overthrew the July Monarchy, and aspects of the slavery debate in the United States, such as the Free-Soil Party Convention in Buffalo, New York.

In REDBURN, the protagonist encounters a Chartist youth haranguing a crowd in St. George's Square in Liverpool. Clarel also contains allusions to Chartism and revolutionary movements.

Chase, Jack   Character in WHITE-JACKET. Jack Chase, whom WHITE-JACKET elevates nearly to the status of a god, is modeled on John J. Chase, an Englishman and captain of the foretop when Melville met him aboard the frigate U.S.S. UNITED STATES in 1843. Although there are differences between John J. Chase and his fictional counterpart, similarities abound. Like the fictional character, John J. Chase had deserted his ship in Callao, Peru, to fight in the civil war there, then signed on board the United States as an ordinary seaman. The real Chase spoke five languages and could recite long passages from The Lusiads by Luíz Vaz de Camões in the original Portuguese. He was a brave man who had fought with Sir Edward Codrington at the Battle of Navarino during the Greek War of Independence, and he was a literate man whose friendship clearly meant a great deal to Melville. When White-Jacket bids Jack Chase goodbye at the end of their voyage together, he kisses the hand of the man he had so often referred to as his noble captain. Melville devoted his last work, BILLY BUDD, to "Jack Chase, Englishman, / Wherever that great heart may now be, / here on Earth or harbored in Paradise, / Captain of the Main-Top in the year 1843 / in the U.S. Frigate United States."

Chase, Owen (b. 1796–7)   Author of Narrative of the Most Extraordinary and Distressing Shipwreck of the Whale-Ship Essex (1821). Chase's tale of how his ship was rammed by an angry sperm whale formed the basis of MOBY-DICK. Aboard the ACUSHNET, Melville met William Henry Chase, Owen Chase's son, who gave Melville a copy of his father's book.

"Chattanooga. (November, 1863.)" (1866)   Poem in BATTLE-PIECES. The CIVIL WAR Battle of Chattanooga took place over three days and nights. Melville describes the night battle on Lookout Mountain in a poem of the same name, but this poem focuses on Union general Ulysses S. Grant's oversight of the assault that ended in a Confederate rout:

> Grant stood on cliffs whence all was plain,
> And smoked as one who feels no cares;
> But mastered nervousness intense
> Alone such calmness wears.

This poem first appeared in the June 1866 issue of HARPER'S NEW MONTHLY MAGAZINE.

Chaucer, Geoffrey (c. 1343–1400)   English poet, born near London. He traveled extensively in service of the royal court and is best known for his unfinished but brilliant picaresque poem The CANTERBURY TALES. Melville was drawn both to Chaucer's worldliness and to the searching, even ironic, treatment of religion and human character that makes Chaucer an enduring author. The Canterbury Tales provide important stimulus for both The CONFIDENCE MAN and CLAREL.

"The Chipmunk" (1924)   Poem in WEEDS AND WILD-INGS. Apparently intended as part of section of the volume titled "The Year," "The Chipmunk" compares a sweetly ephemeral autumn sighting of the rodent with an infant who vanishes almost as quickly as it appears at "our hearth." Although the poem is seemingly lighthearted, the reference to the baby, startled "By some inkling / Touching Earth," hints at early death.

Chips ("Beauty")   Minor character in OMOO. Chips is the ship's carpenter aboard the Julia. A decidedly ugly individual, he also carries the nickname "Beauty." Together with his cohort Bungs, the cooper, Chips manages to indulge his taste for liquor by literally tapping into the ship's stores. Like Bungs and virtually every other member of the crew, Chips signs the round robin, a petition signed in a circular manner so that no leader can be singled out.

Christodulus   Minor character in CLAREL; the abbot of MAR SABA, he represents the certainty of the believer.

Civil War, the (1861–65) Melville was too old to serve in the American Civil War, and his weak eyes and back trouble would have been further disqualifications for active service. His name, however, did appear on militia rolls. In private, he was a staunch supporter of friends and family fighting the war on the Union side. He was proud of their fight for a good cause, but he also abhorred the brutality of war and of military service, which he had seen firsthand as a young man aboard the man-of-war UNITED STATES. During most of the Civil War, Melville remained in New York. Unlike Walt Whitman, who served as a nurse, Melville had no direct contact with soldiers except for one visit to a relative stationed at a battlefield in Virginia. Melville's sequence of poems, BATTLE-PIECES, reflects his keen observation of the war's progress and its devastation. Melville met Abraham Lincoln just before the war began. He observed the draft riots in New York City, and his poems deal with those riots, as well as addressing a range of other Civil War subjects, including the Armies of the Wilderness, the Battle for the Mississippi, the *Cumberland*, the fall of Richmond, a former slave, the Battle of Fredericksburg, the March to Virginia, Lee's threat against the capitol, John BROWN, Shiloh, the fight between the *Monitor* and the *Merrimac*, and Antietam.

Claggart, John Character in *BILLY BUDD, SAILOR*. He is the master-at-arms. Little is known about Claggart's background except that he seems to have been educated to a station in life far above what he now enjoys aboard ship. He takes an almost obscene joy in finding ways to undermine Billy Budd even while treating the young man with the utmost courtesy. Claggart is portrayed as evil incarnate; no reason is ever given for his antipathy to Billy Budd. Billy seems to represent goodness and innocence, virtues that Claggart seems to abhor. Claggart plans his attack on Billy carefully, playing up to Captain VERE's fear of mutiny and suggesting that Billy is a conspirator against the order of the ship. When he is made to confront Billy with his alleged crime, Claggart calmly repeats his false charge and Billy strikes him dead.

Clarel: A Poem and Pilgrimage in the Holy Land (1876) Melville's 10th book, a narrative poem that grew out of his own voyage to the Middle East and the Mediterranean in 1856–57. Nathaniel HAWTHORNE's comment on Melville, when Melville visited him in Liverpool at the beginning of his pilgrimage, is an apt summary of *Clarel*'s tone and temper: "He can neither believe, nor be comfortable in his unbelief." The single greatest influence on Melville's composition of *Clarel* is Matthew ARNOLD's great poem "DOVER BEACH." That work's evocation of a world shaken by a loss of religious belief, which is embodied in the image of a retreating "sea of faith," governs Melville's vision of a humanity

that has lost a sense of conviction and is seeking to regain it.

Melville would travel for five months and cover 15,000 miles, visiting three continents and nine countries. He traveled by himself, keeping a journal that formed the basis of his long poem. He was in a sort of no-man's-land, since he was no longer a popular novelist and had not yet received the critical attention that would put him into the canon of American literature. Yet Melville's ambition never relented. He conceived of an epic poem as serious and broadly based as Geoffrey CHAUCER's poem of pilgrimage, *The CANTERBURY TALES*, and as searching as John Milton's *PARADISE LOST*.

Melville divided *Clarel* into 150 cantos and four parts: "Jerusalem," "The Wilderness," "Mar Saba," and "Bethlehem." This huge poem (nearly 18,000 lines) progresses from the pilgrim's eager but disappointed arrival in JERUSALEM, where so much of the history of Christ's agony has been obliterated, to the wilderness of the Dead Sea (part two), where the desolate landscape becomes a metaphor for the despair and search for salvation that stimulate the pilgrimage. The quest is renewed in part three, where the pilgrims rejuvenate themselves in scaling the heights of MAR SABA, with its twin towers which evoke something of the grandeur of man's spiritual quest. If the pilgrims do not gain spiritual fulfillment and remain as thwarted as Melville himself, part four, ending in BETHLEHEM, honors the grandeur and necessity of the quest as well as offering a vision of the abiding ancient faith in the town of Christ's birth.

The quality of Melville's poetry has received mixed reviews by his contemporaries and by later scholars of his work. On the one hand, he relies heavily on "poetic" words such as "anon," "fro," "boon," "oft" that give his work a derivative, cliched, old-fashioned flavor. He pads lines with words that fit the meter or the rhyme scheme with awkward results: e.g., "ungladsome," "arborous," "chanceful." Walter Bezanson, one of the great authorities on the poem, has called these words "loppings and stretchings." On the other hand, fine modern poets such as Robert Penn Warren have lauded *Clarel*'s ambition, its modern tone, and its moving passages. Bezanson cites lines such as "Wear and tear and jar / He met with coffee and cigar" to suggest Melville's direct and colloquial style. Bezanson argues, in fact, the colloquial and the antique are meant to clash in *Clarel* just as the traditional and modern interpretations of religion do.

Similarly, Melville's choice of iambic tetrameter (a line of four metrical feet, two syllables per foot, with the emphasis usually falling on the second syllable) has seemed problematic to scholars. A line of eight syllables rather than 10 (the number found in the blank verse of Shakespeare, for example), tends to make for disjointed reading. The lines do not flow. On the other hand, Melville's rhymes are strengthened by the

Mount Olivet in Jerusalem is one of the major sites in Clarel, *Melville's long narrative poem.* (Library of Congress)

shorter lines, and sometimes the abruptness of the line startles and arrests the reader with its meaning.

SYNOPSIS

Part One: "Jerusalem"

Cantos 1–2: "The Hostel"; "Abdon"

Clarel is introduced as a student sitting in an old chamber, alone and brooding. He has fine, pale features "all but feminine," with an "eye and serious brow." Saturated with his studies, he feels the need to relieve his "bookish vapors" and to explore the Holy Land for himself, since "the books not all have told." He longs to see the "actual visage of a place," to examine the source of faith.

Clarel comes under the spell of his host, ABDON, an orthodox Jew. Abdon has come to Jerusalem and the Jewish homeland from Amsterdam, "less to live than end at home / One other last remove!"

Cantos 3–11: "The Sepulchre"; "Of the Crusaders"; "Clarel"; "Tribes and Sects"; "Beyond the Walls"; "The Votary"; "Saint and Student"; "Rambles"; "Lower Gihon"

As Clarel approaches the Church of the Holy Sepulchre, he thinks of Christ's humanity and how it has inspired the pilgrims who visit the site of his crucifixion. He marks its spot where Christ was scourged, where "Mary paled." He thinks of the generations of pilgrims who have come to this very spot, "or false or true / As an historic site." Clarel approaches not as a believer but as a quester, probing the meaning of pilgrimage.

The narrator wonders at the motivations of the Crusaders who invaded the Holy Land. Even if they were brigands, were they not moved by what they saw ("Grant them the worst—is all romance / Which claims that the crusader's glance / Was blurred by tears?")? Do not these large movements of men to holy sites suggest the "intersympathy of creeds," the desire for "exalted thought or groveling dream"?

Yet different religions and peoples hardly see the resemblances between their spiritual quests, and the Holy Land has become the site of conflict between religions and peoples: "Contentions for each holy place, / And jealousies how far from grace: / O, bickering family bereft, / Was feud the heritage He left?" Christ's message of peace has not united the human family.

Beyond the walls of the Holy Sepulchre, Clarel meets NEHEMIAH, who asks the young scholar where his guide is. Nehemiah simply identifies himself as a "sinner." He will become for Clarel the purest example of the human devotion to the divine, of a man who tries to live exclusively by the commandments of his religion. Nehemiah has left his native Narragansett to travel to the Holy Land dispensing religious tracts. When Clarel identifies himself as "a traveler—no more," Nehemiah replies: "'Me let be guide whose guide is this,' / And held the Book [the Bible] in witness so." Clarel, won by Nehemiah's "primal faith" and "mystic saintly way," agrees.

Clarel and Nehemiah "rove the storied ground," examining the historic sites of Jerusalem, which Clarel finds disheartening: "But of the reign / Of Christ did no memento leave / Save soil and ruin?" Meanwhile, Nehemiah speaks in certain terms about Christ's return.

Cantos 12–15: "Celio"; "The Arch"; "In the Glen"; "Under the Minaret"

Coming from Rome, CELIO seeks inspiration in the Holy Land, yet in "chapel service . . . he shows no zest / Of faith within, faith personal." As he confesses, "This world clean fails me; still I yearn. / Me then it surely does concern / Some other world to find. But where?" Clarel catches something of Celio's mood. Although the two do not exchange words, their "meeting eyes / Betrayed reciprocal surmise / And interest." Celio, contemplating Christ's despairing words ("My God, my God, forsakest me?") wonders if he too is marked out for suffering and destruction: "Am *I* the Jew?" Retracing Christ's route on Mt. Olivet, Celio wonders about the Christ's return, yet he resists: "Weak am I, by a myth abused."

Clarel and Celio pass each other under a minaret near Mt. Olivet, yet they still do not meet, although again they exchange meaningful glances. Some days later Clarel learns the name of the young man he has encountered twice, but it is too late for them to meet, for Celio has gone away.

Cantos 16–17: "The Wall of Wail"; "Nathan"

Clarel resumes his exploration of Jerusalem in the Jewish quarter, where he meets NATHAN, an American Zionist (see ZIONISM) who comes from "worthy stock— / Austere, ascetical, but free." He is from a Christian family and has tried various faiths. After marrying AGAR, a Jew, he decides to settle her and their daughter RUTH in the Holy Land. In an era of crumbling faith, Nathan has gone "rearward" to the "crag of Sinai" to find the origins of faith and to "reinstate the Holy Land." Like his ancestors fighting the Indians, Nathan battles the Arabs, who to him are no better than slaves "imperiling his state."

Cantos 18–20: "Night"; "The Fulfillment"; "The Value of Ashes"

Clarel stands in his "vaulted room" thinking of Nathan's story and of his daughter Ruth. Celio's image, however, "strangely underrun[s]" hers, "Celio—sought / Vainly in body—now appeared / As in the spiritual part, / Haunting the air, / and in the heart." Feeling haunted by Celio, he asks Abdon to stay with him when the two encounter each other at the inn.

Clarel's obsession with Celio reflects his "inquietude of fears." All questions on the "primal ground" of Jerusalem are "laid bare by faith's receding wave," the narrator says. Treading the ground Celio has covered, Clarel is met by Nehemiah, who, sensing his companion's troubled mind, invites him to his room.

Cantos 21–23: "By-Places"; "Hermitage"; "The Close"

The narrator points out that pilgrims follow their obsessions to the native soil of the myths that master them, and as "visionaries of the World / Walk like somnambulists abroad." Thus Nehemiah and Clarel ("saint and student") continue their tour of Jerusalem arriving at Nathan's home or "hermitage." There Clarel sees Ruth, who seems a symbol of purity in her "snowy robe." Ruth thrills Clarel with "life's first romance." He falters, but Nehemiah provides the introduction. Little is said, but "To Clarel's heart there came a swell / Like the first tide that ever pressed / Inland, and of a deep did tell."

Cantos 24–25: "The Gibe"; "Huts"; "The Gate of Zion"

Climbing Mt. Zion, Nehemiah and Clarel are accosted by a merry stranger asking them where he is and what the prices are in the market. The short, rugged, iron-gray man disturbs Clarel, who moves away only to encounter the beggars and lepers coming out of their huts. Nehemiah scarcely seems to notice the "sad crew," so fixed is he on his "mystic day." He approaches the legendary gates of David in Zion, the site of David's palace and tomb. Finally commenting on the lepers and beggars, Nehemiah simply says that in paradise they will be "re-clad / Transfigured like the morning glad."

Cantos 27–30: "The Matron and the Maid"; "Tomb and Fountain"; "The Recluse"; "The Site of the Passion"

Clarel visits Agar and Ruth often. Both women grow fond of him, even though he does not share their

Jewish blood. He observes how the "family feeling of the Jew, / Which hallowed by each priestly rite, / Makes home a temple." In his vision of Ruth, Clarel seeks paradise, "to try to realize the unreal!" The narrator says that Ruth and Clarel are like a vision of Eden won back.

At the tomb of the Holy Sepulchre, Clarel sees "a funeral [somber] man, yet richly fair," a shy figure who salutes Clarel when he realizes he has been "discerned." Later, Nehemiah and Clarel encounter the stranger again, and he and Clarel exchange sympathetic glances.

The stranger's name is VINE, the narrator reveals, although to say much about his background would not explain much about him. Vine has a magnetic appeal, although the narrator hastens to add that he is no saint. He is a recluse whom Clarel wishes to approach but does not know how. Nehemiah and Clarel are in the garden of Gethsemene, near the foot of the Mount of Olives, just east of Jerusalem, the site of Christ's agony and betrayal. As Nehemiah reads from the Bible, Clarel feels a numbness coming over him as he waits to see whether Vine will acknowledge him. As tourists begin to replace the more serious pilgrims, Clarel sees a "ripple . . . Of freakish mockery" on Vine's face.

Canto 31: "Rolfe"

Nehemiah and Clarel meet a second stranger, ROLFE. He looks like an outdoorsman and seems out of place in the Holy Land. His tanned face and marble brow are matched by a "genial heart, a brain austere." He is a man "given to study," but he is not a scholar or academic. He "supplemented Plato's theme / With daedal life in boats and tents, / A Messmate of the elements." He is sensitive and frank to the point of indiscretion. Clarel compares Vine and Rolfe, concluding that they are "peers" (equals). Vine withdraws—not in order to shun Rolfe, but instead "Ready, if need were, to accord / Reception to the other's word." Rolfe speaks at length about his convictions, pointing out "long as children feel affright / In darkness, men shall fear a God." Science can help bring man out of his ignorant state and "deepen, enlarge" his consciousness. "But though 'twere made / Demonstrable that God is not— / What then? it would not change this lot: / The ghost would haunt, nor could be laid," Rolfe concludes. Doubts about God and religion are nothing new, Rolfe continues: "Caesar his atheism avowed / Before the Senate." Like a tide Rolfe's ideas overwhelm Clarel, while Vine holds back.

Canto 32: "Of Rama"

The narrator invokes Rama, the epic hero of the Indian *Ramayana*, the Sanskrit epic that tells the story of Rama, the incarnation of Vishnu who appears on Earth to do battle with Ravana, a great demon threatening mankind. Like Christ, Rama is both man and god, although he does not recognize his divinity. Are there such men as Rama, the narrator asks, who lead unspotted lives and yet like him are forced into "outlawry": "May life and fable so agree?" Can there be, in fact, an innocent self? Perhaps only in verse can such a conception of man be sustained, the narrator speculates.

Cantos 33–34: "By the Stone"; "They Tarry"

Looking over Jerusalem the narrator tries to imagine the "fair scene" of Christ's day, but "*now*—a vision here conferred / Pale as Pompeii disinterred." Rolfe and the others see a wasteland. Clarel listens to Rolfe's lament over the scene, but he watches Vine's face for changes of expression, a "face indeed quite overlaid / With tremulous meanings, which evade / Or shun regard, nay, hardly brook / Fraternal scanning."

Surveying the city once again, Rolfe remarks: "All now's revised / Zion, like Rome, is Niebuhrized. / Yes, doubt attends. Doubt's heavy hand / Is set against us." Rolfe's reference is to Barthold Niebuhr (1776–1831), a renowned German historian who sought to establish the historical basis of revealed religion. This critical analysis of religion, Rolfe suggests, deprives faith of its authority.

Canto 35: "Arculf and Adamnan"

Arculf, an eighth-century French bishop, made one of the first pilgrimages to the Holy Land. Adamnan, the abbot of St. Columba monastery (in the Scottish Hebrides), sheltered Arculf when his ship was wrecked on the way back from his pilgrimage. Adamnan then recorded an account of Arculf's pilgrimage. Commenting on their story and the faith they shared in miracles, the narrator observes:

> The abbot and the palmer rest:
> The legends follow them and die—
> Those legends which, be it confessed,
> Did nearer bring them the sky—
> Did nearer woo it to their hope
> Of all that seers and saints avow—
> Than Galileo's telescope
> Can bid it unto prosing Science now.

Cantos 36–38: "The Tower"; "A Sketch"; "The Sparrow"

The pilgrims ascend a tower that gives them a good view of Jerusalem and the Dead Sea. Climbing down, they are met by Nehemiah, who wishes to take them to Bethany. He gazes expectantly at them. Vine seems embarrassed by Nehemiah's simplicity, and so is Clarel, who thanks Nehemiah, but Rolfe speaks for the group, saying "Some other day." Nehemiah turns away in disappointment, and Rolfe asks Clarel what he knows about Nehemiah's past. Clarel knows nothing, and Rolfe says that Nehemiah reminds him of a mariner, "one whom grim / Disaster made as meek as he / There plodding." Vine, taking an interest, asks Rolfe to recount his story. Rolfe describes a man who is master of his ship, a believer in free will and scornful of the idea of fate, which his subaltern clings to "in humble way / That still heaven's over-rulings sway / Will and event." The victim of a shipwreck, the master holds on and is rescued. "'Strong need'st thou be,' the rescuers said, / 'Who has such trial sole survived.' / 'I *willed* it,'" gasps the master. Aboard a sealing ship, the master is once again wrecked—this time by a whale. Is he, then, master of his fate, or a Jonah? Rolfe asks. The master, Rolfe concludes, "Praised heaven, and said that God was good, / And his calamity but just." Observing Nehemiah, Rolfe says, "Look, the changed master, roams he there? / I mean, is such the guise, the air?" The narrator alludes to "Laocoön's serpent" which seems to twine its coils about Rolfe, Vine, and Clarel. In Rome, Melville had seen the statue of Laocoön and his two sons writhing in agony as the serpent strangles and crushes them, and commented on it as the "very semblance of a great and powerful man writhing with the inevitable destiny which he cannot throw off."

Clarel now wonders if he should sound out Nehemiah about his background, yet Nehemiah seems so guarded about his past that Clarel decides not to question him.

Canto 39: "Clarel and Ruth"

Clarel's love for Ruth grows every day and is perhaps spurred by the fact that he was "bereft while still but young, / Mother or sister had not known." Ruth, unhappy in exile, seems open to new vistas, and Clarel tries to hide his own anxieties in her presence.

Cantos 40–41: "The Mounds"; "On the Wall"

Clarel is at Celio's grave, for the young Italian has committed suicide. He held "Faith's candle in Doubt's dying hand." Clarel meets Rolfe at Celio's grave and is told that Rolfe once knew Celio "far from here." Rolfe laments that to "moderns death is drear, / So drear: we die, we make no sign, / We acquiesce in any cheer— / No rite we seek, no rite decline." This nonchalance, he suggests, is indicative of modern indifference to the claims of faith and conviction.

Clarel himself is caught between doubt and the desire to believe. His quest is defined, in a sense, by the writing he finds on a wall—references to the works of David Friedrich Strauss (1808–74), Ernest Renan (1823–92), and Pierre Joseph Proudhon (1809–65). Strauss and Renan wrote lives of Jesus Christ that furthered the analytical tradition that called into question his divinity. Proudhon, a philosophical anarchist, was active in the 1848 revolution in Paris. Each writer contributes to the growth of skepticism and the eroding of the religious basis of civilization. Clarel scans their volumes hoping to "construe / the lines their owner left on the wall."

Cantos 42–44: "Tidings"; "A Procession"; "The Start"

Clarel, unsure of what next to do, looks to Rolfe and Vine for guidance. Although he is deeply attached to Ruth, he yearns to accompany these two men and the "journeying band" of pilgrims. He is left in his "hermitage of mind," declaring he will "waver now no more" and stay with Ruth. Yet he rebukes himself and resolves once more to join the pilgrimage. Part one ends with everything yet to be established: "In heart what hap may Clarel prove? / Brief term of days, but a profound remove."

Part Two: "The Wilderness"

Cantos 1–3: "The Cavalcade"; "The Skull-Cap"; "By the Garden"

The narrator explicitly compares his pilgrims to Chaucer's, noting: "Another age, and other men, / And life an unfulfilled romance." There is no "franklin, squire," no "wit and story good as then." A new character is introduced: DERWENT, an Anglican priest who affects both the "secular and cleric tone." He has the "emblems of that facile wit, / Which suits the age—a happy fit." Derwent, in other words, tends to rationalize his own times and is far less skeptical than Rolfe and the other pilgrims. Other new pilgrims include a "solid stolid Elder" and a BANKER from the Levant. The most important addition is MORTMAIN, a man of "rigorous gloom." Nehemiah follows this group with his religious tracts as Clarel looks on with "earnest face." Rolfe, seated on a horse, is the very picture of an Indian.

The banker travels with his prospective son-in-law, GLAUCON, a genial, rather flighty companion. Derwent comments on the young man's high spirits. "Folly, folly— / But good against the melancholy," the banker replies. In contrast, Clarel is preoccupied with thoughts about Ruth, and Mortmain (offended by Derwent's "easy air") asks "Who he that with a tongue so nimble / Affects light heart in such a pass?" Taken aback, Derwent sizes up the glum Mortmain, who points out that the pilgrims have their backs to the garden of Gethsemene, where Judas betrayed Jesus. Derwent asks Mortmain if he is a priest. "Methinks, good friend, too much you chide." In Derwent's view, the Christ story "can give / A hope to man, a cheerful hope." Mortmain is "unsolaced" by Derwent's view that it is better for man to know he cannot be happy on Earth and that his salvation lies elsewhere. To Mortmain, the crucifixion only reveals how deep human hatred is and how fiercely men betray each other. Derwent tries to pass off Mortmain's despair as a temporary mood—"Thou'rt ill to-day"—which Mortmain answers only with silence.

Canto 4: "Of Mortmain"

From Rolfe, Derwent learns about Mortmain's background. A Swede, the illicit son of a noble lady and a father who does not acknowledge him, he grew up isolated and settled in Paris. He becomes involved in the revolutionary cause as a conspirator and pamphleteer. He has had his experience with Judases who betray the revolution of 1848. In Rolfe's view, Mortmain discovers that he cannot change history. "Behind all this still works some power / Unknowable, thou'lt yet adore. / *That* steers the world, not man," Rolfe tells Derwent: "In the dust / Of wisdom sit thee down, and rust." But rather than simply withdrawing from the world and finding a cloister, Mortmain travels, apparently seeking nature's secrets. Derwent responds: "There's none so far astray, / Detached, abandoned, as might seem, / As to exclude the hope, the dream / Of fair redemption."

Cantos 5–7: "Clarel and Glaucon"; "The Hamlet"; "Guide and Guard"

The giddy Glaucon tells Clarel all about his plans to marry the banker's daughter. Derwent comments: "This lad is like a land of springs . . . he gushes so with song." Rolfe, too, marvels at Glaucon's unresponsiveness to the pilgrimage. As the pilgrims approach a hamlet, Clarel thinks of Christ's painful journey to his crucifixion. The group is guided by DJALEA, a Druze from Lebanon. Rumored to be the son of an emir (a prince or chieftain), he has a dignity and self-contained quality that make him a fascinating figure, the representative of a religion that combines Eastern and Western elements but which is little understood by the pilgrims. Djalea has six companions, old Arab Bethlehemites, with BELEX, a tough old Turkish warrior, in command.

Canto 8: "Rolfe and Derwent"

As the journey continues, Derwent "invoked his spirits bright." He suggests to Rolfe that Belex represents the "inherent vigor of man's life." But Rolfe is not taken by this one example, asking "Prone, prone are era, man and nation / To slide into a degradation? / With some, to age is that—but that." Derwent finds such sentiments "pathetic."

Cantos 9–10: "Through Adommin"; "A Halt"

The pilgrims pass through Adommin, presumed to be the place where Christ spoke the parable of the Good Samaritan (Luke 10:30–37), which Nehemiah proceeds to retell. The singing Glaucon, completely out of tune with the pilgrimage, provokes the banker's outburst: "Have done with this lewd balladry!" During a halt in the journey, Derwent and Rolfe discuss its significance as Mortmain sits "aloof" and "all disarmed." Nehemiah fascinates both Derwent and Rolfe, who says "And shall

we say / That this is craze? or but, in brief, / Simplicity of plain belief? / The early Christians, how did they? / For His return looked any day." Clarel ponders Rolfe's words and then Rolfe himself, wondering at the man's "bluntness" and whether it is right to be put off by it or to accept it as truth.

Canto 11: "Of Deserts"

The narrator explores the nature of deserts as a metaphor for the forsakenness of the human heart. DARWIN quotes SHELLEY, the narrator notes, referring to a passage in Charles Darwin's journal in which he quotes Percy Bysshe Shelley's poem "Mont Blanc": "None can reply—all seems eternal now. / The wilderness has a mysterious tongue, / Which teaches awful doubt." The lines recall the feeling of emptiness, of lack of meaning, that deserts can evoke. In *Clarel*, the immensity of the desert attracts the pilgrims, but also defeats them: "men here adore this ground / Which doom hath smitten. 'Tis a land / Direful yet holy—blest tho' banned."

Cantos 12–13: "The Banker"; "Flight of the Greeks"

Rolfe wonders why the banker is on the pilgrimage, since it seems an unlikely activity for a worldly man concerned with money. Clarel, meanwhile, turns from Rolfe and Mortmain, whom Clarel finds disturbing, to Vine, whose "level sameness" remains comforting and intriguing. When a band of 10 armed Turks crosses the paths of the pilgrims, the banker along with Glaucon arranges to leave the pilgrims, clearly having had enough of the journey in the desert.

Canto 14: "By Achor"

The Druze leads the pilgrims into the valley of Achor, the site of the slaughter related in chapter seven of the Old Testament book of Joshua. Joshua and his band of 3,000 were defeated, and Achan the thief was "made to die." His children were stoned and burned, the narrator recalls. Rolfe surveys the scene and speaks of "Nature . . . in region roundabout / She's Calvinistic, if devout / In all her aspect." This invocation of predestination, a feature of CALVINISTIC religion, is not commented on by the others. Vine, for example, rides in "thought's hid repast." Clarel is "receptive, saw and heard, / Learning, unlearning, word by word." Mortmain is remote. And Rolfe goes on speaking, not giving Derwent an opportunity to interrupt.

Cantos 15–18: "The Fountain"; "Night in Jericho"; "In Mid-Watch"; "The Syrian Monk"

Finally, Derwent finds something in the scene to praise, "truly, the fount wells grateful here," he remarks to Clarel. Yet Mortmain remains "aloof abiding in dark plot, and leaves the pilgrims for a while." No one takes up Derwent's message of hope.

The pilgrims pass the Crusaders' Tower "on the waste verge of Jericho." Rolfe evokes the story of Elijah who went up by a whirlwind into heaven" in a chariot of fire (2 Kings 2:11). He also mentions John the Baptist who preached by the Jordan, a figure dressed in "raiment of camel's hair" (Matthew 3:4). These biblical characters are contrasted with C. F. Volney (1757–1820), Vicomte de Chateaubriand (1768–1848), and Alphonse de Lamartine (1790–1869). Each of these modern men contributes to the secular world that is now juxtaposed against the Holy Land. Volney brought a critical mind to the study of imagination and illusion. Chateaubriand defended Catholicism against atheists, setting scenes of a historical novel in Jerusalem, along the Jordan, and by the Dead Sea. Lamartine wrote of his voyage to the Holy Land and was minister of foreign affairs in the French government of 1848. Its fall signals the death of a certain idealism. Rolfe's references to these thinkers and doers, as well as to the Septembrists who took part in the massacre of royalists on September 2–6, 1792, all contribute to his sense of "waste," of the futility of human efforts. Derwent counters: "Omit ye in citation, pray, / the healthy pilgrims of times old? / Robust they were; and cheery saw / Shrines, chapels, castles without flaw, / Now gone." Rolfe rejoins: "Man sprang from deserts: at the touch / Of grief or trial overmuch, / On deserts he falls back at need." He points to the example of Mortmain, who flees civilization to take this "wild plunge" into the wilderness of the Holy Land. Derwent diverts the argument by observing the moon "in pearl-cloud; look, her face / Peers like a bride's from webs of lace." Watching the fading image of the moon, a "discouraged" Rolfe "sat as rebuked," confessing "My earnestness myself decry; / But as heaven made me, so am I." Vine recalls to Rolfe that he spoke of Mortmain, and Rolfe responds: "In gusts of lonely pain / Beating upon the naked brain— / God help him, ay, poor realist!"

Disturbed by the debate, Clarel has troubled dreams and awakes at night. Rolfe joins him, and Clarel again considers whether he can learn something from his frankness, or whether a deeper truth resides in Vine, who "could lure / Despite reserve which overture / Withstood."

Early in the morning Clarel, Rolfe, and Vine happen on a "strange wayfarer," the SYRIAN MONK. Grown thin from his fasts, he looks like a latter-day John the Baptist. Sin—the sin of doubt—has driven him out into the desert, the monk explains. Rolfe wonders what the monk has accomplished by self-denial: "Surely, not all we've heard: / Peace—solace—was in end conferred?" Vine and Clarel sit in silence, and Rolfe continues: "And this but ecstasy of fast?" Clarel turns to Vine, expecting an answer. Vine remains silent.

Cantos 19–22: "An Apostate"; "Under the Mountain"; "The Priest and Rolfe"; "Concerning Hebrews"

The pilgrims watch MARGOTH, a Jewish geologist who denies the divine history of the Holy Land and sees only material for scientific study. Margoth is ascending the Crusader's Tower. To Derwent, Margoth is the epitome of the "self-satisfied" modern who needs no support from religion. Rolfe and Derwent debate the merits of modern science, with Rolfe conceding that science does not provide all the answers. Vine gives Derwent a sidelong glance, as if envying the clergyman's gift for lightly disposing of weighty issues. Clarel honors Rolfe's skepticism, but he is also wary of Rolfe's "illogical wild range / Of brain and heart's impulsive countercharge." Vine deems it significant that Margoth is a Jew, and Derwent canvases what it means to be a Jew—at once the inheritor of an ancient tradition and in the forefront of the "liberal sciences." Rolfe consults his own knowledge of freethinking Jews, from Heinrich HEINE to Moses MENDELSSOHN to Baruch SPINOZA. Tiring of the back-and-forth debate, Clarel observes: "And whose the eye that sees aright, / If any?" When Derwent tries to cheer Clarel and instill "some saving truth," Clarel thinks, "What wouldst prove? / Thy faith an over-easy glove."

Cantos 23–24: "By the Jordan"; "The River-Rite"

As they are about to cross the Jordan River, Rolfe and Derwent continue their jousting as Nehemiah approaches, riding an ass. Margoth sneers at the sight of Nehemiah, but the other pilgrims ignore Margoth. Nehemiah represents "true feeling" and "steadfast faith" while the pilgrims experience "at best . . . / A transient, an esthetic glow."

Cantos 25–27: "The Dominican"; "Of Rome"; "Vine and Clarel"

The pilgrims meet with a DOMINICAN (one of the orders of the Catholic Church, founded in 1216 to fasten teaching and preaching), who debates with Derwent. The Dominican is willing to concede Derwent's Protestant point of view, but then he adds: "Reform was needed, yes, and came— / Reform *within*." But in a world where "this riot of reason" is "quite set free," "Rome is the Protestant to-day." Similarly, he acknowledges but modifies Derwent's vision of a rigid Catholic Church: "Rome being fixed in form, / Unyielding there, how may she keep / Adjustment with new times? But deep / Below rigidities of form / The invisible nerves and tissues change / Adaptively." No matter what the pilgrims believe, the Dominican observes that "If well ye wish to human kind, / Be not so mad, unblest, and blind / As, in such days as these, to try / To pull down Rome. If Rome could fail/'Twould not be Rome alone, but all / Religion."

Observing the departing Dominican, Margoth says: "All, all's geology I trow. / Away to you POPE JOAN—go!" He mocks the church by alluding to the legend of a woman who was pope. Rolfe rises to challenge Margoth, but Derwent restrains him. Derwent gives the Dominican his due, and Rolfe objects, suggesting the Church draws away "rich minds" who might otherwise explore the nature of the world more deeply. Rolfe exaggerates Rome's importance, counters Derwent. It is not the "oceanic" force he portrays. "The world is now too civilized for Rome," Derwent claims. On the contrary, Rolfe replies, who has gained from the failures of Europe's revolutions? Protestants? Liberals? Hardly. "Rome and the Atheist have gained."

Rolfe does not explain himself, and perplexed Clarel looks to Vine for help, but Vine says nothing. When Clarel leans beside him, Vine says he rejects the "moralizing" he finds around him. He does not commit himself to a creed, but, rather, seems to open his mind to nature and to the quest for knowledge. He seems somehow above the debate: "Of true unworldliness looked Vine."

Cantos 28–33: "The Fog"; "By the Marge"; "Of Petra";
"The Inscription"; "The Encampment"; "Lot's Sea"

The pilgrims move south through the biblical sites of Sodom and Gomorrah, and westward along the shore of the Dead Sea, passing by the ancient fortress city of Petra. Derwent discovers a strange cross with an inscription: *"By one who wails the loss, / This altar to the Slanting Cross."* Rolfe supposes this is a "mad freak" of Mortmain's. Derwent disagrees. Then Margoth chalks his own legend on the cross: *"I, Science, I whose gain's thy loss, / I slanted thee, thou Slanting Cross."* But the sun and rain almost immediately obliterate the chalked message.

The pilgrims drive farther south still in expectation of meeting up with Mortmain. They fear for him. Derwent denies Mortmain would "Do his life a wrong— / No, never!" Rolfe, on the other hand, sees Mortmain as a man driven by inner demons. Clarel is hard pressed to "reconcile Rolfe's wizard chord / And forks of esoteric fire, / With common-place of laxer mien." Is Derwent's tolerant, accessible tone more persuasive than Rolfe's complicated, abstruse arguments? Clarel cannot say, and the narrator uses his doubt to express the greater mystery of the pilgrimage: "But if in vain / One tries to comprehend a man, / How think to sound God's deeper heart!" Meanwhile, Rolfe and Margoth debate whether the biblical sites were formed by supernatural or natural forces.

Cantos 34–35: "Mortmain Reappears"; "Prelusive"

The pilgrims are relieved to see Mortmain moving toward them. But no one knows how to approach him. The narrator speculates on the mysterious depths of the human mind, invoking PIRANESI's "rarer prints," which portrayed vast Roman ruins, often projections of the painter's imagination rather than depictions of actual sites.

Cantos 36–37: "Sodom"; "Of Traditions"

Passing through Sodom, the pilgrims make Mortmain their "theme." If Mortmain is mad, "'Tis indignation at the bad," Rolfe contends. Unlike most men, Mortmain cannot get used to seeing evil. Meanwhile Margoth is busy doing some kind of chemical experiment, calling forth from Rolfe the phrase "reason's sorcerer."

Cantos 38–39: "The Sleep-Walker"; "Obsequies"

Nehemiah is aroused by his journey in the Holy Land. His brain throbs at his contact with the origins of Christianity. He imagines Christ's promise of eternity, and yearns for union with God: "Would God I were in thee!" Rising from his sleep, this "somnambulist" leaves the pilgrim encampment. The next morning, the innocent and sinless body of Nehemiah is discovered. How and why he has died is not explained. Mortmain withdraws deeper into his armored self. Margoth just sees the death as part of the natural process. Clarel bows and kneels. Derwent says a quiet prayer, and Vine only *"In pace* [peace]." Rolfe addresses the pilgrims and asks them: "How fare we *now?"* But he receives no reply. The pilgrims bury Nehemiah, and as Derwent says a prayer, even Margoth bends down. Rolfe insists that Nehemiah be buried with his Bible, "thy friend and guide."

Part Three: "Mar Saba"

Cantos 1–3: "In the Mountain"; "The Carpenter"; "Of the Many Mansions"

The pilgrims enter the pass of Mar Saba. Mortmain erupts over his experience in Europe, the failed revolutions, the way science "can so much explode, / Evaporated is this God?" Nehemiah's death still plagues the pilgrims' minds. Rolfe raises the issue of an eternal home for mankind, an Elysium, as the Greeks imagined it. Where do such visions of paradise come from? he wonders. Acknowledging the appeal of religion, of the story of a god come down to earth, Mortmain arouses the pilgrims who are wary of answering him. Like Vine, they respect the "Swede's wild will."

Canto 4: "The Cypriote"

The pilgrims encounter a singing CYPRIOTE. This young, good-looking man evokes wonder in the pilgrims, who hope "That heaven would brim his happy years / Nor time mature him into tears."

Canto 5: "The High Desert"

The narrator meditates on the pilgrims' debate and asks "Science and Faith, can these unite?" Is "faith dead *now,* / A petrifaction?" If so, what will take its place?

This is an infidel age, even while so many still profess Christianity. How can religion survive in the world of science, democracy, and Mammon? Clarel gazes at the Druze and admires his restful pose. Vine remains aloof, siding with no one. He is alert, yet the constant argument among the pilgrims wearies him.

Canto 6: "Derwent"

Mortmain confronts Derwent: "Who sends for thee to act thy part / Consoling—not in life's last hour / Indeed—but when some deprivation sore / Unnerves, and every hope lies flat?" Derwent, troubled by Mortmain's doubts, worries about being trapped in controversies: "Oft I've said / That never, never would I be led / Into their maze of vanity." Derwent's philosophy that "All turns or alters for the best" does not persuade the disconsolate Mortmain, who hangs his head: "Twas SHAFTESBURY first assumed your tone, / Trying to cheerfullize Christ's moan." Clarel marvels that it is not the other outspoken pilgrims but the mild Derwent who most clearly provokes Mortmain's anger and despair.

Cantos 7–10: "Bell and Cairn"; "Tents of Kedar"; "Of Monasteries"; "Before the Gate"

Canto 7 begins with Jesus's cry, "Eloi Lama Sabachthani!" It is his famous lament, "My God, my God, why hast thou forsaken me?" Mortmain's words somehow conjure in Clarel the image of the abandoned Christ. Rolfe, hearing chimes, urges the pilgrims on: "'Tis Saba calling, yea . . . Saba, Mar Saba, summons us: / O, hither, pilgrims, turn to me, / Escape the desert perilous; / Here's refuge, hither unto me!"

They scale the heights of Mar Saba. Derwent tries to cheer Mortmain with an encouraging look but he is answered with a "withering retort." Comparing Mar Saba with other mountain retreats, the narrator notes that "Saba abides the loneliest" as the weary pilgrims approach the gate of the monastery.

Cantos 11–14: "The Beaker"; "The Timoneer's Story"; "Song and Recitative"; "The Revel Closed"

The pilgrims encounter the ARNAUT, a massive Albanian who serves as their escort. He is an impressive figure, this "lion of war" who is so outside their experience. Then the pilgrims meet AGATH, a timoneer or pilot, who tells them of his troubles at sea and how he survived them. He becomes a symbol of human endurance.

The LESBIAN (a Greek from Lesbos) breaks out into song. Rolfe wonders if he should protest against this "true child of the lax Levant, / That polyglot and loose-laced mother? / In such variety he's lived / Where creeds dovetail into each other." The Lesbian's lack of seriousness and conviction offends Rolfe. The Lesbian calls on the startled Derwent to sing a song, which he does, provoking general merriment.

Cantos 15–16: "In the Moonlight"; "The Easter Fire"

Mortmain spends a restless night. Rolfe rises and shakes him. Clarel also cannot sleep. Clarel and Rolfe speak with the Druze, coaxing him to say something about his religion. "No God there is but God," the Druze replies. Rolfe remarks: "There's politesse! we're left behind. / And yet I like this Prince of Pith; / Too pithy almost." He is so different from Derwent, who seeks to mediate between science and faith. Clarel finds Rolfe's candor distasteful, but he tries to master his disapproval. Rolfe is a conundrum for Clarel: "Earnest he seems: can union be / 'Twixt earnestness and levity? / Or need at last in Rolfe confess / Thy hollow, Manysidedness!"

Cantos 17–18: "A Chant"; "The Minster"

Approaching the monastery, the pilgrims hear chanting voices speaking of God's wrath, the destruction and rebuilding of Jerusalem, and God's mercy. The library and church of the monastery are described. Derwent admires the Greek cross but feels drugged by all the incense.

Cantos 19–20: "A Masque"; "Afterward"

A masquer (an actor in a pageant or play) dramatizes the legend of the Wandering Jew: "My fate! / Cut off I am, made separate." The Jews wander from Spain to Rome and back to the Holy Land. The masquer is followed by a song that troubles Clarel, who feels "bantered" and who is full of sad questions.

Canto 21: "In Confidence"

Derwent joins Clarel and they gaze over the valley of the Kedron. But Derwent's expectant air does nothing to dispel Clarel's brooding over the "Swede's dark undelight," the company of the Arnaut, the Lesbian, and the "calm, grave Druze," as well as Belex (the tough old Turkish warrior), and Rolfe and Vine. To Clarel, "Derwent bred distrust / Heavier than came from Mortmain's thrust." It is the din of "clashed belief / So loud in Palestine" that captures Clarel's attention. "No one opinion's steadfast sway . . . so the churches strain, / Much so the fleet sectarian meet / Doubt's equinox." But Derwent rallies: "Shall everything then plain be made?" Clarel is tempted into a personal comment but holds his tongue—as does Derwent, who wants to say, "Throw all this burden upon HIM." Derwent feels a paternal closeness to Clarel and wishes Clarel could draw strength from faith. Clarel seems to want a rational explanation of the universe. Derwent advises him: "do you know / That what most satisfies the head / Least solaces the heart?" Acknowledging that faith has retreated from the modern scene, Derwent nevertheless observes: "Christ built a hearth: the flame is dead / We'll say, extinct; but lingers yet, / Enlodged in stone, the hoarded heat. / Why not nurse that?" "Sorely tried," Clarel cannot find comfort in Derwent's words. Derwent continues: Has Clarel considered that his "swarm of buzzing doubts" might be no more than a "selfish introverted search, / Leaving the poor world in the lurch?" This is not the example Christ set. Why take the extreme? "Midway is best." Why is Clarel torturing himself? Rolfe and Vine will be of no help, Derwent suggests, because they are like "prints from plates but old." No longer able to bear Derwent's argument, Clarel turns on him and says "Forebear!" Derwent's last words are "Alas, too deep you dive." Clarel thinks of Nehemiah, who was sustained by simple faith. With his "freighted heart," Clarel thinks: "Ah, Nehemiah, alone art true? / Secure in reasons's wane or loss? / Thy folly that folly of the cross / Contemned by reason, yet how dear to you?"

Cantos 22–23: "The Medallion"; "Derwent with the Abbot"

Derwent is fascinated with an emblem that shows a victorious knight, who seems reverent and earnest. The inscription is an evocation of the "friendly manifested Spirit!" It is the spirit that saved the warrior and renewed his strength in battle. A brother of the monastery describes it as a "memorial of grace." "Travel teaches much that's strange," Derwent muses. Derwent remarks to the ABBOT that he leads a life far away from "din and strife." But what news does the abbot need of the world, since what is important is to focus on eternity, on the promise of Christ? What about new books and authors? Derwent asks. The holy books are enough, the abbot assures Derwent. Seeing the abbot grow tired, Derwent asks his blessing and leaves.

Cantos 24–27: "Vault and Grotto"; "Derwent and the Lesbian"; "Vine and the Palm"; "Man and Bird"

In contrast to Derwent, Clarel seeks no companion, no "sprightly frame" in which to put his thoughts. He broods rather on Ruth and imagines her "glance of love . . . / Reproaching him: *Dost tarry, tarry yet?*" The question is why Clarel hesitates to return to Ruth.

The Lesbian, singing love songs, encounters Derwent, and both are shocked to see a great bird snatch Mortmain's skull cap away from him. The Lesbian observes that something similar happened to him while mountain riding, and he sits down with Derwent to tell him a story.

On one of the mountain ledges Vine considers his position: "And is it I / . . . that leave the others, / Or do they leave me?" Vine loves the past and finds it difficult to accept the plebeian present. He observes a palm, "witness to a watered land," a tree that "intimates a Paradise!"

Meanwhile, the Lesbian continues with his story about man and bird. Agath, the timoneer has told him about an incident in which a big bird, a "thing demoniac," tries to steal his hat. Enraged, Agath tries to cuff it, but he cannot

take good aim, since his other hand is holding a spar. Eventually, the two fall into the sea and the bird makes off with the wool cap. What a strange story, Derwent comments. Was it really a fight between man and bird, or was it the devil trying to carry off a soul?

Cantos 28–29: "Mortmain and the Palm"; "Rolfe and the Palm"

Mortmain wonders at the palm's resilience. It remains steady whereas Mortmain's knowledge is a curse: "*Knowledge is power:* tell that to knaves; / 'Tis knavish knowledge." On the one hand, Mortmain is transfixed by the idea of the crucifixion; on the other hand he sees it as a "legend, dream . . . with rumors of *No God* so rife!"

Rolfe is vexed by the palm, seeing it a symbol of calm nature, of simple joy which man, descendant of Adam, has abjured for the "briny world."

Cantos 30–32: "The Celibate"; "The Recoil"; "Empty Stirrups"

Clarel thinks steadfastly of Ruth. Her image is before him like a star. He recognizes the peace and comfort of the monastery, but he longs for "life domestic." Can there be a bond "passing the love of woman fond?"

Clarel evokes Mary, the mother of God, and asks, "[S]prang she from Ruth's young sisterhood?" What does love of woman portend? "Ah, love, ah wherefore thus unsure? / Linked art thou—locked, with Self impure?" Is there a love that is pure? "Is naught then trustworthy but God?" The narrator notes that the musing Clarel takes "self to task."

The pilgrims await Mortmain so that they can resume their journey. Feeling apprehensive, Clarel searches for Mortmain and finds him hanging from a tree. It comes as no surprise to pilgrims who have believed him to be overburdened: "That such a heart could beat, and will— / Aspire, yearn, suffer, baffled still, / And end."

Part Four: "Bethlehem"

Cantos 1–3: "In Saddle"; "The Ensign"; "The Island"

The pilgrims ride toward Bethlehem, escorted by the Arnaut and Djalea, the Druze. Agath points the way, and as he does so reveals a tattoo or ensign of the crucifixion—what Derwent calls a "living fresco!" The trickling blood drops make it look as though Agath's arm is bleeding. He got the tattoo when quite a young man, and he tells the pilgrims that it is supposed to be a "charm . . . 'gainst watery doom." Rolfe says that in ancient times all pilgrims wore such tattoos, but now the tradition has faded out except among the "boatswains of the brine." Derwent urges the pilgrims on, saying the tattoo's star of Bethlehem, discovered when Agath stretched out his arm, now guides them, like wise men, to Christ's birthplace. The pilgrims do not see how Vine carefully watches Agath, regarding the sailor as one of "Nature's mint," that is, an "authentic; man of nature true, / If simple; naught that slid between / Him and the elemental scene." Vine asks him if he has seen any land to compare "with Judah here." Agath replies that a "far isle" he visited in his youthful days reminds him of "this stricken land." The pilgrims crowd around him to hear more. The volcanic island had a beach of cinders and a "wasted look." It had no vegetation or fruit and seemed barren. Clarel ponders this account and of what man can make of the world. Men build, destroy, invent new creeds, change their vocabulary, but they cannot "solve the world!" It is "too wild . . . too wonderful" and baffling, whether made by nature (Agath's island) or by man (Judah).

Cantos 4–5: "An Intruder"; "Of the Stranger"

Agath is startled by a scorpion, which Rolfe first calls an "epitome of evil," and then corrects himself, saying "But speak not evil of the evil: / Evil and good they braided play / Into one cord." Derwent is surprised at Agath's fright, given that he is a sailor who has seen the "wonders of the deep." Rolfe rescues the embarrassed Agath by pointing out that soldiers going into battle have been startled by seeing spiders.

While Agath continues with his story, Rolfe and Clarel consider the new stranger in their midst. UNGAR has the look of a frontiersman and a refugee. What is he doing roaming abroad?

Cantos 6–10: "Bethlehem"; "At Table"; "The Pillow"; "The Shepherd's Dale"; "A Monument"

The excited pilgrims speed toward Bethlehem. When Derwent turns back to share his enthusiasm with the others, he finds that they have been struck dumb and are subdued. Rolfe is overwhelmed by their welcome in Bethlehem, where "Mary found no room at inn." The focus shifts to Ungar, "islanded in thought" and to Rolfe, who contrasts the life of the sea with the "cloistral" people of Bethlehem.

The next morning, the pilgrims rise with gusto, and Derwent leads them on into the morning's light. They descend into the Valley of the Shepherds, a place where the light has a holy resonance. Rolfe suggests the valley must be near the site of Eden, and he feels a "link with years before the Fall." The disaffected Ungar dampens the mood, condemning the crusaders who came to the Holy Land like pirates, who "in the name of Christ and Trade . . . Deflower the world's last sylvan glade!" Derwent counters with praise of Christian charity. "Your alms-box, smaller than your till, / And poorhouse won't absolve your mill," Ungar replies. Seeking to change the subject, Derwent points ahead and wonders what "yonder object" is—a fountain? shrine? But Ungar refuses to quit the argument, contrasting the simplicity and purity of ancient religious belief with

"your sects" that "nowadays create / Churches as worldly as the state." He speaks, the narrator emphasizes, as a "wandering Ishmael from the West."

Cantos 11–12: "Disquiet"; "Of Pope and Turk"

At breakfast, Ungar withdraws, and Derwent feels "less ill at ease." Clarel thinks of Mortmain, another harsh critic of contemporary man. Rolfe, in the meantime, chafes Derwent about Protestantism's poor record in defending Christian countries like Poland when they were dismembered by czarist Russia. The pope and the Turks protested. Derwent replies that the pope was simply worried that Russia would try to make Poland a Russian Orthodox country, and is Rolfe trying to prove that Turks are better than Protestants? The argument breaks off as the pilgrims prepare to journey on.

Cantos 13–17: "The Church of the Star"; "Soldier and Monk"; "Symphonies"; "The Convent Roof"; "A Transition"

Agath leaves the pilgrims at this point. A silver star is set in the pavement before the church, supposedly marking the site where the Magi came to see the Christ Child. They are shown around the church by an ardent monk. There is an inscription in a semicircular recess that identifies this as the place where "THE VIRGIN BROUGHT FORTH THE SON."

Ungar watches the votary (a monk) with keen, sympathetic attention. Derwent seems amused by the monk's enthusiasm, finding something almost feminine in it. MACHIAVELLI hinted something of the same about Christ, Rolfe tells Derwent. And what does it mean to be manly? Derwent throws out his chest and says "man at his best!" Rolfe counters: "But even at best, one might reply, / Man is that thing of sad renown / Which moved a deity to come down / And save him." Derwent seems to ignore the point, expressing his enthusiasm for a "delicate drapery." Clarel and Vine seem momentarily enraptured by the celebration of Christ that is so palpable in the church.

The pilgrims then ascend to the convent roof to get a broader view of Bethlehem, and they agree to spend a second night in the city. Out in the open air, Rolfe feels less inspired by what he has seen below.

Rolfe asks Clarel his opinion of Ungar. Clarel is at a loss, for "he's most strange; / Wild, too, adventurous in range; / And suffers." Ungar bears some kind of cross, Clarel speculates.

Canto 18: "The Hill-Side"

Climbing up a hillside, Derwent meets up with Ungar and asks him to look on the glorious sight. A discussion ensues about Bethlehem's impact on "Western natures." Rolfe thinks the site of Christ's birth should have been Tahiti, a place of peace and shelter "[f]or Christ in advent." Ungar dissents, since he regards Christ's birth as, in part, a rebuke to man. It was fitting that Christ should be born in the "land of Pharisees and scorn." Although Derwent acknowledges that the Holy Land sites have been "gilded," they still serve to renew faith. Rolfe scoffs at taking the sites so seriously. But Derwent insists that they are aids to the spiritual imagination; else, "Tell Romeo that Juliet's eyes / Are chemical; e'en analyze / The iris; show 'tis albumen— / Glue—fish-jelly mere. What then? / To Romeo it is still love's sky: / He loves; enough!" Faith is built on just such use of material to evoke the immaterial or spiritual. Ungar rejects the argument, saying "there is callousness in clay." It cannot be used as symbolic of the divine.

Canto 19: "A New-Comer"

Derwent discovers his old friend, Don HANNIBAL, who introduces himself as a "*reformado* reformed." That is, he has participated in the Mexican Revolution (1858–61) but has been disappointed in its outcome and in the very idea of reform. Ungar takes a keen interest in this disappointed reformer. Having lost an arm and a leg in the revolution, Don Hannibal exclaims: "But what's in this Democracy? / Eternal hacking! Woe is me, / She lopped these limbs, Democracy." Ungar agrees, and dreads the future of a world where democracy is dominant.

Canto 20: "Derwent and Ungar"

Derwent refuses to accept Don Hannibal's antireform talk. He tells the pilgrims not to accept half of what Don Hannibal says. He is a "secret agent of Reform; / At least, that is my theory." Reform movements have unintended consequences, Ungar points out. Derwent disagrees; reform means "belief revised / Men liberated—equalized / In happiness." Ungar is unpersuaded: "the world cannot save the world." On the contrary, Derwent argues: "Howbeit, true reform goes on / By nature; doing, never done. / Mark the advance: creeds drop the hate; / Events still liberalize the state." Does human nature really change, Ungar wonders. Is there no such thing as development? Derwent asks. Undeterred, Ungar presents a catalogue of revolutionary change like the FRENCH REVOLUTION of 1789 which has furthered evil.

Canto 21: "Ungar and Rolfe"

Rolfe asks Ungar if his vision of the future is really so grim. Is Satan weak? Ungar replies. Isn't progress a refutation of God, a claim that man can find better ways? To Rolfe, Ungar argues in "void abstractions." Ungar continues: "For man, like God, abides the same / Always, through all variety." Ungar notes that "One demagogue can trouble much: / How of a hundred thousand such? / And universal suffrage lent / To back them with brute element / Overwhelming?" Each new event merely brings "new confirmation of the fall / of Adam." Although they do not share what even Ungar calls his "monomania," the pilgrims have misgivings about the future and worry that "Columbus ended earth's romance: / No New World to mankind remains!"

Canto 22: "Of Wickedness the Word"

Out of charity, no pilgrim wants to "upbraid" the exile Ungar. Rolfe asks Vine, "Is wickedness the word?" Vine says only the word itself has been overlaid with so many meanings. Derwent looks rather to nature for inspiration, for he cannot believe that Ungar's "jarring theme" really reflects all that is available to man. Clarel, who has not been impressed with Derwent's arguments, nevertheless finds Ungar's deeply disturbing, for man is reduced to a creature of the senses and with no prospects for the future.

Canto 23: "Derwent and Rolfe"

Derwent slips his arm into Rolfe's, assuring him that they share a bond. "Man has two sides," Derwent tells Rolfe, "keep on the bright." But Rolfe answers that two sides imply one is not right. He wonders if large hopes can countermand Ungar's jeremiads. Ungar is wise, although he is also "too vehemently wise! / His factious memories tyrannize."

Cantos 24–27: "Twilight"; "The Invitation"; "The Prodigal"; "By Parapet"; "David's Well"

At twilight, Clarel is beguiled by a tropical song, while Derwent seeks his Mexican friend. He shares a room with the LYONESE Frenchman, whose love songs seem to have inspired in Clarel erotic dreams and fantasies. Clarel appears to be in a state of sexual confusion brought on by the Frenchman's "paganish" songs and stories. At David's Well, Clarel is "[i]n travail of transition rare." Confronting a crisis in his pilgrimage, Clarel asks himself a series of questions: Will he content himself with a "common uninquiring life?" Is he "sick of strife"? Would he really be content with a worldly routine? Would he be happy as a "fugitive" from his own "nobler part"? Should Clarel, in other words, simply accept the world and not strive to understand the meaning of life?

Cantos 29–31: "The Night Ride"; "The Valley of Decision"; "Dirge"

On the day before Lent, Shrove Tuesday in England, the pilgrims ride toward the Cistern of the Kings, where the Magi watered their camels. With a piercing cry, Clarel recognizes two familiar figures: the bodies of Ruth and Agar, who have died in grief over Nathan's death by drowning. "O blind, blind, barren universe!" Clarel cries out. "Take me, take me, Death! / Where Ruth is gone, me thither whirl. / Where'er it be!"

Cantos 32–33: "Passion Week"; "Easter"; "Via Crucis"; "Epilogue"

Several days pass, and on Good Friday, Clarel has a vision of all the dead—of Nehemiah, Celio, Mortmain, and Nathan, with Agar grieving for her husband and Ruth "how estranged in face!" Clarel does not know where to go or what to do. The Easter story of the risen Christ clashes with the vision of the dead Ruth. It is the *via crucis,* the way of the cross, the road of human suffering which Clarel has followed.

The last lines of the poem urge Clarel to "keep thy heart, though yet but ill-resigned . . . like a crocus budding through the snow— / That like a swimmer rising from the deep— / that like a burning secret which doth go / Even from the bosom that would hoard and keep; / Emerge thou mayst from the last whelming sea, / And prove that death but routs life into victory."

PUBLICATION HISTORY

Clarel was published in two volumes on June 3, 1876. It cost three dollars. There was no British edition, but Putnam, Melville's American publisher, distributed the book in England. With help from his family, Melville paid for the entire publication. The critical reception was poor. Reviewers were perplexed, understanding neither the content nor the style of the book. It seemed ambiguous and even without a point. A few reviewers praised Melville's powers of description, but most of the important magazines did not even mention the poem. The English critics were not much better pleased, finding it unintelligible or at best "interesting."

Like most of Melville's work, *Clarel* was rediscovered in the 1920s in a climate better disposed to appreciate his irony, although many critics, like Lewis Mumford, nevertheless considered it a failure as a poem. Since the 1930s, however, critics have grown to appreciate Melville's modern vision, which some have compared to such poems as T. S. Eliot's *The Waste Land.* The poem was reprinted in 1924 as part of the 16-volume Constable edition of Melville's work. The first scholarly edition appeared in 1960, published by Hendricks House, with a superb introduction by Walter Bezanson. Bezanson's essay is reprinted in the Northwestern University Press edition of *Clarel* (1991), part of its collected edition of Melville's work. The Northwestern text, available in paperback, is indispensable. It includes several essays by Melville scholars and detailed notes about the composition, historical context, and reception of the poem. Given Melville's detailed references to history, travel narratives, myths, the Bible, and other literary works, the Northwestern edition's annotations are the single best available source for a study of the entire poem.

Clarel   Clarel is the title character of Melville's great poem (see CLAREL). He is a young scholar searching for a religious awakening. Although he is a modern man who has his doubts about revealed religion, he is obsessed with visiting the sites in the Holy Land and with learning from other pilgrims. He tries to keep an open mind and is swayed by believers and nonbelievers alike. He becomes a kind of sounding board for the views of others. At times he debates with his fellow pilgrims, but he comes to no definitive conclusions. In this respect, he is rather like ISHMAEL in *MOBY-DICK*, a center of consciousness who stands somewhat apart from the action even though he is so closely involved in it.

Claret, Captain   Character in *WHITE-JACKET.* Claret is the captain of the man-of-war *NEVERSINK.* The son of a veteran of the Revolutionary War Battle of Brandywine Creek, Claret is a rotund man whose alcoholism sometimes clouds his judgment—as when he nearly loses the ship off CAPE HORN by giving the wrong command. A stickler for naval discipline, he is also something of a sadist, pitting two black cook's helpers against one another in a head-butting contest for his own amusement. Claret is probably modeled in part on James Armstrong, who was captain of the U.S.S. *UNITED STATES* during Melville's service. Like Claret, Armstrong had a weakness for the bottle. He also published a memoir, *Narrative of the U.S. Exploring Expedition during the Years 1838, 1839, 1840, 1841, 1842* (1845), which Melville may have drawn on when writing his book.

Clootz, Jean-Baptiste du Val de Grace, Baron, a.k.a. Anacharsis Cloots (1755–1794)   A French political activist who traveled across Europe to advocate the union of all nations into one family. He saw the FRENCH REVOLUTION as the fulfillment of his dreams. He called himself an "orator of the human race." But he fell afoul of Robespierre, the French Revolutionary leader, and was guillotined. In *The CONFIDENCE MAN,* Melville refers to the passengers aboard the *FIDELE* as a "piebald parliament, an Anacharsis Cloots [sic] congress of all kinds of that multiform pilgrim species, man." BILLY BUDD is described as a specimen of universal humanity whom Clootz would have favored.

"Clover" (1924)   Poem in *WEEDS AND WILDINGS.* Part of the section of the volume "The Year"—probably meant to follow another poem concerning robins, "THE LITTLE GOOD FELLOWS"—"Clover" is a quatrain that praises the contrast afforded by fields of clover, which point up the rosiness of the dawn and the redness of the ruddock's (or robin's) breast. Melville seems to have taken his inspiration from the popular British poet Thomas Campbell (1777–1844), whose "Field Flowers" is quoted under the heading "Clover" on a loose leaf found among Melville's papers after his death: "Ye field flowers! the gardens eclipse you, 'tis true, / Yet wildings of nature I doat upon you." Such optimistic lines form a marked contrast with the dirge from John Webster's *The White Devil* that apparently served as a source for "The Little Good Fellows."

"Cock-A-Doodle-Doo! Or, The Crowing of the Noble Cock Beneventano" (1853)   First piece of mature short fiction Melville published. In the spring or summer of 1853, Melville delivered "Cock-A-Doodle-Doo!" to HARPER'S NEW MONTHLY MAGAZINE, which printed the piece anonymously the following December. It was among the first short fiction he had written specifically for magazine publication since the humorous sketches that appeared in YANKEE DOODLE in 1847. The narrator of the story, a melancholy man beset by monetary and other disasters, is cheered when he hears the crowing of a magnificent cock. With some effort, he tracks down the bird, only to find that it is owned by a poor wood-sawyer named MERRYMUSK, whose wife and child lie dying. Still, Merrymusk refuses the narrator's offer to buy Trumpet—as the glorious rooster is called—demanding, "Don't the cock *I* own glorify this otherwise inglorious, lean, lantern-jawed land? Didn't *my* cock encourage *you?*" Soon, however, Merrymusk and his family all lie dead, whereupon the rooster itself expires. The narrator calls the magnificent bird Beneventano, after the opera singer Ferdinando Beneventano, whom Melville twice heard sing in Gaetano Donizetti's *Lucia di Lammermoor* in 1847. Contemporary readers also would have recognized this as an allusion to the then current craze for fancy chickens. And some commentators at the time saw something more in the story: a critique of TRANSCENDENTALIST optimism.

Coffin, Peter   In MOBY-DICK, landlord of the Spouter Inn, in NEW BEDFORD, Massachusetts. Coffin provides ISHMAEL with his roommate, QUEEQUEG.

Colbrook, Corporal   Minor character in WHITE-JACKET. It is Colbrook, a handsome, gentlemanly marine aboard the NEVERSINK, who first steps forward to defend WHITE-JACKET when Captain CLARET accuses the seaman of being absent from his station and threatens to flog him for the offense.

Cole, Thomas (1801–1848)   Born in Bolton-le-Moor, England, Cole emigrated to the United States in 1819 and studied at the Pennsylvania Academy of Fine Arts. Considered part of the Hudson River School of landscape painters, he is a painter best known for his epic painting series *The Course of Empire*, which Melville saw on May 4, 1847. In late 1847, Melville's friend Evert DUYCKINCK took him to an exhibition featuring Cole's painting at the just opened American Art-Union. Cole's blending of the historical and the allegorical in his landscapes appealed to Melville and influenced books such as MARDI and MOBY-DICK.

Coleridge, Samuel Taylor (1772–1834)   Born in Ottery St. Mary in Devon, England, Coleridge is one of the great poets and critics of the Romantic Age. He first came to attention for his collaboration with William Wordsworth. Coleridge explored the darker side of human nature in much of his work, and his great poem *The RIME OF THE ANCIENT MARINER* informs Melville's own brooding over destiny in MOBY-DICK, CLAREL, and other works.

"The College Colonel" (1866)   Poem in BATTLE-PIECES. The colonel of the poem was William Francis Bartlett, a Harvard graduate who had lost a leg in the CIVIL WAR and was famous for leading his troops into battle while carrying a crutch across his saddle. Having recently organized the Berkshire regiment of the Massachusetts 57th, Bartlett paraded with his men through PITTSFIELD, MASSACHUSETTS, on August 22, 1863. Melville doubtless saw Bartlett then, as well as again that evening at an engagement hosted in his honor by Sarah MOREWOOD, which Herman and his wife Elizabeth attended. For Melville, Bartlett possessed the kind of stoicism that has allowed the human race to prevail:

> A still rigidity and pale—
> An Indian aloofness lones his brow;
> He has lived a thousand years.

collegian, the   A character in *The CONFIDENCE MAN*. The collegian is reading TACITUS when the MAN WITH A LONG WEED approaches him, advising him to throw the book overboard since the Roman historian teaches nothing but cynicism. The collegian must learn to have confidence in mankind, the man with the weed assures him.

colonialism   In the 19th century, America expanded into an imperial power with colonialist aspirations. Early on, Melville took against this aggressive American and Western desire to "civilize" the rest of the world. He detested the arrogance of missionaries in the South Seas and in HAWAII. Under whatever guise—religion or politics—Melville despised the idea of appropriating the persons or property of others. Both his antislavery and his antimilitaristic views stemmed, in part, from his belief that it was unjust to try to dominate others, especially when the forms of domination led to hypocritical protests of spiritual or democratic values. Thus Melville satirized the cant of democratic and revolutionary politics in ISRAEL POTTER and *The CONFIDENCE MAN* and explored the futility of politics and the ambiguity of the religious quest in CLAREL. Even his earlier, more light-hearted narratives such as TYPEE express his disdain for colonializing Westerners. PIERRE constitutes a direct attack on his own family history, for the novel exposes the extent to which his family's success in the Revolutionary War, for example, simply led to their political dominance and sense of entitlement that was the opposite of a true democratic spirit.

"'The Coming Storm': A Picture by S. R. Gifford, and owned by E. B. Included in the N. A. Exhibition, April, 1865." (1866)   Melville saw the painting that inspired this poem in an exhibition at the National Academy in NEW YORK CITY. The property of the actor Edwin Booth (the brother of Abraham LINCOLN's assassin, John Wilkes Booth), the painting of the gathering storm seemed to presage the personal tragedy to come. A great Shakespearian actor, Edwin Booth could not have been utterly surprised by his brother's fateful actions because John Wilkes was so unstable and such a fanatic. Melville urges sympathy for Edwin Booth's personal loss in the face of the nation's grief over its dead president.

"Commemorative of a Naval Victory" (1866)   Poem in BATTLE-PIECES. One of the "Verses Inscriptive and Memorial" in Melville's collection of CIVIL WAR poetry, this poem speaks to a subject close to Melville's heart. The poem opens, "Sailors there are of the gentlest breed / Yet strong, like every good thing." One of these men is a survivor, much honored, who nonetheless remembers those who "Sleep in oblivion." Even amidst celebration, he cannot be happy, recalling that "The shark / Glides white through the phosphorus sea."

commodore, the   Character in WHITE-JACKET. Because the narrator of the book serves on the NEVERSINK, the flagship of the fleet, he shares space with the commodore. In the book, the commodore is not named, but he seems to have been modeled on Thomas ap Catesby Jones, a hero of the War of 1812 who had commanded the Pacific Squadron, including the U.S.S. UNITED STATES, from 1841 to 1842. Thomas was not on the *United States* at the same time as Melville, but for two and a half months in 1843 Melville's ship was detained in Callao, Peru, where Thomas was paying an official visit. There is no evidence that his and Melville's paths ever actually crossed. The commodore in the book is wizened and old, and rumored to be brave and virtuous, but his command of the ship is virtually nonexistent.

Confidence Man, The   Melville's ninth book, a novel, is a kind of absurdist comedy remarkable for its foreshadowing of much 20th-century literature that questions the stability of human identity. As the critic R. W. B. Lewis notes in his afterword to the Signet classic edition of the novel, it "takes place on the first of April between dawn and midnight on the Feast of All Fools." The book was published, moreover, on April 1, 1857. Like ISRAEL POTTER, *The Confidence Man: His Masquerade* excoriates and lampoons American connivery and energy. The novel's structure, in fact, is based on the confidence man's tricks, disguises (masks), and sophistries. In many ways, the novel is an all-out attack on the American belief in the perfectibility of man.

In the summer of 1850 Melville took a trip on a Mississippi steamboat like the one advertised here, garnering material he would later put to use in The Confidence Man. *(Library of Congress)*

Taking place aboard a Mississippi riverboat, *The Confidence Man* is, like Melville's epic poem CLAREL, the story of a pilgrimage, with the ship's passengers seeking to understand the meaning of life when they are not bilking each other out of their ideas and their purses. Like the poem, the novel is about mixed motivations. Melville certainly does not deny the impulse toward human perfectibility, but he finds that impulse shot through with corrupt and corrupting motivations. Nothing is as it first appears in the world of *The Confidence Man*. As in *Clarel*, the novel's world is a fallen one, with man impossibly struggling to recover his state of grace and fitfully yearning for his salvation. But *The Confidence Man* is a much less earnest work than the poem, and the novel is filled with a kind of ribald cynicism worthy of Mark Twain.

SYNOPSIS

Chapter I: "A Mute Goes Aboard a Boat on the Mississippi"
The confidence man boards a Mississippi riverboat, although he is not identified as such. Rather, he is called a "stranger," a fair-cheeked, flaxen-haired fellow with no baggage. The steamer *FIDELE* is docked at St. Louis and is about to embark for New Orleans. The mute stranger passes a placard near the captain's office that offers a reward for the "capture of a mysterious imposter." The imposter is, of course, the confidence man himself, although, again, this may not be apparent on a first reading of the chapter. The stranger/imposter produces a small slate on which he writes, "Charity thinketh no evil," and places the slate next to the placard. Then he writes a succession of messages about charity—that it "suffereth long, and is kind," "endureth all things," "believeth all things," and "never faileth." Charity, indeed, will become the principal topic of discussion aboard ship as the confidence man in his various disguises tries to convince his interlocutors that they should trust him. Opposed to the stranger's messages is the barber's sign: "No trust."

Chapter II: "Showing That Many Men Have Many Minds"
The mute stranger excites much curious discussion. "Who can he be?" asks one passenger. Is he a humbug, a spiritualist, a pickpocket, an escaped convict? The mute stranger sits peaceably as the speculation builds among this heterogeneous group of passengers, whom the narrator compares to CHAUCER's pilgrims, a "variety of mortals" embodying the "dashing and all-fusing spirit of the West."

Chapter III: "In Which a Variety of Characters Appear"
The confidence man enters in his first disguise—as a "NEGRO CRIPPLE." Speaking in a thick dialect, the "poor old darkie" (as he calls himself) solicits the charity of his fellow passengers. He is challenged by a "limping, gimlet-eye, sour-faced person," with a wooden leg (see WOODEN-LEGGED MAN)—perhaps a "discharged custom-house officer," the narrator speculates. Along with other passengers, he suspects the old Negro is an imposter. Where is the old Negro's proof that he is who he says he is? Where are his documents? He replies he has no "waloable [valuable] papers." But there are several people aboard who can confirm his identity. He describes them but gives no names. A young Episcopal clergyman goes off in search of them. A debate ensues between the wooden-legged man and a METHODIST MINISTER, who declares that the old Negro should be treated with charity. "Charity is one thing, and truth is another," retorts the wooden-legged man. To the Methodist, the old Negro looks honest. "Looks are one thing, and facts are another," the wooden-legged man persists. The exercised Methodist finally says to the

wooden-legged man, "If charity did not restrain me, I could call you the names you deserve." To the wooden-legged man, this is a "ship of fools!" Sounding the other important word in the novel, the old Negro regrets that the passengers have "no confidence in dis poor ole darkie."

Chapters IV–V: "Renewal of Old Acquaintance"; "The Man With the Weed Makes It an Even Question Whether He Be a Great Sage or a Great Simpleton"
A MAN WITH A LONG WEED on his hat strikes up a conversation with a Mr. ROBERTS. "Don't you know me?" the man with the long weed asks Roberts. "No, certainly," Roberts replies. The man with the long weed (it is the confidence man) says that surely Roberts remembers his name, John RINGMAN. Roberts draws a blank, even though the confidence man begins to describe a business transaction he had with Roberts, supplying details about Roberts's life that draw Roberts deeper into the conversation. Finally, the confidence man says he has a story to tell Roberts, one of calamities he has suffered. As the confidence man continues with more unhappy revelations, the "good merchant" Roberts takes out larger and larger banknotes which he puts into the stranger's hands. When Roberts does raise the possibility that the stranger is at fault for some of his troubles, the confidence man professes deep humiliation, wondering that Roberts could "reproach a penniless man with remissness." Roberts relents, secure in his good opinion of himself and of the stranger.

The man with the weed is next seen leaning over a railing on the boat's side, reflecting on the sorrow of the world but also on its goodness. Near him is a "COLLEGIAN," a swan-necked young man wearing a "lady-like open shirt collar, thrown back, and tied with a black ribbon." He is reading the Roman historian TACITUS. The man with the weed advises the collegian to throw the book overboard, because even if Tacitus tells the truth, his history is "moral poison." Tacitus teaches cynicism. "Without confidence himself Tacitus destroys it in all his readers," the confidence man points out. The collegian does not throw the book overboard, but he does become fascinated with the stranger.

Chapter VI: "At the Outset of Which Certain Passengers Prove Deaf to the Call of Charity"
The man with the weed is now referred to as a "a man in a gray coat and white tie" (see MAN IN GRAY). He is seen trying to persuade a passenger to contribute to an Orphan Asylum recently founded among the Seminoles. When he is rebuffed, he urges his fellow passenger: "Give you more charity, sir." Then the young clergyman, looking for proof of the old Negro's claims, spots the man in gray, who exclaims "Ah, poor Guinea! have you, too, been distrusted?" The wooden-legged man is still skeptical. The man in gray asks, "Do you really think that a white could look the negro so? For

one, I should call it pretty good acting." "Not much better than any other man acts," responds the wooden-legged man. Are we all performers then? the man in gray wants to know. Certainly, the wooden-legged man answers: "To do, is to act; so all doers are actors."

Chapters VII–VIII: "A Gentleman with Gold Sleeve-buttons"; "A Charitable Lady"
The man in gray successfully solicits funds from a GENTLEMAN WITH GOLD SLEEVE-BUTTONS, who then confides his plan to systematize charity, to build an organization called "The World's Charity." Its one object will be the "methodization of the world's benevolence," so that the need for charity will be eliminated once and for all.

The man in gray then approaches a lady seated on a sofa. He asks her if she has "confidence." Could she, for example, place her confidence in him? He calls himself a wandering stranger in whom no one will place their confidence. The lady becomes interested. When he despairs, calling himself a fool, she gives him the $20 he asks for. He departs, saying to her, "You have confidence."

Chapters IX–XII: "Two Business Men Transact a Little Business"; "In the Cabin"; "Only a Page or So"; "Story of the Unfortunate Man, From Which May Be Gathered Whether or No He Has Been Justly So Entitled"
The collegian is approached by a man identifying himself as the PRESIDENT OF THE BLACK RAPIDS COAL COMPANY. He is looking for the man with the weed in order to give him $10 for his charity. The business executive begins to inveigh against Wall Street bears who do not have confidence in stock. They are the "destroyers of confidence." His use of the phrase confirms a suspicion that the bank president, like the man in gray and the man with the weed, are all the same confidence man. Soon the collegian is inquiring about investment opportunities, and the confidence man tells him about the "New Jerusalem," a thriving city in northern Minnesota. There are lots for sale. But it is the coal company that most interests the collegian.

Passing through the ship's cabin, displaying a book with the title "Black Rapids Coal Company," the confidence man enlists the interests of a "good merchant" who expresses his desire to invest, having already heard about the company aboard ship. "How can you have confidence in me?" asks the confidence man. The good merchant replies: "If you were other than I have confidence that you are, hardly would you challenge distrust that way." The merchant does not even care to examine the company's books. He is ready to buy stock. "Your logic I will not criticize, but your confidence I admire," says the confidence man.

The transaction is concluded, and the good merchant tells the confidence man about other passengers he has observed—an old MISER, an old Negro (a disguise of the confidence man)—who suffer a life far different from those seated at the "gay tables" gambling. The confidence man observes of the Negro cripple: "The alleged hardships of that alleged unfortunate might not exist more in the pity of the observer than the experience of the observed." The good merchant persists, however, in believing in the misery he has seen, especially that of the man with the weed, now called the "unfortunate man."

The unfortunate man had a wife, GONERIL, "lithe and straight," a hard woman with features that looked baked on. She had deep rich chestnut hair and an Indian figure. Her mouth would have been pretty if she had not had a trace of a moustache. She is taciturn and blunt when she does speak. Her words can seem like an "icicle-dagger." She is an enigma who disturbs her husband, the unfortunate man, by the way she touches young men. Since Goneril will "brook no chiding," the unfortunate man cannot speak to her about his feelings.

Then the "devil of jealousy" enters Goneril and she begins tormenting her seven-year-old daughter. Realizing he cannot control Goneril, the unfortunate man decides to withdraw his daughter from her mother's company. Goneril brings suit against her husband, simultaneously bankrupting him and winning custody of the child. His reputation ruined, the unfortunate man is also threatened with incarceration in a lunatic asylum. He flees, later discovering that Goneril has died. He wears a weed in his hat to conform to the "prescribed form of mourning in such cases," and he is now seeking funds to return home to claim his daughter. To the good merchant, this is a very hard case indeed.

Chapters XIII–XIV: "The Man With the Traveling-Cap Evinces Much Humanity, and in a Way Which Would Seem To Show Him To Be One of the Most Logical of Optimists"; "Worth the Consideration of Those To Whom It May Prove Worth Considering"
Now called the "MAN WITH THE TRAVELING-CAP," the confidence man asks the good merchant if the unfortunate man did "despond or have confidence?" Moreover, the man with the traveling-cap thinks the unfortunate man may have acted hastily, and that there were probably "faults on both sides." As the two men talk and drink champagne together, the merchant suddenly bursts out with the question: "can wine or confidence percolate down through all the stony strata of hard considerations and drop warmly and ruddily into the cold cave of truth?" The man with the traveling-cap points out how inconsistent with his previous line the merchant's words are. Perhaps he should not drink champagne. Taken aback, the merchant feels rebuked. The man with the traveling-cap says he hopes his companion's confidence has been restored.

The narrator comments on the merchant's inconsistency, arguing that only in books are characters expected to be consistent. Human nature is itself inconsistent, the narrator points out.

Chapters XV–XX: "An Old Miser, Upon Suitable Representations, Is Prevailed Upon To Venture an Investment"; "A Sick Man, After Some Impatience, Is Induced To Become a Patient"; "The Herb-doctor"; "In Quest Into The True Nature of the Herb-doctor"; "A Soldier of Fortune"; "Reappearance of One Who May Be Remembered"
The man with the traveling-cap, now referred to as "the stranger," encounters an ailing miser and asks what he can do for him. "How can I repay you?" the miser asks. "By giving me your confidence," the stranger replies. He then asks the miser for $100. It is a rather high price to put on confidence, the miser suggests. Listening to the miser's dreadful cough, the stranger recommends his "Omni-Balsamic Reinvigorator." The miser is reluctant to invest with the stranger, although he is curious as to how the stranger will make good on his claim to triple his investors' profits. Without confidence, such questions cannot be answered, the stranger maintains. After making a show of doubting the miser's now earnest desire to show his confidence, the stranger reluctantly accepts the miser's gold.

A sick, "unparticipating man" is approached by an HERB-DOCTOR (another disguise of the confidence man). The herb-doctor makes no claims that are not nature's claims to cure. Distrust only weakens the invalid, the herb doctor points out to the sick man. It is "time to get strength by confidence." The mind acts upon the body, so a confident mind will help to heal a sick body. Moreover, "hope is proportioned to confidence." Yet the herb-doctor cannot promise a radical, successful cure in this case. Lack of confidence is evil; it wears a man down. The herb-doctor makes his sale.

In an antecabin, the herb-doctor touts his "Samaritan Pain Dissuader," a natural product made from vegetable extract. A rustic-looking giant of a passenger from the Carolinas challenges the herb-doctor, calling him a "profane fiddler on heart-strings! Snake!" The bruised herb-doctor says he will not seek redress: "Innocence is my redress." He continues to sell his product.

Two passengers discuss the attack on the herb-doctor. One calls the confidence man a fool, another admires his glib talk. Other passengers find the doctor suspect; indeed, one of them thinks he must be a Jesuit conspirator.

The herb-doctor then approaches a "singular character in a grimy old regimental coat." His legs are paralyzed. The herb-doctor offers to sell him his "Natural Bone-setter." To the skeptical soldier, the doctor decries his lack of confidence. The soldier replies by telling the whole sad tale of his misfortunes. The doctor says he cannot believe it and that the cripple should show more charity and confidence in regard to the world. When the cripple continues to scoff, the doctor gives him a box of the Natural Bone-setter. Suddenly the cripple wants to know if the treatment will really work. "Now, have you no confidence in my art?" the doctor asks. He mildly tells the cripple that "there is no harm in trying" the remedy. The cripple then asks for three more boxes and hands over his money. "I rejoice in the birth of your confidence," the doctor says.

The miser returns, coughing and asking where the coal company man (now identified as John TRUMAN) is who is selling stock. The doctor tells him that he has also invested and already tripled his money. But Truman has apparently left the ship. The herb-doctor recommends his Omni-Balsamic Reinvigorator for two dollars a box. The miser tries to haggle, but in the end makes the purchase, trying to use false coinage.

Chapters XXI–XXVIII: "A Hard Case"; "In the Polite Spirit of the Tuculan Disputations"; "In Which the Powerful Effect of Natural Scenery Is Evinced in the Case of the Missourian, Who, in View of the Region Roundabout Cairo, Has a Return of His Chilly Fit"; "A Philanthropist Undertakes to Convert a Misanthrope, but Does Not Get Beyond Confusing Him"; "The Cosmopolitan Makes an Acquaintance"; "Containing the Metaphysics of Indian-hating, According To The View of One Evidently Not So Prepossessed as Rousseau in Favor of Savages"; "Some Account of a Man of Questionable Morality, but Who, Nevertheless, Would Seem Entitled to the Esteem of That Eminent English Moralist Who Said He Liked a Good Hater"; "Moot Points Touching the Late Colonel John Moredock"
A MISSOURIAN approaches the miser, telling him that herbs are as likely to do him harm as to cure him. The herb-doctor overhears the conversation and says the Missourian takes his distrust of nature "pretty far." Nature is unpredictable; it ruined his crops, the Missourian points out. "I have confidence in distrust; more particularly as applied to you and your herbs." The Missourian says the miser might as well lie down in his grave as have confidence in herbs. The herb-doctor departs.

Then the Missourian is accosted by a "chance stranger" (another of the confidence man's disguises) who tries to interest him in the "Philosophical Intelligence Office." The stranger promises to supply a boy who will help the Missourian with his business. The Missourian does not want a boy. He is looking for a machine to do his work for him, "as I told that cousin-german of yours, the herb-doctor." But the stranger, who now identifies himself as "PITCH," persists in saying he can supply all manner of boys. All boys and men are "rascals," the Missourian retorts. Pitch suggests that his feelings have been hurt. "Truth is like a thrashing-machine; tender sensibilities must keep out of the way," the Missourian maintains. But all the Missourian's objections only amount to the fact that he lacks confidence, Pitch points out. He has not given boys their due, has not the patience to watch them mature. He therefore is not prepared to understand the "scientific procuring of good servants of all sorts." If the Missourian has struck a "bad vein of boys, so much the more hope now of your hitting a good one," Pitch argues. This puts a new light on the matter, the Missourian confesses. Could he have a "degree of conditional confidence" in a boy Pitch recommends? "Candidly, you could," Pitch assures him. So, "for the sake of a purely scientific experiment," the Missourian agrees to hire the boy.

Stopping at Cairo, Illinois, the Missourian thinks over the "social chat" he has had with Pitch. "Was the man a trickster?" And if so, his elaborate methods would seem to show more than a "love of the lucre." What to make of that "threadbare TALLEYRAND, that impoverished MACHIAVELLI, that seedy Rosicrucian"? (See ROSICRUCIANISM.)

While engaged in musing, the Missourian is approached by a stranger (the confidence man) who confesses he has overheard "something of your chat with the Intelligence-office man; a rather sensible fellow, by the way." The stranger advises the Missourian to "mix in, and do like others." He continues, "Sad business, this holding out against having a good time. Life is a picnic *en costume;* one must take a part, assume a character, stand ready in a sensible way to play the fool." This last comment refers to the stranger's own rather motley, colorful clothing, which the Missourian has mocked. "This austerity won't do," the stranger says to him *"en confidance."* The Missourian is captivated by the argument, if not entirely convinced by it. "This notion of being lone and lofty is a sad mistake. Men I hold in this respect to be like roosters; one that betakes himself to a lone and lofty perch is the henpecked one, or one that has the pip." Evidently the Missourian has been reading too much HUME on suicide or BACON on knowledge. But the Missourian detects in the stranger-philanthropist's argument a measure of misanthropy: "You are DIOGENES, Diogenes in disguise." Aghast at the suggestion, the philanthropist withdraws.

About to retire for the evening, the Missourian is greeted by yet another stranger, who mentions that he has also had an encounter with the philanthropist, a "queer coon" who would be entertaining if he were not so analytical. Something the philanthropist said reminds this stranger (yet another disguise for the confidence man) of what he heard about Colonel John MOREDOCK, an Indian hater of Illinois. The Missourian is shocked. Why should anyone hate Indians? He admires them. He has many Indian heroes. As background, the stranger gives a long lecture on the enmity between backwoodsmen and Indians, emphasizing the stories about Indian scalpings and other atrocities. An intenser HANNIBAL, the Indian hater takes no vacation but maintains his vow to remain in the forest primeval to hunt Indians.

Having lost most of his family in an Indian attack, Moredock has the sentiments of an Indian hater *par*

excellence, although he does not spend all his time killing Indians. But he did forgo certain ambitions to maintain his status as Indian hater.

And the point of the Moredock story? "Charity," counsels the stranger to the Missourian. "If ever there was such a man as Moredock, he, in my way of thinking, was either misanthropic or nothing." With a sense of charity Moredock consigned a whole race of men to destruction. The Missourian should beware. His uncharitable comments about the philanthropist may have done the man an injustice, says the stranger (now called the COSMOPOLITAN). "In either case," the cosmopolitan points out, "the vice consists in a want of confidence." The two men agree in their opposition to misanthropy, and the cosmopolitan proposes that they drink to their new friendship.

Chapters XXIX–XXXIII: "The Boon Companions"; "Opening With a Poetical Eulogy of the Press and Continuing With Talk Inspired by the Same"; "A Metamorphosis More Surprising Than Any in Ovid"; "Showing That the Age of Magic and Magicians is Not Yet Over"; "Which May Pass for Whatever It May Prove To Be Worth"

The Missourian now introduces himself as Charles Arnold NOBLE and the cosmopolitan calls himself Francis GOODMAN. Frank and Charlie, as they call each other, talk over Frank's complaint that too many people fail to show confidence in each other. There are even those, Frank claims, who distrust the press. A shocked Charlie exclaims "I hold the press to be actually—Defender of the Faith!—defender of the faith in the final triumph of truth over error, metaphysics over superstition, theory over falsehood, machinery over nature, and the good man over the bad." The two men then debate the sincerity of Polonius's speech in *Hamlet,* with Charlie finding it "false" and Frank urging him to bring more charity to his interpretation of the lines. The argument advances to the stage where it is unclear to them whether Shakespeare intends to enlighten men with Polonius's words or to corrupt them. Is Shakespeare a god not to be questioned, or a man to be suspected of his motives? Polonius is a "time-serving old sinner," Charlie contends. "Now charity requires that such a figure—think of it how you will—should at least be treated with civility," Frank replies.

Toward the end of their conversation about Polonius, Charlie senses that Frank wants to confide something to him. "What, then, my *dear* Frank? Speak—depend upon me to the last. Out with it." Frank says he is in "urgent want, of money." He needs $50. Charlie is outraged, calling Frank a beggar and an imposter.

The narrator deals with objections that Frank, also known as "the COSMOPOLITAN," is a fantastic figure not to be believed. But is not fiction supposed to evoke scenes and characters different from what the "same old crowd round the custom-house counter, and the same old dishes on the boarding-house table"? We look to fiction not only for entertainment but for "more reality, than real life itself can show." Fiction presents "another world, and yet one to which we feel the tie."

Chapters XXXIV–XXXV: "In Which the Cosmopolitan Tells the Story of the Gentleman-madman"; "In Which the Cosmopolitan Strikingly Evinces the Artlessness of His Nature"
CHARLEMONT, a young merchant of French descent in St. Louis, suddenly changes from an affable man to a morose one and goes bankrupt. He withdraws from society and vanishes. Then one spring, many years later, he returns. He resumes his old life. According to rumor he has spent nine years in France acquiring a second fortune. When a friend dares to ask him what happened, he refuses to say, and no one is able to penetrate the enigma of his case.

The cosmopolitan suggests that if this is a strange story, the strangeness is in the telling, and the telling is but for his auditor's entertainment. But given what Charlemont thinks of the nature of society, how would Charlie react to him? "Would you, for one, turn the cold shoulder to a friend—a convivial one, say, whose pennilessness should be suddenly revealed to you?" Charlie feels aggrieved by the question: "You know I would scorn such meanness," says Charlie, who retires for the night.

Chapters XXXVI–XLI: "In Which the Cosmopolitan Is Accosted by a Mystic, Whereupon Ensues Pretty Much Such Talk as Might Be Expected"; "The Mystical Master Introduces the Practical Disciple"; "The Disciple Unbends, and Consents to Act a Social Part"; "The Hypothetical Friends"; "In Which the Story of China Aster Is at Secondhand Told by One Who, While Not Disapproving the Moral, Disclaims the Spirit of the Style"; "Ending With a Rupture of the Hypothesis"
The cosmopolitan is approached by a stranger who warns him not to see Charlie again. The stranger says that Charlie is no more to be trusted than a rattlesnake. The cosmopolitan does not seem very worried. He asks the stranger what he takes Charlie for. "What is he?" To which the stranger says, "What are you? What am I? Nobody knows who anybody is. The data that life furnishes, toward forming a true estimate of any being, are as insufficient at that end as in geometry one side given would be to determine the triangle." But the cosmopolitan is no nearer to understanding why he should not consort with Charlie, and he marvels at the stranger's distrustful temperament. The stranger finally says that Charlie is suspected of being a "Mississippi operator," a man of "equivocal character." The stranger has been moved to speak to the cosmopolitan because "if I am not mistaken, you also are a stranger here (but, indeed, where in this strange universe is not one a stranger?) and that is a reason why I felt moved to warn you against a companion who could not be otherwise than perilous to one of a free trustful disposition."

The stranger (now called the master) introduces EGBERT, his disciple who has reduced to practice the principles of Mark WINSOME (the master's name). But what are these principles, the cosmopolitan wants to know. The two agree the best way to find out is for Egbert to play the part of Charlie and for Frank to be Frank.

Frank asks Charlie for money, and Charlie declines to give it. Charlie and Frank advance various reasons why the money should or should not be lent. There is no humiliation between friends, Frank assures Charlie, who believes that lending money ruins friendships. Friendship should mean extending a helping hand, Frank continues. What if Charlie needed money from Frank? Charlie (Egbert) answers that this question puts him in mind of the story of China Aster.

China Aster, a young candle maker, is offered a loan of $1,000 by his friend, Orchis, the shoemaker. Aster is reluctant to be obligated for this sum, but Orchis assures him that he does not have to pay it back until he has earned $10,000 from the expansion of his business. "Why don't you have confidence, China Aster?" Orchis asks. China Aster meets reverse after reverse in his business affairs, and Orchis finally demands full payment. Aster eventually collapses and dies. His gravestone contains the inscription "He was ruined by allowing himself to be persuaded, against his better sense, into the free indulgence of confidence." Later another phrase is added by Aster's friend, OLD PRUDENCE: "The root of all was a friendly loan."

Frank rejects the moral of the story. He refuses to let the story destroy his confidence. Charlie (Egbert) asks Frank to consider the "folly, on both sides, of a friend's helping a friend." It would be better that Frank approach him as a beggar than as a friend. Frank says he has had enough of Mark Winsome's philosophy as put into action by Egbert playing the role of Charlie. It is an inhuman philosophy. Frank departs and Egbert thinks of these "familiar lines" from Shakespeare's *Hamlet*: "All the world's a stage, / And all the men and women merely players, / Who have their exits and their entrances, / And one man in his time plays many parts."

Chapters XLII–XLIV: "Upon the Heel of the Last Scene the Cosmopolitan Enters the Barber's Shop, a Benediction on His Lips"; "Very Charming"; "In Which the Last Three Words of the Last Chapter Are Made the Text of Discourse, Which Will Be Sure of Receiving More or Less Attention From Those Readers Who Do Not Skip It"
The cosmopolitan looks at the barber's sign: "No trust." Does that really mean the BARBER has no confidence, the cosmopolitan asks. There is a standoff between the two men. The cosmopolitan points out: "you have confidence, and then again, you have none. Now, what I would ask is, do you think it sensible standing for a sensible man, one foot on confidence and the other on

suspicion?" The barber replies: "Sir, I hope you would not do me injustice. I don't say, and can't say, and wouldn't say, that I suspect all men; but I *do* say that strangers are not to be trusted, and so," pointing up to the sign, "no trust."

The barber takes the cosmopolitan for a philanthropist. "I am Philanthropos and love mankind. And, what is more than you do, barber, I trust them." After more debating about whether the barber is consistent and charitable, the barber points out: "What, sir, to say nothing more, can one be forever dealing in macassar oil, hair dyes, cosmetics, false moustaches, wigs, and toupees, and still believe that men are wholly what they look to be?" But how can the barber so "contentedly deal in the impostures" he condemns? "Ah, sir, I must live," the barber replies. And he does not think that taking up another occupation would change him or the world he does business with. Finally, the cosmopolitan draws up an agreement with the barber. The barber agrees to remove his "no trust" sign, and Frank Goodman, philanthropist, agrees to reimburse him for any losses the barber incurs for trusting mankind. Then the barber demands $50, since he is certain he will sustain losses. The philanthropist deplores this lack of confidence and walks away. The narrator notes that, in talking about this incident with his friends, the barber will employ the phrase "quite an original" to describe the philanthropist.

The barber's phrase provokes a meditation from the narrator on why there are, in fact, few original characters in fiction. "To produce such characters, an author, beside other things, must have seen much, and seen through much; to produce but one original character, he must have had much luck."

Chapter XLV: "The Cosmopolitan Increases in Seriousness"
The cosmopolitan approaches an OLD MAN to speak of his "confidence in man." After much conversation about how wisdom can curdle the blood and how it is better to trust, they are interrupted by a boy who tries to sell the old man a "Counterfeit detector." After the old man purchases one, the cosmopolitan urges him to throw it away because the device only promotes a distrust of mankind. The old man asks the cosmopolitan to lead him (it is dark) to his stateroom, and as the two move on, the narrator ends the book with the comment "something further may follow of this Masquerade."

PUBLICATION HISTORY

The Confidence Man was published simultaneously in New York and in London. In England, the book was well received. Melville was praised for his vivid, fresh story and appreciated for his "sarcastic humor." American reviewers also valued the book's wit, but they were troubled by his dark vision of America. They pre-ferred the earlier Melville who entertained them with sea stories and adventures. Some reviewers were plainly baffled by the book, failing to penetrate the confidence man's elaborate masquerade. There were also some outright rejections of a book that was deemed "bitter, profane and exaggerated."

The Confidence Man did not generate large sales. Less than half the 1,000 copies of the English first edition were sold. The novel was not reprinted in Melville's lifetime, although he asked his publisher to save the plates for future editions. This poor showing only confirmed Melville's decision to turn away from fiction, since he could satisfy neither the critics nor the reading public.

confidence man, the   The character in Melville's novel by the same title. He appears in a number of guises as the MUTE, the STRANGER, a "NEGRO CRIPPLE," the MAN WITH A LONG WEED, John RINGMAN, the MAN IN GRAY, PRESIDENT OF THE BLACK RAPIDS COAL COMPANY, the UNFORTUNATE MAN, the MAN WITH THE TRAVELING-CAP, the HERB-DOCTOR, John TRUMAN, PITCH, a philanthropist, the COSMOPOLITAN, and Francis Goodman.

"The Conflict of Convictions. (1860–1.)" (1866)
Poem in BATTLE-PIECES. This poem is written in a kind of counterpoint of hope and despair. In the end, though, death is the only certainty. The CIVIL WAR is not, the speaker says, a noble crusade, but "man's latter fall," a turn of human history that God cannot—or will not—change:

> YEA AND NAY—
> EACH HATH HIS SAY;
> BUT GOD HE KEEPS THE MIDDLE WAY.
> NONE WAS BY
> WHEN HE SPREAD THE SKY;
> WISDOM IS VAIN, AND PROPHESY.

"The Continents" (1947)   One of more than 40 poems Melville left uncollected or unpublished when he died, "The Continents" reflects Melville's wonder at the city of Stamboul (Istanbul), which he visited in 1856. He describes the waterway that divides Europe from Asia there as

> . . . the cleaving Bosphorus [which] parts
> Life and Death.—Dissembling hearts!
> Over the gulf the yearning starts
> To meet—infold!

Cook, Captain James (1728–1779)   The celebrated explorer and sea voyager who published books and journals about his adventures. He was the first man to sail around the Horn and the Cape of Good Hope. He wrote of his voyage to the South Pole and of his trip to

Melville called James Fenimore Cooper "our National Novelist."
(Library of Congress)

Hawaii, where in 1779 he was murdered by the natives. Cook is mentioned in *BILLY BUDD,* when Billy is compared to one of the natural, unaffected Tahitians Cook described in his books.

Cooper, James Fenimore (1789–1851)   American novelist. Born in Burlington, New Jersey, Cooper grew up in Cooperstown, New York, a town founded by his own father. After he was expelled from Yale in 1805, Cooper went to sea with the merchant marine and then with the U.S. Navy. He began his writing career in 1820 and had his first success a year later with publication of *The Spy,* a novel about the American Revolution. He then launched a series of five novels that became known as the Leatherstocking Tales, which included his most well-known book, *The Last of the Mohicans* (1826). Cooper also grew into a historian and social critic, publishing a *History of the Navy of the United States of America* (1839). In 1842 he became involved in the controversy surrounding the *SOMERS* MUTINY. Despite press criticism of Cooper's extreme conservatism, his many works of fiction, history, and travel literature remained popular, and his reputation as the first great writer of American fiction remains intact.

Cooper's and Melville's paths often crossed—at least figuratively. Cooper was a friend of Melville's uncle Peter GANSEVOORT, and during the *Somers* affair, Cooper was an outspoken critic of Captain Alexander Sidell Mackenzie and Melville's cousin Guert GANSEVOORT. Later, Melville would review several Cooper works, usually with great sympathy. In an 1849 review of Cooper's *The Sea Lions,* Melville called the older writer "our National Novelist." Although Melville's 1850 review of *The Red Rover* was written tongue-in-cheek as "A Thought on Book-Binding," he would later borrow many of the novel's motifs for development in his masterpiece, *MOBY-DICK.* Cooper's novels appealed to Melville because they captured the romance of the sea and of ships. At the same time, in such works as *Moby-Dick,* Melville aspired to go well beyond Cooper's adventure tales to present a profound, symbolic, and Shakespearean probing of what he calls the "watery world."

"Cooper's New Novel" (1849)   Book review. In early 1849, finding himself somewhat at loose ends after completing *MARDI,* Melville undertook to do some more reviewing for his friends Evert and George DUYCKINCK's magazine, the *LITERARY WORLD.* The second of these reviews was of James Fenimore COOPER's *The Sea Lions; or, The Lost Sealers: a Tale of the Antarctic Ocean* (1848). Melville's comments this time were brief, offering a short plot summary and general praise for the man he calls "our National Novelist." Perhaps his unwillingness to say more was a reaction to the tide of criticism he had experienced in the wake of *Mardi,* or perhaps he was preoccupied with plans for his own ideas for a new novel about the sea: *MOBY-DICK.* The unsigned review, "Cooper's New Novel," appeared in the April 28, 1849 issue of *Literary World.* Another, even briefer review of a Cooper book—this time a reprint—would appear in the magazine the next year under the title "A Thought on Book-Binding."

copyright   Body of laws that protects, for a limited time, the rights of creators of products—customarily artistic in nature—against unauthorized use of their works. In Britain, copyright law was first codified in 1710 in the Statute of Anne. In the United States, copyright and patent protections found their way into Article I of the Constitution, which gives Congress the power to "promote the progress of science and the useful arts, by securing for limited times to authors and inventors the exclusive right to their respective writings and discoveries." In 1790, Congress did indeed pass the first Copyright Act, but this law provided only limited protection to authors like Melville who published both at home and abroad. Because American publishers refused to endorse international copyright regulations, Melville suffered many rejections from British publishers, who feared their editions would lose out to other British publishers who pirated American editions. In 1852, Melville added his signature to those of such literary lights as Washington IRVING and William Cullen

BRYANT on a petition requesting that Congress enact legislation governing international publishing agreements. A major revision of U.S. copyright law followed, but the bill was not passed until 1891, the year of Melville's death.

cosmopolitan, the   One of the many names used by the confidence mam. The cosmopolitan debates with the MISSOURIAN (Charles Arnold Noble) about the need for people to trust each other. He also asks the aghast Missourian for $50. The cosmopolitan also tells the strange story of Charlemont.

Coulter, William and Martha   Characters in "POOR MAN'S PUDDING AND RICH MAN'S CRUMBS." William Coulter is the poor woodcutter whom the narrator visits in order to test the thesis that, owing to nature's bounty, the poor man's lot is no worse than the rich man's. But when the narrator tastes Martha Coulter's bitter and mouldy pudding, he knows without doubt that this thesis is false.

Crash, Captain   Minor character in OMOO. A foreigner who, since losing his armed brig on the coast of New Zealand, has lived the life of an omoo, or roving man about town, in the South Pacific. When the narrator and LONG GHOST encounter him on Taloo, Captain Crash makes his living as a smuggler of French wine and brandy, but is on trial for instigating a riot and for corrupting a 14-year-old girl. Finding him guilty as charged, the native judge banishes Captain Crash from the island.

crippled soldier, the   A character in *The CONFIDENCE MAN*. He is approached by the HERB-DOCTOR (the CONFIDENCE MAN) who says the "Natural Bone-Setter" will heal the man's legs. The soldier is skeptical but eventually succumbs to the herb-doctor's pleas to have confidence in him and in the remedy.

"Crossing the Tropics (from 'The Saya-y-Manto')" (1888)   Poem in *JOHN MARR*. In this love poem, a sailor longs for his "bride but for one night" as he sails southward, away from the Pole Star and toward the Southern Cross. The "saya-y-manto" of the title is a Peruvian woman's costume and is probably meant, at least in part, to be the name of the speaker's ship.

"The Cuban Pirate" (1924)   Poem in *WEEDS AND WILD-INGS*. Like other components of the "This, That and the Other" section of the volume, this poem opens with a prose prologue. Melville's subject here is a humming-bird, and before launching into a description of this "flying spark of Paradise," he notes that "Some of the more scintillant West Indian humming-birds are in frame hardly bigger than a beetle or bee."

***Culture and Anarchy* (1869)**   A collection of essays in which Matthew ARNOLD argues for the importance of the intellectual (Greek) and spiritual (Hebrew) roots of Western culture. Melville drew on Arnold's ideas in the discussions between characters in CLAREL.

"The Cumberland. (March, 1862.)" (1866)   Poem in *BATTLE-PIECES*. On March 8, 1862, the Confederate ironclad *Virginia* (formerly the U.S.S. *Merrimac*) rammed and sank the Union ship *Cumberland* in an attempt to break the blockade of Chesapeake Bay. Melville's poem, which first appeared in the March 1866 issue of *HARPER'S NEW MONTHLY MAGAZINE*, extols the sunken vessel, proclaiming that her name and fame will not be forgotten.

Cupid   Character in "THE PARADISE OF BACHELORS AND THE TARTARUS OF MAIDS." Cupid is the "dimpled, red-cheeked, spirited-looking, forward little fellow" who shepherds the narrator around the paper mill that is the "Tartarus of Maids."

When this portrait of Melville was done in 1868, he had just begun work in the Custom House, where he would spend almost 20 years laboring without a pay raise. (Berkshire Athenaeum)

Custom House, the   Site of Herman Melville's employment from 1866 to 1886, localed near the North River in Manhattan. On December 5, 1866, Melville became a civil servant, taking the oath of office as the District Inspector of the United States Customs Service for the port of NEW YORK CITY. He worked six days a week and earned $4.00 per day, a salary that never increased in all the years he held the position. Melville's job consisted mainly of checking docking certificates and bills of lading for all incoming ships and inspecting cargoes for prohibited imports. He was also responsible for itemizing all provisions before they were loaded onto outgoing vessels. His was primarily an administrative position that involved filling out and filing the same reports year after year. He divided his time between the docks and his offices, which he shared with another customs inspector. The job was a political appointment, and as such was subject to the vicissitudes of scandal and economic cycles. Melville often feared that he would be let go, but owing to his reputation for honesty, he always survived the cutbacks that periodically beset the customs service. Melville was in good company in this role: several of his relatives had served as customs inspectors, as had his good friend Nathaniel HAWTHORNE. Still, the routine of the job wore him down and depressed him. After his wife came into a considerable inheritance in the late 1880s, Melville retired voluntarily.

Cuticle, Cadwallader   Character in *WHITE-JACKET*. Cuticle is the surgeon of the American fleet in which White-Jacket's frigate, the *NEVERSINK*, serves as flagship. Melville based Dr. Cuticle on Dr. Thomas Johnson, who in his day had a fine reputation. Melville seems, however, to have borne Johnson a grudge: Cuticle, as his name suggests, is a caricature of a physician—vain, inhumane, and physically grotesque. Against the advice of the other doctors in the fleet, Cuticle amputates the leg of a sailor who has been shot. The result is predictable: although the surgery is brilliantly performed, the patient dies.

Cylinder   Minor character in *WHITE-JACKET*. Cylinder is a bad-tempered, stuttering, club-footed gunner's mate aboard the *NEVERSINK*.

Cypriote, the   Character in *CLAREL*, a rather romantic figure, a singer of love songs. The pilgrims meet this young man on the way to MAR SABA, where he is taking flagons of wine to his mother. He shares none of Clarel's doubts about religion or the pilgrims' awareness of suffering.

Cyril   Character in *CLAREL*. He is described as a "mad" monk. This former soldier, living by himself in a grotto at MAR SABA, dresses in a shroud. When he accosts Clarel and others, demanding the countersign (a secret sign) of "Death," he is treated as a figure of pity, a maniac fixated on mortality.

D

Daggoo Minor character in *MOBY-DICK*. A mate on board the *PEQUOD*, a "gigantic coal-black negro-savage," he has the manner of king, and he has thrived on the courage and hardiness needed for whaling vessels. Curiously, he acts as the squire (attendant) to little FLASK.

"The Dairyman's Child" (1924) Poem in *WEEDS AND WILDINGS*. Part of the section titled "The Year," this lovely seven-line verse describes its subject with a series of similes that address the child's softness, sweetness, and purity, expressing a benediction.

Dana, Richard Henry, Jr. (1815–1882) Sailor, lawyer, and author. Born in Cambridge, Massachusetts, Dana spent two years (1834–36) at sea before completing his

Richard Henry Dana's autobiographical novel, Two Years Before the Mast, *influenced Melville's own writing about the sea.* (Library of Congress)

Harvard degree in 1837. He attended law school (1837–40) and was admitted to the bar in 1840. An outspoken political activist, he defended fugitive slaves in the early 1850s when a federal law required their return to their Southern slave masters. He served as U.S. district attorney for Massachusetts from 1861 to 1866. His autobiographical novel *Two Years Before the Mast* (1840) heavily influenced Melville. The two men knew each other, although Dana seems not to have warmed to Melville or to have understood the import of his work. Both *WHITE-JACKET* and *MOBY-DICK* profit from Dana's vivid narratives and striving for authenticity.

Danby Minor character in *REDBURN*. Danby, an American and a dissolute former mariner, is the keeper of the Baltimore Clipper boarding house where the crew of the *Highlander* stays while in port in LIVERPOOL.

Dansker Character in *BILLY BUDD*. An old seaman, he tries to warn BILLY BUDD that John CLAGGART is out to get him. Dansker has served with Horatio NELSON and understands the antipathy that Claggart bears toward Billy as the handsome sailor. But Dansker has learned to be circumspect, and his oblique advice is difficult for Billy to understand, especially since Claggart seems so pleasant to Billy.

Dante (Dante Alighieri) (1265–1321) An Italian poet and member of a noble family in Florence. He was exiled from the city in 1301 for criticizing the Pope. Steeped in the writing of the Greeks and Romans, Dante brought his learning and spiritual passion to his masterpiece, *The Divine Comedy.* Melville cites Dante in many of his books, including *MOBY-DICK, PIERRE,* and *CLAREL.* Dante's devotion to his ideal love, Beatrice, is echoed in Pierre's attachment to his putative sister Isabel. Moreover, Dante's concern with the man's fate, with the themes of salvation and damnation, clearly affected Melville, most especially in *Clarel,* in which his pilgrim characters seem to reestablish their faith or to ascertain once and for all the futility of the religious quest.

Darby and Joan Minor characters in *OMOO*. This loving old couple offers the narrator and LONG GHOST some generous Polynesian hospitality during their journey to see Queen POMARE. Long Ghost dubs the couple Darby and Joan, giving them the archetypal name of such a pair taken from an 18th-century English ballad.

Darwin, Charles (1809–1882) English naturalist; author of *On the Origin of Species*, which promulgated the idea of the evolutionary development of species, including humankind, by natural selection. Nature or the environment selected species that survived. Darwin's theory of evolution contradicted Christianity's belief in special creation, in the idea that all things were created all at once in their entirety by God. Darwin, on the contrary, envisaged creation as a process occurring over thousands and thousands of years. Believers in the Bible, particularly in the story of the earth being created in six days, were shocked and appalled by Darwin's ideas. In *CLAREL*, Darwin is invoked as a modern thinker who expanded human consciousness but also made it more difficult to believe in religion—at least in traditional terms.

Dates Servant to the Glendinnings in *PIERRE*.

"The Death Craft" (1839) Short story attributed to Melville. "The Death Craft" was published on November 16, 1839, in the LANSINGBURGH, NEW YORK, *Democratic Press,* the same newspaper that published Melville's pseudonymous "FRAGMENTS FROM A WRITING DESK" in 1838. "The Death Craft," too, is pseudonymous, bearing the name "Harry the Reefer," which has been attributed to Melville largely because of the work's subject and style. It is a highly stylized piece of marine Gothic about the dream of a haunted ship in which the narrator walks the decks of a vessel with a corpse at the helm and skeletons on the yards; the sailors who are alive seem not to see him. He wakes from his nightmare clutching his bride, whom he had left a year before. "The Death Craft" probably owes something to Edgar Allan Poe's "MS. Found in a Bottle" (1833) or John W. Gould's "The Haunted Brig" (1834)—and perhaps to Melville's maiden voyage aboard the *St. Lawrence,* from which he had returned in late September 1839.

de Deer, Derick Minor character in *MOBY-DICK*, captain of the German whaling ship the VIRGIN (*Jungfrau*).

Delano, Amasa (1763–1823) Nineteenth-century American ship's captain and character in "BENITO CERENO." Melville borrowed details of chapter 20 of Amasa Delano's autobiographical *A Narrative of Voyages and Travels* (1817) for "THE ENCANTADAS" and took from chapter 18 of the book the outlines for "Benito Cereno." In relating the latter from Captain Delano's point of view, but telling the story in the third person, Melville contrived to make Delano a credulous

observer who only belatedly comes to understand that aboard the *San Dominick* the masters have been forced to change places with the slaves.

Delight In chapter CXXI of *MOBY-DICK,* the PEQUOD meets the *Delight*. The *Delight* has lost five men to the whale, and AHAB is told that there is no weapon that can kill Moby-Dick. Ahab answers by brandishing a harpoon and vowing that he will triumph.

Dempsey, Jane Louisa *See* MELVILLE, JANE LOUISA DEMPSEY.

Derwent Character in *CLAREL*. An Anglican priest and one of the pilgrims, he is a kind, mellow man, inclined to be tolerant of others' opinions and of other religions. He sees the world as gradually evolving, with humankind gradually coming to understand God and nature. He tries to deflect the harsh arguments and doubts of his fellow pilgrims. His confidence verges on complacency.

Descartes, René (1596–1650) A towering figure in Western philosophy, Descartes sought to incorporate the findings of modern science into metaphysics. The physical laws of the universe governed everywhere, he argued, breaking down the distinction between celestial and terrestrial worlds. It was a homogenous universe in which he situated man as thinker. His famous maxim, *Cogito ego sum* ("I think, therefore I exist") actually led him back to God as he tried to establish a foundation for the reliability of human knowledge. Unlike the English philosopher Thomas HOBBES, Descartes wished, however, to separate mind from body, arguing that thought did not take its character from the body. This Cartesian dualism has bothered critics who suggest that he fails to account for the way the human body does influence feelings and ideas. It is the mind-body problem that agitates Melville, especially in *PIERRE*, where his hero's fellow artists become preoccupied with "Descartian vortices"—that is, with the motions of the universe that Descartes said would lead both to human knowledge and to the source of knowledge—God. Pierre's problem is that he is surrounded by "apostles" or theorists of knowledge who have no actual knowledge to offer him.

"The Devotion of the Flowers to Their Lady" (1924) Poem in *WEEDS AND WILDINGS*. This is the last of the "As They Fell" sequence that forms the first part of the second section, "A Rose or Two." The poem begins with a prose passage attributing the title to Clement Douron, an 11th-century Provençal monk who began life as a troubadour and a "devotee of Love and the Rose." The poem itself, "To Our Queen," is addressed to Eve, who is sympathetically portrayed by the flowers which "decked her nuptials with man" and are now cast out of Eden. But just as Eve is "blessed in banishment," the flowers constitute a "voucher of Paradise, visible pledge, / Rose, attesting it spite of the Worm."

Diderot, Denis (1718–1784)   French philosopher best known for his monumental *Encyclopédie* (1751–65), which demonstrates the depth and breadth of Enlightenment learning. He also published plays, satires, essays, and letters. He is mentioned in *BILLY BUDD* as one of the French philosophers for whom ships have been named.

Diogenes (412–323 B.C.)   In *The CONFIDENCE MAN* the MISSOURIAN accuses the philanthropist (a disguise of the confidence man) of being a "Diogenes in disguise." Diogenes belonged to the "cynic" school of Greek philosophy. He advocated a life based on the laws of nature, since he distrusted the ways of men. Melville seems to have in mind a story often told about Diogenes—that he wandered through Athens with a lantern "looking for an honest man." The confidence man accuses the skeptical Missourian of lacking faith or confidence in his fellow man.

"A Dirge for McPherson, Killed in front of Atlanta. (July, 1864.)" (1866)   Poem in *BATTLE-PIECES*. This work was written to honor General James Birdseye McPherson, the highest-ranking Union officer killed in the CIVIL WAR. Born in poverty, McPherson attended West Point, where he taught for a time before rising through the Union ranks to become Ulysses S. Grant's chief engineer during the war. During William Tecumseh Sherman's march through Georgia, McPherson was leading a flanking action against the Confederates when he was shot off his horse and died. For Melville, McPherson was *"Sarpedon of the mighty war"*—a reference to a figure out of Greek legend who, in Homer's *Iliad,* dies in battle during the Trojan War and is afterward given a hero's burial. Melville urges that McPherson receive the same honors.

"Disinterment of the Hermes" (1891)   Poem in *TIMOLEON*. Part of the "Fruit of Travel Long Ago" section of the volume, this work was inspired by the statue of the god Hermes executed by the Greek sculptor Praxiteles (4th century B.C.), which was discovered at Olympia in 1877. This is the only known work by Praxiteles to have survived, and Melville, who had probably seen copies of other works by the sculptor while in Rome in 1857, was doubtless thrilled by the discovery. Here, he avers it is better to dig for divine old statues "in adamant fair" than to search for gold in "arid sands."

"The Ditty of Aristippus" (1876)   Poem from *CLAREL*. This drinking song sung by the CYPRIOTE describes the

gods at their ease, indifferent to man. It is not one of Melville's more significant poetic efforts, but it is notable for its biographical importance. In 1888, after Melville was asked by Clarence Stedman, a Wall Street broker turned editor, for a contribution to the anthology *Poets of America,* he sent Stedman a handwritten copy of "The Ditty of Aristippus," a minor chord in the great epic poem Stedman himself had reviewed negatively a dozen years before. Melville proved to be even less forthcoming when Stedman's son, Arthur, and Nathaniel HAWTHORNE's son-in-law, George Parsons Lathrop, attempted to wrest biographical information from him.

Dix & Edwards   American publishing firm. Joshua Dix declined to publish *ISRAEL POTTER*, but the firm of Dix & Edwards did publish *The PIAZZA TALES*. In spite of the volume's poor sales, the firm also published *The CONFIDENCE MAN.* Sales of this second book were not much better, and Dix & Edwards went out of business shortly thereafter.

Djalea   Character in *CLAREL*. A *DRUZE* from Lebanon, Djalea guides the pilgrims. He has the serene confidence that befits the son of an Emir. Both the man and his religion are a mystery to the pilgrims. Clarel finds it impossible to engage him in discussion, yet Djalea's self-contained quality earns him respect from everyone who meets him.

Dominican, the   Character in *CLAREL*. This French Catholic friar meets the pilgrims by the Jordan. The Dominican manages to embody the authority of the church and seem a modern man at the same time. His openness attracts the pilgrims, who see a man comfortable in the material world without forsaking his religious principles.

"Donelson. (February, 1862.)" (1866)   Poem in *BATTLE-PIECES*. The Union victory after a siege at Fort Donelson, on the Cumberland River in Tennessee, was a turning point in the CIVIL WAR, as Melville's poem states:

> The spirit of old defeat is broke
> The habit of victory begun;
> Grant strikes the war's first sounding-note
> At Donelson.

In this lengthy piece, Melville achieves some nearly modernist effects, interspersing the comments of those waiting at a bulletin board for news of the Union siege at Donelson with newspaper headlines and telegraph messages. In praising the Confederates who cared for injured Union soldiers, he provided an example of the kind of reconciliation between North and South that would be required to bind up the nation's wounds.

Don Hannibal Character in CLAREL. A friend of DER-WENT's. He is a Mexican whom the pilgrims meet in BETHLEHEM. Don Hannibal has lost an arm and a leg fighting for the liberation of Mexico, but he has turned into a doubter of democracy, especially its emphasis on the masses. He literally has been maimed by modern political life, and he thus becomes a symbol of the disaffected activist.

Donjalolo ("Fonoo") Minor character in MARDI. King of the island of Juam, Donjalolo is referred to as "Fonoo," meaning "the girl," because of his feminine appearance. Arbitrary and dissolute, he is first seen reclining on a sedan borne by 30 men. His head rests on the bosom of one beautiful maiden, while another sits at his side fanning the air around him. Donjalolo may have been modeled on KAMEHAMEHA III, who ruled HAWAII in degenerate fashion during the period Melville served aboard ships that plied the South Seas.

Douglass, Frederick (c. 1817–1895) A former slave who, in the years leading up to the CIVIL WAR, electrified the North with his speeches against the evils of slavery. Douglass had learned to read in Baltimore under the guidance of a female owner, who was later told it was dangerous to educate a slave. Hearing these words, Douglass realized how valuable his command of reading and writing could be. He taught his fellow slaves how to read. He rebelled against a brutal overseer. Eventually he was able to escape from bondage. In the North, he became a favorite of ABOLITIONISTS, and once he rose to speak, he discovered he had unusual abilities to sway his audiences. He published his autobiography in 1845 and revised it several times during his long, distinguished career. This articulate man refused to participate in John BROWN's assault on Harper's Ferry, but he had far more faith in the future of African Americans than did any of his fellow abolitionists, most of whom were white and condescended to AFRICAN AMERICANS, then deemed so backward that it would take generations to grant them all the rights and privileges of citizenship. Douglass opposed such gradualism and felt that African Americans, given their complete freedom and rights, would be able to take a respected place in a democratic nation. After the Civil War, Douglass continued to agitate on behalf of African Americans. He also held several U.S. diplomatic posts, including minister to Haiti (1889–1891).

"Dover Beach" This great poem by Matthew ARNOLD (1822–88) had a profound impact on Melville's creation of CLAREL. In the poem, the speaker addresses his lover, urging

> let us be true
> To one another! for the world, which seems

> To lie before us like a land of dreams,
> So various, so beautiful, so new,
> Hath really neither joy, nor love, nor light,
> Nor certitude, nor peace, nor help for pain;
> And we are here as on a darkling plain
> Swept with confused alarms of struggle and flight,
> Where ignorant armies clash by night.

The poem's expressions of doubt about the meaning of human existence, and its lament for the retreating "sea of faith," stimulated Melville's exploration of skepticism in his narrative of pilgrims seeking religious inspiration in the Holy Land. CLAREL, the poem's earnest student and seeker after truth, also addresses himself to a beloved, RUTH, who dies before Clarel is able to consummate his love. Other characters debate the nature of the ancient and the modern world, alluding to many thinkers, historical events, and biblical stories. Like "Dover Beach," *Clarel* yearns for meaning even as it regretfully acknowledges the difficulties of attaining knowledge that is secure.

Doxodox Minor character in MARDI. This supposed sage lives on an island west of Hamora, where he dispenses opinions to all comers. He is revealed as an imposter by the philosopher BABBALANJA, who is every bit as verbose but certainly wiser.

Druze A religious sect of Muslim origin concentrated in Lebanon, with small groups in Syria and Israel. (Also, a member of this sect.) The Druze broke away from the Shiite Muslims in the 11th century in a dispute about leadership. They are considered heretics by the larger Muslim community. The Druze believe that God has been incarnated into a living person. The last incarnation was al-Hakim, who announced himself at Cairo c. 1016. His followers believe that through Hakim, humans have been called upon to redeem themselves. The Druze have often attracted the fascinated attention of Westerners because the religion combines elements of Judaism, Christianity, and Islam. Certainly the dignified, noble DJALEA, the Druze in CLAREL, becomes a figure of mystery for the pilgrims who are themselves trying to sort out the different religious traditions which have contributed to the sites of the Holy Land. Djalea says little, in keeping with the Druze prohibition of proselytizing; they believe that God cannot be really understood or defined in words. The Druze have been subjugated in various periods of history, and yet as a people and as a religion they have remained stubbornly aloof and secretive—qualities that Djalea represents quite well.

Dupetit-Thouars, Abel Aubert (1793–1864) French naval officer who appears in both TYPEE and OMOO. Dupetit-Thouars played a major role in the coloniza-

Duyckinck, Evert A.   57

tion of French Polynesia in the 19th century. At the outset of an around-the-world voyage between 1836 and 1839 as captain of the *Venus,* he was able to reinforce French influence in the Sandwich Islands (HAWAII) by forcing King KAMEHAMEHA III to quash the authority of American Protestant missionaries, and in Tahiti (see SOCIETY ISLANDS) by obtaining favorable trading rights from Queen POMARE IV under threat of bombardment. After installing Jacques-Antoine Moerenhout as French consul in Tahiti in 1838, Dupetit-Thouars returned to France, where he recommended that British sway in the Marquesas be countered by an increase in the French military presence there.

Promoted to vice admiral and commander of the French station, Dupetit-Thouars returned to the South Pacific aboard the *Reine Blanche* in 1841. After seizing two islands in the Marquesas group, he sailed to Tahiti, which he proclaimed a French protectorate in 1842. The next year he returned to depose Queen Pomare and officially annex Tahiti for France, installing Armand-Joseph BRUAT as governor and Moerenhout as director of internal affairs.

France rescinded many of Dupetit-Thouars's actions in Tahiti and replaced him as commander in the South Pacific. Nevertheless, the ramifications of what he had done lingered, and anti-French feeling remained high in Tahiti for decades. Melville observes as much in *Typee* and *Omoo.* In the former he conjures up a meeting between the French admiral and an old Marquesan king that makes it clear where the author's sympathies lie: "[I]nsensible as he is to a thousand wants, and removed from harassing cares, may not the savage be the happier man of the two?"

"Dupont's Round Fight. (November, 1861.)" (1866) Poem in BATTLE-PIECES. On November 7, 1861, Union fleet commander Samuel F. Dupont captured two Confederate forts on opposite sides of Port Royal Sound, South Carolina. The strongholds surrendered after Dupont steamed up the channel between them, his vessels traveling in two columns which then turned and steamed back down, firing as they went. The maneuver was later said to have been performed in a circular fashion, as Melville's title indicates. Dupont's success, Melville says, is the result of having followed enduring rules, so that he "prevailed / In geometric beauty curved."

"The Dust-Layers" (1947) Poem. One of more than 40 poems Melville left unpublished or uncollected when he died, "The Dust-Layers" is the fruit of Melville's travels in Egypt in 1856. Here he describes the "dust-layers," whose job is to spray water on the ground to keep dust levels down in a town near the Nile. Thus has modern life corrupted what was sacred

in times past: the "atoms," which are all that remain of the noble Thotmes (a 15th-century B.C. pharaoh also known as Thutmose III) are "blown about in powder, / Or made a muddy clay!"

"A Dutch Christmas up the Hudson in the Time of the Patroons" (1924) Poem in WEEDS AND WILDINGS. In this last poem in the section titled "The Year," Melville describes a bounteous Christmas such as one that might have been enjoyed by his Dutch forbears, or portrayed in one of the paintings he had viewed and made careful notes about in Amsterdam's Trippenhuis Gallery in 1857. The Dutch patroons inhabit a world where "poor hereabouts there are none"; nonetheless, Christmas Day is a "Happy harvest of the conscience" that inspires generosity even toward the snow-birds and the "one man in jail."

Duyckinck, Evert A. (1816–1878) A New York literary figure, editor of the LITERARY WORLD (1847–53) and of the *Cyclopaedia of American Literature* (1855), Duyckinck recommended TYPEE to Nathaniel HAWTHORNE and shortly became one of Melville's confidants and chief supporters. Soon Melville was reviewing books for the LITERARY WORLD. He showed Duyckinck the manuscript of OMOO before it was published and asked for his private opinion. The two men played cards, attended par-

Evert A. Duyckinck was Melville's friend and editor of the Literary World. (Library of Congress)

ties, and visited art exhibitions together. Duyckinck lent Melville his collection of works by Elizabethan dramatists. The critic and editor's Dutch name meant "diving duck," and Melville complimented him by saying "I love men who dive. Any fish can swim near the surface, but it takes a great whale to down stairs five miles or more." Melville hosted Duyckinck at MELVILL HOUSE. Duyckinck got close enough to Melville to observe his volatile moods, noting in one letter how his friend, returning to the city, appeared "fresh from his mountain charged to the muzzle with his sailor metaphysics and jargon of things unknowable." It was a "good stirring evening," Duyckinck commented, "ploughing deep and bringing to the surface some rich fruits of thought and experience" seasoned with cigars and brandy. The two shared gossip and ribald stories. They were estranged for some years after the conservative Duyckinck wrote a two-part review of *MOBY-DICK* in the *Literary World,* chiding Melville for indulging in the "piratical running down of creeds and opinions, the conceited indifferentism of Emerson, or the run-a-much style of Carlyle." Melville cancelled two subscriptions to the journal—his own and the one he had taken out for his friend Eli FLY.

Duyckinck, George (1823–1863) Brother of Evert A. DUYCKINCK. He collaborated with his brother on the *Cyclopaedia of American Literature* (1855). George took a skeptical view of *TYPEE,* doubting its factuality. George's reaction worried Evert because he wanted his journal, the *LITERARY WORLD,* to be above reproach and the equal, if not the superior, of publishers in BOSTON, New York's chief rival for eminence in periodical and BOOK PUBLISHING. Both Evert and George visited Melville at ARROWHEAD; with Melville and Nathaniel HAWTHORNE, they visited a Shaker colony nearby.

"The Eagle of the Blue" (1866) Poem in BATTLE-PIECES. Melville's note on the poem indicates that several Union regiments in the CIVIL WAR took eagles into battle with them to serve as mascots and rallying points. In the poem itself, he explains why this raptor meant so much to the soldiers in blue: "The pride of quenchless strength is his."

Egbert Character in *The CONFIDENCE MAN*. He is the disciple of Mark WINSOME, who explains his master's principles to the COSMOPOLITAN.

elder, the Character in CLAREL. A Scottish Presbyterian and rigid fundamentalist, he clashes repeatedly with his fellow pilgrims until he decides to leave their company. His doctrines alienate the travelers, even as his desire to survey and measure religious sites threatens to destroy or "disenchant" the holy land.

Elijah A dockside sailor in MOBY-DICK. He asks ISHMAEL and QUEEQUEG about the state of their souls just before they enlist as whalers on the PEQUOD. Ishmael is irritated at this prophet's dire warnings about the ship and its captain, yet he cannot shake off the feeling that the voyage is a fateful one. Like the biblical Elijah, who was rewarded with heaven for his fierce faith in God, the sailor may speak for a divine will.

Emerson, Ralph Waldo (1803–1882) Born in Boston, the writer Ralph Waldo Emerson was one of the founders of American transcendentalism (see TRANSCENDENTALISTS). Emerson began his career as a Unitarian minister. Finding traditional religion too confining for his free-ranging thought, Emerson drew inspiration from Greek and German philosophers such as PLATO and HEGEL to develop a thoroughly American philosophy in such classic essays as "Nature," "The American Scholar," and "Self-Reliance." Melville had mixed feelings about Emerson, calling him a Plato who spoke through his nose. Yet he was pleasantly surprised when he heard Emerson lecture, finding the transcendentalist sensible and comprehensible. Emerson's more mystical notions are satirized in MOBY-DICK. Melville was distrustful of any philosophy that departed too far from man's terrestrial experience. The image of ISHMAEL in *Moby-Dick,* mesmerized by the sea and almost falling from the mast in his daydream, may be a comment on Emerson, whose philosophy seemed to Melville a kind of daydreaming. On the other hand, Emerson's quest for the meaning of the universe, a meaning that surely went beyond the day-to-day experience of human beings, found in Melville a sympathetic sensibility.

"The Encantadas, or Enchanted Isles" (1854) Series of Melville short sketches. The organizing principle of this 10-part series is the Encantadas, or Galápagos Islands. Melville visited the islands or sailed near them on several of his sea voyages: in 1841 and 1842 aboard the whaler ACUSHNET, and in 1843 aboard both the CHARLES & HENRY and the frigate UNITED STATES. Nevertheless, his knowledge of the place was sketchy at best, and in writing "The Encantadas" he drew on several published sources, including chapter 20 of Amasa DELANO's *Narrative* (1817; chapter 18 of which also supplied the plot for "BENITO CERENO"), Charles DARWIN's *Zoology of the Voyage of the H.M.S. Beagle* (1839), and James Burney's *A Chronological History of the Discoveries in the South Sea or Pacific Ocean* (1803–17; also used later as a source for Melville's lecture "THE SOUTH SEAS"). Melville names none of these sources in "The Encantadas," but he does name others: William Cowley's *Voyage Round the Globe* (1699), Captain David Porter's *Journal of a Cruise Made to the Pacific Ocean* (1815—a work Melville had used repeatedly since TYPEE), and Captain James Colnett's *A Voyage to the South Atlantic and Round Cape Horn into the Pacific Ocean* (1798). In addition, each sketch opens with an epigraph, quoted variously from Edmund Spenser, Thomas Chatterton, William Collins, and Beaumont and Fletcher's comic play *Wit Without Money* (1639).

SYNOPSIS

Sketch First: "The Isles at Large"
Melville describes the Galapagos in general, stressing their desolateness. They are, he says, uninhabitable and changeless. He notes, however, that they have earned their moniker "the Enchanted Isles" because of the mysterious currents that surround the islands as well as the giant tortoises—allegedly transmogrified sea officers—that inhabit their shores.

Sketch Second: "Two Sides to a Tortoise"
The narrator describes how the dark upper shell of a giant tortoise contrasts with its bright undershell. He offers other observations about the three seemingly ageless creatures that a hunting party brings back from Albemarle Island. That night in his hammock he hears the tortoises resolutely crawling about the deck, pushing stubbornly against immovable objects. The next night he and his mates sit down to a meal of tortoise steaks and stews, afterwards fashioning the creatures' shells into tureens and salvers.

Sketch Third: "Rock Rodondo"
The narrator and his sailor companions visit the rocky promontory, which rises 250 feet straight out of the sea. Fishing at its base, they are covered by a canopy of flying sea birds. Farther down they see other avian inhabitants of the island, including penguins, pelicans, albatrosses, and storm petrels. As the sun rises, the men ascend the rock.

Sketch Fourth: "A Pisgah View from the Rock"
Alluding to Mount Pisgah on the Dead Sea, the narrator describes the view from atop Rock Rodondo. After situating the Galapagos in splendid isolation north of Antarctica, 600 miles west of Quito, Ecuador, and 5,000 miles due east of the Kingsmills, he turns his attention to nearby islands that make up the Galapagos archipelago, describing four of the islands in detail.

Sketch Fifth: "The Frigate, and Ship Flyaway"
Beginning with this sketch, instead of merely describing the Enchanted Isles, Melville begins to relate stories connected with them. Here the narrator discusses the near wreck of the frigate U.S.S. *Essex* on the cliffs of Rock Rodondo while giving chase to an apparently "enchanted" English ship during the War of 1812.

Sketch Sixth: "Barrington Isle and the Buccaneers"
Legend has it that, beginning in the 17th century, Barrington was a pirates' hideaway. The narrator points to a reported sighting of carved stone seats and the rusted remains of cutlasses and daggers as evidence of the truth of this legend.

Sketch Seventh: "Charles' Isle and the Dog-King"
Charles' Isle is said to have been inhabited by a Cuban Creole who, having fought for Peruvian independence from Spain, was granted ownership of the island as payment. Now king of the island, the Creole surrounds himself with "a disciplined cavalry company of large grim dogs" who help him maintain absolute rule over the immigrants to his kingdom—among them, deserters from whaling ships. When his subjects revolt, the Creole is forced back to Peru as his former kingdom devolves into a "riotocracy."

Sketch Eighth: "Norfolk Isle and the Chola Widow"
Hunting tortoises, the narrator and his companions visit Norfolk Island, where they come upon a woman in distress, a Chola (mixed-race Indian) woman from Peru named Hunilla. Three years earlier, Hunilla had traveled to the island from her home in Payta with her husband and brother aboard a French whaler. Their object was to hunt tortoises for their highly prized oil. The captain of the French whaler promised to pick the small party up from Norfolk Island in four months' time, but he never reappeared. After Hunilla's husband and brother are drowned, the widow stays on alone in the rude hut they have built, her only company the ever-increasing pack of dogs descended from the two that originally accompanied her little party. Rescued at last, she is forced to leave behind her husband's remains and all but two of her dogs. The narrator's ship carries her to Tombez in Peru, where the ship's captain sells Hunilla's tortoise oil and returns the proceeds to her, together with a contribution from the sympathetic ship's crew.

Sketch Ninth: "Hood's Isle and the Hermit Oberlus"
Some 50 years earlier, the narrator reports, a deserter named Oberlus arrived at the black lava beach on Hood's Isle, where he cultivated pumpkins and potatoes to sell to passing ships. Oberlus is a misanthropist, but he nevertheless longs to rule over others. After one abortive attempt to kidnap a sailor, he succeeds in capturing two unfortunates and makes them his slaves. Armed with an ancient blunderbuss, a short musket, and a vicious will, he manages to outwit some others who have stopped for provisions, destroying three of their boats and stealing away in the fourth to Peru, where he nearly manages to convince a young beauty to return with him to Hood's Island. Before he can leave he is jailed on suspicion of attempting to sabotage a small boat just ready to be launched.

Sketch Tenth: "Runaways, Solitaries, Grave-Stones, etc."
The isolation of the Encantadas has made them attractive to solitaries like Oberlus. Some of these individuals have left crude post-and-bottle "post-offices" as traces of their passing, while others have left only grave markers.

PUBLICATION HISTORY

After some discussions, first with HARPER & BROTHERS and then with G. P. PUTNAM & CO. about the publication of a "Tortoise Hunting Adventure" or "Tortoise Book," Melville published "The Encantadas" in three installments in *PUTNAM'S MONTHLY MAGAZINE* in 1854. The installments appeared under the pen name "Salvator R[osa] Tarnmoor," but Melville was known to be the author of the work even before the first installment appeared. None of the sketches was reprinted during his lifetime other than in *The PIAZZA TALES* (1856).

Enderby, Samuel In *MOBY-DICK*, he is the head of a firm that outfits whaling vessels. The ship *Samuel Enderby,* owned by Enderby, meets the *PEQUOD* on its quest for the white whale.

"The Enthusiast" (1891) Poem in *TIMOLEON*. The epigraph for this poem, *"Though He slay me yet will I trust in Him,"* is taken from Job 13:15, which also supplies the text for Father MAPPLE's sermon in *MOBY-DICK*. In the original Greek, an "enthusiast" was one possessed by the gods, and here the speaker clearly falls into that category, urging:

> Walk through the cloud to meet the pall,
> Though light forsake thee, never fall
> From fealty to light.

Not himself an "enthusiast," Melville nevertheless found such persons sympathetic, and in *PIERRE,* he devoted a novel to a young man destroyed by idealism.

"The Enviable Isles (from 'Rammon')" (1888) Poem in *JOHN MARR*. This poem was once part of a projected longer work ("Rammon"), an experimental piece that combined prose and verse and concerned the religious belief in immortality. The islands in the poem recall Melville's many descriptions of the South Seas, but these Enviable Isles are clearly located in the land of dreams, which may also be death itself.

Episcopal clergyman Character in *The CONFIDENCE MAN*. He is doubtful about the truthfulness of the NEGRO CRIPPLE, and he goes off to find the man the cripple says can vouch for his identity and story.

"Epistle to Daniel Shepherd" (1938) Poem. One of more than 40 poems Melville left uncollected or unpublished at his death, "Epistle to Daniel Shepherd" is a tongue-in-cheek pastoral written to a friend who was once Allan MELVILLE's law partner. Shepherd, the poet says, has "such a pastoral name" and should "come and rove" with him along the Housatonic River. The poem serves as an invitation to this "Wall-Street scholar" to visit Melville in the country, share some wine, and renew their friendship.

"An Epitaph" (1866) Poem in *BATTLE-PIECES*. One of the "Verses Inscriptive and Memorial" in Melville's collection of CIVIL WAR poetry, "An Epitaph" speaks of the reaction of a soldier's widow to news of his death. So firm is she in her faith that "priest and people borrowed of her cheer."

"Etchings of a Whaling Cruise" (1847) Book review. This review of J. Ross Browne's *Etchings of a Whaling Cruise, with Notes of a Sojourn on the Island of Zanzibar. To which is appended, a Brief History of the Whale Fishery; its past and Present Condition* (1846) and Captain Ringbolt's *Sailors' Life and Sailors' Yarns* (1847) was Melville's first published effort in this genre. When he wrote it he was already celebrated as the author of *TYPEE* and had completed its successor, *OMOO*. His friend Evert A. DUYCK-INCK was just beginning his job as editor of a new weekly called the *LITERARY WORLD,* and he asked Melville to review Browne's book (and perhaps Ringbolt's) for the journal. Melville's largely positive review not surprisingly contained numerous autobiographical references. It was published anonymously and without a title in the March 6, 1847 issue of the *Literary World,* for which Melville would review other books.

"The Fall of Richmond. The tidings received in the Northern Metropolis. (April, 1865.)" (1866) Poem in BATTLE-PIECES. In a prefatory note to his volume of CIVIL WAR poetry, Melville wrote, "With few exceptions, the Pieces in this volume originated in an impulse imparted by the fall of Richmond [Virginia]," which took place in April 1865, four years after the opening shots of the war were fired on Fort Sumter. The fall of Richmond spelled the end of a long, bloody war, and in this poem Melville appears to exult with other Northerners in their mutual victory. Upon closer examination, however, the excesses of the language in the poem—for example, the Confederacy is referred to as "helmed dilated Lucifer"—indicate that he was at odds with the sentiments of those Unionists who would not just glory in their victory, but also seek to destroy their former foe. Other components of *Battle-Pieces* make it clear that Melville's volume was intended to honor the heroism shown by both sides in the conflict and to mourn the loss of Americans from both North and South.

The fall of Richmond, Virginia, during the Civil War inspired Melville's poem in Battle-Pieces *that satirizes the shallow patriotism of war poetry.* (Library of Congress)

Falsgrave, Mr. Character in *PIERRE*. The equivocal clergyman visits Mrs. GLENDINNING and refuses to be drawn into PIERRE's arguments about whether it is always appropriate to honor the father, even when he has fathered both legitimate and illegitimate children.

"Falstaff's Lament Over Prince Hal Become Henry V" **(1947)** Poem. One of more than 40 poems left uncollected or unpublished when Melville died, "Falstaff's Lament" apparently was written much earlier. The poem reads, however, like many of the others written late in Melville's life when he, like Shakespeare's Falstaff, is left to consider old age and the fleeting nature of fame and glory.

"Far Off-Shore" (1888) Poem in *JOHN MARR*. In this spare, eight-line poem, Melville conjures up the image of a deserted raft, over which sea birds hover, crying "'Crew, the crew?'" As in "THE ÆOLIAN HARP," here Melville's vision of the sea includes a kind of ghost ship.

Farnoopoo Minor character in *OMOO*. Farnoopoo is one of three lovely Polynesian damsels whom the narrator and LONG GHOST meet on the beach near Imeeo. Her name translates as "Night-born," and in company with FARNOWAR ("Day-born") and MARHAR-RARRAR ("Wakeful, or Bright-eyed"), she prefigures the three sister Polysyllables or Vowels, A, I, AND O, in *MARDI*.

Farnowar Minor character in *OMOO*. Farnowar is one of three lovely Polynesian damsels whom the narrator and LONG GHOST meet on the beach near Imeeo. Her name translates as "Day-born," and in company with FARNOOPOO ("Night-born") and MARHAR-RARRAR ("Wakeful, or Bright-eyed"), she prefigures the three sister Polysyllables or Vowels, A, I, AND O, in *MARDI*.

fate A key concept in Melville's work, which often focuses on the extent to which human beings exercise free will. Melville's characters, such as AHAB and PIERRE, seem to have a destiny they cannot deflect, yet especially in such works as *CLAREL*, Melville seems to argue against determinism, or at least to consider the concepts of fate and free will as open questions.

Fayaway Character in *TYPEE*. The narrator and protagonist, TOMMO, is romantically linked with the daughter of his native hosts. Tommo, after telling us about the legendary beauty of the Marquesans, presents us with as fine an example as any romantic could dream up. Fayaway is olive skinned and blue eyed, possessing the whitest of teeth. Her facial tattooing is minimal, as is her clothing: we usually see her dressed in little other than the flowers she wears in her hair. In one memorable scene, however, while riding in a canoe with the narrator, she stands up and opens her TAPA cloth mantle to the wind, transforming herself into a sail. This was an image that seized the popular imagination and helped to account, in part, for the popularity of Melville's first novel. At the turn of the century, the painter John La Farge would make this imaginary picture of Fayaway the subject of one of his famous South Seas watercolors.

Fedallah Character in *MOBY-DICK*. One of the aboriginals AHAB brings aboard the *PEQUOD*, Fedallah piques the curiosity of the crew, who watch him atop the main mast every night. He is a PARSEE who seems to embody Ahab's struggle with the forces of light and darkness. In Arabic, *Fedallah* means "sacrifice or ransom of God." He remains a mysterious figure, one of Ahab's special crew yet somehow removed from and perhaps even opposed to Ahab's quest.

"The Fiddler" (1854) Short story. With the critical and popular failure of *PIERRE* in 1852, Melville found himself unable to find a publisher for his next proposed long work. In order to continue making a living as a writer for himself and his family, he began writing short fiction for magazines. His first three efforts, probably written in the summer of 1853, were "The Fiddler," "The Happy Failure," and "Cock-A-Doodle-Do!" The first two are moralizing sketches that reflect not only Melville's amateur status as a writer of short fiction, but also his disappointment in his literary career. Of the two, "The Fiddler" deals most directly with the plight of the unappreciated artist, beginning, "So my poem is damned, and immortal fame is not for me! I am nobody forever and ever. Intolerable fate!" The narrator, a poet named HELMSTONE, is introduced by his friend STANDARD to a happy, youthful, but clearly middle-aged fellow called HAUTBOY. Although he admires his new acquaintance's cheerfulness, Helmstone at first thinks Hautboy a sort of happy idiot; he cannot understand why Standard compares Hautboy with Master Betty (William Henry West Betty), an English child actor who made a fortune when young but retired, disillusioned, at 33. Then Hautboy takes out his violin and begins to play with extraordinary skill. Standard explains that Hautboy, like Betty, had been a prodigy but grew tired of its demands, changed his name, and now happily teaches violin. The story ends with Helmstone destroying his manuscripts, buying a fiddle, and taking violin lessons with Hautboy. "The Fiddler," probably written during the summer of 1853 and submitted to *HARPER'S NEW MONTHLY MAGAZINE* not long after, was not published until September 1854, when it appeared anonymously in the magazine.

Fidele The name of the Mississippi riverboat on which the CONFIDENCE MAN tries to trick passengers out of their money. The French word *fidèle* means "faithful", "loyal", "accurate". The confidence man is, of course, none of these things, and there is precious little evidence of these virtues aboard the ship.

"Field Asters" (1924) Poem in *WEEDS AND WILDINGS*. In this autumnal poem from "The Year" section of the collection, Melville entertains the conceit that even as man looks on nature, in the form of wild asters (from the Greek word for *star*), nature returns our gaze. We cannot, however, guess the meaning of this examination "When so inscrutably their eyes / Us star-gazers scrutinize."

"The Figure-Head" (1888) Poem in *JOHN MARR*. In this sentimental poem about the figurehead of the *Charles-and-Emma,* likenesses of the ship owner and his bride, many readers have seen a tribute to the lasting—if careworn—marriage of Herman and Elizabeth Melville. Once a "lad and lassie gay," the two parts of the figurehead are buffeted by wind and waves, and one night, their "hug relaxed with the failing glue," they slip into the sea when their ship crashes.

first lieutenant Character in *BILLY BUDD*. He is part of the drumhead court that must decide Billy's fate. Although he has qualms about putting the good-natured seaman to death, he bows before Captain VERE's arguments, not wishing to show any dissension between the captain and his officers.

Flask Character in *MOBY-DICK*. The third mate on the *PEQUOD* hails from Martha's Vineyard, Massachusetts. A small, solidly built man, he is a feisty character and fierce about hunting whales. He is immune to the majesty and mystery of the sea and treats whales as though they are water rats.

Fleece Minor character in *MOBY-DICK*. At *STUBB*'s command, Fleece, an old black cook, gives a sermon to the sharks, urging them to cease the racket they are making while they try to devour the whale secured to the *PEQUOD*.

flogging Corporal punishment administered by beating with a whip or a rod. Corporal punishment was the norm in the U.S. military in the 19th century, but in the

Melville published White-Jacket's *highly critical attack on flogging in the United States Navy at a time when the subject was a major public controversy.* (Library of Congress)

navy, where the risk of mutiny was ever present, it seemed to be imposed for nearly every offense—however minor. Punishment in the navy generally took the form of flogging, in which the victim was stripped of his shirt and tied at the ankles and wrists to a ship's hatch covering. Ordinarily the entire crew would be called on deck to witness as a set number of lashings with a cat-o'-nine-tails (a short-handled whip with nine knotted leather thongs) was administered to the miscreant's naked back, usually by the boatswain's mate.

Such punishment often left a man scarred for life—emotionally, if not physically. The degradation of flogging so impressed and enraged Melville during his stint in the navy in 1843–44 that the book detailing his naval service, *WHITE-JACKET,* is filled with diatribes against this particular form of punishment.

Melville published *White-Jacket* during a period of intense public controversy about flogging in the navy. The book appeared in the United States in March 1850, during Congressional debates about the practice. Some, like Rear Admiral Samuel Franklin, claimed that Melville's book "had more influence in abolishing corporal punishment in the navy than anything else." In fact, the book probably appeared too late to have had any decisive influence, but it certainly helped to create the consensus that led to passage of a bill outlawing flogging in the navy not long after the book was published.

Fly, Eli James Murdock (1817–1854)   Friend of Herman Melville. Eli Fly's family lived in Greenbush, New York, not far from the Melville home in LANSING-BURGH. He attended the Albany Academy, where he was a classmate of Melville's brother Gansevoort, and he served an apprenticeship in the law office of Melville's uncle Peter GANSEVOORT in ALBANY. In 1838, after Melville received his engineering certificate from Lansingburgh Academy, he briefly courted Eli's sister, Helen. In the spring of 1840, Fly, having turned down Peter Gansevoort's offer of a promotion, accompanied Melville—then at loose ends—on his trip west in search of adventure and, possibly, a job working for his cousin Robert MELVILL in Galena, Illinois. Hiking and hitching rides along the Erie Canal, the two friends visited Rome and Buffalo in New York State before taking a steamship across the Great Lakes to Detroit and Chicago and traveling on to Galena, perhaps by stagecoach.

In Galena, Melville and Fly helped Robert with farm work, staying until after the harvest was in. After returning east only to find that there was no work in Lansingburgh, Melville and Fly moved together to NEW YORK CITY, where they found rooms that cost $2.50 per week. Fly landed a job as copyist, but Melville decided to sign aboard a whaler.

In March 1851, learning that Fly was ill, Melville took time out from work on *MOBY-DICK* to visit his old friend, accompanying him from Greenbush to Springfield,

Massachusetts, where Fly caught a train to Brattleboro, Vermont, to take the waters. By this time Fly was an invalid, worn down by prolonged illness and a series of terrible jobs. Melville would use some of Fly's experiences and characteristics when writing his allegory of alienation, "BARTLEBY, THE SCRIVENER."

Ford, William   The narrator of "JIMMY ROSE," who inherits a once grand old townhouse formerly occupied by his once grand friend Jimmy Rose.

"'Formerly a Slave.' An idealized Portrait, by E. Vedder, in the Spring Exhibition of the National Academy, 1865." (1866)   Poem in *BATTLE-PIECES.* Inspired by Elihu Vedder's portrait, "Jane Jackson, Formerly a Slave," which he saw at the National Academy in April 1865, Melville wrote this poem about African American enslavement, the issue that ignited the CIVIL WAR. It is the only such poem in *Battle-Pieces.* Jane Jackson was a Broadway peanut vendor in NEW YORK CITY when Vedder painted her. Melville makes her out to be "Sibylline, yet benign," a prophetess for whom deliverance has come too late, but whose descendants will know "the good withheld from her."

"The Fortitude of the North under the Disaster of the Second Manassas." (1866)   Poem in *BATTLE-PIECES.* One of the "Verses Inscriptive and Memorial" in Melville's volume of CIVIL WAR poetry, this piece compares the defeat of Union troops at the Second Manassas on August 29–30, 1862, with a storm off the Cape-of-Storms (CAPE HORN). Despite wild winds and wilder waves, "The black cliffs gleam through rents in sleet / When the livid Antarctic storm-clouds glow."

Fort Stanwix   Site of the heroic Revolutionary War victory of Peter GANSEVOORT, Herman Melville's grandfather. First a French trading center on the site of modern-day Rome, New York, Fort Stanwix was rebuilt in 1758 by the English general John Stanwix. Afterward, however, the fort fell into a state of disrepair until it was again rebuilt early in the Revolutionary War, this time by the patriots, who called the site Fort Schuyler. In 1777, while in command of the fort, Peter Gansevoort and his 750 men defended the strategic outpost from a siege by 1,700 Tories and allied Indians, thus preventing the British from reinforcing General John Burgoyne's troops before the Battle of Saratoga. In later days, the site was renamed Fort Stanwix and accorded the status of a national monument.

Fourier, Charles (1772–1837)   French social theorist who argued for the reorganization of society into scientifically based, self-sufficient communities. In these communities, such institutions as marriage and the family would be radically redesigned to ensure the maximum of self-fulfillment and cooperation among individuals. His thinking usually has been called utopian; it projects an ideal community without taking into consideration the vagaries of history. In *The CONFIDENCE MAN* the man in the gold sleeve buttons explains his plan to create the World's Charity, one that will eliminate the need for charity once and for all. When he is met with skepticism, he replies: "I am no Fourier, the projector of an impossible scheme, but a philanthropist and a financier setting forth a philanthropy and a finance which are practicable."

Fra Angelico (c. 1387–1455)   This Dominican friar of Fiesole (outside of Florence), born Guido Di Pietro, is most famous for painting 50 exquisite frescoes in the convent of San Marco. His work is especially praised for its sense of joy and elegant simplicity. BILLY BUDD is compared to a Fra Angelico seraph because he seems in his beauty and in his innocent manner like an "angel of God," to quote Captain VERE.

"Fragments from a Writing Desk" (1839)   Two-part Melville juvenilia. These two short pieces, published in May 1839 in the *Democratic Press* of LANSINGBURGH, NEW YORK, constitute the earliest-known examples of Melville's imaginative writing. (He had published three letters about a local debating society in the ALBANY *Microscope* in 1838). The two sketches are numbered, suggesting that Melville and his editor anticipated more in the series. No more appeared, however. The manner of both is precious and allusive: the author seems keen to show off his refinement and his learning. In his later writings, Melville would pay little heed to the first concern, but density of allusion remained an integral part of his style. "No. 1," written in the form of a letter to "My Dear M———," is fairly static, with the narrator describing his own admirable qualities and those of three local belles. "No. 2" opens with the narrator seated on a river bank on an April evening when he is approached by a muffled figure who hands him a note signed "Inamorata," which asks him to follow its bearer. He follows the figure to a lavish villa, where he meets a beautiful, white-robed woman. He professes his love to her, then kisses her passionately, only to find that she is deaf and mute. He rushes from the scene. Both sketches were signed with the pseudonym "L.A.V."

"Fragments of a Lost Gnostic Poem of the 12th Century" (1891)   Poem in *TIMOLEON*. The first "fragment" asserts that all man's endeavors are vanity, as "Matter in end will never abate / His ancient brutal claim." Similarly, the second fragment suggests that the aim of life should be "indolence," for "The Good Man pouring from his pitcher clear, / But brims the poisoned well." Gnosticism was a mystic religion that arose at the same time as Christianity but was characterized by dualism, a belief in the positive power of evil and the limitations of goodness. Such ideas clearly held a powerful attraction for Melville, who addressed them not just here, but also in such fully realized works as "BARTLEBY, THE SCRIVENER" and *BILLY BUDD*.

Frank   Minor character in *WHITE-JACKET*. Frank is an ordinary seaman, about 16 years old, who serves on the *NEVERSINK* with the narrator. Once the ship arrives in Rio de Janeiro, Frank sinks into a deep depression, confessing to WHITE-JACKET that the supply ship that will restock the fleet carries his brother, a midshipman. So ashamed is Frank of the difference in their stations that he does all in his power to hide himself from his brother. Frank's attitude may reflect Melville's own toward his cousin Stanwix GANSEVOORT, a midshipman aboard the store-ship *Erie,* which did in fact resupply the *UNITED STATES* when Melville was a member of the crew.

Franklin, Benjamin (1706–1790)   This famous American appears in *ISRAEL POTTER,* where, in his post as the American ambassador, he finds the fugitive American seaman a hiding place in Paris. Franklin is portrayed as a rather hypocritical, sententious conniver who rationalizes his selfishness by employing logic and the maxims of Poor Richard, the famous character he created in pamphlets that made him wealthy as the publisher of the *Pennsylvania Gazette.* Melville openly mocks Franklin as a "household PLATO."

French Directory (1795–1799)   One of the interim governments established during the French Revolutionary period (see FRENCH REVOLUTION). This government lasted until 1799, when Napoleon overthrew it in a coup. The Directory is mentioned in *BILLY BUDD* as a threat to the discipline of the British navy, which has been suffering from mutinies thought to be inspired by French ideas of the rights of man.

French Revolution (1789–1799)   One of the greatest events of the 18th century, it resulted in the execution of the king and queen of France, the radical reform of French political institutions and culture, and the transmission of French revolutionary ideas of freedom, equality, and fraternity across the continent of Europe. The revolution also led to the Reign of Terror, in which many leaders of the revolution were themselves executed, and the rise of Napoleon, a revolutionary general who became an emperor and the symbol for many in Europe of a new kind of tyranny.

In *CLAREL,* the character MORTMAIN typifies a revolutionary who has lost faith in the human effort to radically change society, and the ex-Confederate soldier, UNGAR, specifically invokes the French Revolution as an example of the desire for human improvement gone awry and transformed into evil. BILLY BUDD is executed during the period when the British are fighting the French navy. Billy is sacrificed as part of the British war effort to stop the spread of mutiny and the propaganda of the French Revolution.

"The Frenzy in the Wake. Sherman's advance through the Carolinas. (February, 1865.)" (1866)   Poem in *BATTLE-PIECES*. This poem follows "THE MARCH TO THE SEA," which presents a Northern view of William Tecumseh Sherman's destructive march through the South. In "The Frenzy in the Wake," Melville adopts the persona of a Southerner to voice the bitterness that would stain the peace that followed the end of the CIVIL WAR: "even despair / Shall never our hate rescind." Melville was profoundly critical of Sherman's tactics, but he was also careful to distance himself from the sen-timents voiced here. In a note to the poem, he tells readers that it was written while reports of Sherman's return from Savannah were still filtering north, and that "it is needless to point out its purely dramatic character."

"The Frigate, and Ship Flyaway."   Sketch Fifth of "THE ENCANTADAS."

"Fruit and Flower Painter" (1924)   Poem. One of more than 40 poems Melville left uncollected or unpublished when he died, "Fruit and Flower Painter" concerns an impoverished artist starving in a garret. Through art, she is able to transcend the grimness of her surroundings. The December wind whistling through her garret becomes flute music as, lacking a seasonal plum-pudding, she "paints the plum!"

Gabriel Minor character in *MOBY-DICK*. He is a member of the "crazy" Neskyeuna Shaker colony who goes to sea on the *JEROBOAM,* announcing that he is the angel Gabriel (who in the Bible foretells the births of John the Baptist and Jesus). He manages to convert several crew members to a belief in his sacredness. The captain finds it impossible to control Gabriel or to put him off the ship. Gabriel solemnly warns the captain not to attack Moby-Dick.

Gansevoort, Catherine ("Kate") *See* LANSING, CATHERINE GANSEVOORT.

Gansevoort, Catherine Van Schaick ("Caty") (1751–1830) Herman Melville's maternal grandmother. Married to Peter GANSEVOORT in ALBANY, NEW YORK, in 1778, she bore him six children. The youngest—and the only girl—was Melville's mother, Maria. The Gansevoorts were pillars of the Dutch Reformed Church and members of the Dutch patrician class that ruled Albany. When her husband died in 1812, Caty was left with a young daughter still at home, a sizable estate to manage, and a profound depression to overcome. After Maria married Allan MELVILL in 1814, however, Caty Gansevoort revived—even to the extent of violating the social prohibition on women traveling alone. She remained a powerful figure throughout her life, and when she died in her 79th year, 400 people attended her funeral.

Gansevoort, Guert (1812–1868) Herman Melville's cousin. Guert was one of seven children born to Maria Gansevoort Melville's brother, Leonard Gansevoort, and his wife, Mary. Guert joined the U.S. Navy as a midshipman when he was only 10 years old and first went to sea in 1824, three years after his father died. Guert was promoted to lieutenant and served aboard the brig *Somers* during a mutiny (see *SOMERS* MUTINY). His commander, Captain Alexander Slidell Mackenzie, asked Guert to convene a summary drumhead court-martial which, at Mackenzie's insistence, hanged the three main conspirators. Guert would later be commended for his behavior throughout the notorious *Somers* affair, but he suffered a depression afterward. His younger cousin, Herman, was also deeply affected by the case, which many years later provided the inspiration for *BILLY BUDD.*

The *Somers* case continued to haunt Guert, who turned to drink for solace. He acquitted himself well during the MEXICAN WAR (1846–48) and was subsequently promoted to commander, earning a commendation in 1856 for defending the port of Seattle against attacks by Native Americans. Still, his propensity to drink while on duty led, the same year, to his being relieved of his command. Promoted to captain in 1862, he was court-martialed that year for negligently running the *Adirondack,* his sloop of war, into a rock in the Bahamas. Eventually he was reprimanded and given the option of returning to his ship, the steam frigate *Roanoke,* as a crew member rather than the commander, or taking a desk job in the Brooklyn Navy Yard. Too proud to accept demotion, he went to the Brooklyn Navy Yard, from which he retired in 1867.

Guert never married, and after he retired he lived with his sister Catherine Gansevoort Curtis in Schenectady, New York, where he died. His cousin Herman, who shared his propensity for drink and depression, evinced mixed emotions about Guert's career, but probably Herman had his cousin in mind when he created Guert Gan, a brave naval officer in the poem "BRIDEGROOM-DICK."

Gansevoort, Henry Sanford (1834–1871) Herman Melville's cousin. Henry Gansevoort was the son of Maria Gansevoort MELVILLE's brother Peter GANSEVOORT and his wife, Mary. Henry's parents were well-to-do, and he was able to obtain degrees from Princeton University and Harvard Law School. He practiced law briefly, but he preferred literature and politics, and when the CIVIL WAR broke out, he immediately joined the upper-class ranks of New York's Seventh Regiment. With his father's help he obtained a commission, and he rose to become a brevet brigadier general, seeing action in the battles of Gainesville, Second Bull Run, South Mountain, and Antietam, before capturing the camp of Colonel John Singleton Mosby in 1864.

Earlier that year, Herman and his brother Allan paid a visit to Henry Gansevoort at his military encampment at Vienna, Virginia. Although Allan declined to join a scouting party sent to locate the hidden camp of the guerilla band known as Mosby's Raiders, Herman went along, gleaning material that later went into "THE SCOUT TOWARD ALDIE," published in *BATTLE-PIECES*.

Moody and arrogant, Henry never married, although for a time he courted a Southern belle named Rachel Turner, who was a friend of Allan Melville. During the war, Henry suffered from chronic venereal disease and contracted malaria. He never truly recovered from either disease, but his death in 1870 was ultimately caused by tuberculosis.

Gansevoort, Herman (1779–1862)   Herman Melville's uncle. Herman Gansevoort—for whom Herman Melville was named—was the oldest brother of the author's mother, Maria Gansevoort MELVILLE. Herman Gansevoort inherited his father's lumber and gristmill interests in 1813, and he and his wife, Catherine Quackenbush (or Quackenboss), built a home near the mills that eventually grew up into the hamlet of GANSEVOORT, NEW YORK.

After Maria was widowed in 1832, she frequently asked her brothers Herman and Peter for financial assistance. Peter was better able to help, as Herman was often in dire financial straits himself. In addition, Herman's wife seems to have been an eccentric character who harbored less than tender feelings toward Maria and her children. Nonetheless, Maria's son Herman seems not to have harbored ill feelings toward his uncle Herman: in 1847, Melville dedicated his second novel, *OMOO*, to "Herman Gansevoort of Gansevoort, Saratoga County, New York." As his aunt Catherine lay dying in 1855, Herman Melville sat by her deathbed. In return, upon his own death Herman Gansevoort left his namesake an elegant old clock, which Herman Melville cherished and passed along in turn to his daughter, Frances.

Gansevoort, Maria   *See* MELVILLE, MARIA GANSEVOORT.

Gansevoort, New York   Hometown of Herman Melville's uncle and namesake, Herman GANSEVOORT. In 1813, when Herman Gansevoort married Catherine Quackenbush (or Quackenboss) and took over his late father's lumber and gristmill interests, he built a homestead not far from his mills, located near ALBANY, NEW YORK. The town of Gansevoort grew up around this place. Gansevoort was also the site of Stanwix Hall, a hotel that Herman's brother Peter built in 1832 on the site of his grandfather's home and brewery after those buildings burned down.

Gansevoort, Peter (1749–1812)   Herman Melville's maternal grandfather. Peter Gansevoort was a descendant of Harmen Harmense Van Gansevoort, a master brewer who emigrated from Groningen in the Netherlands around 1656 and settled in Fort Orange, New York, which was later renamed ALBANY. The family

brewing business prospered there, and the Gansevoort family rose in status to become a part of the local Dutch aristocracy.

Peter Gansevoort, who would become known as the "hero of FORT STANWIX," joined the New York regiment during the Revolutionary War. After participating in the invasion of Canada in 1775, he was promoted to lieutenant colonel, then to colonel, and given the command of Fort Schuyler, later renamed Fort Stanwix. From August 3 to August 12, 1775, Peter Gansevoort and his 750 men defended the fort against 1,700 Tories and their Indian allies, eventually driving the enemy back and preventing them from reinforcing troops led by General John Burgoyne at the Battle of Saratoga.

Gansevoort became a legendary hero. After the war, he was granted a large tract of land near Lake George, New York. Named a brigadier general, he wore his full uniform when the artist Gilbert Stuart painted his portrait. When Gansevoort died, he was director of the New York State Bank. He left behind his widow, Catherine Van Schaick Gansevoort, and five children (one more had died in infancy), the youngest of whom, Maria, would become Herman Melville's mother.

Although Herman Melville never knew his grandfather, he was duly proud of his forebear and named his younger son Stanwix in his grandfather's honor. In *PIERRE,* Melville would also base the grandfather of his protagonist on Peter Gansevoort. In 1870, Melville complained to his mother that few residents of NEW YORK CITY knew that the Gansevoort Hotel, on the corner of Little West 12th Street and West Street, was named for the "hero of Fort Stanwix." The Gansevoort Hotel had been constructed in 1833 by the general's sons, Herman and Peter Gansevoort, for the then astronomical sum of $100,000.

Gansevoort, Peter (1788–1876)   Herman Melville's uncle. The younger Peter Gansevoort was the fifth and last son of Peter and Maria Van Schaick GANSEVOORT, whose sixth and last child, Maria, would become Herman Melville's mother. The Gansevoorts were Dutch aristocrats in the town of ALBANY, NEW YORK, where Peter was born, and they had enough money to send their intelligent youngest son to college. After leaving Williams College without taking a degree, Peter graduated from the College of New Jersey (now Princeton University) and studied law at the Litchfield Law School, the only law school of its day.

Peter returned to Albany to practice law, eventually going into politics and becoming a judge. When his father died in 1812, he became the head of the Gansevoort household. One of his primary responsibilities in this role was to see that his sister Maria was well married. His concern for her and her family never ended. When her husband, Allan MELVILL, got into financial difficulties in 1826, he asked Peter to help him secure a loan. After Allan died in 1832, Maria repeatedly turned to her brother for financial assistance. She was not the only one to do so. The widow of Peter's brother Leonard also appealed to him for money, as did one of her sons.

Peter Gansevoort was usually able to help. Although he had four children of his own by his first wife, Mary Sanford, until the panic of 1837 he was well-to-do. (After Mary's death, Peter's second marriage to Susan Lansing produced no offspring.) Peter Gansevoort helped the young Herman Melville secure a job as a bank clerk, and he let Herman's brother Allan read law with him. Although he and Allan had a falling-out, Peter remained close to Herman, and in August 1875, shortly before he died, he sent Herman a check for $1,200 to help pay the publication costs for CLAREL. Although Peter did not live to see it in print, Herman Melville gratefully dedicated his epic poem about man's search for meaning to his uncle.

Gansevoort, Stanwix (1822–1901) Melville's first cousin. The youngest son of Maria Gansevoort MELVILLE's older brother Leonard, Stanwix was Herman Melville's junior; but in 1844, when Stanwix's supply ship, the *Erie,* arrived in Rio de Janeiro to restock the American fleet, Stanwix outranked his cousin. Because Stanwix was then a midshipman and Herman merely a common sailor, Stanwix was prohibited by naval regulations from acknowledging his cousin. The snubbing apparently stayed with Melville, for in WHITE-JACKET, the book that grew out of his naval experiences, Melville transfers his feelings of shame to a sympathetic young man, FRANK, and repeatedly assails midshipmen as spoiled, arrogant tyrants in training.

The navy seems to have turned Stanwix, like many men, into an alcoholic. After resigning his commission, he became a recluse, dying from shock after a fall from the roof of his house broke his ankle.

"The Garden of Metrodorus" (1891) Poem in TIMOLEON. The Metrodorus of this poem is probably the Greek philosopher Metrodorus of Chios, known for the radical version of skepticism displayed by such statements as "We know nothing, no, not even whether we know or not." Melville's poem employs a silent, overgrown garden as a metaphor for man's inability to achieve certainty:

> Here silence strange, and dumb seclusion dwell:
> Content from loneness who may win?
> And is this stillness peace or sin
> Which noteless thus apart can keep its dell?

Gardiner, Captain Minor character in MOBY-DICK. He beseeches an unmoved AHAB to help him search for his lost whaleboat, which contains his son, a member of the crew that tried to capture Moby-Dick.

"The 'Gees" (1856) Sketch. Often paired in Melville criticism with "BENITO CERENO," "The 'Gees" is, like the longer tale, taken as a critique of prejudice. "The 'Gees" is narrated in the first person by a sailor who provides his assessment of a race of crossbreeds that resulted when a group of Portuguese convicts were sent to Fogo, one of the Cape Verde Islands, where they interbred with the aboriginal black population. The narrator, under the pretense of providing a "scientific" description of this distinctive group, takes the opportunity to degrade them with racist jokes and false sympathy. He reports that they can, however, make excellent sailors, providing that they are not permitted to work their wiles on gullible western sea captains. One Captain Hosea Kean of Nantucket has learned that he can pick up the finest specimens by surprising 'Gees in their beds at night.

Melville probably wrote this and another story, "JIMMY ROSE," in the summer of 1854. It was published anonymously in the March 1856 issue of HARPER'S NEW MONTHLY MAGAZINE, a year and a half after he submitted it.

gentleman with gold sleeve buttons Character in *The CONFIDENCE MAN.* His plan is to systematize charity so that the whole world will be taken care of and the need for charity itself will disappear.

George III (1738–1820) King of Great Britain from 1760 to 1820. He was popular in the American colonies until English taxation became a crucial issue that led to the American Revolution. Thereafter, in America he became a symbol of tyranny. In ISRAEL POTTER, Israel becomes the king's gardener and even has the opportunity to exchange some words with George III. The king realizes he has a rebellious American in his employ, one who will not refer to him by his proper title. Although the king is ruffled, he also respects Israel's integrity for speaking up. Indeed, Melville treats the British monarch more sympathetically than he portrays such American heroes as Benjamin FRANKLIN and John Paul JONES.

"Gettysburg. The Check. (July, 1863.)" (1866) Poem in BATTLE-PIECES. This patriotic and rather conventional poem first appeared in HARPER'S NEW MONTHLY MAGAZINE in July 1866, before it was reprinted in Melville's collection of CIVIL WAR verse. The battle is briefly rehearsed in heroic terms ("Pride was repelled by sterner pride, / And Right is a strong-hold yet"). The speaker then proclaims that some of the preexisting graves that have been disturbed by the conflict will be replaced with a newer one that "[s]hall soar transfigured in loftier light."

Ginger Nut Minor character in "BARTLEBY, THE SCRIVENER." Ginger Nut is the 12-year-old office boy employed by the lawyer-narrator. His moniker is related to his job, which consists in part of fetching ginger cakes for the lawyer's scriveners, or copyists.

Girard, Stephen (1750–1831) This French-born financier and philanthropist settled in Philadelphia, and as an American he named many of his ships after progressive philosophers such as VOLTAIRE and DIDEROT, a fact mentioned by the narrator of BILLY BUDD when he discusses the name of the ship the RIGHTS OF MAN.

"Give Me the Nerve" (1924) Poem. One of more than 40 poems Melville left uncollected or unpublished when he died, "Give Me the Nerve" is a kind of prayer for courage and peace not only in extreme situations but also because "life is to safety a stranger."

Glaucon Character in CLAREL. The traveling companion of the BANKER, Glaucon comes from a wealthy family in Smyrna and will soon marry the banker's daughter. He seems rather superficial and unmoved by the pilgrimage. He is very young and utterly incapable of seeing the gravity of the issues the pilgrims debate.

Glendinning, General Character in PIERRE. Pierre's grandfather, a Revolutionary War hero, is one of an illustrious line of Glendinnings who have established the privileged place of the family in the community of SADDLE MEADOWS.

Glendinning, Mary Character in PIERRE. She is Pierre's mother, an arrogant, unforgiving, and domineering woman who forms an intense bond with her son. Unfortunately, their closeness is based on her contrivance of an aristocratic and solipsistic world that contains virtually no room for other people. When Pierre tries to question her assumptions, she disinherits him.

Glendinning, Pierre The main character in Melville's novel PIERRE. He is a young man torn apart by the ambiguities of life—his love for Lucy TARTAN, his love for his putative sister, Isabel BANFORD, and his roles as writer and man. A failed poet beset by romantic illusions, yet trying to plumb reality, Pierre becomes lost in the labyrinth of his own sensibility.

Goethe, Johann Wolfgang von (1749–1832) German poet, dramatist, novelist, and scientist. Considered one of the great writers of world literature, he studied law in Leipzig and completed his studies in Strasbourg. Deeply read in literature, including classic English authors such as Shakespeare, Goethe also drew on German folk tales and songs to produce a masterpiece,

Faust, a dramatic poem published in two parts in 1808 and 1833. He is also famed for his novels *The Sorrows of Young Werther* (1774) and *Wilhelm Meister's Apprenticeship* (1796), both of which established the genre of the *bildungsroman,* the story of a young man's education. Goethe held several government positions, including chief minister of state at Weimar and director of the state theater.

Goethe's encyclopedic grasp of life inspired the author of *MOBY-DICK,* a novel that endeavored to present a reading of the universe. Between 1811 and 1832 Goethe published a series of autobiographies that emphasized the experiences that shaped his imagination. In his novels and nonfiction, Goethe provided Melville with a model of how the artist creates himself, a model that is most apparent in PIERRE, which resembles Goethe's bildungsroman novels.

"Gold in the Mountain" (1924) Poem. One of more than 40 poems Melville left uncollected or unpublished when he died, "Gold in the Mountain" is a five-line meditation on greed, which leaves "Heaven having no part, / And unsatisfied men."

Goneril The wife of the UNFORTUNATE MAN, an identity assumed by the CONFIDENCE MAN. Goneril was a hard woman who took a dislike to her own daughter and who made life hell for her husband, even attempting to get him declared insane. She ended up ruining his reputation. He is now seeking funds to return home to claim his daughter, who is all alone since Goneril has died.

"The Good Craft 'Snow-Bird'" (1888) Poem in JOHN MARR. This piece is a song of praise for the brave merchant ship "from sunny Smyrna" that has withstood the perils of an ocean crossing carrying figs to Boston harbor.

Goodman, Francis In THE CONFIDENCE MAN, The COSMOPOLITAN calls himself Francis Goodman when he debates with Charles Arnold Noble (a.k.a. The Missourian) about the value of people placing confidence in each other.

"A Grave near Petersburg, Virginia." (1866) Poem in BATTLE-PIECES. Buried with the Confederate soldier Daniel Drouth in a grave located near the CIVIL WAR battlefield in Petersburg lies a gun. In a note to the poem, Melville tells readers that before evacuating Petersburg, the Confederates buried many of their arms along with their dead with the intention of retrieving the guns later. The poem asks that the grave stay green and prays, "May none come nigh to disinter / The—*Buried Gun.*"

Graveling, Captain   Minor character in *BILLY BUDD*. He is captain of the *RIGHTS OF MAN*, the merchantman on which Billy Budd serves until he is impressed into the British navy. Graveling regards Billy as his best man, a peacemaker, and tries to tell Lieutenant RATCLIFFE how devastating Billy's loss will be to his ship.

Great Heidelburgh Tun, the   In chapter 77 of *MOBY-DICK*, ISHMAEL describes the tapping of the Heidelburgh Tun (named for a famous wine cask at Heidelberg holding nearly 50 thousand gallons), the upper part of the sperm whale's head, which can yield as much as 500 gallons of valuable sperm oil.

"The Great Pyramid" (1891)   Poem in *TIMOLEON*. Part of the "Fruit of Travel Long Ago" section of the collection, "The Great Pyramid" reflects the sentiment Melville expressed in his travel diary after seeing the pyramids in Egypt in 1857: "something vast, indefinable, incomprehensible, and awful." His reaction, to judge by the poem, was similar to those of many who have looked on these wonders of the ancient world: no product of human hands, the great pyramid's creation remains a mystery, a "blind surmise." Here, as elsewhere in *Timoleon*, Melville emphasizes the tenuousness of man's grasp of reality, his sheer inability to know any certainty.

"Greek Architecture" (1891)   Poem in *TIMOLEON*. Part of the "Fruit of Travel Long Ago" section of the collection, this short poem reflects the satisfaction Melville garnered from viewing Greek architecture in situ, where the site itself dictated the form, thus revealing its archetypal significance. Outside this context, the ruins lack meaning.

"Greek Masonry" (1891)   Poem in *TIMOLEON*. Part of the "Fruit of Travel Long Ago" section of the collection, "Greek Masonry" is a three-line poem that emphasizes the ancient Greeks' mortarless construction. The poem reveals that what Melville, like others, found so compelling about buildings like the Parthenon was not just their magnitude but also their symmetry, achieved through thoughtful application of a pervasive aesthetic.

Greene, Richard Tobias (1819–1892)   Friend of Herman Melville and model for Toby, the narrator's sidekick in *TYPEE*. Hailing from Buffalo, New York, Greene was one Melville's 25 shipmates aboard the whaler *ACUSHNET* in 1841–42. Together with Melville, Greene jumped ship in Nuku Hiva in the MARQUESAS on July 9, 1842. Despite the attractions of life among the natives, after a short while both men wanted to return to their former lives. Following the rigors of their escape from Nuku Hiva, Melville developed an injured leg, and Greene used this as a pretext for leav-

Richard Tobias Greene was the model for the narrator's friend Toby in Typee. *(Berkshire Athenaeum)*

ing the Typee Valley. He did not, however, return with the promised help, and it was only with the publication of Melville's first novel in 1846 that Greene resurfaced, himself publishing an account of his adventures that same year as "Toby's Own Story."

This was not be the last time Greene capitalized on his association with Melville and his popular book. Living in Sandusky, Ohio, in the 1850s, Greene published a series of articles concerning his South Sea exploits in the Sandusky *Daily Mirror*, for which he worked as an editor and columnist. In 1855, he also went on tour with a lecture titled "Typee: Or Life in the South Pacific." He often referred to himself publicly as "Toby of Typee," and in 1857 he published a note in *PUTNAM'S MONTHLY MAGAZINE* discounting a reviewer's reference to him as Melville's valet and "Man Friday." Richard Tobias Greene was probably not the only member of his family to benefit from his association with *Typee*. Someone named John Wesley Greene, who was possibly Richard Tobias's brother, also impersonated Toby on the lecture circuit.

It is therefore surprising, perhaps, that Melville and Greene remained friends. After what Melville jokingly referred to as Toby's "resurrection" in 1846, the two men began a correspondence; when Greene and his wife had a son in 1854, they named him Herman Melville Greene. Greene also had a nephew named Richard Melville Hair. Melville and Greene continued to correspond during the CIVIL WAR. Greene served with the Union army, seeing combat in such famous battles as Shiloh and Vicksburg and perhaps contributing to Melville's later evocation of the war in BATTLE-PIECES.

Greenlander, the   Minor character in REDBURN. The Greenlander, a fellow crew member aboard the *Highlander,* helps cure Redburn of his initial bout of seasickness by giving him a portion of rum. The character is probably based on a man from Greenland named Peter Brown who sailed with Melville aboard the *St. Lawrence* in 1839.

Greylock, Mount   Berkshire mountain near PITTS-FIELD, MASSACHUSETTS. Mount Greylock was a presence in Melville's life from the time when, as a boy, he began visiting his uncle Thomas MELVILL's farm near Pittsfield. Later, when Herman and Elizabeth MELVILLE bought their own Pittsfield farm, ARROWHEAD, he would build a piazza from which to enjoy the view of the mountain. Just how strong a hold Greylock held on his imagination is clear from reading "THE PIAZZA," but as critics have pointed out, the view of the white, rolling shape of the mountain as seen in winter from Melville's writing desk at Arrowhead doubtless contributed to his masterwork, as well: the white whale in MOBY-DICK is described as "one grand hooded phantom, like a snow hill in the air." Melville would dedicate his next novel, *PIERRE,* "To Greylock's Most Excellent Majesty."

Griggs, Helen Maria Melville (1817–1888)   The eldest of Herman Melville's sisters. The second of Allan and Maria Melvill's children, Helen Maria was born in August 1817, while her parents were living in Boston. She was lame from birth, but in 1854 she underwent an operation that allowed her to walk normally. As a child she attended Elizabeth Sedgewick's private boarding school in Lenox, Massachusetts, where among other subjects she studied Latin and French. A friend of Elizabeth Knapp Shaw, who would later become her sister-in-law, Helen would in later years occasionally substitute as her brother's copyist and proofreader, working on REDBURN and MOBY-DICK. Helen did not marry until January 1854, when she became the wife of Boston attorney George Griggs. The Griggses had no children, although in 1855 Helen delivered a stillborn boy. When George Griggs died in May 1888, Helen was herself already suffering from the cancer to which she succumbed seven months later.

"A Ground Vine Intercedes with the Queen of Flowers for the Merited Recognition of Clover" (1924)   Poem in WEEDS AND WILDINGS. The last poem in the "This, That and the Other" section of the volume, "A Ground Vine" gives voice to the same sort of democratic sentiments that inform Walt Whitman's *Leaves of Grass* (1855):

> O Rose, we plants are all akin,
> Our roots enlock; Each strives to win
> The ampler space, the balmier air.

A lowly clover, "ranked with grass," is cousin to the regal rose, and the creeping vine, already familiar with the delights of the "lowlier Eden," is capable of scaling the garden wall in order to peer at the queen.

"Gun-Deck"   Minor character in REDBURN. A young former man-of-war's man, "Gun-Deck" constantly regales his fellow crewmates aboard the *Highlander* with tales of his adventures in the navy.

Guy, Captain   Character in OMOO. The sickly captain of the *Julia* is despised by his crew, who refuse to honor his command. He is based on Henry Ventom, captain of the LUCY ANN, on which Melville sailed to Tahiti in 1842.

Habbibi Character in *CLAREL*. DERWENT and the LESBIAN visit the cell of Habbibi, a Greek monk long since dead. The inscriptions on his grotto wall reveal a man obsessed with life as a record of human depravity and rapaciousness.

"The Haglets" (1888) Poem in *JOHN MARR*. The poem first appeared in a shorter form as "The Admiral of the White," which was dedicated to Melville's recently deceased brother Tom, and which was published on May 17, 1885, in both the *New-York Daily Tribune* and the *Boston Herald*. It retold a story Melville had heard during his trip to the Levant in 1856–57, when in Greece the captain of his ship had told of another's ship's compass being thrown off by a concealed arms cache. The story would also appear in *CLAREL* as "The Timoneer's Story."

The poem's original title refers to the white ensign with the red cross of St. George flown by a British admiral's ship while part of a squadron. The new title refers to the birds called haglets, or kittiwakes, that fly above the doomed ship as she hurries toward her fate. As "The Haglets" opens, the poet imagines the admiral, recumbent, describing his last homeward voyage in a frigate filled with Spanish loot. The proud admiral pays no heed to the sharks circling his ship below or the haglets flying overhead like "shuttles hurrying in the looms"; in his indolence, he does not notice that his frigate has been thrown off course by hidden "blades whose secret thrill / Perverts overhead the magnet's polar will." The doomed ship hits a reef and sinks to the bottom of the sea, where the admiral, in an "Unfathomable sleep," asks: "Must victors drown?—Perish, even as the vanquished do?" But in the end, the poet concludes, man cannot see the pattern of existence "that blend[s] in dream / The abysm and the star."

"Handsome Mary" Minor character in *REDBURN*. The English wife of a "broken-down American mariner" named Danby, forty-ish "Handsome Mary" runs the Baltimore Clipper, the LIVERPOOL boarding house where Redburn and the rest of the *Highlander* crew stay.

Hannibal (247–182 B.C.) Carthaginian general. In the Second Punic War, he defeated the Gauls (218 B.C.), and in a mighty feat of military campaigning crossed the Alps in 15 days. He marched on Rome and defeated the Romans (217 B.C.). Scipio defeated him at Zama (202 B.C.). Hannibal eventually committed suicide to avoid Roman capture. Colonel John MOREDOCK, the Indian-hater in *The CONFIDENCE MAN* is called an "intenser Hannibal."

Happar Indigenous tribe of the MARQUESAS Islands. The Happar were one of three tribes—the others were the Typee and the Teii—that dominated the Marquesas during the 19th-century colonization period. Europeans and Americans who came to the islands during this period customarily allied themselves with one or another of these tribes, declaring the others to be bloodthirsty cannibals. All three tribes, who continually struggled with one another for dominance, denied such allegations about themselves.

When Melville arrived in Nuku Hiva in 1846, the Happar were widely assumed to be most friendly to white men, with the Typees thought to be hostile. When TOMMO and TOBY find themselves in the domain of the Typee in *TYPEE*, they naturally experience some trepidation. For his part, Tommo, although never free from such worries, begins to feel that it is the destructive western missionaries who are the true enemies. The Typee, he finds, are more than hospitable, and so long as he and Toby dwell among them, the two white men are, understandably, considered enemies by the Happar.

"The Happy Failure. A Story of the River Hudson" (1854) Short story. With the critical and popular failure of *PIERRE* in 1852, Melville found himself unable to find a publisher for his next proposed long work. In order to continue making a living as a writer, he began writing short fiction for magazines. His first three efforts, probably written in the summer of 1853, were "THE FIDDLER," "COCK-A-DOODLE-DO!", and "The Happy Failure." "The Happy Failure" seems to have been one of his first efforts in this form, for it is little more than a sketch and uses stock characters borrowed, perhaps, from Edgar Allan Poe's "The Gold Bug." In Melville's tale, the young first-person narrator tells how he and his uncle, together with the uncle's old black servant, Yorpy, try out the uncle's "Great Hydraulic-Hydrostatic

Apparatus." Needless to say, the contraption—designed to drain swamps and marshes, converting them to fertile fields, and thereby make the inventor's fortune—is an utter failure. At first undone by his failure, the old man soon comes to regard it as a blessing, one his nephew heeds. Melville seems to have submitted the story to HARPER'S NEW MONTHLY MAGAZINE in 1853, but "The Happy Failure" did not appear in print until the July 1, 1854 issue, when it was (as was the magazine's custom) published anonymously.

Hardy, Lem Minor character in OMOO. Hardy is an Englishman who has "gone native" on La Dominica in the MARQUESAS, where he leads a small "army" of natives. When the *Julia* sails into the bay of Hannamanoo, it is met by Hardy—whose forehead bears a TATTOO of a blue shark—and a band of his warriors.

Harper & Brothers Publishing firm founded by four brothers: James Harper (1795–1869), John Harper (1797–1875), Joseph Wesley Harper (1801–70), and Fletcher Harper (1806–77). The family moved from Long Island to New York City in 1816. The brothers gained experience in the printing trade, establishing the family name as a publishing firm in 1833. They were the most successful publishers of their generation. Their list of authors included Richard Henry DANA, Jr., Mark Twain, William Makepeace Thackeray, and Thomas Hardy.

This distinguished American publishing firm rejected TYPEE on the grounds that it could not be an accurate record of what Melville experienced. Nevertheless, they unhesitatingly accepted OMOO without even first reading the manuscript. The firm published MARDI in an edition of 3,000 copies, which took seven years to sell out. The book was reprinted only once during Melville's lifetime, in an edition of 500 copies. Harper's advanced Melville $500 for WHITE-JACKET and printed 5,000 copies, half of them paperbound, half in hardcover. The book sold well in its first year, but then sales dropped off dramatically. Harper's refused Melville an advance for MOBY-DICK and presented him with a bill for $700 (representing what the firm already had advanced him set against faltering sales of his books). Harper's set a high price ($1.50) for its edition of PIERRE, which sold poorly in England and America (fewer than 1,500 copies). Melville received only $58.25 for these sales, and he owed Harper's a balance of $300. Harper's also published BATTLE-PIECES AND ASPECTS OF THE WAR in an edition of 1,260 copies. Two years after publication, only 486 had been sold. Altogether, Melville lost $400.

Harper's New Monthly Magazine Founded in 1850 by HARPER & BROTHERS under the supervision of Fletcher Harper, this magazine began by pirating and serializing British novels. It also published essays, stories, and travel narratives. This general circulation magazine published several of Melville's stories between 1853 and 1856. He earned about $100 for "COCK-A-DOODLE-DOO! OR THE CROWING OF THE NOBLE COCK BENEVENTANO," "THE FIDDLER," and "THE HAPPY FAILURE: A STORY OF THE RIVER HUDSON." Four of Melville's CIVIL WAR poems also appeared in the magazine.

Hatch, Agatha NANTUCKET woman whose story was probably the source for Melville's lost novella, "The Isle of the Cross." In July 1852, Melville traveled to Nantucket Island with his father-in-law, Lemuel SHAW. On Nantucket they met lawyer John Clifford, who told Melville the tale of Agatha Hatch, a Falmouth, Massachusetts, lighthouse keeper's daughter who had saved a sailor named James Robertson from drowning after his ship was wrecked. Robertson married Agatha, and the couple moved to Nantucket, where Agatha became pregnant. Robertson left again to go to sea, and Agatha did not hear from him until 17 years later, when he showed up once more and saw his daughter for the first time. Robertson disappeared again, but he kept in touch with his daughter; on the eve of her marriage, he reappeared, bringing with him a gold watch for the bridegroom and three shawls for the bride. After noticing that the shawls were worn, Agatha learned that Robertson had married for a second time. Agatha neither sued him for bigamy nor accepted his invitation to move west with him and the newlywed couple. After Robertson left again, she learned that he had married for a third time without divorcing either her or his second wife.

Melville was touched by Agatha's story and deeply moved by the "unaffected sympathy" with which Clifford told it. Clifford would later send him a transcript of the narrative. Nevertheless, Melville's initial inclination was to offer the "Agatha story" to his friend Nathaniel HAWTHORNE for literary exploitation because, as he wrote Hawthorne in August 1852, "in this matter you would make a better hand at it than I would." Hawthorne declined the suggestion, instead offering Melville the notes he had made during a visit to the Isles of Shoals in the Gulf of Maine and suggesting Melville set his version of Agatha Hatch's story in that locale. In December 1852, Melville wrote to Hawthorne indicating that did indeed plan to develop the "Agatha story." Melville finished "The Isle of the Cross," a novella based on Agatha Hatch's life story, the following spring and offered it to HARPER & BROTHERS, but the manuscript was never published and is now lost.

Hauser, Kaspar (1812?–1833) Referred to as Casper Hauser in BILLY BUDD. A German foundling, he was rumored to be the son of the Grand Duke of Baden.

He died of a knife wound. Some accounts attribute his death to a political assassination, others to suicide. For Melville, Hauser, like Billy Budd, is a mysterious, ambiguous figure, possibly of aristocratic origin.

Hautboy Character in "THE FIDDLER." Hautboy is the title character in this short story, a cheerful man of about 40 who appears—as his name suggests—to be an overgrown boy. As it turns out, "Hautboy" is not his given name, but instead one he adopted when he turned his back on a celebrated career as a violin prodigy. He then happily began to earn his living as a violin teacher. In the story, he is compared with the English child actor Master Betty (William Henry West Betty), a child actor who retired at 33 after making a fortune. Melville may have based Hautboy on Master Joseph Burke, an English violin prodigy who finally settled in ALBANY, NEW YORK, where as a child Melville may have heard him play.

Hautia Character in MARDI. The queen of Flozella-a-Nina, Hautia plays dark sister to YILLAH, the white goddess—the two may in fact be one and the same. Preceded by handmaidens who communicate, albeit cryptically, through the LANGUAGE OF FLOWERS, Hautia first approaches TAJI after he has consummated his relationship with Yillah. After this first encounter with the menacing seductress, Taji discovers that Yillah is missing and begins his quest to recover her. During his travels he is often approached by Hautia's messengers, and finally he finds himself on her island paradise. He enters her bower of bliss, only to be granted a vision of Yillah drowned. Fleeing Hautia's attractions, Taji sets out alone "over an endless sea" seeking either his beloved or oblivion. Hautia, who shares her name with an exotic hibiscus, is modeled along the lines of a stock romantic figure: the alluring but evil dark lady who is the embodiment of sexual knowledge.

Hawaii An archipelago of islands in the central Pacific which Herman Melville visited in 1843. Once called the Sandwich Islands, Hawaii consists of eight major islands and numerous smaller islets. Its largest island is also named Hawaii. Other islands in the group are Maui, Kahoolawe, Lanai, Molokai, Oahu, Kauai, and Nihau. Volcanic in origin, the Hawaiian Islands are sometimes called "the paradise of the Pacific" because of their innate beauty. The first Europeans to visit Hawaii came with the British explorer Captain James COOK in 1778, when Cook named the islands for the English Earl of Sandwich. At the time, the islands were ruled by a variety of warring kings; they were not united until 1810, when King KAMEHAMEHA I became their sole ruler. Kamehameha was friendly to foreigners and, as a result, American traders exploited the islands' riches. This development brought prosperity to the islands, but it also brought devastation in the form of imported diseases, firearms, and liquor.

Around this time, the native religion also went into decline, and when the first Christian missionaries arrived in 1840 they found fertile ground for their evangelism. The missionaries were given a free hand by Kamehameha III, who ruled from 1825 to 1854 and was in power at the time Melville was writing TYPEE, in which the king is criticized for being lazy, fat, and alcoholic—and not incidentally, for handing his kingdom over to the British at the urging of G. P. Judd. In OMOO, Melville again mentions the debasement of Kamehameha III (whom he calls Tammahamaha) by foreign influences.

Hawaii was declared a constitutional monarchy in 1840. From 1842 to 1854, Judd, an American, served as prime minister. During this period, in fact, ties between the islands and the United States increased. In 1887, a treaty between the two countries was ratified when the U.S. was given the exclusive right to establish a naval base at Pearl Harbor. In 1893, Queen Liliuokalani was overthrown amid agitation for constitutional reform, and the country was declared a U.S. protectorate. The next year, when the U.S. government tried to reinstate Liliuokalani, the provisional Hawaiian government refused to give up power, instead establishing a republic with Sanford B. Dole as its president. In 1898 Hawaii was annexed by the U.S.; in 1900 it became a territory; and in 1959 it was granted statehood.

Melville came to the Sandwich Islands just as Lord George PAULET, who had recently sailed into Honolulu Harbor with the British navy, was claiming the country for the British. Many islanders welcomed this development, as they—along with Melville—regarded the influence of moralistic American missionaries to be deleterious to the native way of life. Melville's open hostility to the missionaries brought him the unwelcome attention of Judd. Concerned that he might be revealed as a deserter from the ACUSHNET and the LUCY-ANN, Melville quit his job as a bookkeeper and left the islands on the U.S.S. UNITED STATES, enlisting as an ordinary sailor.

Hawthorne, Nathaniel (1804–1864) American novelist and friend of Herman Melville. When Melville first met Hawthorne in 1850, he believed he had discovered a kindred soul and a writer the equal of Shakespeare. In works like *The Scarlet Letter,* Hawthorne was willing to tell the dark, subversive truths about human nature and American life that Melville was beginning to essay in his work leading up to MOBY-DICK. Hawthorne was close to nature and yet a critic of society, a posture that gave his work the organic, universal breadth that appealed to Melville's encyclopedic sense of art. The two men spent many hours talking together; Melville had a unique ability to draw out the taciturn

Melville met Nathaniel Hawthorne on August 5, 1850, thus beginning an intense friendship. He wrote an admiring review of Hawthorne's Mosses from an Old Manse *for the* Literary World. (Library of Congress)

Hawthorne. Melville's intense attraction to his handsome colleague, as many commentators have subsequently noted, had a romantic, erotic quality.

In 1851, Melville dedicated his most significant work, *Moby-Dick,* as follows: "IN TOKEN OF MY ADMIRATION FOR HIS GENIUS THIS BOOK IS INSCRIBED TO **NATHANIEL HAWTHORNE.**" Melville never lost his reverence for Hawthorne, but the friendship between the two men cooled when Hawthorne seemed unable to return Melville's passionate feelings and failed to defend Melville publicly when the latter's later writings came under serious attack.

Born in Salem, Massachusetts, Hawthorne was descended from a prominent Puritan family, the Hathornes, one member of which had served as a judge at the Salem witch trials. In an effort to distance himself from this notorious forebear, Hawthorne added a *w* to the family name. He began his literary career writing historical sketches and allegorical tales, and by the time Melville met him when they were neighbors in the Berkshires he had written what was to

be his most famous work, *The Scarlet Letter* (1850), a brooding romance that dwelt on the Puritan dilemma that haunted his past. He had been working as a customs official; but after he wrote a campaign biography of his friend Franklin Pierce, he was rewarded with a consular appointment to LIVERPOOL, England, when Pierce was elected president. By that time, Hawthorne and Melville had grown somewhat estranged, and when Melville visited Hawthorne in Liverpool in 1856, the differences between their sensibilities were more pronounced than their similarities.

Melville never forgot his friend, however, and after Hawthorne died in 1864, Melville visited his grave. The visit took place during the winter of 1864–65, and it was probably then that Melville composed his poem "MONODY," which is almost certainly about Hawthorne. "Monody" was finally published in TIMOLEON in 1891, the year of Melville's own death.

Hawthorne, Sophia Amelia Peabody (1809–1871) Wife of Herman Melville's friend Nathaniel HAWTHORNE. Although it is her husband who is best known as Melville's friend and literary equal, Sophia Hawthorne was herself a good friend to Melville and not an inconsiderable writer. The younger sister of the more famous Peabody sisters, Elizabeth Palmer Peabody and Mary Tyler Peabody, known for their work in the field of educational reform, Sophia began her career as an artist and made a living as a copyist. It was her illustrations for Hawthorne's story "The Gentle Boy" that brought the two together in 1837. They were married in July 1842 and had three children together. In the early 1850s, when the friendship between Melville and Nathaniel Hawthorne was most keen, Melville also formed a close bond with Sophia, who, unlike her husband, appreciated both Melville's artistry and his sensuality. While grateful for the insight into Hawthorne provided by Melville in "HAWTHORNE AND HIS MOSSES," Sophia also expressed delight in Melville's novels, from TYPEE to MOBY-DICK. (She was, Melville said, the "only woman" who liked the latter.)

Left destitute by her husband's death in 1864, Sophia Hawthorne moved to Europe, where she could live more cheaply than in the United States. In 1868, she published her own travel diaries as a means of supporting herself. She died in London in 1871.

"Hawthorne and His Mosses" Herman Melville's review of a short-story collection by Nathaniel Hawthorne. Posing as a "Virginian Spending July in Vermont," Melville published a two-part review in the LITERARY WORLD (August 17 and 24, 1850) of Hawthorne's short story collection, *Mosses from an Old Manse,* which first appeared in 1846. When Hawthorne's wife, Sophia, read Melville's review, she claimed that he was the "first person who has ever in *print* apprehended Mr Hawthorne"—it was as if Melville had spoken her "secret mind." Melville lauded Hawthorne for disguising his tragic sense with an extraordinary charm, setting his fiction amid scenes of "perennial green" and "ruddy thoughts." Into this beautiful, bracing world Melville said Hawthorne introduced a "Calvinistic sense of Innate Depravity and Original Sin, from whose visitations, in some shape or other, no deeply thinking mind is always and wholly free." As many critics have observed, the complexity that Melville found in this fellow writer was also characteristic of his own work, which veered from ravishing scenes of beauty to visions of "blackness, ten times black," such as those Melville's review ascribed to Hawthorne.

"Hearth-Roses" (1924)   Poem in *WEEDS AND WILDINGS.* Part of the second half of the collection, called "A Rose or Two," "Hearth-Roses" presents the image of two aged lovers, "dying the death of the just." The poet prays that in death their dust will "vie with the Hearth-Roses" in their sweet smell.

"Hearts-of-Gold" (1924)   Poem. Among the more than 40 poems Melville left uncollected or unpublished at his death were a number devoted to the "BURGUNDY CLUB," an imaginary society of convivial, sometimes bibulous individuals that included some of the "hearts-of-gold" mentioned here: the Persian lyric poet Hafiz, the Roman poet Horace, and the 18th-century French poet Pierre Jean de Béranger. As the speaker dreams by the firelight, these three appear to him as "Dextrous tumblers eluding the Fall," the memory of whom has only mellowed, "Embalmed and becharmed."

Hegel, Georg Wilhelm Friedrich (1770–1831) German philosopher. Born in Stuttgart, the son of a government clerk, Hegel was educated in theology at Tübingen. After working as a private tutor at Bern and Frankfurt, he became, in 1805, a professor at the University of Jena. His first major work is *Phenomenology of Mind* (1807). He edited a newspaper in 1807 and 1808, and then became rector from 1808 to 1816 of a *gymnasium* (a German high school). Later he held professorships at Heidelberg (1816–18) and Berlin (1818–31). Among his other important books are *Encyclopedia of the Philosophical Sciences* (1817) and *Philosophy of Right* (1821). He also published books on aesthetics, history, and religion.

Hegel is best known for his development of the idea of dialectical logic, in which a particular idea (thesis) inexorably leads to its opposite (antithesis), resulting in a conflict that concludes in synthesis. History was composed of this constant dialectic, with one set of ideas giving way to another set, ad infinitum. Hegel made history a great drama, a kind of debate that informs the back-and-forth speeches of *MOBY-DICK*, which teems with opposing ideas and broods over the significance of history as a whole. The search in Hegel, as in Melville, is for a higher, unifying truth.

Hello   Minor character in *MARDI.* Hello is the ruler of half of the island of Diranda, whose subjects he lightheartedly destroys in war games with the ruler of the other half of Diranda, PIKO.

Helmstone   Character in "THE FIDDLER." Helmstone, a poet, is the narrator of the story. Deeply discouraged by the critical failure of his latest work, he takes a figurative lesson from the former violin prodigy, HAUTBOY, who has turned his back on fame and happily teaches violin for a living. At the end of "The Fiddler," Helmstone tears up his manuscripts and—literally, this time—begins taking lessons from Hautboy.

Heine, Heinrich (1798–1856)   German poet, celebrated for his lyrical poetry and his outspoken liberal attacks on nationalism. Although Heine converted to Christianity in 1825, he was often cited as an example of freethinking Jew, and he is alluded to as such in *CLAREL.*

"Herba Santa" (1891)   Poem in TIMOLEON. For Melville, tobacco was the "sacred plant." In "I AND MY CHIMNEY," one of the things the narrator and his beloved chimney have in common is their shared habit of smoking. In *MOBY-DICK,* ISHMAEL and QUEEQUEG mark their brotherhood pact by sharing a smoke from Queequeg's tomahawk pipe. Melville himself was powerfully addicted to tobacco, and in this hymn of praise to it he even goes so far as to associate the holy herb with Christ, the "Love supreme" that may come again "in likeness of a weed."

herb-doctor, the   Another false identity created by the CONFIDENCE MAN. He approaches various passengers on the *FIDELE* and offers remedies based on natural cures.

Hine, Ephraim Curtiss   Melville met Hine, a novice poet aboard the U.S.S. *UNITED STATES,* in 1843. In WHITE-JACKET he was transformed into "Lemsford the Poet," who hides his poems in a cannon barrel which later explodes when it is used for firing practice. Hine published *The Haunted Barque and Other Poems* in 1848.

Hivohitee   Minor character in *MARDI.* Designated the "MDCCCXLVIII," he is the reigning pontiff of the isle of Maramma, supposedly an exalted being who is—through an unbroken succession of 1,847 unions—a direct descendant of the divine Hivohitee I. When TAJI and his party finally encounter the pontiff, they find him to be an old man, dwelling alone in silence and darkness.

Hoadley, Catherine Gansevoort Melville ("Kate") (1825–1905) The third of Herman Melville's four sisters. Kate Melville was born when her parents were still living in NEW YORK CITY. In 1830, when the family moved to ALBANY, NEW YORK, she was enrolled with her sisters at the Albany Female Academy. Other than the fact that she joined the Presbyterian Church in 1843, not much more is known about her early life. In September 1853, in PITTSFIELD, MASSACHUSETTS, Kate Melville married John Chapman Hoadley, who worked for a locomotive and textile loom manufacturer in Pittsfield. Herman Melville initially disapproved of the marriage because of Hoadley's status as a widower, but Hoadley proved himself to be, in Melville's words, a "man of worth" with "much cultivation of mind." The couple moved to Lawrence, Massachusetts, where they had three children and Hoadley made a small fortune by inventing a portable engine.

Hobbes, Thomas (1588–1679) Philosopher considered the founder of English moral and political philosophy. A controversial figure, Hobbes supported the king against the English Parliament, yet he denied the divine right of kings. He usually found a way to make himself unpopular with all sides in political and philosophical controversies. His most important work is *Leviathan*, in which he promotes a materialist view of reality. For Hobbes, human psychology, ideas, and the whole realm of the imagination can be explained in terms of the human body and its constituents. He believed, for example, that breathing and blood circulation had a profound effect on thinking and feeling. In *PIERRE*, Melville situates his hero's struggles to know himself and to get on with the world between Hobbes's materialism and Immanuel KANT's idealism. Pierre's problem is that neither alternative seems satisfying enough to pursue.

Hoffman, Charles Fenno (1806–1884) Writer and editor. Hoffman had worked in journalism for many years before he succeeded Melville's friend Evert DUYCKINCK as editor of the *LITERARY WORLD,* a journal long associated with Melville and his works. In 1849, Hoffman suffered a psychotic breakdown and was permanently hospitalized. Learning of Hoffman's state, Melville wrote movingly to Duyckinck about their mutual friend, acknowledging the "madness" he himself had experienced.

"Honor" (1924) One of more than 40 poems Melville left uncollected or unpublished when he died,

"Honor" is a meditation in the form of a parable. The King of India marshals all his grandeur and all those under his command to meet "the Diamond from Golconda, / The Great Find of Cathay." The narrator muses that this august assemblage would have little more to say than *"How-de-do?"* to the more common "Little Pearl of Price."

"Hood's Isle and the Hermit Oberlus" Sketch Ninth of "THE ENCANTADAS."

"The House-top. A Night Piece. (July, 1863.)" (1866) Poem in *BATTLE-PIECES.* In his single-stanza poem, the speaker is a New Yorker who looks down from his roof onto rioters violently protesting the federal draft during the CIVIL WAR. During the summer of 1863 the city was suffocatingly hot, and Melville manages to capture the sense of claustrophobia that contributed to the outbreak of civil violence:

No sleep. The sultriness pervades the air
And binds the brain—a dense oppression, such
As tawny tigers feel in matted shades,
Vexing their blood and making apt for ravage.

The First Conscription Act, passed in March 1863, permitted those who were financially able to do so to purchase immunity from or a substitute for the draft for $300. New York's poor responded with violence, rioting in the streets, looting, burning, and lynching African Americans, whom they blamed for the war. The draft riots were eventually put down when militia units were called in, an action which the city praised but which causes the speaker to declare that such intervention implies a "grimy slur on the Republic's faith" which holds "that Man is naturally good."

Hume, David (1711–1776) British philosopher and historian. His major works are *A Treatise on Human Nature* (1739–40) and the six-volume *History of England* (1746–62). Hume was known as a skeptic, placing emphasis on the importance of reason in evaluating man's relationship with nature, his understanding of history, and his adherence to religion. As an empiricist, he insisted on validating knowledge through the evidence of one's senses. As such, he opposed the platonic tradition in which ideas, in their eternal form, preceded any human experience of them. The CONFIDENCE MAN accuses the MISSOURIAN of reading Hume—that is, of taking the skeptical view too seriously. Consequently, the Missourian is not able to take ideas on trust, and without taking certain notions as truth, without having faith in human nature, the Missourian cannot have confidence.

Hunilla Character in "THE ENCANTADAS." Hunilla is the half-breed Indian widow from Peru in Sketch Eighth, "Norfolk Island and the Chola Widow." Hunilla, her new husband, and her brother contract with a French sea captain to carry them to the Galápagos to hunt tortoises. The captain agrees to return for them in four months' time, but he never does. Hunilla loses both her husband and brother to the sea. She lives on, alone but for her dogs, for three years, until she is rescued by the narrator's ship.

"I and My Chimney" (1856) Short story. Probably written in the spring of 1855, "I and My Chimney" bears some resemblance to another story written around the same time, "THE APPLE-TREE TABLE." Both feature narrators whose households consist of a wife, two daughters named JULIA and ANNA, and a maid named BIDDY. The same configuration also appears in another "domestic" tale, "JIMMY ROSE," written the year before, although in this story the daughters are not named and the narrator is an old man who has recently removed to the city. In "I and My Chimney," as in "THE PIAZZA," probably composed early in 1856, the narrator lives in a house that borrows much from Melville's farmhouse, ARROWHEAD.

As at Arrowhead, the farmhouse in "I and My Chimney" is dominated by a central, pyramid-shaped chimney, 12 feet wide at its base, that impractically precludes a central hallway. The narrator's wife chafes at the inconvenience and consults with a master mason named Hiram SCRIBE about removing the chimney. Scribe agrees that it can be done, even going so far as to speculate that the chimney contains a secret compartment filled with hidden treasure. The conservative narrator, who wants nothing in his house to change, vows that he and his chimney shall not budge. He succeeds in buying off Scribe, who retracts his speculation about a secret chamber and provides a certificate of the chimney's soundness. It has now been seven years since the narrator has left his house; he feels obliged, he says, to stand guard over his chimney, for "it is resolved between me and my chimney, that I and my chimney will never surrender."

In "I and My Chimney" the narrator calls his old chimney the spine of his house, which it continues to support even as the house settles over time. The narrator, himself afflicted with sciatica and "sometimes as crippled up as any old apple-tree," clearly identifies with his chimney. The story had personal import for Melville, too, who suffered acutely from spinal rheumatism and sciatica during the period he was writing this story, a period during which he was trying, like the narrator, to preserve his home, his health, and his sense of himself. "I and My Chimney," which appeared anonymously in the March issue of *PUTNAM'S MONTHLY MAGAZINE*, constitutes one of Melville's last efforts to make his living as a professional writer.

"Immolated" (1924) Poem. One of more than 40 poems that Melville left uncollected or unpublished when he died, "Immolated" refers to the poet's "Children" whom he has "sealed . . . in a fate subdued," thus saving them from

Theft and ignoring which need be
The triumph of the insincere
Unanimous Mediocrity[.]

These "children" are doubtless Melville's poems, many of which he had written and discarded during his years at ARROWHEAD, writing his brother Thomas in 1862 that he had "disposed of [them] at a great bargain. . . . a trunk-maker took the whole stock off my hands at ten cents the pound."

imperialism *See* COLONIALISM.

impressment The practice of compelling men to serve in military forces. In both the American and French revolutionary wars, the British navy pursued an active policy of boarding ships at sea and taking sailors for the purposes of serving in the British navy. Both BILLY BUDD and ISRAEL POTTER serve as impressed seamen.

"In a Bye-Canal" (1891) Poem in *TIMOLEON*. One of the poems in the subsection "Fruit of Travel Long Ago," "In a Bye-Canal" apparently relates to an experience Melville recorded in his travel diary for 1857: being rowed through the canals, he sees "[t]he vision from a window at end of long, narrow passage." In the poem, the "long, narrow passage" translates into a series of sexual puns as the narrator makes his escape from the siren who looks out at him from a latticed window. He is an experienced man, one who has swum between "the whale's black flukes and the white shark's fin," and he is thus capable, like the legendary Ulysses, of eluding temptation. Originally the poem carried this parenthetical subtitle: "(How it fared with a reputed libertine, as told me by himself.)."

"In a Church of Padua" (1891) Poem in *TIMOLEON*. Part of the "Fruit of Travel Long Ago" section, this poem probably grew out of Melville's visits to three churches while in Padua on April 1, 1857. What seems to have interested him in retrospect is the confessional, where the sinner plunges deep into the metaphysical mystery of evil. Melville likens the confessional to a diving bell, where the priest descends into "consciences / Where more is hid than found."

"In a Garret" (1891)   Poem in TIMOLEON. At one time Melville considered alternative titles for this four-line poem: "Ambition," "Schiller's Ambition," and "The Spirit of Schiller" (see SCHILLER). The title he eventually settled on is far more evocative, but it still shows evidence of the German romantic's influence, particularly of Melville's reading of "The Diver." In Schiller's poem, it is an ambitious squire who risks (and loses) his life diving for a golden chalice, but for Melville the goal is "to grapple from Art's deep / One dripping trophy!" The artist, dreaming in his garret, apparently has already sacrificed much.

"In a Nutshell" (1947)   Poem. One of more than 40 poems Melville left uncollected or unpublished when he died, "In a Nutshell" sums up life as neatly as its title implies. The last two lines of this eight-line verse present Melville's rather jaded view of existence: "And Grief, the sad thief/Will forever Joy's pocket be picking!"

Indomitable   The British man of war in BILLY BUDD, on which Billy Budd serves as an impressed sailor.

"Inscription" (1924)   Poem in WEEDS AND WILDINGS. Like other poems in the "This, That and the Other" section of the volume, "Inscription" opens with a prose segment, in this case a dedication: "For a Boulder near the spot where the last Hardhack [a woody plant] was laid low By the new proprietor of the Hill of ARROWHEAD." One of several poems in Weeds and Wildings that recall Melville's pastoral life at Arrowhead, "Inscription" is meant to conjure up a paradise lost, where heaven grants even a lowly weed "leave to live / And idle . . . in the sun."

"Inscription for Marye's Heights, Fredericksburg." (1866)   Poem in BATTLE-PIECES. One of the "Verses Inscriptive and Memorial" in Melville's volume of CIVIL WAR poetry, this piece commemorates the December 13, 1862, battle near Fredericksburg, Maryland, where Union General Ambrose Burnside was forced to withdraw from a poorly planned attack that resulted in 12,650 Northern casualties. The poem proposes that a stone be erected to commemorate "more than victory."

"Inscription for the Graves at Pea Ridge, Arkansas." (1866)   Poem in BATTLE-PIECES. One of the "Verses Inscriptive and Memorial" in Melville's volume of CIVIL WAR poetry, this poem takes the form of a monologue delivered by a pro-Union Arkansan who fought and died under General Samuel R. Curtis during a battle that took place March 6–8, 1862. The soldier would have been one of at least 1,380 Union casualties, but Curtis's victory won Arkansas for the North for the next few years of the war.

"Inscription for the Slain at Fredericksburgh" (1864)   Poem. This verse first appeared in *Autograph Leaves of Our Country's Authors*, edited by Alexander Bliss and John P. Kennedy and published in 1864. Melville probably chose not to include the poem in BATTLE-PIECES because of its similarity in subject and tone to another he did include, "INSCRIPTION FOR MARYE'S HEIGHTS, FREDERICKSBURG," which he might have thought better executed.

"In Shards the Sylvan Vases Lie" (1924)   Poem. One of more than 40 poems Melville left uncollected or unpublished when he died, "In Shards the Sylvan Vases Lie," like "IN THE HALL OF MARBLES," laments civilization's failure to appreciate and preserve the past. In the modern climate, art and its eternal verities are ignored as "Apollo's bust / Makes lime for Mammon's tower."

"In the Desert" (1891)   Poem in TIMOLEON. Part of the "Fruit of Travel Long Ago" section, "In the Desert" is among several poems in this volume that grew out of Melville's journey into the Egyptian desert to see the pyramids in 1857. It was an experience that affected him powerfully; in his travel diary he noted, "Desert more fearful to look at than ocean." In this penultimate poem in his last published collection, Melville's begins with darkness—the Egyptian Plague of Darkness described in Exodus 10:21—which builds gradually, like the sun rising over the dunes, into dazzling light. Into a "blank ocean in blue calm," "God flings his fiery standard out" until it reaches such a level of intensity as to become "the effluence of essence" of God. It was here in the Egyptian desert, Melville says in the last line of the poem, that Moses discovered the "Shekinah [in Jewish theology the visible manifestation of the divine presence] intolerably bright." This is the mystical notion that such holy light is a manifestation of the deity's feminine aspect as she embraces her exiled people.

"In the Hall of Marbles (Lines Recalled from a Destroyed Poem)" (1924)   Poem. One of more than 40 poems Melville left uncollected and unpublished when he died, "In the Hall of Marbles" is, like "THE NEW ANCIENT OF DAYS," a statement of Melville's skepticism about evolution as progression. As the world waxes richer, it also becomes narrower: "This plaint the sibyls unconsoled renew: / Man fell from Eden, fell from Athens too."

"In the Jovial Age of Old" (1924) Poem. Unlike many of the more than 40 poems Melville left uncollected or unpublished when he died, "In the Jovial Age of Old" makes light of modern man's amnesia about the past.

"In the Pauper's Turnip-field" (1924) Poem in WEEDS AND WILDINGS. Melville seems to have placed this poem in the section of the volume he titled "The Year," although he may actually have written this nine-line verse years before he assembled his last poetry collection. The farm imagery of the poem, together with its evocation of a crow atop a charred hemlock and the heavy hoe "[t]hat earthward bows me to foreshow / A mattock heavier than the hoe," seem at odds with the other poems that make up "The Year." In 1860 Melville had written a number of poems on domestic themes inspired by Dutch genre paintings glimpsed in the homes of relatives and in European museums, and "In the Pauper's Turnip-field" may date from that period.

"In the Prison Pen. (1864.)" (1866) Poem in BATTLE-PIECES. In April 1864, Herman Melville and his brother Allan accompanied Allan's law partner, George Brewster, when Brewster (or "Bruce," as he was called) reported for duty to Henry GANSEVOORT's CIVIL WAR regiment in Vienna, Virginia. At the end of that year, Bruce was captured and sent to the Confederate Libby Prison near Richmond, Virginia, from which he later escaped. In honor of Bruce and other prisoners of war, Melville wrote this poem about the horrors endured by Union prisoners, whom he pictures as a swarm of

> . . . plaining ghosts
> Like those on Virgil's shore—
> A wilderness of faces dim,
> And pale ones gashed and hoar.

"In the Old Farm-House: The Ghost" (1924) Poem. One of more than 40 poems Melville left uncollected or unpublished when he died, "In the Old Farm-House" pictures the speaker sitting up in the "dead of night" with the ghost of Shakespeare and "Falstaff in view." The setting of the poem suggests that it was written while Melville was still living at ARROWHEAD.

"In the Turret. (March, 1862.)" (1866) Poem in BATTLE-PIECES. On March 9, 1862, during the CIVIL WAR, in the first such battle in naval history, the Union ironclad *Monitor* attacked the Confederate ironclad *Virginia* (formerly the *Merrimac*). The battle proved indecisive, but the commander of the *Monitor*, Lieutenant John Lorimer Worden, performed heroically, confining himself in a small turret amidships from which he could fire on the enemy and where he sustained serious eye injuries. Melville compares Worden's courage with that of Alcides, or Hercules, who went to hell and back to save King Admetus's bride.

"Iris (1865)" (1924) Poem in WEEDS AND WILDINGS. Part of the "This, That and the Other" section of the volume, "Iris" apparently was written much earlier than most of the other poems in *Weeds and Wildings*. "Iris" was meant to honor Rachel Turner (later Rachel Turner Pond), a lovely Southern belle who was a friend of Herman Melville's brother Allan, and, at various times, the object of the affections of both Melville's cousin Henry GANSEVOORT and Allan's law partner, George Brewster. If composed in 1865, it did not find a place among the more militaristic verse in BATTLE-PIECES, but its floral conceit made a nice fit with the other poems in this later collection devoted to flora. A reference to a gravestone in the last stanza indicates that the poem could have been revised following the death in 1874 of Rachel Turner Pond.

Irving, Washington (1783–1859) American man of letters and early supporter of Herman Melville's literary efforts. In January, 1846, when Herman Melville's older brother, Gansevoort, first approached him about TYPEE, Irving was serving as the American minister in Madrid, Spain. Already well established as one of America's premier writers (his 1819–20 *Sketch Book* earned him $10,000 in two years), Irving was serving in the last of several diplomatic posts when he was introduced to Melville's work while on a mission to London. After reading sections of Melville's first novel, Irving recommended it to George Palmer Putnam, the London agent of the American publisher WILEY & PUTNAM, which eventually brought out *Typee* in the United States. Irving's influence was no doubt important in getting the book into print, and doubtless Melville was grateful. Like many young writers, however, Melville in some sense resented his literary forebear and used his own writing to mock Irving. In "HAWTHORNE AND HIS MOSSES," signing himself as the "Virginian" and calling Irving a "grasshopper," Melville criticized Irving as a writer who "perhaps owes his chief reputation to the self-acknowledged imitation of a foreign model, and to the studied avoidance of all topics but smooth ones." In taking a swipe at Irving and other members of the so-called Knickerbocker School who originated in New York and strove to emulate the superficial sophistication of European satirists, Melville was setting himself apart from his literary heritage. Because Irving's name was associated with the New York Dutch about whom he wrote, Melville was also divorcing himself from his actual heritage as a scion of the Dutch aristocracy that settled New York.

Irving was one of the first American writers who could make a living from writing. Nonetheless, starting with the War of 1812 he served in a variety of governmental posts, many of which involved foreign travel. Never married, Irving spent the last 13 years of his life at his country estate, Sunnyside, located on the Hudson River near Tarrytown, New York, the area that figured so prominently in his story "The Legend of Sleepy Hollow."

Ishmael   Narrator of MOBY-DICK. In the Bible, Ishmael is the son of Abraham by the slave Hagar. This Ishmael is an Old Testament wanderer, sent into the wilderness because Sarah, Abraham's wife, favors her own son, Isaac. An angel prophesies that Ishmael will become the ancestor of a great nation but also be subjected to conflict and violence: "And he will be a wild man; his hand will be against every man, and every man's hand against him." (Genesis 16:12, 17:18–25, 21:6–21, 25:9–17.)

Melville emphasizes his character's restlessness and isolation, as well as his willingness to seek out circumstances in which the biblical prophecy is likely to occur. Ishmael is an observer, not a character deeply involved in the novel's central events, except insofar as he is a member of the ship's crew who falls under AHAB's spell even while fearing the captain's monomania. In Melville's work, Ishmael represents the alienated wanderer and survivor, a type he explores again in CLAREL and PIERRE, although these characters do not narrate their own stories. In American literature, Ishmael has become the very symbol of the modern observer/participant reflecting on the ambiguities of existence and the human quest for meaning.

"The Isle of the Cross"   *See* HATCH, AGATHA.

"The Isles at Large"   Sketch First of "THE ENCANTADAS."

isolato   In MOBY-DICK, ISHMAEL's term for himself and other members of the PEQUOD's crew, who are like biblical wanderers that have forsaken or lost home and family. They are lured to sea after having become alienated from the land.

Israel Potter: His Fifty Years of Exile   Melville's eighth book, a novel, is a reworking of the memoirs of a Revolutionary War veteran published in 1824. Potter tells the remarkable story of how he left America at the age of 31 and suffered through an extraordinary number of adventures that delayed his return to his homeland by 48 years. Ineradicably American in spite of his long residence abroad, Potter tells of his work as a hired laborer, farmer, chain bearer, hunter, trapper, Indian trader, merchant sailor, whaler, soldier, courier, spy, carpenter, and beggar. This itinerant life of shifting identities appealed to Melville, especially because

John Paul Jones is one of the historical figures Melville satirizes in Israel Potter. *(Library of Congress)*

Potter seems not to have been daunted by a world that had rendered him obscure and powerless.

Melville also saw in Potter's career an opportunity to satirize American values and American heroes such as Benjamin FRANKLIN and John Paul JONES. The skeptical, philosophically prone author of MOBY-DICK and PIERRE did not hesitate to skewer American idealism and self-promotion. Yet the sheer energy of the characters in the novel constitutes a tribute to American ingenuity and indomitability. The novel is great fun precisely because Melville refuses to take American virtues at face value. Absent from *Israel Potter* is the novelist's brooding, metaphysical side. Yet his indictment of American ambition, greed, and lust for power remains as savage as in any work he produced.

SYNOPSIS

Melville begins *Israel Potter* with a dedication "To His Highness the Bunker Hill Monument" (see Battle of BUNKER HILL). This dedication, Melville biographer Laurie Robertson-Lorant points out, reflects Melville's belief that the "history of the ruined patriot Israel

Potter epitomized America's betrayal of her Revolution." Potter was not rewarded for his services to the Revolution. Presenting himself as an "editor," Melville admits to having rearranged some scenes and made some additions to Potter's story, which he compares to retouching an old tombstone. The editor addresses the monument because, like Potter, other "anonymous privates" may have received no commemoration other than the "solid reward of your granite."

Chapter 1: "The Birthplace of Israel"
The narrator briefly describes the area of the eastern Berkshires in Massachusetts where Israel Potter was born. Speculating about the arduous efforts it must have taken Israel's ancestors to establish settlements in a wilderness, the narrator suggests that Israel's stalwart temperament—like that of other figures from the Revolutionary era—reflects the hardiness of his forebears.

Chapter 2: "The Youthful Adventures of Israel"
The narrator skips the earliest period of his hero's life, childhood, saying that its rural setting can be easily pictured. Plunging into Israel's adolescence, the narrator explains that Israel determines to leave home after his father opposes his marriage to a young woman he loves. Fearless and self-reliant, Israel travels and trades furs, spending time in Connecticut and Canada before shipping out from Providence, Rhode Island, to the West Indies. After many voyages around the world, Israel, sick of the sea, returns to his native land.

Chapter 3: "Israel Goes to the Wars; and Reaching Bunker Hill in Time to Be of Service There, Soon After is Forced to Extend His Travels Across the Sea into the Enemy's Land"
In 1774, Israel, working on a farm in Windsor, Connecticut, enlists in an American regiment, which marches off to war after hearing of the Battle of Lexington, fought on April 18, 1775. He enlists on the brigantine *Washington*—a patriotic choice, since the country lacks for able seamen and Israel has no yearning to return to the sea. Unfortunately his ship is captured by the British gunship *Foy*, and Israel becomes a prisoner of war. Put in irons after an unsuccessful revolt, he nevertheless manages to escape as soon as the ship reaches the British shore. Captured again as a runaway, Israel again escapes at night, eluding his sleepy, drunken guards. He then resumes his original plan: to travel toward London, where he expects he can lose himself in the crowds and then figure out a way back to America.

Chapter 4: "Further Wanderings of the Refugee; with Some Account of a Good Knight of Brentford Who Befriended Him"
After three days of hard travel on foot, Israel is within 16 miles of London. Having exchanged clothing with a ditcher (ditch digger), Israel wearing a seaman's shirt, is apprehended by soldiers who think him a sailor who

has deserted the British navy. This time he saws his way out of prison and takes refuge on the estate of Sir John Millet, who proves sympathetic to Israel's plight as an escaped prisoner of war. Grateful to the knight, Israel nevertheless cannot find it in his democratic soul to call him Sir John. Acclimated to his environment, Israel nevertheless has to be constantly vigilant that his true identity is not discovered. Sensing he is about to be recaptured, he once again sets off for London.

Chapter 5: "Israel in the Lion's Den"
Using Sir John as his reference, Israel obtains employment as a gardener in King George III's gardens at Kew. Encountering Israel in the garden, GEORGE III immediately realizes he has employed a Yankee. "You are one of that stubborn race," the king says, asking Israel how he came to be in the garden. "The fate of war, sir," Israel replies. When the monarch notices that Israel does not address him by his title, Israel says ("firmly, but with deep respect") "'I have no king.'" Although George III feels rebuffed, he respects Israel's honesty and promises him protection. "God bless your noble Majesty!" A pleased king concludes "I thought I could conquer ye—conquer ye." But discharged from the king's service along with others at the end of the season, Israel again is on the lookout for a safe haven.

Chapters 6–9: "Israel Makes the Acquaintance of Certain Secret Friends of America, One of Them Being the Famous Author of the 'Diversions of Purley.' These Dispatch Him on a Sly Errand Across the Channel"; "After a Curious Adventure Upon the Pont Neuf, Israel Enters the Presence of the Renowned Sage, Dr. Franklin, Whom He Finds Right Learnedly and Multifariously Employed"; "Which Has Something to Say about Dr. Franklin and the Latin Quarter"; "Israel is Initiated into the Mysteries of the Lodging-Houses in the Latin Quarter"
Hiding out on a farm, Israel is approached by John WOODCOCK, who tells him that, along with Horn TOOK and James BRIDGES, he has formed a conspiracy to aid the American Revolution. Israel is entrusted with papers that he is to deliver to Benjamin Franklin in Paris.

After an altercation in Paris with a man who wants to shine his shoes, the uncomprehending Israel makes his way to Franklin, finding a man in a "rich dressing-gown" who proceeds to lecture him about all manner of things, including his high heeled boots—until Franklin realizes that the boots' heels contain the secret papers Israel is carrying to him. The sententious Franklin sounds a good deal like his book, *Poor Richard's Almanac*, urging Israel to be more sensible and to use logic. But Franklin secures a hiding place for Israel and promises to help him on his way back to America.

The narrator notes that the frugal Franklin lives not in the aristocratic precincts of Paris but, instead, in the

Latin Quarter, the haunt of writers and philosophers. Franklin is presented in his everyday, unpretentious guise: "Seeking here to depict him in his less exalted habitudes, the narrator feels more as if he were playing with one of the sage's worsted hose, than reverentially handling the honored hat which once oracularly sat upon his brow."

Every time Franklin enters Israel's secret hiding place, he removes something from the apartment, telling Israel that it is not really needed for his comfort. A perplexed and nettled Israel comments: "Every time he come in he robs me . . . with an air all of the time, too, as if he were making me presents." When Israel tries to read Franklin's Poor Richard pamphlet, he exclaims: "Oh, confound all this wisdom! It's a sort of insulting to talk wisdom to a man like me. It's wisdom that's cheap, and it's fortune that's dear. That ain't in Poor Richard, but it ought to be."

Chapters 10–11: "Another Adventurer Appears Upon the Scene"; "Paul Jones in a Revery"
John Paul Jones arrives, accosting a servant girl and badgering Franklin about getting a proper ship with which to fight the British. "Everything is lost through this shillyshallying timidity, called prudence," Jones complains. He is chagrined to learn that Israel has never heard of him.

Sharing Israel's apartment with him, Jones begins reading the Poor Richard pamphlet, finding sayings like "God helps them that help themselves," which pretty much sums up his attitude toward life. The restless sea captain paces the floor all night, preventing Israel from sleeping.

Chapter 12: "Recrossing the Channel, Israel Returns to the Squire's Abode—His Adventures There"
Franklin sends Israel back across the channel, remarking that if he only had the time, he could design a better false heel for the courier. Back in England, Israel is placed in a secret compartment behind Squire Woodcock's chimney. Although the squire promises to look in on him, several days pass by with no visit, and Israel finally emerges from his hiding place to learn that Woodcock has died and that he must search again for refuge.

Chapters 13–19: "His Escape from the House, with Various Adventures Following"; "In Which Israel is Sailor under Two Flags, and in Three Ships, and All in One Night"; "They Sail as Far as the Crag of Ailsa"; "The Expedition That Sailed from Groix"; "They Fight the Serapis"; "Continued They Fight the Serapis"
On the run, changing into clothes that make him look like a beggar, the desperate Israel cries out, "Ah! what a true patriot gets for serving his country!" Looking for Horn Took's residence, he is recaptured by men employed to round up runaway sailors.

Hardly aboard one ship, Israel is picked to serve on a revenue vessel, which is itself attacked by an American warship commanded by none other than John Paul Jones. The two men recount their adventures. Israel remarks, "Ah, Captain, you sleep so little and scheme so much, you will die young." Jones agrees, replying, "I mean to. Who would live a doddered old stump?"

Israel is appointed a quartermaster on Jones's ship, which roves through British waters looking for targets, and descends on Whitehaven, which Jones daringly invades. He follows this triumph up with a brazen visit to the home of the Earl of Selkirk on the Scottish shore. Although the nobleman is not at home, Jones is received by his wife, whom he treats with elaborate courtesy. Jones becomes celebrated for his feats of war, but Israel is no nearer to home and has yet to receive any reward for his service to his country.

In spite of his success, Jones finds it difficult to maintain discipline in his fleet and retires to Groix. He recoups his reputation, however, when he is challenged by the *Serapis* in a battle that is witnessed on a moonlit night by thousands on the cliffs of Yorkshire. There is no hiding on the sea during a battle, the narrator points out, so that the captains' maneuvers become a sight for all to see. When Jones drives his ship into the *Serapis*, it is as though the battle has become one of Siamese twins. The crews on both ships, moreover, imitate their captains in recklessly exposing themselves to gunfire. When asked to surrender, Jones utters the immortal line, "I have not yet begun to fight." Both ships seem about to sink in defeat. So ferocious is the fighting that the narrator observes, "In view of this battle one may ask—What separates the enlightened man from the savage? Is civilization a thing distinct, or is it an advanced stage of barbarism?" At any rate, Jones ultimately triumphs and becomes the very symbol of the American character.

Chapters 20–22: "The Shuttle"; "Samson Among the Philistines"; "Something Further of Ethan Allen"; "with Israel's Flight Towards the Wilderness"
After victory, Israel accompanies Jones on his return to America, but when Jones engages yet another ship in battle, Israel is caught boarding the enemy ship just as Jones's vessel is pulling away. Once again he finds himself in enemy hands. He tries to pretend he is part of the British crew, but no one will give him a place aboard ship. Although he is under suspicion, Israel is appreciated for his "qualities, both as a sailor and man," and he comes under the captain's protection.

On shore in England again, Israel has the opportunity to see Ethan ALLEN, taken prisoner by the British but undaunted. Indeed, Allen taunts the British as Turks who have never seen an "unconquered soldier." But in the British crowd Potter is spotted by an Englishman and immediately arrested. Although he talks his way out of this jam, he is again a fugitive, dressed in beggar's clothes, on his way to London yet again.

Chapter 23: "Israel in Egypt"; "Continued Israel in Egypt"
In his beggar's rags, Israel decides that his safest course is to seek work as a bricklayer, and thus he spends a desolate 13 weeks laying brick. He ponders his "enigmatic" fate, serving the very people his country has revolted against. He concludes, "All is vanity and clay."

Chapters 24–25: "In the City of Dis"; "Forty-Five Years"
Having earned enough to buy a decent suit, Israel resumes his journey to London, where he will spend 40 years wandering like the "outcast Hebrews under Moses." He marries a "Kentish lass" during a period when London is unsafe for him, but even after the two governments repair their relations, he finds it impossible to embark for America, given his family responsibilities. He and his wife produce 11 children. After years of hard existence, one of Israel's sons persuades an American consul to hear his father's story. Thus, in 1826, a half century after Israel left his native land, he finally returns.

Chapter 26: Requiescat in Pace
Little remains for Israel in the new land. The family homestead has been destroyed long ago, his efforts to secure a pension are repulsed by "certain caprices of the law." His scars are his medals, the narrator remarks. Israel's only legacy is the small book he writes about his adventures. The novel concludes: "He died the same day that the oldest oak on his native hills was blown down."

PUBLICATION HISTORY

Israel Potter was first serialized in PUTNAM'S MONTHLY MAGAZINE. Melville assured the magazine's owner, George Palmer Putnam, that the work was an adventure story. He requested five dollars a page for magazine rights and a $100 advance, which Palmer apparently agreed to pay. He also published the novel in book form. The reviews of the book were surprisingly favorable. Rather than reacting to the novel as satire, reviewers praised its comic episodes, its vigorous style, and even its patriotism. Of course, some reviewers did note Melville's sarcastic tone and anti-imperialist attitude, but the book's deeper ironies escaped attention.

Altogether Melville received $421.50 (based on a 12 1/2 percent royalty) for sales of the 75-cent book. It sold almost 3,000 copies in the first six months. This modest success, however, did not prevent the novel from being forgotten. Indeed, the distinguished critic Alfred Kazin chose *Israel Potter* for the Warner Paperback Rediscovery Series; this edition was published in 1974. Kazin identifies the novel's main theme and what drew the solitary Melville to Potter's memoirs: "What Israel shares with Herman Melville is 'exile' seemingly perpetual, exile as a lifetime experience, exile as a feeling about life unexplained by the circumstances of exile."

Italy Melville visited Florence, Milan, Naples, Rome, and Venice in 1857 on his way back from the Middle East. He thought Naples the "gayest city in the world," (Robertson-Lorant) although he also recognized the tyranny of its Bourbon rulers. He visited Mount Vesuvius and climbed down into the crater, noting that its lava looked like "frozen licorice." He went on to Rome by stagecoach to visit the Capitol, the Colosseum, and other sites. During several weeks in Rome he also visited many art galleries, churches, and the Vatican Museum. In Florence, he toured the Pitti Palace and the Uffizi Gallery, and visited the American sculptor Hiram POWERS, whose statue *The Greek Slave* (1843) was shown at the Great Exhibition in New York in 1851. In Venice, he went to St. Mark's Cathedral and toured the Ducal Palace. He admired the city's energetic street life and enjoyed riding in gondolas. Toward the end of his Italian journey he stopped in Milan, visiting its great cathedral and the church of Santa Maria della Grazia, where he saw Leonardo's *The Last Supper* and remarked, "The glow of sociability is so evanescent, selfishness so lasting." At Turin, he departed for Bern, Switzerland.

"Jack Roy" (1888) Poem in *JOHN MARR*. The gallant Jack Roy—truly a noble seaman—is meant to recall Jack CHASE, the captain of the maintop on the U.S.S. *UNITED STATES*, with whom Melville served in 1843–44. Chase made a profound impression on Melville, who featured him in *WHITE-JACKET*. In addition, Melville dedicated his last work, *BILLY BUDD*, to "Jack Chase, Englishman, / Wherever that great heart may now be, / here on Earth or harbored in Paradise, / Captain of the Main-Top in the year 1843 / in the U.S. Frigate *United States*." In his incarnation as Jack Roy, Chase is not only manly and brave, but "Heroic in . . . levity."

Jackson Character in *REDBURN*. Jackson is a physically weak but psychologically astute sailor aboard the *Highlander* who seems to dominate the rest of the crew and who takes a special dislike to young Wellingborough REDBURN. On the return voyage from LIVERPOOL, Jackson, grown mortally ill, coughs up blood while climbing the riggings and falls overboard to his death. He is doubtless based, in part, on Robert Jackson, a 31-year-old New Yorker with whom Melville sailed to Liverpool and back aboard the *ST. LAWRENCE* in 1839.

Jarl ("The Viking," "The Skyeman") Character in *MARDI*. Jarl is the narrator's companion at the beginning of the novel. A taciturn Scandinavian, Jarl joins the narrator in deserting their New England whaler, the *Arcturion,* and setting out by night in a stolen whaleboat for distant western isles. For the next 16 days the pair lives amicably enough together on the whaleboat, the *Chamois;* then they encounter the runaway brigantine, the *Parki,* inhabited only by the Upoluan islander SAMOA and his shrewish wife, ANNATOO. After Annatoo is washed overboard in a storm that also destroys the brigantine, the three men continue on together in the *Chamois.* They remain together during the first leg of the journey through the Mardian archipelago, but both Jarl and Samoa are jettisoned after the narrator, now a demigod called TAJI, acquires new traveling companions. When Taji next has news of Jarl, it is that the old salt has been killed by an arrow, probably shot by one of ALEEMA's sons seeking to avenge their father's death.

Jermin, John Character in *OMOO*. Jermin is the first mate of the *Julia;* he is based on John German, the first mate of the *LUCY-ANN*, the real-life model for the *Julia*. German was in actuality a drunkard, and this fact is reflected in Melville's fictional transformation of him. Nonetheless, John Jermin is not without his merits: even inebriated, he manages to navigate his ship, and his seamanship, together with his ability to take charge of the ship when the captain is incapacitated, earns him the respect of his crew.

Jeroboam In chapter 71 of *MOBY-DICK*, the *PEQUOD* meets the *Jeroboam*. This ship includes a crew member, GABRIEL, who has issued a warning to stay away from Moby-Dick. In fact, one of the *Jeroboam*'s crew, MACEY, has died in pursuit of the whale.

Jerusalem The holy city of the Jews, Christians, and Muslims. It was a Canaanite stronghold captured by David (c. 1000 B.C.). It became the capital of the Jewish state. When Solomon built his temple in the city, it also became ancient Israel's religious capital. It was destroyed by the Babylonians in 586 B.C. and by the Romans in A.D. 70. It was rebuilt by the Roman emperor Hadrian in A.D. 135. For centuries it has been the battleground of warring nations and religions. Jerusalem is the starting point for Melville's pilgrims in *CLAREL*, and the first part of the poem is titled "Jerusalem." The poem alludes to many of the events that mark Jerusalem's history, and Jerusalem itself stands for man's religious aspirations as well as his hostile, divisive tendencies. Melville spent eight days in the city—January 7 to 17, 1857. He wrote in his journal that he had come to saturate himself in the environment. He rose at dawn and walked around its walls. He visited the biblical sites of Mount Olivet (east of the city) and Gethsemane. Much of *Clarel* is set in Jerusalem's Kedron valley, which leads through a wilderness (described in part two of the poem) and to Marsaba (part three) and the Dead Sea. Melville wandered the areas around the city for hours. It was an arid climate with hillsides filled with detritus—a depressing landscape for the spiritual quester. Jerusalem's bleakness is often mentioned in *Clarel*. Its desolate quality was noted not only by Melville but also by many visitors seeking an uplifting experience from the Holy Land. Even the Church of the Holy Sepulcher was a disappointment, since it was rather garishly crowded with relics of the crucifixion. Melville visited it often and was repelled by its moldy smell and the filth of the neighborhood around it. Yet, as *Clarel* reflects, he was also impressed with the constant stream of pilgrims drawn to the site, still seeking their inspiration from Christianity.

"Jimmy Rose" (1855) Short story. Set in NEW YORK CITY, "Jimmy Rose" is narrated by William FORD, now an old man with a younger wife, two daughters, and a maid. Unexpectedly, Ford inherits a faded old house in the city. The house, which has remained largely unchanged for 90 years, is filled with reminders of one of its owners, the once handsome, once hospitable, always charming Jimmy Rose. In particular, the wallpaper in the parlor, with its peacocks and roses, reminds Ford of Jimmy with his always blooming cheeks. Jimmy fell on hard times when two of his ships sank, but he continued to live in New York, a pauper who traded on his fine manners and his friends' long memories in order to keep going. Living on $70 year and all the sandwiches he could cadge during teatime visits, he carried on, always courteous, always smiling, always rosy cheeked. When he died, he was attended by an "opulent" alderman's daughter.

"Jimmy Rose" is replete with autobiographical matter. The details of the narrator's house correspond with those of several houses that Melville himself inhabited over the years. And Jimmy Rose himself—who, like Melville's father, lost his fortune—almost certainly is based on Melville's grandfather, Major Thomas MELVILL, the subject of Oliver Wendell Holmes's poem "The Last Leaf," concerning a superannuated figure whose cheek is "like a rose / In the snow." Melville probably wrote this and another story, "THE 'GEES," in the summer of 1854, although it bares a closer resemblance to the domestic tales "I AND MY CHIMNEY" and "THE APPLE-TREE TABLE," both probably composed a year later. Like these two stories, "Jimmy Rose" features a narrator whose household consists of his wife and two daughters and a maid named BIDDY. "Jimmy Rose" was not published until nearly a year after he sent it off to HARPER'S NEW MONTHLY MAGAZINE, where it appeared anonymously in November 1855.

Joan, Pope Legend has it that in the ninth century, there was a female pope. Variously described as English or German, she fell in love with and married a Benedictine monk. After her husband died she entered the priesthood and eventually was elected Pope John VIII (847–855). This myth was established in the 13th century, and although it was challenged many times, it was not exposed as a myth until 1863. In *CLAREL*, MAR-GOTH alludes to Pope Joan in his ridicule of the Roman church.

"John Marr" (1888) Poem in *JOHN MARR*. The first work in this collection, "John Marr" opens with a long narrative monologue in prose relating the unhappy story of this former mariner who, disabled by a "crippling wound," moves west, where he first loses his wife and child to illness and then loses his house. Isolated from those around him—most of them farmers—he mourns not only his personal losses, but also the loss of wilderness and the progress of civilization. A picture of isolation, he lives now on memories of former shipmates, all dead—or at least dead to him. The piece ends with a verse segment in which John Marr tries to conjure up the only people who mean anything to him, his old companions.

John Marr and Other Sailors with Some Sea-Pieces (1888) Collection of poetry with some prose sketches. Throughout the 1880s, Melville devoted the bulk of his writing time to poetry, much of it concerning the sea and little of it reaching the public. In May 1885, "The Admiral of the White," a long narrative poem dedicated to his brother Tom, who had recently died, was published in both the *New-York Daily Tribune* and the *Boston Herald*. Expanded and revised, the poem would reappear as "THE HAGLETS" in *John Marr*, which was privately published in 1888 by Theodore L. De Vinne & Company in a limited edition of 25 copies. The title page of the book did not bear Melville's name, as all copies were intended for distribution to friends and relatives. Melville dedicated his book to the British maritime novelist and historian W. Clark Russell, who had written an appreciation of Melville earlier in the decade, calling him "the greatest genius" in America.

The volume is divided into two sections. The first of these consists of four monologue-narratives—the first delivered mostly in prose—concerning erstwhile mariners: "John Marr," "Bridegroom Dick," "Tom Deadlight," and "Jack Roy." (Another piece, "Billy in the Darbies," based on a sea lyric, perhaps had a similar genesis, eventually metamorphosing into *BILLY BUDD, SAILOR*. The second section, called "Sea Pieces," includes two longer poems concerning tragedies at sea, "The Haglets" and "THE ÆOLIAN HARP." Other poems in the volume include "THE BERG," "CROSSING THE TROPICS," "THE ENVIABLE ISLES," "FAR OFF-SHORE," "THE FIGURE-HEAD," "THE GOOD CRAFT 'SNOW-BIRD'," "THE MALDIVE SHARK," "THE MAN-OF-WAR HAWK," "OLD COUNSEL," "PEBBLES," "TO NED," "TO THE MASTER OF THE *METEOR*," and "THE TUFT OF KELP." All are bound together by their common element, the sea.

Johnson, Dr. Minor character in *OMOO*. Dr. Johnson is the resident British physician in Papeetee who examines sick crew members on board the *Julia* and later in the CALABOOZA BERETANEE. His original was Dr. Francis Johnson, who was living in Tahiti in 1842 at the time of Melville's voyage there.

Jonah Hebrew prophet discussed in *MOBY-DICK*. In the biblical book of Jonah, the prophet is thrown overboard in a storm, swallowed by a big fish, and then, three days later, cast up on shore unharmed. He takes his salvation as a sign to fulfill the divine command to go to Nineveh to preach repentance. *Moby-Dick*'s narrator, ISHMAEL, implies that his own story, too, is one of survival and of a tale to bear on behalf of higher truth.

Jones Minor character in *REDBURN*. Jones, a NEW YORK CITY friend of Redburn's older brother, introduces the protagonist to CAPTAIN RIGA of the *Highlander* and helps the boy to secure a place aboard ship.

Jones, John Paul (1747–1792) Born in Kirkbean in Kirkcudbrightshire, Scotland, John Paul took the name of Jones after incidents at sea involving the deaths of two men aboard vessels he commanded. He settled in Philadelphia in 1773 and in 1776 entered the American navy, taking command of 40 merchant vessels. He defeated three British warships and won his only victory on British soil on April 23, 1778, when he captured Whitehaven. He was awarded a gold medal from Congress in 1778, the only naval officer to achieve such a distinction. He took command of the Russian fleet in 1788–89 at a time when Russia employed Western officers to modernize its military. Then he retired to Paris.

Jones appears as an egotistical, rowdy character in *ISRAEL POTTER*. He is a self-invented American on the make, pursuing his ambition with relentless gusto and bravado, hectoring Benjamin FRANKLIN, the American ambassador in France, to obtain better ships for him.

Jones, Mr. Minor character in REDBURN; *see* BRADFORD, ALEXANDER WARFIELD.

Jones, Thomas ap Catesby (1790–1858) Naval officer. A hero of the War of 1812, Jones in 1820 was promoted to the rank of commodore. Five years later he was given command of the Pacific Squadron, which he resigned in 1837 after a dispute with the secretary of the navy. In 1841, however, Jones was reassigned this command. Two years later, when Melville was serving aboard the man-of-war UNITED STATES, then weighing anchor at Callao, Peru, Commodore Jones paid an official visit to the port and was slated to inspect the ships in his fleet. Melville never saw the commodore aboard the *United States,* but in his fictional recreation of his experiences there in *WHITE-JACKET,* the *Neversink,* as flagship of the fleet, carries an unnamed commodore. During an 1847 trip to Washington, D.C., Melville attended a ball at the Russian embassy, where he spotted his former commander, who makes another appearance in "Bridegroom-Dick," a poem Melville wrote years later for *JOHN MARR.*

Judd, G[errit] P[armele] (1803–1873) Missionary and statesman. Judd first went to HAWAII in 1828 as a medical missionary. In short order, however, he ingratiated himself with King KAMEHAMEHA III and discontinued his missionary work in order to serve in the Hawaiian government. His involvement escalated over time, and for a decade in the mid-1800s he served as de facto prime minister. Many credit Judd with helping to establish Hawaii as a sovereign nation, rather than a colonial outpost. To Melville, however, he was a "sanctimonious apothecary-adventurer." Fearing that Judd would take revenge for his public denunciations of the foreign missionaries and colonizers who he felt were degrading the native Hawaiians, Melville ended his employment in Honolulu and left the islands in August 1843 aboard the U.S.S. UNITED STATES.

Julia Character in "I AND MY CHIMNEY" and "THE APPLE-TREE TABLE." In both stories she is one of the narrator's two daughters. Julia plays a more active role in the second story. Her response to the ticking sound emitted by the table shifts from spiritualistic to more traditionally Christian when she discovers the source of the sound. As a beautiful bug emerges from a hole in the table, Julia pronounces a kind of benediction on the whole affair, making the bug into an emblem of resurrection.

Jungfrau *See VIRGIN.*

Kamehameha Name given to five Hawaiian kings who ruled from 1810 to 1872. Kamehameha I (c. 1758–1819), known as Kamehameha the Great, ruled Hawaii from 1795, when he united all of the Hawaiian islands by conquest, until his death. Although he opened his kingdom to foreign trade and permitted outsiders to settle in Hawaii, he managed to maintain Hawaiian sovereignty at a time of aggressive colonial expansion on the part of Western European nations. Because of the order his rule brought to Hawaii, the islands knew real prosperity for the first time, but he also insisted upon the importance of observing ancient customs and religious beliefs. On his death, he was succeeded by his son, Kamehameha II (1797–1824), who ruled until his own death from measles, which he contracted during a visit to London, England. He was succeeded by his brother, Kamehameha III (1814–54), who ruled Hawaii until his death.

Kamehameha III's reign coincided with the period of Melville's South Seas voyages. Kamehameha III proved to be a degenerate king, and in *TYPEE*, Melville refers to him (spelling his name Kammahammaha) in unflattering terms, adding that the monarch was gulled into surrendering his kingdom to the British. Although this was not entirely true, during Kamehameha's reign Hawaii was inundated with Western missionaries, barely withstood the threat of annexation by the United States, and evolved from a feudal society into a constitutional monarchy. In *OMOO*, Melville refers to Kamehameha III as Tammahamaha, once again emphasizing his corruption by foreigners.

Upon his death, Kamehameha III was succeeded by his son, Kamehameha IV (1834–63), who ruled until his own death, when he was in turn succeeded by his brother, Kamehameha V (1831–72), who tried to reinstate old tribal customs. During his reign, he proclaimed a new constitution that gave power back to the monarch, and the foreign missionaries lost power. He died without an heir, and the legislature chose his successor, thus ending the Kamehameha dynasty.

Kannakippers Tahitian natives who function as "religious police." In *OMOO*, the narrator describes the duties of these worthies—whose appellation he presumes to be a corruption of the English word "constable"—in ironic terms, citing their interference with their fellow natives' private lives and interruption of the traditional Tahitian way of life. An invention of Western Protestant missionaries, they are much resented by the other islanders, who refer to the kannakippers behind their backs as "Pray-to-Gods."

Kant, Immanuel (1724–1804) German metaphysician, one of the greatest figures in the history of philosophy. Born and educated in Königsberg, Kant first worked as a private tutor, and then began lecturing in philosophy in 1755 at the University of Königsberg. In 1770 he became a professor of logic and metaphysics and began to achieve renown for his writing. His most important writing is contained in *Prolegomena to Any Future Metaphysics* (1783) and *Critique of Practical Reason* (1788). His *Religion Within the Limits of Reason Alone* (1793) provoked a government warning to Kant not to publish on the subject of religion again. Kant is generally credited with infusing philosophy with a fresh sense of skepticism later adopted by other philosophers such as David HUME.

Kant's masterpiece, *Critique of Pure Reason* (1781), argued that our concept of knowledge does not derive from an external reality independent of our minds, but rather that the structure of our minds helps to constitute the nature of reality. This idea was an important discovery for Melville, who believed in the shaping power of the mind, a notion he explores in great depth in *MOBY-DICK*.

Karakoee Minor character in *TYPEE*. Karakoee is a TABOO native who comes from Oahu in the Sandwich Islands (HAWAII). He appears toward the end of novel, acting as the agent for TOMMO's escape. He has learned of Tommo's presence among the Typee from another taboo native, MARNOO, and is eager to shanghai Tommo for service aboard the Australian ship *Julia*, which is desperately short of hands. After first trying unsuccessfully to purchase Tommo's freedom from the Typee chiefs, Karakoee provides the boat that finally escorts Tommo to the *Julia* and his freedom.

Karky Minor character in *TYPEE*. Karky is the master Typee TATTOO maker, whom TOMMO calls a "professor of the fine arts." Seeing Tommo's vast expanse of white skin, Karky is filled with delight. Tommo at first accedes to having his arm tattooed, but recoils in horror when Karky, following local custom, wants to work on the white man's face. Fearful of being scarred for life, Tommo escapes before any damage can be done.

Kean, Captain Hosea Character in "THE 'GEES." Kean is a wiley old Nantucket whaling captain supposedly expert at outwitting the stratagems of the half-Portuguese, half-African natives of the Cape Verde islands, who are likely to misrepresent themselves in their desperation to sign on as sailors.

Kolory Minor character in *TYPEE*. Kolory is a Typee soldier-priest, a sort of "Knight Templer," whom TOMMO observes communing with a religious idol called Moa Artua, a doll-like graven image. After caressing the idol, Kolory cuffs it, thus presaging the behavior of QUEEQUEG toward his own fetish in *MOBY-DICK*.

Kooloo Minor character in OMOO. Kooloo is a Tahitian Christian convert who attaches himself to the narrator, who becomes in turn Kooloo's "tayo karhowree nuee," or special white friend. After Kooloo relieves the narrator of the contents of his sea chest, the native turns his affections elsewhere, even while continuing to wear some of the clothing the narrator had given him.

Kory-Kory Character in *TYPEE*. Kory-Kory appears as a combination valet and chaperon to the protagonist TOMMO, hauling the injured white man about on his back, explaining native customs to him, and generally ministering to his every need. The son of Tommo's hosts in the Typee Valley, MARHEYO and TINOR, Kory-Kory serves as an older brother who guides his infantilized charge through the local culture.

Kostanza, the *See* LOMBARDO.

"Lamia's Song" (1891) Poem in *TIMOLEON*. Lamia, a mythological vampire who lives off the blood of young men, tempts the traveler with a siren's song to come down from his "lonely Alp" to the "myrtles in valleys of May." The traveler longs to succumb to this "downward way."

"language of flowers" A romantic conceit wherein different types of flowers are meant to symbolize different thoughts or emotions. The "language of flowers" was exceedingly popular among the young during the Victorian era. In 1846, on one occasion when Herman Melville went to Boston to court his future wife, Elizabeth ("Lizzie") Shaw, he took with him a lavishly illustrated, terrifically expensive book titled *Floral Tableaux* as a gift. This was an extravagant, romantic gesture. Melville did not himself know much about the "language of flowers" at the time, but he soon learned from Lizzie. When they were newly married, he not only read aloud to her from *MARDI*, the book he was working on, but also wove into its narrative an array of flower symbols, which he associated with YILLAH and HAUTIA, the light and dark ladies of the tale. Over the years, the Melvilles became estranged. Lizzie at one point even considered leaving her husband, but toward the end of Melville's life, they once again grew close. One indication of their reconciliation can be found in the references to the "language of flowers" that made their way into Melville's last major literary production, a book of poetry titled *WEEDS AND WILDINGS CHIEFLY: WITH A ROSE OR TWO*, which was not published until after his death in 1891.

Lansing, Catherine Gansevoort ("Kate") (1839–1918) Cousin of Herman Melville. The daughter of Peter GANSEVOORT, Melville's well-to-do maternal uncle, Kate Gansevoort was a wealthy woman in her own right. She and Melville were close all their lives, but occasionally her money came between them. Peter Gansevoort, to whom Melville dedicated his long narrative poem *CLAREL,* had supported the book both morally and financially. After his death in 1876, however, Melville discovered that the $1,200 his uncle had given him did not cover publication costs. Writing to Kate, Melville asked if the $100 he had been billed for advertising costs came "within the scope of Uncle Peter's design."

Kate responded by sending him a personal check for the amount, which Melville returned, thinking it to be charity. Kate, equally offended, sent him another check, which he donated to charity. Later, Melville wrote her a letter of apology.

Kate remained single until 1873 when, after an 11-year engagement, she married the lawyer Abraham Lansing of ALBANY, NEW YORK. She was 34 at the time; she suffered a number of miscarriages in subsequent years, and she and her husband remained childless. She showered her relatives—particularly Bessie and Fanny Melville, Herman's daughters—with gifts, and remained close to both Herman and his wife, Elizabeth. (*see* Elizabeth MELVILLE, Frances Melville THOMAS, and Elizabeth Knapp Shaw MELVILLE). After Abe Lansing's death from cancer in 1899, Kate became increasingly eccentric. Upon her death, the Gansevoort family estate was valued at $350,000.

Lansingburgh, New York Herman Melville's home from May 1838 to October 1847. Located across the Hudson River and just 10 miles north of ALBANY, NEW YORK, Lansingburgh was founded by the Albany businessman Abraham Jacob Lansing, who in 1763 purchased a large home on what the Dutch settlers had called Tascamasatik, or "Steen Arabia." After having the land around him surveyed, in 1771 Lansing recorded a map of his new town with the Albany County clerk and proceeded to build homes for himself and his family, and to sell lots. By 1786 the village had grown large enough to support its own newspaper, churches, music hall, and inns. In 1790, it was incorporated.

By the time Maria MELVILLE moved there with her eight children, Lansingburgh consisted of about 500 families and boasted several fine schools, including the Lansingburgh Academy and the Female Seminary, where she sent her sons and daughters, respectively. The Melvilles had moved to Lansingburgh from Albany in order to save money, and they shared a two-family house. Melville began his writing career in the attic of his mother's house there, starting with his 1839 magazine pieces, "FRAGMENTS FROM A WRITING DESK," and ending when he moved to NEW YORK CITY in the midst of writing his third novel, *MARDI*.

Larry Minor character in *REDBURN*. An ordinary seaman aboard the *Highlander*, Larry has spent his seagoing life aboard whalers sailing in exotic waters. This experience has made him contemptuous of civilization, as he demonstrates one night by demanding of Redburn, "And what's the use of bein' *snivilized?*"

L.A.V.   Melville pseudonym. Melville used these initials when he published his two "FRAGMENTS FROM A WRITING DESK," the earliest known Melville imaginative writing.

Lavender   Minor character in REDBURN. Formerly a barber on West Broadway in NEW YORK CITY, Lavender is a handsome mulatto man who serves as the ship's steward aboard the *Highlander*. When Redburn first sees him, Lavender, more than a bit of a dandy, is wearing a gorgeous turban. Lavender's moniker is taken from the cologne he wears as an accompaniment to his richly colored suits.

"Lee in the Capitol" (1866)   Poem in BATTLE-PIECES. This is the second of two long narrative poems that appear toward the end of the "Verses Inscriptive and Memorial" section of Melville's collection of CIVIL WAR poetry. Summoned to testify before the United States Senate after the war, Robert E. Lee acquits himself well, voicing one of Melville's most profound worries:

> Push not your triumph; do not urge
> Submissiveness beyond the verge.
> Intestine rancor would you bide,
> Nursing eleven sliding daggers in your side?

Lee is pictured as a worthy foe, and in a long note to the poem Melville admits to taking "poetical liberty" in putting words in Lee's mouth, but justifies this practice by citing Shakespeare's use of similar methods in his history plays. At the poem's end, the senators are "Moved, but not swayed" by Lee's testimony, but Melville ends on a positive note:

> Faith in America never dies;
> Heaven shall the end ordained fulfill,
> We march with Providence cheery still.

Lemsford   Character in WHITE-JACKET. Lemsford is a member of the after-guard on board the NEVERSINK and a particular friend of WHITE-JACKET. Lemsford is a gentlemanly young poet who spends every spare moment, improbably enough, attempting to write poetry aboard the man-of-war on which he serves. He stores his works in a casket inside the seldom-used guns on deck; but one day, when the guns are fired in a ceremonial salute, his works are "published" or distributed to the world. Lemsford was clearly modeled on Ephraim Curtiss HINE, an aspiring poet when he served with Melville on

board the U.S.S. UNITED STATES and later the author of *The Haunted Barque and Other Poems* (1848).

Lesbian, the   Character in CLAREL. A supply merchant from Lesbos, this cheerful, middle-aged businessman mingles with the pilgrims during their stay in MAR SABA.

"L'Envoi."   *See "THE ROSE FARMER."*

"L'Envoi: The Return of the Sire de Nesle, A.D. 16—" (1891)   Poem in TIMOLEON. An envoi is a short concluding stanza in some French verse forms. It often summarizes what came before or serves as a dedication. In the "envoi" to his last published work, Melville chooses as his mouthpiece the Sire of Nesle, a knight-errant who returns home to his faithful wife after years of wandering. It is a fitting conclusion to a collection of poems about long ago and far away, and also to Melville's own history of restless travels and alienation. By 1891, it seems, Melville had finally found a measure of peace at his own fireside with his own patient wife. His next projected collection of poetry, WEEDS AND WILDINGS CHIEFLY: WITH A ROSE OR TWO, was to be dedicated to his wife, Lizzie.

"The Lightning-Rod Man" (1854)   Short story. While the narrator takes shelter in his house to escape a thunderstorm that is just beginning to break overhead, he is visited by a lightning rod salesman, who brandishes a long wooden staff to which are attached a copper rod with two glass balls encircled by copper bands. Delivering a speech about the dangers of lightning in the area, the stranger offers to sell the narrator his lightning rod. When the narrator declines, accusing the salesman of preying on those who fear divine punishment, the salesman attacks him with his rod. The narrator then seizes the rod and breaks it, tossing it and the salesman out. He warns, however, that the salesman is still peddling fear—and his wares—in the neighborhood.

The rather obvious phallic overtones aside, the story seems to be mocking those who would have us believe in an angry, arbitrary God. "The Lightning-Rod Man" first appeared in PUTNAM'S MONTHLY MAGAZINE in August 1854 before being reprinted as one of the PIAZZA TALES in 1856. And it was one of only three stories—other than those in this collection—that were reprinted during Melville's lifetime: it appeared in William E. Burton's *Cyclopedia of Wit and Humor,* first printed in 1857 and reprinted through 1898. "The Lightning-Rod Man" was thus the only one of Melville's tales to be continuously in print while he was alive. It was also the only one of his signed works to appear with an original illustration (in Burton) during his lifetime.

Lincoln, Abraham (1809–1865)   The 16th president of the United States. He was born in Kentucky and made his career in Illinois, serving one term (1847–49) as a Congressman before being defeated by Stephen Douglas in a campaign for the U.S. Senate in 1858. Elected president as a Republican in 1860, Lincoln wished to preserve the Union even if it meant tolerating slavery in some form. But he opposed the expansion of slavery beyond the Southern states, and his election was perceived by the slave states as sealing their doom within the Union. Lincoln was assassinated on April 14, 1865, shortly after the South's surrender and his second inauguration.

Melville met Lincoln once, shortly after he was inaugurated president for the first time. In Washington, D.C., Melville attended one of Lincoln's receptions and shook his hand. He was impressed with Lincoln's direct, conscientious, democratic manners, and he found Lincoln's wife, Mary Todd, an attractive woman. Melville supported Lincoln's policies during the war.

Literary World Under the editorship of Evert DUYCKINCK, this weekly journal promoted Melville's work and gave him the opportunity to review books. As Melville biographer Laurie Robertson-Lorant observes, the journal reached the "largest and most critical audience of any periodical in America." It published excerpts from WHITE-JACKET. Attention to Melville in the *Literary World* meant that his work would be widely reviewed by other prominent periodicals and newspapers. Melville broke with Duyckinck after the editor, preferring the earlier, more light-hearted Melville of TYPEE and OMOO, ran a two-part negative review of MOBY-DICK.

"The Little Good Fellows" (1924) Poem in WEEDS AND WILDINGS. Probably intended as part of the section titled "The Year," "The Little Good Fellows" concerns those harbingers of spring, robins. The birds are pictured first as guardians of the dead, whom they cover "with buds and leaves," then as bridegrooms surrounded by the "bridal-favors" of the orchard. They are, in effect, a conduit between man and nature, whose only plea is to be given "leave to rove." One of Melville's sources for this seemingly optimistic poem is the English dramatist John Webster (c. 1578–c. 1632), whose tragedy *The White Devil* (1612) contains a dirge that begins

> Call for the Robin Red-brest and the wren,
> Since ore shadie groves they hover,
> And with leaves and flowers doe cover
> The friendlesse bodies of unburied men.

Liverpool City in northwest England and setting for part of REDBURN. When Herman Melville's father, Allan MELVILL, traveled to Europe on business in 1818, his ship docked at Liverpool, then a thriving port city with a population exceeding 100,000. It was then, perhaps, that Allan Melvill employed his copy of the guidebook *The Picture of Liverpool* (1803), which his second son would use in turn on his first voyage to Liverpool in 1841 and in the novel that grew out of that voyage, *Redburn*. In 1841, Liverpool, situated near the mouth of the Mersey River on the Irish Sea, was one of the busiest commercial ports in the world. It owed much of its prosperity to the slave trade, however, which Melville found brought wealth to some but also brought abject poverty to others. This disparity made its way into *Redburn,* as did a dismissal of Adam Smith's *The Wealth of Nations* (1776), the bible of 19th-century laissez-faire capitalism.

Liverpool was also the center of the cotton trade, and with the advent of the CIVIL WAR in the United States, its two primary sources of revenue were choked off. When Melville revisited the city in 1856 on his way to the Levant, doubtless he found it much changed. Still later, the advent of container ships and the shift of British trade from America to the European continent would bring ruin to what had once been Britain's greatest port.

Locke, John (1632–1704) English philosopher and founder of philosophical empiricism, which contends that knowledge is built through sensory data. Educated at Christ College, Oxford, he became a lecturer there in Greek, rhetoric, and philosophy. He also studied medicine, which influenced his writing. Locke served as friend, physician, and adviser to Anthony Ashley Cooper, later the first Earl of Shaftsbury. Locke held several diplomatic and civil posts, then later traveled to France, where he consulted with scholars of science and philosophy. Thereafter he returned to Oxford, although he also traveled to Holland, where he completed his most famous work, *Essay Concerning Human Understanding* (1690). This work and others led to his unofficial status as the "philosopher of freedom." Locke's most famous idea is probably that of the tabula rasa, the blank slate, which is what he termed the human mind before it is exposed to the world of experience from which ideas are formed.

Locke thus repudiated the notion of innate ideas. In MOBY-DICK, Melville contrasts Locke with Immanuel KANT (symbolized as hanging heads of the sperm and right whales that balance the PEQUOD). That is, knowledge as derived from the senses and experience of the world is countered by knowledge as derived from mental forms or ideas inherent in the mind.

"The Loiterer" (1924) Poem in WEEDS AND WILDINGS. Probably meant to appear in the section titled "The Year" and possibly as the first poem in the volume, "The Loiterer" was also labeled "The Late-Comer" and much reworked in draft form. The subject of the poem is spring, which arrives belatedly, but blessedly, for the "Old folks" behind "the weather-beat door / That was sunned thro' the skeleton-tree."

Lombardo "Character" in *MARDI*. Lombardo, the long-dead author of an ancient Mardian literary masterpiece, the *Koztanza*, was in life poor and unrecognized. Much discussed by later generations of Mardians like BABBALANJA, who venerates the *Koztanza*, Lombardo is thought to be a tongue-in-check portrait of Melville, who had good reason for seeing himself as a genius unheralded in his own time. In 1849, when his sister Augusta had finished reading the proof sheets for Melville's latest work, she wrote to Elizabeth Shaw MELVILLE: "'Mardi's' a book!—Ah my own Koztanza!"

"Lone Fonts" (1891) Poem in *TIMOLEON*. The speaker urges that one look beyond youthful optimism, cynical worldliness, and the tenor of the times. Instead,

> Stand where Posterity shall stand;
> Stand where the Ancients stood before,
> And, dipping in lone fonts thy hand,
> Drink of the never-varying lore.

Melville considered two other titles for this short, pithy poem: "Counsels" and "Giordano Bruno." The import of the first is obvious, but the second provides insight into Melville's meaning. Bruno was a 16th-century Italian monk who was excommunicated and burned at the stake during the Inquisition for his radical philosophy of skepticism, born from his adoption of Nicolaus Copernicus's theory that Earth—and by extension, man—is not the center of the universe. Bruno's philosophy was later adopted by such philosophers as Baruch SPINOZA and Gottfried Leibnitz (1646–1719). This pantheistic sense of the unity of all things was plainly attractive to the questing, doubting, heretical Melville, who managed to create, in *MOBY-DICK*, a tragedy with a happy ending: Ishmael emerges from the maelstrom on a coffin, which has become a life buoy.

Long Ghost, Dr. Character in *OMOO*. When the narrator meets Long Ghost, the latter is serving as the ship's doctor aboard the *Julia*. Given his status, the doctor initially is accorded privileges not enjoyed by the rest of the crew. Long Ghost, a rebellious but apathetic sort, soon quarrels with the captain and takes up life among the common sailors. In the forecastle he befriends the narrator, all of whose subsequent adventures he shares. When the pair decides finally to leave the SOCIETY ISLANDS aboard the *Leviathan,* however, the American captain of the whaler rejects Long Ghost, declaring him to be a "Sydney bird"—an untrustworthy Australian. When the narrator ships out, he shares his salary advance with his friend, then shakes Long

Ghost's hand one last time, never to see him again. Melville based Long Ghost on John B. TROY, the steward of the *LUCY-ANN*.

Loo Minor character in *OMOO*. A precocious nymph, not more than 14 years old, Loo is the voluptuous but petulant daughter of pious Deacon Eremear PO-PO and his wife AFRETEE, with whom the narrator and LONG GHOST stay in Partoowye. When the latter grows amorous and makes advances toward the indolent Loo, she stabs him with a thorn.

"Look-out Mountain. The Night Fight. (November, 1863.)" (1866) Poem in *BATTLE-PIECES*. On November 23, 1863, during the CIVIL WAR, the Union army, under Generals Joseph Hooker, William Tecumseh Sherman, and George Henry Thomas, advanced against Confederate troops on Lookout Mountain on the bluffs above Chattanooga, Tennessee. The Union troops succeeded in routing the Southerners, under General Braxton Bragg, and their victory vertically bifurcated the Confederacy. In Melville's poem celebrating the victory, the "lurid light" that "is rolled about with thunders" in the night changes to joy as the day breaks; "God has glorified the Mountain / Where a Banner burneth bright."

"The Lover and the Syringa Bush" (1924) Poem in *WEEDS AND WILDINGS*. In this component of section of the volume, titled "The Year," nature and love—of a decidedly heterosexual and erotic sort—lead the poet to "Eden's gate," where he lingers, "Love's tryst to keep, with truant Eve." To the lover the lowly syringa bush appears

> Like a lit-up Christmas Tree,
> Like a grotto pranked with spars,
> Like white corals in green sea,
> Like night's sky of crowded stars—

Love, he declares, has such "heightening power" that it can so transform the world that a flowering bush can seem to contain the sea, the sky, and all between.

Lucy-Ann The Australian whaler on which Herman Melville escaped the MARQUESAS in 1842. At the end of *TYPEE*, when Melville describes his narrator's escape from Nuku Hiva, he calls the ship on which TOMMO departs the *Julia*—which is also its name in *OMOO*, the sequel to *Typee*. In *Omoo,* the narrator deserts the *Julia* because of the ship's poor conditions and the captain's bad attitude. In life, Melville's reasons for leaving the *Lucy-Ann* seem to have been much the same. The whaler was badly neglected, and the failure of the crew to capture more than two whales in many long months had taken its toll in drunkenness and desertions. The men were dispirited also by the tyranny of the skipper, Captain Ventom, and by the continual inebriation of his first mate, John German. When the crew revolted, Ventom steered toward Tahiti (*see* SOCIETY ISLANDS), where Melville and his companion, John B. Troy, jumped ship—much as their fictional counterparts do in *Omoo*.

"Lyon. Battle of Springfield, Missouri. (August, 1861.)" (1866)   Poem in *BATTLE-PIECES*. In this poem, dedicated to General Nathaniel LYON, a Union martyr and one of Melville's neighbors in PITTSFIELD, MASSACHUSETTS, the speaker is one of Lyon's men and a survivor of a CIVIL WAR battle near Springfield, in which Lyon led a preemptory attack against a Confederate force nearly double the size of his own contingent. Lyon died in the assault, leaving his considerable estate to the federal war effort. He is pictured here the night before the battle writing his will by candlelight, leaving "his all / To Her for whom 'twas not enough to fall."

Lyon, Nathaniel (1818–1861)   Union army officer. Lyon was a Connecticut native and a neighbor of Melville's in PITTSFIELD, MASSACHUSETTS. A West Point graduate, Lyon served with the army during the Seminole War (1835–42) and the MEXICAN WAR. During the 1850s he was stationed at Fort Riley, Kansas, where he saw firsthand the bloody rivalry between the abolitionists and those who wanted to preserve the institution of slavery. Lyon cast his lot with the former, attempting to drive Governor Claiborne F. Jackson, a supporter of the Confederacy, from the state. Lyon, by then a general, was the first great Union hero to fall after war was declared, leading his outnumbered troops against the Confederates near Springfield, Missouri, on August 10, 1861. Melville memorialized the battle, and its hero, in "LYON," one of the poems in *BATTLE-PIECES*.

Lyonese, the   In CLAREL, a French Jew from Lyons. He is a salesman of luxuries who shares a room for the night with CLAREL in BETHLEHEM. He is not religious; indeed, he seems to know little about his people's faith. Very much a man of this world, the Lyonese is ignorant of spiritual conflicts and is devoted to the realm of the senses.

Macey Minor character in *MOBY-DICK*. He is chief mate of the *JEROBOAM*. Ignoring Gabriel's warning not to chase the whale, he engages in a pursuit and is thrown from his ship by the whale and drowns.

Machiavelli, Niccolò (1469–1527) Italian statesman and political philosopher. In his classic book *The Prince* (1532), he describes the methods by which a ruler can attain and maintain power. For Machiavelli, it is only power that counts, and thus he has been accused of immorality, of founding a political policy based only on expediency, not on any principles. Machiavelli is invoked in *CLAREL* for his rather slighting references to Christ, a "feminine" man, not one of the powerful. The CONFIDENCE MAN, in his disguise as PITCH, the huckster who tries to sell property in the "New Jerusalem," is called an "impoverished Machiavelli." Melville seems to have in mind the confidence man's cynical exploitation of people in order to acquire money and to achieve power over them.

"Madam Mirror" and "The Wise Virgins to Madam Mirror" (1947) Poems. Among the more than 40 poems Melville left uncollected or unpublished at his death, "Madam Mirror" is one of a pair, a counterpoint to "The Wise Virgins to Madam Mirror," another unpublished verse. The speaker of the former has surpassed her usefulness, stranded with "wrecks in a garret." Despite her withdrawal from society, she finds comfort in her solitude, "Content to escape from the anguish / Of the Real and the seeming in life." The "wise virgins" dismiss her, blithely declaring, "'Tis the elderly only grow old!" They cannot entertain even her reflections as they "whirl in youth's waltz."

Mad Jack Character in *WHITE-JACKET*. Mad Jack is one of the lieutenants aboard the *NEVERSINK*. One of the few officers whom WHITE-JACKET respects, Mad Jack has a weakness for the bottle but a profound love of the sea. Furthermore, he knows what he is doing. When the frigate gets into trouble rounding CAPE HORN, Mad Jack countermands the captain's orders and, in doing so, saves the ship. Later, when the captain's arbitrary order that the men shave off their beards nearly causes a mutiny on board, Mad Jack's confident, scolding manner turns the tide. Mad Jack was probably partly based on Latham B. Avery, a lieutenant who served on board

the U.S.S. *UNITED STATES* during the same period Melville did.

"Madcaps" (1924) Poem in *WEEDS AND WILDINGS*. One of the poems apparently intended for the section titled "The Year," "Madcaps" is related from the point of view of the poet, who watches two "children" frolic out of doors. The children, named Lily and Cherry, may be flowers—or they may be Melville's oldest granddaughters, Eleanor and Frances Thomas, born, respectively, in 1882 and 1883.

"Magian Wine" (1891) Poem in *TIMOLEON*. This obscure poem seems to have something to do with the Old Testament Song of Solomon, an erotic ode sung by a woman to a man that was adopted into the biblical canon from the mystical Apocrypha. It seems also to have something to do with the Magi, Zoroastrian holy men from Persia, as well as with the notion that Buddhism came to Palestine during King Solomon's reign (10th century B.C.) via the princess of Sheba, who imported this philosophy from the Arabian peninsula. "Magian Wine" clearly has erotic overtones, with the wine turning Solomon's "Syrian charms" opaline for Miriam, who is perhaps intended to be the speaker of the "Song of Solomon," or the Princess of Sheba, or both. The Christian sacrament of communion also seems to play a part in this poem, which may be Melville's attempt to address his own version of PANTHEISM.

"Magnanimity Baffled" (1866) Poem in *BATTLE-PIECES*. Melville pictures the victorious North after the CIVIL WAR as "The Victor," magnanimously offering his hand to his defeated foe, who lies silent upon a cot, turned toward the wall. When the Victor reaches for his former enemy's hand, he finds him already dead. Melville clearly was chary of those who wanted to wreak retribution upon the South after the war. He believed that if Reconstruction did not truly reconstruct, the South would perish.

"The Maldive Shark" (1888) Poem in *JOHN MARR*. The shark conjured up here is a denizen of the Maldives, an archipelago in the Indian Ocean, but he is closely related to the white sharks of *MARDI* and *MOBY-DICK*. The Maldive shark has a symbiotic relationship with the "sleek little pilot-fish" that guides him to his prey. In their relationship Melville sees a paradigm of good and evil, forces that seem to coexist in similar fashion. The pilot fish are "[e]yes and brains" to "the dotard lethargic and dull," who unwittingly acts as their protector. One cannot exist without the other.

"Malvern Hill. (July, 1862.)" (1866) Poem in BATTLE-PIECES. Melville here revisits the CIVIL WAR Battle of Malvern Hill, in which General George B. McClellan led his Union forces against Confederate soldiers near Richmond, Virginia. Malvern Hill was a turning point in the war, for it was the first time that the North had been able to withstand assault during the Seven Days' Battles that resulted from McClellan's Peninsula campaign in eastern Virginia. The next day, the Confederate army withdrew toward Richmond. In Melville's poem, the elms in Malvern Wood remember the bravery and the suffering of the Union soldiers, but, he concludes, "Wag the world how it will, / Leaves must turn green in Spring."

Mandeville Minor character in WHITE-JACKET. Mandeville is brought on board the NEVERSINK in Rio de Janeiro when the man-of-war falls short of crew members. Mandeville, a former naval officer, dares to speak to the first lieutenant, who upbraids the now common sailor. Apparently Mandeville had been demoted after leaving his command while drunk, and apparently he learned little from this experience: hardly a week after coming aboard the Neversink, he is flogged for becoming intoxicated on smuggled spirits.

man from the Carolinas, the Character in The CONFIDENCE MAN. He attacks the HERB-DOCTOR for recommending the "Samaritan pain dissuader" to the sick, unparticipating man. The man from the Carolinas calls the herb-doctor a snake who takes advantage of peoples' feelings.

man in gray, the Character in The CONFIDENCE MAN. One of the several names given to the confidence man. He approaches a passenger aboard the FIDELE asking for a contribution to the orphan asylum the man in gray has recently set up among the Seminoles. The passenger refuses to contribute. The man in gray then encounters the young Episcopal clergyman who has been looking for him to corroborate the story of the NEGRO CRIPPLE. The man in gray laments that evidently the Negro cripple, like himself, has been doubted—which leads the clergyman to believe that the man in gray has corroborated the cripple's story.

"The Man-of-War Hawk" (1888) Poem in JOHN MARR. We "low-flyers" cannot hope to gain the perspective—even in thought—of the "placid supreme" heights attained by the man-of-war hawk. Once again, for Melville, nature remains supremely inscrutable.

man with a long weed, the Character in The CONFIDENCE MAN. One of the personae of the confidence man. He vouches for the integrity of the NEGRO CRIPPLE, who is also one of the guises assumed by the confidence man aboard the FIDELE on its way from St. Louis to New Orleans.

man with the traveling cap, the Character in THE CONFIDENCE MAN. A disguise of the confidence man. He approaches the good merchant, Mr. ROBERTS, aboard the FIDELE to question him about the UNFORTUNATE MAN. He wonders whether the unfortunate man acted too quickly and did not try to reconcile with his wife, GONERIL. Perhaps the unfortunate man did not show enough confidence.

Mapple, Father Character in MOBY-DICK. "A sailor and harpooner in his youth," this vigorous old man ministers to seamen and their families, using their vernacular to explain how faith in God can bring them through their suffering and loss. A man of strong personality, he nevertheless counsels his congregation to abjure pride and the strength of their own will. They must submit to the divine will and plan. Like Melville's novel, Father Mapple's story gathers power through his ability to take the details of human experience and shape them into an allegory of the quest for meaning and salvation.

Marbonna Minor character in OMOO. Marbonna is a Marquesan at the court of POMARE IV who cares for the queen's children. Because the narrator is able to speak with him in his native tongue, Marbonna arranges for him and his companion, Dr. LONG GHOST, to be admitted to the inner sanctum, where they essay an audience with the queen.

"The March into Virginia, Ending in the First Manassas. (July, 1861.)" (1866) Poem in BATTLE-PIECES. Before the first battle at Manassas, during the CIVIL WAR, Union soldiers had been confident of their victory over the Confederates, whom they greatly outnumbered. The speaker pictures these boy soldiers heading into battle like picnickers or youths bound for a berry picking party: "So they gayly go to fight / Chatting left and chatting right." But the Union will be defeated in this battle, and those who do not die will know a Second Manassas.

"The Marchioness of Brinvilliers" (1891) Poem in TIMOLEON. Marie Madeleine Marguerite d'Aubray, marquise de Brinvilliers (c. 1630–76), was a childlike French aristocrat who was publicly executed for poisoning her father and brothers. Melville may have seen a famous drawing of her ascending the scaffold, drawn by Charles

Le Brun, on display in the Louvre when the writer was in Paris in 1849. What interests Melville about the marquise is the disparity between her innocent appearance and the nefariousness of her crimes, which he sums up with a reference to her "fathomless mild eyes."

"The March to the Sea (December, 1864)" (1866)
One of two poems Melville wrote about William Tecumseh Sherman's march through Georgia, "The March to the Sea" is told from the Northern point of view. Even though the poem begins by celebrating Sherman's march, however, his troops turn into "foragers" who "helped themselves from farm-lands." Melville's concern about the viability of a peace achieved at the price of such wholesale destruction is clear in the poem's final stanza:

> For behind they left a wailing,
> A terror and a ban,
> And blazing cinders sailing,
> And homeless households wan,
> Wide zones of counties paling,
> And towns where maniacs ran.
> Was it Treason's retribution—
> Necessity the plea?
> They will long remember Sherman
> And his streaming columns free—
> They will long remember Sherman
> Marching to the sea.

"The March to the Sea" was first published anonymously in HARPER'S NEW MONTHLY MAGAZINE in February 1866.

Mardi   Herman Melville's third novel, which appeared in 1849 as *Mardi: And a Voyage Thither*. Melville probably began working on the book that would become *Mardi* almost immediately after he finished reading the proofs of his previous work, OMOO, at the beginning of 1847. This third book was apparently originally intended to pick up where its predecessor had left off, as *Omoo* had with TYPEE. But this was a turbulent time in Melville's life—and in his literary career—and he had difficulty settling in with his new project.

For one thing, Melville had fallen in love with Elizabeth ("Lizzie") Shaw, and he was spending a great deal of time shuttling back and forth between LANSINGBURGH, NEW YORK, where he was living with his mother, and Lizzie's home in Boston. He wanted to marry her, but her father, Judge Lemuel SHAW, doubted Melville's ability to support a wife on the meager income he made with his literary efforts. Melville responded by attempting—unsuccessfully, as it turned out—to obtain a civil service position at the Treasury Department. Nonetheless, Herman and Lizzie married on August 4, 1847, and began their married life under his mother's roof in Lansingburgh.

Melville soon grew restive, however, and he and his brother Allan (see Allan MELVILLE, Jr.) pooled their resources to purchase a brownstone in NEW YORK CITY. In October, they moved the entire household—including their wives, their mother, and their sisters—to Manhattan.

At the same time, Melville's intellectual life was in ferment—both because of the stimulus of living in the metropolis and because of the books he was borrowing from his friend Evert DUYCKINCK's 16,000-volume library and from the New York Society Library, which he had recently joined. When it finally appeared, *Mardi* would evince the influence of such sophisticated, even recondite, writers as Edmund Spenser, Jonathan Swift, Sir Thomas BROWNE, Robert BURTON, and François Rabelais.

In his preface to *Mardi*, Melville says that when the veracity of his first two narratives of his voyages in the Pacific was called into question, he conceived the idea of transforming his Polynesian adventures into romance to see if fiction would be read as fact. Although it is true that he was annoyed by critical assaults on his accuracy—his English publisher, John MURRAY, had continued to nettle him with requests for evidence of the incidents detailed in *Typee* and *Omoo*—Melville seems to have had no clear plan for his third book. *Mardi* had a life of its own, and its chaotic tone and structure not only reflect the turmoil of Melville's life, but also point the way toward a new artistic vision that would only be fully realized in *MOBY-DICK*.

SYNOPSIS

Chapters 1–8: "Foot in Stirrup"; "A Calm"; "A King for a Comrade"; "A Chat in the Clouds"; "Seats Secured and Portmanteaus Packed"; "Eight Bells"; "A Pause"; "They Push Off, Velis et Remis"
Mardi begins conventionally enough, with the unnamed narrator, an American sailor, making up his mind to desert the *Arcturion* after three years of an unsuccessful whaling voyage. One day, when the ship is off the Galapagos coast, the narrator reveals his plans to another crewman, a steady old "Viking" from the Isle of Skye named JARL, in order to induce him to come along. Jarl at first points out the folly of the plan—they are at least 1,000 miles from land—but then concedes. They make their plans, setting aside a larder and a wardrobe.

Before heading off, the narrator pauses to recount that in doing so, he and his companion saved themselves from a certain death, for the *Arcturion*, headed to the Arctic to hunt right whales, was never heard from again. Late one night, the pair of deserters call out that a man has fallen overboard, and in the disarray that follows, they lower one of the whaler's small open boats and row off.

Chapters 9–18: "The Weary World Is All Before Them"; "They Arrange Their Canopies and Lounges and Try to Make Things Comfortable"; "Jarl Afflicted with the Lockjaw"; "More About Being in an Open Boat"; "Of the Chondropterygii and Other Uncouth Hordes Infesting the South Seas"; "Jarl's Misgivings"; "A Stitch in Time Saves Nine"; "They Are Becalmed"; "In High Spirits, They Push On for the Terra Incognita"; "My Lord Shark and His Pages"

Jarl and the narrator set their craft in order, fixing their compass and putting up a canopy to gain some relief from the tropic sun. The narrator finds the taciturn Jarl to be a dull companion, and he grows desperately lonely gazing at the endless horizon. He discourses on sharks and other fish they encounter and describes the daily routine of life in a small open boat. Then they are becalmed for five straight days. When the wind finally picks up again, Jarl takes the shark and pilotfish that accompany their boat as good omens indicating they will come to no harm.

Chapters 19–22: "Who Goes There?"; "Noises and Portents"; "Man Ho!"; "What Befell the Brigantine at the Pearl Shell Islands"

On the 16th day after their desertion, Jarl and the narrator spot a brigantine on the horizon. As they approach the ship, they find it to be in a state of utter chaos, apparently abandoned. Boarding the ship, they find the decks awash in litter. Searching the ship below decks, they find no one. When the next day dawns, however, they discover a native hiding in the maintop. When the stranger descends, they see he has a mutilated arm. He identifies himself as SAMOA and reveals that his wife, ANNATOO, is also aboard.

Samoa reveals that the name of the brigantine is the *Parki,* and that she is out of Lahina on the island of Maui (which Melville spells "Mowee"), one of the Hawaiian islands. Four months earlier, carrying a crew made up of Europeans and Polynesians, it had sailed south in search of pearls. Samoa, as the ship's navigator, was a highly respected member of the crew, and he was able to bring his wife along on the cruise.

While harvesting pearl shells among some islands, the crew of the *Parki* encountered some Cholos (half-Spanish) deserters, who had risen to positions of authority among the natives with whom they took up residence. They made friends with the captain, and one day lured him and the two other white crew members away. In their absence, the Cholos' native henchmen boarded the brig and overpowered its Hawaiian crew. Annatoo escaped to the fore-topgallant sail, and in the fray Samoa's arm was mangled. Still, he and his wife managed to prevent their foes from steering the brig onto a coral reef, killing them and the pursuing Cholos in the bargain.

Chapters 23–27: "Sailing from the Island, They Pillage the Cabin"; "Dedicated to the College of Physicians and Surgeons"; "Peril a Peacemaker"; "Containing a Pennyweight of Philosophy"; "In Which the Past History of the Parki *Is Concluded"*

Samoa tells how he and Annatoo pillaged the captain's wardrobe, with the bellicose Annatoo taking the lion's share of the loot. By this time, Samoa's wound had grown much worse, so Annatoo helped her husband amputate his arm with a blunt cook's ax. The wound was then cauterized and seemed to trouble Samoa no further. During the next several days, the *Parki* continued to sail aimlessly about as Annatoo jealously guarded her stores, occasionally adding to them by stealing from her husband's booty. Finally the pair are discovered by the narrator and Jarl.

Chapters 28–37: "Suspicions Laid, and Something About the Calmuc"; "What They Lighted Upon in Further Searching the Craft, and the Resolution They Came To; Hints for a Full Length of Samoa"; "Rovings Alow and Aloft"; "Xiphius Platypterus"; "Otard"; "How They Steered on Their Way"; "Ah, Annatoo!"; "The Parki *Gives Up the Ghost"; "Once More They Take to the Chamois"*

The narrator takes command of the ship. Finding no navigational instruments, they decide to keep to a westerly course. The narrator describes Samoa, a native of the island of Upolu of the Samoan group. With his noble bearing and amputated arm, he reminds the narrator of Lord Horatio NELSON. He is far less generous toward Annatoo, whom he regards as both a pack rat and a termagant.

For a time nothing momentous happens to the *Parki.* The narrator lands an impressive swordfish. He discovers the captain's store of prime aged liquor. Annatoo's pilferings serve to impede the ship's progress, so she is locked up at night. Then, after a period of calm, the *Parki* encounters a sudden storm. In a freak accident, Annatoo is washed overboard and disappears into a whirlpool. Abandoning the sinking brigantine, the three male survivors board the small chamois (called so because it leaps "from watery cliff to watery cliff") that Jarl and the narrator had used to escape the *Arcturus.*

Chapters 38–40: "The Sea on Fire"; "They Fall In with Strangers"; "Sire and Sons"

That night, the chamois encounters marine phosphorescence and a pod of whales that threatens to upturn the little boat. On the ninth day of sailing westward in the chamois, they run across enormous flocks of sea birds, a sign that they are not far from land. Off on the horizon they see dark purple land haze.

In jubilant spirits, they spy a sail. As the craft approaches, they see that it consists of two canoes that have been lashed together to hold up a center platform and a tent. The canoes are manned by burly islanders, who assume hostile attitudes and then row swiftly away when the chamois gets too close. Hoisting its sail, the little lifeboat soon overtakes the unwieldy canoe contraption, and the narrator makes it clear to the natives that he and his two companions have only friendly intentions.

Chapters 41–42: "A Fray"; "Remorse"

The narrator soon discovers that the brawny warriors are all brothers sired by the old priest, ALEEMA, who commands their catamaran. Furthermore, he learns that the mysterious tent contains a beautiful maiden, who is being carried to an island where she will be offered as a sacrifice to the islanders' pagan gods.

Upon discovering this last bit of information, the narrator resolves to save the innocent girl. He and Samoa board the catamaran and ply the priest with gifts in an effort to ingratiate themselves with the old man. Quickly, however, the old man's sons surround them as the priest warns that they must either leave or die.

They are vastly outnumbered, but the narrator, intent on his purpose, lunges at the priest with his sword and kills the old man. He and Samoa then jump back into their boat with Jarl and quickly sail off, taking two of the sons as hostages. Shortly thereafter, they row back to the canoes, where they find the remaining sons mourning their loss. The narrator experiences a moment of doubt about what he has done, but quickly shakes it off. Brandishing their superior weapons, he and Samoa make it known that all they want is the occupant of the tent.

Chapter 43: "The Tent Entered"

Dividing the folds of the tent, the narrator discovers crouching within a beautiful blond, blue-eyed girl. Eager to know her history, the narrator questions her in English, then in Polynesian. The girl answers haltingly, indicating that she is more than merely mortal. Her name is YILLAH. Born in a place called Amma, when still an infant she was spirited to Oroolia, the Island of Delights, where the water washed her olive skin white and turned her hair golden. Walking one day in a woodland in Oroolia, she was snared by a vine, which drew her in and gradually turned her into a blossom. After hanging in a trance on the vine, the blossom that is Yillah snapped off and was borne by a soft wind to the sea, where it fell into a shell. Yillah, like Venus, was thus borne across the waves, until the shell washed up on the sands of the island of Amma.

These events had been revealed to the priest Aleema in a dream. He opened the bivalve and retrieved the bud within, which in turn unfolded to reveal Yillah, wearing a rose-colored pearl at her bosom. Aleema quickly locked her up in the sacred temple of the god Apo, where no other eyes could behold her. Then, just four days previous to encountering the survivors of the *Parki*, Aleema had told her that she was being called home via Tedaidee, where she would descend into a whirlpool.

Chapters 44–51: "Away!"; "Reminiscences"; "The Chamois with a Roving Commission"; "Yillah, Jarl, and Samoa"; "Something Under the Surface"; "Yillah"; "Yillah in Adair"; "The Dream Begins to Fade"

Fearful of alarming her, the narrator tells Yillah that Aleema has left on an errand to Oroolia, leaving her in his care. Transferring the tent to the chamois, the narrator, Jarl, and Samoa spirit Yillah away. Although haunted by thoughts of his murder of the priest, the narrator glories in the knowledge that Yillah is his.

The next day he tells Samoa and Jarl to steer for the island of Tedaidee. He wants, he tells us, to have more time to contemplate Yillah before reaching land. He thinks she might be one of the albino Polynesians known as the Tulla. She tells him something more of her life in the temple of Apo, a paradisal but lonely place where she one day conjured up a beautiful youth whom she could reach. Aleema brought her a shell and a bird that become her only companions.

The narrator muses that Yillah has lived so long in her own fancies that she believes herself to be unearthly. Then, as his intimacy with her grows, Yillah's dreams begin to fade. She saddens, while her new lover begins to take on her dreams, which prefigure his loss of her.

Chapters 52–64: "World Ho!"; "The Chamois Ashore"; "A Gentleman from the Sun"; "Tiffin in a Temple"; "King Media a Host"; "Taji Takes Counsel with Himself"; "Mardi by Night and Yillah by Day"; "Their Morning Meal"; "Belshazzar on the Bench"; "An Incognito"; "Taji Retires from the World"; "Odo and Its Lord"; "Yillah a Phantom"

After five days, the boat reaches shore, where the four passengers are greeted exuberantly by the native inhabitants of these islands, which are known collectively as Mardi. Their joy, it seems, results from a notion that the narrator is a superior being resembling one of their demigods, TAJI. With Samoa's encouragement, the narrator declares that he is indeed Taji. A group of chiefs approaches, and one of them challenges the narrator's identity. Once satisfied that the stranger is indeed Taji, MEDIA, the king of the island Odo, introduces himself.

The entire party sails to Odo, where, as guests of Media, they lead a lavish life, disturbed only by the cruel indifference Media exhibits towards his subjects. Many visitors come from the other islands, and one day Taji receives a call from three black-eyed damsels who are handmaidens of Queen HAUTIA. As gifts from their ruler they give Taji three flowers, which seem to carry some mysterious meaning he cannot discern.

Yillah, meanwhile, has grown pensive, muttering in her sleep about whirlpools and spending her days gazing into the lagoon. One day Taji wakens in their bower of bliss to discover Yillah gone. Visitors—including Hautia herself, once more bringing flowers—continue to come, but are sent away to search for Yillah. When they have no success, Taji announces to Media that he must leave Odo and roam throughout Mardi in search of his lost love.

Chapters 65–102; "Taji Makes Three Acquaintances"; "With a Fair Wind, at Sunrise They Sail"; "Little King Peepi"; "How Teeth Were Regarded in Valapee"; "The Company Discourse, and Braid Beard Rehearses a Legend"; "The Minstrel Leads Off with a Paddle Song, and a Message Is Received from Abroad"; "They Land Upon the Island of Juam"; "A Book from the Chronicles of Mohi"; "Something More of the Prince"; "Advancing Deeper into the Vale, They Encounter Donjalolo"; "Time and Temples"; "A Pleasant Place for a Lounge"; "The House of the Afternoon"; "Babbalanja Solus"; "The Center of Many Circumferences"; "Donjalolo in the Bosom of His Family"; "Wherein Babbalanja Relates the Adventure of One Karkeke in the Land of Shades"; "How Donjalolo Sent Agents to the Surrounding Isles, with the Result"; "They Visit the Tributary Islets"; "Taji Sits Down to Dinner with Five and Twenty Kings, and a Royal Time They Have"; "After Dinner"; "Of Those Scamps the Plujii"; "Nora Bamma"; "In a Calm, Hautia's Heralds Approach"; "Braid Beard Rehearses the Origin of the Isle of Rogues"; "Rare Sport at Ohonoo"; "Of King Uhia and His Subjects"; "The God Keevi and the Precipice of Mondo"; "Babbalanja Steps in Between Mohi and Yoomy, and Yoomy Relates a Legend"; "Of That Jolly Old Lord Borabolla and That Jolly Island of His, Mondoldo; and of the Fishponds and the Hereafters of Fish"; "That Jolly Old Lord Borabolla Laughs on Both Sides of His Face"; "Samos a Surgeon"; "Faith and Knowledge"; "The Tale of a Traveler"; "'Marnee Ora, Ora Marnee'"; "The Pursuer Himself Is Pursued"; "The Iris"; "They Depart from Mondoldo"

Media proposes to travel with Taji, providing him with three royal canoes and three companions: MOHI (also called "Braid Beard"), the historian; BABBALANJA, the philosopher; and YOOMY, the poet. Jarl and Samoa—as well as a complement of retainers that includes Media's fool, VEE VEE—round out the company of searchers.

Their first stop is Valapee, the Isle of Yams, which is ruled by King Peepi, a boy of 10. Peepi's arbitrariness is said to result from his possession by the souls of his dead forebears, who take turns dominating him. For his own part, Peepi seems most interested in human teeth, begging that Media extract for his pleasure the dentals of one of the Odoan attendants. Media demurs, and the party sails on, discoursing as they go—Media having declared a relaxation in the usual courtly etiquette. Their discussion ends abruptly, however, when

they are overtaken by Hautia's heralds, once again bearing flowers for Taji. As Yoomy interprets their message, Babbalanja warns Taji to beware of the queen.

The company next comes to the island of Juam, ruled by the comely King DONJALOLO. Nicknamed "Fonoo," meaning "the girl", Donjalolo is effeminate and willful, living like a Turkish pasha in splendor with his harem. The party from Odo revel in his luxurious hospitality, but as Yillah is not be found in Juam, they move on.

Back afloat, Mohi entertains them with stories about the Plujii, invisible imps of the perverse. They pass Nora Bamma, the Isle of Nods, which is inhabited by dreamers, hypochondriacs, and somnambulists. Becalmed, they are once again accosted by Hautia's heralds, bearing enigmatic messages.

They land on Ohonoo, the Isle of Rogues, which like Australia was settled by those exiled from other lands. Ohonoo is ruled by UHIA, who embodies the imperialist ambitions of absolute monarchs in his desire to be king of all Mardi.

On their way to the next port of call, Mohi and Yoomy quarrel and are separated by Babbalanja, whom they then turn on. Babbalanja, they declare, is not a true philosopher, but, rather, a filcher from old BARDIANNA, an ancient Mardian authority. The ships then land on Mondoldo, which is ruled by old King BORABOLLA. The mood on Mondoldo is jolly—even after Samoa's unsuccessful attempt to perform brain surgery on an injured diver. The patient dies, but all agree that the procedure was marvelous.

The fun is spoiled when three of Aleema's sons arrive, seeking revenge. To Borabolla, Taji denies their allegations that he is a murderer, but he is nearly undone to discover that they know nothing of Yillah's disappearance. The reappearance of Hautia's messengers only deepens the gloom. Leaving Jarl and Samoa behind, Taji and Media and their court push off again in search of Yillah.

Chapters 103–141: "As They Sail"; "Wherein Babbalanja Broaches a Diabolical Theory and in His Own Person Proves It"; "Maramma"; "They Land"; "They Pass Through the Woods"; "Hivohitee MDCCCXLVIII"; "They Visit the Great Marae"; "They Discourse of the Gods of Mardi, and Braid Beard Tells of One Foni"; "They Visit the Lake of Yammo"; "They Meet the Pilgrims at the Temple of Oro"; "They Discourse of Alma"; "Mohi Tells of One Ravoo, and They Land to Visit Hevaneva, a Flourishing Artisan"; "A Nursery Tale of Babbalanja's"; "Landing to Visit Hivohitee the Pontiff, They Encounter an Extraordinary Old Hermit with Whom Yoomy Has a Confidential Interview, but Learns Little"; "Babbalanja Endeavors to Explain the Mystery"; "Taji Receives Tidings and Omens"; "Dreams"; "Media and Babbalanja Discourse"; "They Regale Themselves with Their Pipes"; "They Visit an Extraordinary Old Antiquary"; "They

Go Down into the Catacombs"; "Babbalanja Quotes from an Antique Pagan, and Earnestly Presses It upon the Company That What He Recites Is Not His, but Another's"; "They Visit a Wealthy Old Pauper"; "Yoomy Sings Some Odd Verses, and Babbalanja Quotes from the Old Authors Right and Left"; "What Manner of Men the Taparians Were"; "Their Adventures upon Landing at Pimminee"; "A, I, and O"; "A Reception Day at Pimminee"; "Babbalanja Falleth upon Pimminee Tooth and Nail"; "Babbalanja Regales the Company with Some Sandwiches"; "They Still Remain upon the Rock"; "Behind and Before"; "Babbalanja Discourses in the Dark"; "My Lord Media Summons Mohi to the Stand"; "Wherein Babbalanja and Yoomy Embrace"; "Of the Isle of Diranda"; "They Visit the Lords Piko and Hello"; "They Attend the Games"; "Taji Still Hunted and Beckoned"*

Just out of Maldondo, the royal canoes are almost swamped by the mad prince TRIBONNORA, who delights in such sport. They manage, finally, to land at Maramma, seat of the Mardian pontiff, HIVOHITEE. Although a blind man promises them that surely here they will find the lost Yillah, such is not to be—despite their pilgrimage to Ofo, the highest peak on the island.

As they sail on, they are met by a messenger from Borabolla, who informs them that Jarl is dead. The three arrows found in Jarl's heart, Taji is sure, were meant for him. As he dreams, Media and Babbalanja discourse—the latter explaining that he is sometimes possessed by an internal imp named Azzageddi. The others join in, as all indulge in smoking.

They land at Padulla, where they visit an old collector of relics named Oh Oh, who bears more than a slight resemblance to Melville's contemporary P. T. BARNUM, the impresario of oddities. As they sail on, Babbalanja discusses the relative merits of fame and goodness, and Yoomy sings of love. They land at Pimminee, an island that had been purchased by the clothes-conscious Tapparians, or Men of Tappa, who then set up a separatist community whose legal code dictates the minute particulars of dress. The most elevated citizen of Pimminee is a man named NIMNI, who is married to an old woman named OHIRO MOLDONA FIVONA, with whom he has had three daughters, named A, I, AND O, collectively referred to as the Polysyllables or the Vowels. At a reception the next day, the foreigners meet the remaining members of the Pimminee aristocracy, who bear similarly foolish names, such as the Lol Lols and the Dedidums. It almost goes without saying that the most pronounced characteristic of these people is their self-importance.

As they leave Pimminee, they are pursued by the avenging sons of Aleema, who shoot arrows bearing Taji's name. Taji confesses his crime to his companions, but claims that he only murdered the priest to save Yillah. Babbalanja notes that it is perhaps no wonder that Yillah is now lost, given the price of her rescue. Like a dark refrain, Hautia's heralds appear yet again.

They approach Diranda, an island divided between the lords HELLO and PIKO, who constantly engage in war games that destroy their subjects. On Diranda, Taji is wounded by one of three arrows, after which he is beckoned by three mysterious maidens. He resists their blandishments, as well as Yoomy's offer to distract him from his woes.

Chapters 142–156: "They Embark from Diranda"; "Wherein Babbalanja Discourses of Himself"; "Of the Sorcerers of the Isle of Minda"; "Chiefly of King Bello"; "Dominora and Vivenza"; "They Land at Dominora"; "Through Dominora They Wander After Yillah"; "They Behold King Bello's State Canoe"; "Wherein Babbalanja Bows Thrice"; "Babbalanja Philosophizes, and My Lord Media Passes Round the Calabashes"; "They Sail Round an Island Without Landing, and Talk Round a Subject Without Getting at It"; "They Draw Nigh to Porpheero, Where They Behold a Terrific Eruption"; "Wherein King Media Celebrates the Glories of Autumn; the Minstrel, the Promise of Spring"; "In Which Azzageddi Seems to Use Babbalanja for a Mouthpiece"; "The Charming Yoomy Sings"

As the group leaves Diranda, Babbalanja and Mohi deliver parables about man's follies. Thus far the voyage has touched on places and people who illustrate a broad range of these foibles. From now on, however, the royal canoes will land on islands that embody the foolishness of nations.

The first of these is Dominora (England), ruled by old BELLO the Hump, whose deformity is meant to signify the British national debt. The ambitious, imperialist Bello has designs on Porpheero (Europe) after having been defeated in a war with Vivenza (America). In his own country he successfully put an end to an internal revolt, just as the English monarchy put a stop to the Chartist rebellion (see CHARTISM).

Failing to find Yillah in Dominora, they sail on towards Kaleedoni (Scotland), "a country integrally united to Dominora." A strong wind sweeps them away from Kaleedoni toward Verdanna (Ireland), "a stepchild" of King Bello. They do not stop there, however, instead pointing their prows towards Porpheero, where they try to visit Franko (France), only to have it erupt like a volcano. Taji is consoled by Yoomy: surely Yillah would prefer to dwell in the new wilderness of Vivenza rather than in the old vineyards of Porpheero. Babbalanja, however, adds a note of caution.

Chapters 157–162: "They Draw Nigh unto Land"; "They Visit the Great Central Temple of Vivenza"; "Wherein Babbalanja Comments upon a Speech of Alanno"; "A Scene in the Land of Warwicks, or Kingmakers"; "They Harken unto a Voice from the Gods"; "They Visit the Extreme South of Vivenza"

Approaching Vivenza, they pass Kanneeda (Canada), to the north, which is rocked by violent gusts that result from its differences with Dominora. When they approach Vivenza the next day, they spy in a lagoon a temple made of canes containing a helmeted image of Vivenza's guiding spirit. An inscription over the temple reads: "In-this-re-publi-can-land-all-men-are-born-free-and-equal. " Below this, in smaller letters, is inscribed a codicil: "Except-the-tribe-of-Hamo"—a reference to the belief that Africans are descended from the tribe of Ham, Noah's third son, whom God cursed.

They are greeted by throngs of happy citizens of Vivenza, who insistently call their visitors' attention to their strength and virtue. Asked who is the king, they scoff. All are kings here, they say, and lead the foreigners to their Temple of Freedom. As the visitors approach, they see a man with a collar around his neck and red stripes on his back raising a striped flag. Other collared menials wait upon the chiefs, who lounge around in the amphitheater inside, some napping, some posturing, some chewing tobacco. This, a bystander informs the visitors, is the grand council, and at that moment Alanno of Hio Hio (Senator William ALLEN of Ohio) delivers a diatribe against King Bello and his threat to the northwest of Vivenza.

Failing to find Yillah in the north of Vivenza, the group departs for the south. The northerners had warned them that they would find much in the south repulsive, and indeed, their first view of the southern region is of hundreds of collared men toiling under the hot sun, overseen by men unlike them bearing whips. The travelers approach the foremost one of these overseers, NULLI, a "cadaverous, ghostlike man with a low ridge of forehead; hair, steel-gray; and wondrous eyes: bright, nimble as . . . twin corposant balls." This fellow, who is modeled along the lines of John C. CALHOUN, declares that the slaves have no souls and are content with their lot—and besides, their treatment is no worse than that meted out to slaves in the north of Vivenza. While acknowledging that there is some truth to this claim, the travelers nonetheless all condemn slavery, and Mohi the historian predicts that "These South savannas may yet prove battlefields."

Chapters 163–168: "They Converse of the Mollusca, Kings, Toadstools, and Other Matters"; "Wherein That Gallant Gentleman and Demigod King Media, Scepter in Hand, Throws Himself into the Breach"; "They Round the Stormy Cape of Capes"; "They Encounter Gold Hunters"; "They Seek Through the Isles of Palms and Pass the Isles of Myrrh"; "Concentric, Inward, with Mardi's Reef, They Leave Their Wake Around the World"

After sailing to the southwest of Vivenza, where they witness laborers shoveling earth they have brought from other islands onto their own land in order to enlarge it piecemeal, the group travels on down the eastern shore of Kolumbo (South America) and around the Cape of Capes (CAPE HORN). Sailing north along Kolumbo's western shore, they encounter gold

miners. They sail west across the "blue lagoon," encountering group upon group of isles, until they reach Orienda (the Orient), "Mardi's fatherland." Passing Hamora (Africa), they reach an inland sea; but not finding Yillah there, they turn to face the universe once more.

Chapters 169–189: "Sailing On"; "A Flight of Nightingales from Yommy's Mouth"; "They Visit One Doxodox"; "King Media Dreams"; "After a Long Interval, by Night They Are Becalmed"; "They Land at Hooloomooloo"; "A Book from the Ponderings of Old Bardianna"; "Babbalanja Starts to His Feet"; "At Last the Last Mention Is Made of Old Bardianna, and His Last Will and Testament Is Recited at Length"; "A Death Cloud Sweeps by Them as They Sail"; "They Visit the Palmy King Abrazza"; "Some Pleasant, Shady Talk in the Groves Between My Lords Abrazza and Media, Babbalanja, Mohi, and Yoomy"; "They Sup"; "They Embark"; "Babbalanja at the Full of the Moon"; "Morning"; "L'Ultima Sera"; "They Sail from Night to Day"; "They Land"; "Babbalanja Relates to Them a Vision"; "They Depart from Serenia"

They are, in fact, embarking on the metaphysical phase of their journey. Taji confesses that he has traveled without a map or compass, but maintains that had he employed such guides he never would have found Mardi. It is better, he declares, to keep up the quest and risk sinking than to follow merely familiar routes.

They come upon a wooded isle inhabited by a supposedly wise man named DOXODOX. Doxodox is every bit as prolix as Babbalanja, but the philosopher bests him, revealing him to be an imposter. They land next at Hooloomooloo, the Isle of Cripples, ruled by King YOKY, where the travelers are made to ask whether they or their hosts are monsters. On their way again, Babbalanja recites Bardianna's last will and testament, which bears a close resemblance to the celebrated will of millionaire financier John Jacob ASTOR.

They next visit ABRAZZA, king of Bonovona, a man filled with empathy who cannot bear to look on anything unpleasant. Babbalanja lectures him about the *Koztanza*, the ancient masterwork of the greatest poet of Mardi, LOMBARDO. Abrazza's protestaton—"the *Koztanza* lacks all cohesion; it is wild, unconnected, all episode"—may in fact be Melville's attempt to forestall critics of *Mardi* itself.

After a lavish supper with Abrazza, the party sets sail again. When all insist that they bypass the island of King Klanko, whose slaves toil endlessly in the mines, Babbalanja protests, "[M]ust we shun the unmitigated evil and only view the good, or evil so mixed therewith, the mixture's both?"

At their next stop they do encounter the good. Serenia is, as its name implies, a land as free from evil and folly as it is free of government. Here dwells Alma, a Christ-like figure whose teachings emphasize love and charity. Serenia is so compelling a place that Media is moved to renounce his old ways and his status as a demigod, and the philosopher Babbalanja even decides to stay on there. The others decide to press ahead, however, for even in this happy land, Yillah cannot be found. For a moment Taji contemplates giving up the quest and returning to Serenia, only to hear Yillah calling to him from the sea.

Chapters 190–195: "They Meet the Phantoms"; "They Draw Nigh to Flozella"; "They Land"; "They Enter the Bower of Hautia"; "Taji with Hautia"; "Mardi Behind, an Ocean Before"

At midnight, the canoes are approached by sirens bearing the iris flag of Hautia, as well as the message that through their queen, Taji may find his Yillah. At dawn the travelers arrive at Hautia's land, Flozella a Nina, which the narrator also calls the "Last Verse of the Song." Here, at last, Taji meets the evil seductress herself. For a time, he resists her, but at last surrenders, hoping that through her—by gaining knowledge of evil through familiarity with her—he will discover his lost love.

Taji enters Hautia's bower and drinks her wine. He is on the point of embracing her when she vanishes. Mohi tells a parable about a youth named Ozonna, who in vain sought the beautiful Ady among Hautia's handmaidens, all of whom look alike. All urge Taji to leave, but he remains, convinced that he must experience evil to find good.

When the others leave, Hautia draws near, urging Taji to come sin with her. Just as he is losing his will to resist, Taji begs Hautia to reveal the mystery of life and death. She responds by holding up Yillah's rose pearl. As Taji snatches it from her hand and calls for his lost love, Hautia mocks him, telling him that Yillah cannot answer because she "lies too deep . . . bubbles are bursting round her."

Taji rushes out, passing a lake where he sees a vision of Yillah beneath the surface. He plunges in after her, but her shadow slips away. When Mohi and Yoomy find him again, he is more dead than alive. When they question his spectral figure, he responds: "Taji lives no more. So dead, he has no ghost. I am his spirit's phantom's phantom."

Mohi and Yoomy place him in a canoe and flee from Flozella. They had returned, on Media's orders, to save Taji from Hautia and return with him to Serenia. But Taji insists on steering his own fate. As Mohi and Yoomy strike out for land, Taji points his craft toward the realm of shades, pursued by three specters bearing arrows: "And thus, pursuers and pursued flew on over an endless sea."

PUBLICATION HISTORY

There is some evidence that Melville intended, from a fairly early stage, for his third book to be a departure from its predecessors. What changed was the manner in which it was to differ. Initially, he was most concerned with writing something that would, above all else, make money, suggesting to John Murray on October 29, 1847, that the book not appear, as had *Typee* and *Omoo,* in the Home and Colonial Library series. Instead, he submitted, it could be published "in a different style, so as to command, say, double the price." What he may have had in mind at the time was a romance of the sort that was popular with the voracious female readers of the day—the kind of reader who would appreciate the references to the "LANGUAGE OF FLOWERS" that he wove into the narrative.

By the turn of the year, Melville would write Murray apologetically that his own South Seas material was threadbare. What he was writing, he said now, was a book that "clothes the whole subject in new attractions & combines in one cluster all that is romantic, whimsical & poetic in Polynusia (sic)." Nevertheless, he declared, he was producing a "continuous narrative." But by the spring of 1848, it was clear that even this last statement had to be modified. On March 25, Melville wrote Murray that he had experienced a "change in [his] determinations." Although his new book opened like a true narrative, "the romance & poetry of the thing thence grow continually, till it becomes a story wild enough I assure you & with a meaning too."

John Murray, who had never ceased asking Melville for documentary proof of his exploits in the South Seas, was not disposed to publish a romance. In January 1849, when Melville shipped him the proofs of his new book, together with a request for payment of 200 guineas, it was only too easy for Murray to refuse to meet Melville's terms.

Instead, British publisher Richard BENTLEY happily paid Melville the princely sum he sought and published *Mardi* on March 16, 1849. Publication in the United States by HARPER & BROTHERS, which paid Melville a $500 advance and promised him half the profits, occurred a month later. Reviewers on both sides of the Atlantic were for the most part disappointed and profoundly puzzled by the book. While many found the more realistic opening chapters of *Mardi* worthwhile—and worthy of the author of such entertaining adventures as *Typee* and *Omoo*—most found the allegorical voyage through Mardi unintelligible, affected, and tedious. The reviewer for *Blackwood's Edinburgh Magazine* even went so far as to call the book "trash."

Poor reviews translated into poor sales. In the United States the book sold fewer than 3,000 copies, and even though it was reprinted after a fire at Harper's destroyed most of the unsold copies in 1853, as late as 1887 Melville had realized only $741 in royalties. Sales of only about 1,000 copies of *Mardi* in England meant that Bentley lost money on the project and was unable to pay Melville anything after his advance.

The birth of Herman's and Lizzie's first child, Malcolm, on February 16, 1849, put Melville under more financial pressure than ever. After it was clear that *Mardi* would not be a success, he turned, almost immediately, to more remunerative fact-based fiction, publishing both *REDBURN* and *WHITE-JACKET* by February of the next year. These books were clearly a comedown for Melville, who afterwards dismissed them as "two *jobs,* which I have done for money."

Margoth   Character in *CLAREL*. A Jewish geologist who denies spiritual truth. To him the biblical sites are physical properties, the world a material place only. He appears at various sites in and around JERUSALEM, where CLAREL sees him. In general, Margoth represents those who use modern science to repudiate the religious quest.

"The Margraves's Birthnight" (1891)   Poem in *TIMO-LEON*. Numb peasants gather year after year in midwinter at their lord's castle to celebrate his birthday. But the celebration has lost all meaning, and there is "no host." Melville clearly was addressing what he saw as the debased nature of Christianity and, in particular, the meaningless celebration of Christ's birth. The age of miracles is gone, he laments:

> Ah, enough for toil and travail,
> If but for a night
> Into wine is turned the water,
> Black bread into white.

Marhar-Rarrar   Minor character in *OMOO*. Marhar-Rarrar is one of three lovely Polynesian damsels whom the narrator and LONG GHOST meet on the beach near Imeeo. Her name translates as "Wakeful, or Bright-eyed," and in company with FARNOWAR ("Day-born") and FARNOOPOO ("Night-born") she prefigures the three sister Polysyllables or Vowels, A, I, AND O, in *MARDI*.

Marharvai   Minor character in *OMOO*. This old gentleman of Imeeo hosts a feast for the narrator and LONG GHOST that amply illustrates Polynesian generosity and hospitality.

Marheyo   Minor character in *TYPEE*. Marheyo is TOMMO's host, the head of the household in which Melville's protagonist lives during his time in the Typee Valley. Marheyo appears to be senile and spends much of his time working on a shed without making any discernible progress, but Tommo senses in his host a certain sympathy for the Westerner's need to escape from paradise and return home.

Marianna   Character in "THE PIAZZA." Marianna is the poor, wan seamstress who inhabits the tumbledown shack which the narrator, seeing it sunlit and from afar, imagines to be inhabited by fairies.

Marnoo   Character in *TYPEE*. Melville describes this emissary from another tribe who ventures into the Typee Valley as a "Polynesian Apollo." Marnoo is a "taboo Kannaka," a type of sacred individual who is protected from the animosity that typically characterizes relationships among different Marquesan tribes (see MARQUESAS). Marnoo brings joy to the Typees, as well as news from outside the isolated Typee Valley. He is an appealing individual, and TOMMO describes his physical attributes at some length, evidently attracted to the handsome stranger. When Tommo discovers that Marnoo speaks some broken English, he attempts to enlist Marnoo's aid in getting back to Nukuheva. Marnoo, apparently fearing the displeasure of the Typee and eager to guard his own protected status, refuses, leaving hastily. It is his intervention, however, that finally expedites Tommo's escape. On a second visit to the Typee, Marnoo suggests to Tommo that he watch the way he leaves to return to his own village of Pueearka. Some night, he says, Tommo should follow him, and once he reaches Pueearka in his turn, Marnoo will take him to Nukuheva. Tommo's first escape attempt fails, but the second one succeeds, largely because Marnoo had intervened with KARAKOEE, the Oahu native who rescues Tommo and deposits him with the ship's captain who paid for the rescue.

Marquesas   Setting for much of the action in *TYPEE*. The Marquesas is a group of 12 rugged and mountainous islands situated about 740 miles northeast of Tahiti in the South Pacific. The islands are divided into two groups: the southern group (sometimes called the Mendana Islands) consists of five islands and was first discovered in 1595 by the Spanish explorer Alvaro de Mendana; the northern group (sometimes called the Washington Islands) was discovered in 1791 by the American navigator Captain Joseph Ingraham. The largest of the Marquesas, Nuku Hiva (or Nukuheva, in Melville's spelling), where Melville dwelt among the natives for four weeks in 1842, is among the second group. In 1813, Commodore David Porter claimed Nuku Hiva for the United States; Congress never ratified this claim, however, and in 1842 France took possession of the island. The French abandoned the settlement in 1859, then reclaimed it in 1870. In 1958, together with the other island groups that form what is known as French Polynesia (the Society Islands, the Tuamotu Archipelago, the Gambier Islands, and the Austral Islands), the Marquesas voted by plebiscite for more autonomy, becoming an overseas territory of France. In Melville's time in the Marquesas, the native population of all the islands numbered roughly 20,000, but imported Western diseases cut that number by two-thirds.

Mar Saba Eight miles west of the Dead Sea, the twin towers of Mar Saba rise 1,800 feet above a valley. In Melville's time, the towers were considered the most striking building in Palestine. The towers were part of a Greek church built in the fifth century to honor St. Saba. Attacked many times by various non-Christian peoples, Mar Saba became a symbol of Christian persistence. Mar Saba is the title for part two of CLAREL. The Pilgrims reach Mar Saba on the evening of their fourth day of travel. They see the dawn on their sixth day from Mar Saba's towers, and the next day they depart for BETHLEHEM.

"The Martyr. Indicative of the passion of the people on the 15th of April, 1865." (1866) Poem in BATTLE-PIECES. The assassination of Abraham LINCOLN confirmed Melville's belief that the end of the CIVIL WAR did not mean the end of internecine strife. In this poem, Melville warned: "Beware the People weeping / When they bare the iron hand."

Marvell, Andrew (1621–1678) English poet famed for his metaphysical verse and pastoral poetry. In BILLY BUDD, Captain VERE is said to get his nickname of Starry Vere from a line of Marvell's poetry.

Matthews, Cornelius (1817–1889) Writer, editor, and friend of Melville. Born in Port Chester, New York, he was admitted to the bar in 1837, but he turned almost immediately to a career in literature. As a New York writer and editor he became Melville's friend. In 1840, he founded *Arcturus,* a monthly periodical dedicated to touting American writers. In 1847, Matthews took up the editorship of YANKEE DOODLE, a weekly, called the "American *Punch*" because it featured amusing articles similar to those in the British magazine *Punch.* Matthews was also the author of *Behemoth: A Legend of the Mound-Builders* (1839) and *The Career of Pupper Hopkins* (1841–42), serialized in *Arcturus.* Along with Melville and other prominent writers, he signed a petition defending the right of the English actor William Macready to perform in *Macbeth* in New York while the American actor Edwin Forrest was appearing in an American production in the same city. Forrest's ardent nationalist supporters provoked the ASTOR PLACE RIOTS. Melville later invited Matthews to spend a week at MELVILL HOUSE.

Max the Dutchman ("Red Max") Minor character in *REDBURN.* Although Max has fiery red hair and a temper to match, REDBURN finds his disposition to be better than other members of the *Highlander's* crew. Perhaps his equanimity is due in part to the fact that he has two decent, devoted wives, one in NEW YORK CITY and one in LIVERPOOL.

May-Day Minor character in *WHITE-JACKET.* May-Day is a large black man who serves as an assistant to the ship's cook. When Captain CLARET grows bored on the voyage homeward, he sadistically pits May-Day against the other cook's assistant, a much slighter man called ROSE-WATER, in a head-butting contest. But when the dark skinned May-Day and the mulatto Rose-Water get into a genuine fight inspired by racial one-upmanship, the captain has them flogged for breaching navy discipline.

Mayhew Minor character in *MOBY-DICK.* He is captain of the *JEROBOAM* out of Nantucket.

"The Medallion in Villa Albina & C" (1924) Poem. One of more than 40 poems that Melville left uncollected or unpublished when he died, "The Medallion" compares the "inmost self" revealed by a face in repose to the truths revealed by serious verse written with "candor grave."

Media Character in *MARDI.* Media is king of the isle of Odo, where he is worshipped as a demigod and exercises absolute control. He provides safe harbor for TAJI and YILLAH. After Yillah disappears, Media accompanies Taji on his quest for his lost love. When Taji and his party reach the island of Serenia, however, Media is so taken with the local religion, propounded by a Christlike teacher, that he converts, throwing off his claim to be a demigod and vowing to rule Odo from that time forward with love and charity.

"A Meditation: Attributed to a Northerner after attending the last of two funerals from the same homestead— those of a National and a Confederate officer (brothers), his kinsmen, who had died from the effects of wounds received in the closing battles." (1866) Poem in BATTLE-PIECES. In this, the last poem in Melville's CIVIL WAR collection—and the conclusion of the "Verses Inscriptive and Memorial" section— Melville recollects various incidents that affirmed the brotherhood of Northern and Southern soldiers during the war. The most outstanding example of such moments of reconciliation came "When Vicksburg fell, and the moody files marched out, / Silent the victors stood, scorning to raise a shout." Melville reiterates that in order for peace to prevail, such restraint is called for now.

Mehevi Character in *TYPEE.* Mehevi is the principle chieftain of the Typee tribe among whom TOMMO lives. Melville describes him in grand terms, devoting a great deal of time to detailing his dress and mannerisms. It is Mehevi who controls Tommo's destiny, and the chief makes it clear from the outset that he values his captive and will not permit him to leave.

Melvill, Allan (1782–1832)   Herman Melville's father. Allan Melvill (his wife added the final "e" to the family name after his death) was born in Boston, Massachusetts, one of 11 children of Thomas MELVILL and Priscilla Scollay MELVILL. He was named for his paternal grandfather, a Boston merchant. The Melvill family had been in Boston for many generations, and Allan could trace his lineage back to Scottish warriors of the 13th century. Allan had a genteel education and an aristocratic bearing. After completing the Grand Tour of Europe, he returned to Boston and entered a real estate partnership with his school friend, Lemuel SHAW. The venture did not succeed. After Allan married Maria GANSEVOORT in 1814, the couple moved first to ALBANY, NEW YORK, then to back to Boston, and finally to NEW YORK CITY, where Allan set himself up as an importer of luxury goods.

As Allan and Maria's family grew to eventually include eight children, so Allan's business increased—but only because Allan was borrowing heavily, first from his father and then from his brother-in-law, Peter GANSEVOORT. Finally, in the economic depression of 1830, Allan was forced to liquidate his business and send his family back to Albany. Struggling to establish himself there as retailer, in December 1831 Allan took an ill-fated trip to New York City to solicit customers. On his return, Allan was forced to walk a long distance in extreme cold and arrived home deathly ill. Too restless and pressed for money to allow himself to recuperate properly, he kept working, and early in January he became delirious with fever. He died on January 28, still in the grip of a derangement that would haunt his son Herman for the rest of his life.

After Allan Melvill's death, a number of people approached his family seeking payment. Among these were a Boston milliner named Martha Bent and her daughter, Anne Middleton Bent. The pair apparently made some unspecified claim on Allan Melvill's estate which subsequently led some Melville scholars to speculate (using the plot of *PIERRE* as evidence) that Anne was the product of an illicit liaison between Martha Bent and Alan Melvill. No proof, however, has emerged to substantiate this theory.

Melvill, Anne Marie Priscilla (1810–1858)   Herman Melville's cousin. Anne Marie Priscilla was the daughter of Herman Melville's father's eldest brother, Thomas MELVILL, Jr., and Thomas's first wife, Françoise Lamé-Fleury MELVILL. When Herman was a child, Priscilla, as she was called, lived with his family in PITTSFIELD, MASSACHUSETTS, helping his mother care for her many children. Much later, in the fall of 1853, Priscilla again came to live with Herman and his family at ARROWHEAD after quitting her teaching job. While there, the unmarried Priscilla set herself up as a seamstress in Pittsfield,

where she moved the following spring. She died there from tuberculosis four years later.

Melvill, Françoise Raymonde Eulogie Marie des Douleurs Lamé-Fleury (1781–1814)   Herman Melville's aunt. Françoise Lamé-Fleury was the first wife of Herman's father's oldest brother, Thomas MELVILL, Jr., who married her in Paris in 1802. She was the adopted niece of Madame Récamier, hostess of a renowned Parisian literary salon. Thomas's elopement with Françoise scandalized his family, but when he returned, bankrupt, to PITTSFIELD, MASSACHUSETTS, with her and four of their children in 1811, his father lent him money. Thomas and Françoise had two more children together, the last of whom died, together with his mother and a six-year-old brother, in 1814.

Melvill, Maria Gansevoort   *See* MELVILLE, MARIA GANSEVOORT.

Melvill, Mary Ann Augusta Hobart (1796–1884)   Herman Melville's aunt. In 1815, a year after his first wife's death, Thomas MELVILL, Jr., Allan MELVILL's oldest brother, married Mary Ann Hobart, a widow. The couple farmed in PITTSFIELD, MASSACHUSETTS, and raised 12 children, four from Thomas's first marriage and eight whom they had together. Their nephew Herman visited the farm during the summers of 1837 and 1838 to help out with the chores while his uncle sought greener pastures in Galena, Illinois. Mary later joined her husband in Galena, where she was widowed in 1845. Later, she moved back to Pittsfield, where she turned the family homestead, MELVILL HOUSE, into an inn. It was she who, in July 1850, gave Herman Melville a copy of Nathaniel HAWTHORNE's *Mosses from an Old Manse*, which Melville would explore his seminal essay, "HAWTHORNE AND HIS MOSSES."

Melvill, Priscilla (1784–1862)   Herman Melville's aunt. Priscilla was the younger of Allan MELVILL's two unmarried sisters. When Herman was a toddler, Priscilla lived with his family in NEW YORK CITY, where she suffered an attack of rheumatic fever in 1824. Upon her death in Boston in 1862, she willed the not inconsiderable sum of $900 to her nephew, the writer.

Melvill, Robert (1817–1881)   Herman Melville's cousin. Robert was the first child of Allan MELVILL's brother Thomas and his second wife, Mary. On September 17, 1838, Robert married Susan Bates. In the late 1830s, he joined his father in Galena, Illinois, where Herman visited them in 1840. In 1845, Robert inherited MELVILL HOUSE in PITTSFIELD, MASSACHUSETTS, from his father, and he and Susan and his mother, Mary, turned the family homestead into an inn, which Herman and his family visited in the summer of 1850. That July, Herman accompanied Robert, who was then chairman of the Viewing Committee of the Berkshire County Agricultural Society, on an inspection tour, and a few months later, a report on the tour—apparently ghostwritten by Herman—was published under Robert's name. That September, Herman purchased a farm adjoining the old Melvill property and named it ARROWHEAD.

Robert would return to Galena, where he worked as a steamboat commander, among other jobs. At some point he acquired a boat of his own, which he enlisted in the civilian auxiliary fleet of the Army of the Republic during the CIVIL WAR. In 1863, he participated in a successful naval raid on Vicksburg, Mississippi, led by Admiral David Porter and a Galena native, General Ulysses S. Grant.

Melvill, Thomas (1751–1832) Herman Melville's paternal grandfather. Thomas Melvill was a Boston merchant and a Revolutionary War hero who participated in the Boston Tea Party and distinguished himself at BUNKER HILL. Major Melvill was called back into service during the War of 1812, after which he was given a "permanent" position in the Boston Custom House, which he was forced to give up during the presidency of Andrew Jackson, who preferred to make his own appointment.

In 1774, he married Priscilla Scollay, with whom he had 11 children. His eldest sons, Thomas and Allan, relied heavily on their father for financial assistance throughout their adult lives (see Thomas MELVILL, Jr., and Allan MELVILL). In 1816, Major Melvill purchased a 246-acre property in PITTSFIELD, MASSACHUSETTS, that he leased to Thomas in hopes that it would support his oldest son. But Allan owed his father so much money that after Allan died in January 1832, his widow, Maria, went to Boston to plead with the major not to saddle Allan's oldest son, Gansevoort, with his father's debts. Although the Major assured Maria that he would not do so, he himself died the following September, leaving a will that deducted Allan's loans from the estate.

Melvill, Thomas, Jr. (1776–1845) Herman Melville's uncle. Thomas Jr. was the firstborn son of Thomas and Priscilla MELVILL. As a young man, he pursued a career in international banking in England, Spain, and France, where he married his first wife, Françoise Lamé-Fleury, with whom he had six children. In 1811, however, he returned bankrupt to the United States, where he settled in PITTSFIELD, MASSACHUSETTS. He served in the War of 1812 as an officer. In 1814, he lost his wife and baby and a six-year-old son to illness. One year later, Thomas married Mary Ann Hobart, with whom he had eight children.

During the next phase of his life, Thomas worked as a gentleman farmer, a line of work that proved so unre-

munerative that on more than one occasion he was imprisoned for debt, despite his status as a prominent citizen of Berkshire County. In 1837 he moved to Galena, Illinois, where he worked in—and stole from—a store. Living in what was then considered the uncivilized West, Thomas Melvill never reconciled himself to his surroundings and continued to affect French manners and fashions and to go by the title of "Major Melvill."

Melville Herman Melville's altered family name. Melville's mother added a final "e" to the family name after the death of her husband, Allan MELVILL, in 1832. This may have been an attempt to give her first-born son, Gansevoort, a fresh start in the business world by thus distancing him from the debt and other improprieties associated with his father's business dealings.

Melville, Allan, Jr. (1823–1872) Herman Melville's brother. Allan was the fifth child of Allan MELVILL and Maria Gansevoort MELVILLE. After his father's death in 1835, Allan was permitted to remain in school for a while, but when he was 15 he was put to work in his uncle Peter GANSEVOORT's law office in ALBANY, NEW YORK. Allan fought with his uncle and lost his job, but he found work in other law offices and read law himself in NEW YORK CITY, eventually setting up his own law office there.

In 1847, Allan married Sophia Elizabeth Thurston, a wealthy socialite with whom he would have five daughters. For a time Allan and Sophia shared a household in Manhattan with his brother Herman and Herman's wife, Lizzie, as well as the Melville brothers' mother and four sisters. In 1850, however, Allan moved his family to the Melvill hometown of PITTSFIELD, MASSACHUSETTS.

Allan and Herman remained close, visiting each other during the period both lived in the Berkshires. In 1853 and again in 1861, Allan, a successful lawyer and politician associated with TAMMANY HALL, tried but failed to secure a consular appointment for Herman. Allan also took a lively interest in his brother's literary career, agenting the sale of *TYPEE* to HARPER & BROTHERS in 1846 and helping to negotiate the contract for *MARDI*—which is dedicated to him—in 1848. When Herman left on a voyage in 1856, he left Allan in charge of overseeing the printing of *The CONFIDENCE MAN*. When Herman was once again planning a sea voyage in 1860, he left a manuscript—this time a collection of poems—with his brother. Allan did not meet with success, as this first effort to publish a book of Herman Melville's poetry was rejected by Charles Scribner.

Allan's wife died in October 1858, and the following April he remarried. His new wife was Jane Louisa Dempsey, called "Jennie"—a woman the rest of the Melville clan considered a spoiled and selfish spend-

Allan Melvill, Melville's father. Herman Melville's mother added a final "e" to the family name after her husband's death. (Library of Congress)

thrift. In 1863, when she and Allan were considering buying a country place, Allan purchased ARROWHEAD from Herman and Lizzie for three-quarters of its assessed value of $4,000, while Herman and Lizzie purchased Allan and Jennie's house in New York City for $7,750. Allan and Jennie continued to maintain a Manhattan residence while spending summers at Arrowhead, where they often hosted Herman and his family.

In 1866, Herman, accompanied by Allan, went to visit their cousin Henry GANSEVOORT at his military encampment in Vienna, Virginia, during the CIVIL WAR, an experience that gave Herman material for some of the poems in his collection BATTLE-PIECES.

After combating tuberculosis for a number of years, Allan succumbed to the disease in February 1872.

Melville, Augusta ("Gus") (1821–1876) Herman Melville's sister. Augusta was the fourth child of Allan MELVILL and Maria Gansevoort MELVILLE. Gus, as she was called, never married and was exceedingly attached to her brother Herman. Her life revolved around the Dutch Reformed Church, her women friends, and her brother's literary career. As soon as Herman returned

from the South Seas and started work on his first novel, TYPEE, Gus began serving as his copyist and proofreader. While at times Herman's sister Helen and his wife, Lizzie, would help with the tasks of making fair copies of his manuscripts and proofreading them, it was Augusta who performed these jobs most often for her brother, sometimes also seeing to his correspondence. Augusta lived off and on with Herman and Lizzie and helped care for their children. She had a decided literary bent, and was delighted to make the acquaintance of her brother's friend Nathaniel HAWTHORNE at ARROWHEAD. When Augusta died on April 7, 1876, of an internal hemorrhage, Herman was by her side.

Melville, Catherine Gansevoort ("Kate")   *See* HOADLEY, CATHERINE GANSEVOORT MELVILLE.

Melville, Elizabeth ("Bessie," "Bess") (1853–1908) Herman and Elizabeth ("Lizzie") Knapp Shaw MELVILLE's older daughter and third child. Named for her mother but called Bessie or Bess, she also shared

Augusta Melville, Herman Melville's sister, made copies of his manuscripts and preserved family correspondence. (Berkshire Athenaeum)

Lizzie's hay fever, which they referred to as "rose colds." In an effort to alleviate this malady, she and her mother often spent summers away from NEW YORK CITY. But little could be done about the crippling rheumatoid arthritis that marred Bessie's life. By the time she was 20, Bessie's disease had progressed so far that she could no longer draw or write. By the time she was 26 she needed constant care, which was provided by her mother. Bessie never married, and lived with her parents until both had died. After her mother's death, she hoarded her father's manuscripts in a tin breadbox, which she willed to her sister, Frances Melville THOMAS. Frances's daughter, Eleanor Metcalf, ultimately used the papers for scholarly research, and donated them to Harvard University in 1942.

Melville, Elizabeth Knapp Shaw ("Lizzie") (1822–1906) Herman Melville's wife. Elizabeth Knapp Shaw was the daughter of Judge Lemuel SHAW and his first wife, Elizabeth, who died after giving birth to their daughter. Initially cared for by her paternal grandmother, Lizzie gained a second mother in 1827 when Judge Shaw married Hope Savage (see Hope Savage SHAW). Lemuel Shaw had long been a friend of the Melville family, and his daughter was a friend of Helen Melville (see Helen Maria Melville GRIGGS) before becoming acquainted with her brother, Herman. In 1846, Herman dedicated his first novel, *TYPEE,* "[a]ffectionately" to Judge Shaw. After publishing the sequel, *OMOO,* the next year, Herman proposed to Lizzie. They were married on August 4, 1847.

The couple first set up housekeeping in NEW YORK CITY with Herman's extended family in a house that had been partially financed by Lizzie's father. Eventually they moved to PITTSFIELD, MASSACHUSETTS, where—again with Judge Shaw's help, and with a lien on Lizzie's inheritance—they purchased ARROWHEAD. Throughout their married life, Lizzie had more money than her husband, and their homes usually were held in her name. Nonetheless, Lizzie, who had once been a spirited young woman, evolved into a rather subservient wife whose world revolved around her demanding husband and their four children.

As Herman's literary career foundered, he grew depressed and drank heavily. He also, apparently, became abusive—perhaps physically—toward his wife. In the spring of 1867, Lizzie considered leaving Herman, but any plans she might have had were scotched that September when their eldest son, Malcolm (see Malcolm MELVILLE), committed suicide. This tragedy did not immediately bridge the gap between Herman and Lizzie; but beginning with the marriage of their youngest child, Frances, in 1880, and the birth two years later of their first grandchild, the couple began to draw back together. The death of their younger son, Stanwix (see Stanwix MELVILLE), in 1886, nearly proved Lizzie's

This portrait of Elizabeth Shaw Melville, Melville's wife, dates from the mid-1840s. (Berkshire Athenaeum)

undoing, while Herman reacted stoically to the event. In the late 1880s, Lizzie and Herman recovered the equanimity, and even some of the romance, that had characterized the early years of their marriage. By then Lizzie had inherited a considerable sum of money, an event that enabled her husband to retire from his job at the CUSTOM-HOUSE and write and privately publish poetry. In 1891, Herman planned to dedicate *WEEDS AND WILDINGS CHIEFLY: WITH A ROSE OR TWO* to his wife, for it made use of the same "LANGUAGE OF FLOWERS" that had been so important to their courtship. He died, however, before the book made its way into print.

After her husband's death, Lizzie Melville sold their home on 26th Street in Manhattan and moved with her daughter Bessie to an apartment on 18th Street, where Lizzie died in 1908.

Melville, Frances ("Fanny") *See* THOMAS, FRANCES MELVILLE.

Melville, Frances Priscilla ("Fanny") (1827–1885) Herman Melville's youngest sister. Like her sister

Augusta (see Augusta MELVILLE), Fanny Melville never married, and for a time both women formed part of the extended Melville household lodged with Allan and Herman Melville and their wives in NEW YORK CITY. When her aunt Catherine GANSEVOORT died in 1855, Fanny and her mother, Maria, stayed with Catherine's husband, Herman, in GANSEVOORT, NEW YORK, to comfort and care for the old man. When Herman Gansevoort himself passed away in 1862, Fanny stayed on in his home.

Fanny died in her sister Helen's home in Brookline, Massachusetts, in 1885, leaving her brother Herman a bequest of $3,000, a sum that allowed him to take a cruise to Bermuda in 1888, as well as to subsidize the private publication of several volumes of his poetry.

Melville, Gansevoort (1815–1846) Herman Melville's older brother. Gansevoort was his parents' treasured firstborn. They christened him with a name that would be sure to convey his aristocratic lineage on both sides of the family, and they clearly had high expectations for him. Throughout his brief life, Gansevoort was always his mother's favorite. As a child, he had his father's patrician good looks and a ready wit that contrasted favorably with Herman's more stolid appearance and retiring nature. Gansevoort was given a fine early education, as his mother was preparing him for Harvard.

In 1832, however, Allan MELVILL died bankrupt and insane, and Gansevoort was thrust into the role of head of the household. Two months after his father's death, Gansevoort was obliged to withdraw from Albany Academy and take over his father's fur and cap business. He made a go of it for several years, but with the economic panic of 1837, the venture ended in bankruptcy. The remainder of his mother's inherited wealth went toward paying off Gansevoort's creditors.

It was then determined that Gansevoort should read law in NEW YORK CITY. Like his brother Allan MELVILLE, Gansevoort became a lawyer and politician—although, unlike Allan, he never became caught up in TAMMANY HALL politics. In 1845, Gansevoort was appointed secretary of the American legation in London, England, where he took the opportunity of showing the manuscript of Herman's first novel to the publisher John MURRAY. When Murray accepted TYPEE conditionally, Gansevoort also had a hand in making some of the revisions the publisher requested, and acted as proofreader. In 1846, Gansevoort succeeded in gaining an advocate for *Typee* in America when he showed proof sheets of the novel to Washington IRVING, who was visiting London in a diplomatic role. Irving, in turn, recommended the book to Wiley & Putnam, which would publish *Typee* in the United States.

After the first English reviews of *Typee* appeared, questioning the book's veracity, Gansevoort conferred

Gansevoort Melville, Melville's older brother. (Berkshire Athenaeum)

with John Murray about making more revisions, but he never had the chance to pursue them. Gansevoort's health had always been precarious, and the damp climate of London only exacerbated his chronic pulmonary problems. After writing Herman on April 3, 1846, that he feared he was "breaking up," Gansevoort asked to be relieved of his duties at the embassy. His superiors were only too happy to receive his resignation, as Gansevoort had, on more than one occasion, disgraced himself in public. In retrospect, it appears that his erratic behavior may have stemmed from a brain disorder, for when he died on May 12, 1846, he exhibited signs of derangement indicative of tubercular meningitis.

Melville, Helen Maria *See* GRIGGS, HELEN MARIA MELVILLE.

Melville, Herman (1819–1891) Herman Melville was born in NEW YORK CITY on August 1, 1819, the third child and second son of Allan MELVILL and his wife, Maria Gansevoort MELVILLE. (Maria added a final "e" to the family name after her husband's death.) At the

time, Allan Melvill, the son of an old Boston family, was a fairly prosperous importer of luxury items, and the Melvills lived well. In 1830, however, Allan's business collapsed, and the family was obliged to move to ALBANY, NEW YORK, to seek sanctuary among Maria's relatives. Allan made another attempt at business in Albany, but in 1832 he died, bankrupt and insane. Herman, whom his parents considered "innocent" and "shy," was 12 years old but no longer a child.

Herman had been withdrawn from formal schooling at the Albany Academy the year before; rather than returning to school, he was now obliged to seek employment. After working as a bank clerk and a farmhand, however, he enrolled in the Albany Classical School in order to prepare for a business career. Once there, the young man who had been a nearly inarticulate "slow" child discovered that he had a gift for writing, and resolved to put it to some use by becoming a teacher. After returning to the Albany Academy for six months to obtain the requisite knowledge of Latin, Herman obtained a teaching position in PITTSFIELD, MASSACHUSETTS. He found teaching in a country school unappealing, and in 1838 he enrolled in the Lansingburgh Academy, located only a few blocks from the Melvilles' new home in LANSINGBURGH, NEW YORK. That November he was certified as a surveyor and engineer.

Failing to find paid employment, Melville wrote short pieces for the local newspapers while courting some of the town's young ladies and pining for adventure. In June 1839, he finally commenced his seafaring adventures by signing on as a cabin boy on the *St. Lawrence*, a merchant ship bound for LIVERPOOL, England. He would later transform the experiences of this trip into fiction in *REDBURN*.

Returning to Lansingburgh three months later, Melville found his mother and sisters in serious financial trouble. Desperate for extra income, Melville once again took a teaching job, only to lose it a few months later when the Greenbush & Schodack Academy declared bankruptcy. After a stint of substitute teaching, Melville decided to look elsewhere for work and accompanied his old friend Eli FLY on a trip west.

The American West proved not to be the land of opportunity, so Melville went back east. Failing to find a job in New York City, he determined to go back to sea, and on January 3, 1841, he shipped aboard the whaler *ACUSHNET*.

Melville had signed up for the customary four-year tour, but he grew restless under the harsh conditions imposed by Captain Valentine Pease. When the *Acushnet* made one of its few stops in the port of Nuku Hiva in the MARQUESAS in June 1842, Melville, accompanied by his shipmate Richard Tobias GREENE, jumped ship. The two escaped into the jungle, where they were taken up by members of the Taipi tribe. Tobias Greene

escaped almost immediately, but Melville lived among the Marquesan natives for four weeks before finding his way back to Nuku Hiva, where he went abroad an Australian whaler named the *LUCY-ANN*.

Life aboard the *Lucy-Ann* proved to be even harder than it had been on the *Acushnet*. While the Australian ship was anchored at Papeetee, Tahiti's largest port, the crew rioted. The next day, most of the men, including Melville, were arrested and handed over to the British authorities, who locked them up in a makeshift outdoor jail. Melville and his friend John Troy escaped. After touring the SOCIETY ISLANDS briefly, they signed up on yet another whaler, the *CHARLES & HENRY*.

Melville left the ship on May 2, 1843, in Maui, HAWAII. He traveled to Honolulu, where he went to work as a bookkeeper and angered the American colonial authorities by publicly supporting a British takeover of the islands. In bad odor, he left Hawaii on August 17 and joined the crew of the U.S.S. *UNITED STATES* as an ordinary seaman, retaining the option to quit the navy when the ship returned to port. When the *United States* docked in Boston 14 months later, Melville was discharged, full of dark memories that would later make their way into *WHITE-JACKET*.

Melville then returned to Lansingburgh, where his tales of the South Pacific made him a minor celebrity. Friends and family encouraged him to write about his experiences, and he did, transforming his time among the "cannibals" of the Marquesas into *TYPEE* and his Tahitian idyll into its sequel, *OMOO*. With the help of his brother Gansevoort, *Typee* was published in 1846, and *Omoo* appeared the following year. Herman Melville had finally found his calling.

Around this same time, Melville began courting Elizabeth Shaw, a family friend who lived in Boston (see Elizabeth Knapp Shaw MELVILLE). Flushed with his literary success, Herman married Lizzie on August 4, 1847, and the couple set up housekeeping with his family, first in Lansingburgh, and then in New York City. Herman and Lizzie would eventually have four children together: Malcolm, Stanwix, Elizabeth, and Frances. Although Elizabeth, called Bessie, suffered from rheumatoid arthritis, she and Frances outlived their parents.

Both of the boys died young. Malcolm committed suicide—perhaps in part because of his father's cruelty toward him—in 1867, a time when Herman and Lizzie were estranged. Worn out by years of intensive literary endeavor and bitterly disappointed by the reception of his works, in his 40s Melville suffered from depression and sought solace in drink.

When the veracity of his first two novels was widely questioned, Melville responded with *MARDI*, a highly ambitious allegorical romance in which he turned his exposure to the exotica of Polynesia into material for philosophical speculation. While *Mardi*, which appeared in 1849, proved to be a failure, the more conventional *Redburn,* published the same year, was received more warmly. The popularity of the latter earned Melville an advance on his next book, *White-Jacket,* large enough to permit him to travel to Europe, where he presented his latest novel to his English publishers. In 1850, *White-Jacket* was published. Melville bought a farm he named ARROWHEAD near Pittsfield, and wrote "HAWTHORNE AND HIS MOSSES," an important review of his friend Nathaniel HAWTHORNE's recently published collection of tales and sketches, *Mosses from an Old Manse.*

Melville's friendship with Hawthorne would prove to be a tortured one, but the conversations between the two about literature that took place over the next two years were seminal for Melville and his masterpiece, *MOBY-DICK.* Like *Mardi, Moby-Dick* (1851) failed to find an audience, so Melville, attempting still to live by his wits, wrote *PIERRE,* a metaphysical novel that made use of then-popular Gothic conventions.

When *Pierre* (1852) likewise failed in the marketplace, Melville tried unsuccessfully to obtain a consular appointment. Out of financial desperation he turned to writing shorter pieces that could be serialized in magazines and republished later in bound volumes. This period saw the publication of Melville's historical romance, *ISRAEL POTTER* (1855), and short stories such as "BARTLEBY THE SCRIVENER," "THE BELL-TOWER," "BENITO CERENO," "THE ENCANTADAS," and "THE LIGHTING-ROD MAN," which he later collected in the *The PIAZZA TALES* (1856), as well as other pieces that were not republished during his lifetime. In 1856–57 he once again went abroad, this time to Glasgow, Liverpool, the Holy Land, Greece, and Italy. The critical and popular failure of his satirical novel, *The CONFIDENCE MAN* (1857), essentially ended Melville's career as a professional writer.

During Melville's lifetime, the eight significant novels he had produced between 1846 and 1857 sold only 35,000 copies altogether and earned him a mere $10,400. This was hardly enough money to support a family. After spending the next three years attempting—but failing—to make a living on the lecture circuit, Melville again sought solace in travel, in 1860 sailing with his brother Thomas to San Francisco. Once again he tried to obtain a consular appointment, but failed. In 1863, Herman and Lizzie and their children moved from Arrowhead to New York City, where Melville worked on a series of poems about the CIVIL WAR that would appear in 1866 as *BATTLE-PIECES.*

That same year, Melville became a civil servant, taking a job as a customs inspector, a position he would hold for the next 19 years. This final acknowledgement of the end of his dreams of literary achievement coincided with an increase in drinking and despair that drove Lizzie to thoughts of divorcing her husband in the spring of 1867 and—perhaps—to their son Malcolm's suicide that September.

By this point Melville devoted his writing talents almost exclusively to poetry, publishing CLAREL, his long narrative poem set in the Holy Land, in 1876, and privately printing his collection of sea poetry, JOHN MARR, in 1888, and another collection of poetry, TIMOLEON, in 1891. Melville seemed reconciled to his obscurity (many of his early readers did not know he was still alive) as well as to his marriage. When he died in his own bed on September 28, 1891, he left behind an unpublished collection of love poems, WEEDS AND WILDINGS CHIEFLY, which was dedicated to Lizzie.

Melville left behind one other important unpublished work, BILLY BUDD, SAILOR, a novella he had been working on since 1888. Lizzie put the incomplete manuscript in a tin breadbox for safekeeping, where it stayed until 1924, when Melville's granddaughters, Eleanor Metcalf and Frances Osborne, saw to its publication. The appearance of this ambiguous and richly allusive tale of good and evil sparked a revival of interest in Melville that elevated him to the highest rung of the American literary pantheon.

Melville, Jane Louisa Dempsey ("Jennie," "Madam Jane") (d. 1890) Herman Melville's sister-in-law. Jennie was the second wife of Allan MELVILLE, Melville's younger brother. Although the Melville clan disapproved of Allan remarrying only a year and a half after the death of his first wife, Sophia Elizabeth Thurston MELVILLE, and although they also disapproved of the self-centered "Madam Jane," the couple was married in April 1860. In 1863, Allan and Jennie purchased the ARROWHEAD farm in the Berkshires from Herman and his wife, Lizzie, while Herman and Lizzie bought Allan and Jennie's house in NEW YORK CITY. The couples often hosted one another, in the country and in the city, but Lizzie sometimes grew irritated with "Madam Jane's" highhandedness. Jennie Melville was indeed a headstrong woman. When Herman and Allan proposed to visit their cousin Henry GANSEVOORT's military encampment in 1864, Jennie insisted on coming, too—and bringing Allan's daughter, Milie, along. Ultimately the women did not get beyond Washington, D.C.—either because the Melville brothers were able to convince them it was unwise for them to visit an army camp after a recent military engagement, or because the War Department would not grant them passes.

Melville, Malcolm ("Barny," "Mackie," "Mackey") (1849–1867) Herman Melville's older son. Lizzie Melville picked the name Malcolm for her firstborn, but her husband's family quickly appropriated it. Herman's sister Augusta even claimed that the name came from "Grandma Melville's side of the house—the Scollay family." Malcolm was born on February 16, 1849, in the

Melville and his wife had four children— Stanwix, Frances, Malcolm, and Elizabeth. Only Frances went on to marry and have children. (Berkshire Athenaeum)

Boston home of his maternal grandfather. As a child he was a good student and showed a flair for theatrics, but at 17 he took a job as a clerk at an insurance company. At 18 he joined the New York State National Guard and was issued the pistol that he would use to commit suicide. At the time, Malcolm was earning his own money but still living at home, where he frequently came into conflict with his parents. His father, in particular, treated him harshly, locking him out of the house when he returned home after an 11 P.M. curfew. On the night of September 10, 1867, Malcolm stayed out until 3 A.M., but when he got home, his mother was waiting up for him. After kissing her goodnight, he went upstairs to bed. When he did not come down the next day, Lizzie decided to wait for Herman to come home and deal with their son. Finding Malcolm's door locked, Herman broke the door down, only to find his son lying in bed with his gun in his hand and a bullet in his brain. Malcolm's suicide remains largely a mystery, although its circumstances indicate a desire to wound his parents. Herman and Lizzie Melville's reactions to his death were muted, perhaps because of the strain in their marriage at the time.

Melville, Maria Gansevoort (1791–1872)   Herman Melville's mother. Maria was the last of six children— and the only daughter—born to Peter GANSEVOORT, a hero of the Revolutionary War, and Catherine Van Schaick GANSEVOORT. The Gansevoorts were numbered among the old Dutch families who formed the "Albany Regency" that socially dominated their hometown (ALBANY, NEW YORK), and Maria was educated accordingly in dancing, music, poetry, and religion. A coquettish and self-assured woman, Maria was also a prolific letter writer whose sometimes shaky command of the

niceties of spelling and punctuation (Dutch, not English, was her first language) did not deter her from committing her thoughts to paper.

On October 14, 1814, Maria married Allan MELVILL, and together they had eight children before Allan died, bankrupt and insane, in 1832. After her husband's death, Maria was heavily dependent upon her relatives—particularly her brother Peter—for financial support. When her oldest son, Gansevoort MELVILLE, failed to salvage his father's fur and cap business and he himself became too sick to work, Maria was obliged to move with her children from Albany to a less expensive neighborhood in LANSINGBURGH, NEW YORK, about 10 miles away.

Maria was by all accounts a demanding parent. Family legend has it that she made all eight of her children sit motionless and silent by her bed every afternoon while she napped. Still, she seems to have forged strong bonds with her offspring. When her sons Herman and Allan married, Maria and her daughters moved in with the young couples in NEW YORK CITY. When Herman and his wife, Lizzie, moved to PITTSFIELD, MASSACHUSETTS, in 1850, again Maria and her daughters went with them. Finally, when Herman and Lizzie and their own children moved back to New York

Maria Gansevoort Melville, Melville's mother. (Berkshire Athenaeum)

in 1863, Maria established her own residence in GAN-SEVOORT, NEW YORK.

The death of her favorite child, Gansevoort, in 1846, devastated Maria emotionally and financially. She nevertheless survived—and even thrived—into her 80s. After Gansevoort's death, Herman, who was next in line, became the head of the family, but his mother never entirely approved of either his seafaring or his literary career, both of which she viewed as unstable and unremunerative. In later life Herman Melville would claim that his mother "hated" him. While this statement seems an exaggeration, it is clear that she preferred her son Allan, a successful lawyer and politician, over Herman. When Allan died in February 1872, grief over his passing hastened Maria's decline, and she died just two months later.

Melville, Sophia Elizabeth Thurston (1827–1858)
Herman Melville's sister-in-law. Sophia, a wealthy New York socialite, was the first wife of Herman's younger brother Allan MELVILLE, whom she married in 1847. They had their first child, a girl they named after the family matriarch, Maria Gansevoort MELVILLE, just two days after Herman and his wife's first child was born in 1849. Allan and Sophia had four more children together before she died, of tuberculosis, at 31.

Melville, Stanwix ("Stannie") (1851–1886) Herman Melville's younger son. Stanwix was the second child and second son born to Herman and Lizzie Melville. He was named for his great-grandfather Peter GAN-SEVOORT's great Revolutionary War victory over Indian and Tory troops at Fort Stanwix in the Hudson Valley of New York. Stanwix was underweight when he was born, and throughout his life he suffered from precarious health. After his brother Malcolm (see Malcolm MELVILLE) shot himself in 1867, Stanwix began to experience intermittent deafness. He first worked as a clerk in his uncle Allan MELVILLE's law office, after which he was for a brief time a dental apprentice. His deafness, however, made him unsuited to dentistry, so in 1869 Stanwix decided to go to sea. He returned from a voyage to China 10 months later looking robust and exhibiting a taste for travel.

Shortly after his return from that trip, he set off for Kansas and parts west. He returned home in February 1873, after wandering through Arkansas and Mississippi to New Orleans, where he boarded a ship to Cuba. From Cuba he went to Costa Rica and Nicaragua, where he and some companions—one of whom died—contracted fever. When the ship that was carrying him to Panama broke up in a heavy gale, he lost all his possessions and was hospitalized before returning home. Another go at dentistry was aborted by nearsightedness and the return of his deafness. He left home again, this time for California.

Back in New York again 18 months later, he fell ill, but when he recovered, he moved to San Francisco. In 1877, after losing all his money in an ill-conceived financial venture, Stanwix felt obliged to work as a miner in the Black Hills of South Dakota. His time there was brief, however, as the cold and damp and toxic fumes associated with the work wrought havoc with his congenitally weak pulmonary system. Back in San Francisco, he worked for a short time as a canvasser, then moved to the drier climate of San Rafael, across the bay. Hospitalized in Sacramento with tuberculosis, he died on February 25, 1886.

Melville, Thomas ("Tom") (1830–1884) Herman Melville's youngest brother. Thomas was the eighth and last child of Allan MELVILL and Maria Ganesvoort MELVILLE. Tom idolized his older brother Herman, and when Herman returned from his voyages in the South Pacific, his tales about his adventures apparently made a profound impression on Tom. When he was just 16 years old, Tom signed on with a whaler. He returned to his family briefly in 1848 but shipped out again almost at once, this time on a merchant ship bound for the Orient. When REDBURN was published in 1849, Herman dedicated it to "My Younger Brother, Thomas Melville, Now a Sailor on a Voyage to China."

Tom made a success of his maritime career. By 1860, when Herman accompanied him on a voyage from Boston to San Francisco on board the clipper ship *Meteor,* Tom was the ship's captain. Tom's final commercial voyage was aboard the *Bengal Tiger,* which he captained from 1862 to 1864. In 1867, largely though his brother Allan's efforts, Tom was appointed governor of the Sailor's Snug Harbor, a retirement home for seamen located on Staten Island in New York harbor. Only then did he marry. His wife was Catherine E. Bogart, the daughter of New York's chief medical examiner. They had no children and were married for 18 years, until Tom's death in March 1884 of a heart attack. Tom was Herman's favorite brother, and after his death Herman memorialized him by dedicating a poem, "The Admiral of the White" (see "THE HAGLETS"), to Tom.

Melvill House The Melvill family homestead in PITTSFIELD, MASSACHUSETTS. Herman Melville's grandfather, Thomas MELVILL, purchased the house in 1816 from a privateer named Elkanah Watson. By 1848, the house had been converted into an inn by Herman's aunt Mary Hobart MELVILL after she returned as a widow from Galena, Illinois. The inn provided shelter for several important guests, including the poet Henry Wadsworth Longfellow and his wife, Fanny, and the abolitionist Senator Charles SUMNER, whose stay gave rise to rumors that Melvill House was connected with the Underground Railroad.

Mendelssohn, Moses (1779–1826) A German philosopher and ardent advocate of Jewish rights. Heavily influenced by PLATO, he was often called the German Socrates. He is invoked in *CLAREL* as one of the free-thinking Jews in the debate between MARGOTH (a Jewish geologist) and ROLFE.

"Merry Ditty of the Sad Man" (1924) Poem. One of more than 40 poems Melville left uncollected or unpublished at his death, this is a slight piece that appears to be an exercise in wringing music from verse. The burden of the poem is simply this: "Nothing like singing / When blue-devils throng!"

Merrymusk Character in "COCK-A-DOODLE-DOO!" Merrymusk is an impoverished sawyer who is the proud owner of the magnificent cock called Trumpet. Merrymusk and all his family eventually die, although their deaths, like their lives, are enriched by the crowing of the singular rooster. When all the Merrymusks are finally gone, Trumpet, too, expires.

Methodist minister, the Character in *The CONFIDENCE MAN*. The minister, a passenger aboard the *FIDELE*, is inclined to believe the NEGRO CRIPPLE's story and to extend charity to him. He is countered by the WOODEN-LEGGED MAN and the EPISCOPAL CLERGYMAN, both of whom suspect the cripple to be shamming.

Mexican War (1846–1848) The war with Mexico started over disputed territory in Texas. When President Polk deemed that American forces had been threatened by Mexican forces stationed along the Rio Grande, he sent the American army to attack the Mexicans. This was the first war in American history to provoke significant internal opposition. Congressman Abraham LINCOLN attacked President Polk's war, and many in the Northeast saw the conflict as contrary to American democratic ideals, as a war more befitting an imperialistic power. In this view, the war was little more than a land grab of the Southwest. Melville also was critical, regarding the war as the first sign of empire building that a republic should avoid: "Lord, the day is at hand, when we will be able to talk of our killed and wounded like some of the old Eastern conquerors reckoning them up by thousands . . . the Constitution's timbers [will] be thought no more of than bamboos."

"Milan Cathedral" (1891) Poem in *TIMOLEON*. Part of the "Fruit of Travel Long Ago" section of the volume, "Milan Cathedral" reflects Melville's awe upon seeing the storied *duomo di Milan* in 1857. He wrote about it appreciatively in his travel diary, noting its grandeur and elaborate decoration. Built of white marble in Gothic style, Milan Cathedral is the third largest church in Europe. While others have described it as a wedding cake, Melville's poem likens it to an iceberg rising out of the "light green haze, a rolling sea" that is the "fat old plain of Lombardy."

Millet, Sir John Character in *ISRAEL POTTER*. When Israel is on the run from British authorities, this British gentleman takes him in. Although Millet knows that Israel is a rebel, he finds him work and promises to keep him safe.

Millthorpe, Charlie Character in *PIERRE*. Pierre's friend from SADDLE MEADOWS, Millthorpe provides Pierre with his home with the Apostles (a group of artists) in the city, and he enthusiastically encourages Pierre to apply his philosophy to earning his way in the world.

miser, old Character in *The CONFIDENCE MAN*. The MAN WITH THE TRAVELING-CAP, also identified as the STRANGER, assures the miser that his cough can be cured with the Omni-Balsamic Reinvigorator. The miser wishes to bargain on the price of the remedy but eventually is persuaded to purchase it at the offered price.

"Misgivings. (1860.)" (1866) Poem in *BATTLE-PIECES*. In this, the first of the "battle-pieces" in Melville's collection of CIVIL WAR poems, the poet watches a storm ("Nature's dark side") wreak havoc in his town as he ponders his "country's ills," the result of "the world's fairest hope linked with man's foulest crime." Unlike many in the North—especially ABOLITIONISTS—who felt sure that a decent peace would inevitably result from a war that would rid the country of slavery, Melville wondered if civil war could rectify the nation's ills, for "storms are formed behind the storm we feel."

Missourian, the Character in *The CONFIDENCE MAN*. He is skeptical of the HERB-DOCTOR's remedies, pointing out that nature can kill as well as cure. Nature has ruined the Missourian's crops, for example. He advises the old MISER to lie down in his grave; it would do as good as taking the herb-doctor's products. But then the Missourian himself succumbs to the arguments of a "CHANCE STRANGER," yet another disguise of the confidence man. This stranger eventually convinces the Missourian to hire a boy from the Philosophical Intelligence Office.

"Mr Parkman's Tour" (1849) Book review. In early 1849, finding himself somewhat at loose ends after completing MARDI, Melville undertook to write more reviews for his friends Evert and George DUYCKINCK's magazine, the *LITERARY WORLD*. The first review was of the historian Francis Parkman's *The California and*

Oregon Trail; being Sketches of Prairie and Rocky Mountain Life (1849), which Melville thought mistitled because "there is nothing about California or Oregon in the book." He also disagreed with Parkman's presentation of Indians as savages—his own time among the Polynesians of the South Seas had given him a high opinion of native peoples. In general, however, Melville's review was favorable, and closed, as was the custom with *Literary World* book reviews, with a long extract from Parkman. The unsigned review appeared in the March 31, 1849, issue of the journal.

***Moby-Dick; or, The Whale* (1851)**   Melville's sixth book. As in his previous sea novels, Melville drew on personal experience, particularly his 18 months on board the whale ship *ACUSHNET* and his six months on two other whalers, the Australian *LUCY-ANN* and the *CHARLES & HENRY*, out of NANTUCKET. In retrospect, it is curious that Melville's work up to 1851 did not deal with whaling, although his review of J. Ross BROWNE's "ETCHINGS OF A WHALING CRUISE" (1850) showed how deeply the subject engaged him.

Several events seem to have triggered the writing of *Moby-Dick*. Melville's contacts with figures such as

Richard Henry DANA, author of the stirring sea narrative *Two Years Before the Mast* (1840), and with Nathaniel HAWTHORNE, convinced him that he could do more with his travels as part of his quest to create great literature. Immersing himself in the works of SHAKESPEARE, Melville aspired to outstrip his reputation as an author of adventure tales. Although *MARDI* had been a step toward a symbolic, mythopoeic story, it failed to generate momentum through plot and character development. In *Moby-Dick*, Melville found in the whaling voyage and in the whale itself perfect metaphors for evoking both the world of concrete experience and of the human striving to explore the mysteries of existence.

Just before beginning work on his great novel, Melville set off on a four-month trip to Europe, where he encountered German metaphysics. He read and discussed the work of the philosophers KANT and HEGEL with the new friends he made. In England, France, and Germany he visited the great cathedrals and read works such as ROUSSEAU's *Confessions* and GOETHE's *Autobiography*. When he returned home in February 1850, he was ready for an intense 18-month period of composition that would result in his greatest achievement, now considered one of the world's finest works of literature.

This engraving shows a sperm whale hunt like those undertaken by the **Pequod** *in* **Moby-Dick**. (Library of Congress)

SYNOPSIS

"Etymology"

Etymology is the study of the origin and history of words. In this brief prefatory section, Melville has fun with scholars and teachers who dwell on the minute particulars of knowledge, forsaking the broader world of experience and learning that the reader will undergo in this vast novel. The "Usher" (an obsolete form of a word that once meant assistant teacher) is portrayed as "late" (dead) and "consumptive" (the 19th-century word for a person suffering from tuberculosis), someone barely alive when he constructed the etymology, which with its dry list of words imitates the Usher's own lack of life, spirit, and imagination. In the study of elementary school grammar, students use lexicons (dictionaries of words). Melville's Usher provides a list of words meaning "whale" in different languages. The reference to "Hackluyt" (sic) is to Richard Hakluyt (1552–1616), who devoted himself to collecting and publishing accounts of English explorations. He is considered one of the great travel writers, opening up to his readers a sense of the world's size that is directly counter to the Usher's narrow, dusty, dead experience. The definitions of whales from Webster's and Richardson's dictionaries emphasize shape and motion, suggesting that the word "whale" comes from the creature's curved or vaulted configuration and its arching action when it emerges from the sea.

"Extracts"

Melville continues his satire on pedants (scholars who insist on meticulous accounts of minute details) by supplying passages about whales from a "sub-sub-librarian" or under-librarian. "Sub" means below or inferior to—in this case, a lower rank of librarian or a librarian not quite up to his or her job. "Sub" also alludes to this story about the whale, which is a submarine story, set below the surface of the sea, so to speak. Melville's parody of scholarship (imitating as well as spoofing it) is another effort to attack the confines of the world and its categories. Every definition of the whale breeds other definitions and names for it precisely because the whale cannot be contained in conventional language and learning.

What the sub-sub-librarian lacks, Melville makes clear in his first paragraph, is a unifying imagination. His collection of sayings about whales is just a list of fragments. The whale can be described, but its significance cannot be grasped in this catalogue of statements.

In the second paragraph, Melville refers to Hampton Court and the Tuileries, sites of the English and French courts, evoking the grandeur and beauty of a world that the sub-subs can never master or please, a world of power and magnificence that pedants can never explain simply by collecting details about it. Similarly, before beginning his great narrative of the whale, Melville feels the need to impress on his readers the awesomeness of the adventure they are about to undergo.

The first set of extracts is taken from the Bible, emphasizing the whale's mystery and power, the Leviathan who swallows up Jonah, the monster regarded as an evil besetting the world.

The second set of extracts is from classical literature, concentrating on the whale's malevolence, its deliberate intent to destroy and to terrorize.

The third set of extracts is drawn from early English and Renaissance accounts, which describe whales with some scientific precision while also using them as a metaphor for destruction. In other words, whales have become a part of the imaginative structure of thinking about the dangers of the world. The philosopher Thomas HOBBES (1588–1679) called his great treatise on the state *Leviathan* (1651). For him, the metaphor of the leviathan captured the idea of sovereign or independent and autonomous power, which is used to control the life of man; life, in Hobbes's words, tends to be "solitary, poore, nasty, brutish and short." Hobbes's book, like Melville's novel, asks penetrating questions about human nature and the nature of the world.

At the same time the whale began to acquire this heavy symbolic meaning, whaling—the hunting of whales—became an industry, a commercial enterprise, a business. As several extracts in *Moby-Dick* suggest, whale products were put to medicinal uses. Whale bones even became part of human dress in such garments as corsets, as Alexander Pope notes in the extract from *The Rape of the Lock* (1714). By the 18th century, whales were dissected and studied scientifically, as more than one extract shows. Poems, travel accounts, novels and stories by Melville's contemporaries (notably Nathaniel Hawthorne and James Fenimore COOPER) contribute to a vision of the whale as a universal and ever-present phenomenon in civilization. The sound, the sight, the smell of whales pervade these extracts, making them a kind of prologue to a fictional narrative that seems to arise inevitably out of centuries of human reckoning with the Leviathan of the sea.

In "Extracts," Melville moves from an encyclopedic survey of the world and the way it has viewed whales to his own time and place. He gradually focuses on several references to Nantucket, the starting point of his novel, and the point where the universal story of the whale becomes the particular tale of ISHMAEL, his captain, and his crew.

Chapter I: "Loomings"

The novel begins with one of the most famous lines in literature: "Call me Ishmael." Although the narrator speaks informally and even casually, his quest for meaning in the world is deadly serious. His biblical name suggests he is a wanderer and what Melville will later call an "ISOLATO." Ishmael may be remarkable for acting on his impulses and going to sea, but he also represents every man's yearning to explore the world beyond the boundaries of land.

It is the "watery world" that attracts Ishmael, and he contends that it mesmerizes most men, who stand around the docks in Manhattan dreaming about the sea. To landlocked men who are confined by jobs, routines, and responsibilities, the sea represents a world without bounds. All great bodies of water, Ishmael argues, excite meditation, a desire to dive into the depths, to search out the significance of the world. From the myth of Narcissus, whose fascination with his own reflection causes him to drown in a fountain, to the trips tourists take on rivers and oceans, the desire to merge with water is irresistible, Ishmael suggests. Water is the "image of the ungraspable phantom of life."

Ishmael embarks on his sea journeys not as a passenger but as a "simple sailor." He is resigned to the fact that taking orders, being a slave to someone else, is the fate of most of humanity, but at least as a sailor he is paid for his passage and obtains some healthy exercise. Ishmael admits that to sign on for a whaling voyage is an extreme choice, and suggests that it has to do with the biblical fate connected to his name. He introduces the question of free will by wondering how much the adventure he is about to narrate was truly a choice for him.

Ishmael is attracted to the idea and mystery of the whale itself. The whale represents the "itch for things remote." Like the sea, it also represents the ungraspable phantom of existence, looming "like a snow hill in the air."

Chapter II: "The Carpet-Bag"
Ishmael describes his arrival in NEW BEDFORD, Massachusetts. He is determined to sail on a whaling craft out of Nantucket, the center of the action for whalers, an island full of the lore of man's encounters with the monsters of the deep.

Poorly dressed and without much money, Ishmael seeks a place near the water to sleep for the night. He makes his way down dreary streets and stumbles into a "Negro church," where the preacher's text seems to be about the blackness (evil) of the world, before stopping at the SPOUTER INN, whose proprietor has the ominous name of Peter COFFIN. The name of the establishment and its owner conjure up images of an encounter with a spouting whale that will end in death, but the name Coffin is so common in Nantucket that Ishmael shrugs off its symbolism. Still, he prolongs his meditation, wondering if he has found the site of his salvation or his damnation.

Chapter III: "The Spouter-Inn"
Ishmael finds that the inn's interior resembles that of a whaler, with a mysterious painting that appears to depict a whaling vessel breaking up in a storm as a whale attempts to vault the foundering ship. The destructive scene, of course, foreshadows Ishmael's own adventure.

Ishmael meets his first shipmate, QUEEQUEG, a dark-skinned native with whom he must share a bed at the crowded inn. At first, Ishmael is shocked at Queequeg's purple-yellow tattooed skin, his scalp-knot, and the collection of human heads he sells to the locals in Nantucket. But Queequeg's natural nobility and the landlord's assurances prompt Ishmael to accept his new bedmate, who on further examination seems perfectly clean and companionable. "Better sleep with a sober cannibal than a drunken Christian," Ishmael advises, sounding a theme about a common and universal humanity that pervades the novel.

Chapter IV: "The Counterpane"
Not only does Ishmael sleep well, but he also wakes to the pleasant sensation of Queequeg's embrace—although it takes Ishmael considerable effort to rouse his roommate, who continues to show a charming sense of delicacy and poise. Ishmael watches Queequeg make his morning toilet, and admires Queequeg's skill with a harpoon, which he uses as a razor to shave his face.

Chapter V: "Breakfast"
Ishmael watches Queequeg among his breakfast companions. The native is cool and confident, eating his rare beef steaks while the others (to Ishmael's surprise) eat silently, resembling nothing like the boisterous whalers he had been prepared to meet.

Chapter VI: "The Street"
Ishmael tours the streets of Nantucket, where whalers, exotics like Queequeg and various American types from all over the country, congregate, incongruously placed in a town that also sports great mansions and wealth.

Chapter VII: "The Chapel"
Ishmael visits the whaleman's chapel, which contains tablets commemorating men lost at sea—a grim reminder that his adventure will be dangerous and perhaps even fatal.

Chapter VIII: "The Pulpit"
The "famous Father MAPPLE" enters the chapel. "[A] sailor and harpooner in his youth," he is an old but robust man, and as he mounts his nautical-looking pulpit, complete with side ladder and ropes, he looks like the captain of a ship. This self-contained old salt stands before his congregation as a kind of beacon in the storm of human striving and suffering.

Chapter IX: "The Sermon"
Father Mapple begins his sermon with a hymn that describes the opening jaws of the whale as the "opening maw of hell," and goes on to discuss the saving presence of the Lord who delivers man from this evil. Lacing his talk with whaling and shipboard terms, Father Mapple sermonizes on Jonah and the whale. He preaches exact obedience to God and disobedience to

man's willful desires. Jonah cannot captain his ship without God's help; he errs when he puts his trust in human strength and tries to avoid his mission as God's "pilot-prophet." Father Mapple retells the biblical story with a worldly wisdom and sense of doom that will parallel the story Ishmael is about to tell. Like Jonah, Ishmael will be swallowed by the sea monster and spit out again, thus becoming a survivor like Father Mapple, who must, like an ancient mariner, recount the story of his death and rebirth.

Chapters X–XI: "A Bosom Friend"; "Nightgown"
Returning to the Spouter Inn, Ishmael finds himself more and more attracted to Queequeg's easy ways and serene demeanor. Ishmael says they have become cronies; Queequeg says they are "married." Ishmael and Queequeg retire to their cozy bed like two honeymoon lovers. They are warm and snug together but unable to sleep, so Queequeg begins to tell Ishmael the story of his life.

Chapter XII: "Biographical"
Ishmael explains that Queequeg is a native of Rokovoko, an "island far away to the West and South. It is not down on any map; true places never are." This famous statement evokes the world of imagination as a true place. The son of a high chief, Queequeg, like Ishmael, yearns to travel and to see the world. Although he originally intended to learn from the world of Christendom and then return to his people, Queequeg now feels unfit to return to a land with an unbroken succession of 30 pagan kings. He prefers, instead, to gather more experience. Finding that Ishmael is a wanderer like himself, Queequeg resolves to join him on a whaler.

Chapter XIII: "Wheelbarrow"
Ishmael and Queequeg put their belongings in a wheelbarrow and set off to find employment on a whaler. Along the way Queequeg tells Ishmael more about life on Rokovoko and its curious customs, which Christian visitors often misinterpret. Ishmael witnesses an example of Queequeg's strength when he lifts a young man off the ground for making fun of Ishmael. Queequeg then saves the same young man when he falls off a schooner.

Chapters XIV–XV: "Nantucket"; "Chowder"
Having taken a ship from New Bedford to Nantucket, Ishmael provides a brief history of this whale port. From its earliest days, Nantucket has been a stopping point for "sea hermits" who are more comfortable on the sea than on land.

Ishmael and Queequeg dine well on clam and cod chowder at the Try Pots in Nantucket, an establishment recommended to them by Peter Coffin, the proprietor of the Spouter Inn.

Chapter XVI: "The Ship"
Queequeg's idol (object of worship), YOJO, a "black little god," advises him, contrary to Ishmael's wishes, to let Ishmael alone seek the whaling ship the men will work on. Ishmael picks the *Pequod,* pointing out that its name derives from an extinct tribe of Massachusetts Indians. The old ship exudes an air of the ancient even as it is fitted with the modern equipment necessary to hunt whales. Ishmael is questioned closely about his desire to go whaling, and he replies that he wants to learn about whaling and see the world. He learns in an interview with old Captain PELEG (part owner of the *Pequod*) about Captain AHAB, whose leg was devoured by a monstrous, malevolent whale. Peleg accepts Ishmael for service, although he clearly believes that Ishmael's rather innocent desire to see the world does not take into account the vastness of the sea and the considerable monotony inherent in a whaling voyage, interrupted only by periods of sheer terror that require the sailors to drive harpoons into whale flesh. After a prolonged argument between Peleg and his fellow owner, Captain BILDAD, over the share of the profits from the whale hunt Ishmael should receive (this was a common form of payment for whalers, who earned no salary), Ishmael tells his employers about a friend and veteran harpooner who also wishes to ship on the *Pequod.* They encourage Ishmael to present Queequeg for an interview. Wishing to see his captain, Ishmael is informed that Ahab keeps to himself. He is no common run of captain, but a man who has experienced both colleges and cannibals. Peleg and Bildad ominously mention that Ahab is the name of a wicked king in the Bible, but Peleg assures Ishmael that Captain Ahab is a good, if moody, man. He is married to a young woman, and he has his "humanities." Ishmael leaves his job interview feeling a mixture of sadness, pain, and awe concerning this mysterious captain.

Chapter XVII: "The Ramadan"
Ishmael mentions Queequeg's "Ramadan," or period of fasting and humiliation, which Ishmael finds absurd and yet tolerable. He seems to regard all forms of worship as mere human peculiarities. He apparently believes that all should be tolerated, since different forms of RELIGION expose the irrational behavior of humanity, cannibals and Christians alike. But Ishmael grows alarmed when Queequeg does not stir from his room or answer his call. After much commotion and the breaking down of a door, Ishmael finds his companion meditating with Yojo on his head. Ishmael is finally forced to retire for the night, not having been able to budge Queequeg. At the next dawn, Queequeg announces that his Ramadan is over; Ishmael, incensed at the turmoil his comrade has caused, attempts to argue him out of his religious principles. Ishmael treats Queequeg to a history of religions—a comparative, almost anthropological lecture designed to show his mate how ridiculous and perhaps even harmful such religious exercises can be. What is the point of starving and weakening the body? How do these practices

strengthen the soul, Ishmael asks. On the contrary, he argues, such physical denial leads to a kind of spiritual dyspepsia (an upset of the stomach). Queequeg profits little from Ishmael's sermon, understanding only a portion of what he says. Probably, Ishmael imagines, Queequeg is not even bothered by such scruples as Ishmael raises. The two then set off for their voyage on the *Pequod*.

Chapter XVIII: "His Mark"
Captains Peleg and Bildad seek to bar Queequeg from the ship because he is not a Christian. Ishmael argues that his friend is a member of the "First Congregation of this worshipping world." Peleg and Bildad relent, touched by Ishmael's tolerance and wit. They are especially impressed when Queequeg demonstrates his skill with a harpoon. Bildad cannot resist trying to convert Queequeg and reminiscing about the accidents that have almost sunk the *Pequod*.

Chapter XIX: "The Prophet"
No sooner have Ishmael and Queequeg signed to ship on the *Pequod* than a stranger with the biblical name of ELIJAH inquires about the state of their souls. He refers ominously to "Old Thunder" (Ahab), who lost his leg to a whale. Ishmael scoffs at the man's smugly knowledgeable air; yet he is disturbed, too, especially when Elijah appears to be following him and Queequeg.

Chapter XX: "All Astir"
The *Pequod* puts in stores of food, equipment, and other necessities as Ishmael and Queequeg wait to ship out on their long voyage. The two visit the *Pequod* often and ask about Ahab, for Ishmael is troubled about setting out without some glimpse of his captain.

Chapter XXI: "Going Aboard"
Just as Ishmael and Queequeg are boarding the *Pequod*, Elijah appears again, irritating Ishmael with his mysterious reference to a "warning" he had meant to give the men. They encounter a black servant who tells them the ship is about to sail and that Captain Ahab is aboard.

Chapter XXII: "Merry Christmas"
The *Pequod* gets under way on a cold Christmas day. Peleg and Bildad issue directions to STARBUCK, the first mate, but there is no sign yet of Captain Ahab. Peleg and Bildad seem reluctant to leave a ship in which they have invested much and that represents the life at sea that has shaped their characters. They give last-minute advice and urge the men to mind their prayers. The *Pequod* then plunges "like fate into the lone Atlantic."

Chapter XXIII: "The Lee Shore"
Out in the vast Atlantic, Ishmael thinks of the lee shore—that is, the land toward which the wind is blowing, the land that represents a safe haven. He encounters BULKINGTON, a figure who represents the "intrepid effort of the soul to keep the open independence of

her sea." Bulkington reminds Ishmael of why Ishmael left the "slavish shore,"—to free himself by exploring the world.

Chapters XXIV–XXV: "The Advocate"; "Postscript"
Ishmael undertakes a defense of whaling, seeking to prove that it is not unpoetical or dirty but, instead, cleaner and more noble than many other human occupations. Certainly the butchery of whales cannot compare to the gore of battlefields. Moreover, whaling's contribution to the world economy has been enormous, judging by the care rulers have taken to outfit ships and to pay whalemen handsomely. Whalemen are explorers who have opened up the world for "missionary and merchant." Ishmael concludes that a whale ship has been "my Yale College and my Harvard."

Ishmael points out that before monarchs are crowned, their heads are anointed with oil. After canvassing the various possibilities, he concludes that the only oil fit for a king is that from the whale, which in its unpolluted state is the sweetest of all oils.

Chapters XXVI–XXVII: "Knights and Squires"
Ishmael introduces Starbuck, an earnest Quaker who reveres the watery world. A careful and seasoned seaman, he has the respect of the whole crew. He has lost a father and brother, both whalers, at sea. Foreshadowing his narrative, Ishmael comments that the fallen valor of a man like Starbuck and the failures of humanity in general must be balanced against "man, in the ideal, so noble and so sparkling."

Ishmael describes STUBB and FLASK, respectively the second and third mates on the *Pequod*. Stubb is a cheerful and calm whale hunter. Flask is more fierce about the chase. All three mates—Starbuck, Stubb, and Flask—are the "headsmen" of the *Pequod*, Ishmael says. They are like Gothic knights on a quest. Supporting these mates as "squires" are TASHTEGO, an Indian from Gay Head (the westerly point of Martha's Vineyard), noted for his bravery and noble demeanor, and DAGGOO, a towering "negro-savage" with the grace and power of a king. Ishmael observes that this diverse crew is typical of American enterprises that often rely on the brawn of native peoples. Most of these men are islanders, or what Ishmael calls "Isolatoes."

Chapter XXVIII: "Ahab"
Still awaiting the appearance of Ahab, Ishmael dwells on Elijah's portentous manner, which suggested that the voyage with Ahab was something to dread. The ship's three officers (Starbuck, Stubb, and Flask) seem so well suited to their tasks that Ishmael renews his confidence in his choice to forsake land for this wilder experience. Then Ishmael has his first sight of Ahab on the quarterdeck. The captain stands almost like a piece of bronze statuary, a god born out of violence, or a tree struck by lightning but still standing. He has lost one leg to a whale, and his limb has been replaced with a

white bone taken from a whale's jaw. With his artificial leg stationed in a specially made niche, Ahab seems to plant himself immovably on the rocking ship as the embodiment of unshakable resolve. As the ship journeys farther from land, Ahab makes himself more visible to his crew. The improving weather almost puts a smile on his dour visage, Ishmael observes.

Chapters XXIX–XXXI: "Enter Ahab; to Him, Stubb"; "The Pipe"; "Queen Mab"

In the balmy August weather Stubb encounters his ornery captain, who bids him to go below to his berth. Stubb takes issue with Ahab's contemptuous tone, which only riles the captain more. Stubb retreats, wondering at Ahab's rage, but concludes he must "stash" his own thoughts—that is, give up brooding over Ahab's ferocity.

Ishmael compares Ahab to a leviathan of the sea. After the encounter with Stubb, Ahab takes out his pipe, but it does not soothe him. He throws the pipe into the sea and resumes pacing the planks.

Stubb's brooding over Ahab's insulting behavior takes the form of a dream in which Ahab kicks him with his ivory leg. Stubb reasons, in the dream, that there is no great insult in the kick because it was given by an artificial leg. A merman appears and reinforces Stubb's reasoning. Stubb describes this dream to Flask and advises him to avoid contact with Ahab, who then suddenly appears, shouting that whales have been sighted and that they should "split" their lungs in chase if they spot a white one. Stubb is wary of his "bloody"-minded captain.

Chapter XXXII: "Cetology"

Ishmael decides to provide an introduction to the varieties of whale before the action of the hunt takes over his narrative. He cites several authorities who have claimed it is impossible to classify whales and their behaviors. Ishmael lists famous writers who have commented on whales, and observes that only one of these authorities, Captain Scoresby, has actually seen whales. Ishmael's first contribution to cetology, the study of marine mammals, is to claim pride of place for the sperm whale and to depose the Greenland whale. Only two books do any justice to the sperm whale, whose life is, as yet, unwritten. In the absence of reliable data, Ishmael provides his own classification. He warns his readers that his venture to bottom of the sea, the very ribs and pelvis of the world, is perilous.

Although the whale is warm-blooded and has lungs, Ishmael rejects those authorities who do not classify it as a fish. The men who have hunted it say it is a fish—notwithstanding its differences in anatomy from other fish. Ishmael insists that the definition of a whale as a "spouting fish with a horizontal tail" is the product of much meditation, designed to distinguish the whale from other fish and from amphibious creatures such as walruses.

Ishmael then breaks down the different types of whales into three books: the "Folio" (Sperm), "Octavo" (Grampus), and "Duodecimo" (Porpoise). He then divides each book into chapters, so that the Folio contains the Sperm, the Right, the Fin-Back, the Humpbacked, the Razor Back, and the Sulphur Bottom whales. Each chapter is then described. Book I, Chapter 1 provides the names of sperm whales in different languages. This whale is the largest animal in the world, and the only one from which SPERMACETI is obtained. Book I, Chapter 2 remarks that the Right Whale (known by various names Ishmael lists) has been the most frequently hunted. Book I, Chapter 3 notes that the Fin-Back looks like a Right Whale but is lighter in color. It is distinguished by its pointed tail, single straight lofty jet, and solitary nature. It is a powerful swimmer and hard to catch. Book I, Chapter 4 treats the "Hump-Backed" whale as the sportiest and most gregarious of whales. Book I, Chapter 5 notes that not much is known about the Razor Back except that it is remarkable for its sharp, ridged back. Book I, Chapter 6 reports that the Sulphur Bottom whale has a "brimstone belly." It is a deep diver and is seldom seen or chased.

Book II, Chapter 1 distinguishes the Grampus for its loud, sonorous breathing. This whale swims in herds, and fishermen often regard its presence as a sign that sperm whales are near. Book II, Chapter 2 describes the Black Fish or Hyena Whale, which is a good cheap source of oil. Book II, Chapter 3 reports that the Narwhale or Nostril whale gets its name from its peaked nose. With its leopard-spotted skin and its horn, this whale is often called the unicorn of the sea. Ishmael canvasses speculation about the horn, such as the notion that it is used to scoop up food from the sea bottom or to break ice. Book II, Chapter 4 notes that the Killer Whale is never hunted because of its savagery and that there is little precise information about it. Book II, Chapter 5 reports that the Thrasher uses its tail to whip its foes, but it is otherwise as unknown as the Killer.

In Book III, Chapter 1, Ishmael gives the name "Huzza" to a common porpoise, which he insists is also a whale because it is spouting fish with a horizontal tail. This spirited, frolicking fish always raises cheers, or huzzas, from sailors, who regard its presence as a good omen. The fish is good to eat and yields about a gallon of oil. Book III, Chapter 2 calls the Algerine Porpoise a pirate and a savage. When chased, it acts like a shark and is difficult to capture. Book III, Chapter 3 describes the Mealy-Mouthed as the largest type of porpoise, much less pleasing to look at than the Huzza.

Ishmael confesses that his cetological catalogue is incomplete, but he leaves it as is, much as the architects of Cologne cathedral left their monument unfinished.

Chapter XXXIII: "The Specksnyder"

The Specksnyder, in the early days of whaling, was the chief harpooner, who shared with the captain the management of the ship. Specksnyders ruled the deck while the captain navigated. Even the seemingly all-powerful Ahab, Ishmael observes, has to respect a tradition that singled out the harpooner. Yet Ahab's greatness will derive from his own effort to "pluck" at the skies and to dive into the deep, showing himself to the "unbodied air."

Chapter XXXIV: "The Cabin-Table"

Ahab presides over the dinner table with his three mates, Starbuck, Stubb, and Flask, in attendance. A strict hierarchy is observed as the first, second, and third mates in turn receive their dinners from the silent Ahab. On deck the harpooners, in contrast, observe a rough-and-ready democracy. Ahab stands apart from both sets of men. Ishmael likens him to an old grizzly bear, brooding in his cave of a cabin.

Chapter XXXV: "The Mast-Head"

Ishmael's first mast-head (his first watch from the mast) "comes round." He discourses on the history of mast-head or tower builders, beginning with the Egyptians and advancing to the Christian hermits atop their stone pillars, and then to the statue of Admiral Horatio NEL-SON in Trafalgar Square. The lookout at sea is liable to fall into a languor, entranced by the waves and caught up in a "sublime uneventfulness." The perch on a ship is akin to other forms of isolation that may be obtained in such contrivances as hammocks, pulpits, and coaches. Ishmael admits he made a poor lookout, being a too-dreamy "Platonist"—that is, one who muses on ideal forms and is not observant. The south seas, Ishmael suggests, are particularly conducive to this loss of individuality and perceptiveness and to a desire to merge with nature. Take a step that puts you over the edge of your perch, and you will be brought back quickly to a sense of your self, Ishmael points out. The price of PANTHEISM, he implies, is a loss of identity.

Chapter XXXVI: "The Quarter-Deck"

The crew observes an agitated Ahab pacing the deck. They suspect that he is about to reveal the purpose that moves him. Sure enough, the captain calls for everyone to assemble. He quizzes them on what to do when whales are sighted. Each question drives them to a higher pitch of enthusiasm for the hunt. He promises an ounce of gold to any man who raises the white-headed whale. Tashtego realizes that Ahab means to catch Moby-Dick, the great white whale. The whole crew adds its knowledge of the fierce creature, which already has iron in it from previous hunts. Starbuck asks whether Moby-Dick took off Ahab's leg. Ahab acknowledges that the whale "dismasted" him. While the crew falls in with Ahab's fanaticism, Starbuck holds back, saying he came to hunt whales, not to satisfy his captain's vengeance. It seems ridiculous and blasphemous to Starbuck to blame a dumb creature for what it would do by instinct. Ahab counters that the whale is but an "unreasoning mask" of malevolent forces. Striking the whale is striking through the mask. To Ahab, the whale is the sum of the world's "inscrutable malice." The proud captain admits "I'd strike the sun if it insulted me."

Ahab then shifts the direction of his argument, pointing out that the whole crew sees the whale as a worthy adversary. Would Starbuck oppose the entire ship? An aghast Starbuck retreats, muttering about his faith in God. To seal his hold on the men, Ahab orders a round of drinks, calling the men his "braves." He binds them in a ceremony: filling the hollows in the heads of their steel harpoons with drink. Calling his three mates his cardinals and their new drinking vessels their chalices, he binds them into an "indissoluble league" and has them swear death to Moby-Dick. Only Starbuck, pale and shivering, seems immune to Ahab's power.

Chapters XXXVII–XXXIX: "Sunset [The cabin; by the stern windows; Ahab sitting alone, and gazing out]"; "Dusk [By the Mainmast; Starbuck leaning against it]"; "First-Night Watch [Stubb solus, and mending a brace]"

Ahab's soliloquy, which makes him sound like Shakespeare's Richard III and Macbeth, reveals his willful temperament and desire to dominate. Like Hamlet, he raises the issue of madness, calling himself "madness maddened!" He vows to "dismember my dismemberer."

Starbuck feels "overmanned" by a madman. Although the rational side of Starbuck resists Ahab's adventure and his religious side considers it impious, he nevertheless finds it impossible not to follow his captain's lead.

Stubb sees that like himself, Starbuck has bent his will to Ahab's. There is nothing to be done, Stubb concludes, but to laugh—always the wisest response to all that is queer.

Chapters XL–XLI: "Midnight, Forecastle [Harpooners and Sailors]"; "Moby-Dick"

The crew, caught in a squall, toss around references to Ahab and the whale, excited by the idea of the hunt. Like the rest of the crew, Ishmael finds himself caught up in Ahab's mania about the famous Moby-Dick, even though Ishmael dreads the outcome of the chase. There have been many reports of the whale's malevolence and its taste for human blood. Particularly disturbing to Ishmael are accounts of Moby-Dick that put the whale in different places at once, contributing to the air of the supernatural and the mysterious that the whale evokes. Certain whalemen regard Moby-Dick as immortal. The whale's unusual whiteness adds an eerie quality to its elusive yet ubiquitous presence. Ahab's hunt for the whale has been transformed, Ishmael believes, into an assault on all his "intellectual and spiritual exasperations." Ishmael speculates that the captain's desire to kill the whale only increased during the period he spent recuperating after losing his leg, an experience that made him a stronger man bent on taking his revenge. Ishmael marvels and worries that this motley crew of castoffs, renegades, and cannibals can be too easily molded to fulfill Ahab's quest—one that the ship's owners, concerned with profit, would surely stop.

Chapter XLII: "The Whiteness of the Whale"
Although Ishmael catalogues many examples of whiteness as a symbol of purity, goodness, spirituality, and majesty, when the color is combined with objects frightening in themselves—such as bears, sharks, and tigers—it seems especially menacing. White is also the color of the dead, of fierce storms such as "white squalls." Perhaps the lack of warmth and the indefinite quality of white—as opposed to warmer, richer colors—is what is so upsetting, Ishmael muses. He thinks of the white albatross, "a mystic thing," in *The RIME OF THE ANCIENT MARINER*. This is a particularly grim reference, since the shooting of the bird dooms the ship and crew in Samuel Taylor Coleridge's great poem.

Chapters XLIII–XLIV: "Hark"; "The Chart"
While the crew ponders Ahab's plans, the captain pores over maps and charts in his cabin, hoping to track the whale's route. Ishmael imagines a man completely overtaken by his quest—almost a disembodied spirit whose body is absorbed by his fierce will.

Chapter XLV: "The Affidavit"
Ishmael recounts various incidents in which whales have eluded capture, or have escaped and then been caught. Such whales become identifiable as individuals and bolster the veracity of Ishmael's story of Moby-Dick. Landsmen in particular are in need of such examples, for they have not heard of (and otherwise will not believe) these sea marvels. Ishmael also documents the stories of three ships sunk or severely damaged by whales. He says his readers must not think the story of Moby-Dick is only an allegory.

Chapter XLVI: "Surmises"
Ishmael speculates that Ahab conceals his monomania so that it does not arouse the opposition of Starbuck and the crew. The captain, Ishmael reasons, must continue to hunt for all whales until he meets his prime adversary.

Chapters XLVII–XLVIII: "The Mat-Maker"; "The First Lowering"
In weaving mats, Ishmael falls into a reverie about the weaving of fate and destiny, about the individual and the forces of the world, the role of chance and free will. Then, suddenly, a group of whales is sighted.

Ahab appears with a mysterious group of five "aboriginals," men hitherto hidden from and unknown to the rest of crew. Ahab commands one of them, FEDALLAH, to lower away and pursue the whales. Four boats set off, and Starbuck's closes in on the whales. Queequeg thrusts his harpoon into the white, roiling water, but the grazed whale escapes. With a white squall imminent, the whalers return to the *Pequod*.

Chapter XLIX: "The Hyena"
An astonished Ishmael questions Queequeg and other crew members about the chase. It has seemed so reckless in the face of the storm, yet all tell Ishmael there has been nothing extraordinary in their first day's hunt. Ishmael decides to make out his will, with Queequeg as his executor and legatee.

Chapter L: "Ahab's Boat and Crew. Fedallah"
Stubb is astonished that his one-legged captain should himself man one of the boats that chase whales. Even more surprising is Ahab's marshaling of his own personal crew. Yet whalemen do not spend much time wondering, Ishmael explains—not even about the mysterious, turbaned Fedallah.

Chapters LI–LIII: "The Spirit-Spout"; "The Albatross"; "The Gam"
Fedallah, atop the mainmast, spots a silvery jet, but it is too difficult to hunt this sign of the whale at night, even in moonlight at midnight. The men grow to dread this mysterious presence that beckons night after night. Ahab withdraws into a gloomy reserve. Then the *Pequod* encounters a dilapidated ship, the *ALBATROSS*, a reminder of the ship described in *The Rime of the Ancient Mariner*. Ahab and his crew hail the *Albatross*, but the two ships pass without exchanging an intelligible word about whether Moby-Dick has been sighted. Ishmael speculates that Ahab avoids the gam (a social meeting of whale ships) because he does not want to encounter a captain who may lack news about the whale and sympathy for Ahab's quest.

Chapter LIV: "The Town-Ho's Story [As told at the Golden Inn]"
Ishmael hears the story of this strange ship's mutiny involving STEELKILT and RADNEY. The *TOWN-HO* has been plagued by leaks (using its pumps constantly), yet even Steelkilt and Radney abandon their enmity in the heat of the chase after the elusive Moby-Dick. Radney died chasing Moby-Dick.

Chapters LV–LVII: "Of The Monstrous Pictures of Whales"; "Of the Less Erroneous Pictures of Whales and the True Pictures of Whaling Scenes"; "Of Whales in Paint; in Teeth; in Wood; in Sheet-iron; in Stone; in Mountains; in Stars"
Ishmael surveys the history of how the whale has been pictured in cultures all over the world. None of these inaccurate pictures has been based on actual sightings of the whale in its element. Ishmael believes no true picture of the leviathan is possible, but he cites a few texts that do the whale some justice. He suggests artists have done a better job in capturing the scenes and atmosphere of whaling life.

Chapters LVIII–LX: "Brit"; "Squid"; "The Line"
The *Pequod* moves through brit, a "minute, yellow substance" on which the whale feeds. Ishmael meditates on the mystery and power of the sea, which has swallowed up so many human beings but which also gives rise to the very creatures (even whales) who are born to it.

Then the crew mistakenly thinks it sights Moby-Dick. The creature they see is, in fact, a squid—a large, milky mass rarely visible on the water and the subject of much inconclusive speculation.

Ishmael describes the whale-line, an item that will help explain what happens in the following chapters. The line measures over two fathoms and can bear a weight of about three tons. Understanding how the line is played out and used in pursuit of the whale is crucial to understanding the process of the whale hunt. But the whale line, Ishmael suggests, is also a metaphor for the lines that tangle human beings in life itself.

Chapters LXI–III: "Stubb Kills a Whale"; "The Dart"; "The Crotch"
Standing at the foremast as the ship makes its way across the Indian Ocean, Ishmael falls into a reverie which is then interrupted by sight of a gigantic sperm whale—an event Queequeg predicted would follow after the ship's sighting of the squid. Stubb, in avid pursuit of the whale, succeeds in driving his men to the kill.

In the aftermath, Ishmael discusses the trials of the harpooner and describes the "crotch." The harpooner must row and shout with the rest of the men and yet be ready at a moment's notice to heave his harpoon (iron dart) the length of 20 or 30 feet into the whale. The crotch is a notched stick inserted into the front of the boat. It forms a platform on which to rest harpoons so that they can be picked up quickly to throw at whales. The first and second irons are attached to a rope so that the whale can be hauled in after a successful strike. But often the whale proves elusive, and ships have been endangered by their own harpoons coming back at them in the water.

Chapters LXIV–IX: "Stubb's Supper"; "The Whale as a Dish"; "The Shark Massacre"; "Cutting In"; "The Blanket"; "The Funeral"
The crew struggles to bring aboard the huge whale. The hunt seems to perturb Ahab, who broods on Moby-Dick, his "grand monomaniac object." Meanwhile, the cheerful Stubb dines on whale steak. Ishmael gives an account of the whale's place in the history of dining and of the different ways in which parts of the whale have been prepared for meals. This survey is followed by a short explanation of how dangerous it is to haul even a dead shark aboard, as its jaws can clamp down on a sailor attempting to take off its skin. Ishmael then describes the enormous cutting blocks, tackles, and tables used to take apart the whale. For Ishmael, the wonder and the mystery of the whale persists as he tries to say exactly what part of the transparent surface of the whale can be called a skin. As the whale is hauled into the ship, the birds and sharks make a tremendous din, marking the whale's only funeral service.

Chapter LXX: "The Sphynx"
Just before being hoisted aboard, the whale is beheaded. This is a difficult, arduous procedure because the head meets the body at the thickest part of the creature. The black and hooded head resembles the sphynx of the desert. Ahab is provoked to address it, as though the whale head might yield knowledge of some ancient mystery or the secret of life.

Chapter LXXI: "The Jeroboam's Story"
The *Pequod* meets the *JEROBOAM* and learns of the strange figure of GABRIEL, who had warned the *Jeroboam*'s captain and crew not to attack Moby-Dick. Learning that Ahab means to pursue the whale, Gabriel reminds him of MACEY, the chief-mate of the *Jeroboam*, a "blasphemer" who dared to hunt Moby-Dick and who perished in his pursuit.

Chapter LXXII: "The Monkey-Rope"
Ishmael returns to a description of how the whale is cut up and apportioned. Queequeg is lowered onto the whale's back by a rope attached to a piece of canvas around his waist. The other end of the rope is attached to Ishmael. The rope becomes, in Ishmael's imagination, one of those ties that bind a man to life.

Chapters LXXIII–LXXVII: "Stubb and Flask Kill a Right Whale; and Then Have a Talk Over Him"; "The Sperm Whale's Head—Contrasted View"; "The Right Whale's Head—Contrasted View"; "The Battering-Ram"; "The Great Heidelburgh Tun"
Ahab orders the crew to hunt down a right whale, a creature usually disdained because it lacks the quantities of oil found in sperm whales. According to Flask, Fedallah has said that the heads of the two whales, hanging on each side of the ship, will prevent it from ever capsizing. Fedallah's mysterious knowledge leads to speculation that he is a demon and that Ahab has made a bargain with the devil.

Ishmael then contrasts the two whales' heads and explains the sperm whale's superiority. Speculating on the whale's massive head, which separates its two eyes, Ishmael concludes that each eye must see at a 30-degree angle, providing the creature with two separate pictures and a massive darkness straight ahead. Unlike human beings, in other words, the whale cannot focus on what is directly in front of it. The whale's predicament is the equivalent of human eyes placed near the ears. Ishmael concludes his remarks as the whale is hoisted aboard and the crew inspects the inside of its mouth.

While not as impressive as the sperm whale's, the right whale's head and the interior of its bony mouth nevertheless make a fascinating study when viewed from different angles. To Ishmael, the sperm whale appears platonic (that is, of Plato's school of philosophy), whereas as the right whale seems a stoic.

Ishmael concludes his description of the sperm whale by noting the properties of its massive head, especially the upper part, which Ishmael calls the GREAT HEIDELBURGH TUN—an allusion to the prized wine of the Rhenish valleys which is like the coveted sperm oil found in the upper head. Impervious to sensation, the head will subsequently be used, Ishmael hints, as a battering ram.

Chapter LXXVIII: "Cistern and Buckets"
Queequeg saves Tashtego, who falls into the whale's head as the oil is being extracted. After Tashtego and the head (which falls off its hooks) plunge into the sea, Queequeg dives after them, using his sword to make a slit in the bottom of the head, thus releasing Tashtego from a sure death by drowning in sperm oil.

Chapters LXXIX–LXXX: "The Prairie"; "The Nut"
Ishmael wonders whether PHRENOLOGY or physiognomy can be used to analyze the whale's personality. Can the shape of its face and head yield knowledge of the creature's character? The massive head and the face that does not have typical features such as a nose make the whale hard to read, inscrutable, godlike.

Pursuing his investigation of the whale's anatomy, Ishmael traces the structure of the spinal cord and wonders if the phrenology should not be extended to other parts of the body, especially since the whale's brain is not seated in the head proper but is located some 20 feet away.

Chapter LXXXI: "The Pequod Meets the Virgin"
Ishmael says portentously that on the "predestinated day" the *Pequod* meets the ship *Jungfrau* (the VIRGIN), and its captain, Derick DE DEER, of Bremen. De Deer tells Ahab he knows nothing of Moby-Dick, but their talk is broken off when an old wounded whale is sighted and both ships give chase. The *Pequod's* crew gains the advantage when de Deer's boat nearly capsizes, and Ishmael watches the grisly bloodletting of the old whale as the harpooners drive in their irons.

Chapters LXXXII–LXXXIII: "The Honor and Glory of Whaling"; "Jonah Historically Regarded"
Ishmael relates the history of humans and whales (including myths and legends) before whale hunting became a business. In this context, Ishmael reports the skeptical reactions in Nantucket and among whalemen to the biblical story of Jonah.

Chapter LXXXIV: "Pitchpoling"
Pitchpoling is one of the ingenious devices developed by harpooners, who use a lance (lighter in weight than a harpoon) with a rope that can be used to haul the weapon back into the whaling boat. Ishmael then provides a description of Stubb's effective pitchpoling method.

Chapters LXXXV–LXXXVI: "The Fountain"; "The Tail"
Ishmael describes the manner in which the whale uses its spout, its need for air, and how it lives between the intervals when it surfaces for air. The whale's tail, often measuring 50 square feet and 20 feet in length, excites Ishmael's wonder and admiration. Capable of five great motions (leaping, curving, sweeping, slapping, and plunging), the tail exhibits an elasticity unrivaled in nature.

Chapter LXXXVII: "The Grand Armada"
The *Pequod* is approaching the Java Sea, moving toward the waters that Moby-Dick is known to frequent. Here the ship encounters a fleet of sperm whales, a veritable armada. Chasing the whales, the *Pequod* finds itself chased, in turn, by Malay pirates. Managing to outrace its pursuers, the *Pequod* drives into the wake of the whales, panicking the herding creatures. Negotiating this mass with harpooners who are ready to strike, Ishmael is enchanted by the cows (females) and calves (young whales) who come up to the whaleboats like dogs, curious and docile. Nearly trapped between two masses of whales and finding yet another whale snagged in a harpoon line, the whalemen manage to capture only one whale when the herd regroups and gathers speed, eluding its pursuers.

Chapter LXXXVIII: "Schools and Schoolmasters"
Ishmael explains that whales often travel in schools of 20 to 50, mostly females accompanied by a bull male. This "schoolmaster" protects his harem fiercely with a vigorous show of strength. There are also schools of young males, who act like young collegians, full of fun and fight.

Chapters LXXXIX–XC: "Fast-Fish and Loose-Fish"; "Heads or Tails"
Ishmael explains the protocol that is observed when two whaleboats pursue the same fish. The rough-and-ready rules of the sea dictate that the fast fish—a whale already secured by some means to a whaleboat—belongs to the party fast enough to catch it; a loose fish belongs to whoever is game enough to capture it. Ishmael observes that a loose fish is practically whatever a whaleman says it is. He cites examples from history of how men have always defined what they coveted, whether it be a fish or a country, as "loose," or available for the taking.

English law dictates that for whales caught off the coast of any given country, the head goes to the king and the tail to the queen. Such claims have actually been made on whales beached on England's shores, Ishmael explains, and whalemen have had their catch seized and sold.

*Chapters XCI–XCII: "The Pequod Meets the Rose-Bud";
"Ambergris"*
The *Pequod* encounters the ROSE-BUD, a French ship
that is extracting oil from two old, rotting whales.
Referring to the foul odor of the carcasses that
engulfs the *Rose-Bud,* the contemptuous Stubb notes
the irony of the ship's name. He manages to fool the
French captain into thinking the whales are diseased
and will infect his ship. He offers to tow the lighter
whale away, and on doing so goes for its hidden treasure: ambergris, "worth a gold guinea to any drug-
gist." Ambergris is a soft, waxy material found in the
intestines of sperm whales and used in cosmetics and
perfumery, as Ishmael explains in a brief history of
the substance's use.

Chapter XCIII: "The Castaway"
PIP, the shipkeeper, is called on to replace an injured
oarsman. Poor Pip jumps out of the boat in fright during a whale chase. Admonished not to do so again or
he might be left behind, the frightened man cannot
help himself and jumps again. By the time he is rescued, after floating in the "awful lonesomeness" of the
vast sea, he has gone mad.

*Chapters XCIV–XCVIII: "A Squeeze of the Hand"; "The
Cassock"; "The Try-Works"; "The Lamp"; "Stowing Down
and Clearing Up"*
Ishmael joins the crew in squeezing lumps of sperm
into oil. The sweet, soft substance creates a soothing
atmosphere in which Ishmael is unable to tell whether
he is squeezing the sperm or a crew member's hands, as
everyone is enveloped in the "very milk or sperm of
kindness." The scene excites in him an image of paradise.

Ishmael then describes the work of the mincer
(dressed in black like a priest or minister), who with
two assistants skins the whale, turns its pelt inside out,
and stretches it.

Ishmael then describes the try-works, an open kiln
that contains large try-pots used to collect the liquid
from the rendered whale fat or blubber, which is fed
into the furnace of the kiln. Thus the *Pequod* becomes a
"burning ship" carrying a cargo of boiling oil. Ishmael
conjures up an image of the fires of hell and suddenly
is overcome with dread. Still, he reasons, it is the lamp
oil that lights the whaleman's darkness.

With the oil put away in casks, the crew turns to
scrubbing the ship and removing the residue from the
burning oil and the slaughter of the whale. The crew
turns merry, exchanging stories. Such a brief moment
of rest on a whaler is usually interrupted by a sighting
of whales, meaning that the whole business of the chase
and the slaughter begins again—a fact not only of whaling but of much of life, Ishmael observes. The old routines of the world prompt Ishmael to think of the
Greek philosopher Pythagoras (see PYTHAGOREAN) and

his notion of metempsychosis (the transmigration of
souls).

Chapter XCIX: "The Doubloon"
Ahab pauses while pacing the deck to contemplate the
Ecuadorian gold doubloon riveted to the main mast.
He interprets the mountain peaks and towers on this
"gold sun" as symbols of his volcanic self. While Ahab
sees in the doubloon a sanction for his own enterprise,
Starbuck dreads its portent, thinking it might signify
evil. Stubb scoffs at both of them for brooding on the
coin. To Stubb and Flask, the coin signifies only the
reward for capturing Moby-Dick.

Chapter C: "Leg and Arm"
The *Pequod* encounters the *Samuel Enderby* of London,
and Ahab asks about Moby-Dick. For reply, the *Enderby*'s
Captain BOOMER waves his prosthetic arm made from
sperm-whale bone, provoking Ahab to board the
English boat. Boomer describes sighting the whale,
emphasizing its milky whiteness and wrinkled head.
The whale, already harpooned (Ahab interjects that
the irons were his) and in a rage, struck Boomer's boat
and then plunged down into the sea. Caught in a harpoon line that was still attached to the whale, Boomer's
arm was severed when the iron drove back at him. Keen
to learn more about the pursuit, Ahab learns from
Boomer that the captain did not wish to tangle again
with the whale. "Ain't one limb enough?" the mild-
mannered Boomer asks. Ahab breaks off their conversation, feeling the heat of the chase rising in him.

Chapter CI: "The Decanter"
Ishmael describes the history of the *Enderby,* the ship of
an English firm involved in whaling since the 18th century, which leads to an account of Dutch and European
whaling methods.

*Chapters CII–CV: "A Bower in the Arsacides"; "Measurement
of the Whale's Skeleton"; "The Fossil Whale"; "Does the
Whale's Magnitude Diminish?—Will He Perish?"*
Ishmael claims to have acquired much of his whale lore
from King TRANQUO of Tranque, one of the Arsacides,
who had examined a dead sperm whale on the shores
of his island. With the king of Tranque, Ishmael was
able to visit the whale skeleton and examine its parts
for himself. Ishmael then proceeds to give his estimate
of the full length of a sperm whale, the shape and other
details of its skull, jaw, teeth, forehead, fins, tail, and
other parts. This catalogue leads to a consideration of
fossil records and the whale's place in the record of the
earth's development. Indeed, Ishmael goes so far as to
call himself a geologist, implying that his theme is no
less than a study of creation—a mighty theme for a
mighty book.

Whales today, Ishmael continues, are even greater in
size than their predecessors, even though ancient
myths and legends may make the earliest leviathans

seem gigantic in comparison with those currently hunted. Unlike other great beasts that have been hunted to extinction, Ishmael predicts that whales—however much they are hunted—will remain the immortals of the sea.

Chapter CVI–CVIII: "Ahab's Leg"; "The Carpenter"; "Ahab and the Carpenter"

Ishmael speculates on Ahab's reclusiveness before the *Pequod* went to sea. He concludes that the loss of the captain's leg promoted an alienation from the rest of humanity, even as the ship's carpenter worked on an artificial limb made according to Ahab's specifications.

Ishmael then describes the carpenter at his vise-bench, an "omnitooled" man apparently prepared for any repair on a long sea voyage—a man in sympathy with the ship he fixes, as though he were part of the very machinery of the voyage.

As the carpenter measures Ahab for his leg, Ahab meditates on the dimensions of man, his makeup and prospects, and on the fact that he ("proud as a Greek god") has to rely on a blockhead of a carpenter. The carpenter, speaking to himself, mentions Stubb's opinion that Ahab is "queer." This hard-driving captain has driven one leg to death already, the carpenter notes, and Ahab is now standing on a leg made out of the very thing that took his natural leg away.

Chapter CIX: "Ahab and Starbuck in the Cabin"

Starbuck announces a serious leak in the casks holding the sperm oil, but Ahab refuses to postpone his quest for Moby-Dick, even though Starbuck reminds him of the shipowners' concern for the oil. When Starbuck continues to protest, Ahab aims a musket at him and reasserts his command of the *Pequod*.

Chapter CX: "Queequeg in His Coffin"

Queequeg develops a fever, perhaps hastened by his work in the damp of the ship's hold, where he sees to the storage of the oil casks. Thinking he is about to die, he requests that the ship's carpenter build him a "coffin-canoe," which will bring him eternal rest. At his own bidding, he is put into the canoe and supplied with his harpoon and ship's biscuits, only to make a remarkable recovery. He explains, simply, that he made up his mind not to die.

Chapters CXI–CXIV: "The Pacific"; "The Blacksmith"; "The Forge"; "The Gilder"

While Ishmael is lulled by the serene Pacific, Ahab thinks only of the bloody white whale. Meanwhile, PERTH, the blacksmith, puts the finishing touches on an artificial leg for Ahab. Ishmael introduces Perth as one of those "isolatoes" who have lost his home and family and gone to sea. In the forge, Ahab watches Perth smooth out seams and dents in metal and asks Perth if he can do likewise with Ahab's ribbed brow. No, it is not possible, Ahab assures Perth, for the

wrinkles go right to Ahab's bones and are ineradicable. He urges Perth to make the harpoons of the sharpest iron in preparation for killing Moby-Dick. Meanwhile, in the calm of the sea, Ishmael feels almost at home, and reports Stubb's and Starbuck's similar reactions.

Chapter CXV: "The Pequod Meets the Bachelor"

The *Pequod* meets the *Bachelor* on its way back from a successful whaling voyage. Boarding the jolly ship, the moody Ahab only wants to know if the captain has sighted Moby-Dick. When the *Bachelor*'s captain says gaily that he has heard of the whale but not seen him, Ahab dismisses his counterpart as a fool.

Chapters CXVI–CXVIII: "The Dying Whale"; "The Whale Watch"; "The Quadrant"

The *Pequod* sails on, killing more whales, and Ahab retreats into a deeper gloom, meditating on his chances of killing Moby-Dick and surviving the deed. He studies his quadrant, checks his latitude, and impatiently searches for a position that will place him near the whale. Rejecting mechanical devices that will never tell him his true position in relation to the whale, Ahab tramples on the instrument and vows to rely on his own will.

Chapter CXIX: "The Candles"

The *Pequod* suddenly finds itself battling a typhoon. For Starbuck, trying to keep the ship from breaking apart, the course Ahab has set for the whale has led inevitably to this storm and other portents of disaster. A baffled Stubb wonders at Starbuck's meaning, while Ahab actually welcomes the storm as a sign that the struggle with Moby-Dick is about to begin.

Chapter CXX–CXXII: "The Deck Towards the End of the First Night Watch"; "Midnight.—The Forecastle Bulwarks"; "Midnight Aloft.—Thunder and Lightning"

Starbuck and Ahab confront each other, the former thinking only of saving the ship, the latter bent on driving forward to the final confrontation with Moby-Dick. Meanwhile, Stubb and Flask argue over the hazards of the voyage and how they should respond to it. Tashtego, on the mainmast, only wants the thunder to stop.

Chapter CXXIII: "The Musket"

The typhoon abates, and Starbuck goes below deck to report a fair wind to Ahab. Starbuck sees the musket that Ahab had pointed at him and considers whether he should use it now against his captain, who seems determined to bring his ship to disaster. Was not Ahab ready to sacrifice ship and crew for his cause, Starbuck asks himself. Would it be murder to stop this madman? Starbuck hears Ahab raving in his sleep, calling out that he has the whale in his clutches at last. Starbuck retreats and asks Stubb to wake the captain.

Chapter CXXIV: "The Needle"
Ahab and Starbuck are startled to discover their compass showing the ship heading east, when they know they are bound west. Ahab attributes the malfunction to the storm. An uneasy Starbuck watches while Ahab claims he is his own compass needle, setting his own course. Stubb, Flask, and the rest of the crew sense perhaps for the first time Ahab's "fatal pride."

Chapter CXXV: "The Log and Line"
It is now hard to tell the *Pequod*'s true course because Ahab not only has destroyed his quadrant and ignored the compass, but also has neglected the log and line that are used to help ships determine their place on the sea. One crew member observes that they have already lost one daft one (Pip) to weakness and will lose another one (Ahab) "daft with strength."

Chapters CXXVI–CXXVII: "The Life-Buoy"; "The Deck"
The *Pequod* travels toward the equator, spurred on by trade winds. It enters the equatorial fishing grounds, and the crew is startled by the cries of seals, foreboding sounds followed by a foreboding event—the loss of a life buoy. Queequeg suggests they use his canoe-coffin as a life buoy, and Starbuck is struck with the irony of the substitution. Ahab questions the carpenter, who is now fashioning the coffin into a life buoy. Ahab accuses the carpenter of a lack of principle, but the carpenter replies that he does not think about the implications of his work: "I do as I do." Ahab then speaks to himself of "dumb" things who do not see the world of symbols and meanings he sees.

Chapter CXXVIII: "The Pequod Meets the Rachel"
Ahab finally learns more about Moby-Dick from the *Rachel*, which has lost a whaleboat that had pursued the whale. The *Rachel*'s captain entreats Ahab to join forces to look for the lost crew. The captain, GARDINER, has lost his son, but Ahab does not heed his plea, even after Gardiner offers to charter the *Pequod* and pay for the expense of the search. Ahab will not countenance any loss of time in his own quest for Moby-Dick.

Chapters CXXIX–CXXX: "The Cabin"; "The Hat"
Pip accosts Ahab, who does not wish to listen to him, fearing that to come too near Pip's madness might cure his own. Ahab will not be diverted from his purpose. The crew senses that the *Pequod* is approaching Ahab's final confrontation with the whale, and they become silent under their captain's "despot eye." A hawk swoops down and snatches Ahab's hat, and Ishmael recalls the legend of Tarquin, who would be king of Rome. In the legend, Tarquin gains his throne only when his hat is restored. Ishmael pointedly notes that Ahab's hat was not returned to him.

Chapter CXXXI: "The Pequod Meets the Delight"
Ahab asks an approaching ship whether it has sighted Moby-Dick. No weapon yet has been made that can kill the whale, he is told. Ahab answers with harpoon in hand, vowing that he holds the whale's death. The "dejected *Delight*," having lost five men to the whale, turns away from the *Pequod*.

Chapter CXXXII: "The Symphony"
On a beautiful, azure day, a tearful Ahab reminisces to Starbuck about catching his first whale. He has known 40 pitiless years on the sea, he exclaims. Past 50, Ahab married a young woman, knowing that in his monomania he had already "widowed her." He refers to himself as an Adam suffering over his lost paradise. Starbuck is moved and urges his "noble captain" to sail home to his wife just as Starbuck would like to sail back to his own wife and child. Ahab replies by citing man's fate, which is to be turned in the wind like a handspike, and Starbuck retreats.

Chapters CXXXIII–CXXXV: "The Chase—First Day"; "The Chase—Second Day"; "The Chase—Third Day"
Moby-Dick is sighted—if only for an instant. The boats are lowered for the chase. Ishmael imagines the whale gliding majestically on, enticing the *Pequod*'s crew. Then the whale arches and shows more of its frightening form. Moby-Dick turns and shows its glistening white teeth and a mouth that looks like a marble tomb. The cunning whale dives beneath Ahab's whaleboat, only to surface and take the boat in its enormous mouth. Ahab, sensing the whale's maneuver, tries to push the boat away from the whale's jaws. The whale withdraws and then swims around the crew members who have spilled out of the boat. Ahab is rescued by Stubb's boat and continues the chase. He promises the gold doubloon to the man who kills the whale. In the grip of the chase, Ishmael explains, a crew of 30 acts as one, pursuing whales day and night.

When the crew sights Moby-Dick again, it charges the three remaining boats, with Ahab in the central position. The whale crosses and recrosses the lines of the three boats, entangling them. As the whale draws back, apparently readying itself to charge the boats, Ahab readies his harpoon line and cuts away the snarled ones. Moby-Dick, in the meantime, drives toward Stubb's and Flask's boats and dashes them against each other. The whale uses its head to strike Ahab's boat from underneath, and Ahab is left hanging onto one half of his broken boat. Hauled onto the deck of the *Pequod*, Ahab has lost all but a sharp splinter of his artificial leg. When the whale appears again, a tormented Starbuck calls on God to show himself and stop this remorseless hunting. He feels he is being towed down into hell. It seems a blasphemy to keep hunting the whale. But to Ahab, "fate's lieutenant," it seems predestined that he will confront Moby-Dick. The chase continues as the carpenter makes Ahab a new leg.

On the third day of the chase, Ahab commands his crew to follow the whale's wake. Boats are lowered as soon as Moby-Dick is sighted. Ahab exclaims to Starbuck that, for the third time, his "soul's ship" is started on its voyage. Ahab and Starbuck shake hands, each knowing that this third encounter may result in their deaths and the loss of the ship. Ahab continues the chase even though sharks are swarming. Starbuck murmurs that the captain has a heart of "wrought steel." Starbuck yearns for his wife and child. For the last time he pleads with Ahab to turn back, but it is too late. Moby-Dick charges the *Pequod,* and Ahab, in fanatical pursuit, is pulled into the sea when the harpoon line catches around his neck. The ship and all hands go down in the whale's attack.

"Epilogue"

Only Ishmael survives to tell the tale. He was some distance from the ship when it went down, and after being sucked down into the whirlpool of its sinking, he reemerges, holding on to the canoe-coffin that had originally been made for Queequeg. Ishmael, describing himself as an orphan, is picked up by the *Rachel.*

PUBLICATION HISTORY

Moby-Dick was widely reviewed both in the United States and in England. Although some reviewers recognized the novel's originality, wit, philosophical depth, and remarkable literary form, others found it verbose, chaotic, and even blasphemous. *Moby-Dick* sold approximately 2,000 copies in the first months of its publication, but by the end of the century it had sold fewer than 4,000 altogether. Sorely disappointed, Melville never again attempted so ambitious a work of fiction. He could not return to his earlier career as travel writer, and the failure of subsequent works, such as *Pierre* (1852), turned him toward poetry and an inward life that would draw less on his career as sailor and traveler. (He would return to the sea one more time with BILLY BUDD, which did not see publication until the Melville revival in the early 20th century.)

Although Melville's literary peers had acknowledged his early promise, by the end of his life the author of *Moby-Dick* had virtually no following, and he died in obscurity. Contemporaries such as the novelist Henry James seem not to have known or followed his later work. Indeed, it was not until the 1920s that critics began to rediscover Melville and hail him as one of the key figures of the "American Renaissance" in literature.

There are, of course, many reasons for Melville's rediscovery and the emergence of *Moby-Dick* as a novel that would have an extraordinary impact on writers emerging in the 1920s, such as William Faulkner and Eugene O'Neill, as well as on post–World War II writers such as Norman Mailer and William Styron. For one thing, Melville seemed modern. His questing spirit, his religious doubts, his alienation from the status quo, and his feeling for nature all made him a kindred spirit

of modernist writers, some of whom considered themselves members of a "lost generation." Above all, Melville's experimentation with literary form and point of view in *Moby-Dick* blends narrative, drama, and symbolic action in a manner that make him a harbinger of 20th-century literature.

modernism   Modernism in literature is usually ascribed to 20th-century works that are experimental and innovative. Certain 19th-century writers, Melville included, often are incorporated into the modernist canon because of their great influence on such writers as William Faulkner, Norman Mailer, and many others. Melville's exploration of ambiguity, of multiple interpretations of events—especially in novels like MOBY-DICK—make him seem modern. Indeed, the rediscovery of Melville's work in the 1920s coincided with the growing artistic maturity of such American writers as Faulkner, Ernest Hemingway, and F. Scott Fitzgerald, who admired Melville as well as the European masters as examples of unconventional writers who found new ways of writing poetic, highly symbolic novels. Modernists have been attracted to Melville because he questions the meaning of literary genres and the stability of history. His radical skepticism and his restless search for new methods of crafting different types of novels make him a precursor of the modernist mentality.

Moerenhout, Jacques-Antoine (1796–1879)   French diplomat. Moerenhout first came to Tahiti by accident, when in 1828 the ship taking him to his first diplomatic post in Valparaiso, Chile, sank near the SOCIETY ISLANDS. He used the following 14 months well, establishing himself in Papeetee as a planter and trader. Over the next six years, he shuttled back and forth between his diplomatic duties in Chile and his commercial interests in Tahiti until, in 1836, he gained a post as United States consul in Papeete. After providing aid and comfort to French Catholic missionaries there, however, he was relieved of this appointment in 1837, only to be appointed French consul the next year. When he was replaced in 1843 by Armand-Joseph BRUAT, Moerenhout became director of native affairs, a post he retained until 1845, when he was sent to California as French consul, first to Monterey, then to Los Angeles, where he died. In OMOO, Melville refers to Moerenhout as the hated French commissioner royal.

Mogul   In MOBY-DICK, the nickname the crew of the PEQUOD uses for Captain AHAB.

Mohi ("Braid-Beard")   Character in MARDI. This bearded historian of Odo accompanies King MEDIA, the philosopher BABBALANJA, and the poet YOOMY when the party joins in TAJI's quest for his lost love, YILLAH.

"Monody" (1891) Poem in *TIMOLEON*. Melville closes the first section of his collection with what is customarily thought to be a lament for his lost relationship with Nathaniel HAWTHORNE. When Melville was in England on the first leg of the long journey that would inspire most of the poems in *Timoleon*, he saw Hawthorne for the last time. Hawthorne was then serving as the American consul in LIVERPOOL, where the two men had what for Melville seems to have been an unsatisfying reunion. When Hawthorne died in 1864, Melville grieved, and possibly at that time set down the first stanza of the poem that would later become "Monody":

> To have known him, to have loved him
> After loneness long;
> And then to be estranged in life,
> And neither in the wrong;
> And now for death to set its seal—
> Ease me, a little ease, my song!

The second stanza, however, broadens outward to include the outside world, wrapped in a wintery embrace.

"Montaigne and His Kitten" (1924) Poem. One of more than 40 poems that Melville left uncollected or unpublished when he died, "Montaigne and His Kitten" shows Melville in an uncharacteristically light-hearted mood. Melville's object here is to praise play and denigrate work, and he chooses the essayist Michel Eyquem de Montaigne (1533–92) as his spokesman, no doubt because of the Frenchman's ability—as revealed in his essays—to keep matters large and small in perspective. Here, addressing his kitten, Blanche, Montaigne considers such weighty matters as immortality and fame. Tying his Order of St-Michel (awarded by Charles IX in 1571) around Blanche's neck, Montaigne declares, "Pish! what fops we humans here."

Mordant, Mr. Character in *BILLY BUDD*. Mordant is the captain of the marines who is instructed by the ship's surgeon (according to Captain VERE's orders) not to disclose to the crew that a drum-head court will be assembled to try Billy for killing John CLAGGART.

Moredock, Colonel John Character in *The CONFIDENCE MAN*. The real Colonel Moredock was a veteran Indian hater and the subject of a book, *Sketches of History, Life and Manners in the West* (1835), by James Hall. Melville inverts Hall's portrayal of Moredock, the only survivor of an Indian massacre. In Melville's book, Moredock is a fanatic who brutally mixes patriotism and murder.

Morewood, John Rowland This NEW YORK CITY hardware factory owner had a summer home in PITTSFIELD, MASSACHUSETTS. There he and his wife Sarah entertained New Yorkers such as the Melvilles at parties and picnics. The conservative John told his wife that he disapproved of Melville's opinions and religious views, and found Melville's conversation much too irreverent.

Morewood, Sarah Wife of John Rowland MOREWOOD. A great hostess, she took the Melvilles in hand for water excursions, costume balls (Herman Melville once appeared as a Turk in robes and caftan), mountain-climbing picnics, and old-fashioned English Christmas parties. She thought Melville cared "very little as to what others may think of him or his books so long as they sell well." She enjoyed his company immensely. He flirted with her, calling her his "goddess" and her home a "paradise." Sarah reciprocated, using language reminiscent of his wife, Lizzie, in the days he was courting her. Even as Sarah was dying of tuberculosis, she hosted a lavish party complete with fireworks. Lizzie Melville was at Sarah's side when she died at the age of 39, and wrote, "I feel that I have lost a very dear and much attached friend—for thirteen years we have been on the most intimate terms without the least shadow of a break in our friendship."

Mortmain Character in *CLAREL*. A Swede marked by his past as a revolutionary leader in Paris in 1848, he seeks a new truth, but his repudiation of an all-consuming devotion to politics isolates and depletes him. He dies at MAR SABA, having descended into the Dead Sea, unable to save himself from despair. His suicide is that of a figure caught between ancient and modern forms of belief. He has failed to find his own form of faith, realizing that Christ's sacrifice only emphasizes man's tragic fate.

"The Mound by the Lake" (1866) Poem in *BATTLE-PIECES*. One of the "Verses Inscriptive and Memorial" in Melville's collection of CIVIL WAR poetry, "The Mound by the Lake" commemorates a dead woman, "So warm her heart—childless—unwed, / Who like a mother comforted." The unnamed woman was modeled on one of Melville's neighbors in PITTSFIELD, MASSACHUSETTS, Mrs. Deacon Curtis T. Fenn, who nursed sick and wounded Union soldiers.

Mowanna Minor character in *TYPEE*. In "The Story of Toby," the sequel to the novel proper, King Mowanna is the ruler of the main Marquesan city, Nukuheva, and an ally of the French colonizers.

Mow-Mow (also, Mow Mow) Character in *TYPEE*. Mow-Mow is a one-eyed Typee chief who makes his first appearance in chapter 32, after the second battle with the HAPPAR, in which he is wounded. In chapter 34, Mow-Mow informs TOMMO that TOBY has returned, but this is apparently part of a ruse to conceal from Tommo the true nature of the whaleboat anchored in the bay below the Typee Valley. Mow-Mow in fact opposes Tommo's leaving on the Australian whaler that takes him to freedom, and when the Typees attempt to ambush the whaleboat as it carries Tommo away, Mow-Mow is in the lead. Tommo insures his escape by throwing a boat hook at the chief, catching him just below the throat. Mow-Mow also makes an appearance in "The Story of Toby," the sequel to *Typee*.

Mudge, Reverend Enoch   In early 1840, Melville went to hear Reverend Mudge preach at Seaman's Bethel on Johnny Cake Hill, a chapel in New Bedford, Massachusetts. In a chapel dedicated in 1832, Mudge preached to all men, believers and unbelievers alike. On the walls of the chapel were plaques commemorating the lives of lost sailors, which Melville regarded as a melancholy reminders of "the fate of whalemen who had gone before me." Mudge is the model for Father MAPPLE in *MOBY-DICK*.

Murphy, Father   Minor character in *OMOO*. Father Murphy is an Irish-born, French-trained Roman Catholic priest who visits the prisoners in the CALABOOZA BERETANEE. He was modeled on James Murphy (1806–44?), who first arrived in Tahiti as a lay missionary in 1835 and, encountering difficulties with George PRITCHARD, the British consul, left almost immediately. He was back in Tahiti the next year but was quickly expelled. After being ordained a priest in 1837 and serving in several other South Seas locales, Father Murphy returned in 1841 to Papeetee, where Melville met him in the fall of 1842. Father Murphy was shortly thereafter recalled to France.

Murray, John (1808–1892)   English publisher. John Murray III was born in London, the son and grandson of publishers. After completing his studies at the University of Edinburgh in 1827, he traveled extensively on the Continent, studying languages and assembling notes on his experiences. When he returned to the family business, he published in 1836 the first of Murray's Handbooks, a series of travel guides. When his father died in 1843, Murray took his place as publisher and began his Home and Colonial Library, a series devoted largely to travel narratives. In 1846 he was approached by Gansevoort MELVILLE, who carried with him to London a portion of his brother Herman's manuscript for *TYPEE*. Murray thought the book would

indeed fit into the Home and Colonial Library, although he was concerned about the book's veracity and requested a number of revisions. In 1846, he published *Typee* and the next year its sequel, *OMOO*—although he still expressed reservations about the truth of what Melville had written. This concern was the rock on which the Murray-Melville connection foundered. John Murray strove to honor his father's wish—one he developed towards the end of his career—that the house publish no poetry or fiction, and when Melville's next book, *MARDI*, proved to be a Polynesian "romance," Murray declined to meet Melville's terms. In 1849, Murray also rejected *WHITE-JACKET*, although he did invite Melville to a dinner party that the author found formal to the point of coldness.

Until his mother's death in 1846, John Murray made his home in apartments above the publishing house offices. In 1847 he married Marion Smith, and together they had three sons and one daughter. The eldest son, also named John Murray, carried on the work of the family firm with his brother Alexander.

"The Muster: Suggested by the Two Days' Review at Washington. (May, 1865.)" (1866)   Poem in *BATTLE-PIECES*. These verses commemorate two parades of CIVIL WAR veterans through the streets of Washington, D.C. On May 23, 1865, General George Meade's Army of the Potomac marched in good trim past thousands of well-wishers. The next day, General William Tecumseh Sherman's troops marched more casually through the capital's streets. Melville's poem exults in the show.

mute, the   Character in *The CONFIDENCE MAN*. The mute, a disguise of the CONFIDENCE MAN, comes aboard a Mississippi river boat posting signs about the need for charity, for human beings to trust each other, to have confidence in each other—which is, of course, the line the confidence man himself takes as he assumes the identities of many different characters to bilk the ship's passengers out of their money.

"My Jacket Old" (1924)   Poem. One of more than 40 poems that Melville left uncollected or unpublished when he died, "My Jacket Old" focuses on a jacket worn during "the dull day's work"—presumably at the CUSTOM-HOUSE. At the end of such a day, the dust from the jacket inspires the poet to dream of faraway places and of "Edenic Leisure's age" before the Fall, when humans were unburdened by labor and vestments.

Nantucket, Massachusetts A town on the island of Nantucket southeast of the Massachusetts mainland, where ISHMAEL visits on his quest to join a whale ship in *MOBY-DICK*. It was a famous whaling center in the 18th and early 19th centuries.

"Naples in the Time of Bomba." *See* "THE BURGUNDY CLUB SKETCHES."

Nathan Character in *CLAREL*. An American farmer whose ZIONISM brings him to the Holy Land. He is the father of RUTH, whom Clarel loves. Nathan has changed his beliefs from Christianity to deism (belief in a God who does not intervene in human affairs) to PANTHEISM. He marries AGAR, a Jew, and converts to Judaism. Zionism then becomes his mission and the focal point of his identity.

negro cripple, the Character in *THE CONFIDENCE MAN*. The cripple, one of the disguises of the CONFIDENCE MAN, excites much discussion aboard the *FIDELE*. Some passengers regard him as a fraud, perhaps even a white man acting so as to provoke sympathy and charity. The cripple says there are many aboard who can vouch for him (all of whom are the confidence man himself in his various masks), and a clergyman goes off in search of these corroborating witnesses.

Nehemiah Character in *CLAREL*. He is a true believer who carries tracts about the Second Coming and the New Jerusalem. Unlike the other pilgrims, Nehemiah never doubts the validity of Christianity and never even considers the arguments against it. He is pure and innocent in his devotion to sacred texts. His sweetness prevents him from exhibiting the harshness of the fanatic. He is a zealot, but of the most gentle kind. His drowning in the Dead Sea causes great sadness in the pilgrims who honor his dedication, even if they cannot emulate his confidence in the new millennium.

Nelson, Horatio (1758–1805) Born in Norfolk, England, Nelson (Lord Nelson; Viscount Nelson) became England's greatest naval commander by defeating the French fleet several times, as in the Battle of the NILE, and then destroying it in the Battle of TRAFALGAR. In *BILLY BUDD, SAILOR*, Admiral Nelson is portrayed as the epitome of the 18th-century naval hero, a figure no longer possible to conceive of in a later time. Captain VERE dies before seeing action in any of Nelson's great victories.

Neoplatonism A philosophy associated first with Plotinus (A.D. 204–270), who sought to reconcile the philosophies of Plato and Aristotle. Like Plato, Plotinus stresses that the ultimate reality is beyond the material world, and that this higher level of reality can be apprehended only through intuition. But Plotinus also tries to incorporate Aristotle's concern with the material world by positing a union between natural and supernatural, replacing Plato's dualism with monism—that is, with the notion that the material and the ideal share a common identity. Melville was strongly drawn to Neoplatonism out of his own drive to unite his experience of the physical world with a strong metaphysical sensibility. He specifically invokes the ideas of the Neoplatonist writers in *PIERRE*, especially in his chapter on the Apostles, the group of writers and artists he associates with in New York City.

Neversink The U.S. Navy frigate that carries the narrator of Melville's fifth book, *WHITE-JACKET; OR, THE WORLD IN A MAN-OF-WAR*. The book draws heavily on Melville's experiences serving as a common sailor aboard the U.S.S. *UNITED STATES* from August 1843 to October 1844.

"The New Ancient of Days: The Man of the Cave of Engihoul" (1947) Poem. One of at least 40 poems left uncollected or unpublished when Melville died, "The New Ancient of Days" was originally titled "The Old Boy of the Cave." A send-up of the theory of evolution, the poem refers to the discovery in 1835 by paleontologist Philippe Charles Schmerling of human remains in the Engihoul cavern in Belgium. Melville compares this evidence of the so-called missing link to a circus side-show. His title, taken from the Book of Daniel 7:9, "I beheld till the thrones were cast down, and the Ancient of days did sit," indicates that he thought the rage to replace religion with science was more than a little misguided.

New Bedford, Massachusetts A seaport in southeastern Massachusetts. New Bedford was a leading whale port in the early decades of the 19th century. In MOBY-DICK, Ishmael lodges there. Melville visited New Bedford on December 26, 1840.

"The New Planet" (1847) Short satiric squib attributed to Melville. Published anonymously in the July 24, 1847, issue of YANKEE DOODLE, it opens with a mock letter to the magazine from a "Prof. of Astronomy and Celestial Trigonometry" at Columbia College in NEW YORK CITY. The professor reports his observation of a strange light in the southern sky, which he cannot identify. He theorizes that the light must be coming from a new planet, "The Barnum," which shines just over P. T. BARNUM's American Museum. The piece describes a number of the attractions in the museum and refers to the Chinese junk (a Chinese flat-bottomed boat) then anchored in New York harbor. Because Melville is believed to have written other unsigned pieces for *Yankee Doodle* about the Barnum Museum and the Chinese junk, there is some evidence that he is the author of this piece as well.

"The New Rosicrucians" (1924) Poem in WEEDS AND WILDINGS. Part of the "As They Fell" sequence in the "A Rose or Two" section of the collection, "The New Rosicrucians" evokes the name of an order of mystics who professed to apply ancient religious principles to modern life. Melville plainly found such beliefs wanting, decrying those "Who have drained the rose's chalice / Never heeding gain or loss" for their inability to recognize the concept of mortal sin. Such esoteric interpretations of Christianity were for Melville no more convincing than orthodoxy.

New York City Herman Melville's birthplace, and his home from 1819 to 1830, 1847 to 1850, and 1863 to 1891. The New York in which Melville was born in August 1819 was a busy seaport that imported goods—including those his father, Allan MELVILL, sold—from all over the world. The house where Melville was born was on Pearl Street near the southern end of Manhattan and had a view of the Battery, the southern tip of Manhattan Island. It was a genteel neighborhood. Most of those who could afford to do so crowded into the downtown area, for uptown was inhabited by freed slaves and laborers living in rundown shanties. Maria Gansevoort MELVILLE and her children often spent time away from the city to escape the heat and smells of summer as well as the epidemics of diseases, such as yellow fever, that spread from the city's docks and tenements.

Such epidemics were exacerbated by the economic depressions that periodically hit the city and ultimately drove Melville's father out of business and out of New York City. Before this misfortune struck them, however, the Melvill (the name was changed to *Melville* after Allan's death) family moved to a more prestigious address on upper Broadway, where people like the Astors (one of New York's wealthiest and most influential families) were their neighbors. They lived there for just over two years before moving back to ALBANY, NEW YORK, where they took up residence with Maria's family.

After Allan Melvill's death in 1832, Maria lived for a time with her children in Albany, then moved to nearby LANSINGBURGH, which remained Herman's home base until after he married. In October 1837, he and his wife, Lizzie, joined with Herman's brother Allan and his wife to buy a brownstone in Manhattan on Fourth Avenue between 11th and 12th Streets, which they also shared with Maria Melville and her daughters. The New York City of the 1840s was alive with cultural opportunities, and this clearly was one of the reasons that Herman, now at work on his third novel, wanted to escape the sleepy backwaters of upstate New York.

Like his mother before him, though, Melville liked to take himself and his growing family out of the city during the summer. His chosen spot for vacations was the Berkshires, and in particular PITTSFIELD, MASSACHUSETTS, with which the Melvill family had a long association. Upon meeting Nathaniel HAWTHORNE there in 1850, Melville found reason to take up residence in the Berkshires year-round, and in 1850 he and Lizzie bought ARROWHEAD farm.

Melville's relationship with Hawthorne deteriorated, as did his marriage to Lizzie. In 1863, finding the work required to run a farm more than he could cope with, Melville exchanged his farm for Allan's house on East 26th Street in Manhattan. Melville would live there for the remainder of his life, close to P. T. BARNUM's stables, Lorenzo Delmonico's famed restaurant, Stanford White's new Madison Square Garden, and the home of Theodore Roosevelt, the future president. By the time Melville moved to East 26th Street, his own celebrity had already faded. By the 1880s, many people presumed he was already dead. But in the waning days of the next century, the block where he spent nearly three decades would be renamed Herman Melville Square.

"The New Zealot to the Sun" (1891) Poem in TIMOLEON. This poem makes a quick march through human history, rehearsing the evils of received religion, from the adulation of Eastern worship to "Calvin's last extreme." But in the poem's final stanza, the speaker is unveiled as a scientist every bit as fanatical and purblind about the efficacy and purity of the tenets of his faith as any religious true believer.

"The Night-March" (1891) Poem in TIMOLEON. "The Night-March" pictures an army marching over "boundless plains" without a visible leader. The "chief" is instead a legend who signals his "mandate" to his armies—which Melville refers to as "that shining host." The import of the poem is ambiguous, but the leader could be Christ or any other religious or, perhaps, political leader; or even some organizing principle in the universe—gravity, or the sun, for example—that, though intangible, yet commands the obedience of a mighty force.

Nile, Battle of the   Famous victory of Admiral Horatio NELSON, who destroyed the French fleet at Abukir Bay in 1798. In *BILLY BUDD, SAILOR,* the narrator mentions that Captain VERE died before he could serve with Nelson in great victories like the Battle of the Nile. Vere, in fact, shares Nelson's unswerving dedication to duty and great compassion for his men.

Nimni   Minor character in *MARDI.* Nimni is the most exalted citizen of the isle of Pimminee and its leading Tapparian. The Tapparians, or Men of TAPPA, are ruled by a legal code that amounts to little more than a dress code, and when Nimni holds an open house in honor of TAJI and his company, the Pimminee aristocracy turns out in all its finery.

Nippers   Minor character in "BARTLEBY, THE SCRIVENER." Nippers, one of the scriveners employed in the narrator's law office, is a young man who chafes at his duties, which cause him to grind his teeth. It is probably this habit that gives rise to his nickname.

Noble, Charles Arnold   Minor character in *The CONFIDENCE MAN.* This is one of the names the MISSOURIAN takes for himself.

Nord   Minor character in *WHITE-JACKET.* Nord is a literate, reserved member of the after-guard on board the *NEVERSINK* who becomes a particular friend of WHITE-JACKET. Nord is a genuine recluse, however, and refuses to warm up to the other men. When the man-of-war finally docks in Norfolk, he leaves the ship without saying farewell to anyone. Nord was clearly based on one of Melville's crewmates aboard the U.S.S. *UNITED STATES,* a man named Oliver Russ who, for mysterious reasons, enlisted as "Edward Norton." Melville called him "Nord," and the two had many long shipboard conversations about literature. These discussions apparently meant a great deal to Norton, for years later Melville learned that he had named his first child Herman Melville Russ.

Nore mutiny   The Nore is a sandbank in the mouth of the Thames River in England. In 1797, a mutiny broke out in the British fleet stationed there. The sailors protested their bad food and poor pay. The mutiny was harshly put down, and its leader was hanged. It is this summary justice that Captain VERE has in mind as he considers the punishment of BILLY BUDD for killing John CLAGGART. Vere is concerned that no matter how compassionate it might be to spare Billy, the result will be a weakening of naval discipline.

"Norfolk Isle and the Chola Widow."   Sketch Eighth of "THE ENCANTADAS."

Nulli   Minor character in *MARDI.* Nulli is a slave overseer in the southern part of Vivenza. In appearance he resembles John C. CALHOUN (1782–1850), the South Carolina statesman who was a leading proponent of states' rights and nullification, the doctrine whereby an individual state declines to recognize federal authority.

Oates, Titus (1649–1705) English conspirator who in 1677 claimed to uncover a "Popish plot" (a cabal of Catholics) supposedly planning to assassinate King Charles II. He was later found to have committed perjury and was imprisoned, but was freed during the Glorious Revolution of 1688. By comparing John CLAGGART to Oates, the narrator in *BILLY BUDD* emphasizes Claggart's scheming personality and his conspiracy to make BILLY BUDD look like a mutineer.

Oberlus Character in "THE ENCANTADAS." Oberlus appears in Sketch Ninth, "Hood's Isle and the Hermit Oberlus," where he appears as a misanthropic deserter who takes over one of the Galapagos Islands, engaging variously in farming, kidnapping, slave-holding, and robbery. Eventually he leaves his island kingdom and is jailed in Payta, Peru, on suspicion of sabotage.

"Off Cape Colonna" (1981) Poem in *TIMOLEON*. Part of the "Fruit of Travel Long Ago" section of the volume, "Off Cape Colonna" concerns a rocky promontory on the Greek coast that has been the site of numerous shipwrecks—among them the one that inspired William Falconer's poem "The Shipwreck" (1762), written from Falconer's own experience there. Atop the promontory sits the ruin of a temple to the God Poseidon, built in the fourth century B.C., making Cape Colonna one of the most arresting sites in all of the Grecian peninsula.

Ohiro Moldona Fivona Minor character in *MARDI*. She is the wife of NIMNI of Pimminee and the mother of three daughters, "the Vowels" A, I, AND O.

Oh Oh Minor character in *MARDI*. Oh Oh is a collector of antiquities, oddities, and curios on the island of Padulla. He resembles P. T. BARNUM, the impresario whose museum, during Melville's time, was known for its exhibition of curiosities.

"Old Age in His Ailing" (1924) Poem. When he died, Melville left more than 40 poems uncollected or unpublished. These date from various periods in his career. "Old Age in His Ailing" seems to be one of his later efforts, focusing on old age's scorn for youth. But this attitude, says the speaker, is like skimmed milk slandering cream, and he will have none of it.

Old Bach Character in "THE PARADISE OF BACHELORS AND THE TARTARUS OF MAIDS." Old Bach—who is, indeed, a bachelor—is the supervisor of the paper mill that is the "Tartarus of Maids."

Old Coffee Minor character in *WHITE-JACKET*. Old Coffee is the ship's cook aboard the *NEVERSINK*. A dignified black man, Old Coffee claims to have been trained at New York's Astor House restaurant.

"Old Counsel of the Young Master of a Wrecked California Clipper" (1888) Poem in *JOHN MARR*. Three lines of this five-line poem read like simple directions on how to sail a ship out of the Golden Gate. But this "young master" has already learned a thing or two and cautions against the overconfidence he apparently felt at one time: "*All hands save ship!* has startled dreamers."

"The Old Fashion" (1924) Poem in *WEEDS AND WILDINGS*. Part of the section titled "The Year," "The Old Fashion" speaks lovingly of a figure named Ver who is eternally youthful and "the same, and forever, / Year after year." "Ver" may be a Latinate reference to the green spring; it may also be a moniker lovingly bestowed on Melville's wife, Lizzie.

old man, the Minor character in *The CONFIDENCE MAN*. He is approached by a young boy who sells him a "counterfeit detector." The COSMOPOLITAN (a guise of the CONFIDENCE MAN) tries to persuade the old man to throw away the device since it promotes a distrust in mankind.

Old Prudence Minor character in *The CONFIDENCE MAN*. He advises China ASTER not to accept offers of loans from friends.

"The Old Shipmaster and His Crazy Barn" (1924) Poem. One of more than 40 poems Melville left uncollected or unpublished at his death, this one bears indications that it was written during—or at least inspired by—the author's years at ARROWHEAD. The speaker of this dramatic monologue is a retired ship's captain who discourses about his creaky old lichen-covered barn, which he refuses to tear down. The site is home to a friendly spirit akin to his own; both he and the spirit would be uprooted if the barn were razed:

Let me keep where I cling!
I am touchy as tinder
Yea, quick to take wing,
Nor return if I fly.

Omoo: A Narrative of Adventures in the South Seas
Herman Melville's second novel, published in 1847. In order to prevent the British pirating of an American edition, *Omoo* appeared first in Britain, where it was titled *Omoo: A Narrative of Adventures in the South Seas; Being a Sequel to the "Residence in the Marquesas Islands"*— the last being a reference to Melville's first book, TYPEE, which had been a popular success. Melville himself wanted to capitalize on his fame in order to further his literary career. Besides, he had more material gleaned from his voyages in the exotic South Seas, enough to write a sequel.

Omoo—the title was taken from a Polynesian word meaning "rover"—is narrated by a character sometimes called, just as his celebrated creator was, "Typee," after the custom of naming sailors for a place with which they are associated. Melville's second novel picks up precisely where his first ended: with the rescue of TOMMO/TYPEE from the hands of his Marquesan captors.

SYNOPSIS

Chapter 1: "My Reception Aboard"
In the middle of a bright, tropical afternoon, the narrator makes his escape from the Typees onto a small, Yankee-built Australian whaling ship, the *Julia*. Wearing native dress, Typee boards the ship, where he recognizes two members of the crew from previous ports of call. He is then summoned to the captain's cabin, where he is asked to sign the ship's articles, or contract. Captain Guy is a pale, sickly young man who immediately hands Typee off to the mate, John Jermin. Jermin doctors Typee's leg, which has plagued him ever since he escaped another ship by finding his way to the Typee Valley. After he has been barbered and provided with a proper sailor's frock, Typee is fed and shown his bunk, where he passes a sleepless night.

Before daybreak, the *Julia* arives off the bay of Nuku Hiva (which Melville calls Nukuheva), where the natives who had delivered Typee to the ship the previous day are sent ashore. This task completed, the ship sails out of the harbor, while Typee learns the history of its voyage thus far.

Chapters 2–3: "Some Account of the Ship"; "Further Account of the Julia"
Typee describes the ship, which is very old and in a state of disrepair. Nonetheless, "brave Little Jule" sails well. Setting out from Sydney, she had carried a crew of 33, now diminished by desertions to 20. Of these, more than half are suffering from illnesses contracted during a long stay in a "dissipated port."

Captain Guy is described in detail. An incompetent captain, he is held in contempt by his crew, who refer to him behind his back as "The Cabin Boy" and "Paper Jack." Guy, in response, leaves most matters in the hands of his mate, Jermin, who is a good seaman except that he is under the influence of alcohol most of the time. The third member of the *Julia*'s ruling class is the ship's doctor, a tall, bony fellow named Dr. Long Ghost, who, having quarreled with the captain, forsook the cabin for the forecastle. Living among the crew, Long Ghost becomes Typee's companion.

Normal discipline seems to have broken down entirely on board the ship. BEMBO, the New Zealand harpooner, speaks only to Jermin. Long Ghost, having resigned as the ship's doctor, holds himself out as a passenger. Stores are running dangerously low, but Captain Guy dares not bring the *Julia* into port to reprovision, for fear that the remainder of his crew will desert. Instead, the ship heads for Hytyhoo, a village on the Marquesan island of St. Christina, where Guy hopes to pick up eight crewmen who had deserted some weeks earlier. The ship has managed thus far to capture only two sperm whales, and the captain is desperate to fill the hold with oil as quickly as possible.

Chapter 4: "A Scene in the Forecastle"
The narrator relates an episode that illustrates the balance of power on board the *Julia*. Jermin's reign appears to be absolute with one exception: he has never gotten the best of the ship's carpenter, a man so ugly he is known as "Beauty"—when he is not called "CHIPS." On Typee's second day aboard, Jermin calls for the carpenter to come up from the forecastle to fix something on deck. When Beauty refuses, Jermin struggles unsuccessfully to haul him up physically. The noise of their battle rouses the captain, whose investigation leads to a cup of tea being thrown in his face. Guy retreats, followed by Jermin, who is heard to upbraid him for failing to force Beauty to bend to the mate's will. Guy responds by promising to flog the carpenter, but nothing comes of this.

Chapter 5: "What happened at Hytyhoo"
As the *Julia* draws near Hytyhoo, she is met by a French man-of-war, which carries two officers and three drunken old native chiefs. The latter have the ship declared TABOO in order to ward off the native girls just then swimming out to meet the whaler.

That night, taking advantage of Jermin's drink-induced slumber while he is supposed to be on watch, several crew members desert. Together with five others who had deserted earlier, they are recovered toward sunset, when a crowd of natives—persuaded by the promise of gunpowder—turns them over to the French. Back on board, the deserters treat the whole episode as a lark.

Chapters 6–8: "We touch at La Dominica"; "What happened at Hannamanoo"; "The Tattooers of La Dominica"

The next day, the *Julia* heads for Hivarhoo, on the nearby island of La Dominica, in search of several English sailors who recently deserted from an American whaler. Finding only a band of spear-carrying natives, Captain Guy fires his pistol at them, providing the narrator with an opportunity to condemn the degraded attitudes of westerners toward native people.

The *Julia* then heads for the bay of Hannamanoo, on the other side of the island. The ship is met by a canoe carrying young native men, as well as a white renegade named Lem Hardy. Hardy makes an immediate impression, largely because of the blue shark TATTOO that embellishes his forehead. An Englishman who deserted from a trade ship, he has "gone native," transforming himself into the military leader of a local tribe. One of his tribesmen, Wymontoo, agrees to join the crew of the *Julia*, which then sets sail.

Hardy's adornment occasions a digression devoted to the art of tattooing as practiced in La Dominica.

Chapters 9–12: "We steer to the Westward. —State of Affairs"; "A Sea-Parlour described, with some of its Tenants"; "Doctor Long Ghost a Wag. —One of his Capers"; "Death and Burial of two of the Crew"

The *Julia* sails westward, its destination kept secret by Jermin who, now that Guy has relapsed into illness, has assumed full command of the whaler. The narrator, himself still suffering from lameness, gets further acquainted with Long Ghost and with his books in the forecastle. The narrator describes this "sea-parlour" at length, with some humorous asides about the cockroaches and rats it harbors and details of Long Ghost's pranks, including his tying an old sailor's ankle to a sea chest.

This jolly episode is followed by a contrasting one devoted to burial at sea. When two of the *Julia*'s sick crew members expire, their corpses are stitched up in hammocks and—as the ship's progress is temporarily halted—rather unceremoniously dumped overboard. The crew are deeply affected by these deaths, which rouse their inherently superstitious natures. Van, a Finn supposedly gifted with second sight, lays his hand on the horseshoe charm nailed to the foremast and solemnly declares that within three weeks less than a quarter of the crew will be left.

Gradually, however, the men begin to recover their spirits—helped, in part, by twice daily dispensations of "tots" of Pisco, an alcoholic drink.

Chapters 13–17: "Our Destination changed"; "Rope-Yarn"; "Chips and Bungs"; We encounter a Gale"; "The Coral Islands"

About a month after leaving Hannamanoo, the *Julia* changes course and heads for Tahiti. Captain Guy has taken a turn for the worse, and Long Ghost convinces

Jermin that rather than officially assume command in the event of Guy's death, the mate is obliged to steer the ship to the nearest civilized port.

Melville then devotes two chapters to some of the other characters who people the *Julia*. A presumably useless landlubber called Rope Yarn, or Ropey, once a journeyman baker in London, performs all manner of disagreeable tasks in addition to serving as the butt of the other sailors' jokes. Chips the carpenter and BUNGS the cooper, his cohort, employ their skills to siphon off Pisco. When the *Julia* encounters a gale, BALTIMORE, the black ship's cook, is dashed about the deck as his cookhouse breaks loose from its moorings. Jermin, despite his drunkenness and rusted quadrant, manages to steer a proper course, which takes them past the Coral Islands, the Pomotu or Low Group, less than 24 hours from Tahiti. The passage provides Melville with an opportunity to discourse on exotica, extolling the beauty of the islands, which produce "pearl-shell" and cocoanut oil.

Chapters 18–22: "Tahiti"; "A Surprise. —More about Bembo"; "The Round-Robin. —Visitors from Shore"; "Proceedings of the Consul"; "The Consul's Departure"

The next dawn sees the *Julia* drawing near Tahiti, which poor Wymontoo at first mistakes for his home. The narrator describes the beauties of this famous island and relates that it was the setting for the infamous mutiny on the *Bounty* in 1789, after which some of the British mutineers, together with Tahitian women, founded a colony on Pitcairn Island, elsewhere in the South Pacific.

The crew gathers on deck, eager to go into port. In the harbor of Papeetee, they see Rear Admiral Dupetit Thouars's flagship, the *Reine Blanche,* firing a salute in honor of a treaty signed that morning that handed control of the island over to the French.

Much to the crew's dismay, Jermin orders them to haul in the sails. The *Julia* and its crew will remain at sea, while only Captain Guy, attended by his mate, will go ashore. Bembo is left in charge, while the angry crew members mutter darkly among themselves, threatening to mutiny. Long Ghost and Typee try to defuse the situation. Typee suggests that they all sign a "round robin" petition describing their plight and send it ashore with Baltimore to the British consul. The men agree, and draw up a list of grievances which 16 sign in circular fashion (Melville provides a drawing) so that no individual can be singled out as the instigator.

Baltimore returns that evening with news that in the consul's absence, the petition was handed to his substitute, an Englishman named Wilson who is, alas, an old friend of Captain Guy. The next morning, Wilson and another Englishman, Doctor Johnson, visit the *Julia.* Jermin musters the crew. Those who are sick are taken below to be seen to by Doctor Johnson, while Wilson proceeds to question the others about Jermin's leadership and about their rations. His hostile manner provokes hostility in the crew, and after one Salem threatens Wilson with a knife, the Englishman retreats—but not before he orders all hands to prepare to leave shortly for a three-month whaling voyage. As the men explode in anger, Wilson and Doctor Johnson depart, soon followed by Jermin, the ship's cook, and the ship's steward—leaving the *Julia,* as before, under the control of Bembo.

Chapters 23–24: "The Second Night off Papeetee"; "Outbreak of the Crew"
That evening Jermin, intoxicated again, returns with the cook and the steward. The crew, likewise intoxicated, listen to his suggestion that they follow Wilson's orders and shove off—after all, there is plenty of Pisco on board, and they need never return to Captain Guy. But the men remain unconvinced and are soon distracted when a fight breaks out between Bembo and Sydney Ben, an escaped convict. The aborigine gets the better of the convict, but is hauled off before he can do any real damage. Typee wakes to find Bembo steering the *Julia* straight toward a coral reef. He wakes the crew members who had been left on watch, and together they manage to change course just in time. Jermin wakes and locks Bembo in the scuttle to prevent the men from murdering the Maori (Melville calls him the "Mowree"), who is never seen again.

Chapter 25: "Jermin encounters an Old Shipmate"
That night, by accident, a schooner bearing a dozen natives and one white man comes alongside the *Julia.* In an episode that brings to mind the reunion of Melville and Richard Tobias GREENE after *Typee*'s publication, the white man turns out to be Viner, a former shipmate of Jermin who was thought to have been lost at sea some 15 years earlier. In an aside probably meant for his doubting publisher, Melville underscored the notion that truth is stranger than fiction: "The meeting of these men, under the circumstances, is one of a thousand concurrences appearing exaggerated in fiction; but, nevertheless, frequently realized in actual lives of adventure."

Chapters 26–29: "We enter the Harbour. —Jim the Pilot"; "A Glance at Papeetee. —We are sent aboard the Frigate"; "Reception from the Frenchman"; "The Reine Blanche"
Not long after midnight, Jermin, grown impatient, decides to take the *Julia* into the harbor of Papeetee. Few of the crew are willing to help with this perilous trip, but Jermin proves his mettle as a navigator. With the assistance of Jim, the native harbor pilot, the ship is steered safely into port.

Papeetee is briefly described. No sooner does the *Julia* drop anchor than Wilson comes alongside. Boarding the ship, he orders that all the "mutineers"— including Long Ghost and the narrator—be rounded up. All (except the cooper) refuse to resume their duties and are transferred to the *Reine Blanche.*

On board the French man-of-war, the prisoners are handcuffed and shackled. The ship itself is an elegant affair, but it is manned by unprofessional sailors who are poorly fed. Melville takes the opportunity to put this tongue-in-cheek evaluation in the mouth of his nearly invisible narrator: "Though I say the French are no sailors, I am far from seeking to underrate them as a people. They are an ingenious and right gallant nation. And, as an American, I take pride in asserting it."

Chapters 30–31: "They take us Ashore. —What happened there"; "The Calabooza Beretanee"
For five days and nights, during which they are badly fed, the mutineers remain on the French ship. On the afternoon of the fifth day, a cutter takes them ashore, where Wilson asks them if they still refuse to serve. All answer yes, whereupon a group of good-natured Tahitians are ordered to escort the men to jail.

The narrator delights in being free of the confines of the frigate and describes in detail the beauties of the Broom Road, a wide avenue that circles the island. The men are marched along this road to the CALABOOZA BERETANEE, as the Tahitians call the jail built by English settlers.

The Calabooza Beretanee proves to be merely a grass shack furnished only with "stocks" consisting of two 20-foot timbers. The jailor, Captain BOB, a rotund old Tahitian, proves to be so companionable that the sailors cheerfully obey his orders to place their ankles between the stocks. Both the sailors and their native guards find the whole affair a farce and behave accordingly. When morning comes, the men are freed from their bonds and permitted to bathe in a local stream. Captain Bob, whose casual grasp of reality is signified by his claim to have known Captain COOK (who last set foot in Tahiti decades before Captain Bob's time), trades his breadfruit for the sailors' despised sea biscuit and permits his prisoners to go into the local orange groves to pick all the delicious fruit they want.

Chapter 32: "Proceedings of the French at Tahiti"
The narrator delivers a history of the French in Tahiti. When French missionaries first tried to establish a Roman Catholic mission there, they were unceremoniously ousted by the natives, who were egged on by the resident English Protestant missionaries. Using the ouster of the priests as an excuse, Rear Admiral Dupetit Thouars then seized the island, which became a French protectorate. The French governor, Armand-Joseph BRUAT, is much hated by the people and feared by their queen, POMARE. In short, no love is lost between the natives and their occupiers, and the animosity has resulted in bloodshed.

Chapters 33–37: "We receive Calls at the Hotel de Calabooza"; "Life at the Calabooza"; "Visit from an Old Acquaintance"; "We are carried before the Consul and Captain"; "The French Priests pay their Respects"

After offering some observations about the physical degeneration of the Tahitians from diseases such as elephantiasis, the narrator extols their physical beauty. Many Tahitians—including a wild and beautiful girl who mocks the narrator—come to visit the captive "Karhowrees," or white men, in the Calabooza Beretanee. When Captain Bob relaxes his vigilance further, the prisoners are allowed to roam about almost at will. They find food in native homes, all of which extend their hospitality.

One day the captives are paid a visit by Doctor Johnson. Many of the sailors feign illness, none so well as Long Ghost, who persuades the doctor to send along some laudanum (liquid opium), of which all partake.

Wilson and a panel of other Europeans, overseen by a convalescent Captain Guy, then conduct a semblance of a hearing. Wilson reads a series of exaggerated affidavits to the prisoners in an attempt to frighten them back into service on board the *Julia*, but they refuse to take the bait and are ordered back to the Calabooza Beretanee. Three French priests come calling, together with a French-trained Irish priest, Father MURPHY. Finding a fellow Irishman, Pat, among the captives, Father Murphy takes pity on them, sending Pat clothing and providing bread for them all. Further attempts to bribe Pat to rejoin the crew of the *Julia* fail, but the narrator jokes that the priest's beneficence—in particular his openhandedness with his liquor—turns them all into Catholics.

Chapter 38: "Little Jule sails without us"

Liquor is common coin among mariners and provides the narrator with material for two more anecdotes. One concerns Jermin, who, with his friend Viner, has been having a high time on board ship. One afternoon, feeling no pain, the mate managed to frighten a group of natives and, as a result, was hauled before Wilson. Rather than punishing Jermin, Wilson and Captain Guy and their bottle of brandy make a night of it.

Wilson's weakness for the bottle, it seems, has often proved his undoing. Formerly, he had tried to shut down the cantina run by an infamous Englishwoman known as "Old Mother Tot," only to have the cagy old woman catch him out when he was carried home drunk one night.

After relating these episodes, the narrator tells how a gang of sailors idling in Papeetee, urged on by the inmates of the Calabooza, make up a new crew for the *Julia*, finally allowing the ship to set sail again. When Captain Bob announces her departure, the former mutineers all rush down to the beach to see her off. Thereafter, the jailor declines to exercise any restraint

but, lacking a better place to go in Papeetee, the sailors stay on at the Calabooza.

Chapters 39–47: "Jermin serves us a good turn. — Friendships in Polynesia"; "We take unto ourselves Friends"; "We levy Contributions on the Shipping"; "Motoo-Otoo. —A Tahitian Casuist"; "One is judged by the Company he keeps"; "Cathedral of Papoar. —The Church of the Cocoa Nuts"; "A Missionary's Sermon; with some reflections"; "Something about the Kannakippers"; "How they dress in Tahiti"

The convicts' stay is made more comfortable by the appearance of their sea chests, which Jermin has sent ashore before departing. The contents of these chests—essentially all the sailors' worldly possessions—prove invaluable, as the Tahitians consider these items riches and their owners infinitely worthy. Each westerner finds himself attached to a native according to the Polynesian custom of "tayos," and the narrator describes his own tayo, a Christian convert named KOOLOO. As soon as the sailor's chests grow empty, however, the tayos shift their affections elsewhere.

Other whalers arrive in due course, and their crews invite the convicts to pilfer rations from the ships. Long Ghost and the narrator make a successful trip out to one of these ships in Captain Bob's "Pill Box," a tiny outrigger canoe. Typee also employs the Pill Box in an attempt to penetrate Motoo-Otoo, an island situated in Papeetee Harbor and belonging to the Tahitian queen. He is rebuffed. Indeed, nearly everyone regards the convicts as a set of lawless vagabonds, as the narrator discovers when he causes chaos among a group of missionaries' wives simply by doffing his turban and drawing attention to himself.

Typee clearly is doing his best to fit in, adopting local garb and attending the principal native church in Papeetee, where an anti-French, pro-British sermon is delivered. This last affords the narrator an opportunity to expatiate about the hypocrisy of the Polynesians, who seem to regard the Sabbath as merely a good excuse to get out of work. He offers up his former friend Kooloo as a primary example of this tendency toward moral laxness, which has to be held in check by religious constables, or "kannakippers." But, he adds, such tendencies—like the Tahitians' motley form of dress—result primarily from European influences that have "denationalized" them.

Chapters 48–49: "Tahiti as it is"; "Same Subject continued"

Omoo is a powerfully antimissionary book, and in these chapters Melville cites a number of different authorities as support for his conviction that these foreign influences have wrecked this South Seas paradise, displacing functioning native institutions with bastardized—and dysfunctional—western ones. In Tahiti and Hawaii both, the missionaries have set themselves apart from—even above—the native population, enriching themselves while degrading their hosts.

"Civilization" has brought the Polynesians alcoholism and smallpox, and as a result, they are a dying breed.

Chapters 50–61: "Something happens to Long Ghost"; "Wilson gives us the Cut. —Departure for Imeeo"; "The Valley of Martair"; "Farming in Polynesia"; "Some Account of the Wild Cattle in Polynesia"; "A Hunting Ramble with Zeke"; "Musquitoes"; "The Second Hunt in the Mountains"; "The Hunting Feast; and a Visit to Afrehitoo"; "The Murphies"; "What they thought of us in Martair"; "Preparing for the Journey"

Returning to the narrative, Typee relates how his friend Long Ghost throws a fit in front of Doctor Johnson in order to obtain more regular meals. This tactic, however, proves fruitless. The captives, who have become an economic hardship for the natives, decide to march off to Wilson to demand adequate maintenance. The interview proves fruitless, and Long Ghost and the narrator, certain now that Wilson simply wants to get rid of the captives, decide to head out to the territory ahead of the rest.

A few days before, the narrator had met two white planters, ZEKE and SHORTY, from Imeeo, the next island over. The planters had been looking for two other white men to serve as field laborers, and Long Ghost and Typee now volunteer their services—although they give their names as Peter and Paul, respectively. They slip away by night and row quickly over to Imeeo to survey the valley of Martair, which will be the setting for their labors.

Peter and Paul are warmly greeted by Zeke and Shorty and their tayo, a local chief named Tonoi. But the physical labor involved in farming in this part of Polynesia involves crude tools and brute force; it is not to the taste of Peter and Paul. Peter, in particular, is subject to malingering, and Paul begins to fear that they will soon come to loggerheads with their employers. Peter and Paul decide to take their leave and search for an easier life elsewhere—but not before the narrator devotes a few chapters to local color. He discusses Queen Pomare's wild cattle, which roam all over Imeeo; goes off on a tangent about the history of Hawaii; reprises a wild hog hunt with Zeke; and describes the flora of Imeeo, as well as an unhappy encounter with the island's multitudes of mosquitoes.

Peter and Paul resolve to go to Tamai, an inland village reputed to have the sweetest fruit and most beautiful women in all the Society Islands. The village is so remote that the narrator hopes to find there the ancient Tahitian way of life.

Chapters 62–66: "Tamai"; "A Dance in the Valley"; "Mysterious"; "The Hegira, or Flight"; "How we were to get to Taloo"

Bidding farewell to the planters, Peter and Paul set off for what they hope will be a paradise. Reaching Tamai, they are welcomed by the villagers, who are only nom-

inally Christian. The white men convince RARTOO, the old chief who acts as their host, to stage a pagan dance for their benefit. Although Long Ghost can barely contain himself during the affair, the narrator contents himself with describing in detail the Lory-Lory, which he calls "the dance of the backsliding girls of Tamai."

The pair of wanderers have another adventure with a hideous little old man whose desire to sell them an ancient pair of trousers serves as a reminder that western ways have polluted even Tamai. Shortly thereafter, the "omoo," or wanderers are obliged to leave on pain of being arrested as runaways by some outsiders who suddenly appear in the village.

They resolve to go to Partoowye, site of a missionary station and also, from time to time, Queen Pomare's residence. The narrator and Long Ghost entertain visions of attaching themselves to her court. The narrator recounts several instances of westerners joining various Polynesian royal households, and the pair feel sure that they would be welcomed by Pomare as bulwarks against the French who threaten to usurp her throne. Long Ghost is confident his facility with the fiddle will appeal to the queen's well-known passion for music as well.

The pair is somewhat concerned, however, about being apprehended along the way, and decide that they need some sort of passport indicating that they are not highwaymen, kidnappers, or—least of all—runaway sailors. Passports, however, are unknown in Imeeo, so they decide to ask Zeke, who is well respected on the island, to draft papers for them. With much fanfare, Zeke complies, and the wanderers make their way on foot around the island.

Chapters 67–72: "The Journey round the Beach"; "A Dinner-Party in Imeeo"; "The Cocoa-Palm"; "Life at Loohooloo"; "We start for Taloo"; "A Dealer in the Contraband"

On the fourth day of what the narrator calls their "Hegira, or Flight from Tamai," the pair come upon the hut of a loving old couple they call Darby and Joan, who extend their typically Polynesian hospitality to the travelers. Continuing along the beach, they next encounter three gay girls named FARNOWAR ("Day-born"), FARNOOPOO ("Night-born"), and MARHAR-RARRAR ("Wakeful" or "Bright-eyed"), who lead them into the village of Loohooloo. The village chief, MARHARVAI, welcomes the strangers with a feast, which is described in detail—as is the Polynesian passion for bestowing humorous nicknames. While Long Ghost and the natives rest after their meal, the narrator walks around the area, observing the glories of the cocoa palm.

The pair of omoo are so comfortable in Loohooloo that they stay a while, passing their time spear fishing, swimming, and lounging in a swing suspended from a coconut tree. When they finally resume their travels, they are accompanied part way by the three gay girls, who finally bid them a sad and ceremonious farewell.

On what the narrator reckons to be the 10th day of their hegira, he and Long Ghost arrive at the shanty of a hermit called VARVY, who appears to be deaf and mute. Varvy has little to offer in the way of food, but he tries to make up for this deficiency by sharing some of his taboo moonshine with his guests. When the narrator turns up his nose at the potent brew, Varvy suddenly finds his voice, protesting his guest's stupidity. After he shows them his still—and his contempt for the missionaries—Long Ghost gets quite drunk with the old hermit. The next morning he wakes with a terrific hangover and cannot find his boots. Still, he and the narrator—who throws away his sandals in sympathy—journey on.

Chapters 73–79: "Our Reception in Partoowye"; "Retiring for the Night. —The Doctor grows devout"; "A Ramble through the Settlement"; "An island Jilt. —We visit the Ship"; "A Party of Rovers. —Little Loo and the Doctor"; "Mrs. Bell"; "Taloo Chapel. —Holding Court in Polynesia"
Finally arriving at Partoowye, they are welcomed by a native convert, Eereemear ("Jeremiah") PO-PO, who shares his home with his wife, AFRETEE, their 14-year-old daughter, LOO, and a number of other relatives. Po-Po nevertheless invites the travelers to join the household, and they do so for several days. They enjoy touring the settlement of Partoowye, which consists of 80 houses and the queen's residence, which they approach but are not allowed to enter. During their jaunt, they encounter an English ship's carpenter who has set himself up in business in Imeeo and fallen in love with a native girl, whom he is forbidden by law to marry.

In the nearby harbor of Taloo, Long Ghost and the narrator spy the whaler *Leviathan* and row out to take a good look at her. The crew is eager to have the two former sailors join them at sea, but the wanderers prefer not to commit themselves. Returning to Po-Po's, they are handed—improbably enough—three volumes of novels by Tobias Smollett, which seem to inspire romance. Before long, the doctor is wooing the beautiful but cool Loo who, when her suitor becomes too insistent, stabs him with a thorn. For his part, the narrator is smitten with the beautiful and equally unavailable Mrs. BELL, an Englishwoman who is married to the proprietor of a nearby sugar plantation.

The narrator and his companion attend a local chapel made of coral, where Po-Po serves as deacon, then visit the court house, where they witness a criminal proceeding against Captain CRASH, a corrupt foreigner who is on trial for despoiling a young native girl, among other offenses.

Chapters 80–81: "Queen Pomaree"; "We visit the Court"
As the adventurers prepare to approach Queen Pomare, the narrator stops to give his readers some background, first rehearsing the history of the Tahitian "Pomarees"—the royal patronymic since the time of Captain Cook. Then he relates something of the current ruler, whose reputation is more than a little tarnished both by her own laxness and by the disturbing influence of foreign colonizers.

Finally, five weeks after they first arrived in Partoowye, the doctor and the narrator gain admittance to Pomare's court. By making friends with MARBONNA, the Marquesan minder of the queen's twin boys, Typee is able to finagle a tour of the palace. Left to their own devices in the inner courtyard, Long Ghost and Typee impress the the queen's retainers with their desire to see her, and their wish is granted. But just as Long Ghost is pressing forward, the queen summarily dismisses the interlopers. The next day, the narrator solemnly reports, Po-Po informs them that he has strict orders to admit no strangers into the palace grounds.

Chapter 82: "Which ends the Book"
Their hopes of gaining the queen's favor dashed, the two old salts decide to return to the sea. The narrator, having liked what he saw of the *Leviathan*, decides to ship with her to Japan. After an interview with the captain during which they present themselves in a light both flattering and false (they are both Americans, they say, who have been working on a plantation in Tahiti), Typee is taken on, but Long Ghost is rejected. Seemingly relieved, Long Ghost declares he will remain on Imeeo for a while.

The next day, Typee returns briefly to shore to bestow half of his advance of 15 Spanish dollars on his friend, and to say goodbye to Po-Po and his family. After a night of celebration aboard ship, the *Leviathan* raises its anchor and prepares to get underway. As the doctor steps over the side into a canoe, he and Typee shake hands one last time, never to meet again. Then the ship pulls away from land, the whole adventure fades as quickly as a dream, and the narrator is restored to what he once was: "Once more the sailor's cradle rocked under me, and I found myself rolling in my gait."

PUBLICATION HISTORY

Although others may have referred to Melville as "Typee," Nathaniel Hawthorne's wife, Sophia, often called her friend "Mr. Omoo." Melville told his British publisher, John MURRAY, that he intended in this sequel to write a book about the "'man about town' sort of life, led, at the present day, by roving sailors in the Pacific." Hence the book's title—*Omoo* being a Polynesian word for "rover"—and hence Sophia Hawthorne's teasing nickname for the dashing former seaman who had so handily transformed his adventures into celebrated literary works. The tone of *Omoo* is entirely tongue-in-cheek, starting with its dedication to Melville's uncle

Herman GANSEVOORT, a man who rarely left his home in the tiny village that bore his name.

The British edition of *Omoo,* which was reset from the type set by the book's American publisher, HARPER & BROTHERS, first appeared on March 27, 1847. The first American printing of the book, which appeared around May 1 of that year, sold out in a week. *Omoo* was in fact more widely reviewed than any of Melville's other books. Most of these reviews were favorable; those that were not largely criticized Melville's antimissionary stance and provoked a controversy that only improved sales of *Omoo.*

Omoo actually did better for its author than his popular first novel had done. By the end of July 1847, the American edition of *Omoo* had sold more than 3,600 copies, netting Melville a total of $718.79 in royalties. The English edition did not fare as well, failing to earn a profit until more than a year after it was first published. (Despite Melville's efforts to protect his English COPYRIGHT, the London publisher George Routledge published a pirated version of *Omoo* in 1850.) For the remainder of Melville's life, the book remained in print in England and in America, and by the turn of the century Murray's and Harper's combined sales equaled more than 15,000 copies.

"On a natural Monument in a field of Georgia." (1866) Poem in *BATTLE-PIECES.* One of the "Verses Inscriptive and Memorial" in Melville's collection of CIVIL WAR poetry, this poem was, Melville explains in an accompanying note, written prior to the establishment of the National Cemetery at Andersonville, Georgia, site of the most infamous Confederate prisoner-of-war military prison. At the time, the only memorials to Union prisoners were items like the "unhewn stone" of Melville's poem, a marker that commemorates not "deeds of men who bleeding die," but rather those who "withering famine slowly wore, / And slowly fell disease did gloat."

"On Sherman's Men who fell in the Assault of Kenesaw Mountain, Georgia." (1866) Poem in *BATTLE-PIECES.* One of the "Verses Inscriptive and Memorial" in Melville's volume of CIVIL WAR poetry, "On Sherman's Men" commemorates a battle on June 24, 1864, between troops commanded by Union General William Tecumseh Sherman and Confederates under the command of General Joseph E. Johnston. Although Sherman's slash-and-burn march through Georgia spelled the end of the Confederacy, a frustrated Sherman, in an effort to deal with Johnston's retreat maneuvers, forsook his customary flanking movements and attacked Johnston's troops directly. The result was failure and Union casualties numbering 3,000. Melville says that Sherman's men braved more than "mailed ones ever knew" and are worthy of the fame accorded ancient heroes.

"On the Chinese Junk" (1847) Series of 13 short satiric squibs and cartoons, some attributed to Melville. Published between July 17 and September 18, 1847, this unsigned series in the humor magazine *YANKEE DOODLE* concerned a Chinese junk then moored in New York harbor. The junk was the subject of great curiosity among the general public and the press—both of which *Yankee Doodle* sought to lampoon. (Installment number one, for example, ends with this postscript: "Yankee Doodle has consulted his lawyer and is now able to inform his readers, that although curiosities are bought and sold on board it, the vessel is not indictable, as has been supposed, as an unlicensed junk shop.") Installment three, "Yankee Doodle's Visit," the longest of the series, describes an inspection of the ship by "Yankee" and "all of his curious friends" and is generally believed to have been written by Melville. Scattered references to a sea serpent seen off Nahant, Massachusetts, and to then Postmaster General Cave Johnson, addressed in another *Yankee Doodle* piece attributed to Melville, "ON THE SEA SERPENT," indicate that Melville probably had a hand in other installments of this series.

"On the Grave of a young Cavalry Officer killed in the Valley of Virginia." (1866) Poem in *BATTLE-PIECES.* One of the "Verses Inscriptive and Memorial" in Melville's volume of CIVIL WAR poetry, this five-line verse tells of an unnamed, and perhaps unknown, soldier with "Beauty and youth, with manners sweet, and friends—" whose given attributes are all surpassed by his glorious death.

"On the Home Guards Who Perished in the Defense of Lexington, Missouri." (1866) Poem in *BATTLE-PIECES.* This is the first of the "Verses Inscriptive and Memorial," a separate section in the collection. The poem commemorates the deaths of 159 guardsmen under the leadership of Union Colonel James A. Mulligan at Lexington, Kentucky, which was besieged by Confederate state guardsmen on September 12, 1861. Mulligan surrendered on September 20, but Melville proclaims that the casualties the Northerners incurred were not in vain: "They by their end well fortified / The Cause. . . ."

"On the Men of Maine killed in the Victory of Baton Rouge, Louisiana." (1866) Poem in *BATTLE-PIECES.* One of the "Verses Inscriptive and Memorial," this poem commemorates dead soldiers from Maine who in the CIVIL WAR fell in "A land how unlike their own, / With the cold pine-grove overgrown." The Battle of Baton Rouge took place August 5, 1862, when Confederates attacked Union troops who had been transported there to recover from fever. Of the 84 men killed in battle in Baton Rouge, 40 percent were Mainers.

"On the Photograph of a Corps Commander." (1866) Poem in BATTLE-PIECES. The poet praises the "manly greatness" of the commander, whose photograph is a "cheering picture." His lineage goes back to those who fought with King Henry the Fifth at Agincourt, with the Knights Templar. Melville's corps commander is probably based on General Winfield Scott Hancock, whom Melville might have seen when he visited a Union army encampment in Virginia in April 1864.

"On the Sea Serpent" (1847) Satiric squib attributed to Melville. This piece, published anonymously in the September 11, 1847, issue of the humor magazine YAN-KEE DOODLE, has been attributed to Melville on the basis of circumstantial evidence. Melville became a regular contributor to the magazine in July 1847, around the time that Evert DUYCKINCK wrote his brother George that Melville "will probably in some shape take care of the sea serpent." *Yankee Doodle* had already published, on June 19, 1847, a cartoon concerning the uproar surrounding the supposed sighting of a sea serpent in Massachusetts Bay off Nahant. The piece attributed to Melville, "$1,000 Reward," consists of a fake advertisement announcing that the postmaster general is offering $1,000 to anyone who can "procure him a private interview with the Sea-serpent," so that he can arrange for the creature to transmit the mail from Boston to Halifax.

"On the Slain at Chickamauga." (1866) Poem in BAT-TLE-PIECES. One of the "Verses Inscriptive and Memorial" in Melville's book of CIVIL WAR poetry, this poem honors both those who have come through the war unscathed and those who experienced defeat: "mischance is honorable too—." At the Battle of Chickamauga, in Tennessee (September 19–20, 1863), several divisions of Union General William S. Rosecrans's Army of the Cumberland were forced to retreat by Rebel troops commanded by General Braxton Bragg.

"On the Slain Collegians." (1866) Poem in BATTLE-PIECES. In the note accompanying this poem, Melville speaks of the enormous number of Northern and Southern college boys who went to war never to return. The poem is an elegy to the young men who never had a chance to fulfill their promise, as "Each bloomed and died an unabated Boy."

pantheism A philosophical or religious belief mentioned in *MOBY-DICK*. In a pantheistic universe, all things are swallowed up in the unity of God. Pantheism is often thought of as a religion of nature, in which human beings, for example, are just another part of nature, another part of God. This belief cancels out the romantic sense of a unique self, or merges that self with nature—a point ISHMAEL makes when he loses himself in a reverie, so mesmerized by the sea that he almost falls off the masthead. Being swallowed up in the sea would make him, of course, literally a part of nature. In *PIERRE,* pantheism is invoked as a kind of binding force that links PIERRE to Isabel BANFORD and the couple to the world. Pierre surmises that finding Isabel seems tantamount to recognizing the mysterious ways in which all things of the world are related to one another.

Paradise Lost (1667) The great epic poem by John Milton (1608–74). The first lines of the poem state the poet's theme: "Of man's first disobedience and the fruit / Of the forbidden tree whose mortal taste / Brought death into the World, and all our woe, / With loss of Eden." Milton wrote in order to justify the ways of God to man, to explain how original sin brought man into this world, and how his confrontation with his own mortality is the only way to win back his state of grace. Milton's powerful exploration of evil, especially in his creation of Satan, informs *BILLY BUDD* and *CLAREL*. In *Billy Budd,* the character of John CLAGGART is clearly influenced by Milton's exploration of malevolence. *Clarel* emulates the ambitiousness of Milton's epic, and it takes up the issues of PREDESTINATION and the fate of man in a world that is fatally separated from God.

"The Paradise of Bachelors and the Tartarus of Maids" (1855) Short story. This story is one of three diptychs, or two-sided stories, that Melville probably wrote between the late summer of 1853 and the early spring of 1854. (The others are "POOR MAN'S PUDDING AND RICH MAN'S CRUMBS" and "THE TWO TEMPLES.") Unlike some of his earlier efforts in the short story form, they do not moralize or attempt to turn misfortune into a boon.

Part one, "The Paradise of Bachelors," concerns the narrator's visit while in London to the Temple cloisters, a cozy old club for deeply satisfied unmarried lawyers. There he enjoys a sumptuous banquet for nine. In part two, "The Tartarus of Maids," the narrator, a "seedsman," travels to a New England paper mill to buy a supply of envelopes to contain his products. To get to this Tartarus, or infernal place, he must ride in his buggy towards Woedolor Mountain, though a dusky pass called Mad Maid's Bellows'-pipe and a narrow gorge known as Black Notch, and finally into a hollow called the Devil's Dungeon, though which runs the Blood River. This is a landscape described in clearly sexual terms, which are further elaborated in the scenes set in the mill itself. The mill is staffed by pale girls—all maidens, according to their overseer, OLD BACH, because married women are not "steady" enough for the stultifying routine. As a boy named CUPID shows him around the mill, the narrator observes the workers chopping rags that are first converted into an "albuminous" mass before being fed into a huge machine housed in a room "stifling with a strange, blood-like, abdominal heat." Nine minutes later, the machine gives birth to perfect foolscap. The mill hands, however, experience no such miracle; instead, "through consumptive pallors of this blank, raggy life, go these white girls to death." The mill is the "very counterpart of the Paradise of Bachelors, but snowed upon, and frost-painted to a sepulchre." As in even his earliest work, Melville is writing here as a social critic, but as in such celebrated pieces as *BARTLEBY,* he is also attempting—through the use of a flawed narrator—to say something about the limits of perception.

Melville had visited the Temple in London in 1849, when he dined with his English publisher's cousin, Robert Francis Cooke (the model for the narrator's host, "R.F.C.," in "The Paradise of Bachelors"). Similarly, he based elements of "The Tartarus of Maids" on a trip he made to a Dalton, Massachusetts, paper mill in the winter of 1851. The story these experiences helped to produce was published anonymously in *HARPER'S NEW MONTHLY MAGAZINE* in April 1855, nearly a year after Melville had submitted it.

Parsee Member of the Zoroastrian religion in India. Parsees are mentioned several times in *MOBY-DICK*. Zoroaster founded the ancient Persian religion, which emphasizes a worldwide, titanic struggle between the forces of light and darkness. FEDALLAH is a Parsee.

155

"The Parthenon" (1891) Poem in *TIMOLEON*. Part of the "Fruit of Travel Long Ago" section of the collection, "The Parthenon" concerns the celebrated Athenian temple, a wonder of the ancient world. The poem is organized into four titled sections. Cleverly, as the poet multiplies meditations inspired by the architecture, he provides a closer and closer look at the building, as if zooming in on it: Part one is titled "Seen aloft from afar"; two, "Nearer viewed"; three, "The Frieze"; and four, "The last Tile."

Paulet, Lord George (1803–1879) British naval officer who appears as a character in *TYPEE*. George Paulet came from a prominent family named for the parish of Pawlett in the English county of Somerset. After studying at the Royal Naval College, he worked his way up through the ranks of the British navy to captain. In 1841, in command of the *Craysfort*, he was ordered by Rear Admiral Richard Thomas, commander of the British Pacific Squadron, to sail into Honolulu harbor to protect British interests in the Sandwich Islands (HAWAII). The British consul to the islands, Captain Richard CHARLTON, had recently resigned, and there was some concern that France or the United States would elbow Britain out of the picture. Paulet believed that his objective was to seize the islands for his country, and he refused even to negotiate with King KAMEHAMEHA or his American spokesman, G. P. Judd. Many among the native population welcomed the prospect of British rule, as they disliked the stern moralism of the influential American missionaries. American residents of the islands feared a British takeover and regarded it as only marginally better than a French one, which seemed the only real alternative to a British seizure. For his part, Melville seems to have regarded Paulet favorably, for he mentions him in *TYPEE* as one of the only responsible British authorities, and one of the only foreign leaders truly approved by the natives.

The British government, however, repudiated Paulet's efforts. Five months after Paulet's arrival in Honolulu, Thomas returned the islands to home rule, provoking massive rejoicing among the Hawaiians. In Melville's view, this was the final act in a charade in which Paulet was cast in the role of dupe. The corrupt King Kamehameha had conspired with his American advisers to pretend to surrender to the British so as to turn world opinion against these foreign interlopers. The British, it seems, never had any intention of appropriating the islands, but only wished to ward off the French.

In July 1844 Paulet went to Tahiti, where he escorted Queen POMARE IV to the island of Eimeo (now Moorea) for her own protection during a period of native resistance to French rule. He returned to Hawaii shortly thereafter and the next year left for England, where he died.

"Pausilippo (in the Time of Bomba)" (1891) Poem in *TIMOLEON*. Part of the "Fruit of Travel Long Ago" section of the collection, "Pausilippo" is a sketch of a Neapolitan hillside famed for its beauty. During the time Melville visited the city, however, it was under the repressive regime of King Ferdinand II of the Two Sicilies ("Bomba"), and in this poem Melville contrasts the beauty of the scenery with the fate of a former political prisoner, a poet once imprisoned for composing a supposedly treasonous song. Melville would revisit "Naples in the Time of Bomba" in the unpublished "BURGUNDY CLUB SKETCHES."

"Pebbles" (1888) Poem in *JOHN MARR*. Melville ends his volume with this series of seven numbered short poems. Melville had thought at one time of calling them "Epigrams," and each is in fact a pithy restatement of themes sounded earlier in the collection. Part one speaks of the superior wisdom of fish and fowl that adapt to nature rather than trying to control it. Part two contrasts man's changeability—in creed, in school of thought—with the changeless sound of a conch shell: "The Seas have inspired it, and Truth— / Truth, varying from sameness never." Part III emphasizes the unyielding character of the sea, which has no echo and does not respond to man's hopes and dreams. Part IV consists of two lines asserting that the ocean merely suffers man's presence as he sails its waters. Part V is spoken by "the old implacable Sea" which is "Pleased, not appeased, by myriad wrecks in me." Part VI asks if storms at sea are evidence that evil exists, given that Christ exists. Part VII is a final benediction upon "the inhuman sea," which heals the speaker's soul.

Pedro II (Dom Pedro II de Alcântara) (1825–1891) Second and last emperor of Brazil. Born in Rio de Janeiro, Pedro II was a member of the ruling family known as the House of Coburg-Braganza. His father, Pedro I, was forced to flee to Brazil from Portugal with the rest of the Portuguese royal family when Napoleon's armies threatened to take over their country in 1807. At age five, Pedro II became regent of Brazil when his father abdicated the throne in 1831. He ruled in his own right from 1840 to 1889, when he was overthrown by a revolution. Pedro II appears in *WHITE-JACKET* when he and his entourage make a state visit to the *NEVERSINK* while the frigate is harbored in Rio. The narrator remarks the emperor's regal clothing, young face, and corpulent body. Mostly, the royal visit provides some respite from the boredom experienced by the man-of-war's crew when at anchor.

Peepi Minor character in *MARDI*. This 10-year-old is the ruler of the island kingdom of Valapee. His lengthy pedigree and diminutive size (to say nothing of his name) are meant to satirize the institution of hereditary monarchy.

Peleg, Captain Minor character in *MOBY-DICK*. Part-owner of the *PEQUOD*, he interviews ISHMAEL, who wishes to ship aboard the whaler.

Pennies, the Misses Minor characters in *PIERRE*. Two kindly spinster sisters invite Pierre to the party where he first sees his putative sister, Isabel BANFORD.

Pequod In *MOBY-DICK*, the whaling ship that ISHMAEL joins. The vessel is commanded by Captain AHAB, whose monomaniac goal is the pursuit and killing of the great white whale, Moby-Dick.

Perth Character in *MOBY-DICK*. The "begrimed, blistered old blacksmith" makes the bolts for Ahab's artificial leg. Perth is another isolated sailor who tells the crew about a family loved and lost. Melville may have modeled his character, in part on Ephraim Walcott, the blacksmith aboard the *ACUSHNET*.

"Philip" *See* "SHERIDAN AT CEDAR CREEK."

phrenology A popular pseudoscience in the 19th century, mentioned in *MOBY-DICK*. Phrenology purported to describe personality by studying the shape and contour of the skull. ISHMAEL refers to phrenology when discussing the whale's head.

"The Piazza" (1856) Introductory story in *The PIAZZA TALES*. Melville wrote "The Piazza" specifically as a sort of preface for the collection of five previously published stories brought out by DIX & EDWARDS in 1856. His model was Nathaniel HAWTHORNE's "The Old Manse," which served the same prefatory purpose in *Mosses from an Old Manse* (1846), about which Melville had so compellingly written in "HAWTHORNE AND HIS MOSSES" in 1850. It is worth noting, however, that Melville seems to have borrowed both the name of one of his characters, Marianna, and numerous details in the story from Alfred, Lord Tennyson's poem "Mariana" (1830), itself inspired by the Mariana in William SHAKESPEARE's *Measure for Measure* (1623). Melville, too, makes use of Shakespeare in his tale, starting with the epigraph taken from *Cymbeline* (1623).

In "The Piazza," an unnamed narrator describes his old farmhouse, modeled on Melville's own at ARROWHEAD, where the narrator, like the author, has built a piazza from which to view Mount GREYLOCK. From the piazza, he sees in the distance a "golden sparkle" of light from the window of a cottage which he dreams is occupied by a charmed creature. Riding over to investi-

gate, he finds instead a tumbledown old gray structure occupied by a pale seamstress, Marianna. Marianna, for her part, has fastened on what she sees as a golden palace down in the valley: the narrator's house. Marianna wonders aloud about the happy lives led by those who occupy such a glorious place, and the narrator declines to disabuse her of her one illusion. Returning to his home, the narrator continues to look on Marianna's abode, but now with different eyes: "[E]very night, when the curtain falls, truth comes in with the darkness. No light shows from the mountain. To and fro I walk the piazza deck, haunted by Marianna's face, and many as real a story."

***The Piazza Tales* (1856)** The only collection of Melville's short fiction published during his lifetime. After the disastrous reception of *PIERRE* in 1852, Melville found himself unable to place a lengthy book manuscript, probably based on the story of Agatha HATCH, with his publishers. Despite Melville's refusal up to that point to write for magazine publication, financial pressures forced him to take up his American publishers' invitations to write short pieces for their magazines, *HARPER'S NEW MONTHLY MAGAZINE* and *PUTNAM'S MONTHLY*. Both were magazines of some stature, but of the two, *Putnam's* was both more prestigious and more responsive. Between 1853 and 1855, *Putnam's* published five of Melville's short stories and serialized *ISRAEL POTTER* before the magazine was sold to the New York publishing firm of DIX & EDWARDS. The magazine's founder, George Putnam, had committed to separate monograph publication of *Israel Potter* before the sale, and in December 1855, Melville proposed that the new owners also bring out a volume tentatively titled "Benito Cereno and Other Sketches" that would contain the remainder of his contributions to *Putnam's*: "BARTLEBY, THE SCRIVENER," "BENITO CERENO," "THE LIGHTNING-ROD MAN," "THE ENCANTADAS," and "THE BELL TOWER." Dix & Edwards agreed, and after Melville wrote a new story, "The Piazza," as an introductory piece, in May 1856 published the collection as *The Piazza Tales*.

Melville had hoped to repay some pressing debts out of royalties from the collection. In the end, however, he earned nothing from the volume. His contract with Dix & Edwards stipulated that he was to receive a royalty of 12 1/2 percent per copy, but only after expenses of publication had been met. They never were. In April 1857, Dix & Edwards went bankrupt, as did its successor firms. In September 1857, the plates for *The Piazza Tales*, together with other inventory of the second successor, Miller & Curtis, were offered at auction. Failing to attract a single offer, they were, with Melville's permission (he himself lacked the funds to purchase them), sold for scrap. *The Piazza Tales* was never reprinted during Melville's lifetime.

The Picture of Liverpool　Anonymous work published in 1803 and cited in REDBURN. Melville inherited his father's copy of this illustrated guidebook and took it with him on his 1839 maiden voyage to LIVERPOOL. Reformulating the experiences of this trip later for *Redburn*, Melville made extensive use of the guide (which Wellingborough REDBURN refers to as the "prosy old guide-book") one of the only things handed down to him by his dead father.

Pierre　Main character in *PIERRE. See* GLENDINNING, PIERRE.

Pierre; or, The Ambiguities　Melville's seventh book. This highly autobiographical novel is a searing exploration of family life, of the writer's plight, and of American history. Pierre's home, SADDLE MEADOWS, draws on aspects of ARROWHEAD and Herman GANSEVOORT's estate in Saratoga County. The setting, Melville biographer Laurie Robertson-Lorant points out, is reminiscent of both the Berkshires and the Hudson Valley. Melville's democratic politics are revealed in the opening chapters, where he demonstrates how the landed upper class holds on to power in ways not much different from those of the gentry in England.

　Pierre's illustrious grandfather is based on Colonel Peter GANSEVOORT. Similarly, Pierre's mother Mary has many of Maria Gansevoort MELVILLE's characteristics, particularly her controlling, coquettish behavior. Laurie Robertson-Lorant also points out that Lucy TARTAN, Pierre's childhood playmate and romantic interest, resembles Herman Melville's wife, Elizabeth Knapp Shaw MELVILLE.

　The novel, however, is not realistic but instead satirical and symbolic. The overblown romantic language exposes the vacuity of Pierre's highly idealized view of the world. His principles seem founded on nothing but imagination, and he comes to a hard end precisely because he cannot adjust to reality. His secluded, indulgent life in Saddle Meadows leaves him unprepared for the shifting competition of urban life, the very life to which Melville had to reconcile himself when he became a customs inspector in NEW YORK CITY.

　Pierre's failures as man and author echo Melville's troubles. Indeed, the novel seems to be a conflicted enterprise: on the one hand, Melville sought another success through writing; on the other, he despaired that such a success was possible, let alone desirable. In writing *Pierre*, Melville confronted his demons, and if the novel itself was not a popular or critical success, it nevertheless helped him to clarify the nature of his own temper and prospects.

SYNOPSIS

Book I: "Pierre Just Emerging From His Teens"
Pierre Glendinning, the "only son of an affluent and haughty widow," grows up in the country on an estate

Melville wrote Pierre *in his study at Arrowhead.* (Herman Melville's Arrowhead)

in Saddle Meadows. Mother and son form a close bond—more like that of brother and sister. Indeed, Pierre calls his mother "Sister Mary." The Glendinnings have an illustrious family heritage, dating back to Pierre's paternal great-grandfather, who, cheering his men to press on, died in an epic battle with Indians. A grandfather, a major general, had earned glory in the Revolutionary War defending a fort. Pierre's mother also presents an idealized portrait of his father. If Pierre feels bereft, it is principally because he has no sister on whom he can confer his fraternal feelings. As the narrator remarks, "He who is sisterless, is as a bachelor before his time." Without a male mentor, Pierre is thrown upon his own resources.

　To situate Pierre in his time and place, the narrator provides an extended commentary on the political and economic landscape of Saddle Meadows. Although America is thought of as a land of new men and of opportunity for the common man, whereas England, for example, is regarded as the home of a privileged, elite class, the narrator argues that the differences between the two societies are not as great as generally assumed. Indeed, many so-called noble families in England are actually of recent vintage, having managed to obtain land and titles without much difficulty. In America, on the contrary, the original Dutch settlers have been remarkably successful in keeping the power and the land to themselves. The narrator points out that pedigree—that is, the line of succession within families—is purer in parts of America than it is in England.

　Thus Pierre grows up in an insular, aristocratic world unused to having its ideas or its power challenged. The narrator makes a particular point about Pierre's isolation: *"it had been the choice fate of Pierre to have been born and bred in the country."* The country is "not only the most poetical and philosophical, but it is the most aristocratic part of this earth," hailed as such by generations of bards.

As if to demonstrate the impact of aristocratic country on Pierre, the narrator notes that his mother expects "homage" from him, and Pierre enthusiastically offers it. Mother and son live in a lover-like complacency, in a "circle of pure and unimpairable delight." Mary, casting Pierre in her image, hopes that he will become a "haughty hero to the world!"

Book II: *"Love, Delight, and Alarm"*
Lucy Tartan, Pierre's childhood playmate and now the beloved of the 19-year-old hero, is devoted to him. She believes he leads a charmed life. A beauty and a charmer herself, she is the daughter of Pierre's father's best friend. Lucy's mother has expected all along that Lucy and Pierre would marry, as though they are "Platonic particles" destined to merge with each other. Pierre thinks of himself as the "bait" in paradise that Lucy is supposed to catch. Lucy is thought of as the perfect mate for Pierre, since she comes from a wealthy family and has already received the Glendinning blessing through her father.

Pierre is bemused by his Glendinning ancestors, especially by his grandfather's military portrait, which Pierre yearns to meet in living form. His love for Lucy only deepens his "glow of family pride." Yet at a party Pierre glimpses a "mysterious face" that for some reason alarms him. He cannot say why, but the disturbing experience colors his next meeting with Lucy. The face reminds him of a character out of DANTE. He resolves to explore what it is about the mystery of that face that so unnerves him.

Book III: *"The Presentiment and the Verification"*
Pierre accompanies Lucy to a social gathering at the home of the two Miss PENNIES, "truly pious spinsters, gifted with the most benevolent hearts in the world." Escorting his mother into the drawing room he is suddenly pierced to the heart by a shriek, although he cannot see the young woman who makes the sound. She recovers and begins looking furtively at Pierre. Something about her face troubles Pierre; it is familiar to him, yet he cannot place it as he wrestles with his "haunted spirit." Musing on her melancholy face, Pierre again thinks of DANTE, "the poet being the one who, in a former time, had first opened to his shuddering eyes the infinite cliffs and gulfs of human mystery and misery."

Mrs. Glendinning, apparently alarmed by Pierre's sudden change of mood, proposes that he marry Lucy soon, even though she has resisted an early marriage. But she acts too late as Pierre begins to feel the "irresistible admonitions and intuitions of FATE." Almost immediately Pierre receives a letter from the young woman with the sad face, informing him that she is his sister, Isabel BANFORD, an "outcast in the world" who dares address him. She asks that he meet her at night-

fall at a little farmhouse three miles from the village of Saddle Meadows.

This devastating letter makes Pierre question the heroic image of his father. Life itself seems blighted by this sudden revelation. Pierre would prefer to believe he is dreaming or that the letter is a forgery, but his intuition tells him that Isabel is indeed the sister he has longed for, and his instinctive reaction is to declare his desire to protect her.

Book IV: *"Retrospective"*
Pierre, a "tender-hearted and intellectually appreciative child," had worshipped his father's portrait. Now he stands before his father's shrine, the father whom he lost when he was 12, and contemplates the "darker, though true aspect of things," which comes earlier to the city dweller than to one like Pierre secluded in the country. Pierre remembers that his father, dying of a fever, had cried out "My daughter! my daughter!" The nurse had attributed the words to a wandering mind, and wondered how "so thoroughly good a man, should wander so ambiguously in his mind." Then Pierre remembers a second portrait of his father, one that portrays not the settled married man but a "brisk, unentangled young bachelor." He remembers his Aunt Dorothea's story about his father's interest in another woman, "a foreigner" who would not have made nearly as good a match as Pierre's mother. Aunt Dorothea told him of a cousin, Ralph WINWOOD, who had secretly painted that second portrait of his father at a time when he was in love with a "French young lady." Having read a work on physiognomy, Pierre's father feared his love for the woman would show in the portrait. At any rate, Pierre knows that his mother has never liked this second portrait. The narrator comments, "love is built upon secrets, as lovely Venice upon invisible and incorruptible piles in the sea." Pierre looks at the first, larger portrait, the one his mother favors, and imagines his father saying that this is the representation of himself that his son should trust, the one that reflects his mature character. Yet Pierre finds in his father's ambiguous smile the ambiguities of life, which makes him think that all has not been as he supposed. As the narrator puts it, "Pierre saw all preceding ambiguities, all mysteries ripped open as if with a keen sword, and forth trooped thickening phantoms of an infinite gloom." All the misgivings and suspicions that Pierre had hardly recognized now emerge, and he remembers lines from Dante:

> "Ah! how dost though change,
> Agnello! See! thou art not double now,
> Not only one!"

Book V: *"Misgivings and Preparations"*
Pierre turns the larger portrait of his father to the wall, symbolizing the "reversed idea" in his soul. "I will no

more have a father," he declares. Pierre's soul is "in anarchy." But he resolves not to "blast my father's blessed memory in the bosom of my mother, and plant the sharpest dagger of grief in her soul." It is in this disordered state that Pierre encounters his mother with Mr. FALSGRAVE, the local clergyman. They are exercised over Ned and Delly ULVER, who have produced an illegitimate child. The haughty Mrs. Glendinning wishes to banish the couple from her estate even as Pierre pleads for charity toward the miserable girl. Pierre argues, "Should the legitimate child shun the illegitimate, when one father is father to both?" Pierre tries to extract Falsgrave's opinion on whether a child should honor a father who has produced both legitimate and illegitimate offspring, since the religion teaches that the father must be honored. Mrs. Glendinning intervenes, chiding Pierre for hectoring Falsgrave, who would rather not commit himself, so that Pierre must retire without an answer to his dilemma.

Books VI–VIII: "Isabel, and the First Part of the Story of Isabel"; "Intermediate Between Pierre's Two Interviews with Isabel at the Farm-House"; "The Second Interview at the Farm-House, and the second part of the story of Isabel. Their Immediate Impulsive Effect Upon Pierre"

Isabel recounts for Pierre her strange, lonely childhood in the country and the woods, telling how she was raised by a undemonstrative couple, an old man and woman who, although they were not cruel in other respects, seldom spoke to her. At about the age of 10 or 11, Isabel was removed from the country house by a pleasant woman, who installed her in a farmhouse. Too young to question her circumstances, Isabel remained lonely and forlorn, but she was also praised for her beauty and was visited by a man who whispered the word "father" to her. She kissed this gentleman and thought him kind. When he ceased his visits, she was told that he had died. Isabel did farm work and consoled herself with a guitar she was able to buy from a peddler.

Pierre responds to her story with the declaration: "Know me eternally as thy loving, revering, and most marvelling brother, who will never desert thee, Isabel."

Pierre broods on the wonder and mystery of Isabel's story. Mrs. Glendinning senses the change in her son's mood and cautions him to "beware of me." Agitated, Mrs. Glendinning rises and unconsciously throws the fork in her hand so that it stabs her portrait. She turns on Pierre, telling him that the silver tines of the fork now buried in the bosom of her portrait are actually the blow he has delivered to her heart. She enjoins him to confess, to unbosom himself of his hurt. When he does not, she concludes: "Shall a mother abase herself before her stripling boy? Let him tell me of himself, or let him slide adown!"

Pierre runs from the house, brooding on whether it is his fate to break his family tie to his mother. He

approaches what he calls the Memnon Stone, which he has named for the young king of Egypt, a rash Hamlet-like character who threw himself into a quarrel and died beneath the walls of Troy.

Putting together the words of his Aunt Dorothea and Isabel's story, Pierre is confirmed in the belief that she is his sister and his father's illegitimate offspring. He decides to keep this secret to himself and to confide in no one. The mystery of existence and the workings of fate now preoccupy him. Isabel becomes for him a symbol of "uncorrupted love."

Isabel resumes her story, telling Pierre how she came to live with Delly Ulver and how she herself, knowing that she is related to the Glendinnings (the last name had been on a handkerchief, a memento of her father's), fainted at the Miss Pennies' party. As he listens to Isabel, Pierre feels himself enveloped in a "Pantheistic master-spell, which eternally locks in mystery and in muteness the universal subject world." Isabel, herself an object of mystery and wonder, seems to link him to the world at large, to its greater ambiguities. That Isabel also found the name Glendinning inscribed in the guitar she bought from a peddler only strengthens Pierre's belief in the hidden yet palpable connections between disparate phenomena. Thus Pierre resolves not only to protect Isabel but to "succor" Delly, in whose home Isabel sought refuge. Similarly, Isabel has visited families in neighboring cottages, offering her help and concern. Indeed, her offer of charity expresses her belief in the links between people and nature. This sense of family urges Isabel to find "some one of my blood to know me, and to own me."

Isabel's words provoke Pierre to confront Reverend Falsgrave. What does he intend to do about Delly Ulver? Pierre asks the clergyman. Falsgrave tries to deflect Pierre's question. Pierre concludes that Falsgrave will let Delly "be driven out to starve or rot." Falsgrave is fatally compromised, Pierre realizes: "I begin to see how thy profession is unavoidably entangled by all fleshy alliances and cannot move with godly freedom in a world of benefices." In other words, Falsgrave, so deeply beholden to Mrs. Glendinning, will not dare to oppose her desire to punish Delly.

Books IX–XI: "More Light, and the Gloom of That Light: More Gloom, and the Light of That Gloom"; "The Unprecedented Final Resolution of Pierre"; "He Crosses the Rubicon"

Pierre, a kind of Hamlet figure, is quoted as suffering from the melancholy of a youthful mind who discovers the world is "out of joint" and that it is his responsibility to "set it right." But how to apply thought to action—this was Hamlet's dilemma, and is Pierre's. Pierre taunts himself with his lamentable lack of initiative. How to withhold from public exposure the actions of his father

so as not to hurt his mother while also acknowledging Isabel, as Pierre deems it only right to do?

Pierre decides that the only way to preserve his father's reputation and his mother's peace is to pretend that he has secretly married Isabel, making her thus an acknowledged member of the Glendinnings without creating a scandal for the family. Of course, he knows that his decision will cause Lucy Tartan tremendous pain, yet he cannot think of another solution, and his previous playacting with his mother, in which he treated her as a sister, has prepared him for this new imposture. Even worse, he resolves not to tell Lucy that Isabel is his sister, so that she will inevitably think he has rejected her for another woman. Yet his mother's "strength and masculineness" makes it virtually certain that Pierre's actions will not please her, and she holds exclusive title to the Glendinning estate.

Pierre approaches Lucy and tells her that he is married. She faints from the shock of his blunt announcement. In an equally abrupt encounter with his mother, he is banished from Saddle Meadows when he tells her of his marriage to Isabel.

Books XII–XIII: "Isabel: Mrs. Glendinning: The Portrait: and Lucy"; "They Depart the Meadows"
Pierre tells Isabel that he has protected her true identity, but she fears he has ruined himself, and she warns him that she has so little experience of the world that he has to be careful with her. To Pierre this turn of events seems fated, and he informs her that he has decided to move with her and Delly Ulver to the City.

Meanwhile, Mrs. Glendinning announces to Reverend Falsgrave that she is disinheriting Pierre, and she has Dates, the family servant, remove her son's possessions from the house as Pierre himself desires.

Pierre broods over his father's portrait, seeing in it Isabel's likeness and the "tyranny of Time and Fate." Isabel becomes all the dearer to him because of what he has had to sacrifice.

Book XIV: "The Journey and the Pamphlet"
Hamlet-like, Pierre tortures himself with doubts about whether he is pursuing the right course, but he is brought out of reverie by the necessity of providing for Isabel and Delly. He is energized to think that he is in charge of their destinies.

In a world of conflicting philosophies—the narrator cites PLATO, SPINOZA, GOETHE, and the Greek and German Neoplatonists—there will be no way for Pierre to find peace, to "reconcile this world with his own soul." On the ride to the city, he reads a pamphlet by Plotinus PLINLIMMON, who posits two basic kinds of minds: the watchmaker, who (like Francis BACON) can see reality only in terms of its immediate, local world, and the chronometer (like Christ), who can intuit right and wrong irrespective of "mere local standards." Plinlimmon argues that the appearance of figures like

Christ express God's unwillingness to leave man to suppose there is no higher authority than nature. Man has a tendency to believe in a world without God because that world seems to function on its own, but in fact the ultimate cause of the world is beyond that world's power to fathom. The individual must learn to distinguish between the terrestrial and the celestial, which means a man should not take upon himself the Christlike role, "making an unconditional sacrifice of himself in behalf of any other being, or any cause, or any conceit." Pierre reads this pamphlet without understanding how such statements apply to his own treatment of Isabel. That he cannot grasp the pamphlet's message is apparent when the chapter ends with the announcement that the pamphlet is torn, making it impossible for Pierre to engage with the whole of Plinlimmon's thought.

Books XV–XVI: "The Cousins"; "First Night of Their Arrival in the City"
Pierre is counting on a stay with his cousin, Glendinning STANLY. Although the cousins have not been close since childhood, they have exchanged letters and Pierre believes he can rely on Glen's good will. Indeed, Glen has extended an invitation for a visit. But this was before the advent of Isabel, and after Pierre has won Lucy's heart, the same Lucy whom Glen once aspired to court. Pierre does not expect Glen to be happy about a visit, but he does believe his cousin will behave decently.

In the event, Pierre finds Glen's house with difficulty, for it is unlighted and unprepared for Pierre's visit. Indeed, when Pierre forces his way into Glen's rooms, his cousin pretends not to know him, and Pierre is forced to leave—now in a desperate quest to find a suitable lodging for himself, Isabel, and Delly.

Books XVII–XVIII: "Young America in Literature"; "Pierre, as a Juvenile Author, Reconsidered"
An exploration of the fate of Pierre, Isabel, and Delly is postponed for digressive chapters on Pierre's reputation as a young author courted by publishers who wish to promote his complete works. He receives many flattering proposals, including one to have his biography written, a premature effort, the narrator implies, for a writer so young and unsophisticated. This is a world full of superfluous ideas and quests for originality when in fact the "truest book in the world is a lie." Only God can claim originality, the narrator emphasizes. So-called transcendentalists—those claiming knowledge of a reality that supersedes the immediate concrete world—seem merely "theoretic and inactive." But the utilitarians are no better, because their "worldly maxims," supposedly founded on everyday experience, are "incomprehensible." In other words, no matter in which direction Pierre turns, he is lost.

Book XIX: "The Church of the Apostles"
Pierre takes refuge with Isabel (who has her own room) in an ancient church, now divided into offices and apartments and occupied by "ambiguously professional nondescripts in very genteel but shabby black." They are artists (painters, sculptors, poets, indigent students, and itinerant teachers), scornful of the material world, of the philosophy of Thomas HOBBES. They favor the "airy exaltations of the Berkeleyan philosophy" (see George BERKELEY) and "cannot but give in to the Descartian vortices" (see Rene DESCARTES). With time on their hands, they turn to the "indispensable Kant," and "digest" his categorical imperatives (see Immanuel KANT). In such passages dense with allusions to western philosophy, Melville emphasizes how far removed Pierre is from life in the city or from any effort to take life on the terms actually offered to urban inhabitants. These "Apostles" offer little help, since they are themselves wallowing in theories of knowledge and have little that is concrete to offer Pierre.

Melville emphasizes Pierre's incapacity by recurring to a description of his pastoral upbringing. There are no pleasures of the country here to sustain him. Examining his youthful writings, he finds them "bungling," for they have not embodied the ideal he has imagined. He tries to take heart from his effort to protect Isabel, vowing to write the deeper secrets of existence, but he gives way to despair, declaring: "for I am a nothing. It is all a dream—we dream that we dreamed we dream." In both his doubts and his desire to overcome his doubts, he resembles the Descartes whom the Apostles revere.

Book XX: "Charlie Millthorpe"
Charlie Millthorpe, the son of a respectable farmer in Saddle Meadows, has been responsible for finding Pierre his place at the Apostles'. The Millthorpes have lived on Glendinning lands for several generations. Charlie has moved to the city after being unable to pay the rent on his property. Indeed, as a boy Pierre learned what little he knew about poverty from his companionship with Charlie and from visits to his family's house. Since the age of 15, Charlie has been possessed with the idea of becoming a poet or an orator. It is this "vagrant ambition" that has brought him to the city. But like Pierre, Charlie is saddled with taking care of his family (his mother and sisters) in the city. Charlie, who is making a living in the law, welcomes Pierre enthusiastically. Ever hopeful, Charlie urges Pierre to "Stump the State on the Kantian Philosophy!"

Books XXI–XXII: "Pierre Immaturely Attempts A Mature Work. Tiding from the Meadows. Plinlimmon"; "The Flower Curtain Lifted From Before A Tropical Author, With Some Remarks on The Transcendental Flesh-Brush Philosophy"
Pierre now devotes himself to the effort of producing a new, major work that transcends his previous writing projects. At the same time, he feels the urgency of writing something that will earn money. He aims to contribute to the great body of literature even as he isolates himself more and more from the world. In the meantime, his mother has died, Saddle Meadows has become Glen Stanly's, and Stanly has become Lucy Tartan's suitor. Pierre is devastated by the news of his mother's death, and he tortures himself with imagining how Glen has taken over his place at Saddle Meadows. It is as if Glen is an imposter who has assumed Pierre's name and possessions.

In his anguish Pierre encounters the philosopher Plotinus Plinlimmon. The two pass each other in a hallway but make no real contact, so that Pierre once again is unable to engage himself with Plinlimmon's arguments. Indeed, this failure to make contact is just one example of Pierre's growing isolation. He becomes the parody of the artist starving in a garret. A wasted body is no guarantee of great thoughts. Pierre has become a victim of the "Flesh-Brush Philosophy" (which mortifies the body in the mistaken belief that the spirit will be strengthened) promulgated by the Apostles. As the narrator puts it, "Nor shall all thy Pythagorean and Shelleyan dietings on apple-parings, dried prunes, and crumbs of oatmeal cracker, ever fit thy body for heaven." Pierre is coming to a realization that he has doomed himself, but it is too late: "For in tremendous extremities human souls are like drowning men; well enough they know they are in peril; well enough they know the causes of that peril; nevertheless, the sea is the sea, and these drowning men do drown."

Pierre spends full eight-hour days trying to write his masterpiece, but the pace of his work seems to kill, not enliven him. He is "rehearsing the part of death." His book, "like a vast lumbering planet, revolves in his aching head."

Books XXIII–XXV: "A Letter for Pierre. Isabel. Arrival of Lucy's Easel and Trunks at the Apostles'"; "Lucy At the Apostles"; "Lucy, Isabel, and Pierre. Pierre at His Book. Enceladus"
Lucy sends a letter to Pierre vowing to remain at his "noble and angelical" side. She will be like a nun dwelling with him in his "strange exile." Upset by Pierre's announcement that Lucy will soon join them, Isabel wonders why she is not enough for her brother. "She shall not come! One look from me shall murder her, Pierre!" Isabel exclaims. But Pierre calms her with the explanation that Lucy will be *"ours"* and that she will "serve *us*."

Lucy arrives, and her devotion to Pierre sets both Isabel and Delly at ease—after some preliminary tension between the women. Then Glen Stanly and Lucy's elder brother Frederic arrive in an attempt to bring Lucy back home. After a struggle on the steps, Pierre manages to wrest Lucy from them and has the two men taken away as trespassers. Not even Lucy's mother's subsequent visit manages to make Lucy abandon Pierre. Isabel is quite taken with Lucy's "unearthliness," her pure devotion to Pierre, especially after Lucy's mother disowns her, just as Pierre's mother disowned him.

With three women devoted to him, Pierre's tension mounts as he thinks of "all the ambiguities which hemmed him in." Isabel is his sister, yet Lucy happens upon them at a moment when they are embracing almost as lovers. Lucy has been his beloved, and yet she now serves him like a cousin. Yet Isabel watches Pierre look at Lucy with an expression "illy befitting their singular and so-supposed merely cousinly relation." Lucy maintains her cousin-like devotion to Pierre, yet "did she seem, hour by hour, to be somehow inexplicably sliding between" Pierre and Isabel. Ironically, with two women deeply attached to him, Pierre feels as "solitary as at the Pole." The more he works on his book the more the truth he seeks seems elusive, a galling experience for an "eager contender for renown." He again feels a "foretaste of death itself . . . stealing upon him."

In a kind of delirium, Pierre has a vision of a rocky mountain which he equates with Enceladus the Titan, "the most potent of all the giants, writhing from out the imprisoning earth." In a dream, the Titan confronts a terrified Pierre, who sees a phantom and then the armless Titan's trunk on which appears Pierre's "own duplicate face and features." The story of Enceladus, retold by the narrator, resembles Pierre's own quest to transcend the earthly for the ideal, the terrestrial for the celestial, the imperfect for the ideal. In the myth the gods chain the world to Enceladus, and in his grief Pierre realizes that he cannot transcend the world that burdens him.

Book XXVI: "A Walk: A Foreign Portrait: A Sail: And the End"
Pierre dreads the outcome of his own life. His book is not finished. He takes Isabel to an art gallery, where they gaze at a copy of Guido Reni's portrait of Beatrice CENCI. The painting of a woman's head combines the physical characteristics of Isabel and Lucy. She has light blue eyes, fair skin, and jet black hair. Another painting, *The Stranger,* shows a youth with an ambiguous smile. His jet-black hair seems to be "just disentangling itself from out of curtains and clouds"—a fit image of Pierre's own state of mind. Isabel sees a resemblance between *The Stranger* and herself. The portrait also reminds her of the man who identified himself as her father in his visits to her so many years before. Isabel tries to get Pierre to see the resemblance to their father, but he dismisses it as a "one of the wonderful coincidences, nothing more." An unnerved Pierre suddenly asks himself if Isabel is really his sister. If the portrait of *The Stranger* is no more than a coincidence, then is Isabel's story anything more than that as well? Why

should the man she describes be his father any more than the figure in the portrait is? Isabel's story now seems no more than a mystery, part of an "imaginative delirium" of the kind he felt while writing his book.

Full of doubt, Pierre is then assaulted by Glen Stanly and Frederic. Armed with two pistols, Pierre shoots both men, wounding them. "A hundred contending hands" seize Pierre. In prison, he is in despair: "Oh now to live is death, and now to die is life." When Lucy collapses and dies at his feet, Pierre commits suicide, taking a vial of poison Isabel has hidden in her bosom. When Frederic and Glen burst in upon the scene and discover the dead Lucy, Isabel collapses, dropping an empty file and falling on Pierre's heart: "her long hair ran over him, and arboured him in ebon vines."

PUBLICATION HISTORY

Pierre proved to be a critical and financial disaster. Contemporary reviewers and critics were put off by the novel's florid language and harsh criticism of American society. As romantic hero, Pierre failed, thus losing for Melville the growing audience of middle-class women readers. Working-class readers who might have been sympathetic to his fierce attack on the economic elite did not seem to have the patience for a novel that was without much dramatic incident or a strong story line. The life of a writer with strange states of mind did not appeal to a mass audience. The "ambiguities" or the unknowable nature of existence explored in the novel made Melville seem an isolated, irrelevant writer in the context of an expanding, largely optimistic culture looking for books that ratified a nation-building spirit. In the end, Melville's work was simply too introspective and brooding, too depressing, for most readers.

The novel sold poorly, with the American and British sales amounting to slightly fewer than 1,500 copies. Melville earned just $58.25 and owed his publisher $300.

With the revival of interest in Melville, which began in the late 1920s, *Pierre* began to assume its place as a key text in the development of Melville's sensibility. Reprinted in paperback in the 1950s, it has been taught in college courses, although few critics have deemed it one of Melville's masterpieces. It is a deeply flawed novel—a fact recognized by Hershel Parker, the dean of Melville critics and biographers. He issued a revised edition of the novel, arguing that an earlier draft—written before Melville added significant material on the publishing industry in New York—is closer to Melville's real intentions and is superior to the book actually published.

Piko   Minor character in *MARDI*. Piko is the ruler of half of the island of Diranda, whose subjects he lightheartedly destroys in war games with the ruler of the other half of Diranda, HELLO.

Pip   Character in *MOBY-DICK*. This black man is called the shipkeeper, for he is placed in charge of the vessel while others go off in smaller boats after whales. Genial and happy in his position, Pip is nervous when he is called on to replace an injured whaleboat oarsman. He jumps from the boat in the heat of a chase, and by the time he is rescued from the sea he has gone mad. John Backus, a black man aboard the *ACUSHNET*, may have given Melville the idea for Pip.

Piranesi, Giovanni Battista (1720–1778)   Italian artist famous for his engravings, etchings, and prints. He transformed Roman ruins into images of the fantastic—huge dungeons, bizarre arcades, and staircases of incredible heights. In *CLAREL*, Melville invokes him as an example of how the human mind can elaborate its ideas and diverge from reality.

"Pisa's Leaning Tower" (1891)   Poem in *TIMOLEON*. Part of the "Fruit of Travel Long Ago" section of the collection, this work grew out of Melville's visit to Pisa on March 23, 1857. Afterward he wrote in his travel diary: "Campanile like pine poised just ere snapping. You wait to hear it crash." In the poem, he couched the source of the tower's fascination in far more dramatic terms:

> It thinks to plunge—but hesitates;
> Shrinks back—yet fain would slide;
> Withholds itself—itself would urge;
> Hovering, shivering on the verge,
> A would-be suicide!

"A Pisgah View from the Rock"   Sketch Fourth of "THE ENCANTADAS."

Pitch   Character in *The CONFIDENCE MAN*. Pitch is the name of the CHANCE STRANGER (actually the CONFIDENCE MAN). He approaches the MISSOURIAN aboard the *FIDELE* and convinces him to hire a boy from the Philosophical Intelligence Office.

Pittsfield, Massachusetts   Seat of Berkshire county, in the western part of the state, long associated with the Melville family. Pittsfield is the site of the family homestead, MELVILL HOUSE, which Herman Melville's grandfather, Thomas MELVILL, purchased in 1816. Melville's uncle, Thomas MELVILLE JR., owned a farm near Pittsfield that Melville visited frequently when he was a boy and a young man. After Melville married in 1847, he enjoyed taking his wife, Lizzie, to the farm, and in the summer of 1850, Herman and Lizzie took their firstborn, Malcolm, to Pittsfield for the whole summer.

For Melville it was a magical season, during which he socialized with literary lights such as Dr. Oliver Wendell Holmes and Catharine Maria Sedgwick and formed a profound friendship with Nathaniel HAWTHORNE, who was living in nearby Lenox, Massachusetts. As the summer came to an end, Melville could not bear the thought of going back to NEW YORK CITY, so he and Lizzie purchased a farm abutting the Melvill property and about one and one-half miles from Pittsfield proper. They would live at the farm, which they christened ARROWHEAD, for the next 13 years.

In modern times, Lenox is part of the Berkshire resort area, which continues to draw a wide variety of artists with such attractions as the Tanglewood Music Festival and Jacob's Pillow dance festival. Pittsfield is somewhat depressed.

Plato (427?–347 B.C.)   Not much is known about this philosopher's early life, but he was probably born in Athens of an aristocratic family. As a youth he had political ambitions, but he abandoned these when his mentor Socrates was condemned and executed in 399. Plato left Greece after Socrates' trial and did not return until 387, when he founded the Academy, a renowned center of philosophical and scientific research. He is best known for his dialogues, which develop different sides of arguments about philosophical ideas.

Plato postulated a harmonious universe composed of ideal forms or archetypes. Only these forms held the truth; the temporal, physical world was but a reflection of the ideal one.

Followers of the Greek philosopher have been called Platonists. Platonists and Platonism are referred to in *MOBY-DICK*. When ISHMAEL refers to himself as a Platonist, he is invoking the image of a man less concerned with the particulars of immediate experience and with observing the world as it is, and more concerned with penetrating the veil or wall that separates the time-bound world from the eternal, ideal world that Plato believed to be the true reality. Similarly, the whale is not just a whale to Ahab, but a symbol or sign of supernatural forces.

In *PIERRE*, Lucy TARTAN and Pierre are referred to as "platonic particles" or ideal forms destined to link together. In *CLAREL*, Plato is represented as a philosopher for whom ideas precede our experience of the world. Similarly, in *The CONFIDENCE MAN*, the philosopher's belief in eternal ideas is contrasted with the "vile uses of life."

Plinlimmon, Plotinus   Character in *PIERRE*. The author of a pamphlet, "EI," that PIERRE reads on his way to the city with Isabel and Delly. Plinlimmon addresses the question of the authority for human actions, exploring those thinkers who take man as developing his own authority for what he does and those who base their concept of authority on the idea of a divinity who created the world. Pierre later passes by Plinlimmon but fails to engage him in conversation. Their failure to actually meet reinforces Pierre's inability to comprehend his own situation, to find a sound basis for his beliefs and actions. Pierre had thrust the pamphlet into a coat and then forgotten about it, then tried in vain to secure another copy from booksellers and from Plinlimmon's friends.

Pomare (also Pomaree) Tahitian dynasty. In chapter 80 of OMOO, Melville rehearses the history of the Pomares. Pomare I (1743?–1803), then called Otoo (sometimes Otou, or Otu), was king of Tahiti when the island was visited by the English explorer Captain James COOK in 1773. Melville reports that when Otoo changed his name to Pomare before his death, "Pomare" became the "royal patronymic."

Pomare II (1774?–1821), his son, became king in 1803. During Pomare II's reign, Tahiti was converted to Christianity by British missionaries and welcomed other Europeans. Although Pomare II was himself baptized a Christian and built an elaborate chapel, he is remembered for his debauchery.

His son, Pomare III (1820–27), was raised by British missionaries. Pomare III was crowned king in 1824 after his father's death, but the boy himself died from dysentery when he was only seven years old. He was succeeded by his half sister, Pomare IV (also called Pomare Vahine IV), who was sovereign during Melville's time in Tahiti in 1842.

Pomare IV (1813–77), whose original name was Aimata, was the illegitimate daughter of Pomare II. In 1824, she married Tapoa II, then the 16-year-old ruler of nearby Bora Bora, whom she rejected as sterile when, after five years, he failed to impregnate her. Then, in 1832, she married one Tenanai, of nearby Raiatea, an event that resulted in a native uprising against her. Queen Pomare was a weak and undisciplined ruler who permitted the British consul, George PRITCHARD, to persuade her to expel two French Catholic missionaries. French naval forces, led by Admiral DUPETIT-THOUARS, responded by threatening to shell the island. Pomare gave in, granting the French control over Tahitian foreign affairs, but this proved not to be enough. In 1843 France formally annexed Tahiti, installing the hated Armand-Joseph BRUAT as governor.

When the native population revolted, British men-of-war sailed into Tahitian waters. One of these ships, commanded by George PAULET, spirited Pomare to safety in nearby Eimeo. In the end, the French prevailed over the British, deporting Pritchard and forcing the British naval officers to salute the French flag. When the unrest quieted in 1847, Pomare IV was returned as sovereign. She had eight children by her second husband. Her eldest son died in 1855, so when Pomare IV died in 1877, she was succeeded by her second son, who became Pomare V.

Pomare IV is mentioned briefly in TYPEE and makes an actual appearance in *Omoo*, when the narrator and LONG GHOST attempt to gain an audience with her—an experience Melville himself seems to have had. In Melville's second novel, Queen Pomare is described as matronly and careworn, looking markedly older than her 30 years.

"Pontoosuce" (1924) Poem. Of the 40 or so uncollected poems still in manuscript when Melville died, "Pontoosuce" is perhaps the most celebrated. Named for a lake north of PITTSFIELD, MASSACHUSETTS, this late poem is both a nostalgic recollection of a place Melville once loved and a meditation on death:

> All dies! and not alone
> The aspiring trees and men and grass;
> The poet's forms of beauty pass,
> And noblest deeds they are undone.

Just as the speaker is entertaining such thoughts, however, he is visited by a female spirit who reminds him of the great cycle of life, in which

> The grass it dies, but in vernal rain
> Up it springs and it lives again;
> Over and over, again and again.

Telling him to "Let go, let go!" she then kisses him with her warm lips while her "cold chaplet" brushes his brow—and then she vanishes. It is a melancholy but still comforting vision that unifies man and nature, male and female, death and rebirth. "Pontoosuce" is clearly the work of an old man, but that of a man who seems at last to have found a measure of peace.

"Poor Man's Pudding and Rich Man's Crumbs" (1854) Short story. This story is one of three diptychs, or two-sided stories, that Melville probably wrote between the late summer of 1853 and the early spring of 1854 (the others are "THE TWO TEMPLES" and "THE PARADISE OF BACHELORS AND THE TARTARUS OF MAIDS"). Unlike some of his earlier efforts in the short story form, they do not moralize or attempt to turn misfortune into bounty. "Poor Man's Pudding" is the least developed of the three diptychs and therefore perhaps the first to have been written.

In "Picture First: Poor Man's Pudding," a nameless narrator provides an audience for his host, a poet named BLANDMOUR, who pontificates about the blessings of the poor. Snow, says Blandmour, is "Poor Man's manure," fertilizing his fields, just as melted snow acts as "Poor Man's Eye-water" and rain as "Poor Man's Egg." The narrator decides to take up Blandmour's suggestion that he test for himself the poet's assertion that a "Poor Man's Pudding" is every bit as delectable as a rich man's. Pleading traveler's fatigue, he introduces himself to a poor woodcutter named William COULTER and his wife Martha, who generously share their sparse rations with him. The narrator declines all but their pudding, which is bitter and mouldy. Taking his leave, the narrator returns to Blandmour's, where he decries the rich and their attitudes towards the poor.

In "Picture Second: Rich Man's Crumbs," the narrator travels to England after the Battle of Waterloo. In London he meets a man who discourses about local charities and tells him about a Guildhall banquet staged the night before by the nobility as a celebration of the victory over Napoleon. Last night's remains, he says, are being made available to poor people who have been issued blue entry tickets. While his companion talks of how fortunate these folk are to be permitted to eat the aristocrats' leavings, the narrator is nearly crushed in the melee. In the end, he concludes, "Heaven save me equally from a 'Poor Man's Pudding' and a 'Rich man's Crumbs.'"

"Poor Man's Pudding" appeared anonymously in the June 1854 issue of HARPER'S NEW MONTHLY MAGAZINE. During Melville's lifetime it was reprinted twice: in the June 19, 1854 edition of the Salem, Massachusetts *Register* and the August 1854 issue of the Buffalo *Western Literary Messenger*.

Po-Po, Ereemear ("Jeremiah")   Minor character in *OMOO*. A Tahitian convert to Christianity, Po-Po is a deacon of his church in Partoowye. This generous fellow, together with his wife, AFRETEE, extends his hospitality to the narrator and LONG GHOST, putting the foreigners up for several days.

"The Portent. (1859.)" (1866)   Poem in *BATTLE-PIECES*. In this first stand-alone poem in the collection, the abolitionist John BROWN is shown swinging from the gallows. Although Melville calls him "weird," Brown is pictured not as a lunatic but instead as a martyr in whose "streaming beard is shown . . . The meteor of the war."

Potter, Israel (1744–1826?)   Revolutionary War veteran who published in 1824 an account of his life which Melville drew on and transformed for his novel *ISRAEL POTTER*. A quintessential American in his industry, Melville's Potter nevertheless exposes the dark side of the American dream as he comes into contact with American heroes like Benjamin FRANKLIN and John Paul JONES, who are distinguished mainly by their connivery, ambition, and vaingloriousness.

predestination   Doctrine that denies free will. Melville uses the word "predestinated" several times in *MOBY-DICK* to suggest that the encounter between the *PEQUOD* and the white whale is a foreordained event. He is drawing upon Calvinist theology, derived from the religious thinker, John Calvin (1509–64), who proposed the doctrine that God predestines the salvation of certain souls. Consequently, certain souls would seem predestined for damnation. Although not a strict Calvinist, Melville borrowed from Calvinism a brooding sense of doom, an awareness that human actions have been somehow foretold (see CALVINISTIC). *BILLY BUDD* may be regarded as an extended consideration of predestination, especially in the depiction of John CLAGGART.

Powers, Hiram (1805–1873)   American sculptor. Born in Woodstock, Vermont, he studied art in a sculptor's studio in Cincinnati, Ohio. Later he made busts of famous Americans, including John Marshall and John C. CALHOUN. He is best known for his controversial statue *The Greek Slave* (1843), which Melville first saw at the Great Exhibition in New York in 1851. The sculpture of a nude woman in manacles and chains affronted those critics who disapproved of nudity and those who thought women should not be depicted in such servile, degrading poses. Melville visited Powers's Florence studio in 1857 and found the artist an "open, plain man" and a "fine specimen of an American."

"Presentation to the Authorities, by Privates, of Colors captured in Battles ending in the Surrender of Lee." (1866)   Poem in *BATTLE-PIECES*. One of the "Verses Inscriptive and Memorial" in Melville's collection of CIVIL WAR poetry, this work reads like a final act. After the victors present their captured flags and lay them before "The altar which of right claims all— / Our country," they gladly return "To waiting homes with vindicated laws."

president of the Black Rapids Coal Company, the   Character in *The CONFIDENCE MAN*. This "character" is, in fact, one of the guises of the CONFIDENCE MAN. He approaches the COLLEGIAN, asking him to make an investment in the "New Jerusalem," a community the president is touting.

Priming   Minor character in *WHITE-JACKET*. Like all members of gunner's gangs, the narrator says, Priming is bad-tempered. But Priming, a nasal-voiced, hare-lipped individual who shares WHITE-JACKET's mess, is a superstitious sort who takes a particular dislike to White-Jacket, whom he views as a sort of pariah. After White-Jacket becomes the 13th member of the mess, Priming blames him for the harm that comes to two other members of the group.

Melville wrote one of his greatest poems, "The Portent," about John Brown's abortive attempt to free slaves, an attempt that resulted in Brown's execution. (Library of Congress)

Pritchard, George (1796–1883)   British missionary and diplomat. Ordained in the Congregational Church, Pritchard became a missionary to Tahiti in 1827. He was an ambitious man. Put in charge of religious life in Tahiti's main population center, Papeetee, he also pursued a variety of commercial interests and sought to become British consul. His missionary work prevented his appointment to this position until 1837, when the Tahitian ruler, POMARE IV, came into conflict with the French. His position came with the proviso that it exclude missionary work, but Pritchard continued to mix religion and business until 1842, when Tahiti became a French protectorate. Back in England, he wrote a book titled *The Missionary's Reward; or, The Success of the Gospel in the Pacific* (1844). He then returned to Tahiti, but was expelled by French authorities for fomenting rebellion among the natives.

Pritchard is mentioned briefly in *TYPEE*, where his wife makes a more pronounced appearance as the consul's wife who stands up to the French. In *OMOO*, Pritchard is mentioned as the absent consul who has appointed one Wilson to serve as acting consul in his absence.

"Profundity and Levity" (1924)   Poem in *WEEDS AND WILDINGS*. Like other poems in the "This, That and the Other" section of the volume, "Profundity and Levity" opens with a prose prologue—this one comparing the profundity of the owl with the levity of the meadowlark. But the poet, meditating on their different natures, is moved to ask:

> Life blinks at strong light,
> Life wanders in night like a dream—
> Is then life worth living?

purser, the   Character in *BILLY BUDD*. He argues with the surgeon about why Billy's body did not go into the spasm that is expected of hanged men. He supposes it might be a question of Billy's willpower—an explanation the surgeon rejects as unscientific. When pressed by the purser, however, the surgeon admits that he has no explanation for the unusual phenomenon.

Putnam's Monthly Magazine Founded in 1853, this periodical appealed mainly to well-cultivated and liberal readers. *Putnam's* published Henry David Thoreau, James Fenimore Cooper, Henry Wadsworth Longfellow, James Russell Lowell, and many other important writers. Melville was paid five dollars a page for his stories, a sum he considered admirable. "BARTLEBY, THE SCRIVENER: a Story of Wall Street" appeared in three monthly installments (October, November, and December of 1853). "THE ENCANTADAS" appeared in *Putnam's* under the pseudonym Salvator R. Tarnmoor, and Melville arranged for serial publication of ISRAEL POTTER at five dollars a page. By early 1855, he had earned over $1,000 from the magazine.

"Puzzlement as to a Figure Left Solitary on a Unique Fragment of Greek Basso-Rilievo" (1947) Poem.

One of more than 40 poems left uncollected or unpublished when Melville died, this work was written in the spirit of others that went into TIMOLEON but never found a place there. A fragment of marble seems to resemble the goddess Artemis; the poet, lacking any other clues, is left to wonder who the flirtatious figure is and why she has been thus carved.

Pythagorean Term referring to a philosophy named after Pythagoras (c. 550–c. 500 B.C.). Little is known about this Greek philosopher, although he was renowned for his strictures about diet, such as his ban on eating certain meats and beans. In PIERRE, the Apostles (a band of urban artists who provide the hero with a home) are Pythagoreans. They encourage PIERRE's tendency to dwell in an ideal world of his own making, seek inspiration in a denial of luxury, and subsist on a poor diet of fruits and nuts.

Q

Queequeg Character in *MOBY-DICK*. Queequeg is ISH-MAEL's shipmate, a tall, brawny, and dark-skinned harpooner. The two share a bed at the SPOUTER INN. Ishmael overcomes his initial repugnance to his comrade and finds him to be noble, gentle, affectionate, and extremely polite. Queequeg becomes one of the stalwarts of the *PEQUOD*. His appearance and character may have been suggested by the description of the easygoing New Zealand chief Ko-towatowa of Kororarika, described by Charles Wilkes in *Narrative of the U.S. Exploring Expedition During the Years 1838, 1839, 1840, 1841, 1842.*

Quoin Minor character in *WHITE-JACKET*. Quoin is the quarter-gunner on board the *NEVERSINK*. He is, the narrator says, typical of all gunners in that he is bad-tempered and whimsical. Quoin at least loves the guns that are his life—he even resembles them physically in his short stature and his "complexion like a gunshot wound after it is healed."

R

Rachel In chapter CXXVIII of *MOBY-DICK,* the *PEQUOD* meets the *Rachel.* Captain GARDINER of the *Rachel* tells AHAB that he lost a boat and some members of the crew (including his son) chasing the whale. Gardiner implores Ahab to help him find his son, but Ahab refuses, even after Gardiner offers to charter the *Pequod.* ISHMAEL is later picked up by the *Rachel* after the *Pequod* sinks.

Radney Character in *MOBY-DICK.* Radney is a mate on the *Town-Ho* who becomes alarmed when the ship begins to leak. Radney is assaulted by STEELKILT after menacing the latter with a hammer and ordering him to perform the demeaning task of cleaning the ship's decks. Steelkilt starts a mutiny, which is quashed by the ship's captain, and Radney dies chasing Moby-Dick. Something of Radney seems to be derived from Jenney, the first officer of the *Nassau,* a New Bedford whaler. In April 1843, in a quarrel with a crew member, Luther Fox, Jenney's leg was cut with a mincing knife, and he bled to death.

Radcliffe, Mrs. Ann (1764–1823) Melville refers to something mysterious and "Radcliffian" about John CLAGGART in *BILLY BUDD, SAILOR.* He has in mind Mrs. Radcliffe's Gothic novels, such as *The Mysteries of Udolpho* (1794), which arouse feelings of terror and the supernatural.

"A Rail Road Cutting Near Alexandria in 1855" (1947) Poem. One of more than 40 poems left unpublished or uncollected when Melville died, "A Rail Road Cutting Near Alexandria" grew out of Melville's travels in Egypt in 1857. Like some other Melville poems that contrast the old world with the new, this one finds the modern age degenerate by comparison. As in "THE DUST-LAYERS," modern practices contaminate "Egypt's ancient dust." The Egyptian engine, inspired by "Watt's his name" (Scottish engineer James Watt [1736–1819], inventor of the modern steam engine), so disrupts the ancient land that the poet fears "The Pyramid is slipping!"

"Rammon" (1947) Prose and poetry. "The Enviable Isles," a poem in *JOHN MARR,* would be the only part of "Rammon" published during Melville's lifetime. Another lengthy segment of prose and poetry from "Rammon" would remain among the more than 40 uncollected and unpublished poetic works he left behind. This segment, which features a questing Prince Rammon, one of King Solomon's sons, was to have been part of a longer work concerning the nature of personal immortality. Rammon becomes interested in the Buddhist teachings concerning immortality that have been imported to Jerusalem by the Princess of Sheba. Setting out on a spiritual journey, Rammon encounters Tardi, a Tyrian importer and poet who professes to love Buddha. Rammon rejects Tardi, however, after the poet tries to convince the prince that he will find happiness in "The Enviable Isles," of which he sings. There the fragment ends.

Rartoo Minor character in *OMOO.* Rartoo is the chief of the inland village of Tamai, which because of its remoteness is supposed to be one of the last bastions of purely Polynesian life. While there, the narrator and LONG GHOST stay with Rartoo, whom they inveigle into staging a native dance for the Westerners' edification and enjoyment.

Ratcliff, Lieutenant Character in *BILLY BUDD.* He boards The *RIGHTS OF MAN* to impress a sailor (see IMPRESSMENT), and BILLY BUDD is his choice.

"The Ravaged Villa" (1891) Poem in *TIMOLEON.* In February and March of 1857, Melville recorded in his travel diary having seen many ruined classical villas in the vicinities of Naples and Rome. He used some of the details he observed then to write this one-stanza condemnation of materialism, in which classicism itself is allowed to crumble into dust and art is sacrificed to greed:

> The spider in the laurel spins,
> The weed exiles the flower;
> And, flung to kiln, Apollo's bust
> Makes lime for Mammon's tower.

"A Reasonable Constitution" (1947) Poem. On the manuscript of this, one of more than 40 poems left uncollected or unpublished when he died, Melville wrote: "Observable in Sir Thomas More's 'Utopia' are First Its almost entire reasonableness. Second Its almost entire impracticality[.] The remark applies more or

171

less to the Utopia's prototype 'Plato's Republic.'" For Melville, in the end, reason cannot govern men. Only government and, above all, art can impose order on man's inherently chaotic nature.

"Rebel Color-Bearers at Shiloh: A plea against the vindictive cry raised by civilians shortly after the surrender at Appomattox." (1866) Poem in BATTLE-PIECES. In a note on the poem, Melville describes how, during the first day of the battle at Shiloh, Tennessee, in April 1862, the Confederate color-bearers displayed so bravely that Union soldiers were ordered not to shoot them. In the aftermath of Appomattox, Melville urges the victors to remember the valor of their former enemies—"Perish their cause! but mark the men"—and, like the Union soldiers at Shiloh, refrain from retribution.

Redburn: His First Voyage, Being the Sailor-Boy Confessions and Reminiscences of the Son-of-a-Gentleman, in the Merchant Service (1849) Melville's fourth novel. Disappointed by the sales and critical reception of MARDI and beset by family obligations that increased with the birth of his son Malcolm in February 1849, Melville determined that he would jettison his artistic aspirations and return to the kind of novel-writing his public seemed to expect of him. To his readers he was, apparently, not a novelist, but instead a sailor who wrote travelogues. He turned, with some bitterness, to his earliest seagoing adventures.

Ten years earlier, finding no success in his search for work as an engineer, the 19-year-old Melville had decided to follow his cousin Leonard Gansevoort's advice and example by going to sea. On June 4, 1839, in NEW YORK CITY, Melville signed on as a cabin boy with the merchant ship *St. Lawrence*, bound for LIVERPOOL, England. Much of what he experienced during the three-month voyage there and back would find its way—often much romanticized—into *Redburn*.

SYNOPSIS

Chapters 1–2: "How Wellingborough Redburn's Taste for the Sea Was Born and Bred in Him"; "Redburn's Departure from Home"
The narrator, Wellingborough Redburn, is a 15-year-old "son-of-a-gentleman" who finds himself in dire straits. Like the young Herman Melville, Redburn has lost his father, an importer, whose death has left the family—now living in a pleasant Hudson Valley village—virtually penniless. Wearing his older brother's shooting jacket and carrying his brother's fowling piece, which Redburn hopes to sell in New York to raise money, the boy bids farewell to his mother and three sisters and sets off for the city.

With only a dollar in his pocket, Redburn boards the Hudson River steamboat for New York. Almost immedi-

ately, he is exposed to the world's cruelty. He is shunned by the other passengers, for "the scent and savor of poverty" is upon him. When the captain's clerk demands Redburn's ticket, the boy responds that he has none—in fact, half the fare, one dollar, is all the money he has in the world.

Chapters 3–4: "He Arrives in Town"; "How He Disposed of His Fowling Piece"
Redburn does carry something of value, however: an introduction to a Mr. JONES, one of his brother's college friends. Mr. Jones not only provides the boy with bed and board, but the next day also takes him down to the docks to help him find employment. They decide upon a ship bound for Liverpool, and when they board the *Highlander*, they are greeted with the utmost courtesy by Captain RIGA. But when Mr. Jones makes the mistake of representing Redburn as a gentleman's son who is only going to sea on a lark, the captain turns this intended kindness to his favor, offering to pay Redburn a mere three dollars a month. This is only the first indication of the captain's duplicitousness.

Redburn is hardly in a position to argue over this pitiful salary, but he hopes to make up the shortfall by selling his fowling piece for a goodly sum. When the first pawnbroker he approaches offers him only three dollars for his gun, Redburn reacts with indignation, but efforts to sell it elsewhere prove fruitless. He is forced to return to the first pawnbroker, who this time offers him only two and a half dollars, which Redburn, learning another hard lesson, is obliged to take.

Chapters 5–6: "He Purchases His Sea-Wardrobe, and on a Dismal Rainy Day Picks Up His Board and Lodging along the Wharves"; "He Is Initiated in the Business of Cleaning Out the Pig-Pen, and Slushing Down the Top-Mast"
Redburn's money does not stretch far. He spends it the very next morning on some stationery he uses to write to his mother, and on a simple sea wardrobe consisting of a sailor's traditional red woolen shirt and a tarpaulin hat. Fortunately, Mr. Jones once again provides him with a good meal and a warm bed.

The next morning Redburn makes his way to the docks, but to his disappointment it begins to rain. Not wanting to impose further on the Joneses, he spends the day walking around in the wet with nothing to eat. After a sleepless night on board the *Highlander* and drinking a glass of water for breakfast, he finds little sympathy among the crew. After the second mate rebuffs his offer of tobacco, the first mate belittles his inappropriate shooting jacket and equally unsuitable name, rechristening him "Buttons."

Redburn's first task is to clean out the pigpen. His second is to learn to follow orders exactly. His third task is harder still: faint from lack of food, he is obliged to climb the rigging up to the top of the mainmast while carrying a heavy bucket. Somehow he survives this ordeal, and as the *Highlander* weighs anchor he is called to supper, only to find that he can eat little.

Chapters 7–8: "He Gets to Sea and Feels Very Bad"; "He Is Put into the Larboard Watch; Gets Seasick; and Relates Some Other of His Experiences"
Young Redburn finds that as the ship glides out of New York harbor, he is struck by the beauty of the land he is leaving behind, and he becomes homesick. His greenness and his alienation from his rough crewmates is pronounced; when the watches are assigned, Redburn is chosen last and given the larboard, or port watch, presided over by the first mate. Before he can assume his duties, however, he is overcome by seasickness, which a Greenland sailor offers to cure with rum. Having taken a temperance pledge, Redburn at first declines, but then accepts the GREENLANDER's offer—but not before delivering a pious aside about how temperance advocates really should make an exception for such circumstances.

Chapters 9–12: "The Sailors Becoming a Little Social, Redburn Converses with Them"; "He Is Very Much Frightened; the Sailors Abuse Him; and He Becomes Miserable and Forlorn"; "He Helps Wash the Decks, and then Goes to Breakfast"; "He Gives Some Account of One of His Shipmates Called Jackson"
The rum proves medicinal, and Redburn stands his first watch. A member of an antismoking society, he declines the Havana cigar sociably offered by another sailor, while confessing that this pledge, too, would be broken before the voyage was done. He is shocked to discover that many of the men are drunk while on duty, and when he begins to inquire about their religious convictions, their patience with the greenhorn cabin boy begins to wear thin.

Redburn is traumatized when a drunken sailor jumps overboard in a suicidal frenzy; and he is yet more traumatized to discover, when the watch is over, that he is obliged to sleep in the very bunk that the drowned man had recently vacated. Below decks, the others taunt Redburn for his fearfulness; one sailor, Jackson, is especially sadistic, threatening to throw the boy overboard if Redburn ever gets in his way.

Redburn goes on to describe Jackson, who serves as kind of nemesis for him. Although thin and sickly, Jackson has a commanding air and manages to hold sway over the others. Because they fear him and he has taken a dislike to Redburn, the boy finds himself friendless and alone, "a sort of Ishmael in the ship."

Chapters 13–14: "He Has a Fine Day at Sea, Begins to Like It; but Changes His Mind"; "He Contemplates Making a Social Call on the Captain in His Cabin"
During his second day at sea Redburn begins to get his sea legs, reveling in the glories of a sunny day and delighting in all the new things he is learning. All too quickly, however, he is brought back down to earth when he is commanded to clean out the *Highlander*'s chicken coops and make up the ship's pigpens. He is, he concludes, no better than a slave.

Casting about for ways to better his situation, Redburn recalls how beneficently Captain Riga had regarded him during their interview. Thinking it strange that the captain has not stopped by to see how he is doing or invited him to his cabin, Redburn sets off to make a social call on his chief superior, disregarding the laughter of his crew mates. On his way, however, he is stopped dead by the first mate, who cuffs him after he declares he will complain to his "friend," the captain.

Throughout the narrative, Redburn presents himself as a credulous youth. Although he confesses that he is beginning to get the idea that a social call on the captain by the lowliest man on board is not customary, he characteristically blames his foolishness on his "ignorance of sea usages." The next day Redburn compounds his error when he sees the captain promenading on the quarterdeck and seizes the opportunity to chat with him. Both the captain and the first mate fly into a rage at this impertinence, and poor Redburn can only conclude that Riga is no gentleman.

Chapters 15–17: "The Melancholy State of His Wardrobe"; "At Dead of Night He Is Sent Up to Loose the Main-Skysail"; "The Cook and the Steward"
Redburn laments the state of his wardrobe, and explains how he was given the monikers "Boots" and "Buttons." When he left home, he had done so wearing his new Sunday boots and his brother's shooting jacket. Very quickly, he learned how unfit these items were for seafaring, but he lacked the money to replace them with more suitable items. His shipmates loved to mock the way his high-heeled boots trip him up on board and to tease him about the many buttons that ornament his jacket and pantaloons.

Despite his lack of preparedness, Redburn still glories in the romance of seafaring, recollecting a mid-sea encounter with a ship from far-off Hamburg. But such joys are balanced by terrors, such as those engendered by his first trip aloft to loosen a sail. Such work is, he is told, "boy's business," but it is business that puts him in a great deal of danger, nonetheless.

Redburn begins to take an interest in his crewmates, some of whom treat the boy kindly. One of these is MAX THE DUTCHMAN, who voices concern about Redburn's poor wardrobe. Another is the ship's black cook, known—like all ship's cooks—as "the doctor." The cook, who calls himself Mr. THOMPSON, is devoted to Bible reading—notwithstanding his cursing. Mr. Thompson is friendly with the mulatto steward, a man known as LAVENDER owing to his habit of perfuming his hair. Lavender is more than a bit of a dandy whose devotion to decadence the cook tries to counteract with frequent readings of such Bible stories as the story of Joseph and Potiphar's wife, a cautionary tale in which the Old Testament hero is falsely accused of licentiousness and loses his employment.

Chapters 18–22: "He Endeavors to Improve His Mind; and Tells of One Blunt and His Dream Book"; "A Narrow Escape"; "In a Fog He Is Set to Work as a Bell-Toller; and Beholds a Herd of Ocean-Elephants"; "A Whaleman and a Man-of-War's-Man"; "The Highlander Passes a Wreck"
For his part, Redburn is also attempting to better himself by reading. Having already read two works lent by Max the Dutchman—a book on shipwrecks and a large black book titled *Delirium Tremens*—Redburn turns to yet another unsuitable tome, Adam Smith's *Wealth of Nations*, which Mr. Jones has given him. Not surprisingly, such fare puts him to sleep.

Redburn then delivers an aside about Jack BLUNT, a curious-looking fellow whose Irish origins seem to underlie his belief in all manner of magic. Blunt's credulousness makes him an easy target for unscrupulous peddlers of nostrums and potions. It also makes him a true believer in the system for success explained in a large red pamphlet titled *The Bonaparte Dream Book*, a method of interpreting dreams said to have secured greatness for Napoleon Bonaparte.

The aside on Blunt's "Dream Book" leads to yet another concerning a night when Blunt's meditations are interrupted as the *Highlander* rams an unknown ship, an accident caused by the drowsiness of those on watch. The ship is sailing through the perilous fogs of the Grand Banks off Newfoundland, conditions requiring the utmost care. Redburn, in fact, is sent aloft to toll the ship's bell repeatedly as a warning to other vessels. While performing this task, he gets his first view of a pod of whales, a sight that proves to be mightily disappointing for the boy. They are so much smaller than he expected them to be that he begins to doubt the biblical story of Jonah.

Recounting this sighting of the whales causes Redburn to remember a crewmate named LARRY, who had previously served on a whaler. Although "blubber-boilers" like Larry are customarily looked down upon by merchant seamen, Larry is the one who exhibits prejudices, asking Redburn rhetorically, "What's the use of bein' *snivelized*?" The *Highlander* also carries a former man-of-war's man known as "Gun-Deck," who could not offer more of a contrast. Unlike Larry, Gun-Deck exhibits a marked preference for the all the trappings of civilization.

Still in the Grand Banks, the *Highlander* weathers a ferocious storm, then passes a drifting wreck of a schooner carrying three decayed, greenish corpses. Redburn is shocked that Captain Riga does not stop to bury them.

Chapter 23: "An Unaccountable Cabin-Passenger, and a Mysterious Young Lady"
Even though it is a merchant ship, the *Highlander* carries a few passengers. Only one of these—a quiet, little man—is a regular cabin passenger. Unobtrusive as he is, he still manages to get into trouble by venturing aloft. Caught out by the mate, the passenger is bound hand and foot in the rigging by the Greenlander, who, following an old merchantman custom, demands that the passenger hand over a fee before being released.

The other cabin passenger is a beautiful, mysterious young girl whom the steward holds to be Captain Riga's ward. The story has it that she is a Liverpool dockmaster's daughter who, for health reasons, had been sent on a "cruise" to America in Riga's care. Even the credulous narrator has some sense that this story rings hollow, however: on board, the girl and the captain flirt in what he calls a "shabby" fashion.

The *Highlander* also carries a number of steerage passengers—20 or 30 people, mostly men—who are returning to England in order to escort their families to their new homes in America. In addition, the ship carries a stowaway, a young English boy who had, with his father, left England for America aboard the *Highlander* some six months before and is now returning home an orphan. The boy brings out the best in the sailors, all of whom, with the notable exception of Jackson, cosset and spoil him.

Chapters 24–26: "He Begins to Hop About in the Rigging Like a Saint Jago's Monkey"; "Quarter-Deck Furniture"; "A Sailor a Jack of All Trades"
Redburn spends his time properly, learning to handle many chores aboard ship, although he regrets not having the opportunity to steer. As a result of his diligence, the crew begins to treat him with more consideration.

Chapter 27: "He Gets a Peep at Ireland, and at Last Arrives at Liverpool"
Thirty days after leaving New York, the *Highlander* comes within sight of Ireland. When a fishing boat draws up next to the ship, an Irish sailor asks the crew to throw down a rope. Thinking he might have important news to convey in person, the crew complies, adding more and more line as the fisherman continues to reel it in. When he has as much as he thinks he can get, the Irishman cuts and runs, prompting Redburn to make another of his sadder-but-wiser observations: "Here, then, was a beautiful introduction to the eastern hemisphere: fairly robbed before striking soundings."

The *Highlander* sails on past Wales, passing Holyhead and Anglesea. Finally, on the third day after sighting land, the ship approaches Liverpool. As a pilot boat leads the ship into the harbor, Redburn studies the passing scene, which falls far short of what his romantic imagination had conjured up. His shipmates, for the most part, seem blasé. One exception is Max the

Dutchman, who is greeted by a fine-looking woman who seems to be his wife. Although he has heard many a tale about the bigamies of sailors, Redburn is nevertheless shocked to actually witness such immorality. Needless to say, when he brings up the subject of the wife Max left behind in New York, the older man is none too pleased.

Chapter 28: "He Goes to Supper at the Sign of the Baltimore Clipper"
After the *Highlander* is berthed, the crew, led by Jackson, goes ashore in search of supper. First stopping off at a tavern, they make their way to an inn under the sign of the Baltimore Clipper. This sign combines the clipper with a British unicorn and an American eagle, by way of signifying that although it is a British establishment it caters to Americans. In fact, it is kept by a former American seaman named DANBY, although his bustling British wife, known as "HANDSOME MARY," really runs things.

But the Baltimore Clipper is a rather sad place, and Redburn finds himself once again disappointed when his fantasies fail to live up to reality. Furthermore, he is beginning to realize that his prospects of actually seeing the world as a sailor are slim, as most of their time is spent aboard ship. He is revived, however, by an ample supper served on a groaning board.

Chapter 29: "Redburn Deferentially Discourses Concerning the Prospects of Sailors"
While the *Highlander* remains in dock over the next six weeks, the crew is obliged to sleep on board and to continue to perform cleaning duties. But with few other responsibilities, the men have a great deal of time, if little money, on their hands. Despite the presence of numerous religious and temperance organizations in the port, many sailors fall victim to dissipation in places like Liverpool.

Chapters 30–31: "Redburn Grows Intolerably Flat and Stupid Over Some Outlandish Old Guide-Books"; "With His Prosy Old Guide-Book, He Takes a Prosy Stroll through the Town"
Redburn, determined to see something of the city, peruses a number of old guidebooks he has brought along from his late father's library. Taking up one of these, a "prosy old guide-book" titled THE PICTURE OF LIVERPOOL, he decides to track down some of the places his father had visited in the city 30 years earlier.

Once again, Redburn is disappointed by what the world has to show him, for as he soon realizes, this now 50-year-old guidebook is of little use. Filled with a sense of Walter Redburn's presence, he searches for the hotel where his father once stayed, only to find it no longer exists. This is a considerable blow; not only is he unable to trace his father's footsteps, he also is without any sort of guidance. As Redburn observes—perhaps without a great deal of self-awareness—"the thing that had guided the father, could not guide the son."

Chapters 32–36: "The Docks"; "The Salt-Droghers, and German Emigrant Ships"; "The Irrawaddy"; "Galliots, Coast-of-Guinea-Man, and Floating Chapel"; "The Old Church of St. Nicholas, and the Dead-House"
Redburn continues his excursions through Liverpool, visiting other docks. In one he meets a skipper who shares with Redburn his supper, ale, and tobacco (Redburn having apparently given up his vows to neither drink nor smoke). In another he witnesses German emigrants boarding ships bound for New York. In Prince's Dock he visits a celebrated Indian merchant vessel and learns much about her from one of her exotic crew members. He observes many other unusual ships, and he attends services at a number of floating chapels.

Ranging farther afield, Redburn visits a venerable old church that he describes as the "best preserved piece of antiquity in all Liverpool." The basement of the Church of St. Nicholas contains the Dead House, where bodies of drowned persons are kept until claimed. Told that rewards are offered for the recovery of drowning victims, he laments that so many individuals make their living off the dead.

Chapter 37: "What Redburn Saw in Launcelotte's-Hey"
Wandering through a narrow street called Launcelotte's-Hey, Redburn is given an opportunity to try to save lives. Hearing a feeble wail issuing from a warehouse cellar, he discovers a destitute woman in rags who clutches a dead baby to her breast even as two shrunken children cling to her skirts. Although Redburn recognizes that the family has gone to that place to die, he tries desperately to get help for them. None of the local people want to come to the aid of this family, and neither do the police or even Handsome Mary.

Redburn manages to steal some bread and cheese from the Baltimore Clipper and takes the food, together with some water he gathers from a fire hydrant, to the vault in Launcelotte's-Hey. While the two girls manage to eat and drink a little, their mother seems past help. Retreating, Redburn briefly experiences an impulse to put the family out of its misery, but he continues to bring them food until, three days later, he believes they have died. Unable once again to obtain any help, he returns later in the day to find them gone, a heap of quicklime in their place.

Chapters 38–43: "The Dock-Wall Beggars"; "The Booble-Alleys of the Town"; "Placards, Brass-Jewelers, Truck-Horses, and Steamers"; "Redburn Roves About Hither and Thither"; "His Adventure with the Cross Old Gentleman"; "He Takes a Delightful Ramble into the Country; and Makes the Acquaintance of Three Adorable Charmers"
Redburn describes the suffering humanity that surrounds the Liverpool docks, including ragpickers and beggars who prey on the sailors. The sailors have little

money or inclination to help, but they are solicitous of an old man with a wooden leg who begs for coppers—he was once a man-of-war's man who lost his limb in the Battle of Trafalgar.

A similar rabble can be found in the seedier parts of town frequented by the sailors, although Redburn declares that propriety forbids him from describing them in detail. He does describe a hodgepodge of impressions, however, including those of military recruiting posters, hucksters, pawnbrokers, thieves, and draft horses and their drivers. Ranging further afield, he observes that, except for the absence of black faces, Liverpool seems a city much like New York. But this perception is undermined one Sunday when, after attending church, he joins a throng of people listening to a Chartist (see CHARTISM) hold forth.

Redburn is booted out of the Lyceum Club, which he attempted to enter after rationalizing that a "poor, friendless sailor-boy" from a foreign land will surely be welcome in such a cultured, liberal atmosphere. Still failing to grasp the finer points of class, Redburn concludes that Englishmen have no manners. On a ramble into the English countryside, however, he finds that he is more than welcome in the house of a stranger who has three lovely daughters.

Chapters 44–46: "Redburn Introduces Master Harry Bolton to the Favorable Consideration of the Reader"; "Harry Bolton Kidnaps Redburn, and Carries Him Off to London"; "A Mysterious Night in London"

After he has been in Liverpool for at least a month, Redburn makes the acquaintance of an exceedingly good-looking youth named Harry Bolton. Redburn first notices Harry standing about in doorways near the Baltimore Clipper, but the naive American has no sense that this pretty young Englishman is trying to pick up sailors. When the two are finally introduced, Bolton tells Redburn that he is an orphan from Suffolk who lost his inheritance when he fell in with the wrong crowd in London. Lacking any better way of making a living, he says, he joined the East India Company as a midshipman. After two voyages to Bombay, he returned to London where, once again, he gambled away his money. Determined now to make his way in America, he has traveled to Liverpool in hopes of signing on with a ship—such as the *Highlander*—bound for the New World.

Redburn is eager to have Harry Bolton join him on his homeward voyage, but he warns his new friend that because of Captain Riga's parsimony, Harry should only ask for a position as a ship's "boy," despite his maritime experience. The captain hires Bolton at once, but Redburn, oddly, experiences some uneasiness about his friend's job qualifications. Something about Harry Bolton just does not ring true. Redburn's suspicions are further aroused when Bolton ducks around a corner to avoid confronting an elegant young man whom he refers to as "Lord Lovely." When Redburn goes back to take a second look at the fellow, he finds him rather unimpressive. "Lord Lovely" is plainly a male prostitute, but Redburn takes him to be only a poor representative of the English nobility.

Nonetheless, Redburn falls under Bolton's spell. When Bolton proposes to underwrite a whirlwind trip to London, it takes little to persuade Redburn to abandon his ship's duty and head for the big city. The youths' 36-hour adventure starts out with a mystery—Bolton claims he has received a remittance and plans to regain some of the money he has lost—and grows steadily stranger. Before they set out to see the West End, Bolton dons a false beard and mustache, which he claims will prevent him from being recognized as he carries out his plan. Bolton then whisks Redburn off to an exotic, luxurious establishment that Redburn calls a "Palace of Aladdin." Upon entering, Bolton disappears.

When Harry Bolton comes back, he discloses nothing about where he has been or what he has been doing, instead bullying poor Redburn into agreeing to wait for him and, should he fail to reappear by morning, to post a letter that Bolton thrusts into his hand. Despite deep misgivings about his friend and about his opulent surroundings, Redburn falls into a fitful sleep, only to awake to find Harry standing pale before him. Apparently Bolton has failed to earn back the money he sought, or has lost all he had to gambling. Either way, he behaves wildly, one minute threatening suicide, the next insisting that Redburn cannot ask any questions about their sojourn in London. They leave almost immediately for Liverpool, having been to London without ever really seeing it.

Chapters 47–48: "Homeward Bound"; "A Living Corpse"

Redburn and Bolton return to Liverpool. Redburn discovers that his absence from the *Highlander* has been noticed, but because the ship is leaving in two days' time, little is made of Redburn's furlough.

In addition to cargo, the ship will be carrying 15 cabin passengers and roughly 500 emigrants, traveling steerage, to New York. Just before the ship leaves the dock, three apparently drunken sailors are brought on board. Two of these men are able to resume their duties four or five hours later, but the third, listed in the ship's papers as Miguel SAVEDA, cannot be roused. As the night wears on, an intolerable smell issues from his bunk. When several of the crew members go to investigate, they discover that he is dead and his body is being consumed by spontaneous combustion. The sailors are terrified; but, bullied by Jackson, they pitch Saveda's body overboard. Afterward, his bunk is ceremoniously cleansed and nailed up, and all but Jackson avoid the spot for the remainder of the journey.

Chapter 49: "Carlo"
Among the emigrant passengers, a 15-year-old Italian boy named Carlo stands out. He is cheerful and good-looking, and he plays the hand organ—as a livelihood, and as an entertainment for the crew and the passengers.

Chapter 50: "Harry Bolton at Sea"
Redburn discovers that his misgivings about his friend Harry Bolton have some foundation, for it is quickly revealed that Bolton is without past experience as a sailor. Despite all his boasting, which alienates the rest of the crew, Bolton insists that he cannot go aloft in the rigging. When he is finally forced to do so, the experience utterly traumatizes him. Afterward he becomes, Redburn tells us, an altered person. When he refuses to repeat the ordeal, he is treated with utter contempt by the others and assigned the most degrading of chores.

Chapters 51–53: "The Emigrants"; "The Emigrants' Kitchen"; "The Horatii and Curiatii"
As Redburn explained earlier, the competition for emigrant passengers, who constitute a highly lucrative cargo, is so great that often ship owners and their agents promise much that they cannot deliver. Promised that the Atlantic crossing will take no more than 20 days, the emigrants often bring far fewer provisions than are necessary for the 40 to 90 days the trip actually takes. When, several days into her westbound voyage, the *Highlander* comes within sight of land, some of the emigrants—many of whom are Irish—are profoundly disappointed to discover that it is the Irish coast, not the New World, that they see.

The steerage passengers are obliged to share a single stove on top of the main hatches, and this stove can only be lighted at certain hours. Competition for cooking time and space is keen. Other feuds are sparked by the handsome young wife of an English tailor, who bristles at the attention she receives from the young bucks on board. Redburn also makes note of two sisters—both widowed, both Irish—who each have a set of male triplets with them.

Chapters 54–55: "Some Superior Old Nail-Rod and Pig-Tail"; "Drawing Nigh to the Last Scene in Jackson's Career"
Redburn delivers a digression on his crewmembers' lack of tobacco, having divested themselves of their stores for a handsome profit in Liverpool. Redburn, assigned the job of picking oakum, a loose hemp used for caulking seams on board, discovers that the "heart" of some old ropes can be substituted for chewing tobacco. He notes, in addition, that of all the crew, only Jackson seems to have a plentiful supply of tobacco. And Jackson, a "tyrant to the last," appears to be dying.

Chapter 56: "Under the Lee of the Long-Boat, Redburn and Harry Hold Confidential Communion"
Redburn and Bolton spend more time together, and Harry confesses that in order to pay for his board in

New York, he will have to sell some clothing. Redburn in turn suggests that Harry, who has a much-admired voice, could sing for his supper. When Harry spurns this idea, Redburn determines that he will help his friend find a job as a clerk.

Chapters 57–58: "Almost a Famine"; "Though the Highlander Puts into No Harbor as Yet; She Here and There Leaves Many of Her Passengers Behind"
The emigrants, many of whom are now out of food, appeal to the mate, who in turn appeals to the captain. Captain Riga responds by issuing rations of one sea biscuit and two potatoes per person per day. When this allocation fails to satisfy their hunger, many of the steerage passengers begin to steal from the ship's provisions, whereupon Riga issues an edict declaring that anyone caught stealing with be flogged.

Some 20 days into the voyage, the *Highlander* encounters rough weather, forcing the emigrants to remain below in quarters so cramped they resemble those used to ship slaves across the middle passage. These conditions, combined with general malnourishment and an inability to come on deck to cook, give rise to cholera. Despite ministrations from the mate, several emigrants die before the heavy weather subsides enough to permit some of the emigrants to come up on deck and the crew to clean out the pestilence below.

Chapter 59: "The Last End of Jackson"
When at last the ship is off Cape Cod, Jackson, who has been lingering for so long, rises from his sickbed and comes up on deck. Although he looks like death itself, he insists on climbing the rigging. Once on the main topsail yard, however, he begins to hemorrhage and plunges into the sea without a trace. Not only do the sailors make no attempt to save him (it would in any event be vain to try), they never refer to him again in Redburn's and Harry's hearing.

Chapters 60–62: "Home at Last"; "Redburn and Harry, Arm in Arm, in Harbor"; "The Last That Was Ever Heard of Harry Bolton"
After four months at sea, the *Highlander* at last approaches home. Off the coast of New Jersey, she is boarded by a pilot. In order to avoid being quarantined, the steerage passengers are obliged to toss overboard all of their bedding and fumigate their quarters. The ship manages to pass through the Narrows into New York Harbor without being boarded by a quarantine officer.

Once the ship is anchored offshore, the cabin passengers are carried to shore by watermen, although the poor emigrants—except Carlo, who pays with song for his ferry ride—must remain on board until the next morning, when the ship is docked.

Redburn and Bolton disembark to enjoy their first day in New York together. Leaving Harry at his new boarding house, Redburn seeks out Mr. Jones, who hands over some letters that indicate Redburn must quickly leave for home. Before doing so, however, he introduces Bolton, now bewailing his lack of funds, to a friend who might help him find employment.

Their maritime service over, Redburn and Bolton approach Captain Riga for their pay. Citing Redburn's absence from the ship in Liverpool and the money advanced to him for tools, Riga insists that Redburn owes *him* money. Riga figures that Bolton is still due a pittance, but Harry flings the coins back on the captain's desk.

The crewmates bid one another farewell, and Redburn tells Harry that he, too, must depart. Harry accompanies Redburn to the steamboat that will carry him back up the Hudson, and after they shake hands goodbye, Redburn never sees his friend again. After several week pass without news from Bolton, Redburn inquires of his welfare from their mutual friend in New York, only to learn that Harry, unable to find employment there, had shipped out with a whaler. Years would pass before Redburn—himself aboard a whaler—learned that Harry had been crushed between a whale and his ship when he fell overboard off the coast of Brazil.

PUBLICATION HISTORY

Melville completed *Redburn* in roughly three months. The novel that followed it, WHITE-JACKET, took about half that time to write. Melville was displeased with both books, writing his father-in-law, Judge Lemuel SHAW, that "[n]o reputation that is gratifying to me, can possibly be achieved by either of these books. They are two *jobs*, which I have done for money—being forced to it, as other men are to sawing wood."

Melville described his latest effort in more flattering terms when writing on June 5, 1849 to Richard BENTLEY, who Melville hoped would publish *Redburn* in England: "I have now in preparation a thing of a widely different cast from 'Mardi':—a plain, straightforward, amusing narrative of personal experience—the son of a gentleman on his first voyage to sea as a sailor—no metaphysics, no conic-sections, nothing but cakes & ale." Bentley offered Melville £100 for the right to publish the book in England in September 1849, using plates that had already been prepared by Melville's American publisher, HARPER & BROTHERS. The American edition, which appeared later in order to forestall COPYRIGHT piracy, appeared the next month. Both editions carried a dedication "To my younger brother, THOMAS MELVILLE, now a sailor on a voyage to China." Thomas MELVILLE was at the time nineteen, the same age Herman had been when he made his trip to Liverpool, and *Redburn* was as seemingly straightforward as Tom himself.

Herman Melville sat for this portrait around the time he published Redburn *and* White-Jacket, *which he called "two jobs, which I have done for money—being forced to it, as other men are to sawing wood."*   (Library of Congress)

Critics on both sides of the Atlantic seemed relieved to welcome the "cakes & ale" of *Redburn* in the wake of *Mardi*'s metaphysical contortions. Soon enough, sales of Melville's fourth novel exceeded those of his third—although that was not saying much. In the United States, the book only sold 3,314 copies its first year. *Redburn* would be reprinted in 1850, 1855, and 1863, but the book found few readers until Melville was "rediscovered" in the next century.

Redburn, Wellingborough ("Buttons," "Boots") The eponymous narrator of Melville's fourth novel. While early readers questioned the veracity of TYPEE and OMOO, REDBURN was long held to be thinly veiled autobiography. Indeed, 15-year-old Wellingborough Redburn has a great deal in common with the young Herman Melville, who first went to sea as a 19-year-old boy. Like his creator, Redburn is the son of a deceased father who had been a gentleman merchant and had once visited LIVERPOOL, England. And poverty resulting from their fathers' early deaths forced both the young

Melville and his narrator to sacrifice their ambitions and go to sea. Redburn's ship, the *Highlander*, closely resembles the *St. Lawrence*, the ship that carried Melville on his maiden voyage—both in its physical description and in many of the characters that make up its crew. Redburn's English friend, Harry BOLTON, may have had no actual counterpart, but the episodes concerning his and Redburn's adventures reveal a psychological truth about their author: it seems clear that as early as his first time at sea, Melville was struggling to define his sexuality. Young Redburn is both drawn to and discomfitted by the effeminate Bolton, who is obliged to prostitute himself in order to get by. For much of the novel Redburn presents himself as a callow, credulous youth, but his inability to recognize the truth about Bolton—and by extension, about himself— seems so remarkable as to be willed.

Melville was careful to distance himself from his protagonist, making use in *Redburn* of all the popular literary conventions of the day. The episode that lies at the heart of Bolton's true character—the night he and Redburn spend at a London pleasure palace—seems to have its origins in the pulp fiction of the day rather than in any excursion Melville made while in England in 1839. The overall form of *Redburn,* the story of a young man's initiation, is itself a convention. But in the shifting point of view of the novel, which vacillates between humorous contemporary credulity and backward-looking disillusion, readers can find the author himself, alternately amused and dismayed by his own loss of innocence.

"The Released Rebel Prisoner. (June, 1865.)" (1866) Poem in *BATTLE-PIECES.* Melville pictures a vanquished Rebel soldier in the CIVIL WAR, looking upon the mighty Union army and slowly coming to a realization of the "deceit" of his lost cause. Longing to go home, he cannot, for it is gone:

> And so he lingers—lingers on
> In the City of his Foe—
> His cousins and his countrymen
> Who see him listless go.

religion Although Melville's work, especially *BILLY BUDD,* is replete with Christian symbolism, Melville was not an orthodox believer in any particular religion. Indeed, as *MOBY-DICK* demonstrates, he took a rather wry and sometimes even comic view of many religious practices. His narrator, ISHMAEL, tolerates QUEEQUEG's idol worship, finding it no more absurd than Presbyterian doctrine. Melville or his work could be said to be religious, however, in that he uses scriptural language, imagery, and metaphors to explore the mystery of the universe (particularly in *Moby-Dick*). He understands the quest for faith and honors the

impulses that undergird religious belief, but he is himself too much of a skeptic, an ironist, to hold to any particular doctrine or form of worship. In CLAREL, debates abound about religion in the modern world, specific religions, and the history of religion.

"Report of the Committee on Agriculture" (1850) Report attributed in part to Melville. The report first appeared in the PITTSFIELD, MASSACHUSETTS, *Culturist and Gazette* on October 9, 1850, over the signature of Herman Melville's cousin, Robert MELVILL. In July of that year Robert Melvill was serving as chairman of the Viewing Committee of the Berkshire Agricultural Society, and Herman Melville accompanied him on one leg of an inspection tour of the local crops. Afterward, when Robert Melvill was required to write a report of his findings, he is believed to have turned to his writer cousin for assistance. The elaborate phrasing and literary and biblical allusions in the report seem to support the circumstantial evidence that Herman Melville ghosted at least parts of this effort.

"A Requiem for Soldiers lost in Ocean Transports." (1866) Poem in *BATTLE-PIECES.* One of the "Verses Inscriptive and Memorial" in Melville's collection of CIVIL WAR poetry, this poem commemorates those "Whose bark was lost where now the dolphins play." This lovely requiem compares the soldiers with other creatures in the natural world, who rejoice after a storm. Unlike them, these men are borne to the "reef of bones," where the light does not shine and from where they will never again witness the flight of "the lone sea bird / Round the lone spar where mid-sea surges pour."

"The Return of the Sire of Nesle" *See* "L'ENVOI."

"The Returned Volunteer to his Rifle." (1866) Poem in *BATTLE-PIECES.* One of the "Verses Inscriptive and Memorial" in Melville's collection of CIVIL WAR poetry, this nine-line poem, couched in the form of an address to a gun, pictures both rifle and soldier back home in their rightful places in the "Highlands blue" above the Hudson River.

Revolutions of 1848 In 1848, a revolt in Paris caused the abdication of the French ruler, King Louis Philippe. In June of that year a worker uprising in the city was followed by the election of Louis Napoleon as president in December. His ascendancy to power effectively stopped the revolutionary movement and hopes for reform in France. Revolutions also occurred in Vienna, Venice, Berlin, Milan, and Parma. During a second uprising in Vienna, Emperor Ferdinand I fled to Innsbruck. In Prague, Czech revolts were suppressed by Austria. In a third revolution in Vienna the emperor abdicated in favor of his nephew, who became Emperor Francis Joseph. There was also a revolt in Rome, during which the pope fled to Gaeta. This widespread turmoil in Europe stimulated hopes that the ancien regime, or old order, would give way to more democratic governments. In each case, these hopes for reform were crushed, often by force. In CLAREL, the pilgrims—particularly MORTMAIN and Don HANNIBAL—become skeptical about the idea of human progress because they have participated in these failed efforts or witnessed the consequences of revolutionary activity, which often has resulted in more intolerance, tyranny, and bloodshed instead of an improvement for humanity. These disappointed men become pilgrims in quest of a higher spiritual truth, a reconnection to the sources of Christianity that might replace their commitment to modern, secular revolutions.

R.F.C.　Character in "THE PARADISE OF BACHELORS AND THE TARTATUS OF MAIDS." In the first part of Melville's story, R.F.C. is the narrator's host at a sumptuous dinner for nine comfortable bachelor lawyers at a private club known as the Temple. R.F.C. is clearly based on Robert Francis Cooke (1816–91), a cousin and partner of Melville's English publisher, John MURRAY. Like his fictional counterpart, Cooke hosted Melville to a dinner at Elm Court, Temple, on December 19, 1849. Afterward, Melville noted in his journal that the setting was a "Paradise of Batchelors" [*sic*].

Riga, Captain　Character in *REDBURN*. Captain Riga is the duplicitous Russian-born skipper of the *Highlander,* the ship on which Wellingborough REDBURN serves as cabin boy during a voyage from New York to LIVERPOOL and back. Riga is probably based in part on Oliver P. Brown, captain of the *ST. LAWRENCE,* the merchant ship on which Melville served as cabin boy during his maiden voyage in 1839.

Rights of Man　BILLY BUDD serves on the *Rights of Man,* a ship named after the motto of the FRENCH REVOLUTION and the subject of a pamphlet by Tom Paine (1737–1809), an agitator for both the American and French Revolutions.

Rigs, Mr.　Minor character in *REDBURN*. Rigs is the second mate aboard the *Highlander.*

Rime of the Ancient Mariner (1798)　A poem in ballad form by Samuel Taylor COLERIDGE (1772–1834), referred to by ISHMAEL in *MOBY DICK*. The poem tells of a sailor haunted by his killing of a white albatross while on board a ship that is drawn toward the South Pole. Everyone on the ship dies except the mariner, who lives to tell his tale because, in his despair, he learns to bless God's creatures and to repent of his cruel act of

destruction. The moral is a pointed one for Ishmael and the crew of the PEQUOD, who are bound up in Ahab's quest to revenge himself on the white whale.

Ringman, John　Character in *The CONFIDENCE MAN*. One of the many names used by the CONFIDENCE MAN. He introduces himself to a merchant, Mr. ROBERTS, aboard the *FIDELE,* claiming to know Roberts from an earlier business transaction. When he tells Roberts of all his misfortunes, Roberts extends to him the money that is exactly the charity the confidence man is looking for.

"Rip Van Winkle's Lilac" (1924)　Section in *WEEDS AND WILDINGS.* Part III of the volume is devoted entirely to this combination of prose and verse. The piece opens with an introductory paragraph titled "To a Happy Shade" and addressed to Washington IRVING. A long prose section titled "Rip Van Winkle" follows, as Rip returns homeward after his long sleep. What most attracts his attention is a lilac, which has taken the place of a gigantic willow that once grew by his doorway. The old man expresses his confusion in the verse that follows, "Rip Van Winkle's Lilac." The lilac tree, it seems, has grown from a slip Rip himself planted years earlier in an attempt to placate his wife. So large and lovely and fragrant is the lilac that neighbors and even strangers are prompted to take cuttings. Rip Van Winkle's legacy—and presumably Melville's as well—is thus perpetuated and propagated. Out of step with his time, Melville clearly cherished the hope that his literary reputation would not only survive him but also spread through the land like Rip Van Winkle's lilac.

Roberts, Mr.　Character in *The CONFIDENCE MAN*. As the MAN WITH THE LONG WEED, the CONFIDENCE MAN approaches Mr. Roberts, a passenger aboard the *FIDELE,* claiming to know him as John RINGMAN. Ringman proceeds to play upon Roberts's sympathies, extracting from him the money that shows Roberts to be a "good merchant." Later, Roberts eagerly invests his funds in the Black Rapids Coal Company when he is approached by its "president" (who is actually the confidence man).

"Rock Rodondo"　Sketch Third of "THE ENCANTADAS."

Rolfe　Character in CLAREL. The restless American quester whom CLAREL and NEHEMIAH first meet on Mount Olivet, Rolfe has been a sailor, a man of the world, but he is also an intellectual prepared to debate philosophy and theology. Of all the pilgrims, he is the most articulate, the most willing to engage others in argument and to consider all sides of a question. He is a skeptic and yet does not discount the claims of faith. In many ways, he serves as Clarel's mentor.

Rope Yarn   Character in *OMOO*. Rope Yarn, or Ropey, is the name given to one of the sailors aboard the *Julia*. A former London journeyman baker and a landlubber, Rope Yarn seems to be one of life's unfortunates. After he moved to Australia and set himself up in the baking business, he took a wife, who promptly ran off with his money and his foreman. Aboard the *Julia*, Rope serves as the butt of the other sailors' jokes and is obliged to undertake all manner of menial and demeaning jobs.

"Rosary Beads" (1924)   Poem in *WEEDS AND WILDINGS*. Part of the "As They Fell" sequence in the "A Rose or Two" section of the volume, "Rosary Beads" is itself divided into three parts: "The Accepted Time," "Without Price," and "Grain by Grain." "Rosary Beads" does indeed read like a series of prayers—or at least a series of less than orthodox exhortations. While the burden of "The Accepted Time" is something like *carpe diem*, "Without Price" urges the enjoyment of the natural world, and "Grain by Grain" the husbanding of one's resources against the incursions of the world.

Rose-Bud   In Chapter XCI of *MOBY-DICK*, the *PEQUOD* meets the *Rose-Bud*, a French ship busy extracting oil from two rotting, foul-smelling old whales. STUBB, the second mate of the *Pequod*, offers to tow away one of the whales from the loaded down ship. Although he has no respect for the *Rose-Bud*, he delights in securing his treasure: a quantity of ambergris used in cosmetics and perfumes.

"The Rose Farmer" and "L'Envoi" (1924)   Poems in *WEEDS AND WILDINGS*. These two poems make up Part II of the "A Rose or Two" half of the volume. "The Rose Farmer" is a long narrative poem about an older man who has taken up rose culture, as Melville did in retirement. On one level the poem functions as an allegory about the literary life, with the narrator wondering whether to sell his flowers as quickly as they blossom or to engage in the slow process of distilling them into precious attar. One of his neighbors, a prosperous Persian "gentleman-rose-farmer," disdains attar as "far from popular," and prefers to sell or give away the living flowers. With contempt he points to his neighbor the Parsee, "Lean as a rake with his distilling," who has no friends and no money as a result of his commitment to the creation of a precious rose essence. The narrator comes away from this encounter determined to emulate the Persian, opting for the sensual gratification of life rather than holding out for its "mummified quintessence":

> Though damask be your precious stuff,
> Spin it not out too superfine:
> The flower of a subject is enough.

The poem that follows, "L'Envoi," appears to reinforce this notion, with its conclusion: "Wiser in relish, if sedate / Come gray-beards to their roses late."

Rose-Water   Minor character in *WHITE-JACKET*. Rose-Water is an assistant to the ship's cook, whom Captain CLARET sadistically pits against the much bigger MAY-DAY, another cook's assistant, in head-butting contests. Rose-Water is a slender, handsome mulatto man who hates the boorish games—which May-Day always wins, in any event. When May-Day begins to insult him in racial terms, Rose-Water answers back in kind, and soon the two fight for real. The captain, adhering stringently if absurdly to naval discipline, orders both men to be flogged.

"Rose Window" (1924)   Poem in *WEEDS AND WILDINGS*. Part of the "As They Fell" sequence in the "A Rose or Two" section of the volume, "Rose Window" takes the form of a vision that comes to a slumbering worshiper during a church service. After dreaming that an angel bearing a rose has led him into "a sepulchral Strait" where the rose lights shrouds with "plaids and chequered tartans red," he wakes to find the light from the church's great rose window transfiguring the dusty pews around him.

Rosicrucianism   The term given to an esoteric movement that developed in Europe in the early 17th century. Inspired by Christian Rosenkreutz (1378–1484), who wrote pamphlets touting his occult powers, Rosicrucians established the Order of the Rosy Cross, inviting men of learning to explore their mystical powers. Melville calls the CONFIDENCE MAN a "seedy Rosicrucian," apparently because the confidence man in all his guises claims powers to heal and to divine the mysteries of nature. Like the Rosicrucians, he actively seeks converts to his rather vague yet intriguing notions.

Rousseau, Jean-Jacques (1712–1778)   A French philosopher noted for his belief in the natural goodness of human nature and the corruption of society. Melville read Rousseau's *Confessions* (1782) in 1850 and was influenced by the philosopher's effort to delve into the uniqueness of his own personality, a self alienated from society—a theme Melville would explore profoundly in both *MOBY-DICK* and *PIERRE*.

"Runaways, Castaways, Solitaries, Grave-Stones, Etc."   Sketch Tenth of "THE ENCANTADAS."

"Running the Batteries. As observed from the Anchorage above Vicksburgh. [sic] (April, 1863.)" (1866)   Poem in *BATTLE-PIECES*. This poem commemorates a daring CIVIL WAR raid on the Mississippi above

Vicksburg, when Admiral David Porter took a flotilla of 11 boats downstream past Confederate batteries in order to supply the army of Ulysses S. Grant. Both Melville's cousin Robert MELVILL and his old friend Richard Tobias (Toby) GREENE played roles in this brave action.

"The Rusty Man (By a Soured One)" (1924)   Poem. One of more than 40 poems Melville left uncollected and unpublished when he died, "The Rusty Man" looks on Don Quixote from Sancho Panza's point of view. To Sancho Panza ("the Soured One"), La Mancha, groping among his books, is dusty, obsolete. Melville's true sentiments, however, lie with the Don, as revealed in the poem's concluding lines:

So he rusts and musts
While each grocer green
Thriveth apace with the fulsome face
Of a fool serene.

Ruth   Character in *CLAREL*. Ruth is the daughter of NEHEMIAH and AGAR. CLAREL meets her in JERUSALEM and falls in love with her. She dies of grief when she hears of her father's drowning. Little is seen of her, and she seems more like an ideal projection of Clarel's than a person.

Saddle Meadows The country estate where PIERRE GLENDINNING grows up (see also *PIERRE*). Melville emphasizes the estate's isolation, an atmosphere that allows the young man to dream and to keep his illusions intact. Saddle Meadows represents the power of the Glendinning family, which rules the countryside almost like a feudal fiefdom.

sailing master Character in *BILLY BUDD, SAILOR*. He forms part of the drum-head court that tries BILLY BUDD for killing John CLAGGART. Although he accedes to Captain VERE's judgment that Billy must hang, he also shares his fellow officers' qualms about the need to punish so quickly and severely.

St. Lawrence Merchant ship on which Melville took his maiden voyage. When Melville boarded on June 4, 1839, in New York, the *St. Lawrence,* a small, three-masted, square-rigged merchant ship, was carrying bales of cotton that would ultimately find their way to the textile mills of Birmingham and Manchester. Melville served as cabin boy during the three-month round trip voyage to LIVERPOOL, returning with experiences that would ultimately find their way into *Redburn.*

Salem Minor character in *OMOO.* Salem—named for the town in Massachusetts from which he hails—is a "beach-comber," or uncommitted sailor, aboard the *Julia.* Such sailors are, Melville says, held in bad repute; Salem proves no exception when he draws a knife on Consul WILSON and fights with BEMBO.

Salvaterra Character in *CLAREL.* Salvaterra is a devout Franciscan guide at the Latin church of the Star in Bethlehem. Born in Tuscany, he has journeyed to the Holy Land to be near Christ's birthplace. His emaciated body reflects his neglect of this world for the next.

"The Same" *See* "THE ATTIC LANDSCAPE."

Samoa ("The Upoluan") Character in *MARDI.* Samoa is the one-armed navigator of the wrecked brigantine, the *Parki,* which the narrator and his companion, JARL, encounter shortly after they abandon their whaling ship at the outset of the novel. A native of the island of Upolu, in the Navigator, or Samoan, group, Samoa was given his name by a sea captain. The Upoluan, like QUEEQUEG in *MOBY-DICK,* is a noble tattooed savage, an excellent sailor who also claims to be a brain surgeon—although the one time he employs his surgical skills, the patient dies. After Samoa's wife, ANNATOO, is washed overboard in a storm, Samoa accompanies Jarl and the narrator on their journey to the Mardian archipelago. Eventually Samoa, like Jarl, is left behind even as the narrator, now a demigod named TAJI, journeys onward with a new retinue. And like Jarl, Samoa is subsequently killed by arrows probably meant for Taji.

Sandwich Islands *See* HAWAII.

Savage, Hope *See* SHAW, HOPE SAVAGE.

Saveda, Miguel Minor character in *REDBURN.* As the *Highlander* leaves LIVERPOOL for home, three intoxicated sailors—apparently new to the ship—are brought aboard. While two of the men recover enough in a few hours to assume their duties, the man listed as Miguel Saveda remains in his bunk, where he has died. Looking on in horror, several members of the crew witness the corpse beginning to burn, apparently the result of spontaneous combustion. The burning corpse is quickly jettisoned overboard.

Schiller, Johann Christoph Friedrich von (1739–1805) German philosopher, poet, and dramatist greatly influenced by Immanuel KANT. Schiller explored the role of art and beauty in man's life. He differed from Kant in arguing that esthetics, not religion, played the most important role in refining man's sense of the moral and the ethical.

Schopenhauer, Arthur (1788–1860) German philosopher inspired by PLATO and Immanuel KANT. Schopenhauer was especially concerned with Plato's ideas. He located the human understanding of ideas, however, not only in perceptions or in *a priori* reasoning, but in the will to live. From human self-knowledge also sprang a certain knowledge of the world. Melville was attracted not only to the philosopher's handling of the material and immaterial aspects of existence, but also to his pessimism. Schopenhauer portrayed the world as a grim place, and man's fate as rather similar to what

PIERRE experiences. At the same time, like Johann SCHILLER, Schopenhauer emphasized art and esthetics as compensating and even redeeming factors. He believed that art has the capacity—at least briefly—to relieve human misery. His writing on free will and determinism also attracted Melville, especially when he was drafting BILLY BUDD, SAILOR.

Scott, Winfield (1786–1866) American general who fought in the War of 1812, but who made his reputation fighting Indians. He also distinguished himself in the Mexican War, and during a long career was still commander of the American army at the outbreak of the CIVIL WAR. In *The CONFIDENCE MAN,* the CRIPPLED SOLDIER says he received his injuries fighting under Scott's command at the battle of Contreras in Mexico.

"The Scout toward Aldie." (1866) Poem in BATTLE-PIECES. This is the first of two lengthy narrative poems in the "Verses Inscriptive and Memorial" section of Melville's book of CIVIL WAR poetry and the only piece in the entire volume based on firsthand experience. In April 1864, Herman Melville and his brother Allan MELVILLE traveled to Washington, D.C., with Allan's law partner, George Brewster, who had just received his officer's commission in Henry GANSEVOORT's regiment in Vienna, Virginia. Herman and Allan missed Henry, but they went to inspect the Company K encampment in Vienna anyway. There they met the camp commander, Colonel Charles Russell Lowell, and his pregnant young wife, Josephine.

Lowell was planning to ferret out the Confederate guerrillas, called "Mosby's Raiders" after their commander, George P. Mosby, who staged commando raids on Union supply lines. Borrowing a horse from Brewster, Herman Melville announced that he planned to accompany the scouting party, while Allan left for home. On April 18–20, Melville joined the ranks of the cavalry patrol as they made their way toward Aldie, Virginia. The party managed to capture only a handful of green recruits to Mosby's Raiders; and when a troop of Union foot soldiers was sent to Leesburg to apprehend Mosby and some of his henchmen, one of Lowell's men was killed.

Melville's experience provided him with a wealth of detail for his lengthy ballad, in which a world of chivalry is opposed by the villainy Mosby represents, and in which a romanticized young Union colonel is killed, leaving behind a grieving young bride. The colonel in the poem is probably based on Lowell, who was in fact killed on October 19, 1864, at the Battle of Cedar Creek.

Scribe, Hiram Character in "I AND MY CHIMNEY." Hiram Scribe is the "master mason" hired by the narra-

tor's wife to see if the chimney can be removed without destroying the house that surrounds it. Scribe and the pyramid-shaped chimney probably owe something to the mysteries of the secretive brotherhood known as the Masonic order, as well as to Melville's perusal of Washington IRVING's *The Alhambra* (1832), which contains, in the "Legend of the Arabian Astrologer," a story about an astrologer who penetrates to the heart of a pyramid in search of a book containing "all the secrets of magic and art." Scribe's measurements of the chimney are also related to the Egyptian explorations of Giovanni Battista BELZONI.

Scriggs Minor character in WHITE-JACKET. Scriggs is an old marine who cooks for the mess that includes the sergeant-at-arms, BLAND. Scriggs clandestinely sells the sailors the liquor Bland smuggles on board the man-of-war. When the two are caught, Bland gets off lightly, but Scriggs is locked up in the brig.

Scrimmage Minor character in WHITE-JACKET. Scrimmage is a sheet-anchor man aboard the *Highlander* who argues with the cooper, BUNGS, about the proper making of buoys.

Selvagee Minor character in WHITE-JACKET. Selvagee is one of the quarterdeck officers aboard the NEVERSINK, used primarily as a foil to that paragon of a naval officer, MAD JACK. Whereas Mad Jack is swift and sure, Selvagee is an aesthete who originally went to sea primarily because he was attracted to naval officers' uniforms. His moniker, bestowed on him by the sailors, refers to a slender, twining piece of rope used to raise a ship's anchor.

Seneca (4 B.C.?–A.D. 65) Roman philosopher, dramatist, and statesman. Seneca is best remembered for his use of rhetoric and for his plays, which emphasize crime, horror, and revenge. As such, he is anathema to the CONFIDENCE MAN, who lists Seneca as among those authors who destroy confidence in human nature and make it impossible for men to trust each other.

Serapis British man-of-war that engaged John Paul JONES in a famous sea battle. Jones rammed the *Serapis* and uttered the immortal line, "I have not yet begun to fight." His victory secured his legend as an indomitable war hero. This victory is dramatized in ISRAEL POTTER.

"Shadow at the Feast. Mrs. B—— (1847)" (1924) Poem. One of the more than 40 poems Melville left uncollected or unpublished when he died, "Shadow at the Feast" remains as mysterious as its title. The setting of the feast is Christmas, and Mrs. B—— is an "elf-child" clothed in white, a kinswoman who has come to the feast. Married in May, by June she was already a

"Child-widow." Surrounded now by gaiety, she "floats, holy lily, / On waters of calm."

Shaftesbury, Anthony Ashley Cooper, third earl of (1671–1713) English moral philosopher. He argued in favor of natural moral sense and believed good actions were in harmony with a larger cosmic order. Neither an orthodox Christian or an atheist, Shaftesbury usually has been deemed a Deist, favoring a belief in God, but one that largely removes God from the scene of human action. In CLAREL, Mortmain accuses Derwent of taking Shaftesbury's line—that is, minimizing the suffering that suffuses the Christ story.

Shakespeare, William (1564–1616) English playwright and poet. Melville discovered Shakespeare in early 1849, having avoided him earlier because the small-print editions of Shakespeare's work strained Melville's weak eyes. His discovery of a seven-volume edition in large, clear print exhilarated him, and he wrote to a close friend deploring his neglect of the "divine William." Shakespeare's influence can be seen in both the content and form of Melville's work, especially MOBY-DICK, in which Ahab appears as a tragic hero with towering emotions that resemble King Lear's, and in which certain chapter headings read like stage directions (for example, chapter XXIX: "Enter Ahab; to Him, Stubb" and chapter XXXVII for Ahab's soliloquy). Melville was so taken with Shakespeare that he sometimes reproduced his predecessor's faults, as when Ahab's speech turns bombastic. But, from Shakespeare, Melville imbibed a love of language, and of revealing human character through speaking styles, that contributed significantly to the greatness of *Moby-Dick*.

Shaw, Elizabeth Knapp   *See* MELVILLE, ELIZABETH KNAPP SHAW.

Shaw, Hope Savage (1793–1879) Herman Melville's mother-in-law. The natural mother of Melville's wife, Elizabeth (Lizzie), died when Lizzie was born in 1822. In 1827, Lizzie's father, Lemuel SHAW, remarried. His new wife, Hope Savage, was from Barnstable, Massachusetts, the daughter of a physician. Hope was a loving mother to four children: Elizabeth and her older brother, and the two boys Hope and Lemuel Shaw had together. Both parents treasured their only daughter, and Hope remained one of Lizzie's prime confidantes throughout her life. Hope Shaw's attitude toward her son-in-law is more difficult to determine, although she seems at times to have disapproved of Melville's failure to care for Lizzie's financial and emotional well-being. When Hope Shaw died in 1879, she left Lizzie part of her $300,000 estate.

Shaw, Lemuel (1781–1861) Jurist who was Herman Melville's father-in-law. Lemuel Shaw was born in Barnstable, Massachusetts, the son of a Congregational minister. Young Shaw graduated from Harvard and then went on to study law. While practicing law in Boston, he also served in a number of political roles: as a representative of the General Court of Massachusetts; as a member of the Constitutional Convention of 1820; and as a state senator. He was also largely responsible for drafting the first charter of the city of Boston. In 1830, he was appointed chief justice of the state of Massachusetts. During his 30 years on the bench, he distinguished himself by introducing the concept of a public utility and the principle of eminent domain, as well as by paving the way for the formation of labor unions. His decision to uphold the 1850 Fugitive Slave Act proved to be highly controversial, but Shaw saw it as his duty not only to adhere to the law, but also to strive for compromise with the South in order to avoid civil war.

Melville's father-in-law, Lemuel Shaw, was chief justice of the Massachusetts Supreme Court. (Library of Congress)

Shaw was a longtime friend of the Melville family, having once been a partner in a real estate venture with Herman Melville's father (see Allan MELVILL) and having been engaged to Herman Melville's aunt. Nancy Wroe Melvill died before they could marry, however, and in 1818 Shaw married Elizabeth Knapp, who bore him two children. She, too, died young, after giving birth to their second child, Elizabeth, who would later become Herman Melville's wife. In 1846, even before they were related by marriage, Melville dedicated his first novel, TYPEE, "Affectionately" to Judge Shaw.

Even though Shaw remarried in 1827 and had two children with his second wife, he remained devoted to his only daughter, Lizzie. In addition to supporting her emotionally, he also was often obliged to provide her with financial assistance. He initially objected to Lizzie's marrying a writer who did not make enough money to support her. After finally acceding to the marriage, Shaw helped to finance Lizzie and Herman's first home, a Manhattan brownstone they purchased with Herman's brother Allan and his wife. When Herman and Lizzie decided to buy ARROWHEAD farm in 1850, Judge Shaw again advanced them funds. In 1856, Shaw loaned them another $5,000 to help them remain solvent.

Judge Shaw also financed several of his son-in-law's trips. Perhaps the most important of these occurred in 1852, when Shaw invited Melville to accompany him on a vacation to NANTUCKET. It was there that Melville met the attorney John Clifford, who related the story of Agatha HATCH, a woman who nursed a shipwrecked sailor to health and married him, only to have him desert her before the birth of their child. Melville in turn offered the story to Nathaniel HAWTHORNE, perhaps in an attempt to mend the rift in their friendship. Hawthorne, however, declined to accept the overture, and Melville later used the material to write a novella, "The Isle of the Cross," which was never published and is now lost.

Shaw also paid for Melville's trip to Europe and the Middle East in 1856–57, which provided him with material for CLAREL. In 1861, when Melville was desperately seeking a diplomatic position as a means of gaining a steady income, Shaw wrote to his friend Richard Henry DANA, Jr., urging him to recommend Melville to Massachusetts Senator Charles SUMNER for a consular appointment. Before Melville could complete his interviews in Washington, D.C., with Sumner, however, he was called back to Boston, where his father-in-law lay dying. Judge Shaw died before either Herman or Lizzie could reach him.

Shelleyan   An epithet used in PIERRE. It refers to the thought of Percy Bysshe Shelley (1792–1822), the great English romantic poet, who in such poems as "Hymn to Intellectual Beauty" evolved a Platonic vision of perfec-tion that deeply influences PIERRE's quest for the ideal life. Shelley is also evoked in CLAREL as a modern free-thinker and atheist whose ideas of the universe challenged traditional believers in Christianity. *See also* "SHELLEY'S VISION."

"Shelley's Vision" (1891)   Poem in TIMOLEON. On a trip to Rome in March 1857, Melville visited the grave of the English Romantic poet Percy Bysshe Shelley (1792–1822), as well as the Baths of Caracalla, which had inspired Shelley's *Prometheus Unbound* (1820). Melville's poem, which perhaps owes something to his tourism, may be having some fun with the Romantic poet, who is first seen wandering alone and dejected. In a pique, Shelley throws a stone at his own shadow, only to see it transformed into an image of St. Stephen, the first martyr, who was stoned to death for refusing to renounce his faith. The transformation of his own shadow moves Shelley to begin worshiping himself—a sequence that tells us something of what Melville thought about this intense, self-regarding poet.

Shenly   Minor character in WHITE-JACKET. Shenly is one of the narrator's messmates, and when he grows ill on the homeward voyage of the NEVERSINK, the captain commands the other members of the group to sit up with Shenly in the airless sickbay. Shenly's complaint is pulmonary, and the stifling atmosphere of the ship's hospital does him no good: when WHITE-JACKET's turn to watch comes around, Shenly expires. With little ceremony, he is buried at sea. His will consists of one sentence, saying that he leaves his wages to his wife in Portsmouth, New Hampshire.

"Sheridan at Cedar Creek. (October, 1864.)" (1866)   Poem in BATTLE-PIECES. Confederate General Jubal Early and his men had prevailed in the Battle of Cedar Creek in northern Virginia until Union General Philip Sheridan made his famous ride from 20 miles away at Winchester. Sheridan's counterattack upon the Confederates won the day, even though the losses were enormous, with more than 5,000 men dead or missing on the Union side and nearly 3,000 Confederate casualties. Melville's poem focuses on Sheridan's ride, and in particular on Sheridan's horse, which, he says, should be shod in silver and draped in ermine for its heroism. This poem first appeared as "Philip" in HARPER'S NEW MONTHLY MAGAZINE in April 1866.

"Shiloh. A Requiem. (April, 1862.)" (1866)   Poem in BATTLE-PIECES. In April 1862, Confederate General Albert Sidney Johnston led his troops in a surprise raid on Union forces at Shiloh in Tennessee. Although the Confederates won the initial round, after Johnston's death and a second day of fighting against reinforced Union troops, they were forced to retreat. The battle of

Shiloh is memorable mostly for the casualty figures, which numbered in the thousands on both sides. Melville's elegant, 19-line elegy consists of a single sentence that wraps the dead in nature's embrace as swallows fly in wheeling circles over the now silent fields.

"A Short Patent Sermon. According to Blair, the Rhetorician" (1847) Satiric squib attributed to Melville. This piece, published anonymously in YANKEE DOODLE on July 10, 1847, is a send-up of the "Short Patent Sermons," popular moralizing meditations written by Elbridge G. Paige, at the time part-owner of the New York *Sunday Mercury*. This mock sermon is based on the nonsense text "One wishy-washy, everlasting flood!" and is divided into six short parts, in which references to subjects such as missionaries and a Sandwich Islander (see HAWAII) perhaps indicate Melville's authorship.

Shorty Character in *OMOO*. Shorty is the shorter of two white planters who are pursuing a joint venture on the island of Imeeo and who briefly employ the narrator and his friend, Dr. LONG GHOST. Unlike his partner ZEKE, an American, Shorty is a Cockney.

slavery *See* AFRICAN AMERICANS.

Society Islands Group of islands in the South Pacific, a part of French Polynesia. The group consists of two sets of coral and volcanic islands, the Windward Islands and the Leeward Islands. The Windward Islands include Tahiti—site of Papeetee, the capital of French Polynesia—Moorea, Mehetia, and Tetiaroa. The Leeward Islands comprise Raiatea, Huahine, Bora-Bora, Maupiti, Tahaa, Maiao, Mopihaa, Motu-iti, Scilly Island, and Bellingshausen Island. The first European known to visit the islands was the English explorer Samuel Wallis, who claimed them as British territory in 1767. The next year, however, the French navigator Louis Antoine de Bougainville claimed them for his country. They were given the name Society Islands in 1769 by the British explorer Captain James COOK, who made two more visits in 1773 and 1777. The islands became a French protectorate in 1843 and then a French colony in 1880. In 1946, the Society Islands were made an overseas territory of France.

Tahiti is unquestionably the most widely known of the islands, in part because it was the site of the famous *Bounty* mutiny in 1788. Melville's own participation in a "mutiny" there in 1842, retold as fiction in *OMOO,* was far less celebrated. Late in the 19th century, Robert Louis Stevenson's visit to Tahiti added to its appeal in the West, as did Paul Gauguin's sensuous paintings of Tahitian life.

Somers mutiny In late 1843, Melville heard that three sailors aboard the *Somers,* a new and fast U.S. Navy brig, had been found guilty of mutiny and hanged without a proper court martial. The case received national attention because the alleged leader of the mutiny, Philip Spencer, was the son of President John Tyler's secretary of war. The ship's commander, Alexander Slidell Mackenzie, directed Melville's cousin, Guert GANSEVOORT, then a lieutenant aboard the *Somers,* to form the drumhead court that convicted the mutineers. Mackenzie was known for his fair and even kind treatment of young seamen. He was also a learned man and the author of several books. Gansevoort was later commended for his conduct during this trying episode. Melville drew upon this case when writing *BILLY BUDD, SAILOR*. In particular, Captain VERE shares many of Mackenzie's qualities and suffers the same criticism: the suspicion that he acted in haste and overrode the rights of his men. But there was no Billy Budd aboard the *Somers*. Indeed, Spencer seems to have been a bad character, and the evidence against him was considerable.

"The South Seas" (1858) Lecture. By the end of 1856, Melville was suffering from the strain of constant financial worries, the exhaustion of finishing *The CONFIDENCE MAN,* and a deep depression over his inability to make a living as a professional writer. Concerned about his health, his wife, Lizzie, and other members of his family urged Melville to take a break, and on October 11, 1856, he boarded the propeller-driven steamer *Glasgow* for a seven-month trip to Europe and the Levant. Upon his return home in May 1857, Melville hoped to obtain a political appointment to the customs service, but when the appointment did not materialize, he decided to raise capital by putting ARROWHEAD on the market and taking advantage of the vogue for visiting lecturers.

His first effort, "STATUES IN ROME," proved to be less popular, and less remunerative, than he had hoped. Although for years he had tried to live down his reputation as the "man who lived among the cannibals," he realized that to make a living as a lecturer, he was obliged to revisit the sites of the adventures he had detailed in *TYPEE,* the book that first brought him to public attention. Although he delivered "Statues in Rome" twice during the 1858–59 lecture season, his primary offering the second time out was "The South Seas," a subject that permitted him to touch on exotic flora and fauna and such provocative subjects as tattooing (see TATTOO) and TABOO. "The South Seas" was certainly less structured than his first lecture, but as he had done his first season, once again he could not refrain from lecturing his audiences about what he saw as the evils of modern civilization. Christian imperialism, he warned, was in danger of corrupting ancient Polynesian cultures and societies.

Melville's second lecture tour took him as far west as Milwaukee, although the bulk of his talks were delivered in New York and the New England states. "The South Seas," like "Statues in Rome," was not published, but newspapers quoted so extensively from both that scholars have been able to reconstruct what Melville said in his first two lectures. Between December 1858 and March 1859, Melville delivered 11 lectures in 10 cities, clearing $518.50, considerably more than he made his first season as a lecturer. He followed "The South Seas" with a new lecture, "TRAVELING: ITS PLEASURES, PAINS AND PROFITS."

spermaceti   A white, waxy, fatty substance extracted from the heads of sperm whales. In *MOBY-DICK*, the narrator, ISHMAEL, explains the many varied uses of spermaceti, or sperm oil, in lamps, cosmetics, ointments, and many other products.

Spinoza, Baruch (1632–1677)   Philosopher. Born in Amsterdam to a Jewish family, Spinoza was educated as an Orthodox Jew but converted to Catholicism and studied Latin and the work of philosophers Thomas HOBBES and René DESCARTES. Excommunicated in 1656 for his independent thinking, he practiced the trade of lens grinding while developing his philosophy. His major works include *A Treatise on Religious and Political Philosophy* (1670) and *Ethics* (1677).

Spinoza sought to unify the empirical idea of the world experienced through the senses with the Platonic notion of a world derived from innate ideas—that is, from ideas preformed in the mind. Spinoza is invoked in *MOBY-DICK* to suggest the conflict between mind and matter. This clash between the world of experience and the world of ideas is most profoundly explored in *PIERRE*, where Spinoza is specifically invoked, and in *CLAREL*, where he is alluded to as one of several freethinking Jews. References to Spinoza also occur in Melville's other poetry.

Spithead   The eastern part of the Channel between Hampshire, England, and the Isle of Wight. Referred to in *BILLY BUDD* as the site of a mutiny in which crewmen forced officers ashore, ran their ship themselves, and secured better wages and working conditions.

"A Spirit Appeared to Me" (1924)   Poem. One of more than 40 poems Melville left uncollected and unpublished when he died, "A Spirit Appeared to Me" is a slight effort: when asked to choose between "the Paradise of the Fool" and "wise Solomon's hell," the poet quickly opts for the former.

spiritualism (also spiritism)   Superstitious belief in after-death manifestations of individual human personalities. Communications from the dead, particularly from deceased loved ones, were thought to manifest themselves as auras and vibrations available only to clairvoyants and mediums, and to ordinary persons through such means as table rapping and spirit photography. The 19th-century American vogue for spiritualism began in 1848 when the Fox sisters of Arcadia, New York, claimed that they heard mysterious rappings in their house that were communications from the spirit world. Soon they began to organize séances, for which they charged admission. The popularity of spiritualism reached its zenith in the wake of the CIVIL WAR, which claimed so many lives and produced countless bereaved individuals. In 1888, Margaret Fox admitted that the effects she and her sister "interpreted" were fraudulent, but later she recanted. Melville lampooned the Fox sisters and table rapping in "THE APPLE-TREE TABLE."

Spouter Inn, The   In *MOBY-DICK*, ISHMAEL first meets his roommate QUEEQUEG, in a room provided by the inn's proprietor, Peter COFFIN. This NANTUCKET establishment features paintings of whaling, including scenes of destruction that foreshadow the fate of the PEQUOD, the ship on which Ishmael and Queequeg enlist.

Squeak   Character in *BILLY BUDD, SAILOR*. He is one of John CLAGGART's accomplices who tries to get Billy in trouble by making it seem as if he is flouting the discipline of the ship.

Standard   Character in "THE FIDDLER." Standard is the mutual friend of the narrator, HELMSTONE, and the titular character HAUTBOY, who introduces the two to one another.

Stanly, Glendinning   Glen Stanly, as he is referred to in *PIERRE*, is Pierre's cousin who inherits SADDLE MEADOWS, the Glendinning estates, after Pierre is rejected by his own mother. Glen Stanly also courts Lucy TARTAN, who loves Pierre. Having contributed to Pierre's downfall, Glen Stanly appears at the Apostles', where Pierre lives, and tries to remove Lucy, who has followed Pierre to the city. But Pierre successfully foils his rival's visit and maintains his precarious household.

Starbuck   Character in *MOBY-DICK*. Chief mate on the PEQUOD, Starbuck is a Quaker, a "good man, and a pious." Although he doubts the wisdom of AHAB's pursuit of the whale, Starbuck finds himself caught up in the captain's spell. Even as the ship approaches disaster, Starbuck cannot deny the grandeur of Ahab's quest. He pleads with his captain to return home to his young wife, but Ahab refuses. Starbuck, himself a husband and father, dreads the result of the quest for Moby-Dick. Except for ISHMAEL, Starbuck is the one member of the crew capable of understanding Ahab in his own terms. The germ of Starbuck's character may be found in Frederick R. Raymond, first mate under the captain of the ACUSHNET, a ship that serves as a partial model for the *Pequod*. Raymond fought with his captain and was eventually banished from his ship.

"Statues in Rome" (1857)   Lecture. By the end of 1856, Melville was suffering from the strain of constant financial worries, the exhaustion of finishing *The CONFIDENCE MAN*, and a deep depression over his inability to make a living as a professional writer. Concerned about his health, his wife, Lizzie, and other members of his family urged Melville to take a break, and on October 11, 1856, he boarded the propeller-driven steamer *Glasgow* for a seven-month trip to Europe and the Levant. He spent three and a half weeks in Rome, where he visited a plethora of museums, galleries, churches, villas, and gardens and made notes in his travel journal.

Upon his return home in May 1857, Melville hoped to obtain a political appointment to the customs service, but when the appointment did not materialize, he decided to raise capital by putting ARROWHEAD farm on the market and taking advantage of the vogue for visiting lecturers. Melville followed the lead of lecturers like George William Curtis (1824–92), who succeeded in converting his travel writing into public lectures, by using his travel diary to write his first lecture, a discourse on history, aesthetics, and art he called "Statues in Rome." He used that piece alone during his first season of lecturing, which lasted from November 23, 1857 to February 23, 1858 and took him as far north as Montreal, as far west as Detroit, and as far south as Clarksville, Tennessee.

In this first of his three lectures, Melville focused on Roman statuary as a means of discussing the dangers of modern industrial "progress," which he felt threatened the reverence for art that existed in the ancient world. Many of his listeners, expecting to hear a travelogue, were disappointed. Nonetheless, his talks seem to have been well attended, if not highly remunerative (his net profit from the first lecture tour was $423.70). They were certainly well reported: although Melville himself did not publish "Statues in Rome," lengthy excerpts quoted in contemporary news accounts have permitted scholars to reconstruct the text of the lecture. Reviews of Melville's subject and his delivery were uneven. For his next two lectures he chose topics that he thought would be more personal and more popular: "THE SOUTH SEAS" and "TRAVELING."

Steelkilt   Character in *MOBY-DICK*. "A Lakeman and a desperado from Buffalo," he gets into a conflict with RADNEY, the first officer, aboard the *Town-Ho*. He attacks Radney, who menaces Steelkilt with a hammer and orders him to sweep the decks—normally a job reserved for young seamen. Steelkilt foments a mutiny with the aid of his fellow canallers (former workers on the Erie Canal). Although the mutineers are imprisoned and most of them submit to the captain's rule, Steelkilt manages to avoid further punishment after his imprisonment, exerting a strange, unexplained power over the captain. Steelkilt bears some resemblance to the actual Luther Fox of the *Nassau*, a whaling vessel. Fox quarreled with his first officer, Jenney, and cut his superior so severely that he bled to death, in April 1843.

"Stockings in the Farm-House Chimney" (1924)   Poem in *WEEDS AND WILDINGS*. Part of the section titled "The Year," this poem seems to have been written at—or in memory of—ARROWHEAD. The time is Christmas Eve, and the scene includes four children, two boys and two girls, probably modeled on Melville's offspring. The speaker prays that they will continue to believe in Santa Claus, as it is "delight to believe in a wight / More than mortal, with something of man."

"The Stone Fleet. An Old Sailor's Lament. (December, 1861.)" (1866)   Poem in *BATTLE-PIECES*. The speaker is an "old sailor" who thinks he has served aboard some of the 16 granite-loaded ships the Union decided to sink at the entrance to Charleston harbor in December 1861. The aim was to blockade the city, but in fact the maneuver only improved the channel and gave ships better access to the Confederate stronghold.

> The waters pass—
> Currents will have their way:
> Nature is nobody's ally.

The "Stone Fleet" stratagem was a complete failure.

"Stonewall Jackson. (Ascribed to a Virginian.)" (1866)   Poem in *BATTLE-PIECES*. In the volume, this piece follows "STONEWALL JACKSON. MORTALLY WOUNDED AT CHANCELLORSVILLE. (MAY, 1863.)," a Northern view of the Confederate stalwart. This second poem, "ascribed to a Virginian," praises Jackson in grander, more heroic terms, as a man who "followed his star." The speaker sees Jackson as singular, above reproach, "Which not the North shall care to slur."

"Stonewall Jackson. Mortally wounded at Chancellorsville. (May, 1863.)" (1866)   Poem in *BATTLE-PIECES*. Something less than an elegy, Melville's poem still praises the Confederate general, who was "earnest in error" and is now as dead as the cause to which he remained true.

"Story of Toby, The"   *See* TYPEE.

stranger, the Character in *The CONFIDENCE MAN*. The stranger is the epithet usually applied to the CONFIDENCE MAN, who keeps appearing aboard the *FIDELE* in different disguises. In another sense, all the characters in *The Confidence Man* are strangers; that is, they inhabit a universe where human character seems ambiguous, fluid, and ultimately unknowable.

Stubb Character in *MOBY-DICK*. Second mate on the *PEQUOD*, he is a native of Cape Cod. This blithe spirit treats whale hunting in a matter-of-fact fashion. He thinks little about his dangerous occupation and simply adjusts himself to the demands of the chase. His calm and good humor are much appreciated.

"Suggested by the Ruins of a Mountain-Temple in Arcadia, One Built by the Architect of the Parthenon" (1947) Poem. One of more than 40 poems Melville left uncollected or unpublished when he died, "Suggested by the Ruins of a Mountain-Temple" bears the hallmarks of a piece written for TIMOLEON. This poem expresses sentiments similar to those perhaps better stated in other verses in that volume. Still, Melville's evocation of the "shattered marbles" "Old in exhaustion, / Interred alive from storms of fortune" is haunting and powerful.

Sumner, Charles (1811–1874) Politician and abolitionist. Charles Sumner was born in Boston and educated at Harvard College and Harvard Law School. For a number of years, he practiced law in his hometown. He became interested in politics and ran for office. In 1850 he was elected to the U.S. Senate as a Free Soiler, favoring admission to the Union of territories that outlawed slavery, and he quickly made a name for himself as a rabid abolitionist. His speech "The Crime Against Kansas," which he gave before the Senate on May 19–20, 1856, was especially incendiary. In it he called the Kansas-Nebraska Act, a compromise between those advocating admission of slaveholding states and abolitionists, "a swindle," but it was his reference to slavery as the "harlot" of South Carolina Senator Andrew P. Butler that earned him a vicious beating in the Senate chamber at the hands of Butler's nephew, Representative Preston S. Brooks. It took Sumner nearly three years to recover from the attack.

After the CIVIL WAR, Sumner's influence faded. In 1866, he married a widow half his age who left him a year later. He devoted his later years to writing and public speaking.

Melville had contact with Sumner just twice: once in 1847, at the home of a cousin of their mutual acquaintance, Richard Henry DANA, Jr., and again when Melville traveled to Washington, D.C., in 1861 to interview for a possible consular appointment. In 1864, Sumner helped Herman and his brother Allan obtain

passes to visit their cousin Henry GANSEVOORT's army encampment during the Civil War.

Sunshine Minor character in *WHITE-JACKET*. Sunshine is one of the cook's assistants aboard the man-of-war *NEVERSINK* and an enthusiastic singer of work songs.

surgeon, the Character in *BILLY BUDD, SAILOR*. Captain VERE calls upon him to verify John CLAGGART's death. Like his fellow officers, the surgeon has doubts about Vere's quick condemnation of Billy. But also like the other officers, the surgeon keeps his opinions to himself, not wishing to contribute to the mutinous atmosphere Vere seeks to dispel.

"The Surrender at Appomattox. (April, 1865.)" (1866) Poem in *BATTLE-PIECES*. In two verses, Melville marks the surrender of General Robert E. Lee to General Ulysses S. Grant at Appomattox Courthouse, Virginia, on April 9, 1865. This formal acknowledgement of the end of the CIVIL WAR is treated in a restrained, even anticlimactic fashion:

> Not Romeo o'ercome by Roman arms we sing,
> As on Pharsalia's day,
> But Treason thrown. . . .

"The Swamp Angel" (1866) Poem in *BATTLE-PIECES*. The subject of this poem is "a coal-black Angel / With a thick Afric lip"—not a person, but instead the Parrot cannon that the Northern army placed in the marshes outside Charleston and used to bombard the city. Union soldiers gave this cannon, which was actually named after its inventor, Robert Parker Parrot, its moniker, but Melville characterized the gun as a powerful black avenger.

Swedenborg, Immanuel (1688–1772) Swedish philosopher and theologian who claimed to have divine guidance and mystical visions. He believed that God was in the natural world, and that the reign of the Christian Church had ended. In *The CONFIDENCE MAN*, EGBERT refers to Swedenborg as one of those thinkers, like SENECA and Francis BACON, who kept "one eye on the invisible" and the "other on the main chance." Egbert attacks the idea of pure, disinterested knowledge, in other words, as the CONFIDENCE MAN in his guise of the "the COSMOPOLITAN" tries to convince Egbert to have confidence in him and to lend him money.

Sydney Ben Minor character in *OMOO*. Sydney Ben, said to be an escaped convict from New South Wales, is one of the narrator's shipmates aboard the *Julia*. He is also called the "Ticket-of-Leave-Man" because, Melville explains, in this part of Australia prisoners often were hired out as servants but were obliged to carry with them identity papers, or "tickets of leave." One night aboard the *Julia*, Sydney Ben gets into a drunken brawl with BEMBO, a Maori from New Zealand who serves as the ship's second mate, when the Australian casts aspersions on the New Zealander's "maternal origin."

"Syra (A Transmitted Reminiscence)" (1891) Poem in *TIMOLEON*. Part of the "Fruit of Travel Long Ago" section of the volume, "Syra" is a vivid recollection of the one island in the Cyclades that Melville had time to explore, having stopped there three times during his 1856–57 trip to Europe and the Levant. The island world is characterized by a nearly carnival-like atmosphere of sun and gaiety, where "life was leisure, merriment, peace" and "love was righteousness."

Syrian monk, the Character in CLAREL. The pilgrims meet a young anchorite near Quarantania, where he is reenacting Christ's 40-day period of temptation. Like SALVATERRA, the Franciscan monk, he is an ascetic who is wasting away, making of his faith a self-torturing exercise.

T

taboo (also tabu) Polynesian word indicating a prohibition. Customarily a taboo bans an act or the use of an object or word on pain of punishment. It can apply to an object, person, place, or word believed to have extraordinary or unnatural power. The person charged with breaking a taboo is usually required to undergo a cleansing ritual or is sometimes even exterminated so that the larger community is not tainted by the offense. In TYPEE, TOMMO discovers that many things in the Typee Valley are taboo, including the Taboo Groves, the scene of native rituals that, he suspects, include cannibalism. Women are not allowed to enter there. Neither are they permitted to be in or even near boats—although Tommo manages to obtain a waiver of the taboo for FAYAWAY, who joins him in his daily canoe trips. Taboos, apparently, are not always absolute. MARNOO, for example, is a taboo native from another tribe who, because of his personal friendships, is permitted to travel unmolested among all the tribes on the island. Although it is not unconditional, his special status—one that he shares with Tommo—shields him from the animosity that would greet any other foreigner.

In *OMOO*, the narrator discovers that many of the things that are taboo among the Typee, such as the proximity of women and boats, are also outlawed by the most Westernized Tahitians.

Tacitus (c. 55–120) Roman historian famous for his studies of Roman corruption. The COLLEGIAN in *The CONFIDENCE MAN* reads Tacitus and is advised by the CONFIDENCE MAN to throw the book away, since Tacitus invites great skepticism about human motivations and undermines the very confidence and trust the confidence man depends on to be successful.

Tahiti *See* SOCIETY ISLANDS.

Taji Character in *MARDI*. "Taji" is the name assumed by the protagonist of the novel after he is declared a demigod by the inhabitants of the isle of Odo. Previously, he had been an unnamed sailor who deserted a whaling ship somewhere in the Pacific and set off for the distant Mardian archipelago. Before reaching Odo, the narrator encounters the beautiful white maiden YILLAH, and, in saving her from being

ceremonially sacrificed, kills the old priest ALEEMA. When Yillah disappears, Taji becomes a perpetual exile, fruitlessly seeking his lost love everywhere while he is pursued by the vengeful sons of Aleema. Taji, while not truly a demigod, is no more three-dimensional than any of the characters in this allegorical, maddeningly elusive romance, but AHAB's obsessive hunt of the white whale in *MOBY-DICK* can be traced back to Taji's all-consuming—perhaps even suicidal—search for his white goddess.

Talleyrand-Périgord, Charles Maurice de (1754–1838) French statesman born in Paris. Educated in the church, Tallyrand nevertheless became known as a rake and cynical wit. He was elected president of the French Assembly in 1790. He also went on several diplomatic excursions for the French government, and was foreign minister in the French government of 1797. Later, he helped solidify the power of Napoleon. During and after the FRENCH REVOLUTION, Talleyrand played a number of different roles, capitalizing on his career in the church and then attacking the church. It is this role-playing that Melville seems to have in mind when he refers to the CONFIDENCE MAN as a "threadbare Talleyrand."

Tammany Hall Popular name of the Democratic political machine that ruled NEW YORK CITY for a century, from 1828 to 1932. The name "Tammany" is a bastardization of "Tamanend," the name of a Delaware chief who was said to have been friendly to William Penn. The name was adopted after the Revolutionary War by several patriotic societies that were founded in New York, Philadelphia, and other cities, with the aim of promoting certain political and economic programs. The Tammany Society of New York, formally known as the Columbian Order of New York City, was the only one of these societies to survive into the 19th century. Founded in 1786, its primarily social function—manifested in pseudo–Native American rituals—gradually became subsumed by the larger political concerns of Jeffersonian republicanism, particularly after 1798, when Aaron Burr assumed leadership of the society.

Tammany came into its own with the election, in 1828 and again in 1832, of Andrew Jackson as president. Like the Jackson administration, Tammany stood for the rights of the common man, but the privileges enjoyed by its leaders provoked splits within the Democratic party in New York City, such as that between the Hunkers (conservatives) and Barnburners (radicals) in the late 1840s—a controversy joined by Melville's brother Allan. Tammany continued to exert control over local politics by purchasing the loyalty of the city's swelling immigrant population with food, fuel, clothing, and jobs.

Corruption within the Tammany machine was most pronounced during the reign of William Marcy ("Boss") Tweed, from 1857 to 1871, a period that saw vote buying, judicial corruption, and the wholesale plundering of the municipal treasury. After Tweed was brought down, the city went through a period of reform that lasted only a few years. Tammany Hall—as the political machine was then known—continued to control New York until the 1930s, when repeated investigations into political corruption, as well as such societal changes as women's suffrage and New Deal reforms, robbed it of its power.

In MARDI, Melville published his own attack on the hypocrisies that have become synonymous with Tammany Hall politics.

tapa (also tappa)   Bark cloth made in Polynesia. Tapa, as the narrator of TYPEE explains at length, is produced by removing the outer bark of certain trees, such as the breadfruit, and then stripping off the inner bark, which is then soaked until it becomes malleable. The bark fibers are then beaten with mallets until they become matted together. This mass is repeatedly soaked and beaten until it becomes thin and flexible. It is then bleached in the sun and sometimes impregnated with dyes before it is put to a variety of uses, from clothing to bedding. The process of tapa-making is so ancient that it has in many cultures assumed religious significance.

In *Typee*, Tommo one day unwittingly violates a powerful taboo when he fingers some tapa being prepared as head coverings for women. When he is picked up by the Australian whaler *Julia* at the beginning of OMOO, the narrator is wearing the tapa cloth robe he donned while living among the Typee.

Tartan, Lucy   Character in PIERRE. Pierre's childhood playmate, she is intended to be his wife. She becomes distraught when Pierre takes up with Isabel BANFORD, whom Pierre calls his wife rather than reveal she is his sister. Finding herself unable to live without Pierre, Lucy pursues him in the city and takes up residence with Pierre and Isabel. She refuses to come home even after her brother and Pierre's cousin some to fetch her. Lucy collapses and dies when Pierre is attacked by Glen Stanly. (*See* GLENDINNING, PIERRE and STANLY, GLENDINNING.)

Tartan, Mrs.   Character in PIERRE. The mother of Lucy TARTAN, she plans for the day when Lucy and Pierre will be married.

Tashtego   Character in MOBY-DICK. A mate on the PEQUOD, he is an Indian from Gay Head, the westerly point of Martha's Vineyard. He has the look and the behavior of a proud warrior. He is rescued by QUEEQUEG when he falls into a whale's head that has slipped off a hook on the side of the *Pequod*.

tattoo   Skin marking achieved by punctures that are rubbed with pigment. The word "tattoo," if not the practice of tattooing, originated with the Tahitians. Tattooing was long a part of the culture of the peoples inhabiting the Pacific Rim, reaching its highest artistic development in the elaborate embellishments of the Maori of New Zealand and the perfection of colored pigments by the Japanese. In these societies tattoos can indicate personal status or group identification, can serve as an indication of religious devotion or as a charm against some evil or disease, or simply act as adornment. In the West, which was introduced to tattooing by sailors, the practice has been considered both vulgar and fashionable. In TYPEE, TOMMO regards native tattooing with suspicion and resists all efforts to mark his skin. For him, extensive tattooing renders KORY-KORY hideous, and the only distraction from FAYAWAY's nearly flawless beauty is the subtle markings on lip and shoulder worn by all Typee maidens. In OMOO, the narrator devotes a chapter to the tatooers of Hivarhoo, in the MARQUESAS, whose mastery of the art is so exceptional that they have achieved almost priestly status. In MOBY-DICK, Ishmael describes QUEEQUEG's extensive tattoos.

Tawney   Minor character in WHITE-JACKET. Tawney is a sheet-anchor man aboard the NEVERSINK who tells the story of how, while working aboard a merchant ship during the War of 1812, he was impressed on the high seas by a British frigate and forced to fight against his countrymen. For Tawney's account of the battle between the H.M.S. *Macedonian* and the U.S.S. *Neversink* (in reality, the U.S.S. UNITED STATES), Melville drew heavily on Samuel Leech's *Thirty Years from Home, or A Voice from the Main Deck* (1843).

tayo   A Polynesian custom whereby a native attaches himself to a Western visitor, becoming the visitor's special friend and helpmeet. As the narrator discovers in OMOO, however, native tayos can be fickle; when the Western visitor runs out of money and gifts, his tayo often has no qualms about seeking another benefactor.

Taylor, Zachary (1784–1850)   Military leader and 12th president of the United States. Born in Montebello, Virginia, Taylor was raised in Louisville,

Kentucky, where his formal education consisted entirely of a brief period under a private tutor. For most of his life, Taylor was a military man, beginning with his service as a volunteer in the Kentucky militia in 1806. Two years later he was commissioned as a first lieutenant with the 7th U.S. Infantry and began a period of Indian fighting, culminating in a victory over the Seminoles in 1837 that brought him a promotion to brigadier general. His career in Texas, however, made his reputation. In 1845, when the U.S. annexed Texas, Taylor was serving in the area, and in 1846, when "Mexico . . . shed American blood upon the American soil" after some provocation by troops under his command, it was Taylor who reported to Washington that "hostilities may now be considered as commenced." In the war with Mexico that followed, Taylor, now promoted to the rank of major general, captured Monterrey despite President James K. Polk's orders to fight only defensively. Both Polk and the army commander-in-chief, Winfield Scott, moved to limit Taylor's aggression and his growing popularity with the American public. But Taylor proved unstoppable, decisively beating the Mexican forces under Santa Anna at Buena Vista in 1847 and the next year capturing the Whig nomination for the presidency. Defeating the Democratic candidate, Lewis Cass, in 1848, the "Hero of Buena Vista" (also known as "Old Rough and Ready") held the office of the presidency only briefly. He died of cholera on July 5, 1850.

Taylor is generally regarded as one of the most uneducated and inexperienced men ever to enter the White House, and Melville seems to have concurred with the notion that his reputation was overblown. Although Melville disagreed with the expansionist policies of the Polk administration, he remained a Democrat. His satiric "AUTHENTIC ANECDOTES OF 'OLD ZACK'" were probably meant to deflate then-current rhetoric about Taylor's exploits and to discourage voters from taking the general seriously as presidential candidate.

"The Temeraire. (Supposed to have been suggested to an Englishman of the old order by the fight of the Monitor and Merrimac.)" (1866) Poem in BATTLE-PIECES. The CIVIL WAR ironclad ships *Monitor* and *Merrimac* remind the English speaker of storied warships of old, such as the *Temeraire* and Admiral Horatio NELSON's *Victory*. But those ships, he says, have been dismantled and superseded, as "The rivets clinch the iron-clad, / Men learn a deadlier lore."

Thomas, Frances Melville ("Fanny") (1855–1938) Herman Melville's second daughter and youngest child. Fanny was the only one of Melville's four children to marry. Until she did so, however, Fanny lived with her parents in PITTSFIELD, MASSACHUSETTS, where she was born, and in NEW YORK CITY. As a child and young woman she led a fairly demanding life. She served as her mother's primary household helper, because her older sister, Bessie, was disabled by arthritis. Fanny also served as copyist for her father when her mother fell behind in the job. She once recalled being wakened at two A.M. by her father and ordered to proofread pages from his epic poem, CLAREL, during the composition process.

On summer holiday in Jefferson, New Hampshire, in August 1877, Fanny met Henry B. Thomas, a young man from Philadelphia, who fell in love with her at first sight. The couple were married in 1880, after which they settled in Orange, New Jersey, where they raised four daughters together. Although the older two girls had fond memories of their grandfather, Fanny seems to have harbored great resentment toward him: late in life, she went so far as to request that Herman Melville's name no longer be mentioned in her presence.

Thompson, Mr. ("the doctor") Minor character in REDBURN. Although the *Highlander*'s black cook prefers to be called "Mr. Thompson," following the maritime custom he is known to the crew as "the doctor." Mr. Thompson is devoted to his shipboard kitchen and to the Bible, which he reads as he cooks the victuals the men regard as the best medicine available.

"A Thought on Book-Binding" (1850) Book review. This essay would be Melville's last for the magazine LITERARY WORLD. The year before, he had reviewed James Fenimore COOPER's *The Sea Lions* for the journal. This time, his job was to appraise not a new work, but instead a new edition of Cooper's *The Red Rover* (1827)—and he did just that, as the tongue-in-cheek title of his essay indicates. In the brief essay, Melville says little about the content of the book, instead dwelling on its externals. The unsigned review appeared in the March 16, 1850 issue of the *Literary World*.

Thurston, Sophia Elizabeth *See* MELVILLE, SOPHIA ELIZABETH THURSTON.

"Thy Aim, Thy Aim?" (1947) Poem. One of more than 40 poems left uncollected or unpublished at Melville's death, this one, like several of the others, addresses the issue of literary recognition. The poet advises that it is unwise to think oneself an exception to the rule that fame, if achieved in this lifetime, lasts no longer than a "flower cut down in an hour." Others, however, achieve fame only after death, when they, too, can expect only a "belated funeral flower."

"Time's Betrayal" (1924) Poem in WEEDS AND WILD-INGS. This apparently was meant to be the first poem in the section titled "This, That and the Other," a kind of miscellany. The poem is introduced by a paragraph of prose arguing that the annual tapping of young maple trees, while promoting glorious early fall leaf color in some trees, surely shortens these trees' life spans. The poem that follows uses the conceit that such stabbing is a "murder," as proved by the maple's red leaves. Such early glory and premature death are likened to Keats's—"stabbed by the Muses."

"Time's Long Ago!" (1947) Poem. One of more than 40 poems Melville left uncollected or unpublished when he died, "Time's Long Ago" is a seven-line verse written in praise of the healing power of the South Seas, which, with their coral isles and blue lagoons, bring joy to "the heart that hope can lure no more."

Timoleon and Other Ventures in Minor Verse (1891) Poetry collection. This volume, privately published during the last year of Melville's life, appeared, like its immediate predecessor, *JOHN MARR*, in a limited edition of only 25 copies, intended to be shared with friends and family. (As late as 1921, a still unclaimed copy was given as a gift.) Melville dedicated the volume to the painter Elihu Vedder, whose portrait of an African American woman, Jane Jackson, had inspired Melville's poem "'FORMERLY A SLAVE,'" which appeared in *BATTLE-PIECES*.

The volume is only loosely organized, with the first 23 poems growing out of Melville's readings in philosophy and history as well as from his meditations about art and his own past: "AFTER THE PLEASURE PARTY," "THE AGE OF ANTONINES," "ART," "THE BENCH OF BOORS," "BUDDHA," "C——'S LAMENT," "THE ENTHUSIAST," "FRAGMENTS OF A LOST GNOSTIC POEM OF THE 12TH CENTURY," "THE GARDEN OF METRODORUS," "HERBA SANTA," "IN A GARRETT," "LAMIA'S SONG," "LONE FOUNTS," "MAGIAN WINE," "THE MARCHIONESS OF BRINVILLIERS," "THE MARGRAVE'S BIRTH NIGHT," "MONODY," "THE NEW ZEALOT TO THE SUN," "THE NIGHT-MARCH," "THE RAVAGED VILLA," "SHELLEY'S VISION," "TIMOLEON (394 B.C.)" and "THE WEAVER."

A second section, titled "Fruit of Travel Long Ago," was inspired by Melville's travels in Europe, the Holy Land, and Egypt in 1856–57. It includes: "THE APPARITION (THE PARTHENON UPLIFTED ON ITS ROCK FIRST CHALLENGING THE VIEW ON THE APPROACH TO ATHENS)," "THE ARCHIPELAGO," "THE ATTIC LANDSCAPE," "THE SAME," "DISINTERNMENT OF THE HERMES," "THE GREAT PYRAMID," "GREEK ARCHITECTURE," "GREEK MASONRY," "IN A BYE-CANAL," "IN A CHURCH OF PADUA," "IN THE DESERT," "MILAN CATHEDRAL," "OFF CAPE COLONNA," "THE PARTHENON," "PAUSILIPPO (IN THE TIME OF BOMBA)," "PISA'S LEARNING TOWER," "SYRA (A TRANSMITTED REMINISCENCE)," and "VENICE." The volume ends with "L'ENVOI: THE RETURN OF THE SIRE DE NESLE, A.D. 16——."

"Timoleon (394 B.C.)" (1891) Poem in *TIMOLEON*. Melville's reading of Plutarch led him to Timoleon, a Corinthian hero misunderstood in his own time. As the second, less favored son of a domineering mother, Timoleon had a family background something like Melville's own. When Timoleon's brother, Timophanes, becomes a ruthless tyrant, Timoleon agrees to his brother's assassination and is in turn denounced by his mother and rejected by his people. Melville devotes the bulk of the poem to the 20 years of semiretirement that followed, during which Timoleon contemplates his fate. In the end he is recalled to lead a campaign to rescue Corinth from Sicily, a role he brilliantly fulfills—although he chooses to remain an exile.

Tinor Minor character in *TYPEE*. Tinor is KORY-KORY's mother and MARHEYO's wife, thus hostess to the narrator, TOMMO, during the four months he spends among the Typee.

"To——" (1947) Poem. Among the more than 40 poems Melville left uncollected or unpublished when he died, "To——" remains one of the most obscure. The mystery of the poem's title is amplified by its content: a haunted, Platonic meditation on the meaning of existence, where people are but dreams and their emotions are "but phantoms." Still, the speaker says, these phantoms have the power to "make the heart quake and the spirit cower."

Toby Character in *TYPEE*. Based on Melville's friend and fellow deserter Richard Tobias GREENE, Toby is an accomplice in *Typee* to the narrator TOMMO, with whom he jumps ship. Toby demonstrates daring, agility, and optimism while the two undertake the perilous journey to the Typee Valley, but he exhibits discomfiture while actually dwelling among people he presumes to be cannibals.

Because of his companion's stubborn leg injury, however, the Typee do permit Toby to leave in search of help. After a temporary setback occasioned by a run-in with hostile HAPPAR warriors, Toby does depart, never to be seen again in the Typee Valley. Tommo does not know whether Toby is dead or has simply given him up for dead, and the narrator's thoughts about his companion's fate constitute the end of the novel proper.

Richard Tobias Greene did survive, however, and made his whereabouts known in the *Evangelist* magazine in July 1846, only months after *Typee* appeared in the United States. When Melville learned the details of his companion's fate, he published a sequel to the novel called "The Story of Toby," which helped quiet those who questioned the book's veracity.

"Tom Deadlight (1810)" (1888) Poem in *JOHN MARR*. "Tom Deadlight" opens with a prose introduction to the grizzled old petty officer who is the speaker of the poem that follows. Tom is "wandering in his mind" in the sickbay of the British ship *Dreadnaught*, where be begins to sing his farewell to his messmates, setting his memories to the tune of a famous old sea chantey.

Tommo The first-person narrator of *TYPEE*. Tommo's temperament as well as his adventures are elaborations of Melville's own. But the writer, looking back on and embroidering his account of his time among the Typee natives, distances himself from his narrator. One of his primary means of doing so is to give Tommo (whose name, Tom, is altered to suit Polynesian speech patterns) a wounded leg. The source of the wound is never specified, and its severity waxes and wanes with Tommo's anxiety about his captivity among cannibals. Perhaps psychosomatic in origin, the injury seems also to be bound up with the youthful narrator's evolving sexuality which, in the free and easy atmosphere of the Typee Valley, causes him to be attracted to both men and women. Melville's own BISEXUALITY has long been a subject of critical inquiry, and Tommo's leg injury is just one example of how the writer used the techniques of literature to both identify with and distance himself from his narrators.

"To Ned" (1888) Poem in *JOHN MARR*. The speaker addresses his friend Ned Bunn, asking what has become of the world they once roamed, the "Marquesas and glenned isles that be / Authentic Edens in a Pagan Sea." They are, alas, overrun by tourists, ironically lured by the tales told by the poet and his fellow "Typee-truant." Ned is clearly meant to be Richard Tobias GREENE, with whom Melville jumped ship in the MARQUESAS in his youth.

Took, Horn Minor character in *ISRAEL POTTER*. He is part of a conspiracy of agents in England who are in league with the American revolutionary government. Took and his comrade George WOODCOCK persuade Israel POTTER to act as a courier to Paris, where Benjamin FRANKLIN will receive him and the secret papers hidden in Israel's shoe.

"To the Master of the *Meteor*" (1888) Poem in *JOHN MARR*. In 1860, Herman Melville traveled to San Francisco with his brother Tom, then master of the *Meteor*. They were originally supposed to travel on together to Shanghai, but when the merchant ship was instead required to sail back around Cape Horn to England, Melville curtailed his trip, returning home via the Panamanian isthmus. One trip around the Cape of Storms (CAPE HORN) had proven to be enough for Melville at this stage of his life, but when he got back to NEW YORK CITY, he missed Tom and wrote sorrowfully of his beloved brother "Off the Cape of Storms," missing Christmas, alone amidst the vast ocean.

"To Tom" (1947) Poem. One of the more than 40 poems Melville left uncollected or unpublished when he died, "To Tom," addressed to his younger brother, is a lesser version of the sentiments described in "To the Master of the *Meteor*," published in *JOHN MARR*.

"Tortoise Book" Melville work that eventually contributed to "THE ENCANTADAS." On November 24, 1853, Melville wrote to his publishers HARPER & BROTHERS to propose a book of "300 pages, say— partly of nautical, and partly—or rather, chiefly, of Tortoise Hunting Adventure." In the same letter he requested an advance for the book of $300, and on December 7, 1853, the publishing firm met this request. After a devastating fire—one that destroyed thousands of bound and unbound copies of Melville's books—at the publishing house on that very day, Melville wrote to G. P. Putnam & Co. broaching the subject of publishing his "Tortoise Hunting Adventure" in their magazine, *PUTNAM'S MONTHLY*. On February 14 of the following year, the *New York Post* announced the upcoming publication of "The Encantadas" in the magazine, and indeed, the first of three installments of this work—the opening sketches of which concern tortoise-hunting—appeared in the March issue of *Putnam's*. Melville, meanwhile, seems still to have been pursuing his "Tortoise Book," although in late February he wrote Harper & Brothers that the book "still requires additional work." A May 25, 1854, letter to Harper & Brothers indicates that he had, by that time, delivered a "'Tortoises' extract" to them, and more extracts were apparently sent on July 25. After that time, there was no further word about the "Tortoise Book," and at least some of it seems to have found its way into the "Encantadas" sketches, although the exact nature of the relationship between the two has never been determined.

Town-Ho In chapter LIV of *MOBY-DICK*, the *PEQUOD* meets the *Town-Ho*, a troubled ship that has experienced a mutiny and the knifing of a crew member. Its chief mate dies hunting Moby-Dick.

Trafalgar, Battle of (1805) Admiral Horatio NELSON's greatest victory. Although Nelson died aboard his ship, the *Victory*, shot by a French marksman who spotted him parading on deck dressed in uniform with his military medals, this battle once and for all made it impossible for Napoleon to invade England. The manner of Nelson's death was lavishly praised and criticized, as Melville notes in *BILLY BUDD, SAILOR*, when he states that Captain VERE did not live long enough to share in Nelson's glory.

Tranquo   King of Tranque, an island in the Arsacides mentioned in *MOBY-DICK*. ISHMAEL reports that the king took him to examine a whale skeleton on the island's shore, and that this visit accounts for Ishmael's detailed knowledge of whales.

Transcendentalists   In American literature, the term is usually applied to Ralph Waldo EMERSON, Henry David Thoreau, and other lesser writers living in and around Concord, Massachusetts, between approximately 1830 and 1860. In the most basic sense, transcendentalism is a form of Platonism—that is, it is a belief in a higher realm beyond that of the physical senses. These writers drew not only on PLATO and Plotinus but also on German mystics, such as Jacob Boehme, and German idealist philosophers, particularly Immanuel KANT. In *PIERRE*, Melville is critical of Transcendentalists for not grounding their philosophy in a direct, clear perception of the world. In short, they are too abstract.

"Traveling: Its Pleasures, Pains, and Profits" (1859)   Lecture. By the end of 1856, Melville was suffering from the strain of constant financial worries, the exhaustion of finishing The *CONFIDENCE MAN*, and a deep depression over his inability to make a living as a professional writer. Concerned about his health, his wife, Lizzie, and other members of his family urged Melville to take a break, and on October 11, 1856, he boarded the propeller-driven steamer *Glasgow* for a seven-month trip to Europe and the Levant.

Upon his return home in May 1857, Melville hoped to obtain a political appointment to the customs service; but when the appointment did not materialize, he decided to raise capital by putting ARROWHEAD farm on the market and taking advantage of the vogue for visiting lecturers. Melville followed the lead of lecturers such as George William Curtis (1824–92), who succeeded in converting his travel writing into public lectures, by using his diary to write his first lecture, "STATUES IN ROME," which he delivered during the 1857–58 lecture season. When that proved to be too impersonal a topic, for the next season he prepared "THE SOUTH SEAS," which did garner more income. For 1859–60, he again prepared a new lecture, "Traveling," but he had few opportunities to deliver it. Whether because of illness or lack of invitations, Melville delivered this third lecture only three times. It was reported by only one newspaper, which gave a brief digest of the talk rather than the customary lengthy quotations. Because Melville did not himself publish his lectures and because no manuscripts survive, "Traveling" cannot be thoroughly reconstructed. It is clear, however, that although Melville spoke of travel as a salutary, liberating activity, he also emphasized the vitality of bedbugs and fleas, and the mean-spiritedness of guides.

Melville's three engagements for "Traveling" brought him a mere $110 in fees. His talk in Cambridgeport, Massachusetts, on February 21, 1860, was his last appearance as a lecturer.

Tribonnora   Minor character in *MARDI*. Heir to three islands near Maldondo, Tribonnora is, as MEDIA declares, a "mad prince" who attempts to swamp the vessels in which TAJI and his party sail.

"Trophies of Peace: Illinois in 1840" (1924)   Poem in *WEEDS AND WILDINGS*. Melville first visited Illinois in 1840, when, at loose ends, he left New York to stay briefly with his uncle Thomas MELVILL in Galena. (He would briefly return to Illinois as part of his 1859 lecture tour.) With this poem, in the section titled "The Year," Melville recalls the look of the American Midwest, with its vast "[f]iles on files of Prairie Maize." Although the growing corn brings to mind the spears that decorated the field of battle at ancient Marathon, these Illinois cornfields are dedicated to Ceres, the goddess of agriculture.

Troy, John B.   Melville's friend and the model for Dr. LONG GHOST in *OMOO*. When Melville met John Troy in 1842 aboard the *LUCY-ANN*, Troy was serving as the ship's steward. Troy was an erudite prankster who could quote Virgil but was not above tying a sleeping sailor's ankle to a line and hauling him up in the rigging. Troy's only medical qualification seems to have been his ability to pilfer pharmaceuticals from the ship's stores. He and Melville became fast friends and partners in most of the adventures described in *Omoo*. In November 1842, they both signed aboard the *Charles & Henry* as a means of leaving Tahiti. When the ship's captain recognized Troy as an ex-convict from Sydney, however, Melville's friend was obliged to leave the ship. He was supposed to have ended up in California mining for gold.

Truman, John   Character in The *CONFIDENCE MAN*. The name of the PRESIDENT OF THE BLACK RAPIDS COAL COMPANY (a fictitious concern invented by the CONFIDENCE MAN). The HERB-DOCTOR (another guise of the confidence man) tells the old MISER that he has already tripled his money by investing with John Truman. The herb-doctor also manages to sell the miser two more boxes of the Omni-Balsamic Reinvigorator.

Tubbs   Minor character in *WHITE-JACKET*. Tubbs was once a whaler, a profession much disdained by other sorts of mariners. Unfortunately, Tubbs has become bellicose in defense of his past profession, and when Jack CHASE invites him up into the main-top for a social visit, Tubbs as usual elevates whalemen at the expense of man-of-war men. Chase's outspoken reaction to

Tubbs's harangue is equally predictable: Tubbs is no longer welcome in the chatty main-top ranks.

"The Tuft of Kelp" (1888) Poem in JOHN MARR. In this quatrain the poet address a tuft of kelp that has been tossed ashore, wondering if the loss of the "lonely sea" has made the insignificant weed "purer" but also "bitterer." So Melville must have thought of the end of his own seafaring days, which—as *John Marr* itself illustrates—have left him solitary and forever brooding about the nature of existence.

Turkey Minor character in "BARTLEBY, THE SCRIVENER." Turkey is one of the lawyer-narrator's scriveners. A Englishman in his 60s, Turkey is reliable only until noon, after which time, his face inflamed, he thrashes about in a most unbusinesslike manner, leaving blots on his copying even as he rages. The lawyer, who in some senses identifies himself with Turkey—as with all his copyists—nevertheless finds him a valuable employee and keeps him on.

"Two Sides of a Tortoise" Sketch Second of "THE ENCANTADAS."

"The Two Temples" (1924) This story is one of three diptychs, or two-sided stories, that Melville probably wrote between the late summer of 1853 and the early spring of 1854. (The others are "POOR MAN'S PUDDING AND RICH MAN'S CRUMBS" and "THE PARADISE OF BACHELORS AND THE TARTARUS OF MAIDS.") Unlike some of his earlier efforts in the short-story form, they do not moralize or attempt to turn misfortune into bounty.

In the first of these paired stories, "Temple First," the nameless narrator attempts to enter a splendid, fashionable new Gothic church (probably Grace Church) in NEW YORK CITY, only to be turned away by a beadle-faced man. The narrator then surreptitiously enters the church through a side door and climbs up the church steeple where, from a ventilation duct, he can view the glittering congregation. The minister first reads audibly from the Bible, but when he ascends the pulpit to preach his sermon, all the narrator can hear is the ironic refrain "Ye are the salt of the earth." When the service ends, the wealthy parishioners flow out of the church "in three freshets," while the narrator finds himself locked in. When he pulls on some bell ropes to draw attention to his plight, he succeeds only in summoning up the beadle-faced man, who has him arrested as a "disturber of the Sunday peace." Fined and reprimanded by a judge, he is at last set free, pardoned "for having humbly indulged . . . in the luxury of public worship."

In "Temple Second," the narrator finds himself a penniless stranger in London on a Saturday night. No churches are open, so he finds his way to a theater,

where at intermission he is handed a reentry ticket by a cheery fellow who appears to be a working man. Reasoning that we all subsist on charity of one kind or other, the narrator enters the theater, ascending to the uppermost balcony. In the company of the generous-spirited working people who can afford such seats, he watches as the famed English actor William Macready plays Cardinal Richelieu, and marvels at the differences between his experience in this "temple" and the one at home: "a stranger in a strange land, I found sterling charity in the one; and at home, in my own land, was thrust from out the other."

Melville dedicated his story to the English actor Sheridan Knowles, who was also thought to be one of the finest dramatists of the day. "The Two Temples" was not published during Melville's lifetime. When he submitted the story to PUTNAM'S MONTHLY MAGAZINE in 1854, the magazine's editor was "very loathe to reject" it but felt obliged to do so because it might offend "some of our church readers." He did not say—and did not need to say—that the parishioners of the fashionable Grace Church would almost certainly recognize themselves and their well-known sexton, Isaac Brown, once one of Melville's neighbors, in the satire of "Temple First."

Typee Native tribe of the MARQUESAS Islands. Melville spent four weeks in 1842 with natives of the Taipivai (which he called the Typee Valley) in the Marquesas. Later he drew on his experiences there to write his first novel, TYPEE. His next novel, OMOO, although set primarily in TAHITI and elsewhere in the SOCIETY ISLANDS, is told by a first-person narrator known as Typee, following the maritime custom of naming sailors after some location with which they are associated. *Omoo* tracks the narrator's adventures after he escaped the Typee by boarding a whaler in need of extra crew members.

***Typee: A Peep at Polynesian Life* (1846)** Herman Melville's first novel. Written shortly after the author returned from his voyages in the Pacific, *Typee* is Melville's first and arguably most accessible novel. On January 3, 1841, Melville, aged 21, set sail from Fairhaven, Massachusetts, on the whaler ACUSHNET. The *Acushnet* came into port only twice during the 18 months that followed, and conditions on board were dirty and dangerous. By the time the ship docked in Nuku Hiva in the MARQUESAS Islands on June 23, 1842, Melville had made up his mind to desert. Together with shipmate Richard Tobias GREENE (the "TOBY" of *Typee*), he escaped.

Typee was meant, Melville wrote in his preface, to convey the "unvarnished truth" about what he experienced during the four weeks (July 9 to August 9) he lived among the Typee (also Taipis). In the winter of 1845, back home in LANSINGBURGH, NEW YORK, he sat down to record his memories of this period. He may have had in mind writing a travel narrative like C. S. Stewart's *A Visit to the South Seas in the U.S. Ship Vincennes* (1831) or William Ellis's *Polynesian Researches* (1833), both of which he consulted, or Richard Henry DANA's *Two Years Before the Mast* (1840), which first inspired Melville to go to sea. What emerged, however, bore a closer relation to fiction than fact—starting with the premise that the first-person narrator, whom Melville calls Tom and the Typees "TOMMO," spent four months (instead of one) going native.

SYNOPSIS

*Chapter 1: "The Sea * Longings for Shore * A Land-sick Ship * Destination of the Voyagers * The Marquesas * Adventure of a Missionary's Wife among the Savages * Characteristic Anecdote of the Queen of Nukuheva"*
After six months at sea, the narrator's whaling ship, the *Dolly,* is ailing and rapidly running out of provisions. The captain, Vangs, decides to change course and head for the Marquesas, prompting the narrator to relate what he knows about the islands. Readers are thus introduced to an engaging travel writer, at once lay anthropologist (the Marquesas are "among the earliest of European discoveries in the South Seas, having been first visited in the year 1595") and low comic ("What strange visions of outlandish things does the very name spirit up! Naked houris—cannibal banquets . . . *heathenish rites and human sacrifices*"). His book is, after all, subtitled *A Peep at Polynesian Life.*

Such a narrator is capable of providing insights into the differences between European and Polynesian cultures, and he does so straightaway. He tells the story of a missionary's wife whom the natives first worshiped, then reviled once a look beneath her voluminous skirts showed her to be no more than a mortal woman. This anecdote is immediately followed by another, in which the queen of Nukuheva hoists her own skirts in order to show the mariners on a visiting American man-of-war the TATTOOS that adorn her backside. We are not told how the Americans reacted, but the queen's French escort is last seen tumbling into their boat as they flee the scene "of so shocking a catastrophe."

*Chapter 2: "Passage from the Cruising Ground to the Marquesas * Sleepy times aboard Ship * South Seas Scenery * Land ho! * The French Squadron discovered at Anchor in the Bay of Nukuheva * Strange Plot * Escort of Canoes * A Flotilla of Cocoa-nuts * Swimming Visitors * The Dolly boarded by them * State of affairs that ensue"*
When the *Dolly* anchors in the Bay of Nuku Hiva (which Melville spells "Nukuheva"), it as well as the rest of the Marquesas is under the control of the French, whom the natives despise. They seem happy to see the Americans, however, welcoming the *Dolly* in an entirely uninhibited fashion. The antics of the unspoiled and

This portrait shows Herman Melville as the successful young author of Typee. (Berkshire Athenaeum)

bare-breasted young Marquesan girls, in particular, prompt the narrator to deliver the first of many tirades against the evils of colonialism. The "unsophisticated and confiding" Polynesians are easily corrupted: "Thrice happy are they who, inhabiting some yet undiscovered island in the midst of the ocean, have never been brought into contaminating contact with the white man."

*Chapter 3: "Some Account of the late operations of the French at the Marquesas * Prudent Conduct of the Admiral * Sensation produced by the Arrival of the Strangers * The first Horse seen by the Islanders * Reflections * Miserable Subterfuge of the French * Digression concerning Tahiti * Seizure of the Island by the Admiral * Spirited Conduct of an English Lady"*
The narrator next indulges in a digression devoted to denouncing the French who, under the leadership of Rear Admiral DUPETIT-THOUARS, deploy seven warships against "naked heathens" who inhabit "huts of cocoanut boughs." This same Admiral Thouars was responsible for dethroning Queen POMARE of Tahiti and had recently pitted one Marquesan tribe against another by naming the French puppet, MOWANNA, king of all Nukuheva. The narrator's attitude toward the French is

unqualifiedly hostile, and he ends the chapter with a satiric anecdote that reveals Thouars's feet of clay: faced with the obstinacy of a British missionary wife on Tahiti, he backs down when she refuses to obey his command to pull down the Union Jack.

*Chapter 4: "State of Affairs aboard the Ship * Contents of her Larder * Length of South Seaman's Voyages * Account of a Flying Whaleman * Determination to Leave the Vessel * The Bay of Nukuheva * The Typees * Invasion of their Valley by Porter * Reflections * Glen of Tior * Interview between the old King and the French Admiral"*

The narrator gives his reasons for wanting to leave the *Dolly*, including the tyranny of the captain, the sorry state of the ship, and the provisions. His choice to desert is hardly frivolous: some of the inhabitants of Nukuheva are reputed to be cannibals, with Typees considered the most fearsome of all.

The narrator goes ashore with a party from the *Dolly*, and when the ship's boat enters the Bay of Tior, he plunges into a nearby grove. He emerges into a beautiful valley, where he witnesses an encounter between the French admiral and the sovereign of the ruling Tior tribe. The encounter provides the narrator with an opportunity to reflect on the differences between Western civilization and the "savage" existence. The latter, he concludes, has produced a happier man.

*Chapter 5: "Thoughts previous to attempting Escape * Toby, a Fellow Sailor, agrees to share the Adventure * Last Night aboard the Ship"*

Having reconnoitered the location where he hopes to make his escape, the narrator returns to the ship, where he confides his plans to a shipmate, Toby. Toby eagerly agrees to accompany him, and the two decide that the next day they will join a party from the *Dolly* on shore leave.

*Chapter 6: "A Specimen of Nautical Oratory * Criticisms of the Sailors * The Starboard Watch are given a Holiday * The Escape to the Mountains"*

The two conspirators prepare themselves for flight. Determined to travel light, they wear only essential clothing. In addition, the narrator stuffs some dry sea biscuits, several pounds of tobacco, and a few yards of cotton cloth into his frock coat. The last two items are meant to purchase the goodwill of the natives.

The boatload of sailors lands in a driving rain. The seamen take shelter in a canoe house, where the steady beat of the raindrops lulls all but Toby and the narrator to sleep. Seizing their opportunity, the two escape into a nearby grove. As they make their way toward the high ridge of the valley, where they plan to wait until their party returns to the ship, their progress is slowed by their rain-soaked coats and by thick stands of reeds. Finally, they make it to the top where, the narrator rhapsodizes, they behold the loveliest view imaginable.

*Chapter 7: "The other side of the Mountain * Disappointment * Inventory of Articles brought from the Ship * Division of the Stock of Bread * Appearance of the Interior of the Island * A Discovery * A Ravine and Waterfalls * A sleepless Night * Further Discoveries * My Illness * A Marquesan Landscape"*

Turning to assess their location, the narrator and Toby discover that they have ascended only the first of many ridges. They will not, as they had hoped, be able to join a band of natives straightaway. There are no breadfruit or coconut trees in sight, and an inventory of their provisions yields only a few handfuls of sweat- and rain-soaked sea biscuit, covered in shredded tobacco. These they divide into six portions, which will have to last for three days.

They make little progress that day, and finally build a leaky hut where they spend a miserable night. The next morning they eat their portions of sodden biscuits before setting out again. Caught in yet another rainstorm, the two take shelter. Toby sleeps, but the narrator begins to suffer alternating chills and fever as one of his legs develops a painful and mysterious swelling. Tossing and turning, he happens to spy nearby a beautiful valley filled with palmetto-thatched huts.

*Chapter 8: "The Important Question, Typee or Happar? * A Wild-Goose Chace * My Suffering * Disheartening Situation * A Night in a Ravine * Morning Meal * Happy Idea of Toby * Journey towards the Valley"*

The escapees are now confronted with a crucial decision: is this valley that lies before them the home of the peaceful Happars or of their enemy, the dreaded Typee? Tired and hungry, Toby argues for the former, but the narrator, urging caution, convinces him to travel on to the next valley. It proves to be a rough trip. Lame, ill, and hungry, the narrator follows Toby's lead from one ridge to another, unable to find an inviting vale. They pass another uncomfortable night in a makeshift lean-to before deciding to return to the inhabited valley they discovered the day before.

*Chapter 9: "Perilous Passage of the Ravine * Descent towards the Valley"*

Entering paradise is not easy. They find their way back by following a stream, which soon becomes a raging river that plunges into a cataract. After passing another night en route and consuming the last of their provisions, the two determine that their only hope of salvation is to swing from the vines that form a network along one side of the rock fissures. At the bottom they discover a sheer cliff, which they are able to conquer by leaping into the branches of a palm tree that reaches nearly to the top of the cliff. When they encounter yet another waterfall, they decide to camp for the night. Finally, on the fifth day after they first saw it, they make their way into the valley.

Chapter 10: *"The Head of the Valley * Cautious Advance * A Path * Fruit * Discovery of Two of the Natives * Their singular Conduct * Approach towards the inhabited parts of the Vale * Sensation produced by our Appearance * Reception at the House of one of the Natives"*

Toby, who had exhibited great physical courage in leading their descent into the valley, now begins to hang back. When they happen upon two natives, a boy and a girl, it is the narrator who approaches them, bearing his cotton cloth as a gift.

The westerners follow the wary natives down to their village, all the while asking the young couple if they are Typee or Happar. As they approach the settlement, they are surrounded by natives, whose identity still remains a mystery. Suddenly inspired, the narrator utters two words—"Typee mokatee" ("Typee good")—and he and Toby are saved.

They have indeed landed among the Typee. The lead chief introduces himself as MEHEVI. The narrator responds by identifying himself as Tom, which the natives translate as "Tommo." "Toby" does not present them with any pronunciation problem. A troop of natives next passes by, and the men introduce themselves to the now welcome guests before the group settles down to a feast of poee-poee (mashed breadfruit) and coconuts. The villagers touch and smell Tommo's and Toby's white skin; but these shipmates are not the first westerners to encounter the Typee, who go on to express their distaste for the French. Finally, the visitors are permitted to sleep side by side with what they still believe to be a tribe of cannibals.

Chapter 11: *"Midnight Reflections * Morning Visitors * A Warrior in Costume * A Savage Æsculapius * Practice of the Healing Art * Body Servant * A Dwelling-house of the Valley described * Portraits of its Inmates"*

Tommo and Toby wake to a roomful of young girls, who offer them food and fan away the insects even as they scrutinize the white men. Toby is outraged by their familiarity, while Tommo expresses shock at the impropriety of their dress and deportment.

The girls are soon replaced by boys, then by a chief in full royal regalia, his body resplendent with tattoos. Tommo then recognizes him as Mehevi.

Mehevi endeavors to talk to his visitors about "Maneeka" (America) and "Franee" (the French), before noticing Tommo's injured leg. A healer is sent for, but his ministrations leave the narrator's leg "much as a rump-steak after undergoing the castigating process which precedes cooking." Plainly, Tommo is still concerned about cannibalism.

Mehevi then assigns a strong native named KORY-KORY to act as a sort of body servant for Tommo. Kory-Kory is the son of the senile old man, MARHEYO, who owns the structure in which Tommo and Toby reside. The narrator spends a good deal of time describing his

exotic hosts for his audience. Kory-Kory, although faithful and ever solicitous, is "hideous" to look at because of the tattoos that cover his body. Marheyo, who often wears the teeth of sea monsters as earrings, spends his days idly assembling a hut that never reaches completion. In contrast, his wife TINOR is "the only industrious person in all the valley." Best of all is Kory-Kory's beautiful young sister FAYAWAY, who has an olive complexion, blue eyes, full lips, and the merest hint of a facial tattoo. Fayaway, the smitten narrator relates, "for the most part clung to the primitive and summer garb of Eden."

Chapter 12: *"Officiousness of Kory-Kory * His Devotion * A Bath in the Stream * Want of Refinement of the Typee Damsels * Stroll with Mehevi * A Typee Highway * The Taboo Groves * The Hoolah-Hoolah Ground * The Ti * Time-worn Savages * Hospitality of Mehevi * Midnight Misgivings * Adventure in the Dark * Distinguished Honors paid to the Visitors * Strange Procession and Return to the House of Marheyo"*

In some respects, Tommo and Toby seem to be living in paradise. Tommo is hand-fed by the attentive Kory-Kory. Upon awakening, the lame man is hoisted onto Kory-Kory's back and carried to a stream, where Tommo is obliged to take an awkward bath with Typees of both sexes. Next, Mehevi escorts Tommo and Toby to the sacred "hoolah-hoolah" grounds, where they, as privileged males, are permitted to tour a temple called the Ti, from which women are banned by taboo. After an evening meal and a shared pipe, the visitors drift off to sleep.

Around midnight, however, Tommo wakes to find only Toby next to him—all of the natives have withdrawn. The sacred groves nearby are lit by flames, which also illuminate dancing Typees. Their old suspicions are aroused; now that they have been fattened for several days, Toby declares, they are ripe for the eating. But when Mehevi and the others return to the Ti, they bear with them morsels of roast suckling pig to share with their guests.

Chapter 13: *"Attempt to procure Relief from Nukuheva * Perilous Adventure of Toby in the Happar Mountains * Eloquence of Kory-Kory"*

Toby continues to insist that, for all their hospitality, the Typees remain cannibals. Tommo, while in agreement, emphasizes their hosts' humanity and gentility. Nonetheless, his reawakened concern seems to aggravate his injury. He convinces Toby that he must go overland to Nukuheva for help, returning by water. The Typee at first oppose this suggestion, but when Tommo pleads his leg, they finally agree.

The next morning Toby sets out with Marheyo, who leads him to the edge of the Happar valley. There Toby is attacked by three members of this enemy tribe. Wounded, he manages to escape, returning to Typee territory.

*Chapter 14: "A great Event happens in the Valley * The Island Telegraph * Something befalls Toby * Fayaway displays a tender Heart * Melancholy Reflections * Mysterious Conduct of the Islanders * Devotion of Kory-Kory * A rural Couch * A Luxury * Kory-Kory strikes a Light à la Typee"*

Toby recovers quickly. The return of his health brings no joy to Tommo, who fears his own disability will prevent him from ever leaving the valley of the Typee. One morning, however, boats appear in the bay below, and Toby proposes to take advantage of the natives' excitement to get help. When the Typees return from the beach, however, Toby is not with them, and Tommo's questions as to his whereabouts elicit conflicting answers. Not knowing his companion's fate, Tommo gives him up for lost.

Ironically, this decision seems to free him. His leg improves, and he gradually goes native, allowing himself to appreciate fully the Typee's solicitude and their way of life. He uses the occasion of watching Kory-Kory strike a light for his pipe to compare Polynesian and European qualities of life. For the narrator, the balance is beginning to tip markedly in the Polynesians' favor.

*Chapters 15–18: "Kindness of Marheyo and the rest of the Islanders * A full Description of the Bread-fruit Tree * Different Modes of preparing the Fruit"; "Melancholy condition * Occurrence at the Ti * Anecdote of Marheyo * Shaving the Head of a Warrior"; "Improvement in Health and Spirits * Felicity of the Typees * Their enjoyment compared with those of more enlightened Communities * Comparative Wickedness of civilized and unenlightened People * A Skirmish in the Mountain with the Warriors of Happar"; "Swimming in company with the Girls of the Valley * A Canoe * Effects of the Taboo * A pleasure Excursion on the Pond * Beautiful freak of Fayaway * Mantua-making * A Stranger arrives in the Valley * His mysterious conduct * Native Oratory * The Interview * Its Results * Departure of the Stranger"*

These chapters are largely given over to travelogue. Tommo gives a full description of the Polynesian staple, the breadfruit, together with recipes for its preparation. He describes his new native TAPA cloth garments. He uses the needle and thread he has brought with him to show the natives how to sew up a tear. He uses his dull razor to shave a local hero's head. In chapter 17, he indulges in a full-blown comparison of so-called civilization with the native way of life, concluding that the latter is far preferable: "There were none of those thousand sources of irritation that the ingenuity of civilized man has created to mar his own felicity." Even the hostility between the Typee and the Happar seems relatively benign: a skirmish produces in the former only a missing finger, a bruised arm, and a punctured thigh.

In chapter 18, Tommo's bliss reaches a kind of apogee when he convinces Mehevi to make an exception to the taboo that bars females from the vicinity of canoes. Fayaway is now free to join him and Kory-Kory on their excursions to a local lake. Melville paints a memorable picture of Fayaway as she removes her tapa robe and, standing upright in the boat, uses her clothing as a sort of sail.

The narrator's peace of mind is temporarily interrupted by the appearance of the taboo MARNOO, a handsome native from a distant tribe who has attained a nearly sacred status that shields him from the Typee's customary hostility towards strangers. Even more astonishingly, he begins to speak English to Tommo. He chats quite amiably with Tommo for a while, but when Tommo begins to question Marnoo about Toby, the native becomes uncomfortable. Tommo's further questions about why he is being kept a prisoner by the Typees elicit more evasion. Finally, when Tommo requests that Marnoo ask Mehevi for his release, Marnoo becomes alarmed and Mehevi angrily dismisses him.

*Chapter 19: "Reflections after Marnoo's Departure * Battle of the Pop-guns * Strange conceit of Marheyo * Process of making Tappa"*

Although thrown temporarily back into despair by his encounter with Marnoo, Tommo resolves to make the best of his situation. If nothing else, it will serve his purposes to at least let the Typee think he intends to remain with them. As part of his effort to make himself winning, he whittles pop-guns out of cane for the Typee children, only to spawn a fad among the whole tribe. The natives evince a fascination with all new things, and when Tommo gives Marheyo the moldy shoes the old man covets, the latter immediately turns them into a chest ornament. The narrator then ends the chapter with a discourse on tapa cloth making.

*Chapters 20–31: "History of a day as usually spent in the Typee Valley * Dances of the Marquesan Girls"; "The Spring of Arva Wai * Remarkable Monumental Remains * Some ideas with regard to the History of the Pi-Pis found in the Valley"; "Preparations for a Grand Festival in the Valley * Strange doings in the Taboo Groves * Monument of Calabashes * Gala costume of the Typee damsels * Departure for the Festival"; "The Feast of the Calabashes"; "Idea suggested by the Feast of the Calabashes * Inaccuracy of certain published Accounts of the Islands * A Reason * Neglected State of Heathenism in the Valley * Effigy of a dead Warrior * A singular Superstition * The Priest Kolory and the God Moa Artua * Amazing Religious Observance * A dilapidated Shrine * Kory-Kory and the Idol * An Inference"; "General Information gathered at the Festival * Personal Beauty of the Typees * Their Superiority over the Inhabitants of the other Islands * Diversity of Complexion * A Vegetable Cosmetic and Ointment * Testimony of Voyagers to the uncommon Beauty of the Marquesans * Few Evidences of Intercourse with Civilized Beings * Dilapidated Musket * Primitive Simplicity of Government * Regal Dignity of Mehevi"; "King Mehevi * Allusion to his Hawaiian Majesty * Conduct of Marheyo* *and Mehevi in certain delicate matters * Peculiar system of Marriage * Number of Population * Uniformity * Embalming * Places of Sepulture * Funeral obsequies at Nukuheva * Number of Inhabitants in Typee * Location of the Dwellings * Happiness enjoyed in the Valley * A Warning * Some ideas with regard to the Civilization of the Islands * Reference to the Present state of the Hawaiians * Story of a Missionary's Wife * Fashionable Equipages at Oahu * Reflections"; "The Social Condition and General Character of the Typees"; "Fishing Parties * Mode of distributing the Fish * Midnight Banquet * Timekeeping Tapers * Unceremonious style of eating the Fish"; "Natural History of the Valley * Golden Lizards * Tameness of the Birds * Mosquitoes * Flies * Dogs * A solitary Cat * The Climate * The Cocoa-nut Tree * Singular modes of climbing it * An agile young Chief * Fearlessness of the Children * Too-Too and the Cocoa-nut Tree * The Birds of the Valley"; "A Professor of the Fine Arts * His Persecutions * Something about Tattooing and Tabooing * Two Anecdotes in illustration of the latter * A few thoughts on the Typee Dialect"; "Strange custom of the Islanders * Their Chanting, and the peculiarity of their Voice * Rapture of the King at first hearing a Song * A new Dignity conferred on the Author * Musical Instruments in the Valley * Admiration of the Savages at Beholding a Pugilistic Performance * Swimming Infant * Beautiful Tresses of the Girls * Ointment for the Hair"*

The last third of *Typee* is devoted, in the main, to the kind of travelogue and exotica Melville may have hoped would appeal to readers. He begins his ruminations on Typee life with this observation: "Nothing can be more uniform and undiversified than the life of the Typees; one tranquil day of ease and happiness follows another in quiet succession; and with these unsophisticated savages the history of a day is the history of a life."

Then follows the narrator's account of a typical day in the Typee valley. After they awake, the Typee bathe in a nearby stream. They eat breakfast, which is accomplished while reclining on mats like Roman emperors. After smoking a pipe or two, the men busy themselves with carving or napping, while the women groom themselves. The remainder of the day is taken up with similar activities, punctuated by more napping, while evenings often include storytelling and dancing. Melville is careful to add, "In truth these innocent people seemed to be at no loss for something to occupy their time."

The narrator then becomes more anthropological in his observations, describing the history, structures, and customs of the land. In chapters 22–24, however, in which he describes the Feast of the Calabashes, Tommo once again becomes a participant in his own tale. The festival lasts for three days and involves slaughtering and roasting a pig, donning special costumes, and drinking an intoxicating beverage which the narrator tells us is also used to combat diseases imported to the South Seas by white men. Clearly the Feast of the

Calabashes has some religious significance, but Tommo is not able to elicit from Kory-Kory any intelligible explanation of its meaning.

Revisiting the feast affords the narrator an opportunity to debunk much of what has passed in the West as scientific accounts of Polynesian religious practices, based on missionary narratives. Most of these practices, such as ritual immolation, Tommo dismisses as humbuggery. For his own part, he professes not to know much about Typee theology, but he does offer up several of his own observations concerning local sacred customs. One is the deference shown an effigy of some dead Typee chieftain, depicted as forever paddling his way toward the realms of bliss. Such deference is almost immediately undermined by Kory-Kory's comment to the effect that this pleasant afterlife probably is not, in the end, much more pleasant than Typee.

Then there is the curious ritual involving a sort of high priest named KOLORY and a diminutive idol called Moa Artua, which Kolory both coddles and cudgels in order to obtain some divine wisdom, as well as a larger icon that Kory-Kory abuses. The narrator concludes that the latter-day Typee are a backslidden people sunk in religious sloth—but given his opinion of Western missionaries, he would probably agree with Kory-Kory's assessment of the afterlife.

The narrator retreats into objectivity to detail the Typees' physical beauty, dwelling on their luminous complexions and white teeth. He admires the apparent democracy of their social organization, as well as their polyandry—the product of a shortage of females. He discusses marriage customs and funeral rites, taking time to rail against Christian missionaries who have ruined what once was the paradise of the Sandwich Islands (see HAWAII). Largely because they have been so removed from civilization, the Typee have been spared the Western obsession with property and wealth.

The pace of the book begins to mimic the tempos of daily life in Typee as the narrator ranges from a natural history of the valley, to meditations on the art of tattooing and taboo, to some thoughts about the Typee dialect. Somewhat sheepishly, he begins chapter 31 by saying, "Sadly discursive as I have already been, I must still further entreat the reader's patience, as I am about to string together, without any attempt at order, a few odds and ends of things not hitherto mentioned. . . ." He has to get it all in quickly: Tommo's fortunes are about to change.

*Chapter 32: "Apprehensions of Evil * Frightful Discovery * Some remarks on Cannibalism * Second Battle with the Happars * Savage Spectacle * Mysterious Feast * Subsequent Disclosures"*

The narrator, who has been lulled into such sanguinity regarding the Typee that he has managed to explain away even their occasional cannibalism, is about to make a "frightful discovery." Suddenly filled with apprehension, he experiences a return of his old malady. One day, returning home unexpectedly, he surprises his hosts in the act of inspecting the contents of three mysterious packages. These contain three preserved human heads, one of which formerly sat on the shoulders of a white man. Although the natives struggle to convince him that all three heads were taken from Happar warriors slain in battle, Tommo is once again seized by fears that the Typee have imprisoned him so as to eat him.

A week later, after the Typee battle again with the Happar, several of whom they kill, another festival is held. Tommo is convinced that cannibalism was part of the celebrations. Now desperate to escape, the same narrator who once decried the influence of the French in Polynesia prays for them to deliver him.

*Chapter 33: "The Stranger again arrives in the Valley * Singular Interview with him * Attempt to Escape * Failure * Melancholy Situation * Sympathy of Marheyo"*

Marnoo returns to the Typee valley; but when Tommo appeals to Marnoo to take him out of the valley, the taboo warrior cuts him off. Still, Marnoo manages in his broken English to suggest a plan of escape to Tommo. Tommo is to note his exit and follow him later to his native village of Pueearka, from which Marnoo will return him to Nukuheva.

The next night Tommo tries to follow this plan, only to be stopped by one of the Typee. This failure nearly robs him of all mobility—and of hope.

Chapter 34: "The Escape"

Three weeks later one of the Typee warriors announces that Toby has returned. As is always their habit when a boat enters their bay, the Typees rush down to greet it. They refuse, however, to take Tommo along. Mehevi finally relents, however, but even as Tommo is carried down toward the water, he learns that Toby has not arrived with the boat. The natives insist that Tommo return to the village. Desperately he argues with them, and finally one of the chiefs relents, but the lame Tommo is left to his own devices.

Old Marheyo seems to be the only one who sympathizes with Tommo's plight, and he orders his son to carry Tommo once more upon his back. At the shore a whale boat awaits, and Karakoee, a renegade taboo native from Oahu, attempts to barter with the Typee for their captive. The Typee angrily refuse. Summoning all his strength, Tommo takes advantage of the commotion and rushes toward the whaleboat. Bidding farewell only to Marheyo, Kory-Kory, and the sorrowful Fayaway, he boards. After the boat pulls away from the shore, several Typee warriors come after it. Tommo, once an ardent admirer of these noble savages, dashes a boat hook into the throat of a Typee chief who threatens to overtake them. Soon the narrator is lifted over the side

of the *Julia,* an Australian whaler sorely in need of crew members.

Tommo then discovers that his rescue was effected on behalf of the captain of the *Julia* by Karakoee, a kind of hired gun acting on information he had been given by Marnoo. Saved by savages, Tommo ends his narrative still wondering about the fate of his fellow runaway, Toby.

Appendix: "Provisional cession to Lord George Paulet of the Sandwich Islands"

As if to underscore the essentially factual nature of his book as well as the evils of colonialism, Melville includes this afterword, which details a temporary takeover of the Sandwich Islands by the British, an event he found to be much misunderstood in the United States. In 1843, Captain Richard CHARLTON was serving there as consul general. Reacting to abuse by the native authorities of British citizens residing in Hawaii, Charlton appealed to the local British commander in chief, who sent in Lord George PAULET to set matters right.

Paulet accepted at face value the Hawaiian king's ruse, whereby the latter provisionally surrendered to British sovereignty while matters between the two countries were resolved in Britain. In fact the king's goal was to turn world opinion against the British. The ploy worked. Although Paulet's reforms—including his attempt to restrain licentiousness—proved to be highly popular with the Hawaiian people, the king and his Methodist missionary advisers (again, Melville cannot forego an opportunity to denigrate them) complained long and loudly about the foreign effort to change native customs. Five months after the cessation, Admiral Thomas was obliged to return to Honolulu to take down the Union Jack and raise in its place the Hawaiian flag.

Riotous rejoicing, sponsored by the king and his missionary advisers, ensued. Melville notes that the natives, freed from foreign blue laws, "plunged voluntarily into every species of wickedness and excess," an eventuality he blames on foreign meddling with a native culture. In America, Paulet was blamed for a Hawaiian fall from grace; but as Melville sees it, the fault lies elsewhere.

Sequel: "The Story of Toby"

In July 1846, months after the initial publication of *Typee,* Richard Tobias Greene published an account of his adventures that verified much of the story Melville had told in his novel. As some critics had attacked *Typee* by questioning its veracity, Melville seized the opportunity to answer them by writing a sequel to his book.

Tommo relates how, according to their plan, Toby had left the Typee Valley for the bay of the Happars, where he paid a sailor named Jimmy to lead him through Happar territory to Nukuheva. Once there, Toby signed on as a sailor in order to obtain the money he needed to pay Jimmy. He also begged his new captain for an armed boat to rescue Tommo. When the boat left it was manned by Jimmy and some taboo natives, but Jimmy managed to convince Toby that his presence would scuttle any chance of success. When Jimmy returned that evening, it was without Tommo. Jimmy promised to try the next day, but before he returned, Toby's ship weighed anchor. Toby left the ship in New Zealand, arriving home some two years after leaving the Marquesas. Until the publication of *Typee,* Greene had presumed Melville dead.

PUBLICATION HISTORY

In July 1845, only months after he had begun his novel, Melville submitted a manuscript to the American publishing firm of HARPER & BROTHERS, which rejected the book on grounds that it seemed too good to be true, too polished—in short, more fiction than fact. Melville took these criticisms to heart, spending the summer revising his text. When his brother Gansevoort, recently appointed secretary to the American legation in England, left for London at the end of July, 1845, he carried with him a portion of Melville's reworked book, which he managed to sell to the British publisher John MURRAY. Murray proposed that the work appear as part of his Home and Colonial Library, a series devoted to travel narratives, and suggested that Melville make further changes to shore up the book's verisimilitude.

The next January, the well-connected Gansevoort shared parts of his brother's work with Washington IRVING. Much impressed, the celebrated author recommended the Melville book to the American publishers WILEY AND PUTNAM.

Several hands in addition to the author's own went into the next set of revisions of the *Typee* manuscript. Removal of some of the more salacious segments of the story, as well as addition of more factual material, was probably performed at the suggestion of John Murray, whose in-house editor also made numerous stylistic changes. Gansevoort, too, had a hand in making both actual revisions of the text and suggestions for making it more "presentable."

Finally, on February 27, 1846, John Murray's British edition of the book was published as *Narrative of a Four Months' Residence Among the Natives of a Valley of the Marquesan Islands; Or a Peep at Polynesian Life.* It was followed on March 17 by the American edition, published by Wiley and Putnam with a different title, *Typee: A Peep at Polynesian Life,* and a somewhat different text. The following August, in response to negative reactions to Melville's condemnation of missionaries, the reemergence of Richard Tobias Greene, and John Wiley's insistence on further expurgations, *Typee* was reissued in yet another American edition that included both the author's Appendix and "The Story of Toby." The same month, Murray issued a revised British edition that retained his original text, but added "The Story of Toby."

Both the revised American edition and the English edition of *Typee* stayed in print during Melville's lifetime. Although the publication of pirated editions in England ate into his profits, it is estimated that he earned approximately $2,000 from his first book. After his death, *Typee* remained his most popular book and was still available in both versions for four decades. In 1968, elements of the first English edition and the revised American edition were combined in a new edition of the novel and published as part of the multivolume Northwestern-Newberry *Writings of Herman Melville,* meant as an authoritative edition of all Melville's works. In 1983, however, a 30-page manuscript fragment of the first draft of *Typee* was discovered, casting new light on Melville's original intentions concerning his book, such as an early attempt to include an exploration of his aesthetics.

U

Uhia Minor character in *MARDI*. Uhia is the ruler of Ohonoo, also called the Isle of Rogues, where he busies himself with plans to become king of all Mardi.

Ulver, Delly Character in *PIERRE*. Delly is cast out from Mrs. GLENDINNING's estate when it is discovered that she has given birth to an illegitimate child. Pierre takes up Delly's case, eventually including her in the household he establishes in New York City.

unfortunate man, the Character in *The CONFIDENCE MAN*. This is another guise of the CONFIDENCE MAN. He tells the "good merchant" ROBERTS about his hard wife, GONERIL, and how she made his life a misery.

"Under the Ground" (1924) Poem in *WEEDS AND WILDINGS*. Part of a sequence titled "As They Fell" in the "A Rose or Two" section of the volume, "Under the Ground" pictures a gardener's boy carrying fresh roses out of an old funeral vault. Questioned about this odd practice, the boy claims that a "charm in the dank o' the vault" helps the roses keep their bloom.

Ungar Character in *CLAREL*. An ex-Confederate officer, he is now a mercenary working for the Egyptians and the Turks. He meets the pilgrims at MAR SABA and accompanies them to BETHLEHEM. Bearing the scars of war, Ungar is a man alienated from 19th-century democratic America, which he believes is in a state of spiritual decay. He denounces American materialism and the debased state of knowledge in the so-called New World. Although he has a religious cast of mind, he finds it difficult to conceive of man's salvation, perhaps because he is part Indian. There is something wild in his makeup, although he has the stoicism often attributed to suffering Indians. CLAREL is disturbed by Ungar's pessimism, which the optimistic DERWENT tries to counteract. The narrator calls Ungar a "wandering Ishmael from the West."

"An Uninscribed Monument on one of the Battle-fields of the Wilderness" (1866) Poem in *BATTLE-PIECES*. One of the "Verses Inscriptive and Memorial" in Melville's collection of CIVIL WAR poetry, this poem concerns a cryptic monument on the battlefields of the Wilderness, an area in northern Virginia where troops commanded by Ulysses S. Grant and Robert E. Lee fought on May 5–6, 1864, to an indecisive conclusion. Union casualties numbered approximately 18,000, while the Confederates suffered 10,000. Melville's poem adopts the point of view of the uninscribed tablet, which indicates, "Thou too wilt silent stand— / Silent as I, and lonesome as the land."

unparticipating man, the Character in *The CONFIDENCE MAN*. A sick man aboard the *FIDELE*, he is approached by a HERB-DOCTOR (a disguise of the CONFIDENCE MAN) who assures him that sick men can be cured by "Samaritan Pain dissuader."

United States U.S. Navy frigate. In August 1843, Melville enlisted in Honolulu, HAWAII, as a sailor on board the flagship of the U.S. Navy's Pacific Squadron. The *United States* was headed home to Boston via CAPE HORN, and Melville would be discharged at the conclusion of this voyage, never again venturing a maritime voyage as a working sailor. The trip took 14 months, with the ship stopping first at the MARQUESAS, then at TAHITI and its neighboring island Imeeo before heading off to South America. Calls were made in Valparaiso, Chile, and Lima, Peru, before the ship anchored for two and a half months in the bay of Callao, Peru. After rounding Cape Horn, the *United States* stopped briefly in Rio de Janeiro, Brazil, before heading for home. It finally arrived in Boston on October 2, 1844. Five years later, Melville would make direct use of his impressions of life aboard a man-of-war in writing *WHITE-JACKET*, in which the *United States* is renamed the *NEVERSINK*.

Ushant, John Minor character in *WHITE-JACKET*. A sexagenarian captain of the forecastle aboard the U.S.S. NEVERSINK, Ushant is the final holdout in "The Great Massacre of the Beards." Approaching home, Captain CLARET suddenly issues an edict that all sailors must trim their beards to meet Navy specifications. Many refuse at first to comply with the order, but only the stalwart, philosophical old Ushant holds on to this last remnant of his individuality. But naval discipline allows for no exceptions, and so the old man is first jailed, then flogged for his disobedience—despite the fact that his three years' service has already expired. His punishment is perhaps the most egregious example Melville provides in *White-Jacket* of the arbitrary and inhumane resort to FLOGGING.

utilitarianism In *PIERRE,* both utilitarianism and transcendentalism (see TRANSCENDENTALISTS) are found wanting. The former is a philosophy that reduces all moral issues to the quest for "the greatest happiness for the greatest number"—to borrow the famous phrase from Jeremy Bentham (1748–1832), the founder of utilitarianism. All that matters is pleasure, happiness, and well-being. For Melville, as for the questing Pierre, utilitarianism is incomprehensible because it refuses to grapple with religious and metaphysical questions.

"A Utilitarian View of the Monitor's Fight." (1866) Poem in *BATTLE-PIECES.* In this, one of several poems Melville wrote about the recently introduced ironclad ships, the speaker uses a modernist, percussive style to describe the ships' practical virtues:

Hail to victory without the gaud
Of glory; zeal that needs no fans
Of banners; plain mechanic power
Plied cogently in War now placed—
Where War belongs—
Among the trades and artisans.

Their main virtue, he declares, is that they make war seem less grand than peace.

Van Minor character in *OMOO*. Van is a Finnish sailor—ostensibly endowed with second sight—aboard the *Julia* who validates his fellow shipmates' superstitions when his declaration that few of them will be left aboard within three weeks turns out to be accurate. The causative factor is not, however, the shipboard plague they fear, but instead their own revolt against authoritarianism.

Varvy Minor character in *OMOO*. Varvy is an old hermit and moonshiner whom the narrator and LONG GHOST encounter during their journey towards the court of Queen POMARE.

Vee Vee Minor character in *MARDI*. Vee Vee is King MEDIA's fool, probably modeled on the Fool in SHAKESPEARE's *King Lear* and certainly prefiguring PIP in *MOBY-DICK*.

"Venice" (1891) Poem in *TIMOLEON*. Part of the "Fruit of Travel Long Ago" section of the collection, "Venice" reflects Melville's trip to that city in April 1857. The poem speaks of the "Pantheistic energy of will" that motivates the construction of reefs in the Coral Sea as well as the "reefs of palaces" that arose in the lagoon that became the city of Venice.

Vere, Captain Character in *BILLY BUDD, SAILOR*. Vere determines the fate of BILLY BUDD, whom he sentences to hang. The story presents a complex picture of a naval officer determined to do his duty even when it conflicts with his innate compassion and belief that Billy did not intend to kill John CLAGGART. Vere's history and subsequent fate is detailed in the novella, suggesting that Melville wished to make the captain a symbol of authority as well as an example of a man willing to stifle his own feelings in order to be ruled exclusively by his sense of duty.

"The Vial of Attar" (1924) Poem in *WEEDS AND WILD-INGS*. Part of the "As They Fell" sequence in the "A Rose or Two" section of the volume, "The Vial of Attar" concerns the Rose's bereaved lover. At first taking comfort in what remains after the beloved's death, he then cries out for what he has lost:

There *is* nothing like the bloom;
And the Attar poignant reminds me
Of the bloom that's passed away.

"The Victor of Antietam. (1862.)" (1866) Poem in *BATTLE-PIECES*. The "victor" of the poem is General George B. McClellan who, as commander of the Army of the Potomac, was first accused of dragging his heels, then relieved of his command after his Peninsular campaign ended in the bloody Seven Days' Battles of June 26 to July 2, 1862. That September, however, he was called back to defend the capital, and led the Union troops to a victory over Confederate soldiers led by General Robert E. Lee at Antietam. As Melville notes, "[o]nly Antietam could atone" for McClellan's earlier failures. Far from condemning McClellan, however, Melville notes that one cannot always distinguish between the "[d]eferred fulfillment" of the "struggler" and the "foundering" of the "ne'er-do-well." For Melville, the blame for McClellan's failures could be found in the federal government's dithering at the start of the war: "The leadsmen quarrelled in the bay; / Quills thwarted swords; divided sway."

"View of the Barnum Property" (1847) Short squib attributed to Melville. Published anonymously in *YANKEE DOODLE* on July 31, 1847, this piece consists of a cartoon caricature of P. T. BARNUM's American Museum, which is billed in the long caption that follows as "an exact likeness of this celebrated storehouse of grotesqueries" created by the magazine's artist. It is meant, the caption says, to save readers the 25¢ admission price to the museum. The caption has been attributed to Melville because of similarities in references and phrasing to the "AUTHENTIC ANECDOTES OF 'OLD ZACK'" series Melville is known to have written for *Yankee Doodle*.

Vine Character in *CLAREL*. Certainly Vine is the most enigmatic figure in the poem. Clarel and NEHEMIAH meet this middle-aged man at the Sepulcher of Kings in JERUSALEM. Unlike the other pilgrims, he divulges little about his past, and the narrator does little to characterize his biography or his thinking. Yet he is a charismatic personality—in part because he seems to have the

The battle of Antietam is the subject of Melville's Civil War poem "The Victor of Antietam (1862)," which extols General McClellan as the "stormer" avenging the defeat of Bull Run. (Library of Congress)

exquisite taste of an artist. His very self-absorption and isolation appeal to the pilgrims, who are drawn to a man who refuses to pander to others or to reveal much about himself.

Viner Minor character in OMOO. John JERMIN last saw his former shipmate, VINER, 15 years before the *Julia* weighs anchor off Papeete. When the two meet again, it is nothing short of a miracle, as Viner was thought to have been lost at sea. He and Jermin have a jolly reunion, after which Viner signs on as third mate aboard the *Julia*.

Virgin In chapter LXXXI of MOBY-DICK, the PEQUOD meets the *Jungfrau*, or the *Virgin*. Its captain, Derick DE

DEER of Bremen, knows nothing about Moby-Dick, but his ship soon competes with AHAB's in chasing after another whale, with the *Pequod* eventually gaining the prize.

Voltaire (François Marie Arouet) (1694–1778) Considered one of the thinkers who inspired the FRENCH REVOLUTION, Voltaire was also the embodiment of the Enlightenment. He wrote many works of philosophy and literature, but he is particularly known for his skeptical attitude toward humanity and his difficult relationships with European monarchs. He spent some years in exile in England. He is named in BILLY BUDD, SAILOR as one of those philosophers whose name is given to ships.

"A Way-Side Weed" (1924) Poem in WEEDS AND WILD-INGS. An entry in "The Year" section of the collection, "A Way-Side Weed" is clearly an autumnal verse, picturing a "charioteer from villa fine" cutting down "Golden Rod," the "sceptre" of "October's god" as he whips his horses along the road.

"The Weaver" (1891) Poem in TIMOLEON. Melville presents a stark picture of a solitary, impoverished artisan in a mud hut eternally weaving a shawl "for Arva's shrine." The import of the shrine is unclear, although evidence points to a connection to the Muslim Holy City of Mecca, which appears in the manuscript (though not in the published poem). Merwa, sometimes spelled "Marva," is a hill near Mecca. The figure of the weaver in this obscure poem seems to bear a greater resemblance to the artist who labors alone and often in poverty to glorify art than to the figure of Fate—although the two interpretations are not mutually exclusive.

Weeds and Wildings Chiefly: With a Rose or Two **(1924)** Poetry collection. This last of Melville's collections of poetry remained unpublished when he died on September 28, 1891, but less than two months earlier, his wife Lizzie MELVILLE had made a fair copy of the volume for the printer. *Weeds and Wildings* was in fact a book of poems for Lizzie, to whom Melville seems to have grown close again toward the end of his life. The collection employs the sort of floral symbolism that the couple favored during their courtship and early marriage, when they had both been interested in the fashionable "LANGUAGE OF FLOWERS." The book is dedicated to Lizzie, whom Melville calls "Winnefred." The "Clover Dedication to Winnefred" speaks of their mutual affection for clover—especially the red clover that grew at ARROWHEAD—and of the four-leaf clover he found on their wedding day. As a headnote to the volume, Melville chose a passage from their friend Nathaniel HAWTHORNE's posthumously published *Dolliver Romance* (1864): "Youth, however eclipsed for a season is the proper, permanent, and genuine condition of man; and if we look closely into this dreary delusion of growing old, we shall find that it never absolutely succeeds in laying hold of our innermost convictions." The poems that follow fall into two sec-

tions. The first, dedicated to "Weeds and Wildings," consists of three parts: "The Year," "This, That and the Other," and "Rip Van Winkle's Lilac." The second section, "A Rose or Two," consists of two parts: "As They Fell" and an untitled section that includes two poems, "THE ROSE FARMER" and "L'ENVOI."

Wellington, duke of (Arthur Wellesley) (1769–1982) British general and statesman. Along with Horatio NELSON, the duke of Wellington was the great warrior of his age. He defeated Napoleon's forces at Waterloo,

In Weeds and Wildings, *his book of mature poetry, Melville showed his affection for his wife, Elizabeth Shaw Melville, pictured here at age 50 in 1874.* (Berkshire Athenaeum)

thus ending the French threat to England and to the European continent. In BILLY BUDD, SAILOR, the narrator compares Nelson and Wellington, suggesting that Nelson is the greater hero because of his greater willingness to risk his own life in battle.

whaling   Captain John Smith received permission from the British Crown to hunt whales in 1614. At first American colonists waited for whales to wash ashore, but soon they emulated the natives by taking off in small boats to chase their prey. By 1650, there was a whaling industry that stretched from Nantucket in the north to as far south as the New Jersey shore. The chief prize was whale oil, especially after the discovery that sperm whales contained so much of it in their huge heads. More than 100 barrels of oil could be extracted from a single sperm whale for use in candles and other lighting as well as in unguents. A substance called ambergris, which is found in the intestines of sperm whales, was used in French perfume and to spice wines and food. In China, it was used as an aphrodisiac. Whalebones were also put to use in such products as women's corsets. In the 1730s huge iron try-pots were encased in brick hearths aboard ships so that the whale blubber could be "tried," or melted into oil. By the early 19th century, a thriving shipyard business in New England was building bigger and bigger ships to explore fishing grounds as far away as Japan. When Melville boarded his first whaler in 1841, he became part of the most prosperous period of whaling (1825 to 1860). Shipowners made enormous profits that seemed to grow each year. Melville biographer Laurie Robertson-Lorant notes that in "1857 alone, 329 vessels, valued at over $12 million and employing twelve thousand seamen, left New Bedford for the Pacific grounds."

Melville's younger brother Thomas became a whaler at the age of 16 in 1846. The idea of adventure at sea, and of possibly acquiring a fortune, was fostered by Richard Henry DANA's book *Two Years Before the Mast*, and by the writings of explorers such as Charles WILKES, who stimulated Melville's imagination and his desire to acquire firsthand experience at sea.

Life aboard a whaler proved an education in itself. Melville had 26 shipmates: four Portuguese, three African Americans, one Scotsman, one Englishman, and the rest Americans of different ethnicities. He slept on a straw mattress underneath bulkheads. The close quarters were stifling and dangerous. A young sailor was a target for sexual advances, and there was precious little room to avoid intimate encounters. Lice, bugs, and rats were the common companions of sailors. The smells of tobacco, trash, liquor, and human waste were unavoidable. Food was barely edible in a form of salted beef cut with pocket knives. There were few vegetables; raw carrots were prized but seldom available. There were various sweet concoctions made from molasses

and flour and raisins, but they were reserved for Sundays and special occasions. Coffee, in anything like a pure form, was never served. Instead, sailors drank a mixture of coffee, tea, and molasses called "longlick." Under these harsh conditions men broke and deserted—as Melville would do on the ACUSHNET.

Yet Melville remained fascinated by whales and the sea, eagerly reading Owen CHASE's *Narrative of the Most Extraordinary and Distressing Shipwreck of the Whale-Ship Essex* (1821), which formed the germ of MOBY-DICK and its account of a malevolent whale that attacks the PEQUOD and destroys it. According to Robertson-Lorant, Melville also read Harry Halyard's pulp novel *Wharton the Whale-Killer!, or the Pride of the Pacific*, in which a whale destroys a ship. During his time on the *Acushnet*, Melville heard a story about a swordfish piercing the hull of a ship.

The technology of the whale hunt, as Melville experienced it off the coast of Brazil in 1841, consisted of a harpoon with a single hooked blade. A tarred line of hemp coiled in a wooden tub was attached to the harpoon. Lines had to be carefully maintained, since many men lost limbs and even lives getting caught in their own lines.

The action of a whale hunt was exciting and terrifying. In among agitated whales, the whalers had to contend with geysers of blood that would attract other whales who would feed on each other. After striking the whale, the whaler had to be prepared to be shot forward in a wild pattern as the panicked whale tried to escape. The process of coralling dead whales and getting them aboard (described memorably in *Moby-Dick*) proved to be exhausting. The exhilaration of the hunt gave way to lethargy.

"When Forth the Shepherd Leads the Flock" (1924) Poem in WEEDS AND WILDINGS. This poem, perhaps intended as the second in the volume and in the section called "The Year," employs the "LANGUAGE OF FLOWERS" to provide the collection with its title:

> When stir the freshening airs
> Forerunning showers to meads,
> And Dandelions prance,
> Then Heart-Free shares the dance—
> A Wilding with the Weeds!

Like Melville's poems themselves, weeds and wildflowers are eschewed by all but a few, who "Love them, reprieve them, / Retrieve and inweave them." Unable to find an audience for his poetic works, Melville still could not stop them from growing wild and free and "[p]rofitless to man."

White-Jacket   The eponymous hero and narrator of Melville's fifth book. Readers never learn the true name of this two-dimensional character, who is known only by the symbolic white jacket, "of a Quakerish amplitude about the skirts," that sets him apart from his crewmates. Twice the jacket nearly causes his death, and in order to be reborn at the end of his voyage aboard the U.S.S. *NEVERSINK*, he must cut himself free of his outer garment.

But White-Jacket himself is never really fleshed out in the book. This is how it should be, in fact, because he is merely a mouthpiece for Melville, who funnels through White-Jacket the impressions he himself garnered during his 14 months of service aboard the U.S.S. *UNITED STATES* during 1843 and 1844. But *White-Jacket* is not in fact solely an autobiography, neither is it a novel per se. Instead, it is an amalgam of elements taken from a variety of genres, including the mariner's reminiscence and the political broadside, and it is altogether fitting that it should be related by a personage who is neither fully three-dimensional nor allegorical. Instead, White-Jacket is something in between, a character who is more than he appears and yet, somehow, still an empty suit.

White-Jacket; or, The World in a Man-of-War Melville's fifth book, published in 1850. During five months in the summer and autumn of 1849, Melville, singed by *MARDI*'s poor reception and spurred by the need to support his wife and newborn son, managed to turn out two books. *REDBURN* and *White-Jacket* are both highly autobiographical, which undoubtedly contributed to the speed with which they were composed and, perhaps, to Melville's disregard for these creations.

Of the two, *White-Jacket* is more closely based on fact. In August 1843, Melville left his job as a clerk in Honolulu, HAWAII, abruptly when the *ACUSHNET*, the whaler he had deserted two years earlier in the MARQUESAS, pulled into port. Enlisting in the U.S. Navy as an ordinary seaman, Melville served 14 months on board the frigate *UNITED STATES* during its homeward voyage to Boston. It would be the last of his working voyages, and it provided him not only with the material for his fifth book, but also with a profound revulsion against the injustices that riddled navy life. Melville originally may have intended *White-Jacket* to be a potboiler, but by making life aboard a man-of-war stand for

Melville spent 14 months on the navy frigate United States *in 1843–44. Later, he drew on his experience to write* White-Jacket.
(Library of Congress)

life in the world at large, and by turning FLOGGING into a symbol of man's inhumanity to man, he contributed to the escalating debate about slavery.

SYNOPSIS

Chapter 1: "The Jacket"
The narrator introduces himself by describing his exterior—specifically, the origins of the white jacket that lends him his moniker aboard the frigate NEVERSINK. As the ship prepares to leave the port of Callao, Peru, for the rough voyage around Cape Horn and up the east coast of the Americas, he finds that he is unable to obtain a regulation sailor's pea jacket. For lack of better materials, he fashions a padded jacket for himself, using a shirt as a foundation. Ill-fitting and odd-looking, the garment sets him apart from his crewmates not only because of its "Quakerish amplitude about the skirts," but also because of its whiteness. Unable to obtain any waterproof "paint" from the ship's paint room, the narrator is obliged to go about wearing a conspicuous outer shell that makes him look, on a dark night, like "the White Lady of Avenel," a supernatural being created by Sir Walter Scott. Before his tale is done, WHITE-JACKET's outerwear will very nearly prove to be his shroud.

Chapters 2–8: "Homeward Bound"; "A Glance at the Principal Divisions into Which a Man-of-War's Crew Is Divided"; "Jack Chase"; "Jack Chase on a Spanish Quarter-Deck"; "The Quarter-Deck Officers, Warrant Officers, and Berth-Deck Underlings of a Man-of-War; Where They Live in the Ship; How They Live; Their Social Standing on Shipboard; and What Sort of Gentlemen They Are"; "Breakfast, Dinner, and Supper"; "Selvagee Contrasted with Mad Jack"
As the *Neversink* weighs anchor, White-Jacket mans his station aloft, loosing the main royal sail. Melville then launches into a description of the hierarchy that shapes the crew aboard a man-of-war. White-Jacket counts himself lucky to be among those assigned to the topsails, a group captained by Jack CHASE, a noble, literate, and gentlemanly fellow who seems almost too good to be true—despite having a real-life counterpart among Melville's shipmates aboard the *United States*. Jack Chase is compared with the garrulous, vulgar TUBBS, whose chief sin seems to be his long association with whaling ships. White-Jacket adds, in an aside, that he was glad never to have spoken of his own whaling experiences.

White-Jacket then tells the tale of Jack Chase's recent desertion from the *Neversink,* turning it into a parable illustrating the man's nobility: he had left the ship to join the civil war in Peru. No more is heard of him until, months later, a Peruvian sloop-of-war, carrying a handsome officer, pulls up alongside the *Neversink.* Captain CLARET of the *Neversink* recognizes the officer as Jack Chase and demands his return. Instead of

receiving punishment, however, Chase is immediately restored to his old command.

The *Neversink,* as the flagship of the fleet, carries a commodore on board. Modeled on Thomas ap Catesby Jones, a hero of the War of 1812, the commodore is never named. The second in command is Captain Claret, his improbable name a clear indication of his probable status as a fictional composite. Various lieutenants and other officers are described. When Melville reaches the ranks of the midshipmen, *White-Jacket* first reveals its status as, among other things, a jeremiad. The midshipmen are privileged boys sent to sea in order to learn to become commodores, and they are permitted to wield power long before they have earned it.

Melville then details another of his many complaints about the navy: the crew, the very men responsible for performing virtually all the real labor aboard, are required to take all three meals within an eight-hour period, while their superiors dine at more regular intervals.

Then, by way of conveying the vast panorama of personalities on board, the narrator describes two of the quarterdeck lieutenants: the effete SELVAGEE, who was drawn to the navy by the romance of the sea, and MAD JACK, a born tar with a weakness for drink.

Chapters 9–13: "Of the Pockets That Were in the Jacket"; "From Pockets to Pickpockets"; "The Pursuit of Poetry Under Difficulties"; "The Good or Bad Temper of Man-of-War's Men, in a Great Degree, Attributable to Their Particular Stations and Duties Aboard Ship"; "A Man-of-War Hermit in a Mob"
White-Jacket describes with some satisfaction the various pockets he has sewn into his jacket. He is thus able to store most of his valuables on his person—until, that is, some of his unscrupulous shipmates discover his secret. Fear of being accosted provokes White-Jacket to rid himself of pockets and Melville to discourse on the generally lax morals of sailors.

White-Jacket describes some of the quirky individuals aboard. One of them is LEMSFORD, a gentlemanly soul who manages to compose poetry on the gundeck. Another is QUOIN, an evil-tempered little man who yet loves the guns he mans together with his mates PRIMING and CYLINDER. NORD, a taciturn, withdrawn main topsail man, is every bit as literate as Jack Chase, and he becomes a particular friend of White-Jacket, as does WILLIAMS, who formerly was a Yankee peddler and pedagogue.

Chapters 14–15: "A Draught in a Man-of-War"; "A Salt-Junk Club in a Man-of-War, with a Notice to Quit"
The American naval custom of allotting a small daily portion of grog, a type of alcoholic beverage, is discussed in the context of a grog shortage on board the *Neversink.* So important is grog to the morale of the

crew that they manufacture their own drink from cologne, sugar, and tar.

The division of the sailors into messes—dining cohorts—is discussed and the ship's dignified cook, OLD COFFEE, together with his assistants, SUNSHINE, ROSE-WATER, and MAY-DAY, is described. The members of the mess themselves take turns making duff (a pudding composed of flour, raisins, and beef fat), but when White-Jacket's turn comes around, the other members' prejudice against him makes itself plain: they dislike his duff and they subsequently expel him from their mess. White-Jacket is fortunate afterward to be welcomed into Jack Chase's mess.

Chapters 16–19: "General Training in a Man-of-War"; "Away! Second, Third, and Fourth Cutters, Away!"; "A Man-of-War Full as a Nut"; "The Jacket Aloft"
White-Jacket describes maneuvers aboard the man-of-war. He details how, on such a ship, two lifebuoys are perpetually manned by individuals armed with hatchets prepared to cut the lifesavers loose. But the lifebuoys on board the *Neversink* are not buoyant, as the drowning of their creator, the cooper BUNGS, demonstrates.

The next night, White-Jacket is himself nearly tossed overboard when he is taken to be the cooper's ghost. In the habit of meditating aloft at night, the glow of his white jacket betrays his presence to the men on watch, who attempt to throw him off the ship. This narrow escape prompts White-Jacket to plead with the first lieutenant for some tar with which to color his jacket, but he is again turned away.

Chapters 20–22: "How They Sleep in a Man-of-War"; "One Reason Why Man-of-War's Men Are Generally Short-Lived"; "Wash-Day and House-Cleaning in a Man-of-War"
White-Jacket describes the closeness of the sleeping quarters aboard a man-of-war, where each man is allowed only 18 inches for the width of his hammock. The subject of hammocks leads him to the subject of watches—and the book once again becomes a broadside, as Melville bewails the lack of sleep suffered by those sailors on duty.

The subject of hammocks gives way to a discussion of cleaning; clean hammocks and laundry and decks all seem to require a general flooding which keeps the sailors perpetually cold and damp—and subsequently ill.

Chapters 23–29: "Theatricals in a Man-of-War"; "Introductory to Cape Horn"; "The Dog-Days Off Cape Horn"; "The Pitch of the Cape"; "Some Thoughts Growing Out of Mad Jack's Countermanding His Superior's Order"; "Edging Away"; "The Night-Watches"
Independence Day comes as the *Neversink* approaches CAPE HORN. Customarily the holiday is celebrated in the navy with a double allowance of spirits, but since there is no grog on board, Captain Claret proposes that the

men substitute theatricals for drunkenness. The men present "The Old Wagon Paid Off!," a nautical drama starring Jack Chase, to roaring applause on all sides. White-Jacket, for his part, delights in the democratic mingling of officers and seamen.

The hilarity and warm feeling fade quickly, however, as the ship approaches Cape Horn. The trip around the Cape is notoriously rough, but as the *Neversink* draws closer, the wind dies even as the weather grows colder. Fearful that the crew will freeze, the officers order the men to "skylark"—that is, to act out in whatever fashion they choose.

The crew sights a ship in full sail, and as she passes her lieutenant calls out a warning about the winds at the Cape. Suddenly, the *Neversink* is caught up in a gale. When Captain Claret's orders nearly cause the ship to go down, Mad Jack countermands him. The ship is saved, and afterward White-Jacket speculates about the captain's sobriety as Melville fulminates about naval officers who rise to the level of their own incompetence.

The glories of Cape Horn are nevertheless extolled—Melville even has some fun with the captain's Polynesian servant, WOOLOO, who believes the hailstones are beads. White-Jacket hails every snowsquall, for snow allows him—but not the other sailors, in dark clothing—to fade into obscurity.

Chapters 30–31: "A Peep Through a Port-Hole at the Subterranean Parts of a Man-of-War"; "The Gunner Under Hatches"
White-Jacket takes readers on a tour of the lower decks of the man-of-war, which provides Melville with an opportunity to indulge in his habit of piling up facts. A chapter devoted to the gunner's duties serves the same purpose.

Chapters 32–37: "A Dish of Dunderfunk"; "A Flogging"; "Some of the Evil Effects of Flogging"; "Flogging Not Lawful"; "Flogging Not Necessary"; "Some Superior Old 'London Dock' From the Wine-Coolers of Neptune"
A humorous interlude concerning the theft of a "dish of dunderfunk"—which the true owner describes as "a cruel nice dish"—precedes three chapters devoted to the incendiary subject of flogging. White-Jacket describes in detail all the sadistic ceremony devoted to making an example of men who have somehow misbehaved. In this case, four sailors, having been imprisoned for fighting, are now brought before the entire crew, stripped, and tied to wooden grates before being whipped with a cat o' nine tails. One of these sailors, a handsome 19-year-old, is utterly humiliated when he is reduced to tears and pleading.

Melville spends the next three chapters making the case that flogging is not only inhumane but also unlawful, and he appeals to Congress to outlaw the practice.

Another humorous bookend follows: the *Neversink* runs across several barrels found to contain port, which is thereafter doled out to the crew twice daily.

Chapter 38: "The Chaplain and Chapel in a Man-of-War"
This chapter, devoted to the chaplain and chapel aboard the man-of-war, points out the hypocrisy of preaching peace aboard a vessel whose job it is to make war. What is more, Melville contends, obligatory attendance at Sunday services violates the First Amendment's prohibition against intermingling church and state.

Chapters 39–40: "The Frigate in Harbour—The Boats—Grand State Reception of the Commodore"; "Some of the Ceremonies in a Man-of-War Unnecessary and Injurious"
The *Neversink* sails into the harbor at Rio de Janeiro. Claret decides to pay a visit on a neighboring English craft, and White-Jacket finds himself recruited as one of the captain's bargemen. The elaborate ceremonies accompanying this trip and the captain's return to the *Neversink* have been handed down from the English navy and serve to underscore the gulf dividing the officers from the men they command. Melville asks that some "discreet, but democratic, legislation" put an end to these degrading and antiquated practices.

Chapters 41–47: "A Man-of-War Library; Killing Time in a Man-of-War in Harbour"; "Smuggling in a Man-of-War"; "A Knave in Office in a Man-of-War"; "Publishing Poetry in a Man-of-War"; "The Commodore of the Poop, and One of 'The People' Under the Hands of the Surgeon"; "An Auction in a Man-of-War"
Time weighs heavily on the crew of the *Neversink*, who have little meaningful work to perform and even less liberty. Stuck on the ship, White-Jacket peruses the ship's library, providing Melville with an opportunity to list several of his favorite books. Other pastimes are described, including tattooing, brightwork polishing, topside promenading, playing checkers, daydreaming, and sleeping. Some of the men engage in illicit gambling and others in smuggling. YARN, the boatswain, manages to smuggle liquor aboard, as does BLAND, the master-at-arms charged with flogging the very individuals who have become drunk on the spirits he brought onto the man-of-war. These episodes constitute, in Melville's words, "the most curious evidence of the almost incredible corruption pervading nearly all ranks in some men-of-war." Bland's accomplice, an old marine named SCRIGGS, confesses all to Captain Claret, with the result that Bland is merely cashiered and then officially reinstated.

Lemsford passes the time writing poetry, whose manuscripts he stores in one of the unused guns on board—unused, that is, until one morning the *Neversink* returns a shore salute, shooting the pages into the air. This, Jack Chase remarks, is certainly one way to publish.

The *Neversink* engages in a bit of friendly rivalry with neighboring ships, seeing which can loosen and furl their sails the fastest. When an ambitious lieutenant shouts at a mizzen-top captain named BALDY, the sailor overexerts himself and falls to the deck. He is never the same. White-Jacket cites another, similar event that happened on an English ship moored nearby. Melville asks rhetorically, "Why mince the Matter? The death of most of these man-of-war's men lies at the door of the souls of those officers, who, while safely standing on deck themselves, scruple not to sacrifice an immortal man or two. . . ."

Another means of relieving the tedium of lying at anchor is the purser's auction, when dead sailors' goods are sold off on board. After witnessing one such event, White-Jacket decides to auction off his cursed outer garment, but the men immediately recognize it for what it is, and no bids are made.

Chapters 48–50: "Purser, Purser's Steward, and Postmaster in a Man-of-War"; "Rumours of a War, and How They Were Received by the Population of the Neversink"; "The Bay of All Beauties"
Melville devotes a chapter to describing the duties of the purser (a kind of ship's accountant), the purser's steward, and the postmaster on a man-of-war. Rumors of war with England reach the ship but do little to inspire the crew, because they, unlike the ambitious officer class, have nothing of gain from the glory of battle and everything to lose. The beauties of Rio are described.

Chapters 51–55: "One of 'The People' Has an Audience with the Commodore and the Captain on the Quarter-Deck"; "Something Concerning Midshipmen"; "Seafaring Persons Peculiarly Subject to Being Under the Weather—The Effects of This Upon a Man-of-War Captain"; "'The People' are Given Liberty"; "Midshipmen Entering the Navy Early"
Jack Chase, determined to obtain at least one day of shore leave for his men, approaches Captain Claret with the request. Just at that moment the commodore happens to be passing by and, charmed by Jack's manner, he grants the men liberty.

The next morning, a particularly egregious flogging takes place. The fact that the poor miscreant was punished on orders from a midshipman provides Melville with an opportunity to inveigh against the imbalance of power aboard a man-of-war. Although Melville is careful to say that not all midshipmen are evil and that Captain Claret, in spite of everything, is a decent enough commander, the very fact that the Articles of War grant these officers absolute power guarantees that they will exercise it—often arbitrarily.

The sailors—whom White-Jacket refers to as "the people"—are given their shore leave. White-Jacket goes ashore with Jack Chase's party, which returns to the ship promptly and in good order. Others, however, are brought back drunk, beaten, and unconscious. From this evidence White-Jacket draws the conclusion that such disorder is inevitable when "the people" are released from the strain of arbitrary discipline. Melville injects an aside here arguing that midshipmen not be sent to sea when they are mere boys, for they are too impressionable not to pick up the prejudices and bad habits of their superiors, which are thus carried into the next generation of officers.

Chapters 56–63: "A Shore Emperor on Board a Man-of-War"; "The Emperor Reviews 'The People' at Quarters"; "A Quarter-Deck Officer Before the Mast"; "A Man-of-War Button Divides Two Brothers"; "A Man-of-War's Man Shot At"; "The Surgeon of the Fleet"; "A Consultation of Man-of-War Surgeons"; "The Operation"

The emperor of Brazil, Dom PEDRO II, pays a call on the *Neversink*. His visit occasions all manner of pomp and circumstance. The sailors are reviewed in their places, and in the process, one of the royal hangers-on is tripped up by his own sword. Shortly afterward, the royal party withdraws.

Somewhat shorthanded, the *Neversink* takes on some men from a U.S. sloop-of-war anchored nearby. One of these, a former officer who had been stripped of his rank when alcohol caused him to abandon his command, claims an acquaintance with the first lieutenant, Mr. BRIDEWELL. This man, named MANDEVILLE, seems not to have improved over the years. Little more than a week goes by before he is flogged for having become intoxicated on smuggled spirits.

Mandeville's shameless behavior contrasts with that of a young sailor he calls FRANK, who tells White-Jacket of his despair that his lowly status will be discovered by his brother, a midshipman aboard a ship bringing provisions to the naval squadron in Rio.

White-Jacket relates the story of another tar, who, forbidden to take shore leave, slips overboard and tries to swim ashore. Spotted by a sentry, the man refuses to stop and is shot in the thigh. The man is brought so low by loss of blood that the surgeon of the fleet, Cadwallader Cuticle, does not immediately attempt to remove the bullet. Instead, the self-involved—even grotesque—Cuticle invites other surgeons from the fleet to consult with him. They are all of the opinion that the leg, bad as it is, should not be amputated. Cuticle goes ahead nonetheless, expatiating on his methods even as the poor sailor lies fainting beneath the saw. The operation is declared a success, but the patient dies shortly thereafter.

Chapters 64–67: "Man-of-War Trophies"; "A Man-of-War Race"; "White-Jacket Arraigned at the Mast"

The order to weigh anchor comes at last, and the *Neversink* races an English frigate and a French man-of-war out of the harbor. With the wind at their backs and

headed for home, the men become giddy. Seeking outlets for their excess energy, they engage in a number of stylized battles. One of these, head-bumping, is a particular favorite of the captain, who repeatedly pits the powerful black cook's assistant, MAY-DAY, against the slender mulatto ROSE-WATER. May-Day prevails, and he begins to develop contempt for Rose-Water, going so far as to call him a "nigger." This insult causes a genuine fight, which results in both men being flogged.

The arbitrariness of shipboard justice eventually touches White-Jacket, who is accused of being absent from his post. Although he has diligently performed what he thought to be his duties, on paper he has been assigned another position. Threatened with flogging for insubordination, White-Jacket determines that he will jump overboard first—taking the captain with him. Fortunately, a marine corporal, COLBROOK, and Jack Chase intervene, daring to inform the captain the White-Jacket has done his duty.

Chapters 68–73: "A Man-of-War Fountain, and Other Things"; "Prayers at the Guns"; "Monthly Muster Round the Capstan"; "The Genealogy of the Articles of War"; "'Herein Are the Good Ordinances of the Sea, Which Wise Men, Who Voyaged Round the World, Gave to Our Ancestors, and Which Constitute the Books of the Science of Good Customs'"; "Night and Day Gambling in a Man-of-War"

White-Jacket returns to his survey of the man-of-war, detailing among other things the scuttlebutt, a sort of shipboard water cooler that is the site of much gossiping. He discusses the mandatory daily prayer sessions and the monthly "muster round the capstan," when the officers review the men. On this last occasion, the Articles of War are also read aloud (which Melville repeats, with commentary).

Melville devotes a chapter to the origins of the Articles of War and another to the manner in which they are abused. As if to underscore the hypocrisy that characterizes the U.S. Navy, White-Jacket next discusses how illicit gambling aboard the man-of-war has given rise to a system of internal spies who curry favor with the officers by reporting on their fellow crew members.

Chapters 74–82: "The Main-Top at Night"; "'Sink, Burn, and Destroy'"; "The Chains"; "The Hospital in a Man-of-War"; "Dismal Times in the Mess"; "How Man-of-War's Men Die at Sea"; "The Last Stitch"; "How They Bury a Man-of-War's Man at Sea"; "What Remains of a Man-of-War's Man After His Burial at Sea"

Lounging on the main-top at night, Jack Chase quotes poetry and others tell tales. An old black sailor named Tawney tells how, during the War of 1812, he was impressed from a merchant ship by the British and forced to fight against his countrymen. Jack Chase adds an account of his participation in the Battle of Navarino, when a combined force of British, French, and

Russians vanquished the Turks during the Greek War of Independence.

White-Jacket contrasts these scenes of battle with the peacefulness he finds among the chains, small platforms outside the hull to which he sometimes retreats. As the *Neversink* approaches the equator, the heat becomes unbearable, and some of the men grow ill. Among them is SHENLY, who is confined to the ship's airless sickbay. His messmates are ordered to take turns sitting with him, but when White-Jacket assumes the watch, he finds Shenly to be dying. Quickly and unceremoniously the corpse is washed, dressed, sewn up in a bit of sailcloth, and dumped overboard.

Chapters 83–90: "A Man-of-War College"; "Man-of-War Barbers"; "The Great Massacre of the Beards"; "The Rebels Brought to the Mast"; "Old Ushant at the Gangway"; "Flogging Through the Fleet"; "The Social State in a Man-of-War"; "The Manning of Navies"
White-Jacket resumes his portrait of the man-of-war world, describing an onboard school for midshipmen and the important role played by the ship's barbers, who are responsible for the grooming of 200 heads of hair and 500 beards. He next launches into an account of what he terms the "Massacre of the Beards," which takes place when Captain Claret, invoking navy regulations, commands that all beards be shaved. Loath to give up this last remnant of their individuality, the men at first resist, then most capitulate. Only a few refuse to obey the captain's order. The final holdout is an old sailor called USHANT, who submits to a flogging rather than a shave.

Horrible as the sight of Ushant's punishment is, there is worse. White-Jacket describes the practice of "keel-hauling," in which the victim is pulled back and forth underneath the ship's hull. Another sadistic punishment is known as "flogging through the fleet," in which the culprit is rowed from one ship in the fleet to another, receiving a flogging on each. This punishment is never inflicted except by authority of a court-martial, and then only for particularly grievous offenses. Still, the inhumanity of the procedure speaks for itself. White-Jacket comments tersely: "While the *Neversink* was in the Pacific, an American sailor, who had deposited a vote for General Harrison for President of the United States, was flogged through the fleet."

White-Jacket adds to his catalogue of evils aboard a man-of-war the marines carried by all American warships. These marines, it seems to the narrator, serve no purpose other than to impose martial discipline on the seamen. And, he adds, the seamen are not honestly recruited. Many, lured by the blandishments of "crimps," who act as sailor headhunters, are so dismayed by what they find on board that they commit suicide. Volunteers, it seems, are hard to come by. Many of the ordinary seamen in the American navy are foreign-ers who had no idea what they were getting into; similarly, black slaves are sometimes forced to serve in warships. The current methods of manning an American warship, he says, are not much different from impressment, the hated foreign practice of kidnapping men and compelling them to serve in the military.

Chapter 91: "Smoking-Club in a Man-of-War, with Scenes on the Gun-Deck Drawing Near Home"
The tone of the book suddenly shifts as White-Jacket trains his focus on more pleasant matters, portraying the ship's galley as a kind of smoking club. As the ship nears land, the conversation shifts from shipboard matters to what the men plan to do with themselves when they reach shore. White-Jacket reports the remarkable fact that nine out of ten of them do not intend to return to the navy.

Chapter 92–The End: "The Last of the Jacket"; "Cable and Anchor All Clear"; "The End"
White-Jacket relates the circumstances of how his jacket, for the second time, nearly becomes his shroud. Mounting to the top-mast, he loses his balance when the ship unexpectedly plunges. Reaching out for what he thinks is the sail, he grasps only the heavy skirts of his jacket, and he is pitched overboard. Plunged into the sea, where his absorbent jacket weights him down, White-Jacket feels himself to be dying. Then he undergoes a kind of birth experience, managing to cut himself free, at last, from the white encumbrance that has marked his existence on board the *Neversink*. He gets free just in time: thinking the white jacket is a white shark who will eat the man overboard, some of the other sailors run it through with harpoons. Minutes later, the sailor who had been White-Jacket is back at his post. Shortly thereafter, the ship arrives in Norfolk, Virginia, the men disperse, and Melville ends his book with a final section comparing the man-of-war with the greater world.

PUBLICATION HISTORY

In writing *White-Jacket*, Melville drew heavily on published sources of information about men-of-war and on the 19th-century convention of the nautical memoir. The book has no real plot other than that provided by the voyage itself, and its narrator is little more than an overstuffed, patently emblematic white jacket. Still, the documentary aspects of the book appealed to readers, and Melville's polemical zeal forwarded the cause of those who sought to outlaw corporal punishment in the navy.

Melville knew that even as he wrote his diatribes against flogging, Congress was debating a bill to outlaw the practice. Perhaps the book's topicality, together with *Redburn*'s then current popularity, were factors that convinced HARPER & BROTHERS to advance Melville

$500 for *White-Jacket* in September 1849. The "Note" that prefaced the American edition certainly emphasized the book's autobiographical basis:

> In the year 1843 I shipped as "Ordinary seaman" on board of a United States frigate, then lying in a harbour of the Pacific Ocean. After remaining in this frigate for more than a year, I was discharged from the service upon the vessel's arrival home. My man-of-war experiences and observations are incorporated in the present volume.

Owing to concerns about COPYRIGHT infringement, *White-Jacket* was published first in England, where Melville himself negotiated with Richard BENTLEY for an advance of £200. The book that appeared in England in January 1850, however, carried a far different author's Preface, which stressed that "the object of this work is not to portray the particular man-of-war in which the author sailed. . . ." In England, apparently, Melville wanted *White-Jacket* to be perceived as fiction; in America, where corporal punishment in the navy was a controversial subject, he wanted his book to be read as a factual account.

In either event, Melville was clear about his goal in turning out two books in such quick succession. As he wrote his father-in-law, Judge Lemuel SHAW, "my only desire for their 'success' (as it is called) springs from my pocket & not from my heart. So far as I am individually concerned, & independent of my pocket, it is my desire to write those sorts of books which are said to 'fail.'" Unfortunately, *White-Jacket* proved to be a commercial failure, selling fewer than 400 copies in England by March 1852 and less than four thousand copies in the U.S. by April 1851. Melville's next book, another nautical tale titled *MOBY-DICK,* represented his best efforts. But it, too, was a commercial failure, as was its successor, *PIERRE.* As Melville's reputation declined, so did sales of all his books. Over the next quarter century, *White-Jacket* would only earn him another $357 in royalties.

Wiley & Putnam Publisher. Successor to the New York publishing firm Wiley & Long, Wiley & Putnam came into being after George Palmer Putnam succeeded George Long as John Wiley's partner in 1838. In 1846, Putnam was acting as the firm's London representative when Gansevoort MELVILLE showed him the manuscript of *TYPEE.* The following March, Wiley & Putnam published the American edition of the novel. The firm of Wiley & Putnam was dissolved the following year, and in 1848 Putnam established his own firm, which had a continuing relationship with Melville, publishing many of his short stories, as well as *ISRAEL POTTER,* in *PUTNAM'S MAGAZINE* and bringing out *CLAREL* in the United States and Britain.

Wilkes, Charles Said to be the model for AHAB in *MOBY-DICK,* Wilkes, a naval officer, wrote *Narrative of the U.S. Exploring Expedition During the Years 1838, 1839, 1840, 1841, 1842,* which was published in five volumes. Wilkes was well known for his fearlessness, arrogance, and anger. He had a mystique and authority that apply to Ahab as well. As sailors, they undertook similar voyages. One of Melville's cousins, Han Gansevoort, was aboard the *Vincennes,* the flagship of Wilkes's 1840 expedition to Antarctica. Officially called the United States Naval Exploring Expedition, it was charged with making scientific observations and collecting data for naturalists. The expedition's zoological and botanical specimens formed the core of the National Museum of Natural History, later incorporated into the Smithsonian Institution. Unquestionably Wilkes's accounts of his voyages helped to stimulate Melville's desire to go to sea.

Williams Minor character in *WHITE-JACKET.* A maintopman aboard the *NEVERSINK,* Williams is a former peddler and pedagogue from Maine whose humorous personality contrasts vividly with the taciturn NORD, who cuts him dead. Williams probably was based on Griffith Williams, a sailor who enlisted on the U.S.S. *UNITED STATES* with Melville.

Wilson Character in *OMOO.* Wilson is the acting British consul in Papeetee and a friend of the much-hated Captain Guy of the whaler *Julia.* Wilson, in his turn, becomes much hated when he incites the riot onboard the *Julia* with his harsh controls, then imprisons and "trie" the "mutineers." Wilson was based on Charles Burnett Wilson, a British missionary's son who replaced George Pritchard as acting British consul in Papeetee when Melville was there in 1842 with the *LUCY-ANN.*

Winsome, Mark Character in *The CONFIDENCE MAN.* The name of the "master" who debates with the CONFIDENCE MAN (a.k.a the cosmopolitan) the wisdom of trusting in other people and of soliciting funds from them.

Winwood, Ralph Character in *PIERRE.* He is Pierre's cousin, who paints the second, smaller portrait of Pierre's father. This picture helps convince Pierre that his father has indeed fathered a girl by a woman other than his mother.

"The Wise Virgins to Madam Mirror" *See* "MADAM MIRROR."

women Melville's earliest depictions of women are fanciful and romantic. Others, like the depiction of

ANNATOO in *MARDI*, have been called misogynistic. Melville playfully wrote to Sarah MOREWOOD about *MOBY-DICK*:

> Dont you buy it—dont you read it, when it does come out, because it is by no means the sort of book for you. It is not a peice (sic) of fine feminine Spitalfields silk—but is of the horrible texture of a fabric that should be woven of ships cables & hausers (sic). A Polar wind blows through it, & birds of prey hover over it. Warn all gentle fastidious people from so much as peeping into the book—on risk of a lumbago & sciatics.

Melville later claimed that the only woman he knew who liked *Moby-Dick* was Sophia HAWTHORNE. Melville biographer Laurie Robertson-Lorant compares many of his women characters to "phantom women conjured up by Edgar Allan Poe, except that Poe's fantasy women are usually dead and Melville's are merely mute and mysterious." Like the absence of African Americans in Melville's work, women are simply not "there" in any substantial sense. However, the idea of the feminine is very much alive in his work—as in his depictions of BILLY BUDD and of the bisexual nature of male relationships.

Woodcock, John   Minor character in *ISRAEL POTTER*. He is a country squire who persuades Israel to carry secret papers to Paris, where Benjamin FRANKLIN receives them as American ambassador to France. When Israel returns to England he is secreted at Woodcock's estate, but he must leave after discovering that Woodcock has died and he thus has lost his protector.

wooden-legged man, the   Character in *The CONFIDENCE MAN*. He is suspicious of the NEGRO CRIPPLE, one of the disguises of the CONFIDENCE MAN. The wooden-legged man engages various passengers in discussions about whether the cripple is a fraud or not. Indeed, the wooden-legged man becomes the ship's resident skeptic, the precise opposite of the confidence man who preaches the gospel of charity and trust.

Wooloo   Minor character in *WHITE-JACKET*. Wooloo is the commodore's Polynesian servant on board the *NEVERSINK*. Wooloo is sedate and earnest, and he has never been outside the tropics before. The sailors have some fun with him when, after the ship rounds CAPE HORN, he thinks snow is flour and hailstones are glass beads. When he is exposed to raisins, he picks them out of his food, thinking they are bugs.

Wymontoo   Minor character in *OMOO*. A native of the island of La Dominica, or Hivarhoo, in the MARQUESAS, Wymontoo joins the crew of the *Julia* shortly after the narrator of the novel does. Aboard the whaler, the Marquesan grows both seasick and homesick.

Y

Yankee Doodle Humor magazine. In July 1847, Melville went to NEW YORK CITY to meet with Charles Fenno Hoffman, who had succeeded Evert DUYCKINCK as editor of the *LITERARY WORLD,* for which Melville had reviewed several books. At the time Hoffman's friend Cornelius MATTHEWS was editing *Yankee Doodle,* a weekly humor magazine founded in 1846 as a spinoff of the *Literary World* and modeled on the British *Punch. Yankee Doodle* lasted only a year; but during 1847, at Matthews's request, Melville wrote a number of short, topical pieces for the magazine: "AUTHENTIC ANECDOTES OF 'OLD ZACK,'" "THE NEW PLANET," "ON THE CHINESE JUNK," "ON THE SEA SERPENT," "A SHORT PATENT SERMON," and "VIEW OF THE BARNUM PROPERTY." All but the first were published anonymously.

Melville also used the term "Yankee Doodle" in "Authentic Anecdotes of 'Old Zack'" as the name of the newspaper boss who commands the writer/reporter to visit General Zachary Taylor. Yankee Doodle appears as a character in "On the Chinese Junk" and "View of the Barnum Property" as well.

Yankee Doodle Character in several pieces written by or attributed to Melville and published in the humor magazine *YANKEE DOODLE.* "ON THE CHINESE JUNK" is written from the viewpoint of Yankee Doodle, and in this piece as well as "AUTHENTIC ANECDOTES OF 'OLD ZACK'" and "VIEW OF THE BARNUM PROPERTY," he is presented as the embodiment of the spirit of the magazine.

Yarn ("Old Yarn," "Pipes") Minor character in *WHITE-JACKET.* Yarn is the boatswain aboard the *NEVERSINK* who smuggles illicit liquor aboard the man-of-war. After some of his brandy is stolen, Yarn has the satisfaction of seeing the thief flogged when he is found to be intoxicated. Yarn may have been based, at least in part, on William Hoff, an alcoholic sailor who served aboard the U.S.S. *UNITED STATES* with Melville.

Yillah Character in *MARDI.* This beautiful white-skinned, golden-haired, blue-eyed maiden was born with dark hair and olive skin on the isle of Amma. While still an infant, she was spirited away to Oroolia, where her coloring was transmuted and she was transformed into a flower, which snapped off its vine. Caught up in a seashell, she was then borne to the island of Amma. There the old priest ALEEMA enshrined her as a goddess in the temple of Apo in the glen of Adair.

When TAJI first encounters Yillah, she is aboard a ship with the priest and his sons, bound for the isle of Tedaidee, where she is to be sacrificed. Entering a tent that looks "as if it contained their Eleusinian mysteries," Taji sees Yillah and immediately falls in love with her. In order to save her, however, he is forced to kill Aleema. Traveling to the island of Odo, Taji and Yillah live together in bliss for a time; but before long, their idyll is interrupted by the appearance of three hand-maidens of the dark queen HAUTIA, who communicate with cryptic flower messages reminiscent of the "LANGUAGE OF FLOWERS." When Hautia herself appears, Yillah disappears. Taji is then doomed to roam the world in search of his lost love, pursued by Hautia and the vengeful sons of Aleema.

Yillah, who may be Hautia's victim, or who may actually be one with the dark queen, remains elusive, her allegorical significance hard to pin down. Her origins doubtless owe something to the eponymous heroine of the German Baron Friedrich Fouqué's 1811 fairy tale, *Undine.*

Yojo In *MOBY-DICK,* Yojo is QUEEQUEG's idol. ISHMAEL watches Queequeg meditate with Yojo on his head, and although Ishmael has little sympathy for idol worship, he finds it harmless and no less ridiculous than many other forms of religion, including those practiced in his own culture.

Yoky Minor character in *MARDI.* Yoky, the king of Hooloomooloo, the Isle of Cripples, is himself deformed.

Yoomy Character in *MARDI.* Yoomy is the poet and minstrel from the isle of Odo who joins with King MEDIA, the philosopher BABBALANJA, and the historian MOHI in TAJI's fruitless search through the Mardian archipelago for his lost love, YILLAH.

Zeke Character in *OMOO*. Zeke is the taller of two white men who have a farming partnership on the island of Imeeo. Zeke, a Yankee, and SHORTY, a Cockney, temporarily employ the narrator and his friend LONG GHOST as laborers. When the two wanderers decide to leave Imeeo, the well-respected Zeke is able to fashion for them a type of "passport" that protects their identity as runaway sailors.

Zimmermann, Johann Georg, Ritter von (1728–1795) Swiss physician and writer best known for his sentimen-

tal book *On Solitude* (1755), which the CONFIDENCE MAN refers to several times in his various disguises. Like the philosophers David HUME and Francis BACON, Zimmermann presents a view of humanity that destroys confidence in human nature.

Zionism A movement that sought to restore Palestine to the Jews. The modern quest to reestablish a Jewish state began in the 19th century. Several characters discuss the idea of a Jewish homeland and the idea of Zionism in *CLAREL*.

GENEALOGY
OF
HERMAN MELVILLE

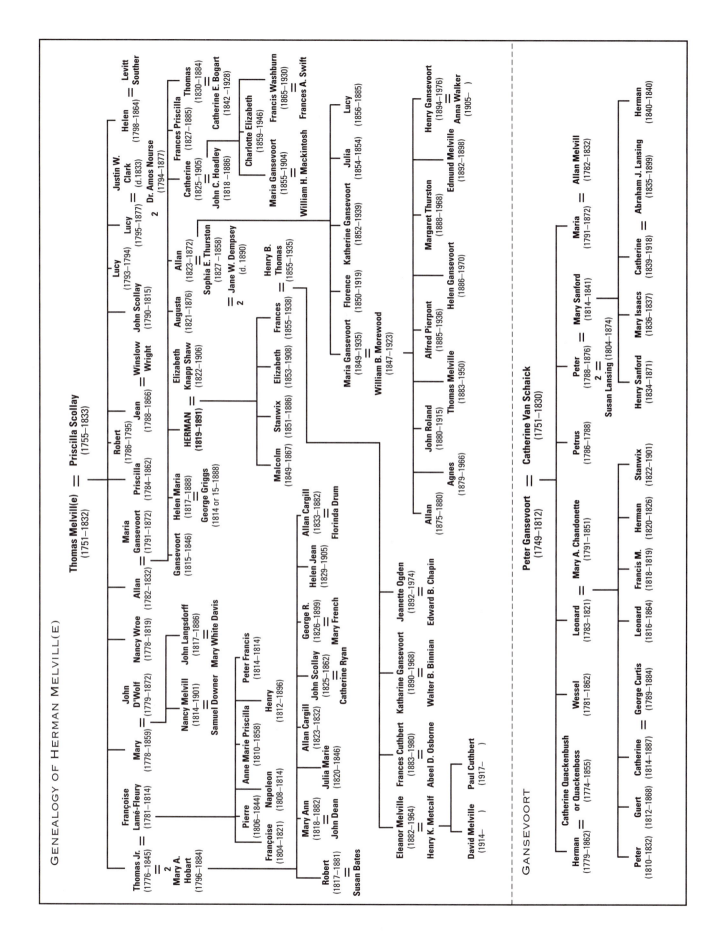

GENEALOGY OF HERMAN MELVILL(E)

227

CATEGORICAL APPENDIX

Characters

A, I, and O ("The Pollysyallables," "The Vowels")
Abbot, the
Abdon
Abrazza
Afretee
Agar
Agath
Ahab
Alanno
Aleema
Almanni
Anna
Annatoo
Antone
Aranda, Alexandro
Arfretee
Arheetoo
Arnaut, the
Aster, China
Atufal
Aunt Dorothea
Aunt Llanyllyn
Azzageddi
Babbalanja
Babo
Baldy
Baltimore
Banford, Isabel
banker, the
Bannadonna
barber, the
Bardianna
Bartleby
Beauty
Belex
Bell, Mr. and Mrs.
Bello ("Bello of the Hump")
Bembo ("the Mowree")
Ben
Biddy
Bildad, Captain

Billy Budd
Black Dan
Bland
Blandmour
Blunt, Bill ("Liverpool," "William"?)
Blunt, Jack
Bob, Captain
Bolton, Harry
Boomer, Captain
Borabolla
Braid Beard
Bridewell, Lieutenant
Bridges, James
Bulkington
Bunger, Dr. Jack
Bungs
captain of marines
Carlo
celibate, the
Celio
Cereno, Don Benito
chance stranger
chaplain, the
Charlemont
Chase, Jack
Chips ("Beauty")
Christodulus
Claggart, John
Clarel
Claret, Captain
Coffin, Peter
Colbrook, Corporal
collegian, the
commodore, the
confidence man, the
cosmopolitan, the
Coulter, William and Martha
Crash, Captain
crippled Soldier, the
Cupid
Cuticle, Cadwallader
Cylinder
Cypriote, the

Cyril
Daggoo
Danby
Dansker
Darby and Joan
Dates
de Deer, Derick
Delano, Amasa
Derwent
Djalea
Dominican, the
Don Hannibal
Donjalolo ("Fonoo")
Doxodox
Egbert
elder, the
Elijah
Enderby, Samuel
Episcopal clergyman, the
Falsgrave, Mr.
Farnoopoo
Farnowar
Fayaway
Fedallah
first lieutenant
Flask
Fleece
Ford, William
Frank
Gabriel
Gardiner, Captain
gentleman with gold sleeve buttons, the
Ginger Nut
Glaucon
Glendinning, General
Glendinning, Mary
Glendinning, Pierre
Goneril
Goodman, Francis
Graveling, Captain
Greenlander, the
"Gun-Deck"

229

Guy, Captain
Habbibi
"Handsome Mary"
Hardy, Lem
Hautboy
Hautia
Hello
Helmstone
herb-doctor, the
Hivohitee
Hunilla
Ishmael
Jackson
Jarl ("The Viking," "The Skyeman")
Jermin, John
Johnson, Dr.
Jones
Jones, Mr.
Julia
Kean, Captain Hosea
Kolory
Karakoee
Karky
Kooloo
Kory-Kory
Larry
Lavender
Lemsford
Lesbian, the
Lombardo
Long Ghost, Dr.
Loo
Lyonese, the
Macey
Mad Jack
Mandeville
man from the Carolinas, the
man in gray, the
man with a long weed, the
man with the traveling cap, the
Mapple, Father
Marbonna
Margoth
Marheyo
Marhar-Rarrar
Marharvai
Marianna
Marnoo
Max the Dutchman ("Red Max")
May-Day
Mayhew
Media
Mehevi
Merrymusk
Methodist minister, the
Millet, Sir John

Milthorpe, Charlie
miser, old, the
Missourian, the
Mpgul
Mohi ("Braid-Beard")
Moredock, Colonel John
Mordant, Mr.
Mortmain
Mowanna
Mow-Mow (also, Mow Mow)
Murphy, Father
mute, the
Nathan
Negro cripple, the
Nehemiah
Nimni
Nippers
Noble, Charles Arnold
Nord
Nulli
Oberlus
Oh Oh
Ohiro Moldona Fivona
Old Bach
Old Coffee
old man, the
Old Prudence
Peepi
Peleg, Captain
Pennie, the Misses
Perth
Piko
Pip
Pitch
Plinlimmon, Plotinus
Po-Po Ereemear ("Jeremiah")
president of the Black Rapids Coal
    Company, the
Priming
purser, the
Queequeg
Quoin
Radney
Ratcliff, Lieutenant
Rartoo
Redburn, Wellingborough
    ("Buttons," "Boots")
R.F.C.
Riga, Captain
Rigs, Mr.
Ringman, John
Roberts, Mr.
Rolfe
Rope Yarn
Rose-Water
Ruth

Sailing Master
Salem
Salvaterra
Samoa ("The Upoluan")
Saveda, Miguel
Scribe, Hiram
Scriggs
Scrimmage
Selvagee
Shenly
Shorty
Squeak
Standard
Stanly, Glendinning
Starbuck
Steelkilt
Stranger, The
Stubb
Sunshine
Surgeon, The
Sydney Ben
Syrian monk, The
Taji
Tartan, Lucy
Tartan, Mrs.
Tashtego
Tawney
Thompson, Mr. ("The Doctor")
Tinor
Toby
Tommo
Took, Horn
Tranquo
Tribonnora
Truman, John
Tubbs
Turkey
Uhia
Ulver, Delly
unfortunate man, the
Ungar
unparticipating man, the
Ushant, John
Van
Varvy
Vee Vee
Vere, Captain
Vine
Viner
White-Jacket
Williams
Wilson
Winsome, Mark
Winwood, Ralph
Woodcock, John
wooden-legged man, the

Wooloo
Wymontoo
Yankee Doodle
Yarn ("Old Yarn," "Pipes")
Yillah
Yojo
Yoky
Yoomy
Zeke

People

Adler, George
Akenside, Mark
Allen, Ethan
Allen, William
Arnold, Matthew
Astor, John Jacob
Bacon, Francis
Barnum, P[hineas] T[aylor]
Bellows, Henry Whitney
Belzoni, Giovanni Battista
Bentham, Jeremy
Bentley, Richard
Berkeley, George
Bradford, Alexander Warfield
Brodhead, John Romeyn
Brown, John
Browne, J. Ross
Browne, Sir Thomas
Bruat, Armand-Joseph
Bryant, William Cullen
Burke, Edmund
Burton, Robert
Calhoun, John C[aldwell]
Carpegna, Edouard Jules Gabrielle de
Cenci, Beatrice
Chase, Owen
Chaucer, Geoffrey
Clootz, Jean-Baptiste du Val de
    Grace, Baron, a.k.a. Anacharsis
    Cloots
Cole, Thomas
Coleridge, Samuel Taylor
Cook, Captain James
Cooper, James Fenimore
Dana, Richard Henry, Jr.
Dante (Dante Alighieri)
Darwin, Charles
Dempsey, Jane Louisa
Descartes, René
Diderot, Denis
Diogenes
Douglass, Frederick
Dupetit-Thouars, Abel Aubert
Duyckinck, Evert A.

Duyckinck, George
Emerson, Ralph Waldo
Fly, Eli James Murdock
Fourier, Charles
Fra Angelico
Franklin, Benjamin
Gansevoort, Catherine ("Kate")
Gansevoort, Catherine Van Schaick
    ("Caty")
Gansevoort, Guert
Gansevoort, Henry Sanford
Gansevoort, Herman
Gansevoort, Maria
Gansevoort, Peter (1749–1812)
Gansevoort, Peter (1788–1876)
Gansevoort, Stanwix
George III
Girard, Stephen
Goethe, Johann Wolfgang von
Greene, Richard Tobias
Griggs, Helen Maria Melville
Hannibal
Hatch, Agatha
Hauser, Kaspar
Hawthorne, Nathaniel
Hawthorne, Sophia Amelia Peabody
Hegel, Georg Wilhelm Friedrich
Heine, Heinrich
Hine, E[phraim] Curtiss
Hoadley, Catherine Gansevoort
    Melville ("Kate")
Hobbes, Thomas
Hoffman, Charles Fenno
Hume, David
Irving, Washington
Jonah
Jones, John Paul
Jones, Thomas ap Catesby
Judd, G[errit] P[armele]
Kamehameha
Kant, Immanuel
Lansing, Catherine Gansevoort
    ("Kate")
Lincoln, Abraham
Locke, John
Lyon, Nathaniel
Machiavelli, Niccolo
Marvell, Andrew
Matthews, Cornelius
Melvill, Allan
Melvill, Anne Marie Priscilla
Melvill, Françoise Raymonde
    Eulogie Maris des Doulours
    Lamé-Fleury
Melvill, Maria Gansevoort
Melvill, Mary Ann Augusta Hobart

Melvill, Priscilla
Melvill, Robert
Melvill, Thomas
Melvill, Thomas, Jr.
Melville, Allan, Jr.
Melville, Augusta ("Gus")
Melville, Catherine Gansevoort
    ("Kate")
Melville, Elizabeth ("Bessie," "Bess")
Melville, Elizabeth Knapp Shaw
    ("Lizzie")
Melville, Frances ("Fanny")
Melville, Frances Priscilla ("Fanny")
Melville, Gansevoort
Melville, Helen Maria
Melville, Herman
Melville, Jane Louisa Dempsey
    ("Jennie," "Madam Jane")
Melville, Malcolm ("Barny,"
    "Mackie," "Mackey")
Melville, Maria Gansevoort
Melville, Sophia Elizabeth Thurston
Melville, Stanwix ("Stannie")
Melville, Thomas ("Tom")
Mendelssohn, Moses
Moerenhout, Jacques-Antoine
Morewood, John Rowland
Morewood, Sarah
Mudge, Reverend Enoch
Murray, John
Nelson, Horatio
Oates, Titus
Paulet, Lord George
Pedro II (Dom Pedro II de
    Alcântara)
Piranesi, Giovanni Battista
Plato
Pomare (also Pomaree)
Potter, Israel
Powers, Hiram
Pritchard, George
Radcliffe, Mrs. Ann
Rousseau, Jean-Jacques
Savage, Hope
Schiller, Johann Christoph Friedrich
    von
Schopenhauer, Arthur
Scott, Winfield
Seneca
Shaftesbury, Anthony Ashley
    Cooper, third earl of
Shakespeare, William
Shaw, Elizabeth Knapp
Shaw, Hope Savage
Shaw, Lemuel
Spinoza, Baruch

Sumner, Charles
Swedenborg, Immanuel
Tacitus
Talleyrand-Périgord, Charles
    Maurice de
Taylor, Zachary
Thomas, Frances Melville ("Fanny")
Troy, John B.
Voltaire (François Marie Arouet)
Wellington, duke of (Arthur
    Wellesley)
Wilkes, Charles
Zimmermann, Johann Georg, Ritter
    von

Places Real and Imaginary

Albany, New York
Arrowhead
Bethlehem
Boston
Calabooza Beretanee
Cape Horn
Custom House, the
Encantadas
Fort Stanwix
Gansevoort, New York
Greylock, Mount
Hawaii
Italy
Jerusalem
Lansingburgh, New York
Liverpool
Marquesas
Mar Saba
Melvill House
Nantucket, Massachusetts
New Bedford, Massachusetts
New York City
Pittsfield, Massachusetts
Rock Rodondo
Saddle Meadows
Sandwich Islands
Society Islands
Spithead
Spouter Inn, The
Tahiti
Tammany Hall

Publications and Organizations

Dix & Edwards
Harper & Brothers
Harper's New Monthly Magazine
Literary World
Putnam's Monthly Magazine
Wiley & Putnam

Yankee Doodle

Ships Actual and Fictional

Acushnet
Albatross
Bachelor
Charles & Henry
Delight
Fidele
Indomitable
Jeroboam
Jungfrau
Lucy-Ann
Neversink
Pequod
Rachel
Rights of Man
Rose-Bud
St. Lawrence
Serapis
Town-Ho
United States
Virgin

Special Topics

abolitionists
African Americans
Astor Place riots
bisexuality
book publishing
breadfruit
Bunker Hill, Battle of
Calvinistic
canallers
Chartism
Civil War, the
colonialism
copyright
Druze
fate
flogging
French Directory
French Revolution
Great Heidelburgh Tun, the
Happar
imperialism
impressment
isolato
Joan, Pope
Kannakippers
Kostanza, the
"language of flowers"
L.A.V.
Mexican War
modernism

Neoplatonism
Nile, Battle of the
Nore mutiny
pantheism
Parsee
phrenology
predestination
Pythagorean
religion
Revolutions of 1848
Rosicrucianism
Shelleyan
Somers mutiny
spermaceti
spiritualiam (also spiritism)
taboo (also tabu)
tapa (also tappa)
tattoo
tayo
Trafalgar, Battle of
Transcendentalists
Typee
utilitarianism
whaling
women
Zionism

Titles

"Adieu"
"The Admiral of the White"
"The Æolian Harp: *At the Surf Inn*"
"After the Pleasure Party. Lines
    Traced Under an Image of Amor
    Threatening"
"The Age of Antonines"
"Always with Us!"
"The Ambuscade"
"America"
"The American Aloe on
    Exhibition"
"Amoroso"
Ancient Mariner
"Apathy and Enthusiasm.
    (1860–1.)"
"The Apparition. (A Retrospect.)"
"The Apparition. (The Parthenon
    uplifted on its rock first challeng-
    ing the view on the approach to
    Athens.)"
"The Apple-Tree Table; Or,
    Original Spiritual
    Manifestations"
"The Archipelago"
"The Armies of the Wilderness.
    (1863–4.)"
"Art"

"At the Cannon's Mouth. Destruction of the Ram Albemarle by the Torpedo-launch. (October, 1864.)"

"At the Hostelry"

"The Attic Landscape"'

"Aurora-Borealis. Commemorative of the Dissolution of Armies at the Peace. (May, 1865.)"

"Authentic Anecdotes of 'Old Zack' [Reported for *Yankee Doodle* by his special correspondent at the seat of War]"

"The Avatar"

"Ball's Bluff. A Reverie. (October, 1861.)"

"Barrington Isle and the Buccaneer"

"Bartleby, the Scrivener: A Story of Wall Street"

"The Battle for the Bay. (August, 1864.)"

"The Battle for the Mississippi. (April, 1862.)"

"Battle of Stone River, Tennessee. A View from Oxford Cloisters. (January, 1863.)"

"A Battle Picture"

Battle-Pieces and Aspects of War

"The Bell-Tower"

"The Bench of Boors"

"Benito Cereno"

"The Berg (A Dream.)"

Billy Budd, Sailor

"The Blue-Bird"

"Bridegroom-Dick"

"Buddha"

"The Burgundy Club Sketches"

"Butterfly Ditty"

"C———'s Lament"

"Camoens 1 (Before)"

Camoens in the Hospital 2 (After)"

Canterbury Tales, The

"A Canticle: Significant of the national exaltation of enthusiasm at the close of the War."

"Charles' Isle and the Dog-King"

"Chattanooga. (November, 1863.)"

"The Chipmunk"

Clarel: A Poem and Pilgrimage in the Holy Land

"Clover"

"Cock-A-Doodle-Doo! Or, The Crowing of the Noble Cock Beneventano"

"The College Colonel"

"'The Coming Storm': A Picture by S. R. Gifford, and owned by E. B. Included in the N. A. Exhibition, April, 1865."

"Commemorative of a Naval Victory"

Confidence Man, The

"The Conflict of Convictions. (1860–1.)"

"The Continents"

"Cooper's New Novel"

"Crossing the Tropics (from 'The Saya-y-Manto')"

"The Cuban Pirate"

Culture and Anarchy

"The Cumberland. (March, 1862.)"

"The Dairyman's Child"

"The Death Craft"

"The Devotion of the Flowers to Their Lady"

A Dirge for McPherson, Killed in front of Atlanta. (July, 1864.)"

"Disinternment of the Hermes"

"The Ditty of Aristippus"

"Donelson. (February, 1862.)"

"Dover Beach"

"Dupont's Round Fight. (November, 1861.)"

"The Dust-Layers"

"A Dutch Christmas up the Hudson in the Time of the Patroons"

"The Eagle of the Blue"

"The Encantadas, or Enchanted Isles"

"The Enthusiast"

"The Enviable Isles (from 'Rammon')"

"Epistle to Daniel Shepherd"

"An Epitaph"

"Etchings of a Whaling Cruise"

"The Fall of Richmond. The tidings received in the Northern Metropolis. (April, 1865.)"

"Falstaff's Lament Over Prince Hal Become Henry V"

"Far Off-Shore"

"Field Asters"

"The Figure-Head"

"'Formerly a Slave.' An idealized Portrait, by E. Vedder, in the Spring Exhibition of the National Academy, 1865"

"The Fortitude of the North under the Disaster of the Second Manassas"

"Fragments from a Writing Desk"

"Fragments of a Lost Gnostic Poem of the 12th Century"

"The Frenzy in the Wake. Sherman's advance through the Carolinas. (February, 1865.)"

"The Frigate, and Ship Flyaway"

"Fruit and Flower Painter"

"The Garden of Metrodorus"

"The 'Gees'"

"Gettysburg. The Check. (July, 1863.)"

"Give Me the Nerve"

"Gold in the Mountain"

"The Good Craft 'Snow-Bird'"

"A Grave near Petersburg, Virginia"

"The Great Pyramid"

"Greek Architecture"

"Greek Masonry"

"A Ground Vine Intercedes with the Queen of Flowers for the Merited Recognition of Clover"

"The Haglets"

"The Happy Failure. A Story of the River Hudson"

"Hawthorne and His Mosses"

"Hearth-Roses"

"Hearts-of-Gold"

"Herba Santa"

"Honor"

"Hood's Isle and the Hermit Oberlus"

"The House-top. A Night Piece. (July, 1863.)"

"I and My Chimney"

"Immolated"

"In a Bye-Canal"

"In a Church of Padua"

"In a Garret"

"In a Nutshell"

"Inscription"

"Inscription for Marye's Heights, Fredericksburg."

"Inscription for the Graves at Pea Ridge, Arkansas."

"Inscription for the Slain at Fredericksburgh"

"In Shards the Sylvan Vases Lie"

"In the Desert"

"In the Hall of Marbles (Lines Recalled from a Destroyed Poem)"

"In the Jovial Age of Old"

"In the Pauper's Turnip-field"

"In the Prison Pen"

"In the Old Farm-House: The Ghost"

"In the Turret. (March, 1862.)"

"Iris (1865)"
"The Isle of the Cross"
"The Isles at Large"
Isreal Potter: His Fifty Years of Exile
"Jack Roy"
"Jimmy Rose"
"John Marr"
John Marr and Other Sailors with Some Sea-Pieces
"Lamia's Song"
"Lee in the Capitol"
"L'Envoi"
"L'Envoi: The Return of the Sire de Nesle, A.D. 16—"
"The Lightning-Rod Man"
"The Little Good Fellows"
"The Loiterer"
"Lone Fonts"
"Look-out Mountain. The Night Fight. (November, 1863.)"
"The Lover and the Syringa Bush"
"Lyon. Battle of Springfield, Missouri. (August, 1861.)"
"Madam Mirror" and "The Wise Virgins to Madam Mirror"
"Madcaps"
"Magian Wine"
"Magnanimity Baffled"
"The Maldive Shark"
"Malvern Hill. (July, 1862.)"
"The Man-of-War Hawk"
"The March into Virginia, Ending in the First Manassas. (July, 1861.)"
"The March to the Sea (December, 1864)"
"The Marchioness of Brinvilliers"
Mardi
"The Margrave's Birthnight"
"The Martyr. Indicative of the passion of the people on the 15th of April, 1865."
"A Meditation: Attributed to a Northerner after attending the last of two funerals from the homestead—those of a National and Confederate officer (brothers), his kinsmen, who had died from the effects of wounds received in the closing battles."
"The Medallion in Villa Albina & C"
"Merry Ditty of the Sad Man"
"Milan Cathedral"
"Misgivings (1860)"
"Mr. Parkman's Tour"
Moby-Dick; or, The Whale
"Monody"

"Montaigne and His Kitten"
"The Mound by the Lake"
"The Muster: Suggested by the Two Days' Review at Washington. (May, 1865.)"
"My Jacket Old"
"Naples in the Time of Bomba"
"The New Ancient of Days: The Man of the Cave of Engihoul"
"The New Planet"
"The New Rosicrucians"
"The New Zealot to the Sun"
"The Night-March"
"Norfolk Isle and the Chola Widow"
"Off Cape Colonna"
"Old Age in His Ailing"
"Old Counsel of the Young Master of a Wrecked California Clipper"
"The Old Fashion"
"The Old Shipmaster and His Crazy Barn"
Omoo: A Narrative of Adventures in the South Seas
"On a natural Monument in a field of Georgia."
"On Sherman's Men who fell in the Assault of Kenesaw Mountain, Georgia."
"On the Chinese Junk"
"On the Grave of a young Cavalry Officer killed in the Valley of Virginia."
"On the Home Guards Who Perished in the Defense of Lexington, Missouri."
"On the men of Maine killed in the Victory of Baton Rouge, Louisiana."
"On the Photograph of a Corps Commander."
"On the Sea Serpent"
"On the Slain at Chickamauga."
"On the Slain Collegians."
Paradise Lost
"The Paradise of Bachelors and the Tartarus of Maids"
"The Parthenon"
"Pausilippo (in the Time of Bomba)"
"Pebbles"
"Philip"
"The Piazza"
The Piazza Tales
The Picture of Liverpool
Pierre; or, The Ambiguities
"Pisa's Leaning Tower"
"A Pisgah View from the Rock"

"Pontoosuce"
"Poor Man's Pudding and Rich Man's Crumbs"
"The Portent. (1859.)"
"Presentation to the Authorities, by Privates, of Colors captured in Battles ending in the Surrender of Lee."
"Profundity and Levity"
"Puzzlement as to a Figure Left Solitary on a Unique Fragment of Greek Basso-Rilievo"
"A Rail Road Cutting Near Alexandria in 1855"
"Rammon"
"The Ravaged Villa"
"A Reasonable Constitution"
"Rebel Color-Bearers at Shiloh: A plea against the vindictive cry raised by civilians shortly after he surrender at Appomattox."
Redburn: His First Voyage, Being the Sailor-Boy Confessions and Reminiscences of the Son-of-a-Gentleman, in the Merchant Service
"The Released Rebel Prisoner. (June, 1865.)"
"Report of the Committee on Agriculture"
"A Requiem for the Soldiers lost in Ocean Transports."
"The Return of Sire of Nesle"
"The Returned Volunteer to his Rifle."
Rime of the Ancient Mariner
"Rip Van Winkle's Lilac"
"Rock Rodondo"
"Rosary Beads"
"The Rose Farmer" and "L'Envoi"
"Rose Window"
"Runaways, Castaways, Solitaries, Grave-Stones, Etc."
"Running the Batteries. As observed from the Anchorage above Vicksburgh. [*sic*] (April, 1863.)"
"The Rusty Man (By a Soured One)"
"The Same"
"The Scout toward Aldie."
"Shadow at the Feast. Mrs. B—— (1847)"
"Shelley's Vision"
"Sheridan at Cedar Creek. (Ocotber, 1864.)"
"Shiloh. A Requiem. (April, 1862.)"
"A Short Patent Sermon. According to Blair, the Rhetorician"

"The South Seas"
"A Spirit Appeared to Me"
"Statues in Rome"
"Stockings in the Farm-House Chimney"
"The Stone Fleet. An Old Sailor's Lament. (December, 1861.)"
"Stonewall Jackson. (Ascribed to a Virginian.)"
"Stonewall Jackson. Mortally wounded at Chancellorsville. (May, 1863.)"
"Story of Toby, The"
"Suggested by the Ruins of a Mountain-Temple in Arcadia, One Built by the Architect of the Parthenon"
"The Surrender at Appomattox. (April, 1865.)"
"The Swamp Angel"
"Syra (A Transmitted Reminiscence)"

"The Temeraire. (Supposed to have been suggested to an Englishman of the old order by the fight of the Monitor and Merrimac.)"
"A Thought on Book-Binding"
"Thy Aim, Thy Aim?"
"Time's Betrayal"
"Time's Long Ago!"
Timoleon and Other Ventures in Minor Verse
"Timoleon (394 B.C.)"
"To ——"
"Tom Deadlight (1810)"
"To Ned"
"To the Master of the *Meteor*"
"To Tom"
"Tortoise Book"
"Traveling: Its Pleasures, Pains, and Profits"
"Trophies of Peace: Illinois in 1840"
"The Tuft of Kelp"
"Two Sides of a Tortoise"

"The Two Temples"
Typee: A Peep at Polynesian Life
"Under the Ground"
"An Uninscribed Monument on one of the Battle-fields of the Wilderness"
"A Utilitarian View of the Monitor's Fight."
"Venice"
"The Vial of Attar"
"The Victor of Antietam. (1862.)"
"View of the Barnum Property"
"A Way-Side Weed"
"The Weaver"
Weeds and Wildings Chiefly: With a Rose or Two
"When Forth the Shepherd Leads the Flock"
White-Jacket; or, The World in a Man-of-War
"The Wise Virgins to Madam Mirror"

BIBLIOGRAPHY

Melville's Books

The Battle-Pieces of Herman Melville. Edited with an introduction and notes by Hennig Cohen. New York: Thomas Yoseloff, 1964.

Billy Budd, Sailor (An Inside Narrative): Reading Text and Genetic Text. Edited by Harrison Hayford and Merton Sealts Jr. Chicago: University of Chicago Press, 1962.

Clarel: A Poem and Pilgrimage in the Holy Land. Edited by Harrison Hayford, Hershel Parker, and G. Thomas Tanselle. Evanston and Chicago: Northwestern University Press and the Newberry Library, 1991.

Collected Poems of Herman Melville. Edited by Howard P. Vincent. Chicago: Packard and Co., Hendricks House, 1947.

The Confidence-Man: His Masquerade. Edited by Harrison Hayford, Hershel Parker, and G. Thomas Tanselle. Evanston and Chicago: Northwestern University Press and the Newberry Library, 1984.

Correspondence. Edited by Lynn Horth. Evanston and Chicago: Northwestern University Press and the Newberry Library, 1993.

Israel Potter: His Fifty Years in Exile. Edited by Harrison Hayford, Hershel Parker, and G. Thomas Tanselle. Evanston and Chicago: Northwestern University Press and the Newberry Library, 1982.

Journals. Edited by Howard Horsford and Lynn Horth. Evanston and Chicago: Northwestern University Press and the Newberry Library, 1989.

The Letters of Herman Melville. Edited by Merrell R. Davis and William H. Gilman. New Haven: Yale University Press, 1960.

Mardi and the Voyage Thither. Edited by Harrison Hayford, Hershel Parker, and G. Thomas Tanselle. Evanston and Chicago: Northwestern University Press and the Newberry Library, 1970.

Melville's Marginalia. Edited by Walker Cowan. New York: Garland, 1987.

Moby-Dick, or The Whale. Edited by Harrison Hayford, Hershel Parker, and G. Thomas Tanselle. Evanston and Chicago: Northwestern University Press and the Newberry Library, 1988.

Moby-Dick, or The Whale. The Northwestern-Newberry text, with introduction by Andrew Delbanco, notes and explanatory commentary by Tom Quirk. New York: Penguin Books, 1992.

Omoo: A Narrative of Adventures in the South Seas. Edited by Harrison Hayford, Hershel Parker, and G. Thomas Tanselle. Evanston and Chicago: Northwestern University Press and the Newberry Library, 1968.

Piazza Tales and Other Prose Pieces 1839–1860. Edited by Harrison Hayford, Alma MacDougall, and G. Thomas Tanselle. Evanston and Chicago: Northwestern University Press and the Newberry Library, 1987.

Pierre, or The Ambiguities. Edited by Harrison Hayford, Hershel Parker, and G. Thomas Tanselle. Evanston and Chicago: Northwestern University Press and the Newberry Library, 1971.

Redburn: His First Voyage, Being the Sailor-boy Confessions and Reminiscences of the Son-of-a-Gentleman, in the Merchant Service. Edited by Harrison Hayford, Hershel Parker, and G. Thomas Tanselle. Evanston and Chicago: Northwestern University Press and the Newberry Library, 1969.

Typee: A Peep at Polynesian Life. Edited by Harrison Hayford, Hershel Parker, and G. Thomas Tanselle. Evanston and Chicago: Northwestern University Press and the Newberry Library, 1968.

Weeds and Wildings Chiefly: with a Rose or Two. Reading Text and Genetic Text. Edited and with an introduction by Robert Charles Ryan. Evanston, Ill.: Northwestern University Press, 1967.

White-Jacket, or The World in a Man-of-War. Edited by Harrison Hayford, Hershel Parker, and G. Thomas Tanselle. Evanston and Chicago: Northwestern University Press and the Newberry Library, 1970.

Books and Articles about Melville

Adler, Joyce Sparer. *War in Melville's Imagination.* New York: New York University Press, 1981.

Anderson, Charles R. *Melville in the South Seas.* New York: Dover Publications, 1966.

Baird, James. *Ishmael: A Study of the Symbolic Mode in Primitivism.* Baltimore: Johns Hopkins University Press, 1956.

Bellis, Peter. *No Mysteries Out of Ourselves: Identity and Textual Form in the Novels of Herman Melville.* Philadelphia: University of Pennsylvania Press, 1990.

Bercaw, Mary K. *Melville's Sources.* Evanston: Northwestern University Press, 1987.

Berthoff, Warner. *The Example of Melville.* Princeton, N.J.: Princeton University Press, 1962.

Bickley, R. Bruce, Jr. *The Method of Melville's Short Fiction.* Durham, N.C.: Duke University Press, 1975.

Blair, John G. *The Confidence Man in Modern Fiction: A Rogue's Gallery with Six Portraits.* New York: Barnes and Noble, 1979.

Bloom, Harold, ed. *Ahab.* New York: Chelsea House, 1991.

Boswell, Jeanetta. *Herman Melville and the Critics: A Checklist of Criticism.* Metuchen, N.J.: Scarecrow Press, 1981.

Bowen, Merlin. *The Long Encounter: Self and Experience in the Writings of Herman Melville.* Chicago: University of Chicago Press, 1960.

Branch, Watson G., ed. *Melville: The Critical Heritage.* Boston: Routledge and Kegan Paul, 1974.

Braswell, William. *Melville's Religious Thought: An Essay in Interpretation.* Durham, N.C.: Duke University Press, 1943.

Brodhead, Richard. *New Essays on "Moby-Dick."* Cambridge: Cambridge University Press, 1986.

Brodtkorb, Paul, Jr. *Ishmael's White World: A Phenomenological Reading of "Moby-Dick."* New Haven: Yale University Press, 1965.

Browne, Ray B. *Melville's Drive to Humanism.* Lafayette, Ind.: Purdue University Studies, 1971.

Bryant, John, ed. *A Companion to Melville Studies.* Westport, Conn.: Greenwood Press, 1986.

Budd, Louis J., and Edwin H. Cady. *On Melville: The Best from American Literature.* Durham, N.C.: Duke University Press, 1988.

Burkholder, Robert, ed. *Critical Essays on Herman Melville's "Benito Cereno."* New York: G. K. Hall, 1992.

Cameron, Sharon. *The Corporeal Self: Allegories of the Body in Melville and Hawthorne.* Baltimore: Johns Hopkins University Press, 1981.

Coffler, Gail H. *Melville's Classical Allusions: A Comprehensive Index and Glossary.* Westport, Conn.: Greenwood Press, 1985.

Chase, Richard. *Herman Melville: A Critical Study.* New York: Macmillan, 1949.

Cowan, Bainard. *Exiled Waters: "Moby-Dick" and the Crisis of Allegory.* Baton Rouge: Louisiana State University Press, 1981.

Crain, Caleb. "Lovers of Human Flesh: Homosexuality and Cannibalism in Melville's Novels." *American Literature* 66 (1964): 25–53.

Creech, James. *Closet Writing/Gay Reading: The Case of Melville's "Pierre."* Chicago: University of Chicago Press, 1993.

Davis, Merrell R. *Melville's "Mardi:" A Chartless Voyage.* New Haven: Yale University Press, 1952.

Delbanco, Andrew. "Melville in the '80s." *American Literary History* 4 (1992): 709–25.

Dillingham, William B. *An Artist in the Rigging: The Early Work of Herman Melville.* Athens: University of Georgia Press, 1972.

———. *Melville's Later Novels.* Athens: University of Georgia Press, 1986.

———. *Melville's Short Fiction, 1853–1856.* Athens: University of Georgia Press, 1977.

Dimock, Wai-chee. *Empire for Liberty: Melville and the Poetics of Individualism.* Princeton, N.J.: Princeton University Press, 1988.

Dryden, Edgar A. *Melville's Thematics of Form: The Great Art of Telling the Truth.* Baltimore: Johns Hopkins University Press, 1968.

Duban, James, ed. *Melville and His Narrators.* Special issue of *Texas Studies in Literature and Language* 31 (1989).

Feidelson, Charles. *Symbolism and American Literature.* Chicago: University of Chicago Press, 1953.

Finkelstein, Dorothy Metlitsky. *Melville's Orienda.* New Haven: Yale University Press, 1961.

Fisher, Marvin. *Going Under: Melville's Short Fiction and the American 1850s.* Baton Rouge: Louisiana State University Press, 1977.

Flibbert, Joseph. *Melville and the Art of Burlesque.* Amsterdam: Rodopi, 1974.

Franklin, H. Bruce. *The Wake of Gods: Melville's Mythology.* Stanford: Stanford University Press, 1963.

Gamer, Stanton. *The Civil War: World of Herman Melville.* Lawrence: University Press of Kansas, 1993.

Gilman, William. *Melville's Early Life and "Redburn."* New York: New York University Press, 1951.

Gilmore, Michael T. *American Romanticism and the Marketplace.* Chicago: University of Chicago Press, 1985.

Goldman, Stan. *Melville's Protest Theism: The Hidden and Silent God in Clarel.* DeKalb: Northern Illinois University Press, 1993.

Hayes, Kevin J., and Hershel Parker, eds. *Checklist of Melville Reviews.* Evanston: Northwestern University Press, 1991.

——— *The Critical Response to Herman Melville's "Moby-Dick."* Westport, Conn.: Greenwood Press, 1994.

Heffernan, Thomas Farel. *Stove by a Whale: Owen Chase and the Essex.* Middletown, Conn.: Wesleyan University Press, 1981.

Herbert, T. Walter Jr. *Marquesan Encounters: Melville and the Meaning of Civilization.* Cambridge, Mass.: Harvard University Press, 1980.

———. *"Moby-Dick" and Calvinism: A World Dismantled.* New Brunswick, N.J.: Rutgers University Press, 1977.

Hetherington, Hugh. *Melville's Reviewers, British and Americans, 1846–1891.* Chapel Hill: University of North Carolina Press, 1961.

Higgins, Brian. *Herman Melville: An Annotated Bibliography, 1846–1930*. Boston: G. K. Hall, 1979.

———. *Herman Melville: A Reference Guide, 1931–1960*. Boston G. K. Hall, 1969.

Higgins, Brian, and Hershel Parker, eds. *Critical Essays on Herman Melville's "Moby-Dick."* New York: G. K. Hall, 1992.

———. *Critical Essays on Herman Melville's "Pierre, or The Ambiguities."* Boston: G. K. Hall and Company, 1983.

Hillway, Tyrus, and Luther S. Mansfield, ed. *Moby-Dick: Centennial Essays*. Dallas: Southern Methodist University Press, 1953.

Howard, Leon. *Herman Melville: A Biography*. Berkeley: University of California Press, 1967.

Inge, M. Thomas, ed. *Bartleby the Inscrutable: A Collection of Commentary on Herman Melville's Tale "Bartleby the Scrivener."* Hamden, Conn.: Archon Books, 1979.

James, C. L. R. *Mariners, Renegades and Castaways: The Story of Herman Melville and the World We Live In*. New York: C. L. R. James, 1953.

Jehlen, Myra, ed. *Herman Melville: A Collection of Critical Essays*. Englewood Cliffs, N.J.: Prentice-Hall, Inc., 1994.

Kaplan, Sidney. "Herman Melville and the American National Sin." *Images of the Negro in American Literature*, edited by Seymour L. Gross and John Edward Hardy. Chicago: University of Chicago Press, 1966.

Karcher, Carolyn. "The Riddle of the Sphinx, Melville's *Benito Cereno* and the Amistad Case." *Critical Essays on Melville's Benito Cereno*, ed. Robert Burkholder. Boston: G. K. Hall, 1996.

———. *Shadow Over the Promised Land: Slavery, Race and Violence in Melville's America*. Baton Rouge: Louisiana State University Press, 1980.

Kelley, Wyn. "Haunted Stone; Nature and City in *Clarel*." *Essays in Arts and Sciences* 15 (1986): 15–29.

———. *Melville's City: Urban and Literary Form in Nineteenth-Century New York*. New York: Cambridge University Press, 1996.

———. *Evermoving Dawn: Essays in Celebration of the Melville Centennial*, ed. John Bryant. Kent, Ohio: Kent State University Press, 1996.

Kenney, Alice P. *The Gansevoorts of Albany: Dutch Patricians in the Upper Hudson Valley*. Syracuse, N.Y.: Syracuse University Press, 1969.

Kenny, Vincent. *Herman Melville's "Clarel": A Spiritual Autobiography*. Hamden, Conn.: Shoe String Press, 1973.

Kier, Kathleen E. *The Melville Encyclopedia: The Novels*. Troy, N.Y.: Whitston Publishing Company, 1990.

Lawrence, D. H. *Studies in Classic American Literature*. New York: Viking Press, 1964.

Lee, A. Robert, ed. *Herman Melville: Reassessments*. London: Barnes and Noble, 1984.

Levin, Harry. *The Power of Blackness: Hawthorne, Poe, Melville*. New York: Alfred A. Knopf, 1958.

Levine, Robert S., ed. *The Cambridge Companion to Herman Melville*. Cambridge: Cambridge University Press, 1998.

Leyda, Jay. *The Melville Log: A Documentary Life of Herman Melville, 1819–1891*, 2 vols. New York: Harcourt Brace and Company, 1951. Reprinted with additional material, Fairfield, Conn.: Gordian Press, 1969.

McCall, Dan. *The Silence of Bartleby*. Ithaca, N.Y.: Cornell University Press, 1989.

McWilliams, John P. *Hawthorne, Melville, and the American Character: A Looking-Glass Business*. New York: Cambridge University Press, 1984.

Markels, Julian. *Melville and the Politics of Identity: From "King Lear" to "Moby-Dick."* Urbana: University of Illinois Press, 1993.

Martin, Robert K. *Hero, Captain, and Stranger: Male Friendship, Social Critique, and Literary Form in the Sea Novels of Herman Melville*. Chapel Hill: University of North Carolina Press, 1986.

Matterson, Stephen. "Indian-Hating in *The Confidence Man*." *Arizona Quarterly* 52 (1996): 21–36.

Matthiessen, F. O. *American Renaissance: Art and Expression in the Age of Emerson and Whitman*. New York: Oxford University Press, 1941.

Mellow, James. *Nathaniel Hawthorne in His Times*. Boston: Houghton Mifflin Company, 1980.

Metcalf, Eleanor Melville. *Herman Melville: Cycle and Epicycle*. Cambridge, Mass.: Harvard University Press, 1953.

Metcalf, Paul, ed. *Enter Isabel: The Herman Melville Correspondence of Clare Spark and Paul Metcalf*. Albuquerque: University of New Mexico Press, 1991.

Milder, Robert. "Melville's 'Intentions' in Writing *Pierre*." *Studies in the Novel* 6 (1974): 186–99.

———. "The Rhetoric of Melville's *Battle-Pieces*." *Nineteenth-Century Literature* 44 (1989): 173–200.

———, ed. *Critical Essays on Melville's Billy Budd, Sailor*. Boston: G. K. Hall, 1989.

Miller, Edwin Havilland. *Melville*. New York: George Braziller, 1975.

Miller, James E., Jr. *A Reader's Guide to Herman Melville*. New York: Farrar, Straus, & Cudahy, 1962.

Miller, Perry. *The Raven and the Whale: The War of Words and Wits in the Era of Poe and Melville*. New York: Harcourt, Brace and World, 1956.

Mumford, Lewis. *Herman Melville: A Study of His Life and Vision*. New York: Harcourt, Brace and World, 1929.

Murray, Henry A. Introduction and Explanatory Notes to *Pierre*. New York: Hendricks House, 1949.

Newman, Lea Bertain Vozar. *A Reader's Guide to the Short Stories of Herman Melville*. Boston: G. K. Hall, 1986.

Olson, Charles. *Call Me Ishmael: A Study of Melville*. San Francisco: City Lights Books, 1947.

Otter, Samuel. *Melville's Anatomies: Bodies, Discourse, and Ideology in Antebellum America*. Berkeley: University of California Press, 1998.

Parker, Hershel. *Herman Melville: A Biography*. Volume 1, 1819–1851. Baltimore: Johns Hopkins University Press, 1996.

———. *Reading "Billy Budd."* Evanston, Ill.: Northwestern University Press, 1990.

———, ed. *The Recognition of Herman Melville: Selected Criticism since 1846*. Ann Arbor: University of Michigan Press, 1967.

———. "Why *Pierre* Went Wrong." *Studies in the Novel* 8 (1976): 7–23.

Parker, Hershel and Harrison Hayford, eds. *"Moby-Dick" as Doubloon: Essays and Extracts (1851–1970)*. New York: W. W. Norton & Company, 1970.

Person, Leland S., Jr. "*Mardi* and the Reviewers: The Irony of (Mis)reading." *Melville Society Extracts* 72 (1988): 3–5.

Phelps, Leland. *Herman Melville's Foreign Reputation: A Research Guide*. Boston: G. K. Hall, 1983.

Pommer, Henry F. *Milton and Melville*. Pittsburgh: University of Pittsburgh Press, 1950.

Post-Lauria, Sheila. "Canonical Text and Context: The Example of Herman Melville's *Bartleby the Scrivener.—A Story of Wall Street*." *College Literature* 20 (1993): 196–205.

———. *Correspondent Colorings: Melville in the Marketplace*. Amherst: University of Massachusetts Press, 1996.

———. "Genre and Ideology: The French Sensational Romance and Melville's *Pierre*." *Journal of American Culture* 15 (1992): 1–8.

———. "Philosophy in Whales . . . Poetry in Blubber: Mixed Form in *Moby-Dick*." *Nineteenth-Century Literature* 45 (1990): 300–16.

Pullin, Faith, ed. *New Perspectives on Melville*. Kent, Ohio: Kent State University Press, 1978.

Quirk, Tom. *Melville's Confidence Man: From Knave to Knight*. Columbia: University of Missouri Press, 1982.

Rampersad, Arnold. *Melville's "Israel Potter": A Pilgrimage and a Progress*. Bowling Green, Ohio: Bowling Green University Popular Press, 1969.

Renker, Elizabeth. "Herman Melville, Wife Beating, and the Written Page." *American Literature* 66 (1994): 123–50.

Reno, Janet. *Ishmael Alone Survived*. Lewisburg, Penn.: Bucknell University Press, 1990.

Reynolds, David S. *Beneath the American Renaissance: The Subversive Imagination in the Age of Emerson and Melville*. New York: Alfred A. Knopf, 1988.

Robertson-Lorant, Laurie. *Melville: A Biography*. Amherst: University of Massachusetts Press, 1998.

Rogin, Michael Paul. *Subversive Genealogy: The Politics and Art of Herman Melville*. New York: Alfred A. Knopf, 1983.

Rosenberry, Edward H. *Melville and the Comic Spirit*. Cambridge, Mass.: Harvard University Press, 1955.

Samson, John. *White Lies: Melville's Narrative of Facts*. Ithaca: Cornell University Press, 1989.

Schultz, Elizabeth. *Unpainted to the Last: "Moby-Dick" and Twentieth-Century American Art*. Lawrence: University Press of Kansas, 1995.

Sealts, Merton M., Jr. *The Early Lives of Melville: Nineteenth-Century Biographical Sketches and Their Authors*. Madison: University of Wisconsin Press, 1974.

———. *Melville as Lecturer*. Cambridge: Harvard University Press, 1957.

———. *Melville's Reading*. Columbia: University of South Carolina Press, 1988.

———. *Pursuing Melville, 1940–1980: Chapters and Essays*. Madison: University of Wisconsin Press, 1982.

Sedgwick, William Ellery. *Melville and the Tragedy of the Mind*. Cambridge: Harvard University Press, 1944.

Seelye, John. *Melville: The Ironic Diagram*. Evanston, Ill.: Northwestern University Press, 1971.

Sherrill, Rowland A. *The Prophetic Melville: Experience, Transcendence, and Tragedy*. Athens: University of Georgia Press, 1979.

Shetley, Vernon. "Melville's 'Timoleon.'" *Emerson Society Quarterly* 33 (1987): 82–93.

Short, Bryan C. *Cast by Means of Figures: Herman Melville's Rhetorical Development*. Amherst: University of Massachusetts Press, 1992.

Shurr, William H. *The Mystery of Iniquity: Melville as Poet, 1857–1891*. Lexington: University Press of Kentucky, 1972.

Spanos, William V. *The Errant Art of "Moby-Dick": The Canon, the Cold War, and the Struggle for American Studies*. Durham, N.C.: Duke University Press, 1995.

Stein, William Bysshe. *The Poetry Of Melville's Late Years: Time, History, Myth, and Religion*. Albany: State University of New York, 1970.

Sten, Christopher, ed. *Savage Eye: Melville and the Visual Arts*. Kent, Ohio: Kent State University Press, 1991.

Stern, Milton R. *The Fine-Hammered Steel Of Herman Melville*. Urbana: University of Illinois Press, 1957.

———, ed. *Critical Essays on Herman Melville's "Typee."* Boston: G. K. Hall, 1981.

Stuckey, Sterling. "The Death of Benito Cereno: A Reading of Herman Melville on Slavery." *Journal of Negro History* 67 no. 4 (1982): 287–301.

Sundquist, Eric J. "Benito Cereno and New World Slavery." *Reconstructing American Literary History*, ed. Sacvan Bercovitch. Cambridge, Mass.: Harvard University Press, 1986.

Thompson, G. R., and Virgil L. Lokke, ed. *Ruined Eden of the Present: Hawthorne, Melville, and Poe: Critical Essays in Honor of Darrel Abel*. West Lafayette, Ind.: Purdue University Press, 1981.

Thompson, Lawrance R. *Melville's Quarrel with God*. Princeton, N.J.: Princeton University Press, 1952.

Tolchin, Neal L. *Mourning, Gender, and Creativity in the Art of Herman Melville.* New Haven, Conn.: Yale University Press, 1988.

Travis, Mildred K. "Fact to Fiction in *Pierre:* The Arrowhead Ambience." *Melville Society Extracts* 15 (1973): 6–8.

Trimpi, Helen P. *Melville's Confidence Men and American Politics in the 1850s.* Hamden, Conn.: Archon Books, 1987.

Updike, John. "Melville's Withdrawal." *Hugging the Shore: Essays and Criticism.* New York: Alfred A. Knopf, 1983.

Vincent, Howard P. *The Tailoring of "White-Jacket."* Evanston, Ill.: Northwestern University Press, 1970.

———. *The Trying-Out of "Moby-Dick."* Boston: Houghton Mifflin, 1949.

Wallace, Robert K. *Melville and Turner: Spheres of Love and Fright.* Athens: University of Georgia Press, 1992.

Weaver, Raymond. *Herman Melville: Mariner and Mystic.* New York: Pageant Books, 1961.

Wenke, John. *Melville's Muse: Literary Creation and the Forms of Philosophical Fiction.* Kent, Ohio: Kent State University Press, 1995.

Wilson, James C. "Melville at Arrowhead: A Re-evaluation of Melville's Relations With Hawthorne and With His Family." *Emerson Society Quarterly* 30 (1984): 232–44.

Wright, Nathalia. *Melville's Use of the Bible.* Durham, N.C.: Duke University Press, 1949.

Yannella, Donald, and Hershel Parker. *The Endless, Winding Way in Melville: New Charts by Kring and Carey.* Glassboro, N.J.: The Melville Society, 1981.

Zoellner, Robert. *The Salt-Sea Mastodon: A Reading of "Moby-Dick."* Berkeley: University of California Press, 1973.

INDEX

Note: **Boldface** numbers indicate primary discussions of a topic. *Italic* numbers indicate illustrations.

A

A, I, and O **1,** 64, 109
abbot (Christodolus) **1,** 28
Abdon **1,** 30
abolitionists **1,** 2, 22, 56
Abrazza **1,** 110
Acushnet (ship) **1,** 73, 119, 199
    conditions on 212
    sailors on, characters modeled on 157, 164, 189
Adamnan 32
"Adieu" (poem) **1**
Adler, George **1–2**
"The Admiral of the White" (poem) **75,** 122
Afretee **2,** 100, 151
African Americans **2**
    enslavement of. *See* slavery
"After the Pleasure Party. Lines Traced Under an Image of Amor Threatening" (poem) **2**
Agar **2,** 31, 40
Agath **2,** 37, 38–39
"The Age of Antonines" (poem) **2**
Ahab **2–3,** 64, 127–137
    Taji compared with 193
    as tragic hero 185
Akenside, Mark **3**
Alanno **3–4**
Albany, New York **3,** 70, 114, 119, 121
Albany Academy 3, 21, 66, 119
Albatross (ship) **3,** 131
Aleema **3,** 107
The Alhambra (Irving) 184
allegory
    in "The Bell-Tower" 12

in "The Paradise of Bachelors and the Tartarus of Maids" 155
Allen, Ethan **3,** 88
Allen, William **3–4,** 110
Alma 110
Almanni **4**
"Always with Us!" (poem) **4**
ambergris 134, 212
"The Ambuscade" (poem) **4**
"America" (poem) **4**
"The American Aloe on Exhibition" (poem) **4**
American editions
    of *Battle-Pieces* 12
    of *Mardi* 111
    of *Omoo* 152
    of *Redburn* 178
    of *Typee* 206
    of *White-Jacket* 218
American Museum, Barnum's 10, 11, *11,* 142
    caricature of 209
"Amoroso" (poem) **4**
Ancient Mariner. See Rime of the Ancient Mariner
Anna **4,** 83
Annatoo **4,** 91, 106
Antarctica, expedition to 219
Antietam, Battle of 209, *210*
Antone **4**
Antonius Pius 2
"The 'olian Harp: *At the Surf Inn*" (poem) **2**
"Apathy and Enthusiasm. (1860–1.)" (poem) **4–5**
Apostles, in *Pierre* 162, 168

"The Apparition. (The Parthenon uplifted on its rock first challenging the view on the approach to Athens.)" (poem) **5**
"The Apparition. (A Retrospect.)" (poem) **5**
"The Apple-Tree Table; Or, Original Spiritual Manifestations" (short story) **5**
    characters in 15, 93
    "I and My Chimney" compared with 83
    "Jimmy Rose" compared with 92
    spiritualism in 5, 188
Appomattox, surrender at
    aftermath of 172
    poem about 190
Aranda, Alexandro **5**
"The Archipelago" (poem) **5–6**
architecture, Greek, poems about 5, 73, 156, 168, 190
Arcturion (ship) 105
Arcturus (periodical) 113
Arculf 32
Arheetoo **6**
"The Armies of the Wilderness. (1863–4.)" (poem) **6**
Arnaut **6,** 37
Arnold, Matthew **6,** 29
    Culture and Anarchy 6, **51**
    "Dover Beach" 6, 29, **56**
Arrowhead **6,** 7
    in "I and My Chimney" 83
    Allan Melville's purchase of 6, 116

Arrowhead *(continued)*
    Herman Melville's purchase
        of 115, 120, 142, 164, 186
    mountain view from 74
    in "The Piazza" 157
    poems inspired by 84, 85,
        145, 189
    vegetation at 211
art
    of Hiram Powers 166
    Italian 89
    lecture on 187, 189
    Melville's theory of 6, 23, 172
    poems about 2, 55
    Schiller on 183
    Schopenhauer on 184
"Art" (poem) **6**
Articles of War 217
Aster, China **6,** 48
Astor, John Jacob **6–7,** 110
Astor Place riots **6–7,** 113
Athens, poems about 5, 73, 156
"At the Cannon's Mouth.
    Destruction of the Ram
    Albermarle by the Torpedo-
    launch. (October, 1864.)"
    (poem) **7**
"At the Hostelry" (poem) 23
"The Attic Landscape" (poem) **7**
Atufal **7,** 14
Aubray, Marie Madeleine
    Marguerite d' 104–105
Augusta. *See* Melville, Augusta
Aunt Dorothea **8,** 159
Aunt Llanyllyn **8**
"Aurora-Borealis. Commemorative
    of the Dissolution of the Armies
    at the Peace. (May, 1865.)"
    (poem) **8**
"Authentic Anecdotes of 'Old
    Zack' [Reported for *Yankee
    Doodle* by his special correspon-
    dent at the seat of War]" (satiri-
    cal sketches) **8,** 195, 221
autobiographical material
    in "Jimmy Rose" 92
    in *Pierre* 158
    in *Redburn* 178
    in *White-Jacket* 213, 219
*Autograph Leaves of Our Country's
    Authors* (Bliss and Kennedy) 84
"The Avatar" (poem) **8**

Avery, Latham B., character based
    on 103
Azzageddi 9, 109

B

Babbalanja **9,** 22, 56, 108–111
Babo **9,** 14
Bach, Old **145,** 155
Bachelor (ship) **9,** 135
Bachelor's Delight (ship) 14
Backus, John 164
Bacon, Francis **9,** 161
Bailey, James A. 11
Baldy **9,** 216
"Ball's Bluff. A Reverie. (October,
    1861.)" (poem) **9**
Baltimore (character) **9,** 147
Baltimore Clipper 175
Banford, Isabel **9–10,** 27, 157,
    159, 160–163
banker **10,** 33–34
Bannadonna **10,** 12–13
barber **10,** 48–49
Bardianna **10**
Barnum, P. T. 8, **10–11**
    American Museum of 10, 11,
        11, 142
            caricature of 209
    character resembling 109,
        145
Barnum & Bailey Circus 11
Barny. *See* Melville, Malcolm
"Barrington Isle and the
    Buccaneers" (sketch) **10,** 60
Bartleby **10**
    model for 66
"Bartleby, the Scrivener: A
    Story of Wall-Street" (short
    story) **10**
    characters in 72, 143, 199
    publication history of 168
Bartlett, William Francis 42
Bates, Susan 114
Baton Rouge, Battle of 152
"The Battle for the Bay. (August,
    1864.)" (poem) **11**
"The Battle for the Mississippi.
    (April, 1862.)" (poem) **11**
"Battle of Stone River, Tennessee.
    A View from Oxford Cloisters.

(January, 1863.)" (poem)
    11–12
"A Battle Picture" (poem) **12**
Battle-Pieces and Aspects of the War
    (poetry collection) **12**
    material for 116, 184
    observations in 29
    poems in 4–5, 6, 7, 8, 9,
        11–12, 26, 28, 42, 43, 49, 51,
        55, 57, 59, 61, 63, 66, 68,
        71, 72, 80, 84, 85, 98, 100,
        103, 104, 113, 123, 138,
        139, 152–153, 166, 172, 179,
        181–182, 184, 186–187, 189,
        195, 207, 208, 209
    publication history of 76
Beauty (Chips) 23, **28,** 146, 147
Belex **12,** 34
Bell, Mr. and Mrs. **12,** 151
Bello ("Bello of the Hump") 4,
    12, 109
Bellows, Henry Whitney 12
"The Bell-Tower" (short story)
    12–13
    characters in 10
Belzoni, Giovanni Battista **13,** 184
Bembo ("the Mowree") **13,** 146,
    147, 148
Ben. *See* Sydney Ben
"The Bench of Boors" (poem) **13**
Beneventano, Ferdinando 42
"Benito Cereno" (short story)
    13–14
    characters in 5, 8, 9, 27, 54
    slavery depicted in 1
Bent, Anne Middleton 114
Bent, Martha 114
Bentham, Jeremy **14,** 208
Benthamites **14,** 16
Bentley, Richard **14,** 20
    contact with 22
    and *Mardi* 111
    and *Redburn* 178
    and *White-Jacket* 219
Béranger, Pierre Jean de 79
"The Berg (A Dream.)" (poem)
    14
Berkeley, George **15**
Berkshires 142, 164
Bessie (Bess). *See* Melville,
    Elizabeth
Bethlehem **15,** 39

Betty, Master (William Henry West Betty) 64, 77
Bezanson, Walter 29
Biddy **15,** 83
Bildad, Captain **15,** 127, 128
Billy Budd **15,** 15–19
    and Claggart 29
Billy Budd, Sailor (novel) **15–19**
    Benthamites in 14
    characters in 15, 26, 27, 29, 53, 65, 73, 138, 167–168, 171, 183, 188, 190, 209
    dedication in 15
    historical setting for 68
    inspiration for 69
    material for 187
    Milton's influence on 155
    predestination in 25, 166
    publication history of 19, 137
    rediscovery of 120
"Billy in the Darbies" (poem) 15, 19
bisexuality **19**
    in *Moby-Dick* 19, 127
    in poetry 2
    in *Redburn* 179
    in *Typee* 197
Black, David 23
Black Dan **19**
Black Rapids Coal Company, president of 45, **166,** 198
Bland **19–20,** 184, 216
Blandmour **20,** 165–166
Bliss, Alexander 84
"The Blue-Bird" (poem) **20**
Blunt, Bill **20**
Blunt, Jack **20,** 174
Bob, Captain **20,** 148
Boehme, Jacob 198
Bogart, Catherine E. 122
Bolton, Harry **20,** 176, 177–178, 179
Bomba (King Ferdinand II) 23, 141, 156
The Bonaparte Dream Book 174
book publishing **20–21.** *See also specific publishers*
book reviews, Melville's 50, 61, 78–79, 123–124, 195
Boomer, Captain **21,** 23, 134
Booth, Edwin 43
Booth, John Wilkes 43

Borabolla **21,** 108
Boston, Massachusetts **21**
Bougainville, Louis Antoine de 187
Bounty mutiny 147, 187
Bradford, Alexander Warfield **21**
Braid-Beard. *See* Mohi
Branch, Watson G. viii
breadfruit **21,** 202, 203
Brewster, George 85, 184
"Bridegroom-Dick" (poem) **21,** 69
Bridewell, Lieutenant **21,** 217
Bridges, James **21,** 87
Brinvilliers, Marie Madeleine Marguerite d'Aubry, marquise de 104–105
British editions. *See* English editions
Brodhead, John Romeyn **21–22**
Brooks, Preston S. 190
Brown, Isaac 199
Brown, John **22,** 56
    execution of *167*
    poem about 12, 22, 166
Brown, Oliver P. 180
Brown, Peter 74
Browne, J. Ross **22,** 61
    Etchings of a Whaling Cruise 22, 61, 124
Browne, Sir Thomas **22**
Bruat, Armand-Joseph **22,** 137, 148, 165
Bruno, Giordano 100
Bryant, John viii
Bryant, William Cullen **22**
"Buddha" (poem) **22**
Buddhism 103
Bulkington **22–23,** 128
Bunger, Dr. Jack **23**
Bungs **23,** 28, 147, 215
Bunker Hill, Battle of **23,** 115
Bunker Hill Monument 86–87
Bunn, Ned 197
Burgundy Club 79
"The Burgundy Club Sketches" **23**
Burke, Edmund **23**
Burke, Master Joseph 77
Burnside, Ambrose 84
Burr, Aaron 193
Burton, Robert **23**
Burton, William E. 98
Butler, Andrew P. 190

"Butterfly Ditty" (poem) **23**
Byrne, Benbow 13

C

Calabooza Beretanee **25,** 148, 149
Calhoun, John C. **25,** 110, 143
The California and Oregon Trail; being Sketches of Prairie and Rocky Mountain Life (Parkman), review of 123–124
Calvin, John 25, 166
Calvinistic (religion) **25,** 34
Camoens, Luis Vaz de 25, 28
"Camoens 1 (Before)" (poem) **25–26**
"Camoens in the Hospital 2 (After)" (poem) **25–26**
Campbell, Thomas 41
canallers **26**
cannibalism 204–205
The Canterbury Tales (Chaucer) **26,** 28
    influence on Melville 29, 33
"A Canticle: Significant of the national exaltation of enthusiasm at the close of the War." (poem) **26**
Cape Horn **26,** 197, 215
captain of marines 18, **26,** 138
Carlo **26,** 177
Carpegna, Edouard Jules Gabrielle de **26**
carpenter
    in *Moby-Dick* 135, 136
    in *Omoo* 26, 146
Cartesian dualism 54
Cass, Lewis 195
Cathy. *See* Gansevoort, Catherine Van Schaick
cat-o'-nine-tails 66, 215
cat's paw 17
Cedar Creek, Battle of 186
celibate **26**
Celio **27,** 31, 33
Cenci, Beatrice **27,** 163
century plant 4
Cereno, Don Benito 14, **27**
cetology 129
Chamois (ship) 91
chance stranger **27,** 46, 123, 164

chaplain
    in *Billy Budd* 18–19, **27**
    in *White-Jacket* 216
charity, theme of, in *The Confidence Man* 44–45, 47
Charlemont **27,** 48
Charles & Henry (ship) **27,** 119, 198
"Charles' Isle and the Dog-King" (sketch) **27,** 60
Charlton, Captain Richard **27,** 156, 205
Chartism **27–28,** 109, 176
Chase, Jack 25, **28**
    dedication of *Billy Budd* to 15
    in *White-Jacket* 198–199, 214, 215, 216, 217
    works inspired by 91
Chase, Owen **28,** 212
Chase, Richard viii
Chase, William Henry 28
Chateaubriand, François Auguste René, vicomte de 35
"Chattanooga. (November, 1863.)" (poem) **28**
Chaucer, Geoffrey **28**
    The Canterbury Tales **26,** 28
    influence on Melville 29, 33
Chickamauga, Battle of 153
Chinese junk, satiric squibs about 152, 221
"The Chipmunk" (poem) **28**
Chips ("Beauty") 23, **28,** 146, 147
cholera 177
Cholos 106
Christianity, Melville on 112. *See also* religion
Christodolus 1, **28**
chronology ix–xxiv
Church of St. Nicholas 175
civilization
    discussion of, in *Redburn* 174
    evils of, Melville on 187, 203
Civil War **29.** *See also Battle-Pieces*
    Battle of Antietam 209, *210*
    Battle of Cedar Creek 186
    Battle of Chickamauga 153
    Battle of Fredericksburg 84
    Battle of Gettysburg 71
    Battle of Lexington 152
    Battle of Manassas
        First 104

        Second 66
    Battle of Mobile Bay 11
    Battle of Murfreesborro 11–12
    Battle of Pea Ridge 84
    Battle of Shiloh 172, 186–187
    Battle of Springfield 101
    Battle of the Wilderness 6
    draft riots in 29, 80
    fall of Richmond, Virginia 63, *63*
    Melville's exposure to 116, 184
    Melville's position on 123
    prisons in 85, 179
    surrender at Appomattox 172, 190
Claggart, John 16, 17, **29,** 53
    comparison to Titus Oates 145
    Milton's exploration of malevolence and 155
Clarel 30–41, **41**
Clarel: A Poem and Pilgrimage in the Holy Land (narrative poem) **29–41**
    Arnold's influence on 56
    characters in 1, 2, 6, 10, 12, 26–27, 28, 52, 54, 55, 56, 59, 72, 75, 101, 112, 138, 141, 180, 182, 183, 191, 207, 209–210
    Chartism in, allusions to 28
    The Confidence Man compared with 43
    criticism on 29
    Dante's influence on 53
    hypocrisy exposed in 42
    influences on 6, 26, 29, 42, 51, 53, 56, 155
    locations in 15, 91–92
    Machiavelli invoked in 103
    material for 186
    Milton's influence on 155
    Platonism in 164
    predestination in 25
    publication history of 41
    rhyming scheme of 29–30
    Spinoza in, references to 188
Claret, Captain **41,** 113, 207, 214, 215, 216, 218
Clifford, John 76, 186

Cloots, Anacharsis 15, **41**
Clootz, Jean-Baptiste du Val de Grace, Baron 15, **41**
"Clover" (poem) **41**
"Cock-A-Doodle-Doo! Or, The Crowning of the Noble Cock Beneventano" (short story) **42,** 64
    characters in 123
Coffee, Old **145,** 215
Coffin, Peter **42,** 126, 127
Colbrook, Corporal **42,** 217
Colburn, Henry 14
Cole, Thomas **42**
Coleridge, Samuel Taylor **42**
    poem modeled after 25
    Rime of the Ancient Mariner 3, 131, **180**
"The College Colonel" (poem) **42**
collegian(s)
    character in *The Confidence Man* **42,** 44, 45
    in Civil War, poem about 153
colonialism **42**
    Melville on 93, 123, 200
"'The Coming Storm': A Picture by S. R. Gifford and owned by E. B. Included in the the N.A. Exhibition, April, 1865." (poem) **43**
"Commemorative of a Naval Victory" (poem) **43**
commodore **43**
A Companion to Melville Studies (Bryant) viii
Confessions (Rousseau) 181
confidence man 3, 44–49, **49**
The Confidence Man (novel) **43–49**
    Bacon in, reference to 9
    characters in 6, 10, 27, 42, 51, 59, 61, 71, 72, 104, 123, 138, 139, 141, 143, 145, 164, 166, 180, 190, 198, 207, 219, 220
    Clarel compared with 43
    hypocrisy exposed in 42
    influences on 26
    Machiavelli in, reference to 103
    Platonism in 164
    publication history of 49, 55

"The Conflict of Convictions. (1860–1.)" (poem) **49**
Conscription Acts 80
"The Continents" (poem) **49**
Cook, Captain James **49–50**, 77, 165, 187
Cooke, Robert Francis 155
    character based on 180
Cooper, James Fenimore **50**, *50*
    Melville's reviews of 195
    publisher of 14
"Cooper's New Novel" (book review) **50**
copyright **50–51**
    infringement on 20, 76, 152, 219
corporal punishment *65*, 65–66
    in *White-Jacket* 104, 113, 207–208, 215, 216, 218
cosmopolitan 47, 48–49, **51**
Coulter, William and Martha **51**, 166
The Course of Empire (epic painting series) 42
Crash, Captain **51**, 151
crippled soldier 46, **51**
criticism, collections of viii
Critique of Pure Reason (Kant) 95
"Crossing the Tropics (from 'The Saya-y-Manto')" (poem) **51**
Crusaders 30–31
"C——'s Lament" (poem) **25**
"The Cuban Pirate" (poem) **51**
Culture and Anarchy (Arnold) 6, **51**
"The Cumberland. (March, 1862.)" (poem) **51**
Cupid **51**, 155
Curtis, Catherine Gansevoort 69
Curtis, George William 189, 198
Curtis, Samuel R. 84
Cushing, William Barker 7
Custom House **52**, 120, 139
Cuticle, Cadwallader **52**, 217
Cyclopaedia of American Literature (Duyckinck) 57, 58
Cyclopedia of Wit and Humor (Burton) 98
Cylinder **52**, 214
Cymbeline (Shakespeare), epigraph taken from 157
cynicism 43

Cypriote 36, **52**
Cyril **52**

D

Daggoo **53**, 128
"The Dairyman's Child" (poem) **53**
Dan, Black **19**
Dana, Richard Henry, Jr. **53**, *53*, 186, 190
    influence on Melville 124
    Two Years Before the Mast 53, 200, 212
Danby **53**, 175
Dansker 17, **53**
Dante Alighieri **53**
    influence on Melville's work 159
Darby and Joan **53–54**, 150
Darwin, Charles 34, **54**
Dates **54**
Dead House 175
death
    meditations on 113, 165
    Herman Melville's 120
    Allan Melvill's 114
"The Death Craft" (short story) **54**
de Deer, Derick **54**, 133
deism 141
Delano, Amasa 14, **54**
    Narrative of Voyages and Travels in the Northern and Southern Hemispheres 13, 27, 54
Delight (ship) **54**, 136
Democratic Press (newspaper), Melville's publications in 54, 67
Dempsey, Jane Louisa. *See* Melville, Jane Louisa Dempsey
depression, Melville's 119, 187
Derwent 33–34, 35, 36, 37–38, 39–40, **54**
Descartes, Ren, **54**, 162
"The Devotion of the Flowers to Their Lady" (poem) **54–55**
dialectic logic 79
Dickens, Charles 20
Diderot, Denis **55**
Diogenes **55**
diptychs 155, 165–166, 199

"A Dirge for McPherson, Killed in front of Atlanta. (July, 1864.)" (poem) **55**
"Disinterment of the Hermes" (poem) **55**
"The Ditty of Aristippus" (poem) **55**
The Divine Comedy (Dante) 53
Dix & Edwards **55**, 157
Djalea 34, **55**, 56
doctor (Mr. Thompson) 173–174, **195**
Dole, Sanford B. 77
Dolliver Romance (Hawthorne) 211
Dolly (ship) 200
    model for 1
domestic themes
    poems on 85
    short stories on 5, 83
Dominican 35, **55**
"Donelson. (February, 1862.)" (poem) **55**
Don Hannibal 40, **56**, 180
Donjalolo ("Fonoo") **56**, 108
Don Quixote, Melville on 182
Dorothea, Aunt **8**, 159
Douglass, Frederick 2, **56**
Douron, Clement 54
"Dover Beach" (Arnold) 6, 29, **56**
Doxodox **56**, 110
draft riots 29, 80
Drouth, Daniel 72
Druze 37, 55, **56**
Dupetit-Thouars, Abel Aubert 26, **56–57**, 148, 165, 200–201
Dupont, Samuel R. 57
"Dupont's Round Fight. (November, 1861.)" (poem) **57**
"The Dust-Layers" (poem) **57**, 171
Dutch aristocracy
    Melville's distancing from 85
    in *Pierre* 158
"A Dutch Christmas up the Hudson in the Time of the Patroons" (poem) **57**
Dutch settlements 3
Duyckinck, Evert A. 42, 50, *57*, **57–58**, 61, 99
    library of 105
    and *Yankee Doodle* publications 153
Duyckinck, George 50, **58**

Dwight, Timothy, influence on Melville 5

E

"The Eagle of the Blue" (poem) **59**
Early, Jubal 186
Egbert 48, **59**
Egypt, Melville's travels in 57, 73, 84, 171
Elijah **59**, 128
Eliot, T. S. 41
Emerson, Ralph Waldo **59**, 198
    and abolitionism 1, 22
    on book publishing 20
"The Encantadas, or Enchanted Isles" 10, **59–61**
    characters in 81, 145
    publication history of 60–61, 168, 197
    sources for 59
Enderby, Samuel **61**
English editions 20, 22
    of *Mardi* 111
    of *Redburn* 178
    of *White-Jacket* 219
"The Enthusiast" (poem) **61**
"The Enviable Isles (from 'Rammon')" (poem) **61**, 171
envoi 98. *See also* L'Envoi
Episcopal clergyman **61**
"Epistle to Daniel Shepherd (poem) **61**
epitaph 1
"An Epitaph" (poem) **61**
Erie (ship) 67, 71
"Etchings of a Whaling Cruise" (book review) **61**, 124
Etchings of a Whaling Cruise (Browne) 22
    Melville's review of 61, 124
etymology, in *Moby-Dick* 125
Europe. *See also* Greece; Italy
    Melville's trip to 29, 124, 186, 187, 191
    Revolutions of 1848 **179–180**
Evils and Abuses in the Naval and Merchant Service Exposed (McNally) 19–20
execution, Billy Budd's 19

existential philosophy 10
extracts, in *Moby-Dick* 125

F

Falconer, William, "The Shipwreck" 145
"The Fall of Richmond. The tidings received in the Northern Metropolis. (April, 1865.)" (poem) 63
Falsgrave, Mr. **64**, 160, 161
"Falstaff's Lament Over Prince Hal Become Henry V" (poem) **64**
family, Melville's 3
    financial difficulties of 3, 70–71, 114, 115
Fanny. *See* Melville, Frances Priscilla; Thomas, Frances Melville
Farnoopoo **64**, 150
Farnowar **64**, 150
"Far Off-Shore" (poem) **64**
Farragut, David 11
fate **64**
    in *Billy Budd* 25, 166
    in *Moby-Dick* 126, 166
    in *Pierre* 159
    predestination 25, 34, 64, **166**
Faulkner, William, Melville's influence on 137
Faust (Goethe) 72
Fayaway **64**, 193, 194, 202, 203
Fedallah **64**, 131, 132, 155
Fenn, Mrs. Deacon Curtis T., character modeled on 138
Ferdinand I (emperor of Austria) 179
Ferdinand II (king of the Two Sicilies) 23, 156
fiction. *See also specific titles*
    discussion of 48
    short 64
"The Fiddler" (short story) **64**
    characters in 79, 188
Fidele (riverboat) 44, **64–65**
"Field Asters" (poem) **65**
"Fifty-Four Forty or Fight" 3
"The Figure-Head" (poem) **65**
financial difficulties, Melville's family and 3, 70–71, 114, 115

first lieutenant **65**
Fivona, Ohiro Moldona. *See* Ohiru Moldona Fivona
Flask **65**, 128, 135
Fleece **65**
flogging *65*, **65–66**
    in *White-Jacket* 104, 113, 207–208, 215, 216, 218
flowers, language of **97**, 107, 211
Fly, Eli James Murdock **66**, 119
    character based on 10
Fonoo (Donjalolo) **56**, 108
Ford, William **66**, 92
"'Formerly a Slave.' An idealized Portrait, by E. Vedder, in the Spring Exhibition at the National Academy, 1865." (poem) **66**, 196
Forrest, Edwin 7, 113
"The Fortitude of the North under the Disaster of the Second Manassas" (poem) **66**
Fort Orange 3, 70
Fort Stanwix **66**, 70
Fouqué, Friedrich 221
Fourier, Charles **66–67**
Fox, Luther 189
Fox sisters 188
Fra Angelico **67**
"Fragments from a Writing Desk" **67**, 98
    publication history of 54
"Fragments of a Lost Gnostic Poem of the 12th Century" (poem) **67**
France, Revolution of 1848 179
Frank **67**, 71, 217
Franklin, Benjamin **67**
    in *Israel Potter* 87–88
Franklin, Samuel 66
Fredericksburg, Maryland, battle near 84
free will
    doctrine denying 25, 34, 64, 126, **166**
    question of 126
French Directory **67**
Frenchman, Lyonese 40, **101**
French Revolution 41, **67–68**
    inspiration for 181, 210
    motto of 180

"The Frenzy in the Wake. Sherman's advance through the Carolinas. (February, 1865.)" (poem) **68**

"The Frigate, and Ship Flyaway" (sketch) 60, **68**

"Fruit and Flower Painter" (poem) **68**

Fugitive Slave Act (1850) 185

G

Gabriel **69,** 91, 132

Gage, Thomas 23

Gal pagos Islands 59–61

gam 3, 131

Gansevoort, Catherine ("Kate"). *See* Lansing, Catherine Gansevoort

Gansevoort, Catherine Van Schaick ("Cathy") **69,** 70, 118, 121

Gansevoort, Guert 21, **69**
  and Cooper 50
  and *Somers* mutiny 187

Gansevoort, Han 219

Gansevoort, Henry Sanford **69–70,** 85
  during Civil War 184

Gansevoort, Herman **70,** 118
  dedication of *Omoo* to 151–152

Gansevoort, Leonard 69, 172

Gansevoort, Maria. *See* Melville, Maria Gansevoort

Gansevoort, New York **70**

Gansevoort, Peter (grandfather) 69, **70,** 121
  character based on 158
  at Fort Stanwix 66

Gansevoort, Peter (uncle) 3, **70–71,** 97
  and Allan Melville 115
  and Cooper 50
  and Eli Fly 66
  financial help provided by 114

Gansevoort, Stanwix 67, **71**

Gansevoort Hotel 70

"The Garden of Metrodorus" (poem) **71**

Gardiner, Captain **71,** 136

Garrison, William Lloyd 1

Gauguin, Paul 187

"The 'Gees" (sketch) **71,** 92
  characters in 96

General Tom Thumb 10

Gentian, Jack 23

gentleman with gold sleeve buttons 45, 67, **71**

George III (king of Great Britain) **71,** 87

German, John 91, 101

"Gettysburg. The Check. (July, 1863.)" (poem) **71**

Gibbon, Edward 2

Ginger Nut **72**

Girard, Stephen 16, **72**

"Give Me the Nerve" (poem) **72**

Glaucon 33, 34, **72**

Glendinning, General **72,** 158, 159

Glendinning, Mary **72,** 158–161

Glendinning, Pierre 15, **72,** 158–163
  Dante compared with 53

Gnosticism 67

Goethe, Johann Wolfgang von **72**

"The Gold Bug" (Poe) 75

"Gold in the Mountain" (poem) **72**

Goneril 45, **72**

"The Good Craft 'Snow-Bird'" (poem) **72**

Goodman, Francis 47–48, 49, **72**

good merchant 45

Gould, John W., influence on Melville 54

Grace Church, New York City 199

Grant, Ulysses S. 28, 115
  victory of 190

Graveling, Captain 15, **73**

"A Grave near Petersburg, Virginia." (poem) **72**

Great Heidelburgh Tun **73,** 133

"The Great Pyramid" (poem) **73**

Greece, poems about 5, 7, 73, 156, 168, 190

"Greek Architecture" (poem) **73**

"Greek Masonry" (poem) **73**

The Greek Slave (Powers) **166**

Greene, Richard Tobias *73,* **73–74,** 119, 199, 205–206

character based on 196
  in Civil War 182
  poem addressing 197
  reunion with 148

Greenlander **74,** 173, 174

Greylock, Mount **74,** 157

Griggs, George 74

Griggs, Helen Maria Melville **74,** 117

"A Ground Vine Intercedes with the Queen of Flowers for the Merited Recognition of Clover" (poem) **74**

Guert Can 69

Gun-Deck **74,** 174

Guy, Captain **74,** 146, 147, 149

H

Habbibi **75**

Hafiz 79

"The Haglets" (poem) **75**

Hakim, al- 56

Hall, James, *Sketches of History, Life and Manners in the West* 138

Halyard, Harry 212

Hamlet (Shakespeare)
  Pierre compared with 160, 161
  references to, in Melville's work 47, 48

Hancock, Winfield Scott 153

Handsome Mary **75,** 175

Hannibal **75**

Hannibal, Don 40, **56,** 180

Happar **75**

"The Happy Failure. A Story of the River Hudson" (short story) 64, **75–76**

Hardy, Lem **76,** 147

Harper, Fletcher 76

Harper, James 76

Harper, John 76

Harper, Joseph Wesley 76

Harper & Brothers **76**
  and *Battle-Pieces* 12
  and *Mardi* 111
  and *Omoo* 152
  and *Redburn* 178
  and *Typee* 206
  and *White-Jacket* 218

Harper's Ferry, raid on 22, 56
Harper's New Monthly Magazine **76**
    Melville's publications in 42,
        64, 71, 92, 105, 155, 157,
        166, 186
Harry the Reefer 54
Hatch, Agatha **76,** 186
Hauser, Kaspar (Casper) **76–77**
Hautboy 64, **77**
Hautia **77,** 107, 108, 111, 221
Hawaii (Sandwich Islands) **77,** 93
    British takeover of 156, 205
    Melville in 119
    rulers of 95
Hawthorne, Nathaniel **77–78,** *78*
    and abolitionism 1
    and "Agatha story" 76
    and bisexuality 19
    comment on Melville 29
    Dolliver Romance 211
    employment of 52
    friendship with 120, 142, 164
    lament for lost relationship
        with 138
    Mosses from an Old Manse
        78–79, 114
    "The Old Manse" 157
Hawthorne, Sophia Amelia
    Peabody **78,** 151, 220
"Hawthorne and His Mosses"
    (review) **78–79,** 120, 157
    criticism of Irving in 85
Hayford, Harrison 19
health problems, Melville's 83
"Hearth-Roses" (poem) **79**
"Hearts-of-Gold" (poem) **79**
Hegel, Georg Wilhelm Friedrich
    79, 124
Heidelburgh Tun. *See* Great
    Heidelburgh Tun
Heine, Heinrich **79**
Hello **79**
Helmstone 64, **79**
"Herba Santa" (poem) **79**
herb-doctor 46, **79**
Hermes, statue of 55
Heth, Joice 10
Highlander (ship) 98, 172–178
Hine, Ephraim Curtiss **79**
    character modeled on 98
*History of the Decline and Fall of the
    Roman Empire* (Gibbon) 2

Hivohitee **79–80**
Hoadley, Catherine Gansevoort
    Melville ("Kate") **80**
Hoadley, John Chapman 2, 80
Hobbes, Thomas 15, **80**
    Leviathan 125
Hoff, William 221
Hoffman, Charles Fenno **80,** 221
Holmes, Oliver Wendell 92, 164
home, Melville's 6, 7, 97. *See also*
    Arrowhead
homoerotic feelings. *See* bisexual-
    ity
"Honor" (poem) **80**
"Hood's Isle and the Hermit
    Oberlus" (sketch) 60, **80**
Horace 79
"The House-top. A Night Piece.
    (July, 1863.)" (poem) **80**
Hudson, Henry 3
Hudson River School of landscape
    painting 42
Hume, David **80**
Hunilla **81**

I

iambic tetrameter 29
"I and My Chimney" (short story)
    5, 79, **83**
    characters in 15, 93, 184
    "Jimmy Rose" compared with
        83, 92
iceberg, poem about 14
idealism, American, satire of 86
"Immolated" (poem) **83**
imperialism. *See* colonialism
impressment 16, **83,** 218
"In a Bye-Canal" (poem) **83**
"In a Church of Padua" (poem)
    83–84
"In a Garret" (poem) **84**
"In a Nutshell" (poem) **84**
Indomitable (ship) 15, 16, **84**
"Inscription" (poem) **84**
"Inscription for Marye's Heights,
    Fredericksburg." (poem) **84**
"Inscription for the Graves at Pea
    Ridge, Arkansas." (poem) **84**
"Inscription for the Slain at
    Fredericksburg." (poem) **84**

"In Shards the Sylvan Vases Lie"
    (poem) **84**
"In the Desert" (poem) **84**
"In the Hall of Marbles (Lines
    Recalled from a Destroyed
    Poem)" (poem) **84**
"In the Jovial Age of Old" (poem)
    85
"In the Old Farm-House: The
    Ghost" (poem) **85**
"In the Pauper's Turnip-field"
    (poem) **85**
"In the Prison Pen. (1864.)"
    (poem) **85**
"In the Turret. (March, 1862.)"
    (poem) **85**
"Iris (1865)" (poem) **85**
ironclad ships, poem about 208
Irving, Washington **85–86,** 118
    The Alhambra 184
    "The Legend of Sleepy
        Hollow" 5
    on *Typee* 206
Ishmael **86,** 125–137
    Clarel compared with 41
    as Platonist 164
"The Isle of the Cross" (novella)
    76, 186
"The Isles at Large" (sketch) 59,
    86
isolato **86,** 125, 128, 135
Israel Potter: His Fifty Years of Exile
    (novel) **86–89**
    characters in 3, 21, 71, 123,
        197, 220
    dedication in 86
    hypocrisy exposed in 42
    publication history of 89, 168
    satire in 86, 89
Italy 89
    poems about 123, 171

J

"Jack Roy" (poem) **91**
Jackson **91,** 173, 176, 177
Jackson, Andrew 115, 193
Jackson, Jane 66, 196
Jackson, Robert 91
Jackson, Stonewall, poems about
    189

Jarl **91,** 105, 106, 109

Jennie. *See* Melville, Jane Louisa Dempsey

Jermin, John **91,** 146, 147, 148, 149, 210

Jeroboam (ship) **91,** 132

Jerusalem 32, **91–92**
 Mount Olivet *30*

"Jimmy Rose" (short story) 5, **92**
 characters in 15
 "I and My Chimney" compared with 83, 92
 narrator of 66

Joan, Pope 92

"John Marr" (poem) **92**

John Marr and Other Sailors with Some Sea-Pieces (poetry collection) **92**
 epigrams in 156
 poems in 2, 14, 21, 51, 61, 64, 65, 72, 75, 91, 103–104, 145, 156, 196–197, 199

Johnson, Dr. **92–93,** 147, 149

Johnson, Dr. Thomas, character based on 52

Johnson, James 20

Johnston, Albert Sidney 186

John VIII (pope) 92

Jonah **93**

Jones **93**

Jones, John Paul *86,* **93,** 184
 in *Israel Potter* 88

Jones, Mr. 21, **93,** 172, 174, 178

Jones, Thomas ap Catesby 43, **93,** 214

Journal of a Cruise Made to the Pacific Ocean (Porter) 59

Judd, G. P. 27, 77, **93,** 156

Julia 5, 83, **93**

Julia (ship) 13, 100, 146, 205
 model for 91

Jungfrau (ship) 133

K

Kamehameha I (Hawaiian ruler) 77, **95**

Kamehameha II (Hawaiian ruler) **95**

Kamehameha (Hawaiian ruler) 56, 57, 77, 93, **95**

Kamehameha IV (Hawaiian ruler) **95**

Kamehameha V (Hawaiian ruler) **95**

Kannakippers **95**

Kant, Immanuel **95**
 influence on Melville 124
 Locke contrasted with 99
 Schiller contrasted with 183
 and transcendentalism 198

Karakoee **95,** 112, 205

Karky **95**

Kate. *See* Hoadley, Catherine Gansevoort Melville; Lansing, Catherine Gansevoort

Kazin, Alfred 89

Kean, Captain Hosea **96**

keel-hauling 218

Kenesaw Mountain, Battle of 152

Kennedy, John P. 84

King Lear (Shakespeare), Fool in, character modeled on 209

Knickerbocker School 85

Knowles, Sheridan 199

Kolory **96,** 204

Kooloo **96,** 149

Kory-Kory **96,** 194, 202, 203, 204

Koztanza 100, 110

Kushner, Tony viii

L

La Farge, John 64

Lamartine, Alphonse de 35

"Lamia's Song" (poem) **97**

language of flowers **97,** 107, 211

Lansing, Abraham 97

Lansing, Catherine Gansevoort ("Kate") **97**

Lansing, Susan 71

Lansingburgh, New York 3, **97–98,** 119, 121

Laocoön, statue of 33

Larry **98,** 174

"The Last Leaf" (Holmes) 92

Lathrop, George Parsons 55

L.A.V. **97**

Lavender **98,** 173–174

Leatherstocking Tales 50

Leaves of Grass (Whitman) 74

lectures, Melville's 187–188, 189, 198

Lee, Robert E. 98
 surrender of 190

Leech, Samuel, *Thirty Years from Home, or A Voice from the Main Deck* 194

"Lee in the Capitol" (poem) **98**

Leeward Islands 187

"The Legend of Sleepy Hollow" (Irving) 5, 86

Leibnitz, Gottfried 100

Lemsford **98,** 214, 216

Lenox, Massachusetts 164

"L'Envoi" (poem) **181**

"L'Envoi: The Return of the Sire de Nesle, A.D. 16—" (poem) **98**

Lesbian (character) 37, 38, **98**

Levant (Middle East), Melville's trip to 29, 186, 187, 191

Leviathan (Hobbes) 80, 125

Leviathan (ship) 151

Lexington, Kentucky, Battle of 152

"The Lightning-Rod Man" (short story) **98**

Liliuokalani, Queen (Hawaiian ruler) 77

Lincoln, Abraham **98**
 assassination of 43, 113
 Melville's encounter with 29, 99
 on Mexican War 123

Lind, Jenny 10

literary recognition, poem about 195

Literary World (journal) **99**
 editors of 57, 80, 221
 Melville's publications in 50, 61, 78, 123–124, 195

literary world, Melville's disgust with 20–21

"The Little Good Fellows" (poem) 41, **99**

Liverpool, England **99,** 119
 guidebook to 158
 Melville's trip to 172
 in *Redburn* 175–176

Lizzie. *See* Melville, Elizabeth Knapp Shaw

Llanyllyn, Aunt 8

Locke, John **99**

"The Loiterer" (poem) **99–100**

Lombardo **100,** 110
"Lone Fonts" (poem) **100**
Long, George 219
Longfellow, Henry Wadsworth
    at Melvill House 122
    publisher of 14
Long Ghost, Dr. **100,** 146, 147,
    150–151
    model for 198
Loo **100,** 151
"Look-out Mountain. The Night
    Fight. (November, 1863.)"
    (poem) **100**
Lory-Lory 150
lost generation, Melville's influ-
    ence on 137
Louis Philippe (king of France)
    179
Louis Napoleon 179
love poems 100
"The Lover and the Syringa Bush"
    (poem) **100**
Lowell, Charles Russell 184
Lucy-Ann (ship) **100–101,** 119
    sailors on, characters based
    on 13, 74, 91, 198
The Lusiads (Camoens) 25, 28
"Lyon. Battle of Springfield,
    Missouri. (August, 1861.)"
    (poem) **101**
Lyon, Nathaniel **101**
Lyonese 40, **101**

M

Macey **103,** 132
Machiavelli, Niccolò 39, **103**
Mackenzie, Alexander Slidell 69,
    187
Mackie (Mackey). *See* Melville,
    Malcolm
Macready, William 7, 113, 199
Madam Jane. *See* Melville, Jane
    Louisa Dempsey
"Madam Mirror" (poem) **103**
"Madcaps" (poem) **103**
Mad Jack **103,** 184, 214, 215
Magi 103
"Magian Wine" (poem) **103**
Magnalia Christi Americana
    (Mather) 5

"Magnanimity Baffled" (poem)
    103
maiden voyage, Melville's 54, 119,
    172, 183
Mailer, Norman, Melville's influ-
    ence on 137
"The Maldive Shark" (poem)
    103–104
"Malvern Hill. (July, 1862.)"
    (poem) **104**
Manassas
    First Battle at 104
    Second Battle at 66
Mandeville **104,** 217
man from the Carolinas **104**
manifest destiny, doctrine of 4.
    See also predestination
man in gray 44, **104**
"The Man-of-War Hawk" (poem)
    104
man with a long weed 44, 45, **104**
man with the traveling cap 45, **104**
Maori
    character in *Omoo* 13, 146,
        147, 148
    tattooing among 194
Mapple, Father **104,** 126–127
    model for 139
    sermon of 61
Marbonna **104,** 151
"The March into Virginia, Ending
    in the First Manassas. (July,
    1861.)" (poem) **104**
"The Marchioness of Brinvilliers"
    104–105
"The March to the Sea
    (December, 1864)" (poem) 68,
    105
Mardi (novel) **105–112,** 119–120
    characters in 1, 3, 4, 9, 12, 21,
        56, 77, 79–80, 91, 100, 113,
        137, 143, 156–157, 163–164,
        183, 193, 198, 207, 209, 221
    Chartism in, allusions to 28
    criticism of, attempt to fore-
        stall 1, 110
    flower symbolism in 97
    influences on 22, 23, 42
    publication history of 14, 76,
        111
    public reception of 172
Margoth 35, 36, **112**

"The Margraves's Birthnight"
    (poem) **112**
Marhar-Rarrar **112,** 150
Marharvai **112,** 150
Marheyo 96, **112,** 202, 203, 205
Marianna **112,** 157
Marnoo **112,** 193, 203, 205
Marquesas **112,** 119, 199, 200
    indigenous tribes of 75, 199
marriage, Melville's 65, 97, 211
Mar Saba 29, **113**
"The Martyr. Indicative of the pas-
    sion of the people on the 15th
    of April, 1865." (poem) **113**
Marvell, Andrew 16, **113**
Mary, Handsome **75,** 175
Masonic order 184
master-at-arms 16, 29
mast-head 130
Mather, Cotton 5
Matthews, Cornelius **113,** 221
Max the Dutchman ("Red Max")
    113, 173–175, 174
May-Day **113,** 181, 215, 217
Mayhew **113**
McClellan, George B. 104, 209
McNally, William 19–20
McPherson, James Birdseye 55
Measure for Measure (Shakespeare)
    157
"The Medallion in Villa Albina &
    C" (poem) **113**
Media 107, 108, 110–111, **113**
"A Meditation: Attributed to a
    Northerner after attending the
    last of two funerals from the
    same homestead—those of a
    National and a Confederate offi-
    cer (brothers), his kinsmen,
    who had died from the effects of
    wounds received in the closing
    battles." (poem) **113**
Mehevi **113,** 202, 203, 205
Melvill, Allan 69, **114,** *116,* 119
    financial difficulties of 3,
        70–71, 115
    marriage of 114, 121
    travel to Europe 99
Melvill, Anne Marie Priscilla **114**
Melvill, Françoise Raymonde
    Eulogie Marie des Douleurs
    Lamé-Fleury **114**

Melvill, Mary Ann Augusta Hobart
    114
Melvill, Nancy Wroe 186
Melvill, Priscilla **114**
Melvill, Robert 66, **114–115,** 179
    in Civil War 182
Melvill, Thomas **115,** 164
    character based on 92
Melvill, Thomas, Jr. 114, **115,** 164
Melville **115**
Melville, Allan, Jr. 85, **115–116**
    and Arrowhead purchase 6,
        116
    during Civil War 184
    as publishing agent 12
    relationship with Herman 69,
        105
Melville, Augusta ("Gus") 100,
    116, *116,* 120
Melville, Catherine Gansevoort
    ("Kate"). *See* Hoadley,
    Catherine Gansevoort Melville
*Melville: A Collection of Critical
    Essays* (Chase) viii
Melville: The Critical Heritage
    (Branch) viii
Melville, Elizabeth ("Bessie,"
    "Bess") **116–117,** *121*
Melville, Elizabeth Knapp Shaw
    ("Lizzie") 74, 97, **117**
    and Henry Bellows 12
    character based on 158
    courtship of 97, 105, 119
    family of 21
    marriage to Herman 65, 97,
        211
    and Sarah Morewood 138
    poem dedicated to 4
    portraits of *117, 211*
    relations with father 186
Melville, Frances ("Fanny"). *See*
    Thomas, Frances Melville
Melville, Frances Priscilla
    ("Fanny") **117–118**
Melville, Gansevoort 3, 21, 22,
    118, *118*
    after father's death 121
    as publishing agent 139, 206,
        219
Melville, Helen Maria. *See* Griggs,
    Helen Maria Melville
Melville, Herman **118–120**

during Civil War 184
depression of 119, 187
employment in Custom
    House 52, 120
female characters of 219–220
health problems of 83
home of 6, *7,* 97
marriage of 65, 97, 211
personality of 10
poetry of 29–30, 120
portraits of *51, 178, 200*
pseudonyms of 54, 60, 97,
    168
rediscovery of 137
relationship with mother 122
sea voyages of 1, 54, 59,
    119–120, 172, 183
smoking habit of 79
teaching career of 119
travel to Europe and the
    Middle East 29, 124, 186,
    187, 191
whaling voyage of 1, 119, 199
Melville, Jane Louisa Dempsey
    ("Jennie," "Madam Jane")
    115–116, **120**
Melville, Malcolm ("Barny,"
    "Mackie," "Mackey") **120–121,**
    121
    birth of 172
    suicide of 117, 119
Melville, Maria Gansevoort 69, 70,
    121, **121–122**
    character based on 158
    financial difficulties of 71
    home of 3
    marriage of 114, 121
Melville, Sophia Elizabeth
    Thurston 115, 120, **122**
Melville, Stanwix ("Stannie") 70,
    117, *121,* **122**
Melville, Thomas ("Tom") 12, **122**
    dedication of *Redburn* to 178
    poems dedicated to 197
    as whaler 212
Melvill House 114, **122,** 164
Mendelssohn, Moses **123**
"Merry Ditty of the Sad Man"
    (poem) **123**
Merrymusk 42, **123**
Metcalf, Eleanor 120
metempsychosis 134

Meteor (ship) 197
Methodist minister 44, **123**
Metrodorus of Chios 71
Mexican War **123**
    Guert Gansevoort in 69
    Zachary Taylor in 195
Middle East (Levant), Melville's
    trip to 29, 186, 187, 191
midshipmen
    Melville's attitude toward 67,
        71
    in *White-Jacket* 214, 216
"Milan Cathedral" (poem) **123**
military
    corporal punishment in *65,*
        65–66, 104, 113, 207–208,
        215, 216, 218
    impressment in 16, **83,** 218
Millet, Sir John 87, **123**
Millthorpe, Charlie **123,** 162
Milton, John, *Paradise Lost* **155**
    allusions to 4
    influence on Melville 29
mind-body problem 54
Miscellany (magazine) 14
miser 45, 46, **123**
"Misgivings. (1860.)" (poem) **123**
missionaries, Melville's criticism of
    149–150
Mississippi steamboat(s)
    advertisement for *43*
    Fidele 44, 64–65
Missourian 27, 46–47, **123**
Mitchell, Maria 2
Mobile Bay, Battle for 11
Moby-Dick; or, The Whale (novel)
    124–137
    bisexuality in, suggestions of
        19, 127
    characters in 2–3, 15, 21,
        22–23, 42, 53, 54, 59, 64, 65,
        71, 103, 104, 113, 157, 164,
        169, 171, 188–189, 190, 194
    dedication in 78
    dialectic in 79
    Duyckinck's review of 58, 99
    Emerson's mythical notions
        satirized in 59
    Father Mapple's sermon in 61
    happy ending in 100
    influences on 23, 42, 53, 72,
        185, 209

Moby-Dick; or, The Whale (novel)
(*continued*)
    Mardi compared with 193
    material for 124, 212
    motivation for writing 124
    narrator of 86
    Platonism in 164
    predestination in 25, 166
    publication history of 14, 76,
      137
    public reaction to 120
    rediscovery of 137
    Shakespeare's influence on
      185, 209
    sources for 28
    Spinoza invoked in 188
    whaling ships in 9, 61, 91,
      157, 171, 181
    works prefiguring 13
modernism **137**
Moerenhout, Jacques-Antoine 57,
  137
Mogul **137**
Mohi ("Braid-Beard") 108, 111,
  137
Monitor (ship) 85
"Monody" (poem) 78, **138**
"Montaigne and His Kitten"
  (poem) **138**
"Mont Blanc" (Shelley) 34
Mordant, Mr. **138**
More, Thomas, *Utopia* 171–172
Moredock, Colonel John 47, 75,
  138
Morewood, John Rowland **138**
Morewood, Sarah 42, **138,** 220
Mortmain 33, 34, 36, 37, 38, 67,
  138, 180
Mosby, George P. 184
Mosby's Raiders 184
Mosses from an Old Manse
  (Hawthorne) 114, 157
    review of 78–79
"The Mound by the Lake" (poem)
  138
Mount Greylock **74,** 157
Mount Olivet, Jerusalem *30*
Mowanna **138,** 200
Mow-Mow **138–139**
Mowree (Bembo) **13,** 146, 147, 148
"Mr Parkman's Tour" (book
  review) **123–124**

Mudge, Reverend Enoch **139**
Mulligan, James A. 152
Mumford, Lewis 41
Murfreesborro, Tennessee, Battle
  of 11–12
Murphy, Father **139,** 149
Murray, John 20, **139**
  and *Mardi* 14, 22, 105, 111
  and *Typee* 118, 206
"The Muster: Suggested by the
  Two Days' Review at
  Washington. (May, 1865.)"
  (poem) **139**
mute **139**
mutiny(ies) 16
  Bounty 147, 187
  Nore 143
  Somers 15, **187**
"My Jacket Old" (poem) **139**

N

*Na Motu; or, Reef-Rovings in the
  South Seas: A Narrative of
  Adventures at the Hawaiian,
  Georgian, and Society Islands*
  (Perkins) 12
Nantucket, Massachusetts 126,
  127, **141,** 186
"Naples in the Time of Bomba"
  (poem) 23, 141
Napoleon III. *See* Louis Napoleon
Napoleon Bonaparte 67
*Narrative of the Most Extraordinary
  and Distressing Shipwreck in
  Whale-Ship Essex* (Chase) 28, 212
*Narrative of the U.S. Exploring
  Expedition During the Years 1838,
  1839, 1840, 1841, 1842* (Wilkes)
  169, 219
*Narrative of Voyages and Travels in
  the Northern and Southern
  Hemispheres* (Delano) 13, 27, 54
Nassau (ship) 171, 189
Nathan 31, **141**
navy
  corporal punishment in *65,*
    65–66, 104, 113, 207–208,
    215, 216, 218
  impressment in 16, **83,** 218
Negro cripple 44, 45, 104, **141**

Nehemiah 31, 32–33, 34, 35, 36,
  141
Nelson, Horatio **141**
  in Battle of Nile 141, **143**
  in Battle of Trafalgar **197**
  glory and idealism epitomized
    by 14
  reference in *Billy Budd* 16
  reference in *Moby-Dick* 130
Neoplatonism **141**
Neversink (ship) **141,** 143, 214–218
"The New Ancient of Days: The
  Man of the Cave of Engihoul"
  (poem) 84, **141–142**
New Bedford, Massachusetts **142**
"The New Planet" (satire) **142**
"The New Rosicrucians" (poem)
  142
New York City **142**
  Grace Church in 199
  as literary capital 21
  Melville family in 105
  Tammany Hall in 193–194
"The New Zealot to the Sun"
  (poem) **142**
"The Night-March" (poem)
  142–143
Nile, Battle of 141, **143**
Nimni 109, **143**
Nippers **143**
Noble, Charles Arnold 47–48, **143**
Nord **143,** 214
Nore mutiny **143**
"Norfolk Isle and the Chola
  Widow" (sketch) 60, **143**
Norton, Edward 143
Nuku Hiva (Nukuheva) 112, 119,
  146, 199, 200–201
Nulli 25, 110, **143**

O

Oates, Titus 16, **145**
Oberlus 60, **145**
observer/participant 86
"Off Cape Colonna" (poem) **145**
Ohiro Moldona Fivona 1, 109, **145**
Oh Oh 109, **145**
"Old Age in His Ailing" (poem)
  145
Old Bach **145,** 155

Old Coffee **145,** 215
"Old Counsel of the Young Master of a Wrecked California Clipper" (poem) **145**
"The Old Fashion" (poem) **145**
old man 48, **145**
"The Old Manse" (Hawthorne) 157
Old Prudence 48, **145**
"The Old Shipmaster and His Crazy Barn" (poem) **145–146**
Old Yarn. *See* Yarn
Olivet, Mount *30*
Omni-Balsamic Reinvigorator 46
Omoo: A Narrative of Adventures in the South Seas (novel) **146–152**
   characters in 2, 4, 6, 9, 12, 13, 19, 20, 23, 28, 51, 53–54, 64, 74, 76, 91, 92–93, 96, 100, 104, 112, 139, 171, 181, 183, 187, 190–191, 209, 210, 219, 220, 223
   dedication in 151–152
   material for 100–101, 119
   political commentary in 95
   prison in 25, 148, 149
   publication history of 76, 139, 151–152
   setting for 25
   taboos in 193
   tattooing in 194
"On a natural Monument in the field of Georgia." (poem) **152**
O'Neill, Eugene, Melville's influence on 137
"On Sherman's Men who fell in the Assault of Kenesaw Mountain, Georgia." (poem) **152**
"On the Chinese Junk" (satiric squibs) **152,** 221
"On the Grave of a young Cavalry Officer killed in the Valley of Virginia." (poem) **152**
"On the Home Guards Who Perished in the Defense of Lexington, Missouri." (poem) **152**
"On the Men of Maine killed in the Victory of Baton Rouge, Louisiana." (poem) **152**

"On the Photograph of a Corps Commander." (poem) **153**
"On the Sea Serpent" (satiric squib) 152, **153**
"On the Slain at Chickamauga." (poem) **153**
"On the Slain Collegians." (poem) **153**
Orange, Fort 3, 70
Oregon Territory, struggle over 3–4
Osborne, Frances 120

P

Paige, Elbridge G. 187
Paine, Thomas 15, 23
pantheism 103, 141, **155**
   in *Pierre* 155, 160
Papeetee 148–149
Paradise Lost (Milton) **155**
   allusions to 4
   influence on Melville 29
"The Paradise of Bachelors and the Tartarus of Maids" (short story) **155**
   characters in 51, 145, 180
Parker, Hershel viii, 163
Parki (brigantine) 106
Parkman, Francis, *The California and Oregon Trail; being Sketches of Prairie and Rocky Mountain Life,* review of 123–124
Parrot, Robert Parker 190
Parsee **155**
Parthenon 5, 73, 156
"The Parthenon" (poem) **156**
Pat 149
Paulet, Lord George 27, 77, **156,** 165
"Pausilippo (in the Time of Bomba)" (poem) 23, **156**
Peabody, Elizabeth Palmer 78
Peabody, Mary Tyler 78
Pea Ridge, Arkansas, battle at 84
Pease, Captain Valentine, II 1, 119
"Pebbles" (poem) **156**
pedants, satire of 125
Pedro II (Dom Pedro II de Alcântara; emperor of Brazil) **156,** 217
Peepi 108, **156–157**

Peleg, Captain 127, 128, **157**
Pennies, Misses **157,** 159
Pequod (ship) 3, 127, 128, **157**
   model for 1, 189
Perkins, Edward T. 12
Perth 135, **157**
Peter and Paul 150
philanthropist 48
"Philip" (poem) 186
phrenology 133, **157**
physiognomy 159
"The Piazza" (short story) 5, **157**
   characters in 112
   material for 74
The Piazza Tales 120, **157**
   publication history of 55
   short stories in 98
The Picture of Liverpool (guidebook) **158,** 175
Pierce, Franklin 78
Pierre. *See* Glendinning, Pierre
Pierre; or, The Ambiguities 120, **158–163**
   Bacon criticized in 9
   characters in 8, 9–10, 72, 123, 157, 164–165, 188, 194, 207, 219
   criticism of transcendentalists in 198
   hypocrisy exposed in 43
   literary world depicted in 20–21
   mind-body problem in 54
   Neoplatonist ideas in 141
   pantheism invoked in 155, 160
   Platonism in 164
   publication history of 76, 163
   setting for 158
   Spinoza invoked in 188
Piko **163–164**
pilgrimage, stories of. *See* Clarel; The Confidence Man
Pimminee 143
Pip 134, 136, **164**
   character prefiguring 209
Pipes. *See* Yarn
piracy, in publishing 20, 76, 152
Piranesi, Giovanni Battista **164**
"Pisa's Leaning Tower" (poem) **164**
Pisco 147
"A Pisgah View from the Rock" (sketch) 60, **164**

Pitch 27, 46–47, **164**
pitchpoling 133
Pittsfield, Massachusetts 42, 142,
    164
    Melville's farm near 6, 7
    Melvill family in 114, 115
    mountain near 74
Plato **164**
Platonism 164
    and Transcendentalists 198
Pleasures of Imagination (Akenside)
    3
Plinlimmon, Plotinus 161, 162,
    164–165
Plotinus 141
Poe, Edgar Allan
    on book publishing 20
    female characters of 220
    "The Gold Bug" 75
    influence on Melville 54
poetry, Melville's 29–30, 120. *See
    also specific poems*
    love 100
    references to Spinoza in 188
politics
    Melville's 95, 158
    revolutionary, satire of 42
    Tammany Hall 194
Polk, James K. 3, 123, 195
Polynesia 187. *See also* Hawaii
    culture of 194, 200
Polysyllables **1,** 64, 109
Pomare (Pomaree) **165**
Pomare, Queen 148, 151, 156,
    165, 167, 200
Pond, Rachel Turner. *See* Turner,
    Rachel
"Pontoosuce" (poem) **165**
"Poor Man's Pudding and Rich
    Man's Crumbs" (short story)
    165–166
    characters in 20, 51
Poor Richard's Almanac (Franklin)
    87, 88
Po-Po, Ereemear ("Jeremiah")
    100, 151, **166**
"The Portent" (poem) 12, 22, **166**
Porter, David 59, 115, 182
Potter, Israel **166**
poverty, Melville's family and 3,
    70–71, 114, 115

Powers, Hiram 89, **166**
Praxiteles 55
predestination 25, 34, 64, **166**
    in *Billy Budd* 25, 166
    in *Moby-Dick* 126, 166
    in *Pierre* 159
Prescott, William 23
"Presentation to the Authorities,
    by Privates, of Colors captured
    in Battles ending in the
    Surrender of Lee." (poem) **166**
president of the Black Rapids Coal
    Company 45, **166,** 198
Priming **166,** 214
prison(s)
    Civil War, poems about 85, 179
    in *Omoo* 25, 148, 149
Pritchard, George 165, **167**
"Profundity and Levity" (poem)
    167
Prometheus Unbound (Shelley) 186
Proudhon, Pierre Joseph 33
Prudence, Old 48, **145**
pseudonyms, Mclville's 54, 60, 97,
    168
publishing **20–21.** *See also specific
    publishers*
punishment, corporal *65,* 65–66
    in *White-Jacket* 104, 113,
        207–208, 215, 216, 218
purser
    in *Billy Budd* 19, **167–168**
    in *White-Jacket* 216
Putnam, George Palmer 85, 89,
    157, 219
Putnam's Monthly Magazine **168**
    Melville's publications in 5,
        10, 13, 60–61, 83, 89, 98,
        157, 197
"Puzzlement as to a Figure Left
    Solitary on a Unique Fragment
    of Greek Basso-Rilievo" (poem)
    168
Pythagoras 134, 168
Pythagorean **168**

Q

Quackenboss, Catherine. *See*
    Quackenbush, Catherine

Quackenbush, Catherine 70
Queequeg 127–128, 131, 132, 133,
    135, 136, **169**
Quoin **169,** 214

R

Rachel (ship) 136, 137, 171
Radcliffe, Mrs. Ann **171**
Radney 131, **171,** 189
"A Rail Road Cutting Near
    Alexandria in 1855" (poem)
    171
Rama 32
Ramayana 32
"Rammon" (prose and poetry)
    171
Rartoo 150, **171**
Ratcliff, Lieutenant 15, **171**
"The Ravaged Villa" (poem) **171**
Raymond, Frederick R. 189
"A Reasonable Constitution"
    (poem) **171–172**
"Rebel Color-Bearers at Shiloh: A
    plea against the vindictive cry
    raised by civilians shortly after
    the surrender at Appomattox."
    (poem) **172**
Reconstruction, Melville on 103
*Redburn: His First Voyage, Being the
    Sailor-Boy Confessions and
    Reminiscences of the Son-of-a-
    Gentleman, in the Merchant Service*
    (novel) **172–178**
    characters in 20, 26, 53, 74,
        75, 91, 98, 113, 180, 183
    Chartism in, allusions to 28,
        176
    dedication in 122, 178
    material for 119, 172
    Melville's opinion of 112, 178
    popularity of 120
    publication history of 14, 178
    setting for 99
Redburn, Wellingborough
    ("Buttons," "Boots") 20,
    172–178, **178–179**
Red Max. *See* Max the Dutchman
The Red Rover (Cooper), Melville's
    review of 195

Red Whiskers 15
Reign of Terror 67
Reine Blanche (ship) 148
"The Released Rebel Prisoner. (June, 1865.)" (poem) **179**
religion **179**
  criticism of
    in "The Margraves's Birthnight" 199
    in *The Two Temples* 199
  discussion of
    in *Moby-Dick* 127–128
    in *Pierre* 155, 160
  Melville and 103, 112
  pantheism 103, 141, **155**
  and science, Melville on 141, 142
Renan, Ernest 33
"Report of the Committee on Agriculture" **179**
"A Requiem for Soldiers lost in Ocean Transports." (poem) **179**
resurrection, theme of 20
"The Returned Volunteer to his Rifle." (poem) **179**
"The Return of the Sire of Nesle" (poem) 98
revolutionary politics, satire of 42
Revolutionary War 23
  Fort Stanwix **66**
  veteran memoirs. *See Israel Potter*
Revolutions of 1848 **179–180**
R.F.C **180**
  model for 155
Richmond, Virginia, fall of 63, *63*
Riga, Captain 172, 173, 174, 177, 178, **180**
Rights of Man (ship) 15, **180**
The Rights of Man (Paine) 15, 23
right whale 132–133
Rigs, Mr. **180**
Rime of the Ancient Mariner (Coleridge) 3, 131, **180**
Ringbolt, Captain 61
Ringman, John 44, **180**
"Rip Van Winkle's Lilac" (prose and verse) **180**
Roberts, Mr. 44, **180**

Robertson, James 76
Robertson-Lorant, Laurie viii, 15, 19, 86, 99, 158, 212, 220
"Rock Rodondo" (sketch) 60, **180**
Rolfe 32–40, **180**
Roman statuary
  in *Clarel* 33
  lecture on 187, 189
  poem about 2
Romantic poets, and 'olian harp 2
Rope Yarn 147, **181**
"Rosary Beads" (poem) **181**
Rose-bud (ship) 134, **181**
"The Rose Farmer" (poem) **181**
Rosencrans, William S. 153
Rosenkreutz, Christian 181
Rose-Water 113, **181**, 215, 217
"Rose Window" (poem) **181**
Rosicrucianism **181**
Rousseau, Jean-Jacques **181**
Routledge, George 152
"Runaways, Solitaries, Grave-Stones, Etc." (sketch) 60, **181**
"Running the Batteries. As observed from the Anchorage above Vicksburg. (sic) (April, 1863.)" (poem) **181–182**
Russ, Oliver 143
"The Rusty Man (By a Soured One)" (poem) **182**
Ruth 31–32, 33, 38, 40, **182**

S

Saddle Meadows 158, **183**
sailing master **183**
Sailors' Life and Sailors' Yarns (Ringbolt), review of 61
St. Lawrence (ship) **183**
  captain of 180
  Melville's voyage aboard 54, 119, 172
St. Nicholas, Church of 175
Salem **183**
Salvaterra **183**
"The Same" (poem) 8
Samoa ("The Utopian") 91, 106, 108, **183**
Samuel Enderby (ship) 61, 134

San Dominick (ship) 14
Sandwich Islands. *See* Hawaii
Sanford, Mary 71
Sarpedon 55
satire
  in *Israel Potter* 86, 89
  in *Moby-Dick* 59, 125
  in *Yankee Doodle* 8, 142, 152, 153, 187, 209
Savage, Hope. *See* Shaw, Hope Savage
Saveda, Miguel 176, **183**
The Scarlet Letter (Hawthorne) 77, 78
Schiller, Johann Christoph Friedrich von **183**
  influence on Melville 84
Schmerling, Philippe Charles 141
scholarship, parody of 125
Schopenhauer, Arthur **183–184**
Schouten, Willem 26
science, and religion, Melville on 141, 142
Scott, Winfield **184**, 195
"The Scout toward Aldie." (poem) **184**
  material for 70
Scribe, Hiram 83, **184**
Scriggs **184**, 216
Scrimmage **184**
The Sea Lions; or, The Lost Sealers: a Tale of the Antarctic Ocean (Cooper), review of 50, 195
Sealts, Merton M., Jr. 19
sea voyages, Melville's 1, 54, 59, 119–120, 172, 183, 199
Sedgwick, Catharine Maria 164
self-promotion, American, satire of 86
Selvagee **184**, 214
Seneca **184**
Serapis (ship) **184**
sexuality
  allegory of, in "The Paradise of Bachelors and the Tartarus of Maids" 155
  female, Melville on 4
  vs. intellectual pursuits 2
  Melville's view of 19
  poems about 83
  in *Typee* 197

"Shadow at the Feast. Mrs. B—
      (1847)" (poem) **184–185**
Shaftesbury, Anthony Ashley
      Cooper, third earl of **185**
Shakespeare, William **185**
      Cymbeline, epigraph taken
            from 157
      Hamlet, Pierre compared with
            160, 161
      influences on Melville's work
            2–3, 64, 124, 130, 157, 160,
            185, 209
      King Lear, Fool in 209
      Measure for Measure 157
      references in Melville's work
            47, 48, 85, 98
Shaw, Elizabeth Knapp. *See*
      Melville, Elizabeth Knapp Shaw
Shaw, Hope Savage 117, **185**
Shaw, Lemuel 1, 76, 105, 114, 117,
      185, **185–186**
Shaw, Sam 12
Sheba, princess of 103
Shelley, Percy Bysshe 186
      "Mont Blanc" 34
Shelleyan **186**
"Shelley's Vision" (poem) **186**
Shenly **186,** 218
Shepherd, Daniel, epistle to 61
"Sheridan at Cedar Creek.
      (October, 1864.)" (poem) **186**
Sherman, William Tecumseh
      casualties incurred by, poem
            about 152
      march in Washington, D.C.,
            poem about 139
      march through Georgia 55
            poems about 68, 105
"Shiloh. A Requiem. (April,
      1862.)" (poem) **186–187**
Shiloh, Tennessee battle at 172,
      186–187
"The Shipwreck" (Falconer) 145
short fiction 64. *See also specific
      short stories*
"A Short Patent Sermon.
      According to Blair, the
      Rhetorician" (satiric squib)
      187
Shorty 150, **187,** 223
skepticism 33

Bruno and 100
Hume and 80
Melville and 84
Metrodorus of Chios and 71
and modernist writers 137
Sketch Book (Irving) 85
*Sketches of History, Life and Manners
      in the West* (Hall) 138
Skyeman 91
slaver (ship) *13*
slave rebellion, in "Benito Cereno"
      13–14
slavery
      abolitionism on 1, 2, 22, 56
      Judge Shaw on 185
      Lincoln's position on 99
      Melville's position on 1, 2, 42
      poem about 66
Smith, Adam 99, 174
Smith, John 212
smoking 79, 109
Smollett, Tobias 151
Society Islands 119, **187**
Socrates 164
Somers mutiny 15, **187**
      and Guert Gansevoort 69
Song of Solomon 103
"The South Seas" (lecture)
      187–188
Specksnyder 129–130
Spencer, Philip 187
spermaceti **188**
sperm whale *124,* 129, 132–133,
      212
Spinoza, Baruch 100, **188**
"A Spirit Appeared to Me" (poem)
      188
spiritualism (spiritism) **188**
      in *The Apple-Tree Table* 5
Spithead **188**
Spouter Inn 126, 127, **188**
Springfield, Missouri, Battle of
      101
Squeak 17, **188**
Standard 64, **188**
Stanly, Glendinning 161, 162,
      188
Stannie. *See* Melville, Stanwix
Stanwix, Fort **66,** 70
Stanwix, John 66
Stanwix Hall 70

Starbuck 128, 130, 131, 135–137,
      188–189
statuary
      in *Clarel* 33
      lecture on 187, 189
      poems about 2, 55
"Statues in Rome" (lecture) 187,
      189
Stedman, Clarence 55
Steelkilt 131, 171, **189**
Stevenson, Robert Louis 187
"Stockings in the Farm-House
      Chimney" (poem) **189**
"The Stone Fleet. An Old Sailor's
      Lament. (December, 1861.)"
      (poem) **189**
"Stonewall Jackson. (Ascribed to a
      Virginian.)" (poem) **189**
"Stonewall Jackson. Mortally
      wounded at Chancellorsville.
      (May, 1863.)" (poem) **189**
"The Story of Toby" 205–206
stranger **190**
Strauss, David Friedrich 33
Stuart, Gilbert 70
Stubb 128, 129, 130, 131, 132,
      135, **190**
Styron, William, Melville's influ-
      ence on 137
"Suggested by the Ruins of a
      Mountain-Temple in Arcadia,
      One Built by the Architect of
      the Parthenon" (poem) **190**
Sumner, Charles 186, **190**
      at Melvill House 122
Sunshine **190,** 215
surgeon 17–18, 19, **190**
"The Surrender at Appomattox.
      (April, 1865.)" (poem) **190**
"The Swamp Angel" (poem) **190**
Swedenborg, Immanuel **190**
Sydney Ben 148, **190–191**
"Syra (A Transmitted
      Reminiscence)" (poem) **191**
Syrian monk 35, **191**

T

taboo (tabu) **193,** 194
Tacitus 44, **193**

Tahiti 187
  dynasty in 165
  French in 57, 137, 148, 165
  George Pritchard in 167
  Kannakippers in **95**
  tattooing in 194
Taipi (tribe) 119. *See also* Typee
Taji 77, 91, 107–111, **193,** 221
Talleyrand-Périgord, Charles
    Maurice de **193**
Tammany Hall 115, **193–194**
tapa (tappa) **194,** 203
Tarnmoor, Salvator R. 60, 168
Tarquin 136
Tartan, Lucy 159, 161, 162–163,
    194
  model for 158
Tartan, Mrs. **194**
Tashtego 128, 130, 133, 135, **194**
tattoo(es) 147, **194**
  lecturing on 187
  maker of 95–96
  in *Typee* 200
Tawney **194,** 217
Taylor, Zachary **194–195**
  satirical sketches of 8
tayo 149, **194**
teaching career, Melville's 119
"The Temeraire. (Supposed to
    have been suggested to an
    Englishman of the old order by
    the fight of the Monitor and
    Merrimac.)" (poem) **195**
Teniers, David, the Younger 13
*Thirty Years from Home, or A Voice
    from the Main Deck* (Leech) 194
Thomas, Eleanor 103
Thomas, Frances 103
Thomas, Frances Melville
    ("Fanny") 97, 117, *121,* **195**
Thomas, Henry B. 195
Thomas, Rear Admiral Richard
    27, 205
Thomas, Richard 156
Thompson, Mr. (doctor) 173–174,
    195
Thoreau, Henry David 198
  and abolitionism 1, 22
  influence on Melville 5
"A Thought on Book-Binding"
    (book review) 50, **195**

Thurston, Sophia Elizabeth. *See*
    Melville, Sophia Elizabeth
    Thurston
"Thy Aim, Thy Aim?" (poem) **195**
"Time's Betrayal" (poem)
    195–196
"Time's Long Ago!" (poem) **196**
"Timoleon (394 B.C.)" (poem)
    196
*Timoleon and Other Ventures in
    Minor Verse* (poetry collection)
  envoi in 98, **196**
  poems in 2, 5–6, 8, 13, 22, 25,
      55, 61, 67, 71, 73, 79, 83–84,
      97, 100, 103, 104–105, 112,
      123, 138, 142–143, 145, 156,
      164, 171, 186, 191, 196,
      209, 211
Tinor 96, **196,** 202
"To——" (poem) **196**
tobacco 79
Toby 75, **196,** 201–203, 205–206
  model for 73, 199
Tom. *See* Melville, Thomas
"Tom Deadlight (1810)" (poem)
    196–197
Tommo 64, 75, 95–96, 193, 196,
    197, 202–205
Tom Thumb, General 10
"To Ned" (poem) **197**
Took, Horn 87, **197**
"Tortoise Book" **197**
"To the Master of the *Meteor*"
    (poem) **197**
"To Tom" (poem) **197**
Town-Ho (ship) 131, 171, **197**
Trafalgar, Battle of 141, **197**
Tranquo 134, **198**
Transcendentalists 2, 10, **198**
  critique of 42
  founders 59
travel, Melville's
  to Europe and the Middle
      East 29, 124, 186, 187, 191
  sea voyages 1, 59, 119–120,
      172, 183, 199
"Traveling: Its Pleasures, Pains,
    and Profits" (lecture) 188, **198**
*Travels in New-England and New-
    York* (Dwight), influence on
    Melville 5

Tribonnora 109, **198**
"Trophies of Peace: Illinois in
    1840" (poem) **198**
Troy, John B. 27, 101, 119, **198**
  character based on 100
Truman, John 46, **198**
Tubbs **198–199,** 214
"The Tuft of Kelp" (poem) **199**
Turkey (character) **199**
Turner, Rachel 70
  poem dedicated to 85
Tweed, William Marcy ("Boss")
    194
"Two Sides to a Tortoise" (sketch)
    60, **199**
"The Two Temples" (short story)
    199
Two Years Before the Mast (Dana)
    53, 200, 212
  influence on Melville 124
Tyler, John 187
Typee (character in *Omoo*)
    146–151, 199
Typee (tribe) 75, **199.** *See also*
    Taipi
Typee: A Peep at Polynesian Life
    199–206
  characters in 64, 95–96, 112,
      113, 138–139, 156, 196
  cultural practices in 21, 193,
      194
  dedication in 117
  Greene's exploitation of 73
  hypocrisy exposed in 42
  indigenous tribes in 75
  material for 1, 73, 119
  narrator of 197
  political commentary in 95
  popularity of 64
  publication history of 76, 85,
      118, 139, 206
  setting for 112, 199
  taboos in 193
  tattooing in 194

U

Uhia 108, **207**
Ulver, Delly 160, **207**
"Under the Ground" (poem) **207**

Undine (Fouqué) 221
unfortunate man 45, 72, **207**
Ungar 39–40, 67–68, **207**
"An Uninscribed Monument on one of the Battle-fields of the Wilderness" (poem) **207**
United States (navy frigate) **207,** 213, *213*
    meeting with *Erie* 67
    Melville's experience on 9, 26, 28, 143
    motivation for enlisting on 77, 93, 119
unparticipating man 46, **207**
Urania 2
Ushant, John **207–208,** 218
utilitarianism 14, **208**
"A Utilitarian View of the Monitor's Fight" (poem) **208**
Utopia (More), Melville on 171–172
Utopian. *See* Samoa

V

Van 147, **209**
Vangs, Captain 200
    model for 1
Varvy 151, **209**
Vavona 22
Vedder, Elihu 66, 196
Vee Vee 108, **209**
"Venice" (poem) **209**
Ventom, Captain 101
Ventom, Henry 74
Vere, Captain 16, 17–19, 143, **209**
    model for 187
"The Vial of Attar" (poem) **209**
"The Victor of Antietam. (1862.)" (poem) **209**
"View of Barnum Property" (short squib) **209,** 221
Viking 91, 105. *See also* Jarl
Vincennes (ship) 219
Vine 32–40, **209–210**
Viner 148, 149, **210**
Virgin (ship) 133, **210**
Virginia (ship) 85

Volney, C. F. 35
Voltaire (François Marie Arouet) **210**
Vowels **1,** 64, 109

W

Walcott, Ephraim 157
Walden (Thoreau), influence on Melville 5
Wallis, Samuel 187
Warren, Robert Penn 29
The Waste Land (Eliot) 41
Watt, James 171
"A Way-Side Weed" (poem) **211**
The Wealth of Nations (Smith) 99, 174
"The Weaver" (poem) **211**
Webster, John 41, 99
Weeds and Wildings Chiefly: With a Rose or Two (poetry collection) **211**
    flower symbolism in 97
    poems in 4, 8, 20, 23, 28, 41, 51, 53, 54–55, 57, 65, 74, 79, 84, 85, 99–100, 103, 142, 145, 167, 180, 181, 189, 195–196, 198, 207, 209, 211, 212
Wellington, duke of (Arthur Wellesley) 16, **211–212**
whale(s)
    cultural representations of 131
    definitions of 125
    right 132–133
    sperm *124,* 129, 132–133, 212
    types of 129
whale-line 132
whaling **212**
whaling voyage, Melville's 1, 119, 199
Wharton the Whale-Killer!, or the Pride of the Pacific (Halyard) 212
"When Forth the Shepherd Leads the Flock" (poem) **212**
The White Devil (Webster) 41, 99
White-Jacket **212–213,** 214–218

White-Jacket; or, The World in a Man-of-War **213–219**
    characters in 9, 19–20, 21, 23, 28, 42, 43, 52, 67, 98, 103, 104, 113, 143, 145, 156, 166, 169, 181, 184, 186, 190, 194, 198–199, 207–208, 219, 220, 221
    criticism of corporal punishment in 66
    criticism of midshipmen in 67, 71
    influences on 53
    material for 119, 194, 207
    Melville's opinion of 112, 178
    publication history of 14, 76, 218–219
    sources for 20
whiteness, symbolism of 131
Whitman, Walt 29
    Leaves of Grass 74
Wilderness, Battle of 6
Wiley, John 219
Wiley & Putnam 85, 118, 206, **219**
Wilkes, Charles 2, 212, **219**
    Narrative of the U.S. Exploring Expedition During the Years 1838, 1839, 1840, 1841, 1842 169, 219
Williams 214, **219**
Williams, Griffith 219
Wilson 147–148, 149, 150
Windward Islands 187
Winsome, Mark 48, **219**
Winwood, Ralph 159, **219**
Wise, Henry Augustus 12, 20
"The Wise Virgins to Madam Mirror" (poem) **103**
women **219–220**
Woodcock, John 87, 88, **220**
wooden-legged man 44–45, **220**
Wooloo 215, **220**
Worden, John Lorimer 85
Wymontoo 147, **220**

Y

Yankee Doodle **221**

Yankee Doodle (magazine) **221**
  editor of 113
  Melville's publications in 8,
   142, 152, 153, 187, 209
Yarn ("Old Yarn," "Pipes") 216, **221**
Yillah 77, 107, 108, **221**
Yojo 127, **221**
Yoky 110, **221**

Yoomy 108, 109, 111, **221**

Z

Zeke 150, **223**
Zimmermann, Johan Georg, Ritter
  von **223**

Zionism 141, **223**
Zoroaster 155